& Seamanship
in the
Bronze Age Levant

ED RACHAL FOUNDATION NAUTICAL ARCHAEOLOGY SERIES

Seagoing Ships
in the

& Seamanship
Bronze Age Levant

SHELLEY WACHSMANN

Foreword by George F. Bass

Texas A&M University Press
COLLEGE STATION

The publication of this book was made possible in part by
the generous support of The Institute for Aegean Prehistory
and The George O. Yamini Family Chair in Liberal Arts
at Texas A&M University.

FRONTISPIECE: Bird-head post ornament, with legs of a man standing on it,
all that remains of a Sea Peoples' ship painted on Late Helladic IIIC 1b sherd
found at Ashkelon (photo by V. Bryant; courtesy of L. E. Stager and the Leon
Levy Expedition to Ashkelon)

Library of Congress Cataloging-in-Publication Data

Wachsmann, Shelley.
        Seagoing ships and seamanship in the Bronze Age Levant / Shelley
    Wachsmann.
        p.   cm. (Ed Rachal Foundation Nautical Archaeology Series)
        Includes bibliographical references and index.
        ISBN 0-89096-709-1
                1. Mediterranean Region—Antiquities.   2. Underwater
    archaelogy—Mediterranean Region.   3. Bronze age—Mediterranean Region.
    4. Seafaring life—Mediterranean Region.   5. Ships, Ancient—Mediterranean
    Region.   I. Title.
        DE61.S43W33   1997   96-49815
        910'9163'80901—dc21   CIP
    ISBN 13: 978-1-60344-080-6 (pbk.)
    ISBN 10: 1-60344-080-1 (pbk.)

For Yonatan & Yishai

Some went down to the sea in ships,
doing business on the great waters;
They saw the deeds of the Lord,
His wondrous works in the deep.

—PSALMS 107: 23–24

CONTENTS

FOREWORD

It was only with watercraft that ancient peoples could discover, explore, colonize, and supply the once uninhabited islands of the eastern Mediterranean, and it was mainly with watercraft that ancient peoples of the bordering African, Asian, and European coasts acquired the raw materials—especially metals and timber—that allowed the rise of Bronze Age civilizations in the Levant.

Of course there were overland caravans and inland caravan cities, but one can scarcely imagine huge cedar logs being hauled overland from Lebanon to the Nile valley or tons of copper and tin being carted from the East across Anatolia to Greece, even had there been a bridge over the Bosporus. It was on the waters of the Red Sea, not across desert and through jungle, that Egyptians sent expeditions to Punt to bring back the exotic goods of tropical Africa.

Maritime commerce turned the eastern littoral of the Mediterranean into a bustling, cosmopolitan entrepôt. Ships sailed from the harbors of Ugarit, Sidon, Tyre, Ashkelon, and Dor, transporting metals, ceramics, resins, and spices southward to Egypt and westward to the Aegean, some at least

as far west as Sardinia. The role of Cyprus within this economic sphere has not yet been determined, but it must have been considerable.

The long-distance exchange of goods and ideas by sea was not always peaceful. We cannot imagine Mycenaean Greeks without the knowledge of writing and art they obtained by naval conquest from the Minoans of Crete. And Mycenaean troops did not march but sailed to Troy. Even the end of the Bronze Age in the eastern Mediterranean was marked by destruction wrought along the Syro-Canaanite coast and on Cyprus by raiding Sea Peoples.

Scholarly interest in the ships and boats of these events has not been lacking. But when I, as a young assistant professor, first offered a graduate seminar on ancient seafaring at the University of Pennsylvania in the middle 1960s, there were few general references to which my students and I could turn for the study of early Near Eastern and Aegean watercraft. M. G. A. Reisner's *Models of Ships and Boats* (*Catalogue général des antiquités égyptiennes du Musée du Caire*) had appeared in 1913, and from the mid 1920s there were M. C. Boreux's *Études de nautique*

égyptienne and August Köster's *Das antike Seewesen* and *Schiffährt und Handelsverkehr des östlichen Mittlemeeres in 3. und 2. Jahrtausund v. Chr.* For pre-Classical ships we read Spyridon Marinatos's "La marine créto-mycénienne" in the *Bulletin de correspondance hellénique* (1933) and G. Kirk's "Ships on Geometric Vases," in the *Bulletin of the British School of Archaeology at Athens* (1949).

More generally, we could consult a few pages each in R. and R. C. Anderson's *The Sailing Ship: Six Thousand Years of History* (1963), James Hornell's *Water Transport: Origins and Early Evolution* (1946), Björn Landström's beautiful but speculative *The Ship* (1961), and the splendid but popular *Illustrated History of Ships and Boats* and *The Ancient Mariners*, both by Lionel Casson.

Mostly, however, we had to seek out depictions and ancient written records on our own, slowly building up a bibliography of several hundred titles, carrying heavy armloads of books from the library to the seminar room, each tome often containing but one relevant illustration of an Egyptian painting or relief or model. Working with such primary sources is essential, but we lacked handbooks like those that had proved so useful to me in learning the basics and bibliographies of subjects I had only recently studied—books like William Dinsmoor's *The Architecture of Ancient Greece,* Gisela Richter's *The Sculpture and Sculptors of the Greeks,* or the many comprehensive works on vase painting and coins.

Since that early and perhaps unique seminar on ancient seafaring, the study of ancient ships has expanded rapidly, largely because of the new field of nautical archaeology that reveals ancient ships themselves, both on land and underwater. Graduate programs in nautical archaeology are springing up around the world, with a growing number of undergraduate introductory courses on the history of ships being offered at various universities.

Publications have kept pace. Specialized periodicals, the English *International Journal of Nautical Archaeology* since 1972 and the French *Archaeonautica* since 1977, are now devoted solely to the archaeology of ships and harbors, with proceedings of conferences on those subjects published regularly from Australia to India to the Americas. Of special interest to scholars of the early Aegean are those entitled *Tropis,* published by the Institut Hellénique pour la Préservation de la Tradition Nautique. Small wonder that 75 percent of the nearly thousand references Shelley Wachsmann has listed in this book have appeared in the three decades since my first seminar.

For the Classical period, especially, there are now three outstanding reference works: Lionel Casson's *Ships and Seamanship in the Ancient World* (1971), J. S. Morrison and R. T. Williams's *Greek Oared Ship: 900–300 B.C.* (1968), and Lucien Basch's *Le musée imaginaire de la marine antique* (1987). These touch on Bronze Age seafaring, as do Marie-Christine de Graeve's *The Ships of the Ancient Near East* (c. *2000–500 B.C.*) (1981) and J. Richard Steffy's essential *Wooden Ship Building and the Interpretation of Shipwrecks* (1994), but none is devoted specifically to it.

For those interested especially in the dawn of seafaring, a book that brings together the earliest writings about and portrayals of seagoing vessels—mixed prudently with ethnographic evidence—has been sorely needed.

When Dr. Wachsmann joined the faculty of the Nautical Archaeology Program at Texas A&M University, he added a seminar on Near Eastern seafaring to those we already offered on pre-Classical, Classical, medieval, and post-medieval seafaring. We soon realized the overlap between his seminar in Near Eastern seafaring and mine in pre-Classical seafaring, for the Near East and Aegean were so closely tied by ships in the Bronze Age that one cannot study the maritime history of one area without studying that of the other. We combined our two classes into one covering the entire Levant—which encompasses the Aegean and the eastern Mediterranean—after which some of our former students, we are told, commented that they especially liked the times when we disagreed, sometimes strongly (but always politely!) in the seminar room.

Now, at last, Dr. Wachsmann's new book pulls together, in a most thought-provoking manner, all the major evidence about Bronze Age seafaring in the eastern Mediterranean. It is another major step toward the day when courses on ancient watercraft can be taught as regularly as are those on ancient architecture, sculpture, and painting. And how welcome that will be. After all, we cannot imagine the Bronze Age without the ships and boats that played such a critical role in its development and demise.

George F. Bass
Abell/Yamini Professor
of Nautical Archaeology
Texas A&M University

ACKNOWLEDGMENTS

This book is a developed, revised, and updated form of my Ph.D. dissertation, submitted to the Institute of Archaeology of the Hebrew University, Jerusalem, in 1989. I owe a particular debt of appreciation for the help and guidance of my dissertation advisors and mentors, Trude Dothan and George F. Bass. To Professor Bass I owe a special thanks for proposing that I turn the dissertation into a book; I am sincerely grateful for his encouragement to do so and for his advice and financial support in seeing this book become a reality.

The writing of my dissertation was made possible by generous grants. For this assistance I sincerely thank the Memorial Foundation for Jewish Culture, particularly its director, Jerry Hochbaum; and the Sarah Rabinovitch Fund. I wrote this book while serving as the Meadows Visiting Assistant Professor of Biblical Archaeology at Texas A&M University's Nautical Archaeology Program. I am grateful to Professor Bass, to the Meadows Foundation of Dallas, to the Institute of Nautical Archaeology, and to Texas A&M University for making this possible. I also thank my parents for their encouragement and assistance during the writing process.

The Uluburun shipwreck is without doubt the single most significant key to understanding Bronze Age seafaring. I have profited greatly from discussions with George Bass and Cemal Pulak. I thank them both for their insights into Bronze Age seafaring, for permitting me to take a small part in their excavation at Uluburun during the 1985 and 1986 seasons, and for their kind permission to publish illustrations from their excavation here.

In a book that deals with such a wide range of cultures and topics, it was inevitable that I would seek advice from experts in various fields of research. I was gratified to discover an openness and unstinting willingness in all the scholars whom I approached to share their knowledge and insights with me. My warm appreciation goes to Amnon Altman for his valuable comments on the Ahhiyawa problem; to Lucien Basch for kindly supplying me with a photo of the Karnak anchor; to Jacqueline Balensi, who told me about the Tel Abu Hawam anchors; to Emmett L. Bennett and John Chadwick for their valuable comments on topics relating to Linear B documents; to Lionel Casson for advising me on numerous nautical matters; to Brenda Conrad for bringing to my attention several important publications on the subject of Minoan archaeology and religion; to Fanouria Dakoronia for permitting me to use illustrations of her discoveries from Kynos in this book; to Michael Fitzgerald for our many stimulating discussions; to Honor Frost and Gerhard Kapitän for sharing with me their understanding of anchors and rigging; to Cheryl Haldane for her insights and comments concerning ancient Egyptian ship construction; to Maria Jacobsen for her assistance with aspects of Ugaritic trade; to Barbara Johnson for her valuable comments on the Late Helladic IIIC 1b sherd from Ashkelon; to Paul Johnston for supplying several illustrations; to V. Karageorghis for his comments concerning the abandonment of Kalavassos; to Christine Lilyquist for information on the tomb of Iniwia; to Ezra Marcus for bringing the Tell el Dabᶜa seal to my attention; to Robert Merrillees for noting the bird-head ship model fragment from Maroni; to Bezallel Porten for supplying me with his revised translation of Elephantine text Cowley 26 (B12) and permitting me to publish it here; to Anson Rainey for his many important insights into many of the texts studied here; to Joe and Maria Shaw for supplying me with information and illustrations on the stone composite anchors from their excavation at Kommos; to Patricia Sibella for a variety of help; to Larry Stager for referring me to the Kamose text and for his many other insightful comments; to J. Richard Steffy for sharing with me his unique perspective on ancient ship construction and his incomparable knowledge of ancient ships; to Frederick van Doorninck, Jr., for his knowledgeable comments; to Michael Wedde for his penetrating comments on the Aegean iconographic material; to Malcolm H. Weiner for reviewing the Aegean chapters and for making numerous valuable suggestions; and to physical anthropologist Joe Zias for his observations on the Anemosphilia material.

As work progressed on the manuscript, it became clear to me that the book would be enhanced by the contributions of other scholars. My sincere thanks go to Frederick Hocker for discussing the question of keels on Hatshepsut's Punt ships as well as for writing the glossary of seafaring terms; to John Lenz for writing an appendix on the question of bird-head ship ornaments in Homer; to Thomas G. Palaima for his commentary on PY An 724 and An 1 as well as for his translation of the latter; and to J. Hoftijzer and Wilfred van Soldt for their translations of the primary Ugaritic and Akkadian texts pertaining to seafaring from Ugarit.

My study of the ship graffiti at Rod el ʿAir was made possible by the gracious permission of the late Raphael Giveon of the Institute of Archaeology, Tel Aviv University. Professor Giveon invited me to take part in his 1972 archaeological survey at Serabit el Khadem and its surroundings and later permitted me to publish the results of my study of the ships from Rod el ʿAir. My thanks goes to Benjamin Sass, then assistant district archaeologist of Sinai, for his help at that time.

I received much welcome assistance in researching the shfifonim of the Sea of Galilee region: the late Pesah Bar Adon, Dan Bahat, Amitzur Bolodo, Moshe Kochavi, the brothers Moshele and Yuval Lufan, and, of course, Mendel Nun. Special thanks are due to Uzi Avner for his penetrating comments on the cultic connotations of the Degania "A" tomb, and to Yizhar Hirschfeld for inviting me to study the fascinating shfifon uncovered in his excavations at Mount Berenice.

I have also learned from my students. My heartfelt appreciation goes particularly to Kyra Bowling for her artwork; to Steven Butler for his assistance during the final stages of the manuscript prior to its publication; to William H. (Bill) Charlton for his valuable editing skills and insightful comments; to Roxani Margariti for making me rethink old interpretations; to Sam Mark for his aid in tracking down obscure references; to Edward Rogers for his comments on the scenes of ship construction in the Old Kingdom tombs of Tí and Mereruka; and to Sam Turner for our stimulating conversations on the Ahhiyawa problem.

We now live in an amazing electronic age. The Internet allows the instantaneous sharing of information among scholars around the globe. Numerous lists deal with archaeological topics. Of these, I have been following the discussions on "Aegeanet," which is owned and operated by John G. Younger. This list has been particularly valuable and stimulating for me in doing this research. I thank Professor Younger and his host of contributors for enabling me to follow developments in the world of Aegean archaeology through their communications.

My past six years at Texas A&M University have been particularly valuable for me. I have had the opportunity to discuss many of the problems dealt with in the following pages with the other faculty of the Nautical Archaeology Program, who are among the foremost experts in the fields of nautical archeology and ancient ship reconstruction. I have learned much from them. Robert K. Vincent, Jr., past president of the Institute of Nautical Archaeology, was a source of encouragement. The staff of the program and of the Institute of Nautical Archaeology, Becky Holloway, Claudia LeDoux, Clyde Reese, and Pat Turner have been most helpful to me in a variety of ways. I thank them all.

I am grateful to the staff at Texas A&M University Press for their considerable efforts in seeing this book through the long and arduous path of publication.

Finally, it is my pleasure to thank Karen, my soul mate, for her endless patience, for her unstinting support, and for her excellent editing skills from all of which I—and this book—have greatly benefited.

Seagoing Ships
& Seamanship
in the
Bronze Age Levant

CHAPTER 1

Introduction

One of the most fascinating and vibrant facets of the Bronze Age—particularly during its latter half—was the expansion and intensification of cultural horizons. These international contacts resulted in an inevitable exchange in material and cultural concepts that measurably enriched the participating civilizations and significantly influenced the course of history.

For the societies ringing the eastern basin of the Mediterranean, contact was established primarily by sea. By the second part of the Bronze Age, the Mediterranean had been transformed from an impassable barrier into a super-highway by which cultures communicated. This new-found freedom primarily resulted from the ability to build vessels capable of standing up to the rigors of open-water travel and from the seafaring knowledge required to use them.

The study of seaborne exploration, trade, migrations, and colonization depends on understanding the nautical capabilities of the various nations. A knowledge of their ships and seafaring practices is a prerequisite for any understanding of the mechanisms and directions of Bronze Age cultural flows.

This raises numerous directions of inquiry. Why did these peoples go to sea? What types of ships did they build? How efficient were the ships and the seafaring practices of those times? And what insights into a culture can be gleaned from studying its ships and the manner in which it interacted with the sea?

Although innumerable studies have dealt with various aspects of Bronze Age ships and seafaring, there is no single monograph that covers the subject comprehensively. This book attempts to do so.

The Mediterranean Bronze Age encompasses the third and second millennia B.C. Yet in order to understand and to place several of the phenomena discussed below in their proper cultural perspective, it is at times imperative to go beyond these chronological restraints. One example of the need to allow for temporal latitude is the study of the phenomenon of bird-head stem and stern devices that appear on the Sea Peoples' ships at Medinet Habu.[1] These have little meaning if they are removed from a cultural continuum that still manifests itself today. Furthermore, the absolute chronology of Egypt, upon which all Near Eastern dating systems are primarily based, is itself problematic.[2]

I have divided the study into two parts. The first discusses sea-going ships of the cultures bordering the eastern Mediterranean, country by country. The order follows the trade routes of antiquity in a counterclockwise sweep of the eastern Mediterranean, beginning in Egypt. The second part deals with seven primary aspects of seafaring: ship construction, propulsion, anchors, navigation, sea trade, war and piracy, and laws pertaining specifically to conduct at sea.

When studying evidence for Bronze Age seafaring, one should keep in mind the limitations imposed by the material—and by the types of materials studied. It is well to ponder the Indian proverb relating what happened to a group of blind men, each of whom was commanded to describe the appearance of an elephant by touching only one part of the animal. Each blind man, depending on which part he had touched—trunk, leg, body, or tail—came away convinced that the elephant was most similar to a snake, a pillar, a wall, or a rope, respectively. There is an important lesson in this parable for those of us who would attempt to reconstruct the past, for we have much in common with those blind men. In a very real sense *we may touch the past, but we cannot see it*. Only by marshaling as many different aspects of the problem as are available to us—metaphorically "touching as many limbs of the elephant as possible" —can we reach conclusions that *may* approach past realities.

The following research tries to collect, describe, and—most importantly—make sense of a wealth of information. This "raw material" must be studied critically, however, as it can rarely be taken at face value and is often of an ambiguous nature. In most chapters the data are subdivided thematically, often followed by a discussion in which specific problems arising from the material are reviewed. The methodological approach I have chosen here is a synthesis based on four available sources of information.

TEXTUAL EVIDENCE. Contemporaneous written evidence dealing with nautical subjects is of varying intrinsic value to this study. Those texts that indicate the nationality, destination, and other information concerning seagoing ships are particularly valuable. Other texts discuss the construction and repair of vessels, but these are rare.

More common are documents that contain references to sea contacts between trading agents or colonies. A third form of textual evidence, of limited interpretational value, is perhaps best termed "miscellany." These consist of personal names or linguistic terms that appear, seemingly out of place, on foreign shores. Although such documents are indicative of some form of sea contact, their interpretation remains open.

ARCHAEOLOGICAL EVIDENCE. Underwater archaeology has made immense strides in the past three decades. The invention of SCUBA, together with the introduction of a proper methodology of underwater research and excavation, has opened up the seabed to serious archaeological exploration. Of particular importance are the actual remains of ships and their cargoes, retrieved from the sea floor. Two coherent wrecks in particular, at Uluburun and Cape Gelidonya in Turkey, have yielded a wealth of information and are discussed in detail below.

The interpretation of wreck sites, however, is problematic. And one of the most difficult things to determine is a ship's home port. What can be accepted as evidence for the ethnic identity of a ship remains a difficult question, particularly when personal objects of a variety of cultures are found on a single wreck, as at Uluburun. At present it is not possible to define the specific ethnic identity of any Bronze Age wreck with absolute certainty. As a result, the archaeological evidence of wrecks is explored in the various thematic chapters in the latter part of the book.

Few artifacts found in foreign archaeological contexts allow us to determine the nationality of the ships that transported them. Cargoes are generally useless in this regard: they indicate that trade had taken place but do not identify the carrier. On occasion, however, an artifact can actually indicate "beyond reasonable doubt" that a ship originating in a specific country brought it to a foreign shore. Because of the limitations of shipwreck archaeology described above, the archaeological evidence is limited to artifacts of this nature as discussed in the chapters dealing with the ships of the various cultures. As we shall see, these artifacts are exceptionally rare.

On a different level, stone anchors, found in large quantities on the eastern Mediterranean sea floor, are an important source of information for the study of ancient seafaring. These bear witness to trade routes and to seafaring practices. Dating and identifying anchors found out of archaeological context, however, remain problematic unless they can be linked to diagnostic anchor shapes found in firmly dated stratified land sites or on shipwrecks.

ICONOGRAPHIC EVIDENCE. Contemporaneous depictions of ships, their construction, and their uses are an invaluable third type of information, particularly for those elements of ships that will not normally be preserved in the archaeological record. Iconographic evidence presents numerous problems of interpretation, however.

Some depictions were created by master craftsmen working under strict artistic canons, while others were no more than simple graffiti or rough models fashioned by unskilled hands. In some depictions, scholars disagree even as to which end is the bow or the stern. When trying to interpret ships drawn by ancient artists, one sometimes feels compassion for the proverbial Martian who was given the task of reconstructing an earthwoman based on a collection of Picasso paintings retrieved by a scout mission.

In discussing the scenes of foreigners in the Theban tombs of Eighteenth Dynasty nobles, Norman de Garis Davies voices a warning that rings equally true for the study of ancient ship iconography:[3]

If the study of written documents and that of excavated objects have their special difficulties and limitations, the interpretation of pictured records, forming a third division of historical research, also offers scope for philological and archaeological knowledge, as well as wide experience and some psychological sense. We may ask then what measure of truth can be reached in this third field. . . .

It is all important, therefore, that an inquiry should be made into the reliability of these pictures, and it is as well to realize at the outset, to prevent disappointment, that modern standards of historical exactness will have to be imported by us into the study of these records. We shall not find them ready for us there. Hence the task cannot consist merely of collecting and arranging the items offered and then deducing the solution, as if by an operation in mathematics or chemical analysis.

In Magritte's famous series of paintings (*Les deux mystères, L'air et le chanson,* and so on), he placed the following statement beneath the painting of a smoker's pipe: "Ceci n'est pas une pipe." When studying ship iconography we must keep in mind the same simple fact: an iconographic depiction is not the object itself.

In ship iconography, we see not ships but *representations of ships* "refracted" through the eyes, culture, schooling, mental attitudes, and skills of their creators. The result at times departs considerably from the prototype.[4] There are a variety of reasons for this: the artist's capability, familiarity with the prototype, sources of information, difficulties in translating the shape and details of the prototype into the chosen medium, and art canons, to name but a few.

Because of these considerations, we should not be surprised if we find that elements of a ship's architecture have been telescoped, compressed, or otherwise exaggerated in a representation. Some details may be portrayed disproportionately small or be totally ignored.

It is basic common sense, therefore, to always turn first to the clearest and most detailed depiction of any given ship type, irrespective of its chronological standing relative to other ship renderings in the group. This aids considerably in deciphering other illustrations that are more difficult to interpret. Although each representation must be studied critically, when this is done we are often re-

warded with valuable insights that cannot be derived from any of the other forms of available evidence.

ETHNOLOGICAL EVIDENCE. The ancients perceived their world in a manner that seems at times inexplicable to the modern mind. Because of this, modern ethnological comparisons are invaluable in helping us enter the conceptual world of the ancients when dealing with ships and seafaring practices. By studying the manner in which traditional ships are built and used today and in the recent past, we are offered possible solutions to seemingly enigmatic pieces of evidence. The ethnological materials are not treated as a separate subdivision of data but are instead incorporated directly into the context of the iconographic evidence or the discussions on seafaring practices.

The purpose for bringing ethnological parallels here is not to argue for a continuation of traditions in these cases. Instead, it is based on the consideration that the psyche of man, given the same problems and similar materials, will tend toward kindred solutions and expressions regardless of their location in space and time.

THE SHIPS
Review of the Evidence

CHAPTER 2

Egyptian Ships

Egyptian civilization developed along the Nile River. It was, therefore, only natural that movement was primarily by water; even the concept of "travel" was expressed as "sail upstream" and "sail downstream."[1]

There are innumerable depictions of *river* boats in Egyptian iconography; here the discussion is limited to seagoing craft, or material that bears directly on them and their uses. Egypt was the only country to trade in both the Mediterranean and the Red Sea during the Bronze Age; much of the extant information on Egyptian seagoing ships derives from the trade with Punt and will be discussed below.

Primitive river craft probably existed on the Nile by Paleolithic times: the earliest Egyptian craft were presumably papyrus rafts.[2] Indeed, the Cheops ship is so technically advanced that development over thousands of years must be assumed.[3] Reed rafts, wedge-shaped bundles of reeds constructed of two conical bundles laid side by side and lashed together at intervals, were still used on the Nile in this century.[4] The modern Nubian rafts consist of pairs of bundles of reeds lashed

together. J. H. Breasted notes how similar this is to the term for raft in the Pyramid texts where it appears in the dual usage ("two *shn*"). Interestingly, apart from the verbs meaning "to hew" and "to make," the most characteristic Egyptian word for shipbuilding is "to bind."[5]

Opinions vary as to whether Egypt can be considered a seagoing culture. T. Säve-Söderbergh argues for a strong Egyptian seagoing presence on the Mediterranean.[6] In doing so, he totally negates Syro-Canaanite seafaring. At the other extreme, A. Nibbi claims a total lack of Egyptian maritime involvement. She argues that the Egyptian term "the Great Green Sea" (*w3d-wr*), normally understood to be the Egyptian term for the Mediterranean, actually refers to the Nile Delta.[7] The reality of pharaonic seafaring probably is to be found somewhere between these two extremes.

The Textual Evidence

The earliest reference to a nautical Egyptian presence on the Mediterranean Sea is a report, recorded on the Palermo Stone, of the importation of wood by Sneferu (Fourth

Dynasty). The text, however, does not indicate the nationality of these transport ships.

> Bringing forty ships filled (with) cedar logs.
> Shipbuilding (of) cedarwood, one "Praise-of-the-Two-Lands" ship, 100 cubits (long) and (of) *meru*-wood, two ships, 100 cubits (long).[8]

Thus, from earliest times, timber for shipbuilding and other purposes was a primary article of trade for Egypt. Pharaonic inscriptions found at Byblos suggest that trade connections may date back at least to Nebka (Khasekhemi), last pharaoh of the Second Dynasty.[9] By the Fifth to Sixth Dynasties, Byblos had become an Egyptian entrepôt for the importation of timber.

Uni, a military commander under Pepi I (Sixth Dynasty), describes the transport of his troops by sea in his cenotaph at Abydos:

> When it was said that the *backsliders* because of something were among these foreigners in *Antelope-Nose,* I crossed over in transports with these troops. I made a landing at the rear of the heights of the mountain range on the

north of the land of the Sand-Dwellers. While a full half of this army was (still) on the road, I arrived, I caught them all, and every *backslider* among them was slain.[10]

The term "Antelope-Nose" apparently refers to a prominent mountain range. Although the identification is not certain, Uni may be referring to the Carmel ridge, which juts out "noselike" into the Mediterranean.[11] If so, Uni perhaps landed his troops north of the Carmel mountains, on the Plain of Jezreel, and found villages and fortified towns there.

During the Twelfth Dynasty considerable quantities of cedarwood were being imported into Egypt: one text mentions "twenty ships of cedar."[12] An inscription from Saqqara describes military expeditions to the Syro-Canaanite coast and possibly to Cyprus (*I3sy*) in which ten ships transported the army returning from Lebanon.[13]

The "Tale of the Shipwrecked Sailor" describes the adventures of an Egyptian who survived the sinking of his ship in the Red Sea while on a voyage to the mines of Sinai.[14] This is the earliest "shipwreck" ever recorded, and, although meager, it also supplies the only textual information on seagoing ships in the Middle Kingdom.[15] The sailor relates that his ship had a 120-man crew and that the craft measured 120 cubits in length by 40 cubits in beam.[16]

Because the entire tale is phantasmagoric, these numbers must be approached with caution, particularly as we know little of the sizes of ships' crews. One Rammeside Nile ship had a crew that varied daily from 26 to 40 men.[17] A ship of Amenhotep II had 200 rowers, but this number might be a convention.[18] The size of the sailor's ship need not be exaggerated, how-

ever. Sahure refers to 100-cubit-long ships that he had built. Furthermore, the beam/length ratio of 1:3 is credible, although it does suggest an extremely beamy and slow craft.

The "Admonitions of Ipu-wer" describe a period of social unrest when foreign trade connections ceased to exist. It was created sometime during the turbulent years between the collapse of the Sixth Dynasty and the rise of the Eleventh.[19] In describing a lack of embalming materials that were normally imported from Byblos, Ipu-wer complains of the lack of trade with Byblos.[20] This assumes that maritime trade had existed previously. Ipu-wer also emphasizes the directionality of the trade: Egyptians had gone north to Byblos.

During the Eighteenth Dynasty, Thutmose III sailed with his army to the Syro-Canaanite shore on his sixth campaign (thirtieth year, ca. 1449 B.C.). This is evident from the ship determinative following the word "expedition" that is used here for the first time.[21] The previous year Thutmose's forces had captured Syro-Canaanite ships. Breasted assumes that these were used to return the army to Egypt.[22] Säve-Söderbergh notes, however, that only two ships were captured and that the reference in Thutmose's annals probably resulted from their valuable cargoes.[23] Two ships would not have been sufficient to carry the army home but could perhaps have transported Thutmose and his staff.

Thutmose soon realized the advantages of transporting his army by sea and improved the logistics involved by organizing and stockpiling the ports on the Syro-Canaanite coast during his seventh campaign (thirty-first year, ca. 1448 B.C.): "Now every port town which his majesty reached was supplied with good bread and

with various (kinds of) bread, with olive oil, incense, wine, honey, fr[uit], ... They were more abundant than anything."[24] References to stockpiling the harbors continue in all the following years for which annals are preserved.[25]

Timber, particularly Lebanese cedar, continued to be a valuable import commodity during the New Kingdom. Senufer, an official under Thutmose III, recorded bringing back a cargo of cedarwood from the Lebanon. Concerning his return trip he wrote, "[I *sailed* on the] Great [Green] Sea with a favorable breeze, land[ing *in Egypt*]."[26]

In one Amarna text, Abimilki of Tyre mentions a contingency plan for abandoning Tyre with all the "king's ships."[27] If these refer to Egyptian ships stationed in Tyre, it suggests that Thutmose's organization of harbor cities, with its emphasis on rapid sea transport, continued to operate into the mid-fourteenth century. Another Amarna text is also best understood in this light.[28] Rib-Addi, the embattled king of Byblos, repeatedly requested an Egyptian ship to take him to Egypt if troops did not arrive.[29] Säve-Söderbergh believes this to be indicative of Egyptian supremacy of the sea lanes during the Amarna period.

Egyptians, some of whom must have been trading agents, are mentioned operating in several Syro-Canaanite cities.[30] The Mycenaean personal name a_3-*ku-pi-ti-jo* (the Egyptian) suggests some form of contact with Egypt.[31] This name is enigmatic, however. Is this an Egyptian living in the Aegean, an Aegean who had some form of contact with Egypt, or does it have some other significance?

In Papyrus Harris I, Ramses III records the building of three types of seagoing ships to transport goods from Canaan to the treasuries of three Egyptian gods:[32]

I made for thee (Amun of Karnak) qerer-ships, menesh-ships, and bari-ships, with bowmen equipped with their weapons on the Great Green Sea. I gave to them troop commanders and ship's captains, outfitted with many crews, without limit to them, in order to transport the goods of the land of Djahi and of the countries of the ends of the earth to thy great treasuries in Thebes-the-Victorious. . . .

I made for thee (Re of Heleopolis) qerer-ships and menesh-ships, outfitted with men, in order to transport the goods of God's Land to thy storehouse. . . .

I made for thee (Ptah of Memphis) qerer-ships and menesh-ships, outfitted with crews of menesh-ships in abundant numbers, in order to transport the goods of God's Land and the dues of the land of Djahi to thy great treasuries of thy city Memphis.

Ramses III dispatched fleets to Punt and to Atika, a land rich in copper:[33]

I sent forth my messengers to the country of the Atika (ᶜ-ty-ka), to the great copper mines which are in this place. Their galleys carried them; others on the land-journey were upon their asses. It has not been heard before, since kings reign. Their mines were found abounding in copper; it was loaded by ten-thousands into their galleys. They were sent forward to Egypt, and arrived safely. It was carried and made into a heap under the balcony, in many bars of copper, like hundred-thousands, being of the color of gold of three times. I allowed all the people to see them, like wonders.

Atika, which could be reached by both water and land, was ten-

tatively located by Breasted in Sinai.[34] An alternate identification, proposed by B. Rothenberg, locates Atika in the copper-producing Valley of Timna near Eilat.[35] Copper was mined at Timna mines by the Egyptians during the Nineteenth and Twentieth Dynasties, including during the reign of Ramses III.[36] If this identification is correct, it would mean that Egyptian seagoing ships were rounding the Sinai peninsula and penetrating the Gulf of Eilat in the early twelfth century B.C.

In the "Renaissance Period," Wenamun sailed to Byblos to bring back timber for the Amun Userhet, the sacred barque of Amun that took part in a yearly procession from Karnak to Luxor and back again.[37] This text indicates that because of Egypt's decline in power, sea trade with Egypt at that time was controlled by the inhabitants of the Syro-Canaanite coast. During his interrogation of Wenamun, Tjekkerbaal, the king of Byblos, speaks of transactions that had no doubt taken place during the Late Bronze Age. He mentions six shiploads of Egyptian goods that previous pharaohs had sent as payment for timber.[38] Presumably, the goods arrived in Egyptian hulls.

The Archaeological Evidence

An axehead belonging to an Egyptian royal boat crew was found in 1911 in the Adonis River (Nahr Ibrahim) on the Lebanese coast, just south of Byblos (Fig. 2.1).[39] It bears the following inscription: "The Boat-crew 'Pacified-is-the-Two-Falcons-of-Gold'; Foundation [gang] of the Port [Watch]." The royal name "Two Falcons of Gold" was a title of both Cheops (Fourth Dynasty) and Sahure (Fifth Dynasty). In form it dates to the Third to Sixth Dynasties.

A. Rowe notes that the axehead must have belonged to one of the ship crews that sailed to Lebanon to acquire cedarwood for either Cheops or Sahure. Both rulers had trade contacts with the Syro-Canaanite coast. In addition to the text discussed above, Sahure also depicted his ships returning from a trip to that region (below). The excavated ship of Cheops is built mostly of Lebanese cedarwood, and his name is recorded on vase fragments at Byblos.[40]

Egyptian-type anchors were found in Middle Bronze Age contexts in temples at Byblos and Ugarit (Figs. 12.28: 21; 33: 11).[41] Presumably, these had been dedicated by Egyptian ship crews who had voyaged with their ships to these cities.

The Iconographic Evidence

The seeming "snapshot" quality of Egyptian wall paintings and reliefs can be misleading. Each picture must be approached with caution and interpreted in light of what is known from other sources.[42] The Egyptian artist did not always include all the same details in two representations of the same ship. For example, in the tomb of Senufer at Thebes, a funerary barge is being towed downstream from Thebes to Abydos.[43] In the scene below it, the barge is being towed back upstream to Thebes. W. F. Edgerton notes that this painting is a unit: the same barge and towing boat are represented in both scenes. Despite this, in one scene the thole bights, scarfs of planking, and through-beams are visible; in the other scene, they are missing.

Similarly, in Ramses III's naval battle scene depicted at Medinet Habu, the ships of both warring sides are stereotyped into one type of craft: the accompanying text,

Figure 2.1. The axe head belonging to a royal boat crew of Cheops or Sahure, found in the Nahr Ibrahim (from Rowe 1936: pl. 36: 1, courtesy of the Israel Antiquities Authority)

however, indicates that at least three varieties of craft took part on the Egyptian side alone.[44] Thus, we are presented with several images of a single ship that is portrayed in varying degrees of detail.

One question that must be asked of the following Egyptian scenes of seagoing ships is whether they are of a narrative nature. That is, do they describe specific events carried out by particular characters in a given location at a determined time, or are they simply pictures meant to transmit an idea?[45]

Finally, it is worth reemphasizing that the following discussion does not deal with actual ships but instead with artists' representations of them. These depictions can deviate from the original craft because of artistic conventions and individual artistic ability.

Old Kingdom
SAHURE. The first definite depictions of seagoing ships in Egypt

are on a relief from Sahure's burial temple at Abusir (Figs. 2.2–3). They appear on the north and south sides of the east wall of the west passage.[46] Both sides of the wall are divided into four registers, the lower two of which depict seagoing craft. The remains of four ships on the north side indicate the moment of departure for the Syro-Canaanite coast; eight ships on the south side represent the return voyage.

M. Bietak suggests that the Asiatics depicted on the seagoing ships of Sahure and Unas represent the ships' crews.[47] This interpretation is unlikely for several reasons:

• The ships used in these scenes are undeniably Egyptian. If Egypt was using Asiatic crews, why not use Asiatic ships?
• In the Sahure scene, the ships departing Egypt are manned solely by Egyptian crews: *Asiatics appear only on the ships returning from over-*

seas. This must indicate that the Asiatics were not the ships' crews.
• Finally, even if the Egyptians were using Asiatic crews, why would a pharaoh wish to communicate this information in his temple complex instead of depicting the impressive importation of valuable tribute? Contrast this, on the one hand, to the importance placed on the ships' cargoes in Hatshepsut's scene of her expedition to Punt (Figs. 2.17–18, 33) and, on the other hand, to Wenamun's embarrassment when he is reminded by Tjekkerbaal that the ship on which he arrived, and its crew, were Syro-Canaanite:

Where is the ship for (transporting) pine wood which Smendes gave you? Where is / its Syrian crew? Wasn't it in order to let him murder you and have them throw you into the sea that he entrusted you to that barbarian ship captain? With whom (then) would the god be sought, and you as well, with whom would you also be sought? So he said to me.

And I said to him: Certainly it is an Egyptian ship and an Egyptian crew that are sailing under Smendes. He has no Syrian crews. And he said to me: Surely there are twenty cargo ships here in my harbor which are in commerce with Smendes. As for that Sidon, / the other (port) which you passed, surely there are another fifty freighters there which are in commerce with Warkatara, for it is to his (commercial) house that they haul.

I kept silent. . . .[48]

G. A. Gaballa considers Sahure's scene an artistic rendition of a specific event of which two moments are recorded: the departure and the return. The home-bound vessels carry a number of Syro-Canaanites accompanied by their

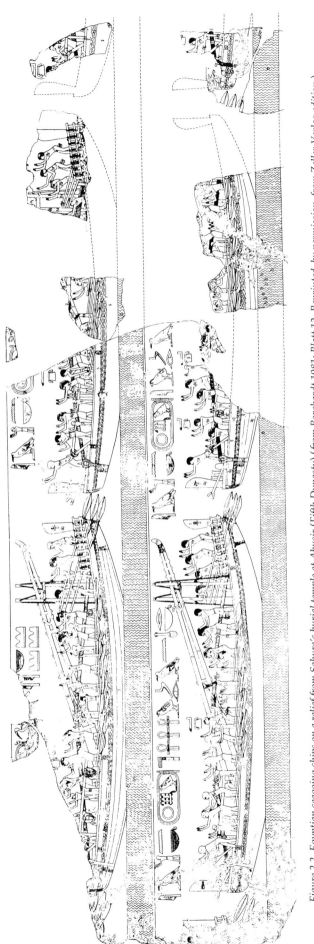

Figure 2.2. Egyptian seagoing ships on a relief from Sahure's burial temple at Abusir (Fifth Dynasty) (from Borchardt 1981: Blatt 12. Reprinted, by permission, from Zeller Verlag edition.)

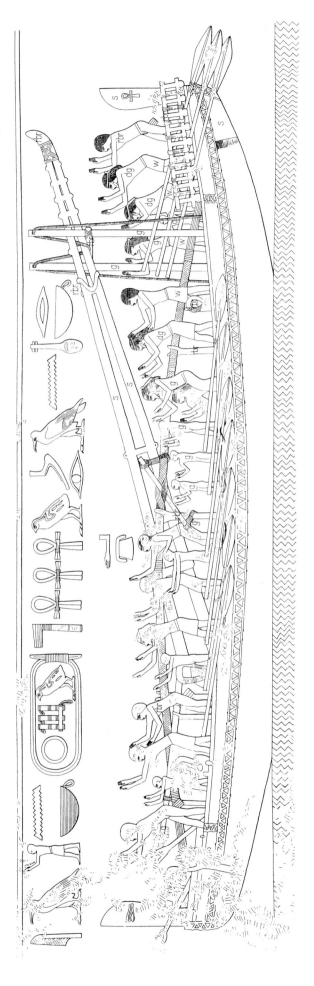

Figure 2.3. One of Sahure's seagoing ships (from Borchardt 1981: Blatt 13. Reprinted, by permission, from Zeller Verlag edition.)

wives and children, all of whom are paying homage to the pharaoh. He assumes that the purpose of the voyage was peaceful and that the scene may represent an Egyptian trading expedition to the Syro-Canaanite coast.

The peaceful nature of the expedition is questionable. In several cases, the Syro-Canaanites are being held by the scruffs of their necks as they raise their arms in adoration, a behavior most inappropriate if the Asiatics were arriving under peaceful circumstances. Most likely the Asiatics were, in themselves, human tribute.[49]

The hulls of Sahure's ships appear to have an exaggerated sheer. The vessels' stems and sterns are finished with vertical posts bearing the Eye of Horus and *ankh* signs. This is the earliest iconographic depiction of an *oculus*.[50] A band of rope lashing runs the length of the hull beneath the sheerstrake. C. V. Sølver suggests that this either hid the ends of the deck planking or connected the sheerstrake to the hull.[51]

Each ship carries a hogging truss connected to cables laid around the stem and stern and supported on stanchions to provide additional longitudinal support. A study of the basic load conditions acting on a seagoing craft explains the need

Figure 2.4. The hull of one of Sahure's ships showing a diagonal scarf (after Edgerton 1922–23: 131 fig. 10)

for a hogging truss on these ships.[52]

A seagoing ship must have the structural strength to head perpendicularly into waves having a length between crests greater than or equal to that of the ship itself.[53] When the crests are at the ship's extremities, its midships section is in a trough. In this case, the upper lateral area is under compression and the lower area under tension.[54] More importantly, when the ship is supported amidships by a single wave, the stresses are reversed. The upper structure is now under tension while the hull's lower portion is under compression. This latter condition is encountered more often because it can be produced by shorter waves. That is, assuming a wave amidships, the previous crest has just left the stern area while the next wave has not yet reached the bow.

Thus, even in a moderate sea, ships lacking sufficient longitudinal support in the form of a devel-

oped keel and framing system and with exaggerated overhang at stem and stern will tend to "hog," or break in two, unless they are given additional longitudinal support. The hogging truss allows for the required tension to be set.[55]

As we shall see, seagoing ships on the Red Sea run to Punt must have been lashed.[56] The Mediterranean ships of Sahure, as well as those of Unas, may also have been lashed, perhaps in a manner similar to the Cheops ship.[57] Edgerton notes three joints on the ships in Sahure's relief where planks were diagonally scarfed instead of abutting squarely (Fig. 2.4). He concludes, "The planks in each strake were held together end to end by flexible bands, possibly of rawhide or metal. But we have to infer that the planks in one strake were secured to those above and below by dowel-tongues or dovetails, *since no bands are visible across the longitudinal seams.*"[58]

The Cheops ship explains why

Figure 2.5. Seagoing ships portrayed on a relief from the causeway of Unas at Saqqara (Fifth Dynasty) (from Hassan 1954: 139 fig. 2)

lashing would have been invisible from the outside: the ropes were transversely lashed through V-shaped mortises cut into the internal surfaces of the strakes and cannot be seen on the hull's exterior (Fig. 10.4). The diagonal planking scarfs on Sahure's ships are also similar to those on the Cheops ship (Fig. 10.5).

On Sahure's ships, three steering oars, lacking tillers, are placed between the stanchions in the stern on the port side. Presumably each ship carried a total of six of these quarter rudders, the number required being indicative of their inefficiency. Seven oars are attached to the hull with lanyards. Sølver suggests that these craft lacked proper decks: in their place the craft may have had removable boards between the deck beams.[59] Each ship is shown with its mast lowered onto a crutch positioned in the stern. The masts are bipod, probably a continuation of the types of masts used originally on papyrus rafts.[60]

UNAS.Two additional Old Kingdom seagoing ships are depicted on a relief from the causeway of Unas's burial temple (Fig. 2.5).[61] These ships are similar in hull form and rigging to those of Sahure; Unas's artists seem to portray the same class of Egyptian seagoing ship depicted by Sahure. The execution of Unas's relief, however, lacks the high quality and detail of that of Sahure. In both cases, the ships are shown with Syro-Canaanites on board (Figs. 2.3, 6).

Unas's ships have tripod masts.[62] These are held in place by cables, wound under tension, that are attached laterally to loops in the ships' hulls (Fig. 2.7). These cables, which also appear on contemporaneous Nile ships, apparently took the place of shrouds (Fig. 2.10).[63] The hogging truss, although shown

Figure 2.6. Detail of the two Syro-Canaanites at the stern of the ship on the right. Causeway of Unas at Saqqara (Fifth Dynasty) (photo by the author)

Figure 2.7. Detail of the lateral trusses supporting the tripod mast of a seagoing ship depicted on a relief from the causeway of Unas at Saqqara (Fifth Dynasty) (photo by the author)

Figure 2.8. The stern of a seagoing ship depicted on the right side of a relief from the causeway of Unas at Saqqara (Fifth Dynasty) (photo by the author)

Figure 2.9. River cargo craft portrayed on a relief from the causeway of Unas (from Hassan 1954: 137 fig. 1)

A

B

C

Figure 2.10. Trusses are used to give lateral support to river ships of the Fourth and Fifth Dynasties (A after Landström 1970: 42 fig. 112; B–C after Goedicke 1971: 107, 111)

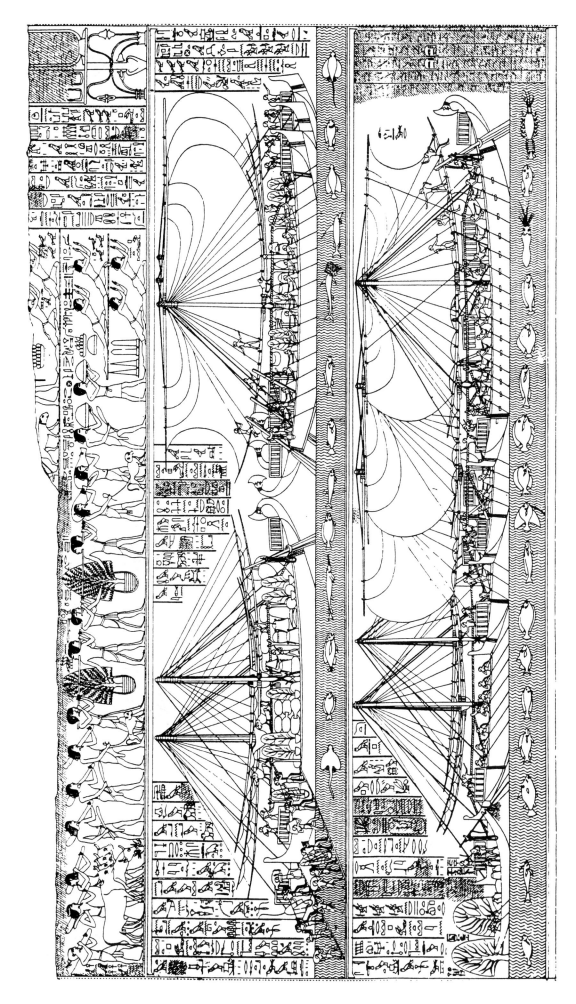

Figure 2.11. Hatshepsut's expedition to Punt, Deir el Bahri (from Säve-Söderbergh 1946: 14 fig. 1)

Figure 2.12. The land of Punt (from Naville 1898: pl. 69)

Figure 2.13. The king and queen of Punt (after Naville 1898: pl. 69)

cause of the longitudinal hogging truss. It is not clear how the boom was connected to the mast.[65]

Calculations concerning the dimensions of the actual ships themselves are untrustworthy. Unas's ships carry the three conventional quarter rudders per side but only four rowers' oars. The number of oars shown may be misleading. Landström considers the Sahure reliefs as scale projections of the ships and calculates their length at 17.5 meters based on the number of rowers. Based on a wooden model of Sixth Dynasty date that may represent a vessel of this type, he postulates their beam at about 4 meters.[66] Prototypes for the ships depicted by Sahure and Unas may have been much larger than generally thought, however, since the human figures are probably shown in a much larger scale than the ships themselves, and it is likely that there were more oars than are portrayed.

Middle Kingdom

There are no known depictions of seagoing ships from the Middle Kingdom, nor from the intermediate periods that preceded and followed it.

New Kingdom

DEIR EL BAHRI. A most detailed depiction of Egyptian seagoing ships is the expedition to Punt portrayed on Hatshepsut's mortuary temple at Deir el Bahri (Fig. 2.11).[67] Hatshepsut emphasized foreign connections and internal affairs over military accomplishments—to which she could hold little claim.[68] Her representation of the Punt expedition suggests that it was a unique voyage. Actually, it was remarkable that Hatshepsut chose to emphasize this accomplishment, because maritime contacts with Punt had been common as early as the Old Kingdom.[69]

in much less detail in Unas's ships, is similar to those on Sahure's ships. In the latter, the truss is connected to the hull by girdles, while Unas's ships have the truss itself passing directly around the hull, a feature probably attributable to artistic license (Fig. 2.8). Nile cargo ships portrayed on Unas's causeway bear multiple vertical posts at stem and stern and a tripod mast (Fig. 2.9).

B. Landström notes that during the Fifth Dynasty, the booms of Nile River ships rested abaft the mast on the caprails (Fig. 2.10: A–C).[64] On seagoing ships, the boom must have been placed higher up and hung forward of the mast be-

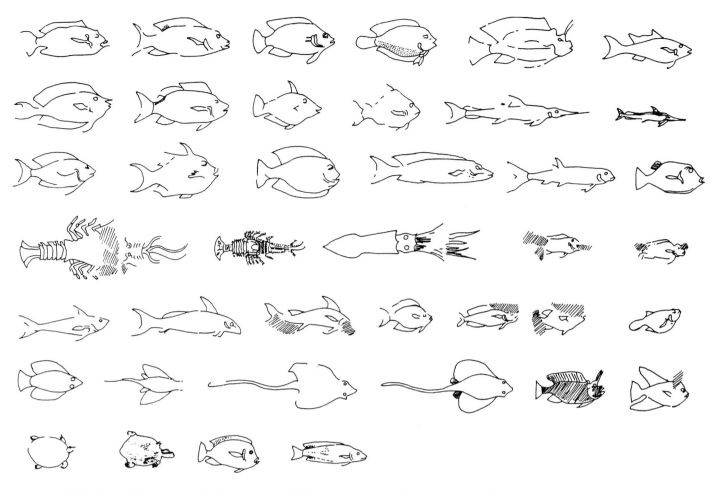

Figure 2.14. Fishes and other marine animals depicted beneath Hatshepsut's seagoing ships at Deir el Bahri (after Naville 1898: pls. 69–70, 72–75)

Punt is first mentioned in the Fifth Dynasty when Sahure lists myrrh, electrum, and wood obtained there.[70] Under Pepi II (Sixth Dynasty), Enenkhet was killed while building a "Byblos ship" for a voyage to Punt.[71] In the contemporaneous inscription of Harkhuf, Pepi II refers to a dwarf brought from Punt.[72] A short historical inscription of Khnumhotep in the tomb of Khui at Aswan (Sixth Dynasty) refers to visits to both Punt and Byblos.[73] Henu (Eleventh Dynasty) recorded the construction of a Byblos ship for a trip to Punt in his Wadi Hammamat inscription.[74]

Hatshepsut's craft are termed Byblos ships (*Kbn*).[75] The name need not indicate that the ship was bound for Byblos but instead that it was of the class normally used on the run from Egypt to Byblos.[76] Apparently, this term originally defined a class of Egyptian seagoing ship that was used on the Byblos run; however, by the end of the Old Kingdom, the term had come to include large seagoing ships, whatever their destination. The ships, probably constructed of cedarwood, may have been built on the Nile and then disassembled for transportation through Wadi Hammamat to Quseir on the Red Sea coast, where they were reassembled.[77] At the completion of the voyage, the craft would have been stripped down and carried back through the desert valley to Koptos. For this to be possible, the craft must have been of lashed construction.

The scene depicts memorable details of the voyage and the land of Punt, its inhabitants, and the sea creatures encountered during the voyage (Fig. 2.12). Note particularly the grossly fat wife of the leader of Punt (Fig. 2.13).[78] The fishes and other marine animals depicted here are, for the most part, indigenous to the Red Sea (Fig. 2.14).[79] Some, however, are fresh-water Nile fish that have been transferred to this scene.[80] Presumably, the marine creatures were recorded after they had been hooked—or netted—by the crew but before they ended up in the pot.[81] The artist did not see the animals in their natural habitat. This is evident from the manner in which they are depicted. All the fish and other creatures are depicted swimming to the right, in-

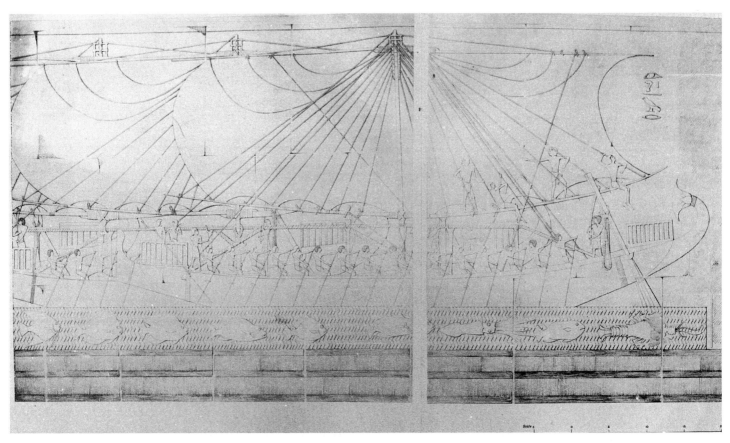

Figure 2.15. *Ships sailing for Punt. Lower right quarter of scene of Hatshepsut's expedition to Punt at Deir el Bahri (from Naville 1898: pl. 73)*

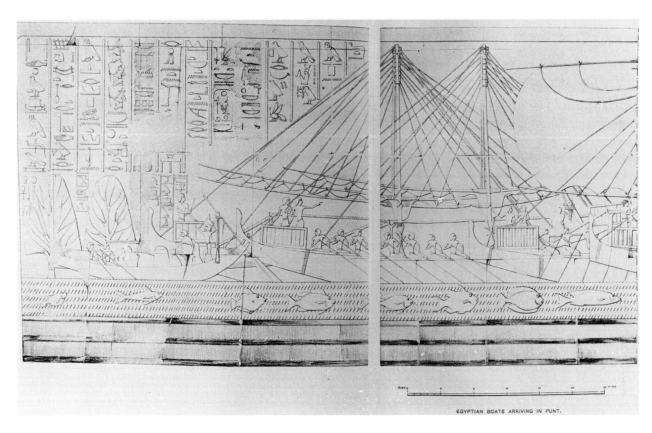

EGYPTIAN BOATS ARRIVING IN PUNT.

Figure 2.16. *Ships arriving at Punt and unloading trade items. Lower left quarter of scene of Hatshepsut's expedition to Punt at Deir el Bahri (from Naville 1898: pl. 72)*

Figure 2.17. Ships loading cargo at Punt. Upper left quarter of scene of Hatshepsut's expedition
to Punt at Deir el Bahri (from Naville 1898: pl. 74)

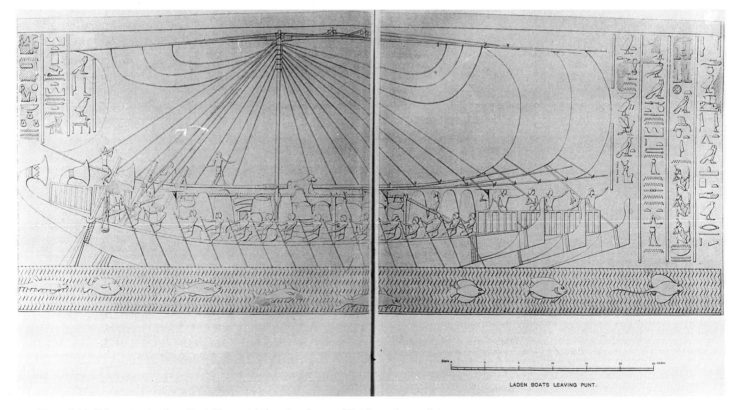

LADEN BOATS LEAVING PUNT.

Figure 2.18. Ships returning from Punt. Upper right quarter of scene of Hatshepsut's expedition
to Punt at Deir el Bahri (from Naville 1898: pl. 75)

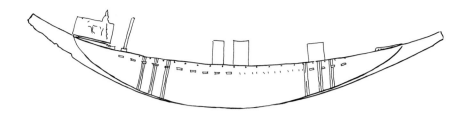

Figure 2.19. Sheer view of a wooden ship model from the tomb of Amenhotep II (Reisner no. 4944) (after Landström 1970: 109 fig. 339)

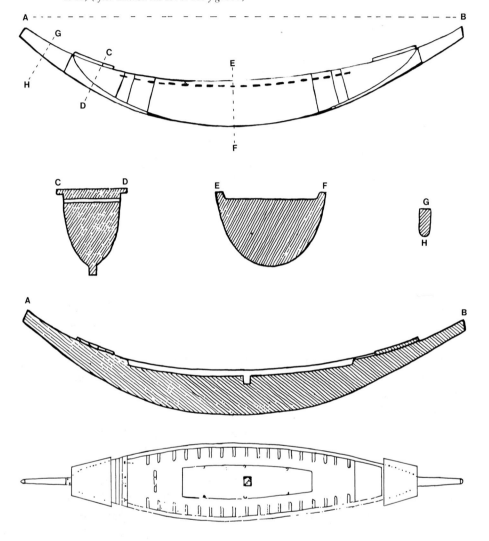

Figure 2.20. Reisner's drawings of the same ship model from the tomb of Amenhotep II (Reisner no. 4944) (after Reisner 1913: 96 figs. 348–49)

trayed only in paint and disappeared with the centuries.[83] The persons involved, whether Egyptian or Puntite, are recognizable and play definite roles in the various events. The development of episodes is clear and comprehensible.[84] The voyage is portrayed in two registers on the northwest wall. The time sequence is clockwise from bottom right to top right and shows four phases of the sea voyage (Fig. 2.11).

Bottom right. The flotilla begins its journey as the ships sail for Punt (Fig. 2.15). The last ship leaving Egypt on the outward journey has, over its stern, the captain's order: "Steer to port."[85] Above the ships is the following inscription: "Sailing in the sea, beginning the goodly way towards God's-Land."[86]

Bottom left. The ships arrive at Punt; using a gangway, trade items are transferred to a launch for further transport to shore (Figs. 2.16, 12.51).[87] These are explained as "(an offering) for the life, prosperity, and health of her majesty (fem.), to Hathor, mistress of Punt ⌈_____⌉ that she may bring wind."[88]

Top left. The produce of Punt is loaded on board the ships. The cargo is depicted on deck (Fig. 2.17). Above the ships is this inscription:[89]

The loading of the ships very heavily with marvels of the country of Punt; all goodly fragrant woods of God's-land, heaps of myrrh-resin, with fresh myrrh trees, with ebony, and pure ivory, with green gold of Emu, (ᶜmw), with cinnamon wood, khesyt wood, with ihmut-incense, sonter-incense, eye-cosmetic, with apes, monkeys, dogs, and with skins of the southern panther, with natives and their children. Never was brought the like of this for any king who had been since the beginning.

cluding two lobsters and a squid. The artist was either unaware that both of these creatures swim backwards or preferred to keep them facing the same direction because of artistic considerations.

These details indicate beyond reasonable doubt that the scenes must be based on the work of an artist (or artists) that accompanied

the expedition.[82] This is of importance vis-à-vis the ships, for it indicates that the source materials used by the Deir el Bahri artists were most likely based on first-hand observation.

The scene was carved in relief and then painted, but only faint traces of the paint still remain. Some details may have been por-

The Puntites ask the Egyptians, "Did ye come down upon the ways of heaven, or did ye sail upon the waters, upon the sea of God's-Land."[90]

Top right. The ships return with their cargo to Egypt (Fig. 2.18). Above the returning ships is the inscription "Sailing, arriving in peace, journeying to Thebes with joy of heart, by the army of the Lord of the Two Lands, with the chiefs of this country behind them. They have brought that, the like of which was not brought for other kings, being marvels of Punt, because of the greatness of the fame of this revered god, Amun-Re, Lord of Thebes."[91]

There is a reason for the direction of the scene. The orientation of Hatshepsut's temple at Deir el Bahri is basically northwest by southeast.[92] Thus, left equates with south while right equates with north. Sailing left signifies sailing south to Punt, which is portrayed on the south wall of the temple.

Gaballa notes the similarity to the Sahure relief at Abusir, where the departure scene is depicted on the north side because the Syro-Canaanite coast was north of Egypt.[93] Thus, both Sahure and Hatshepsut oriented their scenes with respect to the countries involved. The Old Kingdom rendition is more static, illustrating only

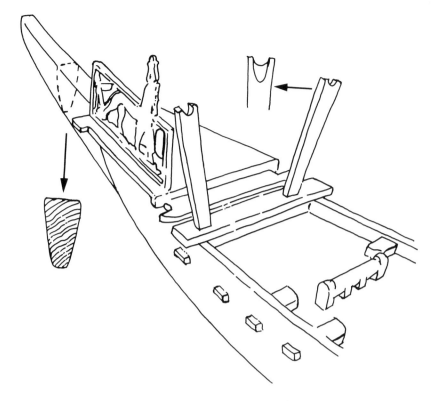

Figure 2.21. Stern of ship model from the tomb of Amenhotep II (Reisner no. 4944) (after Landström 1970: 108 fig. 337)

two points in time, the departure and the arrival; the New Kingdom scene expands this into four scenes. The workmanship of the sculptured relief is so fine that the ships almost seem to be based on scale drawings. This is probably illusionary.[94]

How many ships took part in the expedition? Five ships are shown, but this may be artistic license. Expeditions to Punt, including the crews required to recon-struct the ships on the Red Sea coast, could be quite large. The list of participants of Antefoker's expedition (Twelfth Dynasty) totaled 3,756 men, of which only 500 were sailors.[95]

The ships are portrayed in profile and appear to be long and slender. However, impressions can be deceptive in a two-dimensional aspective portrayal. The hulls of Hatshepsut's Punt ships bear a strong similarity to a particular

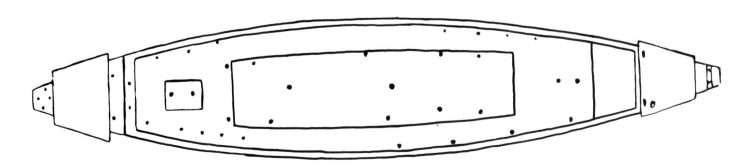

Figure 2.22. Deck plan of a ship from the tomb of Amenhotep II (Reisner no. 4946) (after Reisner 1913: 98 fig. 354)

Figure 2.23. Wooden model of a traveling ship from the tomb of Tutankhamen (after Landström 1970: 107 fig. 331)

Figure 2.25. Bow section and quarter rudder on two of Hatshepsut's Punt ships (detail from Naville 1898: pl. 73)

hull form that appears in the New Kingdom and is known from models found in the tombs of Amenhotep II and Tutankhamen (Figs. 2.19–23).[96] These models have long, nearly horizontal stem- and sternposts. The Punt ships differ in several details from the models: they lack the central cabin, their extremities are finished in a different manner, and they are outfitted with hogging trusses. The models suggest a beam/length ratio of about 1:5 for this ship type.[97]

Only one hull at Deir el Bahri has the rectangular butt ends of through-beams evident (Fig. 2.15). Either the beam ends were painted on the other hulls and have subsequently disappeared, or the artists never bothered adding them. R. O.

Faulkner believes that the through-beams took the place of the truss girdle that appears on Old Kingdom seagoing ships (Figs. 2.2–3).[98] The Old Kingdom vertical sternpost was replaced with a conventionalized recurving papyrus umbel, a decoration also used on New Kingdom Nile traveling ships.[99]

Each ship is portrayed with fifteen rowers to a side. Assuming a standard minimum *interscalmium* of about one meter and allowing another four meters at both stem and stern, the total length of these craft would have been about twenty-three meters—*if the number of rowers is not a convention*. The ships show prominent and no doubt exaggerated overhang, both fore and aft. The waterline is indi-

cated, although it is unconvincingly low. The stempost is vertical with a straight forward face and a curving rear surface. It lacks the Eye of Horus decoration, but with that exception is basically identical to stems on Old King-

Figure 2.24. The bow section of a Punt ship (detail from Naville 1898: pl. 72)

Figure 2.26. A Punt ship's stern (detail from Naville 1898: pl. 74)

dom seagoing ships. The Eye of Horus may have been originally painted on the stems in the relief and subsequently disappeared.

The decking of these ships remains unclear. L. Casson assumes that they were decked only along their center line and that there was an open space for the rowers to sit at their oars.[100] The bows are taken up with a forecastle in which two men are stationed; no figures are portrayed in the sterncastles. These castles are probably similar to those on New Kingdom traveling ships, of which several illustrations exist.[101]

The heavy twisted-cable hogging truss is carried over four crutches. It is not clear how it is attached inside the hull. Perhaps it was connected to through-beams. The multiple cables circling the bow and stern were intended to prevent the planking there from buckling under the strain of the hogging truss (Figs. 2.24–26).

Although the hogging truss is a hallmark of Egyptian seagoing ships without keels, trusses were also used on other craft whenever tension was needed. They appear

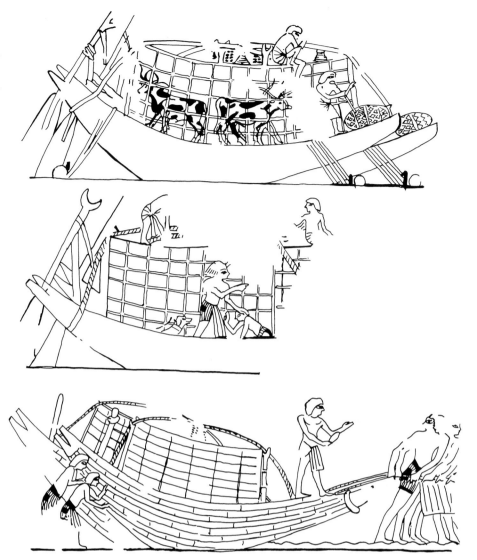

Figure 2.27. Three cargo ships from the tomb of Huy have hogging trusses that are carried over the hull on forked stanchions and are fastened to the stem and stern (Eighteenth Dynasty) (after Landström 1970: 134 figs. 390–92)

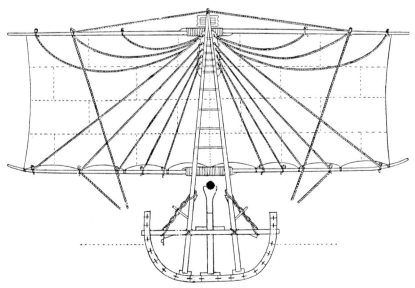

Figure 2.28. Sølver's reconstruction of Hatshepsut's Punt ship with a bipod mast (from Sølver 1936: 458 fig. 10)

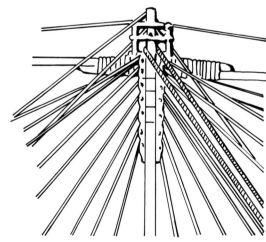

Figure 2.29. Detail of a mast truck on one of Hatshepsut's Punt ships (after Naville 1898: pl. 73)

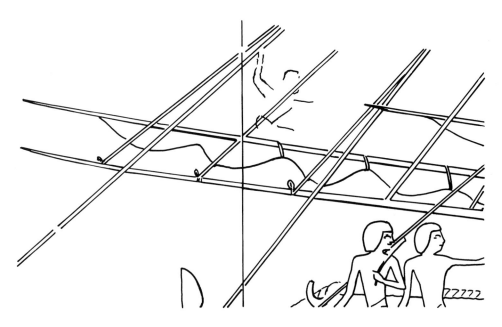

Figure 2.30. Detail of a furled sail (after Naville 1898: pl. 72)

on Hatshepsut's obelisk barge, as support for a ship in the midst of being launched and, on occasion, on Nile ships (Figs. 2.27; 10.9).[102] No anchors are portrayed on these ships.[103] This led G. A. Ballard to the unlikely conclusion that they had none.

The ships have a single pole mast stepped in the ship's center. Sølver reconstructs this as an A-shaped bipod mast like those on Sahure's ships (Figs. 2.3, 2.28).[104] His argument was based on the assumption that the hogging truss always disappears *behind* the mast. This is simple artistic convention, however. It is similar to the bowstring and drawn arrow in Egyptian art passing behind the body of

Figure 2.31. Bows of the ships depicted returning to Egypt (detail from Naville 1898: pl. 75)

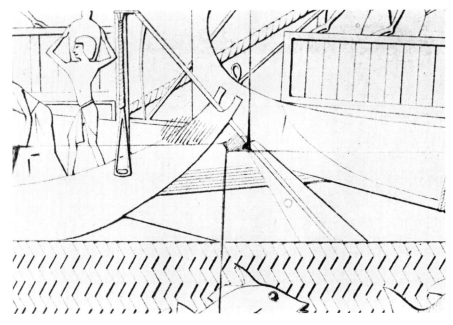

Figure 2.32. Detail of a ship's bow (from Naville 1898: pl. 72)

an archer, as, for example, when Ramses III draws his bow against the Sea Peoples (Fig. 8.1).[105] Had a bipod mast been intended, the Egyptian artist would have indicated it in the normal manner. Furthermore, the bipod mast went out of use in Egypt at the end of the Old Kingdom. There is no reason, or logical explanation, for it to suddenly reappear in the fifteenth century.

The masthead has an elaborate construction to carry the rigging (Fig. 2.29). Faulkner believes the masthead was misunderstood by the artists and that it consisted of a metal cap or sheath with eyes that carried the standing and running rigging.[106] The masthead, seen from behind, had eyes on either side to take the lifts. Above these was a mast cap formed by three horizontal bars connected to the mast and joined at their extremities by vertical side pieces. The halyards ran through the lower part of this construction. The upper part held a single pair of running lifts, used when the sail was in the raised position. This form of masthead seems to have developed from simpler Middle Kingdom forms that lacked the upper mast cap.[107]

The yard is horizontal when in the raised position and curves upward at its extremities when lowered. Both yard and boom were constructed of two timbers lashed together at the center. The boom was lashed to the mast to prevent the spillage of wind; the sail was spread by raising the yard to the masthead. The boom was sturdy: crew are occasionally shown standing and sitting on it (Figs. 2.15, 18, 30).[108]

The sail is low and wide, forming a horizontal rectangle: depicted parallel to the hull, it approximates the ship's length. A boom may have been required for a sail of such large span.[109] The foot of the sail could not have been spread by regular sheets because these would tend to pull inward so much that the wind would have spilled out at the sail's foot. This is not the primary reason for the boom's appearance, however, for it appears earlier on tall, narrow sails (Fig. 2.10: A).[110] When lowered, the sail appears to have been detached from the boom and furled to the yard (Fig. 2.30).

With a following wind the sail was placed perpendicular to the hull, but the exaggerated spread must have been difficult to manage even in moderate seas.[111] When sailing without cargo, these ships must have been heavily

Figure 2.33. Detail of a midship section of one of Hatshepsut's seagoing ships (from Naville 1898: pl. 74)

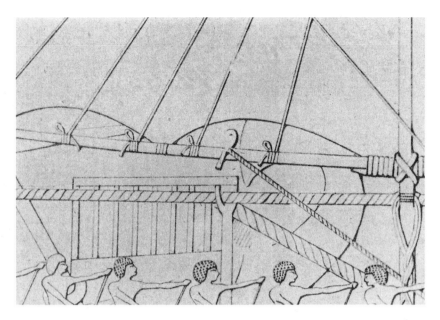

Figure 2.34. Detail of a boom and associated rigging (sheet and lifts) (from Naville 1898: pl. 73)

ballasted to prevent them from capsizing.[112]

Despite the seeming exactness of the relief, not all the rigging is shown. A pair of forestays, a single backstay, and two halyards give the rig longitudinal support. The forward stay is attached to the hull, perhaps by means of a beam, in an area where cables girdle the hull (Fig. 2.31). In several cases the loop of a knot is visible (Figs. 2.31–32). The second forestay seems to have been attached to the same beam as the hogging truss. The lone backstay is fastened to the hull just forward of the quarter rudders (Fig. 2.26). The halyards are portrayed as thick, braided ropes. A detail of the knot attaching the halyards to the yard appears on one ship (Fig. 2.33). Although the knot to the right of the mast is indistinguishable, the one on the left is perhaps a clove-hitch. If so, this is curious, for this knot is poorly suited for such a purpose.

When the yard was in its raised position, running lifts held it horizontal. At Deir el Bahri the running lifts end at the masthead (Fig. 2.29). A painting of a New Kingdom Nile ship shows how these worked,

however.[113] Here, four thick, wavy lines descend from the masthead to the stern. Landström suggests that these represent pairs of halyards *and* running lifts.

The multiple lifts connecting the boom to the yard are the most distinguishing characteristic of this rig. Some of the more detailed representations of the knots attaching the lifts to the boom show the lines turned several times around the yard or boom (Fig. 2.34).[114] The lifts supporting the yard were stretched taut when the yard was lowered (Figs. 2.16–17). When the sail was set they hung loosely in pendant arcs that Hatshepsut's artists depicted in elongated form for aesthetic simplicity (Figs. 2.15, 18).

The purpose for these multiple lifts has been variously interpreted. Ballard and Sølver believe that the lifts served mainly for supporting men aloft in the rigging.[115] R. Le Baron Bowen argues that the lifts were used primarily for *raising* the sail.[116] At that time, in his opinion, they were set up hard, bending the boom up sharply along its entire length. This made the sail slack, easing the weight of

the boom off the sail while it was being raised. Once the sail was in the raised position, the boom lifts were loosened and the weight of the boom pulled the sail taut. The lifts' original purpose may have been to give support to the boom and sail if they dipped in the water when the ship rolled.[117]

Braces and sheets appear on only one ship (Figs. 2.15, 34). The braces are tied to the yard midway between yardarm and mast on either side; the sheets are tied even closer to the mast on either side of the boom.[118] These lines would have been difficult to handle when tied so near to the center of the yard and boom; their positioning may result from artistic considerations.

The ships are steered by a pair of quarter rudders carried on stanchions, operated by vertical tillers (Fig. 2.26). The loom passes through a vertical crutch that is secured by a plain lashing and a rope tackle attached to a stud on the hull's exterior.[119] The manner by which the ships are being rowed has received several interpretations.[120]

Quarter rudders show an interesting development on Egyptian Nile River vessels.[121] The steering oars were originally levered against the side of the stern.[122] The broad overhanging sterns of Nile craft would have aided in this manner of steering. From the Sixth Dynasty, the steering oar was bound in place and was turned on its axis.

Tillers appear slightly earlier, in the Fifth Dynasty. By lengthening the tiller, the helmsman had better leverage over the oar. Because tillers are lacking on Sahure's or Unas's ships, they were probably invented after their reigns. Stanchions also appear first in the Fifth Dynasty. By placing the oar's loom on a stanchion, the helmsman no longer had to hold the loom. The introduction of stanchions and tillers made superfluous the stationing of multiple steering oars on both sides of a vessel. Presumably, this innovation was also adopted on Egyptian seagoing ships at that time.

The ships returning from Punt carry the cargo on deck (Figs. 2.17–18, 26, 33). This may be a result of the artists' desire to illustrate the valuable commodities brought back while, in reality, the cargo would have been stowed lower in the hull.[123] Indeed, the trade items brought to Punt and off-loaded there by the expedition are not shown on the outgoing journey.

These craft, however, may have normally carried their cargo primarily on deck. J. Hornell, describing the hulls of modern Sudanese cargo *nuggars*, notes that they agree in all details of construction with the Dahshur boats.[124] The breadth of both is exceptionally great while depth is reduced to a minimum to facilitate navigation in shallow waters.[125] In section, the hull resembles almost the perfect arc of a circle. This is the counterpart of a shallow, rounded arch in architecture.[126] It affords strength to maintain original curvature when under considerable pressure. It also enables the hull to carry heavy loads without suffering distortion or damage that would otherwise occur due to water pressure exerted on the exterior when the craft was heavily laden.

In Nile *nuggars*, the greater part of the cargo is often stored on and above deck level.[127] Hornell notes that C. D. Jarrett-Bell is theoretically correct in suggesting that the curves of the Dahshur boats indicate that they would have normally carried their load on deck; such also may have been the case with Hatshepsut's Punt ships.[128]

MEDINET HABU. Four Egyptian ships portrayed on Ramses III's mortuary temple locked in a naval

Figure 2.35. Ship E.1 in the naval battle at Medinet Habu (Ramses III) (photo by B. Brandle)

battle with the Sea Peoples' ships are generally considered seagoing vessels (Figs. 2.35–42).[129] This is perhaps due to the misconception that the battle took place at *sea*; in reality it probably took place in the Nile Delta.[130] The ships are portrayed in a summary fashion and lack detail. The scene was painted in colors that have long since disappeared. Because the Egyptian artists did not differentiate between incised and painted detail in their reliefs, and as the scene seems to have gone through several drafts, much information may have been lost (Fig. 2.36: C–D).[131] The ships are apparently four depictions of the same ship with varying detail. In profile they are long and low with a crescentic hull. Above the hull is a light bulwark that protects the rowers.

The impossible manner in which the human figure in ship E.1 is placed, leaning over the line that represents the junction of the sheer and the light bulwark, need not be a result of artist's error (Fig. 2.36: A: A). As H. Schäfer notes, in Egyptian art one sometimes receives the impression that part of a person's body is disappearing behind a structure.[132] At first, this

would appear to be drawn according to modern perspective, directly from a mental image. However, such was not always the case. In one example offered by Schäfer, a man is looking out of the door of a ship's cabin with half his body protruding—but the body begins at the *outside* edge of the door post.[133] The position of the figure in ship E.1 is apparently also a result of this phenomenon in Egyptian art.

Faulkner and Casson consider Ramses's vessels to be influenced by foreign construction and totally different from earlier Egyptian ships.[134] However, Ramses's ships seem to be basically a variant of a type of Eighteenth Dynasty traveling ship exemplified by models from the tombs of Amenhotep II and Tutankhamen (Figs. 2.19–23; 3.18). But none of Ramses's ships in the relief show the differentiation between the posts and the hull that is depicted on Hatshepsut's Punt ships or the models.[135] Either Ramses illustrates a different type of ship or the artists have consistently left out—or depicted in paint, now obliterated—details that would clarify this question. Perhaps the hulls of Ramses's ships were spoon-shaped, like the

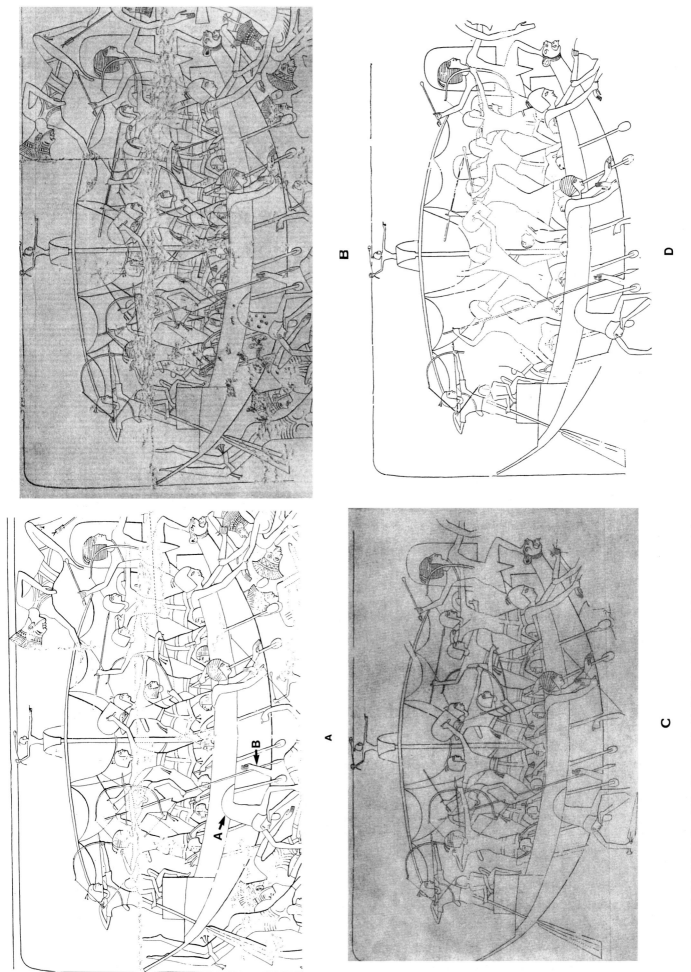

Figure 2.36. (A) Ship E.1, Medinet Habu (Ramses III); (B) ship E.1 with all visible lines depicted; (C) the portion of the ship that appears to belong to a first draft; (D) the parts of ship E.1 that may reasonably be assigned to its revised draft. (A detail from Nelson et al. 1930: pl. 39; introduction © 1930 by the University of Chicago, all rights reserved. Published June, 1930. B–D details from Nelson 1929: 27 fig. 18, 28 fig. 19, 29 fig. 20; © 1929 by the University of Chicago. All rights reserved.)

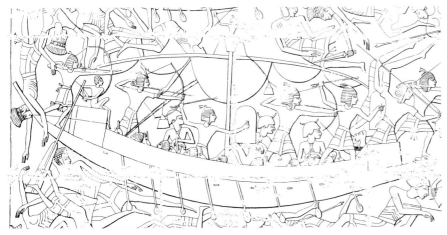

Figure 2.37. Ship E.2, Medinet Habu (Ramses III) (detail from Nelson et al. 1930: pl. 39; introduction © 1930 by the University of Chicago, all rights reserved, published June, 1930)

Figure 2.38. Ship E.2 in the naval battle at Medinet Habu (Ramses III) (photo by B. Brandle)

Figure 2.39. Ship E.3, Medinet Habu (Ramses III) (detail from Nelson et al. 1930: pl. 39; introduction © 1930 by the University of Chicago, all rights reserved, published June, 1930)

Figure 2.40. Ship E.3 in the naval battle at Medinet Habu (Ramses III) (photo by B. Brandle)

hull of several other models from Tutankhamen's tomb.[136]

The stempost of Ramses's ships ends in a lion's head with a Syro-Canaanite head in its mouth; the sternpost continues the curve of the hull. Faulkner thought the ships had a raised gangway.[137] Each of the ships has castles at bow and stern. The sterncastle is at least partially roofed, for the helmsmen are repeatedly shown seated on top of it and the archers stand in it. The butt ends of through-beams appear on three ships, E.2–E.4 (Figs. 2.37–42).

The actual length of these ships is difficult to determine. The figures are clearly depicted at a scale larger than the ships, and the number of rowers varies from eight (ships E.1 and E.2) to eleven men (ship E.4) on each side.

A single helmsman steers each ship with a lone quarter rudder. The rudder is attached to a stanchion that appears on at least one ship (E.3), but the vertical rectangle that constitutes the stern part of the sterncastle on ship E.2 may also be a rudder stanchion (Figs. 2.37–39). The tiller is short and straight, like those used in the Fifth through Eleventh Dynasties.[138] The helmsmen grip the quarter rudder in an unusual manner (Fig. 8.9).[139] The short tiller is always held in the right hand, and on three ships (E.1–E.3), the helmsmen either hold the loom in their left hands or cradle it in their arms. The need for this is unclear.

The rig used by the Egyptian ships is identical to that of the Sea Peoples' ships appearing in the same scene. In place of the boom-footed rig, the ships carry brailed sails.[140] One can only speculate whether the unusual Egyptian custom of attaching the brail fairleads to the after side of the sail began at this time.[141] The mast ends in a crow's nest, from which slingers

Figure 2.41. Ship E.4, Medinet Habu (Ramses III) (detail from Nelson et al. 1930: pl. 39; introduction © 1930 by the University of Chicago, all rights reserved, published June, 1930)

Figure 2.42. Ship E.4 in the naval battle at Medinet Habu (Ramses III) (photo by B. Brandle)

hurl stones at the invaders. This is the earliest depiction of a crow's nest on an Egyptian ship.

Discussion

The Seagoing Vessels of Punt

An unnamed tomb at Thebes (T. 143; Amenhotep II) contains a unique scene of a watercraft from Punt bringing trade items (Figs. 2.43–44).[142] The accompanying text notes, "Making rich provision (?) . . . gold of this district (Punt?) together with gold of the district of Koptos and fine gold (?) in enormous amounts."[143] The items brought by the Puntites include gold, incense, ebony, trees, ostrich feathers and eggs, skins, antelopes (?), and oxen. This scene also shows people of Punt bringing their cargo to an Egyptian port, perhaps Quseir on the Red Sea, where the Egyptians bartered with them. The background of the scene is pink—as is the land of Punt in the Deir el Bahri display. Norman de Garis Davies feels that this represents the inhospitable Red Sea coast.

The hulls portrayed are narrow and rectangular with rounded ends, colored pink like the background. Obviously, these craft were unfamiliar to the Egyptian artists. Davies suggests that they are coracles; alternately, they may depict dugouts. The figures and items of trade are portrayed above the body of the vessel rather than in it, perhaps because of a desire to show them in their entirety.

The rig is very simple and is similar to that used on some Old Kingdom ships.[144] It consists of a single yard with a triangular sail of black cloth or matting. No outrigger is shown, but if these craft were dugouts, an outrigger would have been necessary to prevent them from capsizing when a sail was used. Interestingly, the much later *Periplus of the Erythraean Sea* repeatedly mentions similar small-scale trade taking place in various types of rafts and other small craft in the lowermost area of the Red Sea.[145]

The Egyptian Ship Graffiti at Rod el ᶜAir

Turquoise, the Egyptian *mfk3t*, was considered particularly valuable in pharaonic Egypt. The Egyptians went to considerable effort to mine it in southwest Sinai. During the Middle and New Kingdoms the center of turquoise mining was at Serabit el Khadem, where the Egyptians built a temple to Hathor, the goddess of turquoise.

The Egyptian expeditions reached the plateau of Serabit el Khadem via Wadi Rod el ᶜAir, where a base-camp has been found.[146] The smooth rock faces of the wadi contain numerous hieroglyphic inscriptions and graffiti. These include a unique group of Egyptian ship graffiti that is of particular interest to pharaonic seafaring: it is at present the only such group known that was drawn by Egyptians outside the geographic borders of Egypt and separated from it by a sea.

There are indications that, at times, the Egyptians reached Sinai by ship. The "Tale of the Shipwrecked Sailor" indicates that, in the Middle Kingdom, expeditions were sent to the mines of Sinai by ship. Further evidence of this is found in the various nautical titles that appear at Serabit at that time.[147] The port at Wadi Gawasis was apparently a starting point for

Figure 2.43. *Reception of a Puntite expedition on the shore of the Red Sea. From an unnamed tomb (T. 143) at Thebes (Amenhotep II) (from Säve-Söderbergh 1946: 24 fig. 6)*

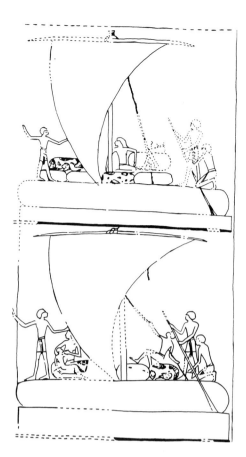

Figure 2.44. *Detail of the Puntite watercraft (after Davies 1935: 47 fig. 2)*

crossing the Red Sea to Sinai during the Middle Kingdom.[148] A New Kingdom port was identified by W. F. Albright at Merkah, south of Abu Zneimeh, on the west coast of Sinai.[149] Therefore, the Rod el ᶜAir graffiti *may* represent the seagoing ships that transported the expeditions across the Red Sea. None of them has been studied in a nautical context; some have never been published. During a visit to the site in 1972, I studied thirteen ship graffiti described below, of which eight have been previously discussed by A. H. Gardiner and T. E. Peet.

SHIP NO. 1. Ship facing left; dated by Gardiner and Peet to the Middle Kingdom (Figs. 2.45, 48: A).[150] This crude graffito has only three elements: the hull, the steering oar, and its stanchion. The hull is crescentic; the long steering oar passes over the sternpost. No tiller is visible.[151] There are several undecipherable hieroglyphic signs over the hull; above it is a Middle Kingdom inscription. This graffito probably represents a Middle Kingdom traveling ship (Fig. 11.3).[152]

SHIP NO. 2. Ship facing right; dated by Gardiner and Peet to the Middle Kingdom (Figs. 2.46, 48: B).[153] The crescentic hull has an unusual tripartite stem. The large steering oar is placed over the sternpost and rests on a large stanchion. A rectangle in front of the stanchion may represent a cabin.[154] In the center of the hull is an enigmatic object that may be either a three-legged oryx or an unsuccessful attempt to portray a lowered mast above a central deck structure. Several obscure signs are incised under the stern. Above the hull is a horn-shaped object that is probably unrelated to the ship.

SHIP NO. 3. Ship facing right; dated by Gardiner and Peet to the Middle Kingdom (Figs. 2.47, 48: C).[155] The graffito is schematic. The hull is crescentic with a steering oar placed over the sternpost and supported on a stanchion. A series of five parallel lines rising in the bow may represent a baldachin like those on ships from the tomb of Amenemhet at Beni Hassan.[156] The graffito apparently represents a Middle Kingdom traveling ship.

Three figures are on and above the boat: an archer stands in the center of the hull and faces the bow, a figure positioned above the steer-

ing assembly faces the prow with staff and scepter in his hands, and a figure to the right of the craft faces the stern and brings an offering of bread and a bird. The last figure bears the inscription "Serving man, (*wbȝ*) Bed, beloved of Hathor."

SHIP NO. 4. Ship facing left; dated by Gardiner and Peet to the Middle Kingdom (Fig. 2.49).[157] This schematic graffito consists of only three lines. The hull is crescentic with a large steering oar supported on a stanchion placed over the sternpost. To the right are several undecipherable signs. Like numbers one through three, this graffito represents a Middle Kingdom traveling ship.

SHIP NO. 5. Two ships facing right; dated by Gardiner and Peet to the New Kingdom (Fig. 2.50).[158] The leftmost ship has a crescentic hull positioned above an elon-

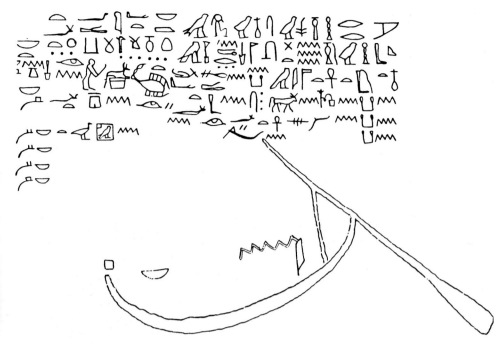

Figure 2.45. Ship graffito no. 1 (Rod el ʿAir) (from Gardiner and Peet 1952: pl. 93: 502–503)

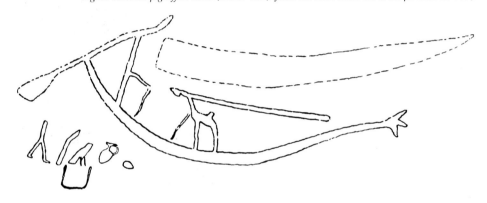

Figure 2.46. Ship graffito no. 2 (Rod el ʿAir) (from Gardiner and Peet 1952: pl. 93: 506)

Figure 2.47. Ship graffito no. 3 (Rod el ʿAir) (from Gardiner and Peet 1952: pl. 93: 507)

gated rectangle (plinth?) that is bisected horizontally in its left half. The mast is stepped amidships and appears through the central deck cabin and bisects the horizontal rectangle beneath the ship. The steering oar is placed over the stern; a tiller is connected to the tip of the loom so that a helmsman would have steered from the roof of the cabin.[159]

The rightmost ship has a crescentic hull with a cabin amidships and a baldachin at the bow. The steering oar is placed on the quarter.

Below the ships are two inscriptions: "Setekhnakhte, true of voice" and "engraver Ḥuy, true of voice." The midships cabin on both ships, the mast stepped amidships in the left ship, and the steering oar placed over the quarter in the right ship support a New Kingdom date for these ships.

SHIP NO. 6. Ship facing right; dated by Gardiner and Peet to the Middle Kingdom (Fig. 2.51).[160] This graffito has a well-drawn crescentic hull. The steering oar is placed over the sternpost and is supported on a tall stanchion. A long vertical tiller is attached to the loom abaft its junction with the stanchion. This is a typical Middle Kingdom feature as is the horizontal quarterdeck for the helmsman beneath the rudder (Fig. 11.3).[161]

A cabin in the stern abuts the rudder stanchion. The mast has been unstepped and lies horizontally on two crutches. In the bow, a quadruped faces forward.[162] To the right of the ship are quarry marks and the figures of a deer and an ostrich. The ship is located beneath a Middle Kingdom inscription, "He who wishes to return (home) in peace says: 'Cool libation, burning offering and incense to the intendant Neferḥotep.'"[163] The graffito depicts a Middle Kingdom traveling ship.

SHIP NO. 7. Ship (facing right?); this graffito is dated to the Middle or New Kingdoms by Gardiner and Peet (Figs. 2.52–53).[164] The hull is a narrow crescent. A vertical line at the left side of the hull probably represents a rudder stanchion. A man standing amidships faces right. Over him is the hieratic inscription "Senwosret." Beneath the hull is the New Kingdom proper name "Sunro"; this is palimpsest over an earlier effaced inscription.

A giraffe is incised to the left of the craft and faces it. A lugged ax has been incised horizontally across the giraffe and the figure in the ship. Lugged axes have a long range of use beginning in the Second Intermediate period and continuing into the Graeco-Roman period.[165] At Rod el ʿAir, this ax graffito must date to the New

Figure 2.48. Rod el ʿAir (photomosaic). (A) Ship graffito no. 1; (B) ship graffito no. 2; (C) ship graffito no. 3 (photos by the author)

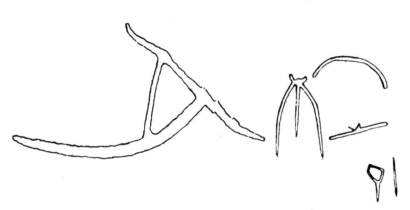

Figure 2.49. Ship graffito no. 4 (Rod el ʿAir) (from Gardiner and Peet 1952: pl. 94: 517)

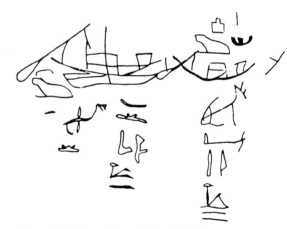

Figure 2.50. Ship graffito no. 5 (Rod el ʿAir) (from Gardiner and Peet 1952: pl. 95: 524)

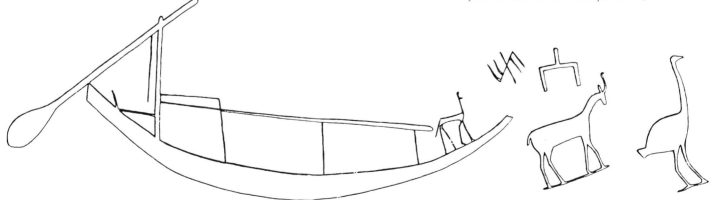

Figure 2.51. Ship graffito no. 6 (Rod el ʿAir) (from Gardiner and Peet 1952: pl. 95: 518)

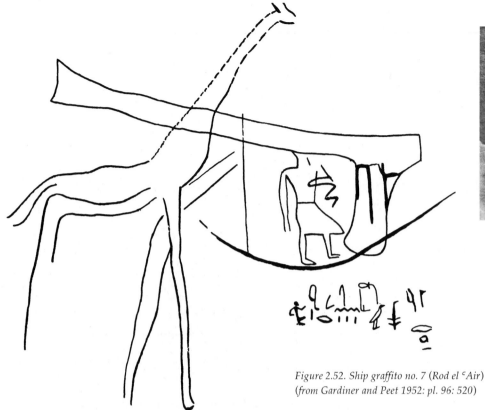

Figure 2.52. Ship graffito no. 7 (Rod el ʿAir)
(from Gardiner and Peet 1952: pl. 96: 520)

Figure 2.55. Ship graffito no. 9 (Rod el ʿAir)
(photo by the author)

Figure 2.53. Ship graffiti nos. 7 (center) and 8 (top right) (Rod el ʿAir) (photo by the author)

Figure 2.54. Ship graffito no. 8 (Rod el ʿAir)
(from Gardiner and Peet 1952: pl. 95: 521)

scription "Stone cutter Khab's son Ameny." A seated figure serves both as the boat's occupant and determinative of the name *Ameny*. The graffito is too schematic to date other than by the accompanying inscription.

SHIP NO. 9. Ship facing right; unpublished. Date: Middle Kingdom (Fig. 2.55). The crescentic hull is steered by a rudder placed over the stern and a tall stanchion. The oar's loom has a long vertical tiller that descends abaft the stanchion, as in graffito number six. A cabin nestles in the stern, forward of the stanchion. The mast is unstepped and lies horizontally. It passes over the cabin in the stern and rests on the stem and a crutch amidships. A small rectangle amidships probably represents the maststep.[167] The ship bears a striking resemblance to two traveling ships in the tomb of Amenemhet, reign of Sesostris I (Fig. 11.3).

SHIP NO. 10. Ship facing right; unpublished. Date: Middle Kingdom (Fig. 2.56). The ship is similar to number nine but lacks a stern cabin. It has a crescentic hull and a steering oar with a long loom resting on the sternpost and a tall stanchion. The vertical tiller is attached to the oar's loom abaft the stanchion. There is an unintelli-

Kingdom period of mining activity. To the right of the craft is a large cross (Fig. 2.53). The only reliable dating evidence for this ship graffito is the tall rudder stanchion that dates it to the Middle Kingdom.

SHIP NO. 8. Ship facing right; dated by Gardiner and Peet to the Middle Kingdom (Figs. 2.53 [upper right], 54).[166] The hull is a long, narrow crescent. Above it is the in-

gible mark near the tiller. The mast is unstepped and placed horizontally from stem to crutch.

Three unpublished New Kingdom traveling ships are carved on a single smooth rock scarp (Figs. 2.57–60). The three are stylistically very similar and may have been carved by the same hand. They are portrayed as being down in the bow.

SHIP NO. 11. Ship facing left (Fig. 2.58). The hull, portrayed in outline, is long and crescentic, narrowing to a line at the stem. There are faint marks of a low stanchion, mast, and yard. Amidships and at the bow, small portions of the hull have been worked, in a manner similar to graffito number twelve. This graffito was apparently never finished.

Beneath the stem is a lugged ax, identical to that above graffito number seven, and a figure, facing left, that holds a crescentic sword (?) and shield. Beneath the stern are two inscriptions:

Khnumḥotep, son of Ameny, born of Iby, living for ever.

his son ———— Woserᶜonkh[168]

SHIP NO. 12. Ship facing left (Fig. 2.59). The hull is long and crescentic; the artist has worked all the surfaces of the ship and its accoutrements. A large steering oar with a wide blade is placed on the quarter and supported by a short stanchion; the tiller is forward of the stanchion. The ship has a small deck cabin amidships and castles at stem and stern. A vertical stanchion of unclear function is located in the bow abaft the forecastle. Above the stem is a #-like sign. This graffito represents a traveling ship, probably with an elongated, spoon-shaped hull; it finds its closest parallels in the Eighteenth Dynasty.[169]

Figure 2.56. Ship graffito no. 10 (Rod el ᶜAir) (photo by the author)

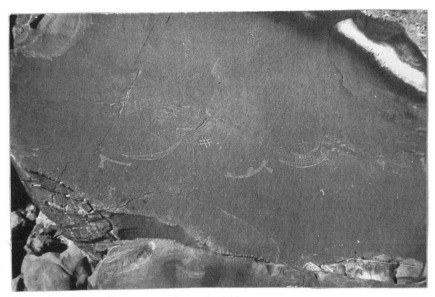

Figure 2.57. Ship graffiti nos. 11–13 (Rod el ᶜAir) (photo by the author)

Figure 2.58. Ship graffito no. 11 (Rod el ᶜAir) (photo by the author)

Figure 2.59. Ship graffito no. 12 (Rod el ᶜAir) (photo by the author)

Figure 2.60. Ship graffito no. 13 (Rod el ᶜAir) (photo by the author)

SHIP NO. 13. Ship facing left (Fig. 2.60). This is the most detailed of the three ships. It has a crescentic, spoon-shaped hull; the lower part of the hull is worked. Apparently the artist intended to work the entire surface of the hull but never completed the task. The hull ends in the stern in a recurving (decorative?) element. A large steering oar is placed on the quarter and supported by a short stanchion. The oar has a very wide blade; the tiller is connected to the loom forward of the stanchion. A large deck cabin, crossed by horizontal and vertical lines, is placed amidships. Landström suggests that deckhouses on New Kingdom traveling ships were made of a timber framework covered by highly decorated tent cloth.[170] This graffito seems to display just such a wooden framework.

The rectangle behind the cabin was probably intended as a flight of steps but was never finished.[171] Castles are located at stem and stern. The forecastle is crossed vertically by one line, the sterncastle by two. The mast is stepped amidships and passes through cabin and hull. The sail has been struck down: the yard, boom, and sail are secured in a crisscross pattern. No rigging is represented.

CHAPTER 3

The Ships of the Syro-Canaanite Littoral

The Iron Age Phoenicians are considered the seafaring merchants par excellence of the ancient world. This is largely because of the respect the Classical Greeks held for them as merchants and seafarers. But the Phoenicians were not new to the sea; their Syro-Canaanite ancestors had already come to know the Mediterranean intimately.[1]

The Textual Evidence

T. Säve-Söderbergh, in lauding Egyptian Mediterranean involvement, leaves little room for the Syro-Canaanites. At the same time, J. D. Muhly downplays the role of the Syro-Canaanite sea traders of the Late Bronze Age, arguing that Homeric references to Phoenicians in Mycenaean Greece must represent an Iron Age reality.[2] A significant role for Syro-Canaanites in maritime mercantile trading during the latter part of the Late Bronze Age was first proposed by G. F. Bass on the basis of the Cape Gelidonya shipwreck and Egyptian iconographic evidence and by J. M. Sasson based on the Ugaritic texts. The many texts dealing with maritime matters found in Ugarit, as well as in Egypt, indicate an in-

tense level of involvement in maritime trade by the Syro-Canaanite city-states among themselves and with other lands and cultures.[3]

Despite long-standing assumptions to the contrary, Homeric references to Phoenician (Syro-Canaanite) sea traders in Mycenaean Greece are entirely compatible with Late Bronze Age realities.[4] A review of the following textual, archaeological, and iconographic materials indicates that the Syro-Canaanites were particularly active—although most certainly not alone—as sea traders in the Late Bronze Age and possibly earlier.

In addition, it is important to emphasize that this seagoing trading ability did not translate into political power. Recent studies indicate that Canaan—modern-day Israel and Southern Lebanon—was politically and financially impoverished during the Late Bronze Age, when Syro-Canaanite sea trade was at its height.[5] The Syro-Canaanites, including the major trading "power" of Ugarit, did so at the pleasure of their Egyptian or Hittite overlords.[6] Thus, terming Ugarit—or any other Late Bronze Age Syro-Canaanite city-state, for that matter—a "thalassocracy" is a misinterpretation of the evidence.[7]

The Syro-Canaanites did not "rule the waves."

Most textual references to their ships refer specifically to heavily laden merchantmen with rich cargoes. During his expulsion of the Hyksos from Avaris, Kamose describes the capture of numerous Hyksos ships in which he found a wealth of trade goods.[8] This is the earliest known reference to trading ships definitely owned, and presumably constructed, by Syro-Canaanites: "I have not left a plank *under* the hundreds of ships of new cedar, filled with gold, lapis lazuli, silver, turquoise, and countless battle-axes of metal, apart from moringa-oil, incense, fat, honey, *itren*-wood, *sesedjem*-wood, wooden *planks,* all their valuable timber, and all the good produce of Tetenu. I *seized* them all. I did not leave a thing of Avaris, because it is empty, with the Asiatic vanished."[9]

Thutmose III supplies the next description of Syro-Canaanite ships when he describes his capture of two cargo-laden Syro-Canaanite merchantmen during his fifth campaign (year twenty-nine; 1450 B.C.): "Now there was a seizing of two ships, . . . loaded with everything, with male and female slaves, copper, lead, *emery,* and every good thing, after his majesty proceeded southward to Egypt, to his father Amun-Re, with joy of heart."[10]

The Amarna texts shed light on the Syro-Canaanite maritime trade in the mid-fourteenth century. Ships of Arwad and Ugarit are mentioned visiting Egypt.[11] Aziru promises to send his messenger, along with gold and various implements, to the pharaoh by ship.[12] The ship referred to presumably belonged to Aziru; i.e., it was Syro-Canaanite. Elsewhere, Biridiya of Megiddo reports that Surata of Acco has taken Labaia and has promised to send him by ship to Egypt.[13]

Documents from Ugarit contain references to traders from Arwad, Byblos, Beirut, Tyre, Acco, Ashdod, and Ashkelon stationed at Ugarit; these indicate significant interstate trade along the Syro-Canaanite coast.[14] One Ugaritic ship was wrecked in a storm near Acco while on a voyage to Egypt; another text mentions a ship that was lost (sank?) with a cargo of copper.[15] Idrimi, in relating the story of his life, tells how, after living among the Habiru for seven years at Ammiya, in the mountains above Byblos, he had ships built (at Byblos?) for his nautical invasion of the land of Muǵisse, thus gaining the throne of Alalakh.[16]

Ugarit's fleet just before its fall is impressive by any measure. One text refers to 150 ships that are to be dispatched.[17] In another, the Hittite king notifies "his son"—a vassal ruler or official—of the arrival of a hundred ships loaded with grain.[18] A third text indicates that during the Late Bronze Age, Syro-Canaanite ships were reaching—and being taxed—for voyages to the Aegean.[19]

The exchange of foreign words and personal names may also suggest contacts, although their meaning and significance are un-

clear. The name *Turios* appearing in the Linear B texts may indicate a connection with the city of Tyre.[20]

Several condiments listed in the Linear B tablets have Semitic names: cumin, kupairos, and sesame seed.[21] An unidentified "Phoenician" spice appears on two Linear B texts at Knossos.[22] Three other Semitic terms appear as loan words: *ki-to* (garment), *ku-ru-so* (gold), and *re-wo* (lion).[23]

The intensity of Late Bronze Age Syro-Canaanite sea trade continued right up to the time that the barbarians were literally at the gates of Ugarit. Some tablets were found adjacent to the "southern archive" in a kiln, in which they were being baked when Ugarit was destroyed.[24] Thus, they must date to the very last days of Ugarit. The tablets reveal a vibrantly active commercial entity, seemingly oblivious to the impending doom.

By the eleventh century, in the aftermath of the migrations that toppled the Late Bronze Age cultures, Egypt lost its political and nautical control over the Levantine coast.[25] Now Syro-Canaanites, perhaps together with the Sea Peoples as well, controlled the maritime trade between Egypt and the Syro-Canaanite coast.

When Wenamun arrived at Byblos, it was on a Syro-Canaanite (Phoenician) ship. This is evident from an argument in which Wenamun claims to have arrived on an Egyptian vessel. However, Tjekkerbaal, the king of Byblos, knew better.[26] Wenamun's comments may also allude to the frequency of ships on the Byblos-Egypt run. When he first arrived in the port, Tjekkerbaal ordered him to leave. Notes Wenamun:

And I sent (back) to him saying: Where should [I go]? . . . ⌈I⌉ go . . . If [you can find a ship] to transport me, let me be taken back

to Egypt. And I spent twenty-nine days in his h[arbor while] he daily [spent] time sending to me, saying: Get out of my harbor!

Now when he offered to his gods, the god took possession of a page (from the circle of) his pages and caused him to be ecstatic. He said to him: Bring [the] ⌈god⌉ up. Bring the envoy who is carrying him. / It is Amun who dispatched him. It is he who caused him to come. For it was after I had found a freighter headed for Egypt and after I had loaded all my (possessions) into it that the possessed one became ecstatic during that night, (this happening) while I was watching for darkness to descend in order that I might put the god on board so as to prevent another eye from seeing him.

The harbor master came to me, saying: Stay until tomorrow, so the prince says. And I said to him: Are you not the one who daily spends time coming to me saying: "Get out of my harbor!"? Isn't it / in order to allow the freighter which I have found to depart that you say: "Stay tonight," and (then) you will come back (only) to say, "Move on!"? And he went and told it to the prince, and the prince sent to the captain of the freighter, saying: Stay until tomorrow, so the prince says.[27]

Wenamun worried, lest he miss his ship and have to wait some time for another opportunity. In a later conversation with Tjekkerbaal, Wenamun refers again to waiting in the harbor of Byblos for twenty-nine days.[28] H. Goedicke suggests that the time periods mentioned by Wenamun may be a literary device.[29] He notes that twenty-nine days is one day short of a month, as the nine days Wenamun spent at Dor are one day short of a decade; thus, a solution arriving on the last day of a time unit might be meant to convey something happening "at the last moment." Even if this is correct, it is apparent that ships were not departing daily from Egypt to Byblos.

SHIP SIZES. *KTU* 4.40 lists the crews of three ships.[30] E. Linder notes that this must refer to rowing crews and points out the similarity with Linear B text An 1.[31] One ship, that of Abdichor, has a complement of eighteen crewmen recruited from three different locations. The crews of the two other ships listed on the tablet are damaged but may be reconstructed as containing eighteen men each. *KTU* 4.689 contains a list of ship's gear.[32] Included in the inventory are nine oars or nine pairs of oars. If the term used here for oars, *mṯṯm*, is indeed in the dual form, then the eighteen oars correspond to the crew of Abdichor's ship—assuming, that is, that each oar was pulled by a single rower.

Taken together, these texts suggest that a type of Ugaritic ship—we cannot determine which specific type as in both cases only the general term for ship (*any*) is used—had a rowing crew of eighteen oarsmen, nine to a side. Each rower would require a minimum *interscalmium* of about one meter. At the very least, an additional three meters in the bow and four in the stern would have been required to bring the hull planking in toward the posts.[33] Thus, a conservative estimate of the length of such a ship is fifteen to sixteen meters.

One text unearthed at Ugarit has been considered evidence for exceptionally large Syro-Canaanite seagoing trading ships. In it, the Hittite king requires the king of Ugarit to supply a ship for the transshipment of two thousand measures of grain from Mukish to Ura.[34] J. Nougayrol notes that the measurement referred to must be the *kor*; this calculates to a total burden of 450 tons.[35] Until recently, a tonnage of this size before the Roman period seemed excessively large. However, the recent discovery and excavation of a large merchantman from the early fourth century B.C., with an estimated length of twenty-six meters and beam of ten meters, require a revision of this assumption.[36]

How far back in time can this "gigantism" in merchant ships be traced? The technological knowledge to build ships of this size existed in the Late Bronze Age; an example was Hatshepsut's obelisk barge. Furthermore, the half-ton anchors found at Ugarit, Kition, and in the sea argue for Late Bronze Age ships of considerable tonnage, particularly considering that these vessels normally carried quantities of anchors.[37]

On the other hand, if traders of these proportions were being built in the Late Bronze Age, their use would have been problematic given the lack of harbor facilities that could have accommodated them along the coast of the Levant. Perhaps the writer of the text intended a form of grain measurement smaller than the *kor*.

The Archaeological Evidence

At the beginning of the Dynastic period, a number of strikingly Mesopotamian influences appeared in Egypt. Scholars have long believed that the Nile was invaded at that time by a seaborne migration.[38] The invasion route, it was argued, followed the Persian Gulf to the Red Sea, and the migrants entered the Nile valley by way of the Wadi Hammamat.

Considerable evidence now indicates that this contact came by way of the Mesopotamian trading colonies that existed in North Syria during the Late Uruk period and that these people must have arrived in Egypt by ship, for no evidence of their cultural equipment exists in Lebanon and Israel.[39] It is difficult to determine which, if any, of the many ship images preserved in Egypt from that period may depict the seagoing ships that carried these immigrants.

Concerning Syro-Canaanite seafarers in the latter part of the Bronze Age, A. Yannai has pointed out the possible significance of the appearance of Levantine Bronze Age smiting-god statuettes found in the Aegean, often in connection with shrines and sanctuaries. She writes:

Firstly, there is no doubt that the figurines have a religious significance. . . . Secondly, the Smiting-god is the only Levantine deity known from the Aegean, although a great variety of divinity figurines, male, female, coupled, seated and so forth are known from the Levant including Cyprus. Thirdly, they do not appear to have occasioned imitation in the Aegean.

An interpretation of the appearance of these votive figurines, like most problems involving religion, is speculative. It is nevertheless tempting to suggest that if the Smiting-god figurines indeed represent Resheph, and that god is connected with uncontrollable disasters which storms at sea most certainly are, and on at least one occasion he is mentioned with tempestuous waters, the god would be a likely candidate to protect seamen. Could then the figurines found in the Aegean be thank-offerings, presented by seamen for a successful voyage? In any case, their origin can again be as likely in Cyprus as further east.[40]

Recent discoveries support Yannai's conclusion. A smiting-god is depicted next to the ship on the Tell el Dab^ca seal, and a female statuette of apparent Syro-Canaanite origin, on the shipwreck off Uluburun, Turkey, may have been the ship's tutelary image.[41]

The Iconographic Evidence

Egypt

TELL EL DAB^CA. A Syrian cylinder seal from the eighteenth century B.C. found at Tell el Dab^ca in the eastern Nile Delta bears a representation of a ship, perhaps not unlike those captured two centuries later by Kamose (Fig. 3.1).[42] The site, identified as the Hyksos capital of Avaris, contains significant Middle Bronze Age II Syro-Canaanite material cultural remains.[43] Porada believes the seal is a copy of an actual Syrian cylinder seal made by a local seal engraver. Next to the ship is a Syro-Canaanite smiting weather god, similar to those discussed above. Porada, echoing Yannai's comments, notes that the god's proximity to the ship may identify him as a guardian of mariners.

The ship's hull is crescentic; one extremity curves gently outward while the other is vertical. The mast is positioned amidships. From the masthead fore and aft stays extend diagonally to the bow and stern. The heads of two figures are visible, one on either side of the mast. Two oars are positioned beneath the hull, adjacent to the figures.

TOMB OF KENAMUN. The tomb of Kenamun (T. 162) at Thebes contains the most detailed known scene of Syro-Canaanite ships (Figs. 3.2–6).[44] The deceased was the "Mayor of Thebes" and "Superintendent of the Granaries" under Amenhotep III.[45]

The scene is divided into three parts. The left third of the scene is a single register with four ships (Figs. 3.3–4). In the scene's center are two registers with seven ships docked at an Egyptian port (Figs. 3.5–6). To the right, the frenetic activities of shore trade are illustrated in three registers (Fig. 14.6).

Although Syro-Canaanite ships were probably reaching Thebes at the time that the scene was painted, the artists lacked actual knowledge of the ships themselves. Kenamun's scene was probably copied from stock scenes.

An understanding of the sources available to the Egyptian artist and of the mechanics involved in the decoration of Egyptian tombs is a necessity, if only to correctly interpret the ships appearing in the tombs. The Theban tombs exhibit numerous cases of scenes and details so similar in context that some form of relationship must have existed between them. There are two possibilities: either artists visited and copied earlier tombs or sets of original drawings existed, collected in some form of "pattern" or "copy"-books. It is possible to demonstrate beyond reasonable doubt that copybooks were indeed used in the creation of wall paintings in the Theban tombs during the Eighteenth Dy-

Figure 3.1. Ship on a Syrian cylinder seal from Tell el Dab^ca (eighteenth century B.C.) (after Porada 1984: pl. 65: 1)

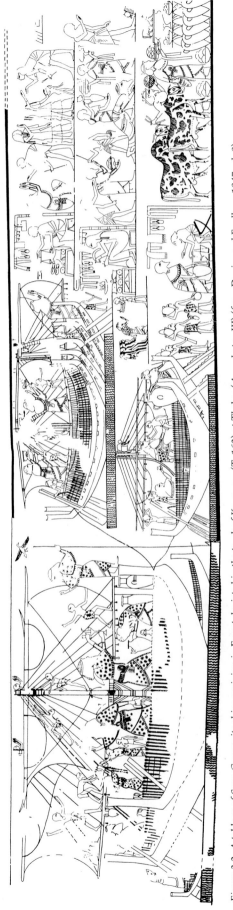

Figure 3.2. A tableau of Syro-Canaanite ships arriving in Egypt depicted in the tomb of Kenamun (T. 162) at Thebes (Amenhotep III) (from Davies and Faulkner 1947: pl. 8)

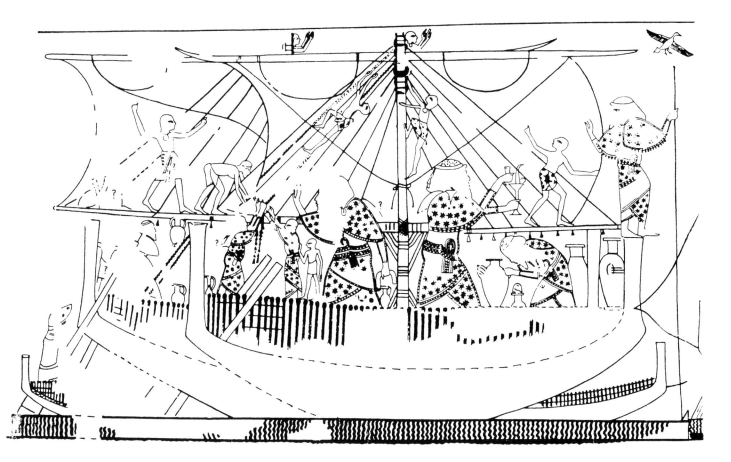

Figure 3.3. Detail of the ships in the left third of the register (from Davies and Faulkner 1947: pl. 8)

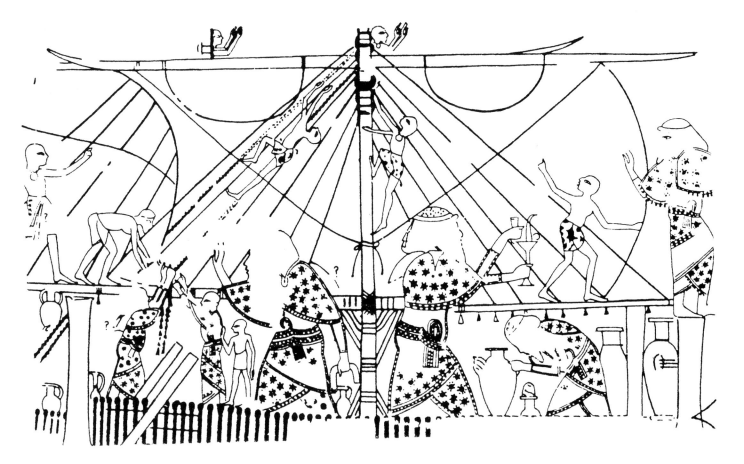

Figure 3.4. Detail of the deck area and rigging of a large ship on the left of the Kenamun scene (from Davies and Faulkner 1947: pl. 8)

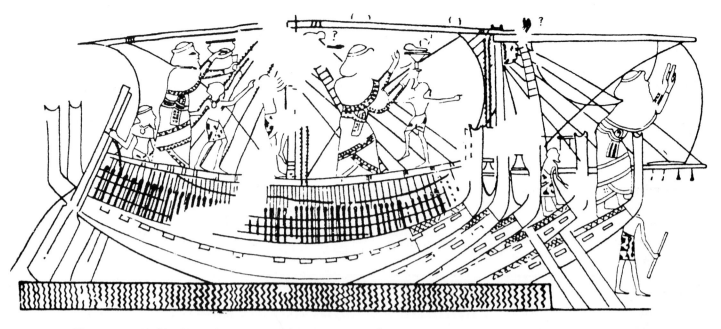

Figure 3.5. Detail of the ships at the upper center of the Kenamun scene (from Davies and Faulkner 1947: pl. 8)

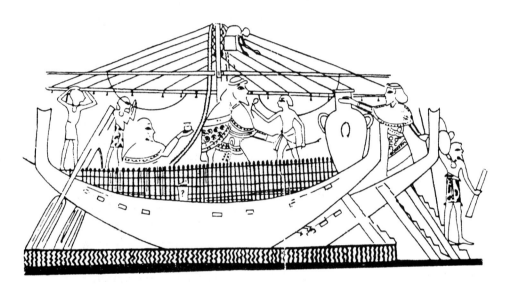

Figure 3.6. Detail of the ships at the lower center of the Kenamun scene (from Davies and Faulkner 1947: pl. 8)

nasty. If so, the artist(s) who painted the ships in Kenamun's tomb was at least once removed from his subject.[46]

The ships are depicted with crescentic hulls and with a particularly severe—perhaps exaggerated—sheer.[47] The vessels at the upper center have the most detailed hulls. The ship nearest the viewer has three strakes delineated with two butt joints: one between the stem finial and the hull, the other between two planks in the middle strake (Fig. 3.5). Butt joints are also visible between the stempost and the hull on the four other ships staggered behind it.

Some ships carry lacing along the sheer (Fig. 3.5). R. O. Faulkner believes this lacing ran the entire length of the ship, as in Sahure's seagoing ships.[48] But similar lacing, positioned at the extremities of the craft, are known from Middle Kingdom wooden ship models.[49] Therefore, this is best understood as an additional Egyptianizing el-

ement introduced by the artist, as, perhaps, are the single rows of through-beams (Figs. 3.5–6).

The stem- and sternposts are vertical with a slight external hollow. The posts' tops are flat or concave.[50] Because of Egyptian artistic conventions, it is not clear if they are portrayed frontally or in profile.[51] Vertical stemposts are known from New Kingdom Egypt on Hatshepsut's seagoing Punt ships as well as on river craft.[52] However, none of these have vertical sternposts. As noted above, vertical posts at stem and stern with straight outer and curving inner faces appear on Old Kingdom seagoing and cargo ships (Figs. 2.2–3, 5, 8, 9).

A screen runs the length of the ships at the sheer. The Uluburun ship seems to have had a wickerwork and post screen of this type.[53] Two rudders with short tillers are hung over the quarters.[54] There are no stanchions, but these must have existed on the actual ships to support the looms.

Säve-Söderbergh, Norman de Garis Davies, and Faulkner consider the ships in Kenamun's tomb to be Egyptian vessels.[55] This conclusion results partially from the many Egyptianizing hybrid elements that the artists infused into the ships.[56] The following compelling considerations indicate that the ships depicted in the tomb of Kenamun are Syro-Canaanite:[57]

• The ships' crews are Syro-Canaanite.[58]

• A similar ship, discussed below, appears in the tomb of Nebamun in a vignette showing the deceased ministering to a Syro-Canaanite. The artist clearly intended to indicate that the ship belonged to the foreigner.

• The ships lack hogging trusses.[59] Säve-Söderbergh believes that they were concealed by the high screen or simply omitted by the artist. The hogging truss may not be a true indicator of a New Kingdom Egyptian seagoing ship, however, if, after Hatshepsut, Egypt adopted keeled hulls. A large mast is stepped amidships. The bindings low on two masts may be wooldings (Figs. 3.4–5). If so, the masts were composite.[60]

The craft carry the typical boom-footed Late Bronze Age rig, best illustrated on Hatshepsut's Punt ships. One mast has a square-shaped crow's nest, and lookouts appear on the other craft, although the crow's nests themselves are hidden by the rigging (Figs. 3.6, 4–5). A row of triangles hanging beneath the boom on several ships may represent toggles for furling sail, or tassels (Figs. 3.3–6).[61]

The artists did not understand the workings of the ships' rigging. On several vessels the lifts appear as pendant arcs—a form these lines take when the yard is raised in this type of rig (Figs. 2.15, 18). Kenamun's artists did not connect the lifts to the mast in three cases; instead, *they are tied to the yard at both ends* (Figs. 3.3–5). In one case, the yard has been lowered (Fig. 3.6). In this position, the lifts would

have been drawn taut supporting the yard (compare Figs. 2.16, 17). The artist, however, has connected the yard and boom with two lifts that form pendant arcs, hopelessly confusing their purpose. Care is clearly required in interpreting these ships.

The ships' yards are straight. This may be an Egyptian hybrid element. Other representations of Syro-Canaanite rigs show yards that curve downward at their tips. The yard was raised and lowered by means of two halyards that are drawn as particularly thick wiggly lines. As in Egypt, when the sail was raised the halyards were tied astern, acting as additional backstays.

Braces appear on four ships (Figs. 3.3–5); once, they are tied to the lower mast. No sheets are visible, and stays are conspicuous by their absence—although the actual ships must have had stays.[62] Shrouds are absent. Cables attached to the lower part of the mast may have served in their place.[63] Rope ladders (?) run from the mastheads forward to the bows on two ships (Fig. 3.5).

Faulkner and L. Basch assume that Kenamun's ships furled their sails by hoisting their boom to the yard.[64] This is unlikely for the following reasons:

• In one case, the yard is shown hanging from its lifts while the halyards are slack (Fig. 3.6). This must indicate that the yard was lowered.

• The halyards of the largest and most detailed ship are held by two men standing in the ship's stern (Figs. 3.3–4). The halyards end at the yard and presumably were attached to it. If the boom was being raised, then the halyards should have continued down the sides of the mast and been tied to the boom.

• In one ship the boom is lashed

to the mast (Fig. 3.4). This would preclude moving it.

TOMB OF NEBAMUN. A second representation of a Syro-Canaanite craft is portrayed in a poorly preserved vignette in the Theban tomb of the physician Nebamun (T. 17). This shows the deceased examining a Syro-Canaanite merchant and probably portrays an actual event (Fig. 3.7).[65]

Nebamun's tomb dates to the reign of Amenhotep II; thus, this scene predates that of Kenamun's tomb by from thirty years to a century.[66] It is unlikely, therefore, that both scenes were painted by the same artist(s). Despite this, the ship is remarkably like those in Kenamun's tomb, raising the possibility that they were derived from a common source.

Two drawings of the ship, different in a number of details, have been published. In W. Müller's reproduction, the hull and other wooden parts are colored yellow, and the brown screen is intersected by a row of vertical lines.[67] The hull is crossed by two horizontal parallel lines that may represent planking seams (Fig. 3.8). These lines are intersected perpendicularly by a row of curved vertical lines. The latter are lacking on the drawing published by Säve-Söderbergh, who notes, however, orange lines on the yellow hull that may indicate the grain of the strakes (Fig. 3.9). The railing, colored red-orange, is identical to those on Kenamun's ships.

The craft's extremities curve smoothly upward from the keel, lacking the angularity of Kenamun's vessels; but, like them, the posts are undecorated. The sheer-line of Nebamun's ship seems more realistic than that of Kenamun's craft. An unusually narrow mast is stepped amidships. A square object situated at the masthead may represent either a crow's nest, like

Figure 3.7. Scene from the tomb of Nebamun (T. 17) at Thebes. A Syro-Canaanite ship appears at the left of the lowest register (Amenhotep II) (from Säve-Söderbergh 1957: pl. 23; © Griffith Institute, Ashmolean Museum, Oxford)

Figure 3.8. Müller's drawing of the Syro-Canaanite ship in the tomb of Nebamun (after Müller 1904: Taf. 3)

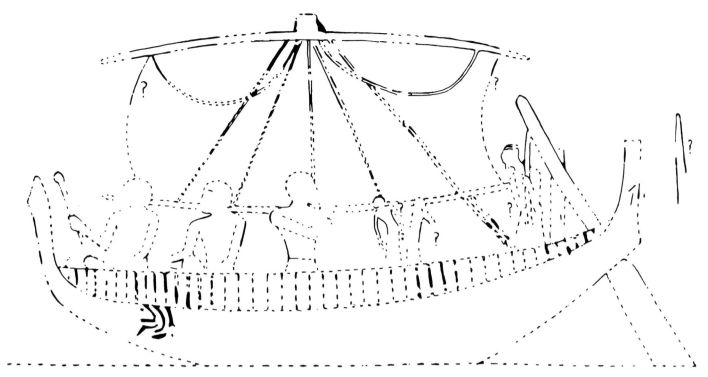

Figure 3.9. Detail of the ship (Säve-Söderbergh) (after Säve-Söderbergh 1957: pl. 23; © Griffith Institute, Ashmolean Museum, Oxford)

those on Kenamun's craft, or simply a mast cap. The raised yard curves down at the tips, a decidedly non-Egyptian trait.[68]

The boom is missing in a lacuna; in Säve-Söderbergh's drawing it is reconstructed. Two lines carried aft are probably halyards. The pendant arc of a single lift is attached to either side of the yard. Three diagonal lifts (two forward, one aft) support the boom. In Müller's reproduction, the port lift is attached to the mast at its lower junction with the yard. The starboard lifts continue up, crossing the yard, and seem to be connected to the square at the masthead.

A single quarter rudder is shown. It rests on a stanchion, an element notably lacking on the Kenamun ships. The tiller is attached above the stanchion, which is identical to the Egyptian New Kingdom form of quarter rudder (Figs. 2.23, 26).[69]

THE MNŠ SHIP. The peculiar determinative for the *mnš* ship, which appears in slightly different varia-

tions in five inscriptions of Ramses III on the temples of Abydos, Karnak, and Luxor, illustrates a ship of the type depicted in the tombs of Kenamun and Nebamun (Fig. 3.10). Säve-Söderbergh assumes that the determinatives depict an indigenous Egyptian ship type, later adopted by the Syro-Canaanites.[70] In fact, as the type appears earlier as distinctly Syro-Canaanite, it is clear that by the times of Ramses

II, this Syro-Canaanite ship variety was being built in Egyptian shipyards.[71] That these ships were merchantmen is clear from an inscription of Ramses II: "I have given to thee (Seti I) a ship (*mnš*), bearing cargoes upon the sea, conveying to thee the great [˹marvels˺] of God's-Land, and the merchants doing merchandising, bearing their wares and their impost therefrom in gold, silver and copper."[72]

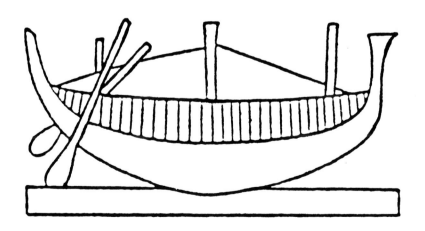

Figure 3.10. Determinative of the word mnš (Ramses II) (from Säve-Söderbergh 1946: 58 fig. 12)

The Syro-Canaanite Coast

DOR. In 1982 an ashlar stone incised with the fragmentary remains of what appears to be a (Syro-Canaanite?) ship's hull and rigging was found at Dor (Fig. 3.11).[73] The stone was in secondary use in a Hellenistic city wall. The rigging has numerous lifts and is clearly of the boom-footed type, giving the graffito a *terminus ante quem* ca. 1200 B.C.[74] It may represent a Syro-Canaanite ship.[75]

TELL ABU HAWAM. A schematic graffito incised on the outer surface of a bowl fragment from Hamilton's Stratum V at Tell Abu Hawam, dated to the fourteenth through thirteenth centuries B.C., is one of only two Late Bronze Age ship representations presently known from Israel (Figs. 3.12–13).[76] Two quarter rudders trailing at the left indicate that the ship is facing right. The bow is missing.

The hull is angled, showing a strong sheer. The four parallel lines that seem to compose it may represent an open bulwark. Alternately, they may be interpreted, from top to bottom, as the boom, the top of an open bulwark, the junction between bulwark and sheer, and the bottom of the hull. In the latter case, however, it is difficult to explain why the mast is terminated at the uppermost line. This horizontal line does not continue forward of the mast.

The graffito may never have been completed. Interpretation of the left extremity of the ship is difficult because of a large piece of grit in the sherd. This part is drawn very lightly, in contrast to the deeply incised lines of the rest of the hull, mast, and most of the yard. The mast is stepped amidships, ending at the first horizontal. The yard curves downward at the tips and seems to be connected in some form (brace?) to the upper two horizontals by their lightly drawn continuations at left. Al-

 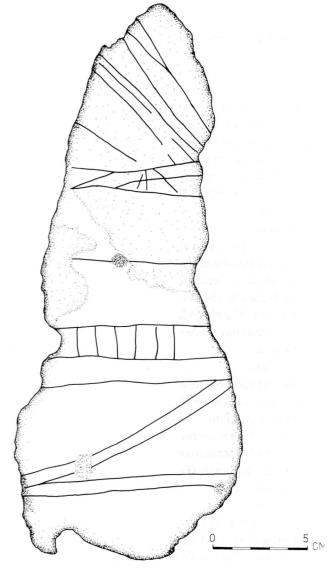

Figure 3.11. Ship graffito carved on plaster from Tel Dor (photo and drawing by the author. Courtesy of E. Stern)

Figure 3.12. *Photo of the Tell Abu Hawam graffito (courtesy of the Israel Antiquities Authority)*

downward. Slanting lines lead from the mast to stem- and sternposts. These may be either stays or lifts. They probably represent the latter, because lifts were the most prominent element in the Late Bronze Age boom-bottomed rig and were the most frequently represented part of the rigging.

The rigging of the second craft is enigmatic. The only vertical (mast?) is off-center, and the upper horizontal (yard?) is twisted in a pretzel-like configuration.

Cyprus

HALA SULTAN TEKE. A limestone ashlar block uncovered in a Late Cypriot IIIA1 context at Hala Sultan Teke bears a rough graffito of a Syro-Canaanite ship (Fig.

though it is unwise to read too much into such a small and schematic portrait, it does agree with other representations of Syro-Canaanite ships.

UGARIT. Two schematic ship representations are reported on a scaraboid seal found at Ugarit. In profile, the hulls appear as narrow rectangles bisected by a single horizontal line. The bottom line represents either the keel or the waterline. The central line probably indicates the sheer; the uppermost line may depict the top of an open bulwark, the boom, or perhaps both. The ships lack quarter rudders but have five oars.

One miniature contains all the main elements appearing on the more detailed representations of Syro-Canaanite craft. C. F. A. Schaeffer compares the two vertical lines of the mast on this ship to bipod masts common on Old Kingdom Egyptian craft (Figs. 2.2–3).[77] However, since bipod masts went out of use in Egypt at the end of the Sixth Dynasty, the double line is better understood as a massive pole mast.[78] The yard's ends curve

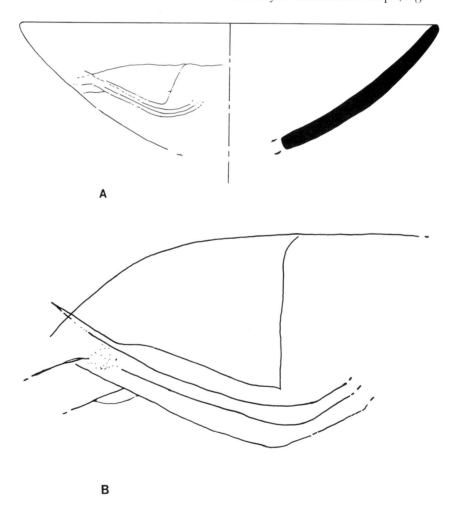

Figure 3.13. (A) *Line drawing of sherds with ship graffito found in Hamilton's excavation at Tel Abu Hawam (fourteenth–thirteenth centuries B.C.); (B) detail of the Tell Abu Hawam ship graffito (courtesy of the Israel Antiquities Authority)*

3.14).[79] At left, the hull curves smoothly upward, while the other end finishes vertically. A horizontal line above the right side of the hull may indicate the top of a screen or a boom, although there is no indication of a mast. In hull shape, this graffito is identical to the *mnš*-ship determinatives and thus represents a ship of that Syro-Canaanite class.

The graffito's particular interest is in its right extremity: it ends in a post with both a vertical internal edge and a decidedly hollow external edge. Although most pronounced in this illustration, this hollow outer post edge is identifiable on the ships of Kenamun, Nebamun, Ramses III's *mnš*-ship determinatives, and a terra-cotta ship model from Enkomi (Figs. 3.3, 8–10).

ENKOMI. The Enkomi model is of Late Cypriot I–II date; it comes from an unknown context at Enkomi (Fig. 3.15). R. S. Merrillees unconvincingly compares it to the three ship models from Kazaphani and Maroni *Zarukas* (Figs. 4.5–6, 8).[80] The model may be patterned after a Late Bronze Age Syro-Canaanite ship, for it bears a striking resemblance to the ship portrayed in the tomb of Nebamun, with a rockered keel and significant hollows on the outer edges of the identical stem- and sternposts. Doubt exists, however, concerning the date of the Enkomi model. Perhaps it is patterned after an Iron Age Phoenician craft. It bears more than a passing likeness to two eighth- or seventh-century B.C. models from Achziv and to Assyrian reliefs of Phoenician ships.[81]

An Iron Age date seems unlikely on archaeological grounds, however. By the eighth through seventh centuries, the great Late Bronze Age city of Enkomi had shrunken into a humble settlement. A single tomb at Kaminia is the only known architectural remains of that date, despite extensive excavations there.[82]

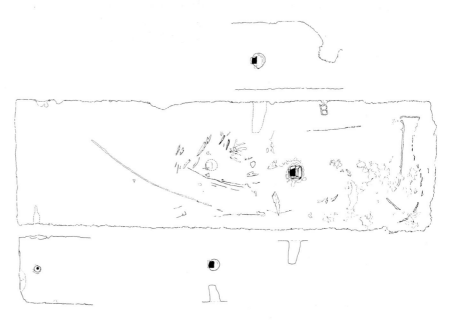

A

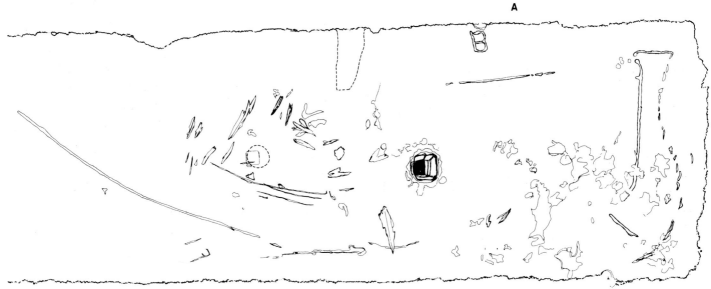

B

Figure 3.14. (A) *Ashlar block from Hala Sultan Teke with a graffito of a ship* (Late Cypriot IIIA1); (B) *detail of the ship graffito* (from Öbrink 1979: 73 fig. 103)

Characteristics of Syro-Canaanite Seagoing Ships

The iconographic evidence allows the following general conclusions about Syro-Canaanite seagoing ships:

• In profile the hulls are crescentic. There is little evidence upon which to base a length-to-beam ratio, although at least two sources —Kenamun and Nebamum—portray a class of trading ships. This argues for a fairly beamy vessel. The Enkomi terra-cotta, the only known model that may represent a Syro-Canaanite seagoing ship, is too problematic for conclusions on hull ratios.

• The ships' stem- and sternposts lack decoration. They may be more or less identical, both vertically oriented (ships of Kenamun and Nebamun, the Enkomi model, and perhaps the Ugarit seal), or the stem may be vertical while the sternpost rises as a gentle curve (*mnš*-determinative, Hala Sultan Teke, and Tell Abu Hawam, in which the bow is lacking). Vertical posts on these ships have a vertical inner edge and a hollow external edge.

• Rudders were placed on the quarters. Both single (Nebamun) and double (Kenamun and Tel Abu Hawam) quarter rudders are represented. The steering oars are fixed on stanchions (Nebamun) and have a tiller (Kenamun and Nebamun), an arrangement identical to that on contemporaneous Egyptian seagoing ships and on some Nile craft.

• A high screen or open bulwark ran the entire length of the craft from stem to stern. This is clearly indicated on the ships of Kenamun, Nebamun, and on the *mnš*-determinative; it may be inferred in the schematic representations from Tell Abu Hawam, Dor, and Ugarit.

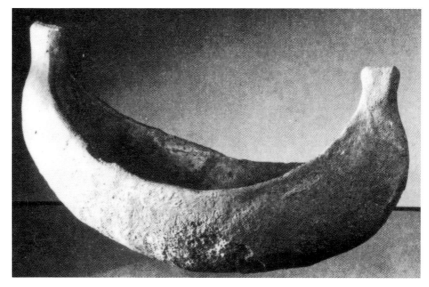

Figure 3.15. Terra-cotta ship model from Enkomi (surface find) (from Merrillees 1968: pl. 37: 1)

• The yard has downward curving ends in three (Nebamun, Tell Abu Hawam, and Ugarit) of the four illustrations that portray rigging. Apart from the yard, Syro-Canaanite craft seem to have used a similar rig, with boom and multiple lifts, as was common in Egypt. The two halyards were tied aft, serving as running backstays when the sail was raised, as was normal practice in Egypt.[83] Lateral cables took the place of shrouds.[84]

• Crow's nests appear first on Syrian ships (Kenamun and perhaps Nebamun). Thus, they seem to be a Syro-Canaanite invention.[85] Subsequently, the idea was borrowed by Egypt and the Sea Peoples (Figs. 2.37–44; 8.3–8, 10–12, 14). Rope ladders, if this is indeed what the Kenamun artists intended, appear in one scene only—and then disappear from sight until Classical times.[86]

• Oars appear on the ships depicted on seals from Tell el Dab^ca (two) and Ugarit (five).

Discussion

The "Keftiu" Ship

In Thutmose III's annals describing the stockpiling of the Canaanite harbors during his ninth campaign (year thirty-four; ca. 1445 B.C.) we read: "Behold, all the harbors of his majesty were supplied with every good thing of that ⌐which⌐ [his] majesty received [in] Zahy (*D^ʾ-hy*) consisting of Keftyew ships, Byblos ships and Sektw (*Sk-tw*) ships of cedar laden with poles, and masts together with great trees for the ⌐_ _ _⌐ of his majesty."[87]

"Keftiu" ships appear in only one other Egyptian text, also dating to the reign of Thutmose III.[88] Several of these craft are being built or repaired at the royal dockyard of *Prw nfr*.[89] S. R. K. Glanville considers them to be a class foreign to Egypt, apparently of Aegean origin.[90] Säve-Söderbergh and E. Vermuele assume them to be a class of Egyptian-built seagoing ships.[91] The origins of this class may be inferred from the following considerations:

• The ships were received as tribute from Canaan, suggesting that they were indigenous to that region.

• There was a distinct Syro-Canaanite presence at *Prw nfr*. Syro-Canaanite shipwrights worked there, and the gods Baal and Astarte were worshipped there.[92] One official was named *śbj-b^cl*, and a "chief workman" was named *Irṯ*—a name that Glanville identified as "the Arwadian." Other Syro-Canaanites at *Prw nfr* are assigned more menial tasks.[93]

There are two reasons for naming a ship class after a geographic area. A ship type may have been built by, copied from, or commonly used by the inhabitants of a specific region—as, for example, in the case of the Roman *liburnian*.[94] Alternately, it may have been used on a particular commercial run to a specific destination, like the "East Indiamen" and "Boston packets" of the recent past.[95] In these cases, the name always refers to a ship's destination.

There is no other evidence for an Aegean ship class being copied in Egypt, and it would be truly re-markable for Syro-Canaanite shipwrights to construct Aegean-style craft in Egypt.

One author assumes that "Egypt's famed Keftiu-ships appear to have ranged northward to Cyprus, Cilicia, Crete, Ionia, the Aegean islands, and perhaps even the mainland of Greece."[96] There is nothing to indicate, however, that Egyptian ships ever sailed farther than the north Syrian coast. On the other hand, Syro-Canaanite ships *were* making the run to the Aegean. This, along with the connection to Canaan and Syro-Canaanite shipwrights and religion in the texts, strongly suggests that the Keftiu ships were a Syro-Canaanite class commonly used on the Aegean run.[97]

Ships Misinterpreted as Syro-Canaanite

The Syro-Canaanite identity of several other ship representations is questionable. These include ship models found by M. Dunand at Byblos and an Egyptian relief. Because the Byblian models come from the Syro-Canaanite coast, they have been thought in the past to represent local craft.

BYBLOS. A terra-cotta model found at Byblos is perfectly symmetrical fore and aft and has a rounded, rather shortened shape (Fig. 3.16).[98] It is painted red and stands on a plinth reminiscent of those found at the base of some Egyptian Middle Kingdom wooden models.[99] A keel runs *inside* the full length of the hull, protruding horizontally at stem and stern (Fig. 3.17).[100] There are castles at both extremities. The ends of four through-beams protrude through the hull-planking on either side.[101] No frames are indicated.

Dunand believes the model represents a small Syro-Canaanite fishing boat. He compares it to Kenamun's ships and the large *mahons* that traded along the Syrian coast in the recent past. The two central through-beams he identifies as benches; the protruding beam ends at the model's extremities he considers *oculi*. He does not offer an identification for the external protrusions of the two central beams. J. G. Février also considers that the model represents a Syro-Canaanite ship and notes that, although internal frames are lacking, the through-beams must have strengthened the hull structurally.[102]

Basch identifies the model as a Late Bronze Age Syro-Canaanite merchantman but then compares it to the Sea Peoples' ships at Medinet Habu (Fig. 8.1). He notes that both the model and the relief depict ships that are symmetrical,

Figure 3.16. Terra-cotta ship model found in the excavations at Byblos (from Dunand 1937: pl. 140, no. 3306)

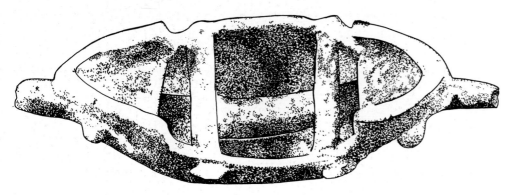

Figure 3.17. The interior of the hull of the ship model from Byblos (after Basch 1987: 67 fig. 122: B)

with castles at stem and stern. Basch concludes that the model's end projections are the continuation of the keel but then compares these prominent elements with undersized spurs that appear at the junction of sternpost and keel on ships N.4 and N.5 (Figs. 8.11: E, 12: A).[103] Basch considers the projections of ship N.4 to be at the ship's bow, while on N.5 it is at the stern. However, the position of the steering oars on the ships indicates that in both cases the projection is at the stern.[104]

I believe that this model copies a known Egyptian ship type, even though it was not made to scale or reduced uniformly in size. If the terra-cotta is "stretched," it bears a remarkable resemblance to the New Kingdom Egyptian traveling ship variety already discussed (Figs. 2.19–23; 3.18).[105] These vessels have long, drawn-out stem- and sternposts, castles at either end, and through-beams. This model, together with the Egyptian wooden models and depictions, suggests that these ships did indeed have keels but that amidships they protruded prominently inward—not outward—beneath the hull.[106]

The second terra-cotta model from Byblos has a flat bottom, a high sheer, and is crudely made (Fig. 3.19).[107] The stern has less overhang than the stem. A rectangular cabin, divided into two rooms, is located in the stern; its roof is flat and decorated in a checkered pattern. The interior of the craft is painted red, and the area of its caprail is ornamented with short incisions.

Dunand theorizes that the model was inspired by Nile boats. He is led to this conclusion by the model's width, its flat bottom, and the checker decoration on the cabin's roof. Février, followed by Sasson, believes that the model represents

Figure 3.18. Bow of a wooden traveling ship model with forecastle and stempost intact (from Landström 1970: 108 fig. 338)

a small but strong seagoing Syrian craft.[108] He tries to calculate the dimensions of the craft on which the model is based, assuming that the cabin was high enough to stand up in. From this, Février postulates a length of from eight to ten meters and a beam of between four and six meters for the model's prototype.

Calculations of this type are extremely tenuous when one is not dealing with scale models—a category that clearly does not include

this terra-cotta. Février further argues against Dunand's nilotic identification. He believes that the cabin was placed inside the hull rather than on a deck, as was customary in Egypt, to provide additional stability in a seagoing craft.

Février's uncritical evaluation and conclusions are unconvincing. The model bears no resemblance to known Bronze Age Syro-Canaanite seagoing boats. The cabin is placed inside the hull, probably more because of the tech-

Figure 3.19. Terra-cotta ship model found at Byblos (from Dunand 1937: pl. 140, no. 6681)

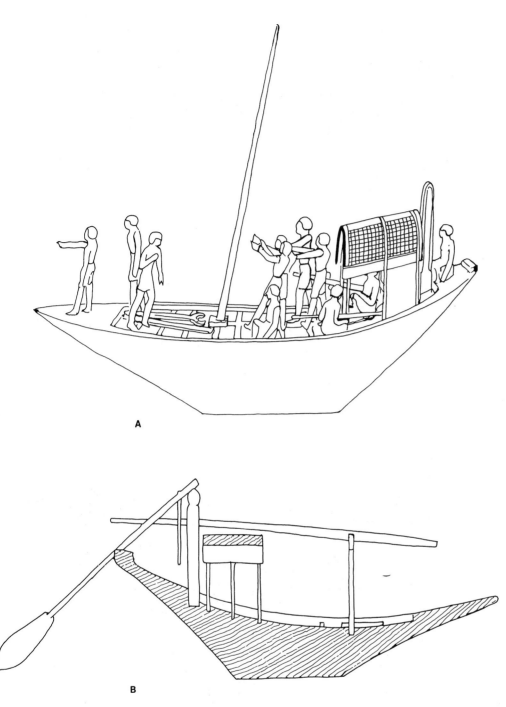

A

B

Figure 3.20. (A–B) Egyptian wooden models of Nile ships (First Intermediate period) (after Landström 1970: 74 figs. 219, 221)

cotta is a copy of an Egyptian river craft raises an interesting question: how was a local Byblian potter familiar with non-seagoing Egyptian craft? One possible explanation is that wooden Egyptian ship models found their way to Byblos through trade, or perhaps as part of the personal baggage of visiting Egyptian officials. Since such models were constructed of perishable materials, they would have left no trace in the archaeological record.

Several metal ship models were found at Byblos in the *Champ des offrandes*.[110] The best preserved of these is a craft of long and narrow dimensions dating to the eighteenth century B.C. (Fig. 3.21).[111] The model's hull is a thin plate of bronze flattened by hammering. The stem is pointed, the stern curved. The posts are not accentuated. Two through-beams are located at the bow and at the stern. Dunand assumes that the through-beam in the bow was used for stepping the mast. The stern beam acts as a base for the steering oar's stanchion. Metal ribbons attach the steering oar to the ship at the stanchion and the stern. The model is either patterned after an Egyptian model or is in itself Egyptian; its closest parallels are representations of Egyptian traveling ships of Middle Kingdom date (Fig. 11.3).[112] Metal ship models are also known from Egypt (Figs. 3.22–23).

In conclusion, Egypt's influence on Byblos during the second millennium is manifest in the ship models from that site, as it is in so many other areas. Unfortunately, these models add nothing to our knowledge of Syrian ships.

THE SHIPS OF INIWIA. A relief from the tomb of Iniwia dating from the Nineteenth to Twentieth Dynasties depicts three ships that have been compared with Hatshepsut's Punt ships (Figs. 3.24, 30: A).[113] These ships raise a number of

nical difficulties of constructing a deck than because of considerations of stability. Terra-cotta ship models with decks are exceptionally rare in the Bronze Age (Fig. 6.37).

The model is so similar to Egyptian traveling boats dating from the First Intermediate and Middle Kingdom periods, however, that Dunand's identification is almost certainly correct (Fig. 3.20). Even the division of the cabin into two compartments finds its exact Egyptian parallels.[109]

The conclusion that this terra-

problems, however. We know that Egyptian artists could combine elements of different objects in their depictions to create nonexistent "hybrid" items.[114] Because of this peculiarity of Egyptian art, objects, human figures, and even entire scenes were composed by uniting elements from two or more sources. For example, Davies, commenting on the decorations seen on several gold vessels taken as booty from Syro-Canaanite kingdoms during the Nineteenth Dynasty, notes that these decorations are unified in a single item (Fig. 3.25: A).

Obvious hybrid copies of these items are found in depictions on booty taken during the Libyan wars of Seti I and Ramses II. The decorations on these vases, albeit clever creations, are variations on the same themes used for the Syro-Canaanite vessels (Fig. 3.25: B). To these decorations the artist has included additional Egyptian and Aegean motives. Davies discounts the validity of these "Libyan" vessels.[115]

Thutmose III's "botanical garden" in the temple of Amun at Karnak is another interesting example of "hybridism" (Fig. 3.26). Some 275 examples of animals, birds, and plants from the Syro-Canaanite littoral are depicted on the walls of this chamber. Although the birds are portrayed with particular accuracy, such is not the case concerning the flora. Some of the plants are depicted accurately, but other "specimens" are either based on imprecise memory or are clever inventions.[116]

Another fascinating example of hybridism is found in the scene of foreign tribute and trade depicted in the tomb of Menkheperresonb, dating to the latter part of Thutmose III's reign.[117] With the exception of the first three figures, who are typical Syro-Canaanites, all the men portrayed in Register I are

Figure 3.21. A bronze (?) ship model from Byblos (ca. eighteenth century B.C.) (from Dunand 1950: pl. 69, no. 10089)

Figure 3.22. Silver ship model from the tomb of Queen Ahhotep, mother of Ahmose (after Landström 1970: 98 fig. 312)

Figure 3.23. Gold ship model from the tomb of Queen Ahhotep (from Landström 1970: 98 fig. 311)

Aegeans (Minoans) with clean-shaven faces, long coiffures, skin of a dark red color, and Aegean skirts like those in the tomb of Rechmire.[118] Beneath this register, however, the tableau is a different matter. Three Syro-Canaanites introduce the register; they are identical in all but minor details and labels to the first three figures in

Register I. Interspersed between the remainder of the row of Syro-Canaanites and their womenfolk are figures that bear both Syro-Canaanite and Aegean attributes.

Figure 3.27: A illustrates a typical red-skinned Aegean of Register I. Figure 3.27: B depicts the head and bust of a typical Syro-Canaanite with light yellow skin,

Figure 3.24. Ship relief from the tomb of Iniwia (Nineteenth–Twentieth Dynasties) (from Landström 1970: 138 fig. 403)

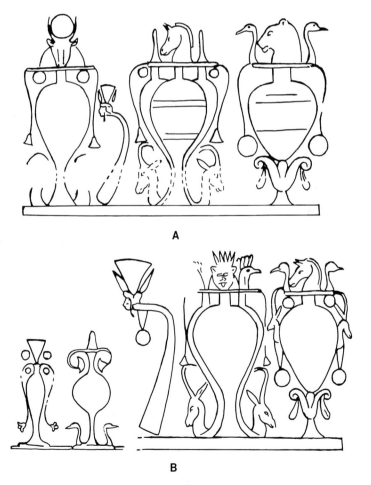

Figure 3.25. Hybrid vessels depicted in scenes of captured spoils from Syria (A) and Libya (B) (after Davies 1930: 36 fig. 6, 37 fig. 7)

bearded face, and straight-cropped hair held in place by a fillet. Figure 3.27: C is a clever combination of the two cultural stock-types. In skin color and kilt he is Aegean; yet his head is that of a Syrian. Clearly, this foreigner is a clever orchestration of details from two entirely distinct ethnic sources.

Hybridism is also at work in the case of the ships of Iniwia.[119] These are based partly on elements taken from the Punt ships of Hatshepsut portrayed at Deir el Bahri (Figs. 2.15–18). The scene's general lay-out, however, and certain other elements of the ships' construction and cargo are derived from a stock scene depicting Syro-Canaanite ships like that portrayed in the tombs of Kenamun and Nebamun (Figs. 3.2, 8–9).

The bows of Iniwia's three ships are best compared to Hatshepsut's seagoing Punt ships. The leftmost of Iniwia's ships carries a hogging truss that crosses the forward overhang and rises aft at an angle (Figs. 3.24, 30: A-arrow). It seems that this hogging truss is derived from Hatshepsut's scene at Deir el Bahri. The interest that this unique monument held for later generations is illustrated by a sketch of the queen of Punt, derived from the relief that was made by a Ramesside artist (Figs. 2.12–13; 3.28).

If the hogging truss were all there was to go on, it would be reasonable to conclude that these are typical New Kingdom seagoing ships. Other elements, however, suggest a Syro-Canaanite identification for the ships. First, the mast carries a basketlike crow's nest attached to its forward side. As noted above, before the twelfth century B.C. this is a feature that appears only on Syro-Canaanite ships. Second, Iniwia's ships have screens above the sheer; and third, each ship has a *pithos* nestled in its bow. All of these elements appear also on the Syro-Canaanite ships in the Kenamun scene (Figs. 3.2–6).

To further illustrate the borrowing that has taken place here, note the portions of the Kenamun scene blocked out in Figure 3.29 and enlarged in Figure 3.30: B. For further clarity, the latter illustration has been reversed right-to-left, and the vertical lines of the fence above the sheer, as well as the zigzag lines of the water, have been excluded.

When the Iniwia relief is compared with this portion of the Kenamun scene, their likeness is striking. There are three ships in the Iniwia scene and only two in the Kenamun scene. But in the latter scene there are three boarding ladders. The Kenamun ships have large jars in the bows and a crow's nest attached to the forward side of the mast. These are the only two scenes in Egyptian art in which a crow's nest of this type appears.

Figure 3.26. A scene from Thutmose III's "botanical garden" in the Temple of Karnak (photo by the author)

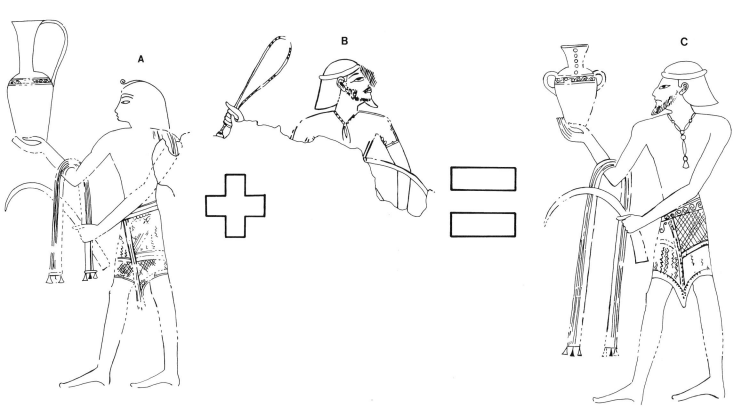

Figure 3.27. Hybridism in human figures. Figure C is a hybrid creation in which the Egyptian artist combined the body, skirt, and red skin color of a typical Minoan (A) with the bearded head and straight-cropped long hair, held in place with a fillet, of a stock yellow-skinned Syro-Canaanite (B). (Tomb of Mencheperresonb [T. 86]; Thutmose III) (figures after Davies and Davies 1933: pls. 5 and 7)

Figure 3.28. Ramesside sketch of the Queen of Punt derived from her depiction in the mortuary temple of Hatshepsut at Deir el Bahri. Limestone flake from Deir el Medina (after Peck 1978: 115 fig. 46)

Figure 3.29. Detail of the scene from the tomb of Kenamun showing the portions depicted in Figs. 3.30:B and 3.31:A-B (from Davies and Faulkner 1947: pl. 8)

Figure 3.30. (A) Line drawing of the relief from the tomb of Iniwia; (B) Line drawing of the scene of Syrian ships from the tomb of Kenamun. For the sake of clarity, this scene has been reversed here (A after Landström 1970: 138 fig. 403; B after Davies and Faulkner 1947: pl. 8)

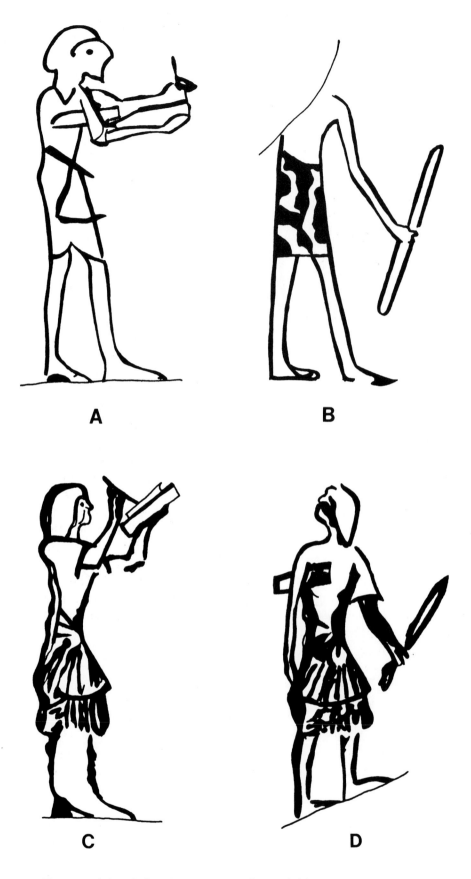

The ships carry the same number of lifts (six) on each side of the mast, instead of the eight carried by Hatshepsut's Punt ships. Furthermore, in both scenes the porters are carrying what appear to be Canaanite jars on their shoulders.

Note the scribe and "headless" man with a staff in Kenamun's scene blocked out in Figure 3.29 and enlarged in Figure 3.31: A–B. The scribe is again reversed here left-to-right for clarity. Compare these figures to the two Egyptian officials facing the ships in the Iniwia scene (Fig. 3.31: C–D). They are identical with the exception of their clothing. Note also that in the Kenamun scene, the Egyptian scribe holds his pen box under his arm (Fig. 3.31: A). Iniwia's scribe has raised his arms, however, making it impossible for the artist to place the pen box under his arm (Fig. 3.31: B). *The pen box was transferred, therefore, to the official with the stick* (Fig. 3.31: D).

In summary, the ships in the Iniwia relief never really existed. They are cleverly contrived hybrid constructions that lived only in the fertile mind of the artist who created them. Attempts to reconstruct an actual ship on the basis of this relief are not valid.[120]

Figure 3.31. (A) *Scribe from the Kenamun scene (reversed);* (B) *man with staff from the Kenamun scene;* (C) *the scribe from the Iniwia scene;* (D) *the official with staff from the Iniwia scene carries the scribe's pen box under his arm* (A *and* B *after Davies and Faulkner 1947: pl. 8;* C *and* D *after Landström 1970: 138 fig. 403*)

CHAPTER 4

Cypriot Ships

Cyprus was being exploited by seafaring hunters ten thousand years ago; it had been settled by the eighth millennium and possibly as early as the ninth.[1] This colonization must have been carried out by means of water transport. From that time on, because of the island's geography, the sea played a significant part in the development of the Cypriot cultures. In the Late Bronze Age, the island flourished as a source of copper. Stone anchors, boat models, and perhaps texts all point to Cypriot seafarers playing a significant role in Mediterranean trade.

The Textual Evidence

Textual evidence for Cypriot Late Bronze Age seafaring depends on whether the term *Alashia* was the island's ancient name. If Alashia was Cyprus (or part of that island), then a considerable amount of textual evidence exists, particularly from Amarna and Ugarit, concerning Cypriot nautical activities.

The "war" over the identity of Alashia has been fought now for a century. Today, the scholarly world seems to lean toward the Alashia-Cyprus equation. Several venerable and vocal proponents

persist, however, in locating Alashia in northern Syria or Cilicia.[2] The *nautical* evidence of Amarna text 114, though, requires that Alashia be located in Cyprus.[3]

Eight Amarna texts, sent to Egypt from Alashia, indicate close trade and diplomatic contacts between them.[4] In one, an Alashian has died in Egypt, and the pharaoh is asked to return his possessions.[5] An Alashian living in Egypt, even for a short time, is best understood as a merchant or trading agent. In another case, the ship may have actually belonged to the king of Alashia.[6]

The cordiality of the letters between the Alashian and Ugaritic kings indicates a very close, if not familial, relationship.[7] Numerous Ugaritic texts refer to Alashian traders. One of them, named Abiramu, received 660 units of oil.[8] Other texts refer to persons simply termed "the Alashian." An extensive list of the names of women and youths who were in several estates has the marginal note "the town of Alashia."[9] Presumably this is a list of the Alashian community at Ugarit.[10] The estate may have belonged to persons with Hurrian and Semitic names.[11] An Alashian ship's inventory, recorded at Uga-

rit, included fifteen talents of copper.[12] The Cypro-Minoan texts found at Ugarit also substantiate a Cypriot presence there.[13]

We lack references to Cypriot ships visiting the Aegean. The term *ku-pi-ri-jo* ("Cypriot"), however, appears in Linear B tablets at both Knossos and Pylos. At the former site, this appears to refer primarily to an ethnic used as a man's personal name.[14] At Knossos the term is used in connection with honey, oil, vases, wool, and the ingredients of salve.[15] There it seems to define an item's origin or, more likely, its ultimate destination.[16]

Cypro-Minoan signs found on some Late Helladic III and Late Minoan III pottery in the Aegean area—primarily at Tiryns and Crete—were incised after firing.[17] These marks seem to be part of a system for designating these items for export to Cyprus, perhaps by Cypriot traders situated in the Aegean.

Wenamun, shipwrecked on Alashia and with the locals about to kill him, tried to communicate with them: "Surely there is one among you who understands Egyptian. And one of them said: I understand."[18] Perhaps the Alashian had learned the language during visits to Egypt?

The Archaeological Evidence

An anchor of typical Cypriot Bronze Age shape—but made of *local* Egyptian stone—was found among architectural fragments in the enclosure of the temple of Amun at Karnak (Fig. 12.44).[19] It may have come from the region of the landing in front of the First Pylon. The inescapable conclusion is that the anchor was made by a seaman familiar with the Cypriot tradition of anchors, presumably from a Cypriot ship that had arrived in Egypt.

The Iconographic Evidence

Unfortunately, neither the Alashians nor their seagoing ships were ever depicted by the Theban tomb painters. Most of our iconographic information on Cypriot Bronze Age ships is limited almost entirely to terra-cotta models. Only a small portion of the many Bronze Age ship representations from Cyprus represent indigenous craft. Those belonging to foreign traditions are discussed in the appropriate chapters.[20]

L. Basch suggests that an Early Cypriot vase from Vounous may be the earliest representation of a Cypriot ship.[21] The earliest definite Cypriot ship model dates to Middle Cypriot I (Fig. 4.1).[22] Of unknown provenance, it is made of local White Painted II Ware. The stem- and sternposts lack decoration and are identical in shape, raking outward. The bowl-shaped hull is deep, with a flat base. It is decorated with a row of cross-hatching with a net decoration beneath, separated from it by two horizontal lines. The sheer is pierced

Figure 4.1. Terra-cotta ship model of unknown provenance (Middle Cypriot I) (from Buchholz and Karageorghis 1973: 471 no. 1718; courtesy of Phaidon Press)

once on either side of the ship, but these holes are not aligned. The hull curves slightly inboard at the sheer, creating a tumble-home. There are no internal plastic decorations. Eight animated figures and two birds surround the ship's caprail, perhaps representing a cult scene. The manner and position of the figures at the ship's extremities suggest that the bow is to the left in the photograph. The figures are apparently represented in a scale larger than the ship itself.

R. Dussaud assumes that the model represents a merchant ship;[23] J. M. Sasson errs in comparing it to one of the Byblos ship models (Fig. 3.19).[24] Basch suggests that it represents a coracle.[25] The model bears comparison to the Late Cypriot ship models that followed; it is so schematic, however, that little can be learned from it.

Several White Painted IV Ware sherds found at Politiko, *Lambertis*, have been identified by K. Westerberg as part of a ship (Fig. 4.2).[26] Remains of five anthropomorphic figures sit on the "sheer" facing "outboard." The "hull" has what

appears to be a tumble-home. This feature may indicate basketry (coracle-curragh) construction.[27] Because the figures are sitting on the hull's exterior facing outward, however, this seems unlikely. Therefore, the identification of these sherds as parts of a ship model is tenuous, in my view.

One model that may suggest the existence of coracles in Bronze Age Cyprus is made of White Painted IV Ware and dates to the Middle Cypriot III period (Fig. 4.3).[28] The outer surface of the model is decorated with a net (basketwork?) design. The bottom of the hull is rounded. Pairs of piercings appear on four sides of the craft. A single anthropomorphic figure sits inside the hull.

A largely reconstructed Red Polished III Ware vessel of Early or Middle Cypriot date may represent a watercraft (Fig. 4.4).[29] The hull and deck are decorated with incisions. The posts, projecting above the sheer, are square. Each post is pierced by a single hole, and there is a rectangular hole in the center of the deck.

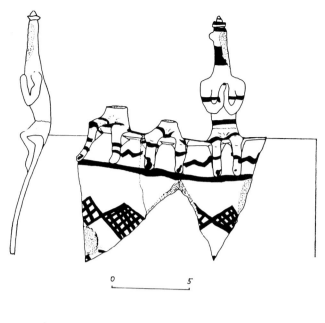

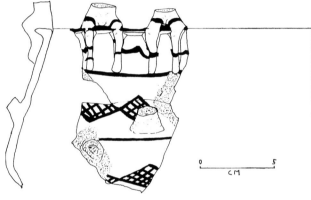

Figure 4.2. Sherds of terra-cotta model boat (?) with human figures from Politiko, Lambertis, Cyprus. The sherds are of White Painted IV Ware (Middle Cypriot II–III) (from Frankel 1974: 44 figs. 1–2)

the hull, thirty-six equidistantly spaced horizontal holes, pierced before firing, are arranged from stem to stern. There is a single narrow plastic ridge, perhaps representing a wale, on either side of the hull (Fig. 4.5: A–B). The stem is flattened frontally. It widens at its upper extremity and is pierced by two holes arranged horizontally.

Although there is no evidence of a keel outside the hull, a narrow molded bar inside, rectangular in section and running the length of the ship, may represent a keel projecting into the hull (Fig. 4.5: C, A).[31] It is perforated amidships by a circular maststep (Fig. 4.5: C, B). The inner side of the sternpost has seven plastic "buttons" that seem to indicate a massive stern construction (Fig. 4.5: C, C). The model's sternpost is now broken but is probably to be reconstructed in a bifurcated manner, as on the following model.

Model A-50 comes from Site A, Tomb 7, at Maroni *Zarukas* (Fig. 4.6).[32] It is surmounted by two tall, narrow, inward-curving prongs set closely together in the same

The most detailed information on Cypriot Late Bronze Age ships consists of three terra-cotta models of Late Cypriot I–II date. Though differing in size, these models are so similar to each other in detail and shape that they all seem to represent the same type of ship. Made in Plain White Handmade Ware, they are markedly different from all other known Bronze Age ship depictions.

The most elaborate model of the group comes from Tomb 2B at Kazaphani *Ayios Andrionikos* (Fig. 4.5).[30] The hull is deep and beamy, with flat-topped incurving sheer. Just below these on either side of

Figure 4.3. Terra-cotta model of a watercraft, provenance unknown. White Painted IV Ware (Middle Cypriot III) (from Westerberg 1983: 78 fig. 3)

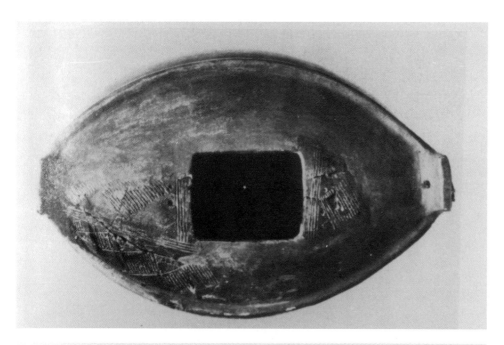

Figure 4.4. Terra-cotta model of a watercraft, provenance unknown. Red Polished Ware III (Early or Middle Cypriot) (from Westerberg 1983: 79 fig. 4)

ships. A narrow, flattened bottom rises at stem- and sternpost, both of which have been broken. A raised mast socket is situated directly amidships (Fig. 4.9). The "caprails" are flattened; beneath them also are eighteen equidistant horizontal holes, made before firing. Four holes cut into the hull after firing may have served to hang the model.

These three models from Kazaphani and Maroni are so similar in shape that they may have originated in the same workshop. The standardized beam/keel ratio of the three models varies between 1:2.19 and 1:2.71. They apparently represent a beamy merchant ship.

The bifurcation at the sternpost perhaps accepted a single steering oar resting on a stanchion. Steering apparatus, placed over the sternpost, was used on Egyptian river craft by the First Intermediate Period and continued in use throughout the second millennium B.C.[35] In Egypt, however, this arrangement was never used on seagoing ships, which are always depicted with rudders hung from their quarters (Figs. 2.3, 5, 8, 11, 15–18, 26, 37–42). Perhaps the bifurcation was a device intended to imitate a bird's (swallow?) tail, like those found on the posts and mastheads of Pacific canoes of the recent past.[36]

The rows of piercings along the sheer are enigmatic. R. S. Merrillees assumes that they are "elaborate provisions for sails and rigging."[37] Although the two upper horizontal piercings on the Kazaphani model may have been used to hold a double forestay, I am not familiar with rigging from the period under discussion (or any other period, for that matter) that would require such an arrangement.[38] Perhaps the holes served to attach to the model an open bulwark—similar to that de-

contour as the keel. Below them, just inside the hull, is a narrow, molded horizontal ledge (Fig. 4.7: A). At either side on the center of the ship are stubby horizontal ledges that are pierced vertically (Fig. 4.7: B–C).[33] On either side of the hull are eighteen equidistant horizontal piercings extending from stem to stern, which were

made before firing. The model is broken; the hull's lower half is missing. This is presumably why, unlike in the case of the other two models, no maststep is reported on this terra-cotta.

The second model from Maroni comes from Site A, Tomb 1, and dates to Late Cypriot I–II (Fig. 4.8).[34] This model is broad amid-

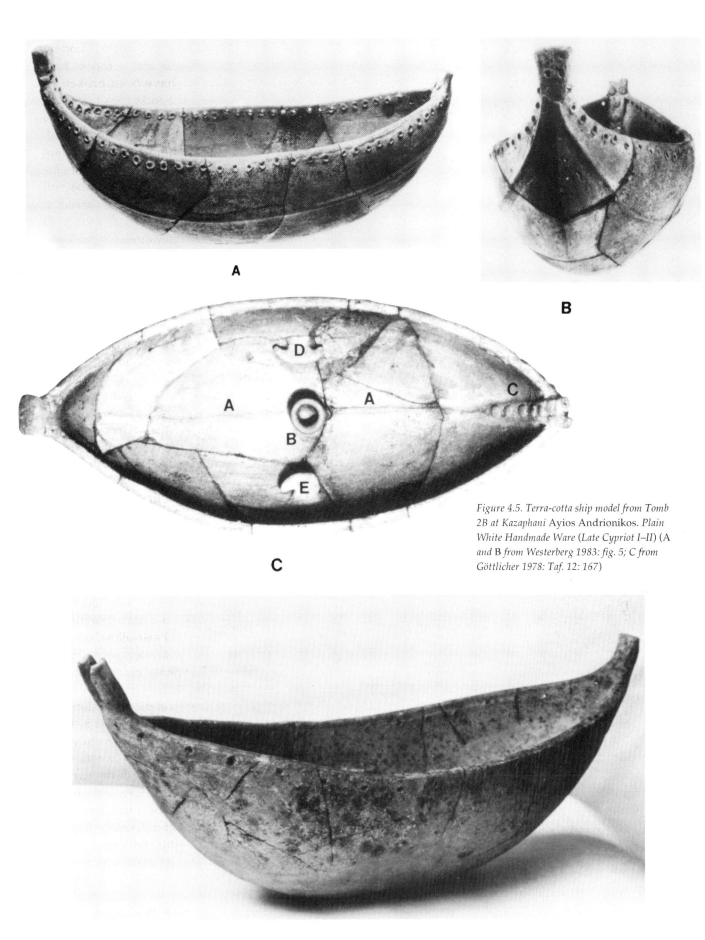

Figure 4.5. Terra-cotta ship model from Tomb 2B at Kazaphani Ayios Andrionikos. *Plain White Handmade Ware (Late Cypriot I–II) (A and B from Westerberg 1983: fig. 5; C from Göttlicher 1978: Taf. 12: 167)*

Figure 4.6. Terra-cotta ship model A–50 from Site A, Tomb 7, at Maroni Zarukas (Late Cypriot I–II) (from Merrillees 1968: pl. 37: 2)

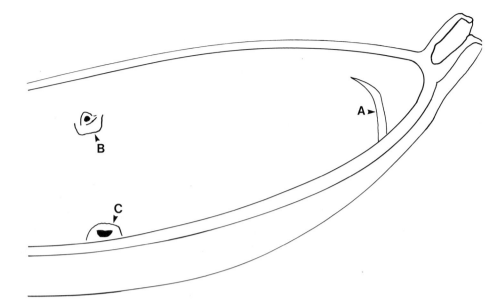

Figure 4.7. Detail of the interior of terra-cotta ship model A-50 from Maroni Zarukas. (after Basch 1987: 74 fig. 145)

Figure 4.8. Terra-cotta ship model A–49 from Site A, Tomb 1, at Maroni Zarukas (Late Cypriot I–II) (from Merrillees 1968: pl. 37: 2)

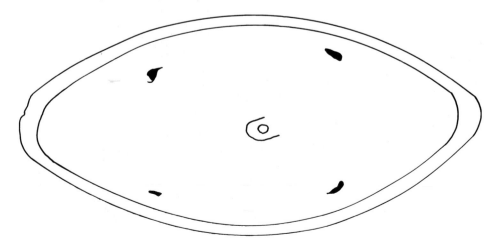

Figure 4.9. Interior of terra-cotta model A49 (after Basch 1987: 73 fig. 144)

picted on Syro-Canaanite ships and perhaps carried by the Uluburun ship—made of organic material that has not survived.[39]

Basch assumes that these models represent skin-covered ships and that the horizontal piercings depict holes through which the skins were connected to the wood framework at the caprail.[40] The hooks, in his opinion, were used to support shrouds. He notes that the narrow plastic ridges on the Kazaphani model's exterior cannot be explained in the context of wood ship construction.

I believe that these models represent beamy wood-planked craft constructed with a keel. The plastic ridges on the hull's exterior would then represent pronounced wales.[41] The massive sternpost on the Kazaphani model is difficult to explain with respect to skin ship construction. Therefore, I believe that the three models from Kazaphani and Maroni probably portray an indigenous class of spacious Late Cypriot seagoing merchant ship for which additional information is lacking at present.

A crescentic ship appears on a cylinder seal dating to the end of the Late Cypriot period (Fig. 4.10).[42] The ship is sailing to the right on the sealing. One of the two crew members depicted is handling the two (?) quarter rudders. The mast is seen through the hull: the identification of the seven other vertical lines crossing the hull is more difficult to interpret.[43] Two lines, representing lifts or stays, lead from the top of the mast to the bow and stern. The mast seems to carry a crow's nest. Horned animals, dots, and oxhide-ingot-shaped objects surround the craft.

A Proto-White Painted amphora from Vathyrkakas has a boat motif on its shoulder (Fig. 4.11).[44] The craft's hull is a crescentic line in which two figures are rowing. The figure at right holds two oars; the object in the left hand of the figure at left may be a fish line instead of an oar since it seems to lead to the mouth of the fish beneath the boat. The drawing confirms the reasonable assumption that small craft also existed in Cyprus during the Late Cypriot period but is too schematic to tell anything more about the craft itself.

The Late Cypriot date attributed to two other models is questionable. Westerberg compares a model found in the sea near Amathus to the Kazaphani/Maroni models, dating it to the Late Cypriot period,[45] but this model finds its closest parallel in a model from the ninth or eighth century B.C. of a merchantman and should be dated accordingly.[46] Another

Figure 4.10. Impression of the Cypriot cylinder seal depicting a ship (end of the Late Cypriot period) (from Westerberg 1983: fig. 16)

model that Westerberg dates to the Late Cypriot period is identified by Basch as a Cypro-Archaic merchantman.[47]

Figure 4.11. Boat on Proto-White Painted amphora from Vathyrkakas (Late Cypriot III) (from Westerberg 1983: fig. 12)

CHAPTER 5

Early Ships of the Aegean

Aegean geography, with its many islands, numerous small natural harbors, and rugged topography, required early on that the cultures inhabiting its rocky shores develop seafaring skills, which were ingrained into their cultural heritage. Fortunately for us, the Aegean region, unlike some of the geographical areas discussed earlier, is exceptionally rich in iconographic materials depicting seagoing ships.[1]

The Archaeological Evidence

The earliest evidence for seafaring in the Aegean—and in the entire Mediterranean, for that matter—is flakes of obsidian originating on the island of Melos that were found in the strata of the Franchthi Cave, located in the southern Argolid.[2] These indicate that the inhabitants of the Greek mainland had the technical skills required to navigate the Aegean by the Upper Paleolithic or Mesolithic periods. Unfortunately, we know nothing about the craft in use at that time.[3]

Navigational skills, however, did not translate into patterns of settlement. Only later, after the in-troduction of agriculture in the Neolithic period, which allowed the immigrants to exploit islands with sparse resources, did settlement of the Aegean islands begin.[4] There is mounting evidence for Late Neolithic settlement on various Aegean islands and for the founding of Crete in the late eighth or early seventh millennium B.C., apparently as the result of a well-organized and concerted effort.[5] The Early Bronze Age, however, experienced the main thrust of Aegean settlement.

The Iconographic Evidence

Iconographic information on Aegean seafaring begins only in the third millennium. *Thus, the period separating the earliest evidence for seafaring from the earliest iconographic representations of seagoing craft is considerably longer than that separating our own time from the Early Bronze Age.* Two distinct types of ships can be defined during this period. The first is a variety of seagoing longship; the other seems to be a fairly small vessel with a cutwater bow and stern. Other types of craft may have existed, but if so, we have no known depictions of them.

Early Bronze Age Aegean Longships

LEAD MODELS FROM NAXOS. As might be expected from the preceding discussion, the earliest iconographic evidence for ships in the Aegean already shows considerable structural development. The clearest indication for the shape of these longships is three lead ship models from Naxos that date to the third millennium B.C. (Figs. 5.1–2).[6] Each of the models is constructed of three lengths of lead. The bow and keel are made from a rod of lead that was flattened by hammering the central two-thirds of its length to form a flat bottom. Two other flat strips form the sides of the hull. One extremity is raised and finishes in a vertical transom, while the other end is narrow and rises at an angle. The models are exceptionally narrow; the largest and best preserved has a beam/length ratio of 1:14. L. Casson believes these to be models of dugouts; L. Basch considers their prototypes to have

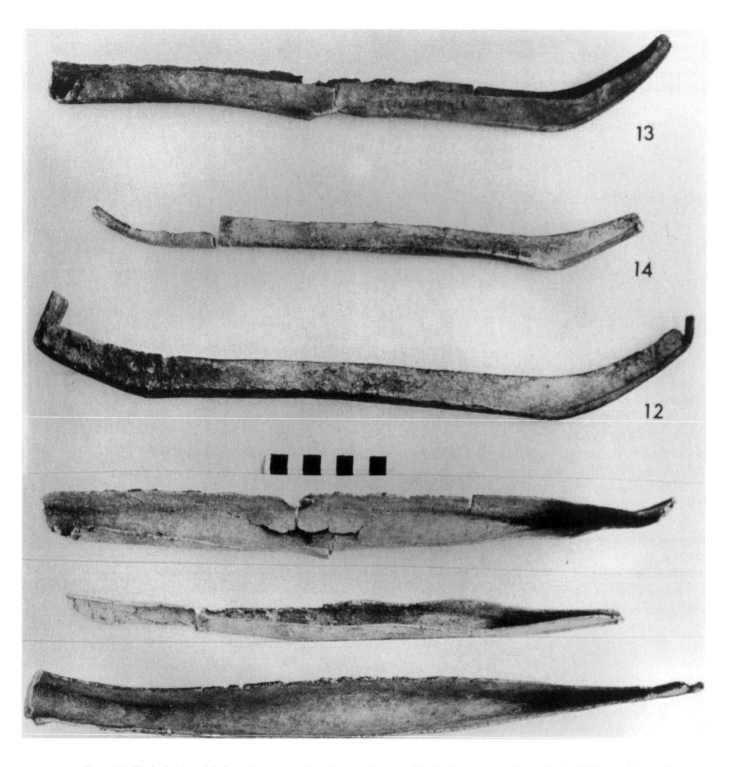

Figure 5.1. The lead ship models from Naxos now in the Ashmolean Museum (third millennium B.C.) (from AJA 71 [1967] pl. 3 [Renfrew])

been planked ships.[7] The largest model is reported to have been discovered in a tomb together with two stone idols.[8]

CYCLADIC "FRYING PANS." Perhaps the best-known examples of this ship type appear on an un-usual group of third millennium terra-cotta artifacts that have been termed generically as "frying pans" because of their odd shape (Fig. 5.3).[9] Frying pans appear throughout a wide area, including mainland Greece and Anatolia, but it is the group from the Cycladic island of Syros, found in the context of the Keros-Syros culture, that has created the most interest for studying ancient seafaring, as only its members bear depictions of ships (Figs. 5.3–4).[10]

The one thing that seems clear about these particular artifacts is that they were probably never intended for use as frying pans. The purpose for which they were made remains enigmatic.[11] The frying pans may have had a cultic or ritual function. This seems to be supported by the occasional depiction of female genitalia just above the two-pronged variety of handles (legs?) (Fig. 5.5).[12] These sometimes have a leafy sprig that later reappears in conjunction with ships and in other, clearly cultic, contexts on Minoan seals (Figs. 6.29: D–E, I, K, 45).

The ships are long and narrow in profile. They obviously depict the same type of ship after which the lead models from Naxos are patterned. One extremity ends in a high post that forms an almost right angle with the hull. The post is decorated with a fish device and tassel placed on a pole. The device invariably points away from the craft. The angle at the other end of the ship, already noted on the Naxos models, also appears in varying degrees on the Syros ships.

Ethnographic parallels of fish ornaments are known from the Solomon Islands, where the device was connected to the stem and faced the stern; and the Moluccas, where it was connected to the stern and faced the stem (Figs. 5.6–7).[13] Tassels are a more common decorative/cultic emblem; parallels are known from antiquity and recent times (Fig. 5.6).[14] The low ends of the ships terminate vertically, apparently ending in a transom-like manner, as on the Naxos models. A horizontal device projects at keel-level abaft the transom.

The short parallel lines on either side of some of the ships are best understood as paddles.[15] The ships are too schematic for the

Figure 5.3. A typical Cycladic "frying pan" decorated with a longship (Early Cycladic II) (photo by the author)

number of strokes on a side (up to twenty-eight) to be taken as the exact number in actual use; clearly a good number is implied, however. Two rock graffiti from Naxos, although of lesser quality, depict the same ship type (Fig. 5.8).[16] Both have horizontal (fish?) devices atop the high extremity. One ship has a horned (?) quadruped above it.

PALAIKASTRO MODEL. A rough

terra-cotta model of this ship type, uncovered in an ossuary dating to the Early Minoan I–II period at Palaikastro in eastern Crete, indicates that these ships were also known in Early Bronze Age Crete (Fig. 5.9).[17] The model has a tear-drop-shaped hull when viewed from above; the same shape is repeated on later models from Christos and Hagia Triada (Fig. 5.10).[18]

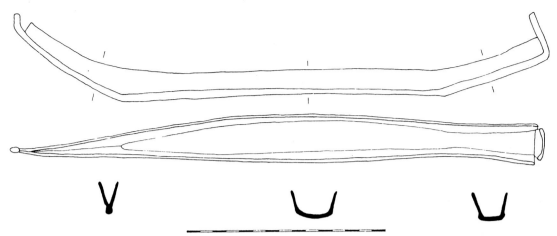

Figure 5.2. The best preserved of the Naxos lead ship models in the Ashmolean Museum (third millennium) (from AJA 71 [1967] pls. 1: 12. [Renfrew])

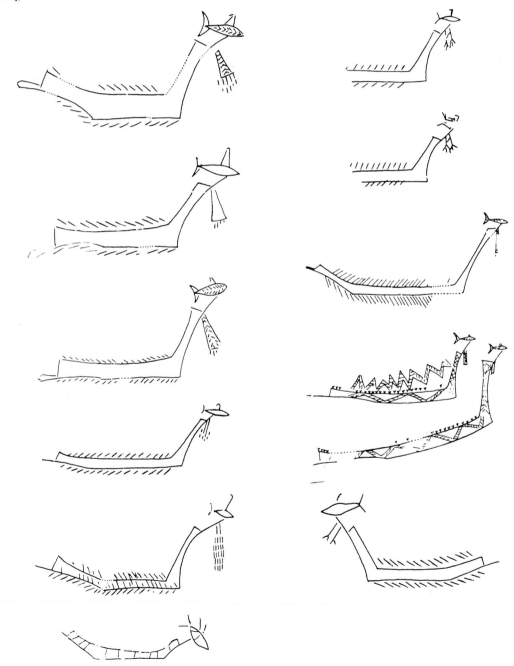

Figure 5.4. Ships incised on Cycladic "frying pans" (Early Cycladic II) (from Coleman 1985: 199 ill. 5)

The pointed end of the "teardrop" finishes in a high post. The rounded end is apparently the terra-cotta equivalent of the stern transom on the Naxos models. The widest part of the hull is well astern of amidships.[19] A blunt horizontal projection extends abaft the stern.

ORCHOMENOS. Another ship of this sort is incised on an Early Helladic vase handle from Orchomenos (Fig. 5.11). Two vertical lines above the hull are probably accidental scratches and are not related to the craft.[20] The line of the keel is slightly longer than the top (sheer) line, forming the familiar horizontal projection. Sixteen short vertical strokes above the sheer are best interpreted as paddles.

PHYLAKOPI. None of the above representations show steering oars. However, the *curving* stern of a ship with a single steering oar appears on a sherd from Phylakopi (Fig. 5.12). A short tiller (?) extends *abaft* the steering oar. The stern projection is absent. Rows of parallel lines above and below the hull again apparently depict paddles.

TARXIEN. The longship class seems to have had a particularly wide area of use. Casson identifies a ship of this class on a stone from

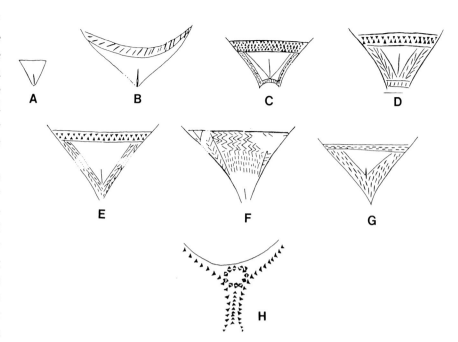

Figure 5.5. *Genitalia appearing on Cycladic "frying pans" (Early Cycladic II) (from Coleman 1985: 196 ill. 4)*

the megalithic temples of Tarxien on Malta (Fig. 5.13).[21] He believes that other graffiti at Tarxien represent merchant craft because of their dumpier proportions.

CHARACTERISTICS OF EARLY BRONZE AGE AEGEAN LONGSHIPS. It has been suggested that the ships depicted in the various iconographic mediums represent different sizes or even classes of longships.[22] Variations of craft probably did exist in the Early Bronze Age Aegean, just as there was a variety of ship types in the

Oceanic region in the more recent past. The iconographic evidence, however, is not sufficiently clear to permit such differentiations. Variations may result from their expression in different mediums—incision on clay, metal/stone/terra-cotta models, and so on—which may significantly change the relative dimensions of the illustrations.[23]

An argument still persists among scholars as to which end of these ships represents the stern and which the bow.[24] There are two compelling arguments for identifying the high end as the stem. Firstly, the lower extremity of the Naxos lead models have a blunt, transom-like ending, strongly suggesting that this end was the stern. Secondly, the ships taking part in the waterborne procession depicted in the miniature frieze at Thera have similar horizontal projections at their sterns (Figs. 6.13–14). This device, unknown outside the Aegean, is so unusual that one may assume it represents the same device in both the Early Bronze Age depictions

Figure 5.6. *A Solima canoe from the Solomon Islands (after Haddon 1937: 88 fig. 59: b)*

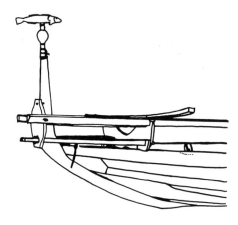

Figure 5.7. Stern of prahu belang, *Moluccas (after Horridge 1978: 43 fig. 31: A)*

and at Thera. Given this consideration, it seems highly unlikely that the horizontal stern projection—whatever its function—would have been transferred from one end of the ship to the other.[25]

Depictions of the Aegean Early Bronze Age longships suggest the following general conclusions:

• The ships are extremely long and narrow and may have descended from monoxylons.[26]

• The high stems were topped on occasion by fish devices and tassels.

• The Cycladic frying pans may be connected with fertility and regeneration.[27] The appearance of ships on these objects also argues for a relationship between the actual ships and the cult.

• Usually—but not in all cases—the stern ends in a horizontal projection at keel level. The craft was finished astern in a transom or was blunt-ended.

• As we have seen in the Byblos archetypes, terra-cotta models have a tendency to shorten the length of ship models to a greater degree than the other dimensions. Therefore, it seems likely that the lead models from Naxos approximate most closely the dimensions of the original craft. If so, these craft would have made a poor showing in high seas: because of

their elongated, extremely narrow dimensions, they would tend to hog. The zigzag lines on two of the Cycladic ships may indicate either some type of decoration, additional strengthening, or perhaps that the ships were lashed (Fig. 5.4).[28]

Perhaps the closest modern ethnological parallel to these Aegean ships is the long, narrow "dragon boats" of the Far East (Figs. 5.14–15).[29] Their beam/length ratio varies between 1:10 and 1:14, thus agreeing with the Naxos models.

Like the Aegean longships, dragon boats are seagoing craft that are manned by rows of paddlers and have no sail. Crews range in size from twenty to one hundred men, depending on the vessel's length, which can vary from twelve to thirty meters. These vessels are definitely seagoing, although because of their long and narrow proportions and lack of internal structure, they tend to hog in even a moderate sea. To prevent this, bamboo hawsers, or on occasion a true hogging truss, are employed (Fig. 5.15:B). C. W. Bishop notes one example of a true hogging truss that ran the length of the hull over its center.

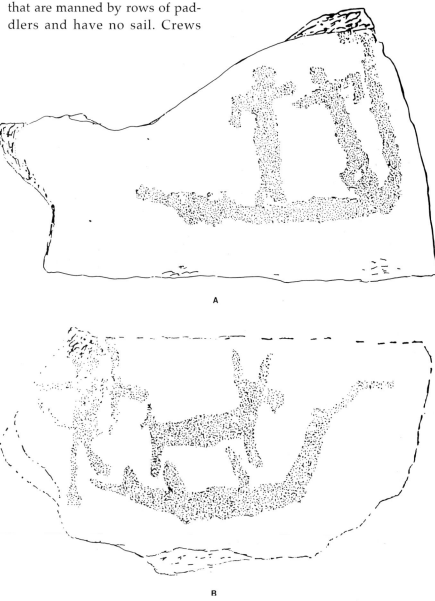

A

B

Figure 5.8. Ship graffiti on rocks from Naxos (after Doumas 1967: 123 fig. 55, 119 fig. 50)

Although today dragon boats are used only for ceremonial purposes, in the recent past these vessels had far more somber functions. They are recorded from the third century A.D. onward used in war and piracy.[30] These boats continued to be used by brigands and water police on the south China coast into the nineteenth century. Imperialist forces used them against the Taiping rebels in "Chinese" Gordon's time, and Burmese ships of similar type were used by opponents of the British.

If the comparison between the dragon boats and the Aegean Early Bronze Age longships is legitimate, it would seem that the Aegean longships were suited primarily for acts of war and ceremony.[31] They were certainly not functionally fitted to be used as merchant craft. Perhaps other ship varieties were used specifically for trading; if so, nowhere have they been revealed in the iconographic evidence of the Aegean Early Bronze Age.[32]

• The large numbers of lines and the narrow beam indicate that *these craft must have been paddled.* There would have been too little inboard room to permit a rower to work his oars. Ethnological parallels of similar long and narrow craft are invariably paddled, not rowed (Fig. 5.15: A).[33]

• C. Broodbank, in discussing the longboat's role, notes that in all but a handful of large sites, the size and social structure of settlements of the Keros-Syros culture were ill-suited to the sort of communal organization required for longboat usage.[34] The evidence suggests that the use of a sole longboat would not only have been beyond the manpower resources of a single settlement but may even have been difficult for the population of an entire island to support during the time of the Keros-Syros culture.

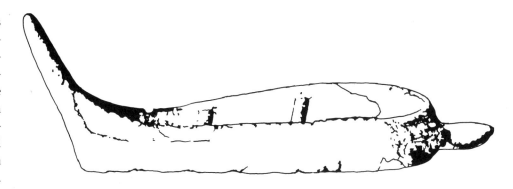

Figure 5.9. Terra-cotta ship model from Palaikastro (third millennium B.C.) (after PM II: 240 fig. 137)

Figure 5.10. Ship model from a tomb at Christos (Messara). End of Early Minoan or beginning of Middle Minoan period (after Göttlicher 1978: Taf. 24: 315)

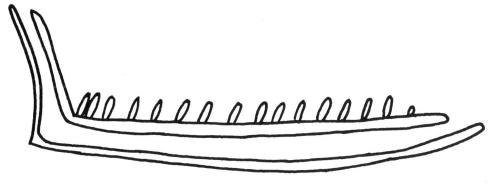

Figure 5.11. Ship on a sherd from Orchomenos (after Marinatos 1933: pl. 13: 9)

Based on a calculation of the synchronous population of Melos, Broodbank notes that, assuming a conservative twenty-five–man crew for a longboat, its manning would have required between 30 to 50 percent of the total male labor force on the entire island.

If these calculations are correct, then, at the very least, the use of longships must have been restricted largely by farming activities. The times of agricultural slack during which voyages could be undertaken within the navigation season were limited to two annual periods of about a fortnight each. Broodbank argues that longships from the Cyclades could have visited and returned from most areas

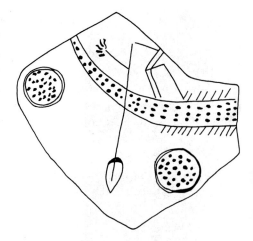

Figure 5.12. Crescentic ship's stern on a sherd from Phylakopi (Melos) (after Casson 1995A: fig. 46)

of the central and southern Aegean within this time span.[35] He believes that their goal would have been primarily to carry out piratical raids, at least in the immediate locality—although longships may have been used for trade over greater distances.

Broodbank emphasizes that, because of the demographical considerations, longships must have been rarities in the Keros-Syros culture. He feels that these ships are best understood in the context of Chalandriani and a few other large sites, for only these centers could have supported the construction and use of such vessels. Interestingly, the majority of the thirteen frying pans on which longships are portrayed either were found in Chalandriani or can be linked to that site.

Early Bronze Age Aegean Double-Ended Craft

Only one other kind of watercraft may be differentiated from the longship class in the iconography of the third millennium. The most detailed representation of this boat-type is a double-ended terracotta model from Mochlos (Fig. 5.16). At stem and stern, the model

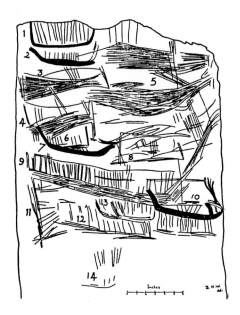

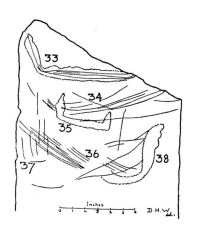

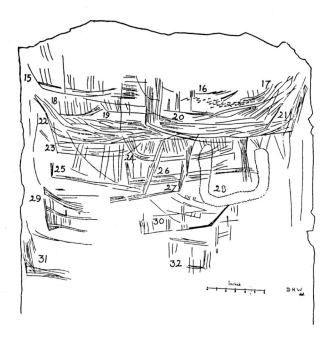

Figure 5.13. Graffiti of ships at the "Third Temple" at Tarxien, Malta (from Woolner 1957: 62 fig. 1, 66 fig. 2, 67 fig. 3; reproduced by permission of Antiquity Publications, Ltd.)

Figure 5.14. Model of a Chinese dragon boat in the J. E. Spencer Collection (NTS) (photo by S. Paris; courtesy Texas A&M University)

has tholes or frames extending above the sheer. This model is generally considered to represent a relatively small vessel.[36] Another terra-cotta fragment from Phylakopi may belong to a similar model.[37]

Double-ended construction with horizontal projections at both extremities may have its roots in monoxylons, skin boats, or bark canoes (Figs. 5.17–22).[38] J. Hornell reports a number of types of modern double-ended craft with horizontal projections at both ends in Indonesia, the Philippines, Bali, the Northern Celebes on the islands of Geelvink Bay, New Guinea, Java, Melanesia, Madura, and the island of Aua (Fig. 5.22: A).[39] Canoes from the island of Aua in the Bismarck Archipelago, ranging in size from 3.5 to 18 meters, are dugouts in which the bow and stern are prolonged into a very long, thin point and have vertical end-pieces added to the hull (Fig. 5.22: B).[40]

This double-ended bifid form is characteristic of vessels of varying dimensions, ranging from the smaller types of outrigger canoes to ships of considerable size. Other modern craft have a horizontal projection at only one extremity.[41]

Cutwater bows were common in Classical antiquity.[42]

The Phaistos Disk

A terra-cotta disk found at Phaistos and dated to the seventeenth century B.C. has a spiral inscription on both sides.[43] The symbols are not related to any known scripts, and the disk itself is believed not to have been of Minoan manufacture.[44] This unique artifact carries the imprints of forty-five different seal stones that were impressed into it while it was wet.[45] Among the signs is a ship, repeated seven times (Fig. 5.23). At one end the ship has a slanting post with a tripartite decoration.

Although not related, being distant in both time and space, an interesting ethnological parallel to the shape and decoration of the Phaistos Disk ship is found in the *Solima* canoe, which was used until recently in the Solomon Islands (Fig. 5.6).[46] The largest recorded *Solima* was nearly fourteen meters long and could carry up to ninety men. The *Solima* had a high stem, which was decorated with a complicated carving of a frigate bird, a fish, and a tassel (Figs. 5.6; 8.60). The tripartite device on the angular stem of the Phaistos Disk ship

and on cultic ships appearing in Minoan glyptic art is reminiscent of the feather stern decorations on the *Solima* (Figs. 6.28 [mast top], 52: A–C). Perhaps the Aegean devices were also made of feathers.

SHIP DEPICTIONS AT AEGINA. A *pithos* from Kolona on the island of Aegina, dating to the Middle Helladic period, is decorated with crescentic ships. The *pithos* is very fragmentary, but it is clear that originally it had four ships painted in a frieze on its shoulder. The figures in the ship are bunched closely together and in one fragment are clearly shown facing the bow, indicating that the ships were paddled and not rowed. The *high* stem ends in an elongated point below a double-curved "stalk" (Fig. 5.24). Vertical stanchions support lances. The best-preserved ship depiction on the *pithos* originally contained about thirty-one men.[47]

A matt-painted drawing on Middle Helladic sherds from the island of Aegina depicts a figure wearing a horned helmet standing on a ship's bow that ends in a bird-head stem ornament (Fig. 5.25). This is the earliest recorded appearance of a bird-head device on an Aegean ship. If they are integral

A

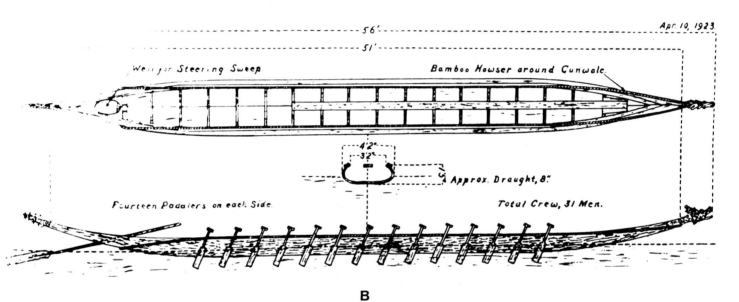

56'
51'
Apr. 10, 1923.

Well for Steering Sweep

Bamboo Hawser around Gunwale.

4' 2"
3' 2"
Approx. Draught, 8."

Fourteen Paddlers on each Side.

Total Crew, 31 Men.

B

Figure 5.15. (A) *Chinese dragon boat,
Yangtze River;* (B) *deck and sheer plans of a
dragon boat, taken off a boat at Itchang;* (C)
*enlargement of the carved dragon's head in B
(from Bishop 1938: pls. 2 fig. 4, 3 figs. 6 and
5; reproduced by permission of Antiquity
Publications Ltd.)*

C

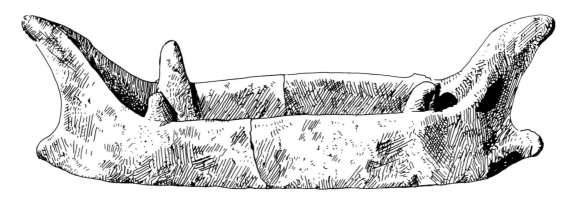

*Figure 5.16. Ship model from Mochlos (*third millennium*) (after Göttlicher 1978: Taf. 24: 313)*

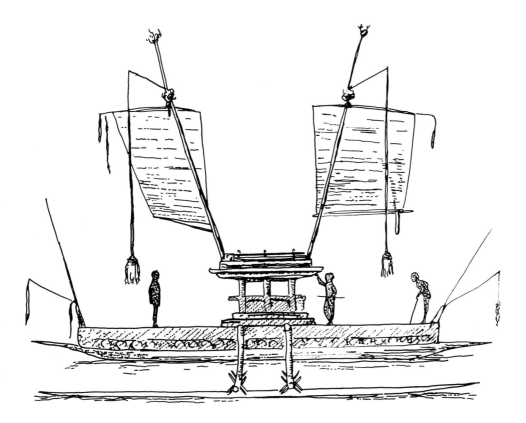

Figure 5.17. Two-masted canoe, Papua (after Haddon 1937: 297 fig. 172)

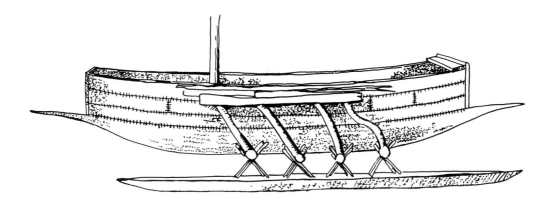

Figure 5.18. Canoe, New Hebrides (after Haddon 1937: 32 fig. 19)

Figure 5.19. Canoe, Cook Islands (after Hornell 1936: 191 fig. 127)

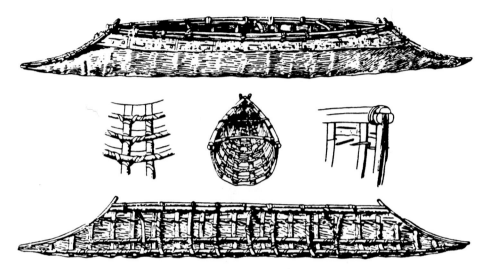

Figure 5.20. A Kutenai bark canoe (from Hornell 1970: 184 fig. 27 [Water Transport, Cambridge University Press])

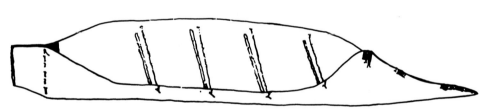

Figure 5.21. Bark canoe from Arafura swamps, Australia (after Thomson 1939: 121 fig. 3; courtesy of the Royal Anthropological Institute of Great Britain and Ireland)

lines are depicted on the ships. In several cases, one line may represent a quarter rudder.

IOLKOS. Designs on painted sherds from a transitional Middle Late Helladic pot found at Iolkos have been identified as a series of oared craft.[49] This reconstruction has been accepted uncritically by some scholars.[50] However, there is insufficient evidence to reconstruct these designs as ships.[51] G. F. Bass notes that the decoration has been compared convincingly with fish painted on a contemporaneous vase in the Archaeological Museum at Nauplion.[52]

The longships of the Aegean Early Bronze Age must have been heirs to a long tradition of seafaring in the Aegean. Toward the end of the third millennium, they disappeared from the iconographic record. In their place we find a different ship type that, for the first time in the Aegean, used a sail for propulsion. The scene is now set for a study of Minoan and Cycladic vessels of the Middle and Late Bronze Age, as exemplified by one of the most exciting discoveries of recent times contributing to our understanding of Aegean ships and their uses.

to the ship, two parallel vertical lines behind the figure may indicate a pole-mast instead of a bipod one. The horizontal lines above the figure may suggest a yard, but this is questionable since no boom appears, nor do the cross-hatched triangles lend themselves to interpretation as an element of a boom-footed rig.

ARGOS. Seven tiny craft are depicted on a vase found in a Middle Helladic Argive tomb (Fig. 5.26).[48] The ships vary in shape from crescentic to rectilinear. Three of them show a recurring extremity at one end; others show one vertical and one slanting post. All the vessels carry a curved structure (cabin?) in the center. Seven, eight, and ten

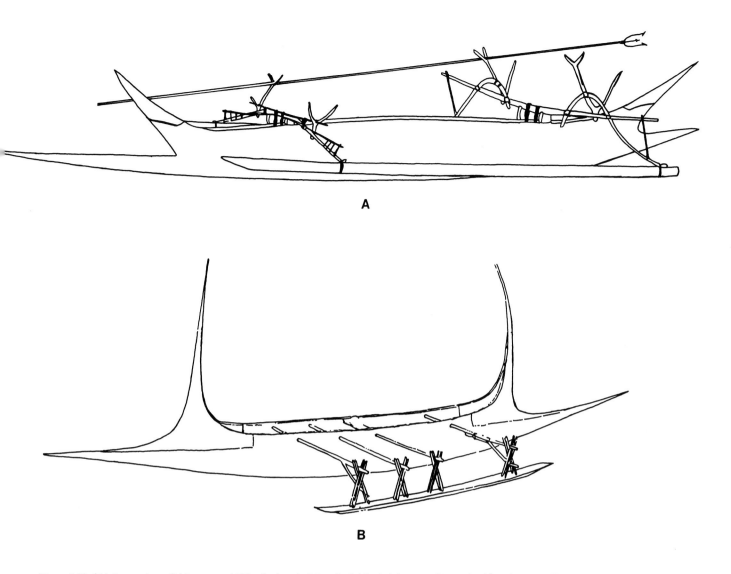

Figure 5.22. (A) *An outrigger fishing canoe, bifid at both ends (Menado Celebes);* (B) *canoe of Aua Island* (*A after Hornell 1970: 210 fig. 39* [Water Transport, *Cambridge University Press*]; *B after Haddon 1937: 177 fig. 109*)

Figure 5.23. Ship represented on the Phaistos disk (after PM I: 654 fig. 485: L)

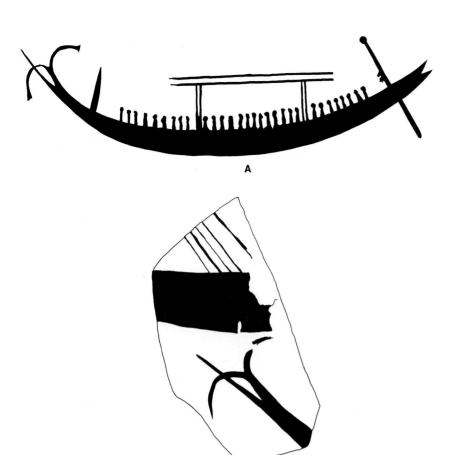

Figure 5.25. Fragment of a ship, with a bird-head device on its stem, painted on sherds from Aegina (Middle Helladic) (after Buchholz and Karageorghis 1973: 301 fig. 869)

Figure 5.24. (A) Basch's reconstruction of a crescentic ship on a pithos from Kolona, Aegina, ca. 1700 B.C.; (B) detail of a stempost decoration (after Basch 1986: 422 fig. 6, 424 fig. 8: D)

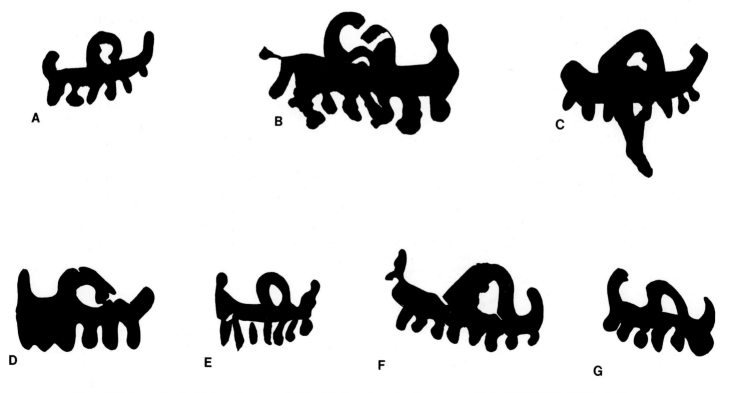

Figure 5.26. Seven ships depicted on a jug from a shaft tomb in Argos (seventeenth century B.C.) (after Deilaki 1990: 126 figs. 1–2)

CHAPTER 6

Minoan/Cycladic Ships

Of all the cultures that flourished around the shores of the eastern Mediterranean during the second millennium B.C., there is none as fascinating—or as enigmatic—as that of the Minoans. Evolving on Crete, these unique people were the quintessential explorers of the Bronze Age. They traded for tin in far-off Mari and presented their wares before the pharaohs. And artisans, schooled in Cretan art forms, decorated Asiatic and Egyptian palaces with Minoan motifs.

But what kinds of ships carried the Minoans on their seafaring journeys of exploration and trade? For decades after Sir Arthur Evans began his excavations at Knossos and discovered the Minoan culture, little was known about their ships. Although a considerable corpus of Minoan ship depictions existed, the quality and detail of these left much to be desired. Most of the evidence was derived from engravings on tiny seals and sealings. A handful of mainly rough and fragmentary models completed the repertoire. Minoan ships remained as enigmatic as the culture that created them.

Then, in 1972, while excavating at the site of Akrotiri on the volcanic island of Thera (Santorini) in the Cyclades, the Greek archaeologist Spyridon Marinatos revealed a well-preserved settlement that had been buried in volcanic ash when the island's volcano exploded, apparently ca. 1628 B.C.[1] One building, a two-storied structure, contained a miniature frieze, depicting in brilliant detail ships taking part in a waterborne race or procession and other nautical activities. The Cycladic ships in the scenes are identical—or at least similar in all discernible details— to vessels depicted in Minoan art.

The Miniature Frieze from Thera has considerably expanded our knowledge of Late Bronze Age Aegean ships and seafaring practices and requires us to study the previously known iconographic evidence for Minoan ships in light of its discovery. Because of the importance of the Theran material for interpreting Aegean seafaring, I have dealt in particular depth with various facets of it in this chapter.

The Textual Evidence

There is considerable and diverse evidence pertaining to the movement of Minoan seafarers and artisans in the eastern Mediterranean during the closing centuries of the Middle Bronze Age II and the beginning of the Late Bronze Age.

Mari

A tin inventory from Mari is the earliest textual evidence for Minoan contact with the Syro-Canaanite coast.[2] The text dates to the first half of Zimri-Lim's reign (ca. 1780–1760 B.C. according to the middle chronology). Among those receiving tin are a Caphtorite (Minoan) and a Carian, apparently from Caria on the western Turkish coast.[3] Ugarit was the port of entry for these Aegean merchants and supplied their dragoman. The fact that an Ugaritian interpreter could converse with Minoans suggests that this contact may have been stronger than the evidence at present allows. Interestingly, a Caphtorite and a Carian are also mentioned in later Ugaritic texts.[4]

The Cypro-Minoan Script

Intimate contacts between the Minoan culture and Cyprus are indicated by the consideration that the Cypro-Minoan script derives from a Minoan, not a Mycenaean, script.[5]

Kom el Hetan

A list of Aegean names in the mortuary temple of Amenhotep III at Kom el Hetan apparently derives from an itinerary of a voyage made in the Aegean.[6] The list begins and ends in Crete, suggesting that the voyage originated there, possibly (but not necessarily) in Minoan times.

Ugarit

Kothar-wa-Khasis, the master-craftsman god of the Ugaritic pantheon who had his home in Caphtor (Crete/Aegean), is linked in one Ugaritic poem with navigation.[7] This mythological attribution may reflect a Syro-Canaanite respect for Minoan navigational skills.

The Archaeological Evidence

Classical Greek historians record that Minos ruled the Aegean (*thalassocracy*)—and particularly the Cyclades—after conquering its indigenous population and establishing his sons as rulers over them.[8] Much has been written concerning the accuracy of these accounts vis-à-vis Bronze Age reality. Archaeological research has indicated a prevalent Minoan influence in the southern Aegean, perhaps driven at least partially by a need for metals.[9] The degree to which this is the result of actual political control or simply "cultural dominance" by a more evolved people over their less-developed neighbors is, in most cases, difficult if not impossible to determine.[10] Some sites, like Trianda on Rhodes during the Late Minoan IA–IB, may have consisted of expatriate Minoans and their descendants.[11] In this respect, more emphasis is now being placed on the simplest items of cultural baggage, such as kitchen wares and weaving implements, instead of luxury items that may reflect little more than what M. Wiener has termed the "Versailles effect."[12]

The topic of Minoan expansion, albeit fascinating, is beyond the scope of the present study. It is worth emphasizing, however, that these contacts presuppose the use of ships on a grand scale over a considerable amount of time. It is reasonable to assume that the ships used were, for the most part, those of the principal players in this drama.

Minoan Artisans Abroad

L. Wooley, in his excavations at Tell Atchana (Alalakh), found a similarity of decoration techniques used there (Stratum VII) and in Crete.[13] Wall paintings imitating marble in the Minoan style were also uncovered at Qatna.[14] From this, Wooley concluded that Near Eastern artisans had decorated Cretan palaces.

In recent years, archaeologists seem to be uncovering Minoan frescoes everywhere along the eastern shores of the Mediterranean. Minoan-style frescoes have been found in at least three, and possibly four, Syro-Canaanite and Egyptian Middle Bronze Age sites. These new discoveries strongly suggest, however, that influences flowed in the opposite direction and that Minoan artisans were visiting and decorating palaces in Asia and Egypt. Frescoes have been uncovered in the Middle Bronze Age palace at Kabri, located in the northwestern corner of the Plain of Acco in northern Israel.[15] There, an entire room was covered with a grid-pattern of red lines. The resultant squares alternate red and white in a chessboard-like pattern imitating stone slabs, a form of decoration used in Crete dating from the Middle Minoan I period and later. The Kabri floor is also decorated with floral designs, including irises and crocuses created in the typical Minoan/Cycladic manner. Additionally, the plastered threshold of a doorway was decorated with a grid system made of red lines. The squares contain remnants of motifs similar to those known from Minoan Crete but unknown from the ancient Near East. Notes W. D. Niemeier: "The Kabri floor and also the fresco fragments from Yarim-Lim's palace at Alalakh do not have only single Minoan motifs foreign to 'Greater Canaan' which could be explained as intrusive or incorporated elements arriving by motif transfer but they show a purely Minoan iconography as well as technique. This can only mean that they were executed by traveling Minoan artisans."[16]

Niemeier's conclusions are strengthened by the discovery at Alalakh of an unfinished red marble basin of a Minoan-style columnar lamp, perhaps made locally by a Minoan artisan.[17] Wooley considered this indicative of its local production, noting that "it would be curious if a Cretan craftsman left unfinished an important piece of work intended for export."[18]

These seem to represent the physical reality behind the Ugaritic myth in which Kothar wa-Khasis, the god of handicrafts, is brought from Caphtor (Crete and/or the Aegean) to construct and furnish with great works of art a majestic palace for the god Baal.[19]

The appearance of a Minoan at Mari may explain the origin of Minoan decorative motifs in the Mari wall paintings and how objects of Caphtorite workmanship found their way to Mari.[20] Of particular interest is a podium, the upper surface of which is decorated with a painting of marble surrounded by a frame of running spirals and flames.[21]

S. Lloyd and J. Mellaart point out the possibility of Minoan elements in the plan and construction of the nineteenth-century B.C. palace at Beyçesultan.[22] If their hypothesis is correct, it suggests a possible presence there also of Minoan artisans during the Middle Bronze Age.

In Egypt, fragments of Minoan-style wall paintings have also been uncovered at Tell ed-Dabᶜa.[23] These paintings, reportedly similar in style and execution to fres-coes from Knossos and Thera, include images of bull-jumping.

The Iconographic Evidence

Minoans in the Theban Tombs
A unique form of graphic evidence concerning Minoan contacts with Egypt consists of tableaus of Aegeans depicted in the tombs of the nobles at Thebes.[24] A study of these Aegean figures and their wares, identified as inhabitants of "Keftiu" (= Caphtor) and the "Isles in the Midst of the Sea" in the accompanying inscriptions, indicates that their ships were arriving in Egypt during the reigns of Hatshepsut and Thutmose III, and perhaps earlier. The term *Isles in the Midst of the Sea* may have been the Minoan name for Crete and the surrounding islands as adopted in translation by the Egyptians.

Scenes of Minoans are discontinued in the Theban tombs after the opening years of Amenhotep

*Figure 6.1. Minoans bringing their wares are depicted for the last time at Thebes, Egypt, in the tomb of Rechmire (*Late Thutmose III; early Amenhotep II*) (*from Davies 1943: pls. 18–20*)

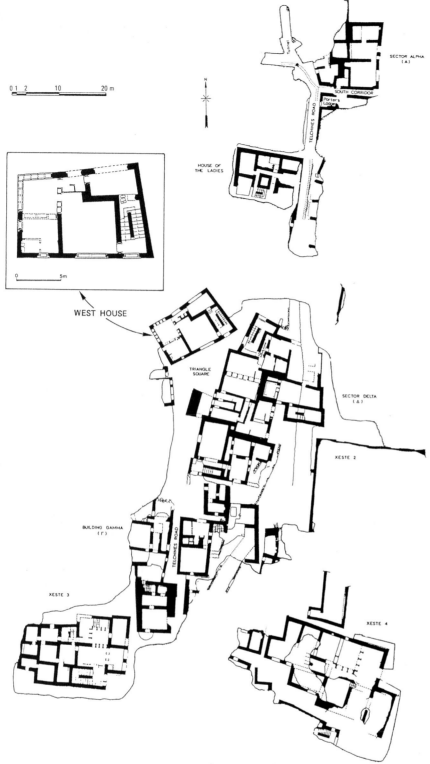

Figure 6.2. *Map of the excavations at Akrotiri. Note the location of the West House (from Morgan 1988: 2 fig. 1)*

II's reign. The tomb of Rechmire, where they appear for the last time, was completed soon after Amenhotep's coronation (Fig. 6.1). This cessation of contact is synchronous with the end of the Minoan culture in Crete at the end of the Late Minoan IB, which seems to have occurred in the latter part of Thutmose III's reign.[25] Apparently the Egyptians ceased to draw the Aegeans in their tombs because direct contact with the Aegean ended when the Minoan culture fell and was not revived by the Mycenaeans after they consolidated their hold on Crete.

Thera

The Miniature Frieze that revolutionized our understanding of Minoan ships was found in a structure at Akrotiri termed the "West House" by Spyridon Marinatos (Fig. 6.2).[26] Only two rooms (4 and 5) on the building's second story were decorated with frescoes; the Miniature Frieze was situated below the ceiling in Room 5 (Fig. 6.3).[27]

Here, windows, doors, and niches in the walls significantly limited the amount of space available to the artists. The lower parts of the walls were covered with a dado consisting of panels imitating stone and wood. At the eastern extremity of the north wall and the southern extremity of the western wall are two nude youths, each over a meter high, who carry fish, seemingly toward the northwest corner of the room.[28] At the vestibule connecting Rooms 5 and 4, a youthful priestess strides into Room 5.[29] This figure wears an unusual sari-like outer garment and holds what appears to be an incense burner into which she drops a yellow ingredient, perhaps saffron.

Although the Miniature Frieze from Akrotiri is the best-preserved example of this Aegean art style, similar miniature wall paintings are known from Late Minoan/Late Cycladic I contexts in Crete—at Knossos, Tylissos, Prasa, and Katsamba—as well as on the islands of Kea and Melos.[30] In all cases, the miniature wall paintings seem to depict cultic activities. The scenes always take place in the open, although adjacent towns or buildings are depicted. For example, in the Knossos miniatures, crowds watch a cultic dance or stand beside a shrine.

The paintings from Kea are perhaps of greatest interest in this regard because they appear to depict a motif similar to the waterborne procession/race at Thera (Fig. 6.4).[31] The Kea painting is badly fragmented, but the many pieces of blue-painted fresco, together with several pieces depicting parts of ships, support this view. Several men are situated beneath wooden struts, paralleling the seated figures in the processional/racing ships at Thera. Diminutive dolphins were apparently painted on the hull of a ship, as at Thera. This may indicate that at Thera and Kea the same festival took place and was recorded.[32] Further connections are the handled tripod-cauldrons being used by men in the Kea frieze.[33] A similar bronze cauldron was found in the debris of Room 4 in the West House.[34]

The Theran Miniature Frieze was painted across the north, south, and east walls of Room 5. The frieze on the east wall depicts a river flowing through clumps of papyrus plants and palm trees in which real and fantastic animals cavort.[35] The waterborne procession/race is portrayed on the

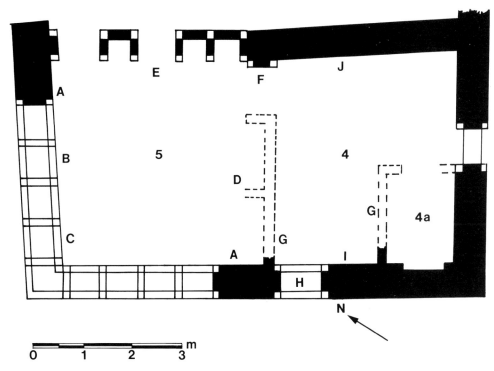

Figure 6.3. Plan of Rooms 4 and 5 in the West House indicating the positioning of the frescoes: (A) fisherman; (B) ships, dead bodies in water, and marching warriors; (C) Meeting on the Hill; (D) waterborne procession; (E) landscape; (F) priestess; (G) two ikria; (H) lilies; (I) one ikria; (J) three ikria (after Morgan 1988: 3 fig. 2)

southern wall (Fig. 6.5). The north wall depicts a group involved in cultic practice on a hilltop as well as additional nautical scenes. The west wall lacked a miniature frieze. It may have borne the continuation of the frieze originally, however. If so, it would have been positioned over openings in the wall and, thus, would have been most susceptible to vibrations caused by earthquakes that preceded the final destruction of Thera.[36] Presumably, these parts of the frieze had been shaken off the wall during the preliminary earth

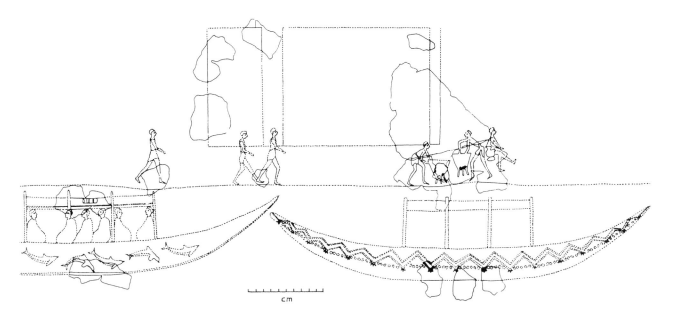

Figure 6.4. Miniature frieze from Kea (provisional reconstruction) (from Morgan 1990: 255 fig. 2)

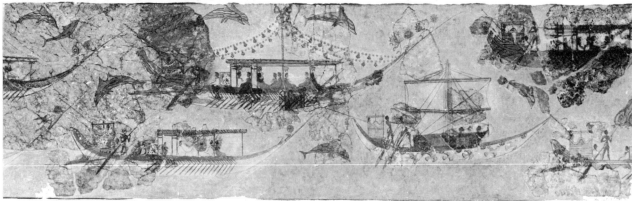

Figure 6.5. The waterborne procession in the south Miniature Frieze (courtesy of the National Archaeological Museum, Athens)

tremors and were removed by the Therans before the settlement's final destruction.

The Miniature Frieze on the northern wall is also badly damaged. Spyridon Marinatos dealt with two elements within this tableau. The first is known as the "Meeting on the Hill," in which a group of men, some wearing robes and others wearing kilts, come together, possibly to worship at a hillside or peak sanctuary over-

looking the sea (Fig. 6.6).[37] The second scene in the Miniature Frieze depicts parts of four ships and a row of soldiers who advance inland in single file (Fig. 6.7). To the left of the soldiers is a settlement in which the inhabitants seem totally oblivious to them.

These ships lack the decorative elements of the processional craft. It is not clear if the ships bear stern cabins (*ikria*) for the area above the sterns of all three is missing. The

oars of one craft are awash in the surf, indicating that they were rowed, not paddled. Two ships have a garland or tassel hanging over the side of the bow. The bow device on one ship is similar to those depicted on the Kolona ships (Fig. 5.24:B).

Three naked dead bodies are floating in the water.[38] Unlike the scene on the "Siege Rhyton" from Shaft Grave IV at Mycenae, to which it has been compared, in the

Miniature Frieze the people in and around the nearby city seem totally oblivious to the detachment of soldiers and the ships.[39] This is a scene of pastoral landscape with the exception of the row of fully armed soldiers.

Since Spyridon Marinatos's publication, additional fragments of the fresco found in Room 5 have been assigned to the north Miniature Frieze.[40] These additions belong primarily to the western and central parts of the northern frieze. There are two ships below and to the left of the "Meeting on the Hill" (Fig. 6.8). One of these is being paddled in the same manner as those taking part in the southern Miniature Frieze. This hints that the waterborne parade/race had continued on the west wall. Beneath it is another ship, of the

Figure 6.6. The "Meeting on the Hill" in the north Miniature Frieze (photo by the author; courtesy of the National Archaeological Museum, Athens)

Figure 6.7. Ships, warriors, and a pastoral scene in the north Miniature Frieze (photo by the author; courtesy of the National Archaeological Museum, Athens)

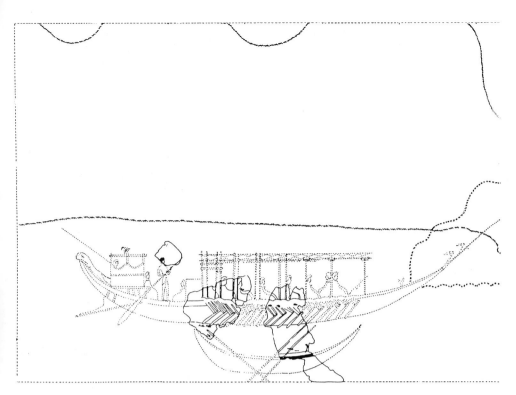

Figure 6.8. Reconstruction (1) of the west part of the north Miniature Frieze (from Televantou 1990: 315, fig. 7)

smaller class. C. A. Televantou plausibly reconstructs another ship beneath the "Meeting on the Hill" in which appear the remains of two figures, one of which holds a staff in an attitude of cultic worship (Fig. 6.9). Two additional ships were located between the "Meeting on the Hill" and the vessels beneath the advancing soldiers (Fig. 6.10).[41] A fragment bearing the bow of yet another ship may be placed to the right of this scene (Fig. 6.11). Thus, the north Miniature Frieze contained at least nine ships of two different types.

THE PROCESSIONAL SHIPS. All the vessels in the Miniature Frieze —from the large ships participating in the procession/race to a small, two-man paddled canoe— have gently curving crescentic hulls when seen in profile. This hull shape is typical of Minoan ship depictions (Figs. 6.12–13, 21, 26, 28, 32–34, 52, 64).

An upcurving crescentic stern

Figure 6.9. Reconstruction (2) of the north Miniature Frieze showing fragments of a processional ship and other vessels, and the Meeting on the Hill (from Televantou 1990: 316 fig. 8)

Figure 6.10. Reconstruction (3) of the north Miniature Frieze from the "Meeting on the Hill" to the bodies in the water (from Televantou 1990: 317 fig. 9)

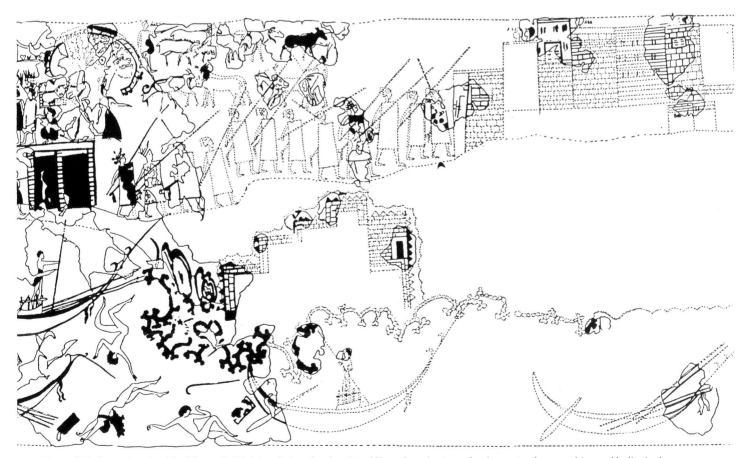

Figure 6.11. Reconstruction (4) of the north Miniature Frieze showing the soldiers advancing toward a city, pastoral scenes, ships, and bodies in the water (from Televantou 1990: 316 fig. 10)

Figure 6.12. *The best-preserved ship in the waterborne parade in the south Miniature Frieze (photo by the author; courtesy of the National Archaeological Museum, Athens)*

Figure 6.13. *Line drawing of the best-preserved ship in the waterborne procession depicted in the south Miniature Frieze at Thera (after Marinatos 1974: color pl. 9)*

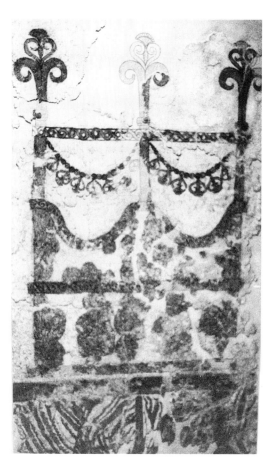

Figure 6.14. The processional ships carry a stylis-*like pole, a horizontal water-level projection, and a small cabin (*ikria*) at the stern (after Marinatos 1974: color pl. 9)*

Figure 6.15. One of the eight painted ikria *in Room 4 of the West House (photo by the author; courtesy of the National Archaeological Museum, Athens)*

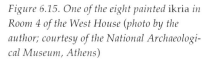

Figure 6.16. The rowed ship accompanying the procession in the south Miniature Frieze (after Doumas 1983: 121 fig. 20)

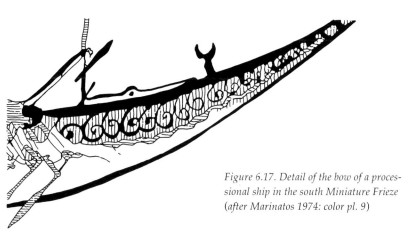

Figure 6.17. Detail of the bow of a processional ship in the south Miniature Frieze (after Marinatos 1974: color pl. 9)

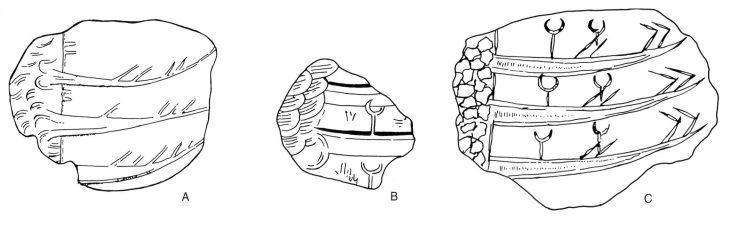

Figure 6.18. Talismanic seals depicting the bows of three ships (after Betts 1968: pl. 61, figs. 1–3)

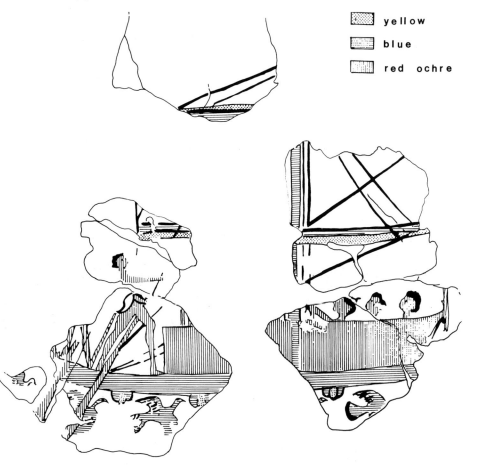

yellow

blue

red ochre

Figure 6.19. The Thera sailing ship without restoration (after Morgan 1988: 124 fig. 70)

cause in the same scene another ship, undecorated and not taking part in the procession, is rowed in the normal manner (Fig. 6.16). All of the ships joining the procession have lowered their sails, and most have unstepped their masts. A study of the figures sitting and standing in the vessels participating in the procession/race suggests that the boats were at least partially decked in the stern.[43]

The ships' bows have a triangular structure that in profile looks like the framework or railing for a splash-guard (Fig. 6.17). It is unlikely that this was its purpose, however. Its true shape and function remain unclear. Next to it, a crescentic object, located in the bow, is identified by Spyridon Marinatos as a *histodoke*, or mast crutch.[44] This interpretation is not valid based on the following considerations:

• These items do not appear together with steering oars at the ships' sterns (Fig. 6.5).

• When lowered, the masts of the Thera ships are shown placed with the rest of the rigging on a row of stanchions along the centerline of the ships.

• The "splash-guard" and the "crescent on a stand" appear in bows of ships depicted on talismanic seals, suggesting that they have a cultic, not a utilitarian, purpose (Fig. 6.18).[45]

first appears in the Aegean on a ship incised on a sherd from Phylakopi, dated to the third millennium (Fig. 5.12). Crescentic hulls are also depicted on the roughly contemporaneous Kolona ships (Fig. 5.24). The ships are profusely decorated and carry horizontal stern devices, ornamental stern cabins (*ikria*), and *stylis*-like poles (Fig. 6.14).[42] Eight large *ikria* are painted on the walls of Room 4 of the West House (Fig. 6.15).

Paddlers propel the ships participating in the race/procession (Figs. 6.13, 42). This is unusual be-

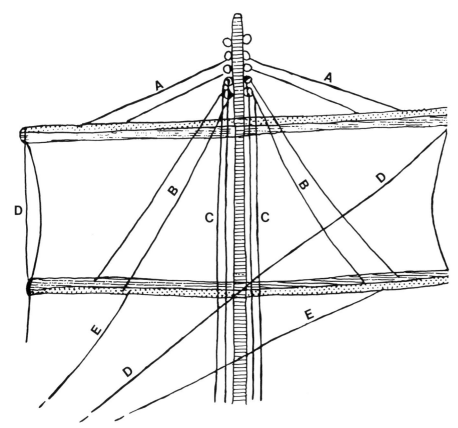

Figure 6.20. The rigging of the sailing ship (after Morgan 1988: 124 fig. 71)

with the Homeric *naúmaha ksustá*.[48] Some pikes are held by the landed contingent of soldiers while others are attached to the bow of one of the ships from which the soldiers presumably have disembarked.

Based on a comparison of the motifs and devices depicted on some of the Theran ships' hulls to Mycenaean decorations, R. Laffineur argues that the ships are Mycenaean.[49] Niemeier, however, has demonstrated that parallels to these exist equally in Minoan Crete.[50] Furthermore, these ships are of the type depicted repeatedly in Minoan glyptic and other art and are, as we shall see, quite distinct from the ships that appear in Mycenaean iconography.[51] Finally, the "Mycenaean connection" is further strained by the late seventeenth-century B.C. date now postulated for the final catastrophe that destroyed Thera.

The lunettes cannot have been a functional feature of the ships.

Some scholars have assumed that the warriors in the ships are sitting under an awning.[46] This, however, would require pairs of stanchions placed abeam in order to allow a sufficient spread to shade the men from the sun. Such pairs of stanchions are lacking for most of the area covered by the lowered rigging, where the only support is a row of fore-and-aft crutches. At the sternmost part of the area below the lowered rig, however, are four stanchions placed in two pairs and connected by horizontal bars at their upper extremities (Fig. 6.13). This may have served as a base structure for a small awning.

The horizontal red lines positioned on the crutches are probably long spears or sea pikes that are seen in use elsewhere in the Miniature Fresco and depicted stowed on the Kolona ships (Figs. 5.24; 6.7).[47] These have been equated

Figure 6.21. Ships under sail depicted on Late Minoan seals (after Casson 1995A: figs. 37–40)

Figure 6.22. Wall painting fragments from Pylos depicting a ship's rigging (from Lang 1969: pl. 113: 19 M ne [M. L. Lang, The Palace of Nestor at Pylos in Western Messenia II: The Frescoes, © 1969 by PUP. Reproduced by permission of Princeton University Press])

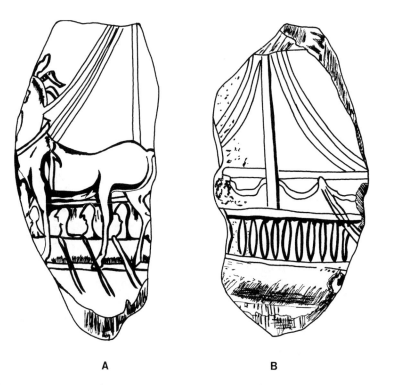

A   B

Figure 6.23. Fragments of clay sealings from Knossos depicting ships (Late Minoan IIIA) (after PM II: 244 fig. 141: a–b)

THE SAILING SHIP AND RIGGING AT THERA. One fragmentary ship accompanying the procession/race is under sail (Fig. 6.19). It has been reconstructed with and without an *ikria*, for which there is no evidence.[52] The ship has a stern deck where the helmsmen stand. The heads of three seamen, just visible above the open bulwark, suggest that the hull was at least partially undecked amidships. The sailing ship, as well as two other vessels in the Miniature Frieze, have open bulwarks similar to those still used in the Aegean (Fig. 6.24).[53] Although missing on the ship under sail, mastheads carrying rows of sheaves to support the lifts and halyards are seen on two ships depicted with their masts stepped (Figs. 6.13, 27 [compare 22]).[54]

L. Morgan assumes that since the ships in the Miniature Frieze lack stays, these were not used on the actual prototype ships.[55] This is most unlikely, however, for stays are required to give a mast longitudinal support. Their absence is probably traceable to artistic convention. Stays normally appear on contemporaneous Egyptian rigs (Figs. 2.11, 15–18, 24, 26, 29–32) and seem to have become more popular in ship iconography after the introduction of the brailed rig (Figs. 7.8: A, 17, 19, 21, 25, 27).

The rig used on the Theran ships has been compared to the contemporaneous Egyptian rig.[56] The area of the sail is mostly lacking in the wall painting. Spyridon Marinatos was able to reconstruct the sail and its rigging, however, based on the remaining fragments and on the rigging shown on the ships that have struck sail (Fig. 6.20).[57] The lines depicted are two pairs of lifts for both the yard and boom (B), halyards (C), braces (D), and sheets (E).[58] The area beneath the raised yard is missing. Presum-

Figure 6.24. The small vessels depicted in the south Miniature Frieze (photo by the author; courtesy of the National Archaeological Museum, Athens)

ably, the concave arcs of the yard's lifts were portrayed here.

The halyards are not secured in the stern as is the case on Egyptian and Syro-Canaanite rigs (Figs. 2.15–18, 26; 3.2–5, 7–9). Instead, they run parallel to the mast and are fastened next to its foot. Two lines are drawn parallel to the mast on its right side; two additional lines are reasonably reconstructed aft of the mast (Fig. 6.20: C). These lines also appear on Minoan seals (Fig. 6.21). Since they cannot represent four halyards, one pair of lines must belong to the running lifts holding the yard when it is in the raised position. Thus, to raise the sail the hands would haul at the halyards; then, when the yard had been raised, they would trim it by pulling on the running lifts, a task perhaps being carried out by the man posi-

tioned forward of the ship's mast (Fig. 6.19).[59]

Unlike the roughly contemporaneous Egyptian and Syro-Canaanite rig where the lifts are shown attached along the entire length of the spars, on the best-preserved of the Theran processional ships the lifts end at the extremities of the yard and boom (Fig. 6.12). This phenomenon is seen on a wall painting from Pylos depicting a ship's mast cap, lifts, and yard, as well as on some Late Minoan seals and sealings that bear ship depictions (Figs. 6.22–23, 26, 28).[60] It may result from artistic license or may mean that lifts had a somewhat different function on the Aegean rig:[61] they supported the yard when it was in its raised position but not when it was lowered. Of course, lifts were not needed on the Minoan rig when

the yard was struck because it was then carried on crutches. As opposed to this, the lifts on the Late Bronze Age ships of Egypt and along the Syro-Canaanite littoral supported the yard when it was lowered, *but not when it was raised.*

The nearest parallels to the Theran rig, with its boom-footed sail, are sails seen on Middle Kingdom Egyptian ships (Fig. 11.3).[62] Similarly, the Theran ships lack the complicated mast cap visible on Hatshepsut's Punt ships and are best compared with simpler Middle Kingdom mastheads.[63]

The breadth of the sail, when shown athwartship, is less than half the length of the ship. This is considerably narrower than the broad sails portrayed on Egyptian and Syro-Canaanite ships, which are normally nearly equal to the ships' length (Figs. 2.11, 15, 18, 35–

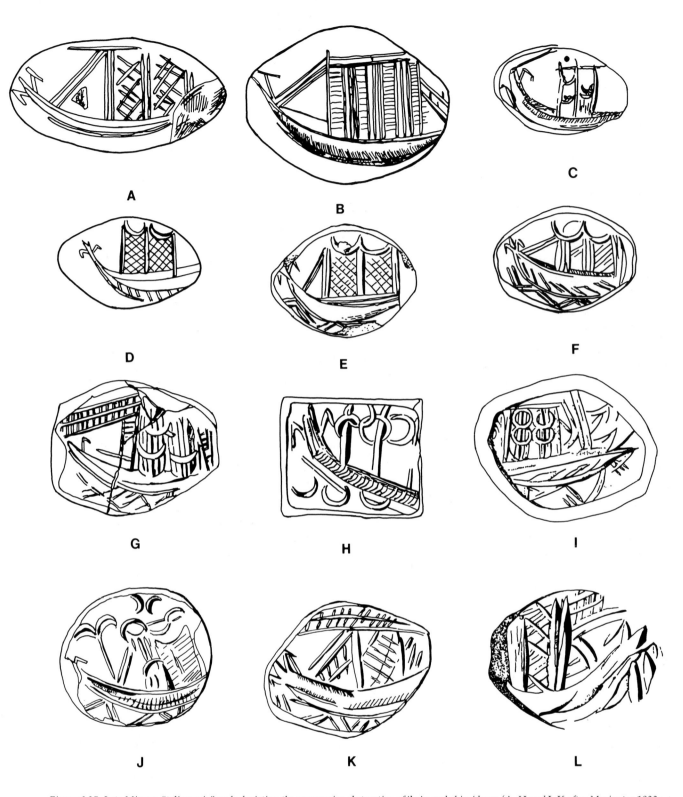

A

B

C

D

E

F

G

H

I

J

K

L

Figure 6.25. Late Minoan "talismanic" seals depicting the progressive abstraction of ikria *and ships' bows (A–H and J–K after Marinatos 1933: pls. 15: 43, 42, 16: 46, 51, 44–45, 49, 48, 50, 47; I and L after Casson 1995A: figs. 44–45)*

42; 3.2–3, 5–6, 8–9, 12–13). The Theran ship carries the boom unusually high on the mast, a detail that is also evident on Late Minoan seals (Fig. 6.21: A–C).

When masts were struck, they rested on a row of crutches; the striped decoration on the masts may represent wooldings.[64] Alternatively, the stripes may be solely decorative. Whatever their meaning, a similar element seems to be depicted on the masts of ships on a Late Helladic IIIB amphoroid krater from Enkomi (Fig. 7.28:A).

SMALL CRAFT. The smallest vessel shown is a crescentic-shaped two-man canoe that is being paddled; five other diminutive crescentic boats are anchored in a bay near the city to the right (Fig. 6.24). Morgan notes that two craft with skeletal awnings depicted in a harbor above and to the right of the canoe, though portrayed on a much smaller scale, are of the same type (and size?) as the rowed ship.[65]

Ships on Minoan Seals

Ships appear on a wide variety of Minoan seals, beginning in the Early Minoan III period.[66] The ships depicted on tiny Minoan seals are often schematic, making it possible to interpret the various representations as different classes of craft.[67] The seals must now be correlated with the evidence from Thera.

TALISMANIC SEALS. A number of seals show the abstract bow of a boat with a bird ornament on the stem; behind this is an object constructed of two or three vertical poles with hatching between them (Fig. 6.25).[68] The motif undergoes a progressive abstraction during the series. This object is interpreted as masts and sails by Spyridon Marinatos, as deck awnings by R. W. Hutchinson, and as a type of pole sail by L. Basch.[69]

The identity is closer at hand, however. H. Van Effenterre identifies this construction as the stern *ikria*.[70] Indeed, in the more realistically portrayed seals, the device is too similar to the *ikria* on the Theran ships for this to be a coincidence (Figs. 6.15, 25: C–F). Furthermore, on a seal from Thebes, the device appears at the stern of the ship, the actual position of the *ikria* on the processional ships (Fig. 6.48). Thus, the seals portray two important elements—bird decorations and *ikria*—that at Thera are specifically connected with the water ceremony. Apparently, *contra* Basch, we are not seeing an entire ship on this seal type.[71]

Figure 6.26. *Ship with festooned lines depicted on a steatite lentoid seal (Late Minoan IIIB)* (*after PM II: 243 fig. 139*)

Figure 6.27. *One of the ships in the procession has rows of garlands running from the mast to the bow and stern* (*from Doumas 1992: 75–76*)

This variety of seal, termed "talismanic" by Evans, dates from the Middle Minoan III to the Late Minoan I periods and ceases to be made after the Mycenaean takeover of Crete.[72] Concerning the uses of this seal type, J. H. Betts notes:[73]

In addition to its incidental artistic attractiveness as jewelry, the sealstone had two main functions as the personal symbol of its wearer. The one was sphragistic: the functional use of a seal to make a mark guaranteeing a document or product as authentic; the vast number of clay sealings from the Cretan and

Figure 6.28. *Minoan crescentic ship depicted on a gold ring from Tiryns (ca. 1300 B.C.)* (*after Casson 1995A: fig. 50*)

Figure 6.29. Ships with mast and rigging depicted on Early Minoan III (A–B) and Middle Minoan (C–K) seals. In all cases, the sails have been lowered (A–B after PM II: 239 figs. 136: a–b; C–E and G–K after Marinatos 1933: pl. 15: 33, 31, 39, 34–35, 32, 36–37; F after Casson 1995A: fig. 48)

Mainland palaces, often found in association with tablets bearing script, indicates the extent of this function. The other was amuletic, the seal being the personal symbol of the individual and so in some way his magical protector. In the case of most sealstones the two uses were not apparently distinct, and it is in general not possible to say that one served as a seal and another as an amulet; *but in the case of those sealstones for which Evans coined the name "talismanic" it seems possible to make such a distinction and to say that their function must have been almost entirely magical.*[74] They are very rarely used sphragistically; clay sealings are not often found bearing impressions made by them. From their earlier and more frequent appearance in eastern Crete in Middle Minoan III, especially in the cemeteries at Mochlos and Sphoungaras, it is probable that they, like the earlier three-sided prisms, originated in eastern Crete. They seem to be almost exclusively Cretan; very few have been found on the Mainland of Greece and their function does not seem to continue much after 1500 B.C. . . . The superstition they were made to serve was Minoan, not Greek. Their magical protective qualities seem to have derived not only from their shape and material, like the normal amulet, but also from the schematic motifs engraved on them and perhaps even from the consistent style of their engraving.

Again, note the link between elements of the procession and cultic significance. This interpretation helps to explain the appearance of the *"Ikria* Wall Paintings" in Room 4 of the West House. Clearly, the *ikria* are not a normal part of the ships' architecture for

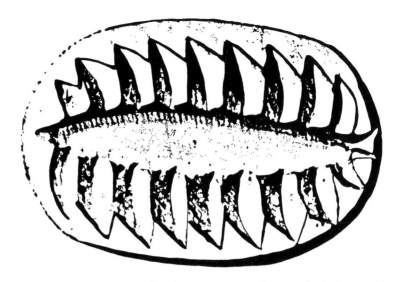

Figure 6.30. Design on a prism seal, perhaps representing a plan view of a ship being paddled (after Basch 1987: 99 fig. B4: B)

they do not appear on the vessels used for functional purposes at Thera.[75]

SHIPS WITH RIGGING. The ships depicted with their rigs lowered on Minoan seals are presumably also shown taking part in a cultic procession like the one at Thera. This is indicated by a seal that shows a ship with its rig down and with a row of garlands running from the masthead to the stem and stern, a decoration par-

alleled on one of the Theran ships (Figs. 6.26–27). Similar devices may appear on a ship portrayed on a gold ring from Tiryns (Fig. 6.28).

When ships first appear on Minoan seals, they are depicted with the sail lowered and with lines running diagonally from the mast to both of the ships' extremities (Fig. 6.29: A–I, K). These are identified as stays by Betts and lifts by Hutchinson.[76] I prefer Hutchinson's identification. On most of

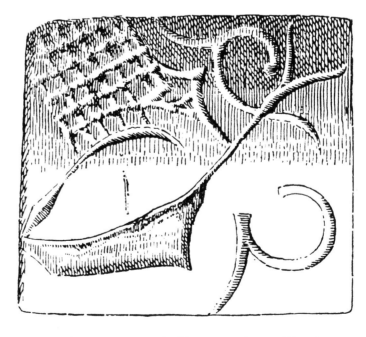

Figure 6.31. Ship shown in perspective view (?) on a Late Minoan seal (from PM II: 243 fig. 140)

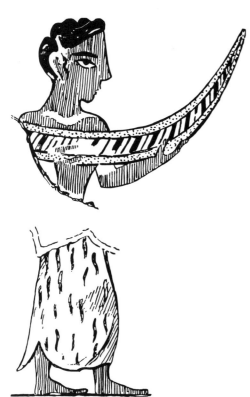

Figure 6.32. Model ship carried by mourner on the Hagia Triada sarcophagus (ca. 1400 B.C.) (after PM I: 439 fig. 316.)

bans).[78] He argues that they must connect to the stern. Considering that all the other seals have these diagonal lines on *both* sides of the mast, however, it seems preferable to assume that the opposing lines are lacking because the seal was never finished.

Crosshatching on the spread sails of ships depicted on Late Minoan seals suggests that the sails were made of sewn panels (Fig. 6.21). Topping lifts appear on one seal (Fig. 6.21: D). The artists' intentions in portraying sets of diagonal lines beneath and on either side of the mast on these seals are unclear; perhaps they are an attempt to depict the boom's lifts in an "exploded view."

BEAM/LENGTH RATIO. One seal may indicate the beam/

length ratio of a Minoan ship.[79] A ship appears on a three-sided Early Minoan III steatite prism seal (Fig. 6.29: I). The craft is well known and has been published repeatedly. The other two sides of the seal are also of interest, however.[80] The second side shows two fish placed head-to-tail.[81] The third side is engraved with an elongated, cigar-shaped object with nine appendages on either side (Fig. 6.30). E. Eccles tentatively identifies this object as a centipede. It also bears a fair resemblance to the bough that appears before the ship's bow. But a third possibility is that the artist has portrayed a bird's-eye view of the ship being paddled. If so, then the boat seems to have been of relatively narrow beam. This is

the seals the lines disappear at the extremities and at first seem to be stays; but on the more detailed depictions at Thera and Pylos, as well as on other seals, these lines are clearly lifts attached to the lowered yard and boom (Figs. 6.13, 22–23, 26, 28).[77]

One ship of this group has four diagonal lines of rigging from the mast to the high extremity of the vessel (Fig. 6.29: J). Basch notes only three of the four lines and interprets them as shrouds (*hau–*

Figure 6.34. Bow section of a bronze ship model from Keos (Late Minoan IB/Late Helladic II or earlier) (from Caskey 1964: pl. 56: c; courtesy of the American School of Classical Studies at Athens)

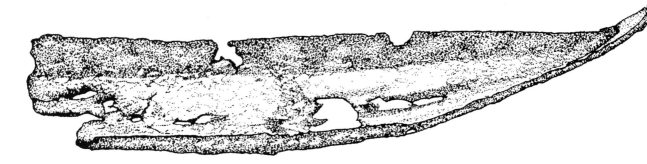

Figure 6.33. Fragmentary bronze ship model from Keos (Late Minoan IB/Late Helladic II) (after Göttlicher 1978: Taf. 25: 335)

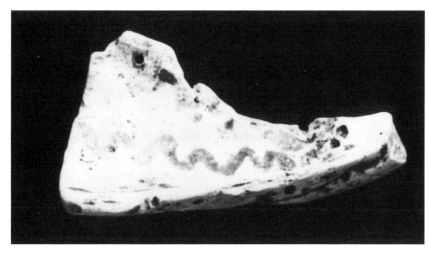

Figure 6.35. Bow of a terra-cotta ship model from Keos (Late Helladic III A2–B1) (courtesy of the Keos Excavations, University of Cincinnati)

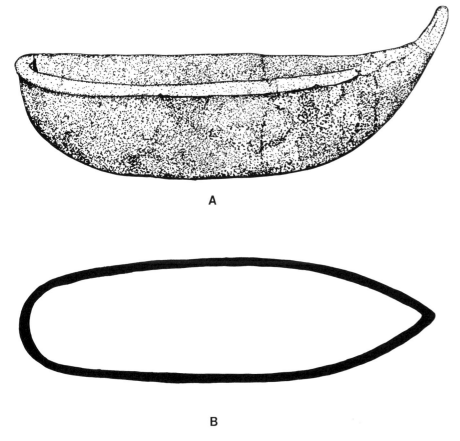

A

B

Figure 6.36. Alabaster or marble ship model from Hagia Triada (Late Minoan I–II) (NTS): (A) profile; (B) plan view (A after Marinatos 1933: pl. 14: 22; B after Göttlicher 1978: Taf. 24: 320)

the similarity here to a ship under sail may be fortuitous.

RAFTS. Basch convincingly shows that rafts supported on skin floats or pots are depicted on Minoan seals.[83] It is not clear, however, whether the rafts themselves actually existed in Minoan times or were anachronistic memories.

BASCH'S TYPOLOGY OF SHIPS ON MINOAN SEALS. Basch concludes that the seals in his groups A–E represent different classes of ships. At times he identifies the pointed end as the stem, at others as the stern. On his class B (le type cycladic), he places the horizontal projection at the bow while the bird decoration is relegated to the stern.[84] Several ships in this group, however, have a vertical element above the extremity with the horizontal projection (Fig. 6.29: B, D). These may represent either the *stylis*-like pole carried at the stern on the Thera processional ships or the exceptionally high loom of a quarter rudder, as on the Kolona ships (Figs. 5.24: A; 6.13–14). Both of these interpretations require the high decorated end to be the stem and the horizontal projection to signify the stern, as at Thera.

THE SIGNIFICANCE OF SHIPS DEPICTED ON MINOAN SEALS. In conclusion, what purpose did the Minoan seals serve by depicting ships and their parts? Summing up the evidence, Betts notes:[85]

This survey of the types of sealstones on which representations of Minoan ships occur will leave a number of nagging problems for the nautical archaeologist, but its central thesis remains clear. Almost all the ships occur on Middle Minoan I–II three-sided prisms and on Middle Minoan III–Late Minoan I talismanic gems. Neither type had much sphragistic use. Both had an amuletic function, apparently

supported by the evidence of Minoan models.[82]

A SHIP IN PERSPECTIVE? Undoubtedly, the most enigmatic and unusual depiction of a ship on a Minoan seal is one in which the vessel is portrayed under sail in what appears to be a one-quarter frontal view (Fig. 6.31). That is, the ship appears to be portrayed in perspective, a form of depiction otherwise unknown until Classical times. This portrayal is also unique in that the foot of the sail is billowing out, as if it were not connected to a boom. I suspect that

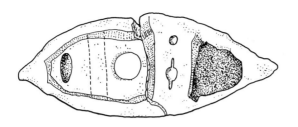

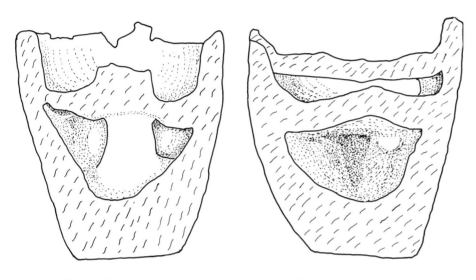

Figure 6.37. Terra-cotta ship model from Hagia Triada (Late Minoan) (NTS): (A) plan view; (B) section at break (courtesy of Paul F. Johnston; drawing by Frederick and Caroline Hemans)

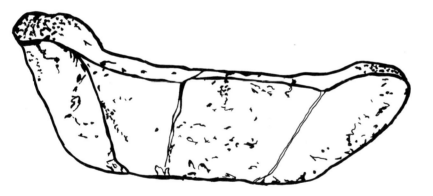

Figure 6.38. Limestone ship model from Melos (date undetermined) (after Göttlicher 1978: Taf. 24: 311)

Figure 6.39. Terra-cotta ship model from a royal tomb at Mycenae (Late Helladic IIIB) (from Göttlicher 1978: Taf. 25: 334)

based as much on their limited range of symbolic motifs as on their material and shape. This curious fact, along with the evidence of boat votives and "bateaux de culte," indicates that, despite Minoan Crete's reputation in later antiquity as a sea power, *the ships which occur in Minoan art almost all have some kind of symbolic, semi-religious or occult significance. The illustrations tend, especially in the Late Minoan period, to be schematic and to overemphasize certain features of the ship, perhaps those which had some special magico-religious significance.*[86] More or less naturalistic representations of ships are rarely found.

Minoan Ship Models

A model ship with the typical Minoan crescentic-shaped hull is carried by a mourner in the Hagia Triada sarcophagus (Fig. 6.32).[87] The repertoire of actual ship models that because of shape or provenance may be realistically considered to be patterned after Minoan or Cycladic ships is somewhat disappointing. Most of these models are of limited value for our study of Aegean ships for they are either fragmentary or crudely constructed. Other Middle and Late Minoan ship models remain unpublished.[88]

A narrow beam/length ratio is suggested by the fragmentary bow-sections of two bronze models from Keos (Figs. 6.33–34).[89] A terra-cotta model fragment of a curving, crescentic extremity similar to the bronze models was also found there (Fig. 6.35).[90] A stone ship model found at Hagia Triada has a rounded stern and pointed bow (Fig. 6.36).[91] It approximates in shape the form of the two bronze models. A hole at the bottom of the model may suggest that it was used as a *rhyton*. The model

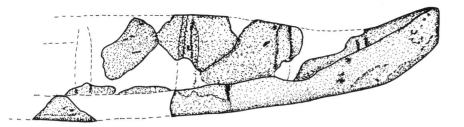

Figure 6.40. Terra-cotta ship model from Kofinas (Proto-Geometric/Early Geometric) (drawing from author's slide)

reaches its greatest beam forward of amidships.

A roughly made terra-cotta model from Hagia Triada, now broken in two, has a deck and the base of a mast. The mast is nearer to one end, identifying that side as the bow (Fig. 6.37).[92] A small hatch at the bow and a larger one at the stern pierce the deck. Two beams, of which only the one in the stern is now preserved, are situated above deck level. This model finds a rough parallel in another poorly made limestone ship model from Melos (Fig. 6.38).[93] Incised lines on the bottom may represent a keel and frames.

Ship depictions with singularly crescentic profiles are the exception rather than the rule in Mycenaean contexts. One such exception is a small, crude terra-cotta ship model from Mycenae itself (Fig. 6.39).[94] Basch discusses a fragmentary terra-cotta model from Kofinas that he dates to the Late Minoan III (Fig. 6.40).[95] The model is apparently of a later date, however.[96] The ship is flat-bottomed and highly reconstructed.

Discussion

Interpreting the Miniature Frieze at Thera

The meaning of the waterborne procession or race at Thera is intriguing, and various explanations have been put forward to explain it. There are two basic theories concerning this procession: military or cultic. Some scholars studying the ships, notably Spyridon Marinatos and Basch, have searched for parallels to the Theran material in Africa. However, before ranging so far afield, it is necessary to evaluate the wall painting against its natural Aegean milieu. Subsequent studies, particularly those by Nanno Marinatos and Lyvia Morgan, have demonstrated that the Miniature Frieze is loaded with Minoan cultic symbolism.[97] This goes hand-in-hand with the clear cultic significance of virtually all

known iconographic representations of Minoan ships. Therefore, the procession is best understood as an Aegean cultic festival that was a direct continuation of earlier practices and that continued, in various forms, into later times.

LOCALE. Spyridon Marinatos argues that the procession (or race) took place in Libya and suggests substantial Minoan-Libyan connections.[98] Basch assumes significant Egyptian influence in the scene. He believes that the city from which the processional ships are departing is located in the Nile Delta while the paddlers are either prisoners or slaves.[99]

Morgan convincingly places the locale in the Aegean.[100] And, indeed, the hypothesis of Minoan-Libyan contacts is faulty, because it presupposes direct two-way traffic between the Aegean and

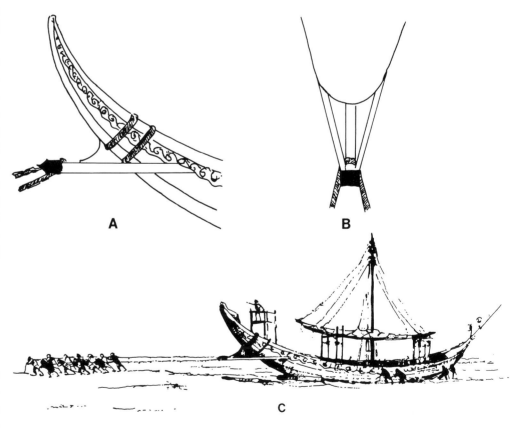

Figure 6.41. De Cervin's reconstruction of the horizontal stern device on the Thera processional ships: (A) the stern device with knee support; (B) plan view of the device; (C) hypothetical reconstruction of a ship being beached using lines attached to the stern device (after de Cervin 1977: 151 figs. 2 and 3)

Libya in the mid-second millennium B.C. This is unlikely to have been the case, however. Although ships could have sailed with relative ease from the Aegean to Libya, returning against the predominant northwest winds that blow throughout the summer sailing season would have been difficult, if not impossible, for a ship using a square sail footed with a boom. Therefore, ships were normally required to make a counterclockwise circuit of the entire eastern Mediterranean to reach the Aegean from Egypt.

Basch suggests that the scene depicts a Minoan military expedition to Egypt in the service of the Egyptian pharaoh. He argues that during their stay in Egypt, the Minoans never reached Thebes. Instead, they visited Lower Egypt and copied scenes of paddling there. In this manner, according to Basch, the paddler motif was adopted in the Theran relief. Basch's scenario does not give sufficient consideration to the evidence for a long tradition of paddling in the Aegean or to the appearance of Minoans in contemporary Theban tombs. There is no reason to doubt that these Minoans were recorded during actual visits to the city of Thebes itself.

The lion figures in the sterns of

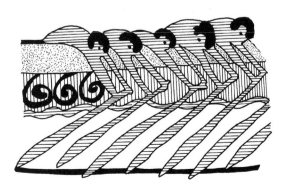

Figure 6.42. Paddlers in the waterborne procession at Thera bending over to complete their stroke (after Marinatos 1974: 51 fig. 6)

the Theran ships and painted on their hulls need not be an Egyptian influence as Basch suggests.[101] Lions have a strong connection with Minoan religion: they appear repeatedly in seals and seal impressions representing the young vegetation god and the mother goddess as the "Mistress/Master of Animals," as well as striding next to armed male figures.[102]

THE HORIZONTAL STERN DEVICE. In the third millennium when it first appears, just as in the time of the Theran frescoes, the horizontal stern device seems to have been optional gear on ships. It is carried by some ship representations: the Cycladic "frying pans," rock graffito of a ship from Naxos, a model from Palaikastro, and an incised sherd from Orchomenos (Figs. 5.3–4, 8–9, 11). It is lacking, however, on the lead models from Naxos and a graffito from Phylakopi (Figs. 5.1–2, 12). This situation admittedly lends itself to a variety of interpretations.

Many ingenious nautical explanations have been proposed to explain the unusual horizontal stern mechanism on the processional ships as well as on the Early Cycladic longships. Evans believes it to be a fixed rudder.[103] Hutchinson suggests that the "projecting keel at the stern" was a carryover from the Early Bronze Age longship type, perhaps resulting from the dugout origins of the hulls.[104] Spyridon Marinatos considers it a landing ladder that also doubled as a ship's head.[105] L. Casson believes that it was used to maintain proper trim.[106] G. B. R. De Cervin suggests that the stern device was used when pulling the ships ashore (Fig. 6.41).[107] T. C. Gillmer identifies it as a stage or platform.[108] C. G. Reynolds considers the stern device to be a landing ramp, or apobathra, used to get the crew quickly off the ship when at-

tacking coastal settlements on piratical raids.[109] D. H. Kennedy believes it served to stabilize the ships, preventing fore and aft rocking.[110] Basch interprets it as an axial fin, located beneath the waterline and used to offset drifting.[111] Morgan identifies the stern device as a landing plank.[112]

These identifications have one thing in common: they all begin with the unstated premise that the horizontal stern device was functional nautical gear. I believe that this basic assumption is wrong, for at Thera *the stern device appears only on those ships taking part in the waterborne procession/race.* All the ships portrayed in functional rig in the Miniature Frieze, on both the south and the north walls of Room 5, lack the stern mechanism.

This can only mean that at the time the Miniature Frieze was painted, the horizontal stern device had a solely ceremonial/cultic use, similar to the other decorations and mannerisms associated in the wall painting with this ceremony. A similar explanation would suffice to explain why some third-millennium ship depictions carry the stern device while others do not.

This connection with ceremonial use at Thera is our sole clue in attempting to identify the nature of the Aegean horizontal stern mechanism. *Because the device is a symbol, it does not need to be explained with reference to a nautical purpose.* In fact, being a symbol, the device may have represented an object that had nothing at all to do with seafaring.[113]

PADDLING. The men paddling the ships in the procession are having a difficult time of it. They have to bend double over the caprails to reach the water with their short paddles (Fig. 6.42).[114] Obviously, they are not going to get far paddling in this manner. It is also clear that the ships in the procession were not normally paddled.

The paddling has received a number of interpretations. Spyridon Marinatos writes that this was necessary because of shallow water.[115] A. F. Tilley and P. Johnstone hold that the ships were being paddled to permit inboard space for the figures sitting in the center of the ship, since rowers take more inboard space than paddlers (Fig. 6.43).[116] Gillmer suggests that paddles were used for short periods to allow "more manoeuverability and speed and were preferred for this work to the more permanent installation of heavier and cumbersome oars."[117]

Paddling, as we have already seen, has a long history in the Aegean. There is further evidence for the continuing practice of paddling during the Late Minoan period. Paddlers appear on a sealing from Knossos that shows part of a ship with a horse engraved on it (Fig. 6.23: A). If the horse is facing the ship's bow, which seems likely, then the men are paddling and not rowing.[118] Similarly, a seal impression and a seal may show men with paddles in hand (Fig. 6.44).[119]

Casson convincingly explains the paddling as an archaic cultic practice:

It is hard to conceive of such craft at this late date being driven in so primitive a way, particularly since it is perfectly obvious that oared ships were in common use. Now, at Athens in Classical times it was the practice to send the embassy to the annual spring festival of Apollo at Delos in a vessel so old fashioned that people were able to say it was the one in which Theseus had sailed to Crete. Why not a similar situation here? That the six ships are an archaic style of craft called into use for a special religious cer-

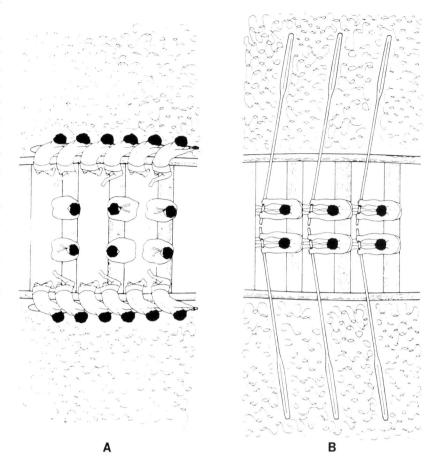

A   **B**

Figure 6.43. Tilley and Johnstone's reconstruction of the midship of a Thera ship being paddled (A) *and rowed* (B) *(from Tilley and Johnstone 1976: 287 fig. 1; courtesy of the* International Journal of Nautical Archaeology)

Figure 6.44. Evans's reconstruction of paddlers/rowers found on a fragmentary seal impression in a palatial deposit at Knossos (Middle Minoan III/Late Minoan I) (after PM IV: 521 fig. 463)

emony? Either that or they are current models which are deliberately being handled in archaic fashion as demanded by the ceremony in which they take part?[120]

ARCHAIC CHARACTERISTICS OF THE PROCESSIONAL SHIPS. The ships participating in the procession in the Miniature Frieze are indeed being handled in an archaic fashion. As we have seen, they exhibit four specific archaic characteristics: they are paddled, they carry horizontal stern devices, they have lowered their sails, and they are profusely decorated. Presumably, these archaic elements

are meant to make the ships taking part in the ceremony / race as similar as possible to a specific type of ship linked in earlier times with this ceremonial occasion. It follows from this reasoning that by studying the archaisms, we may learn something about the archaic ships being simulated by the Therans. The prototype ancestral ships logically must have had the same characteristics attested at Thera. Thus, we may assume that they had been paddled, carried a stern device, lacked a sail, and, at least on occasion, had been decorated.

The last three attributes agree remarkably well with what we

know of the third-millennium Aegean longships, discussed in the previous chapter. These ships also lacked a sail, often appeared with a horizontal stern mechanism, and, at least occasionally, were adorned with fish devices, tassels, and other decorations (Figs. 5.3–4). And if these vessels were as narrow of beam as one is led to believe from the Naxos models, then there may have been insufficient inboard space to work an oar but enough to paddle (Figs. 5.1–2). It is unlikely that a craft of the long and narrow dimensions of the third-millennium longships—as exemplified by the Naxos models—

A

B

C

D

E

F

Figure 6.45. Boughs in cultic scenes (from Nilsson 1950: 171 fig. 73, 172 figs. 75–76, 264 fig. 129, 263 fig. 128, 273 fig. 137)

could carry a sail, even if such was known in the Aegean at that time.

Indeed, as noted above, most open craft of narrow beam are paddled, not rowed. This fact would explain the appearance of the numerous parallel diagonal lines that appear along the sides of the longships depicted on Cycladic frying pans. Spyridon Marinatos believes that the number of lines is purely token.[121] This need not be the case, however, if the lines depict paddles instead of oars.

How far back in time can we trace the practice of a waterborne procession or race? Although the archaisms present on the Theran ships seem to indicate imitation of vessels used in the Aegean during the third millennium, it is possible that this festival has a history in the Aegean as old as seafaring itself.[122] Even though definite conclusions are precluded because of the nature of the evidence, it is interesting to note that many early representations of ships in the Aegean are either connected with cultic items or bear affinities to the processional ships at Thera.

Rigging first appears in the Aegean in Early Minoan III, but at that time, as well as in the Middle Minoan period, ships are always shown with their sails lowered (Fig. 6.29). Why were the sails portrayed in this manner unless the seals depict these vessels taking part in a cultic procession or race? Furthermore, like the Theran ships, they also carry decorations in the bow and usually have a horizontal stern projection. It seems probable, therefore, that the vessels portrayed on the seals represent a recently introduced or evolved type of craft that was capable of carrying a sail. Perhaps these ships were the forerunners of the ships depicted in the Miniature Frieze.

In the Aegean of the third millennium, longships depicted on

Figure 6.46. Dragon boats before the race at Aberdeen, Hong Kong (courtesy Hong Kong Tourist Association)

the frying pans may have played a role in the fertility cult. This is indicated by an attribute of the female pudenda that occasionally appears near the "handles" (legs?) of the frying pans. In some cases, leafy branches are incised at either side (Fig. 5.5: D–F). Identical branches appear on later Minoan seals together with ships (Fig. 6.29: D–E, I, K). The connection is completed when the same kind of branches appears on seals depicting cultic objects, including horns of consecration (Fig. 6.45).

Paddled processions and races find a fascinating parallel in modern dragon-boat races of southeast Asia, mentioned above. In recent times, the main function of dragon boats is to take part in the Dragon-Boat Festival, which falls on the "Double Fifth": the fifth day of the fifth month in the Chinese lunar calendar (Figs. 6.46–47).[123] Dragon-boat races are still held annually in Hong Kong, Singapore, and Taiwan. Similar races take place in Thailand and in some states of the Malay Peninsula. In Japan, the city of Nagasaki holds an annual Pieron Boat Race, the craft used being very similar to dragon boats. More recently, dragon-boat races have gained popularity in the United States as well.[124]

Before the race, the carved head and tail of a monster associated with water, or a fish, are attached to the stem and stern. This custom is widespread and appears to have originated in the belief that by attaching the head and tail to the boat it is changed into the creature itself. The evidence elicited above for the prehistoric Aegean ceremony may be interpreted by this dual usage of the modern dragon boats: for war and piracy on the one hand and for cultic use on the other. C. W. Bishop, speaking of this dual role, writes:

> Wherever this type of craft occurs—from Farther India eastward to Japan, from central China southward to Indonesia—we find it employed in recent or ancient times, mainly for the waging of war afloat. Hand-in-hand

with this use, however, has gone a ritual one, primarily the magical control of the seasons and the securing of bountiful crops by means of canoe races. This latter function has tended to outlast the former—an excellent illustration of the power of religious conservatism.[125]

The similarities between the dragon boats and the third millennium craft are stunning, as is the similarity between the dragon-boat races and the waterborne procession (race?) in the Miniature Frieze. In saying this, I do not wish to imply that any direct connection exists between the procession or race depicted in the Miniature Frieze and the modern dragon-boat races, distant as they are in time and space. However, these races may help us in understand-

ing the Bronze Age mentality behind the ship ceremony. Based on these similarities, I propose the following hypothetical reconstruction of events in the prehistoric Aegean:

• In the third millennium, Aegean seagoing ships of extremely long, low, and narrow lines were in use. Their shape may have been a result of having evolved from dugouts.[126] These craft did not have sails and, like the dragon boats, were paddled, not rowed. Functionally, they were probably better suited to piracy, war, and coastal raids than to trade.[127] Apart from their functional use, whatever it may have been, the longships also served annually in cultic races or processions. Before this cultic act, devices and decorations were added to the stem and stern of each ship and removed at its

Figure 6.47. Dragon boats paddled in the race (courtesy Hong Kong Tourist Association)

completion. The horizontal stern device was probably a cultic object, even at its inception, as is the case with the mechanisms added to dragon boats before the races.

• These third-millennium ships were often, although not always, represented in contemporary art in full regalia, apparently in connection with this cultic event.

• By the beginning of the second millennium, a new class of craft was introduced to the Aegean or developed locally. It is perhaps this variety of ship that is being used in the waterborne procession/race at Thera.

• Even though the type of ship had changed, the waterborne cultic pageant continued. To give continuing tradition to the custom it became customary to make the ships taking part in the procession as similar as possible to the now-defunct longships. Since the latter had lacked sails, these were lowered during the races. Likewise, the ships were paddled in the race, in memory of the manner in which the longships had been propelled in antiquity, even though paddling had been replaced by this time on all but the smallest vessels (Fig. 6.24).

THE CULTIC SIGNIFICANCE OF THE PROCESSION/RACE. The key to interpretation of the procession or race is in a Minoan amygdaloid seal portraying a cultic ship that was found at Thebes (Fig. 6.48).[128] It has a double Minoan bird (swallow?) device at the stem, while beneath the stern is located a typical horizontal device, and above it an *ikria*.[129] Beneath the hull are five diagonal lines, no doubt representing paddles. Thus, the ship bears three elements that, at Thera, are linked only to ships participating in the waterborne procession (race).

Two standing paddlers face the bow. The figures' skirts are composed of vertical lines and are

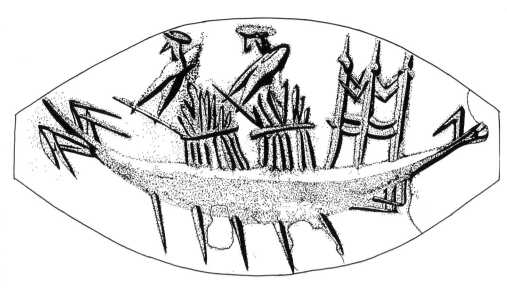

Figure 6.48. Minoan seal from Thebes depicting a ship with two paddlers dressed in sheaves of grain and other cultic accoutrements (after Morgan 1988: 142 fig. 98)

bound at half their height with a horizontal line. These "garments" are quite different from the various other kinds of Minoan skirts (Figs. 6.45: A, 69: D, 72).[130]

The two figures are dressed in sheaves of grain. An excellent parallel to this dress, engraved on a fragment of a stone vessel from Sacke Gözü and dated to the Halaf period, depicts a figure wearing an identical sheaf-skirt, standing in the middle of a reed raft (Fig. 6.49). The figure has upraised hands, and its head and hands are made of ears of grain. A quadruped stands in front of the ship. This motif resurfaces on later Mesopotamian seals in which a god is being paddled in a "living boat," again with a quadruped and other agricultural symbols around it (Fig. 6.50). A similar vegetation god, with head and hands made of grain, appears on an Early Bronze Age II cultic stone from Arad (Fig. 6.51).[131]

The sheaves of grain worn by the figures on the Theban seal seem to imply that the waterborne ceremony was linked to an agricultural cultic festival. To judge from

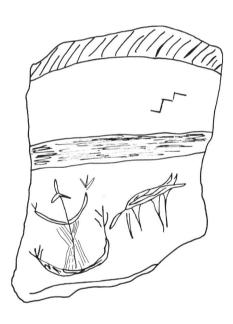

Figure 6.49. Stone bowl fragment from Sacke Gözü bearing a drawing of a cult boat with a figure dressed in a sheaf of grain and a quadruped before it (Halaf period) (after du Plat Taylor, Seton Williams, and Waechter 1950: 118 fig. 29: 7)

the motifs on the bowsprits of the Theran ceremonial ships (swallow, butterfly, and so on), it appears that this was a spring festival. A. Sakellariou and Morgan connect this festival to the inaugura-

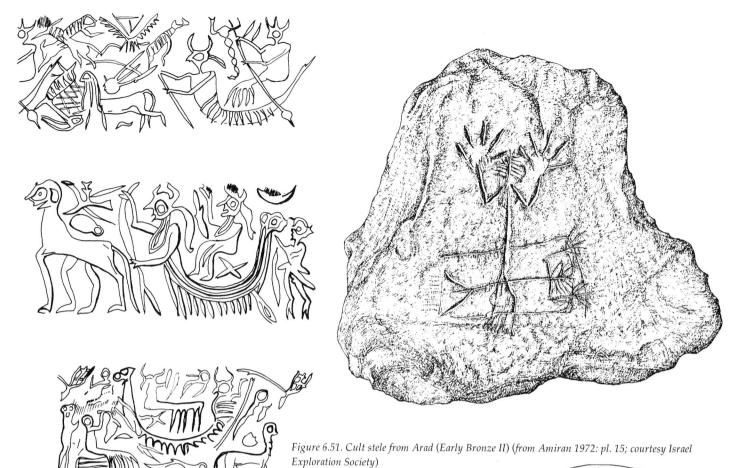

Figure 6.51. Cult stele from Arad (Early Bronze II) (from Amiran 1972: pl. 15; courtesy Israel Exploration Society)

Figure 6.50. The god-boad as it appears on the Mesopotamian cylinder seals (after Amiet 1961: pl.108, nos. 1431, 1440, 1433

Figure 6.52. Minoan cultic boats with zoomorphic stern decorations facing the bow (A–C after PM IV: 950 fig. 917, 952 figs. 919–920; D after Sakellarakis and Sapouna-Sakellarakis 1981:221)

Figure 6.53. Tree-cult scene with dove on the wing identical to birds appearing on one of the processional ships on the north Miniature Frieze (after Nilsson 1950: 268 fig. 133)

tion of the new navigational season in the spring.[132]

Butterflies appear as ships' emblems on at least two of the Theran ships (Figs. 6.13, 27). The butterfly was also linked to the Minoan vegetation cult. A butterfly, like those on the bowsprits of the Theran ships, appears on a gold signet ring from Phourni that was found with the skeletons of a woman and a sacrificed bull.[133] It shows a god-

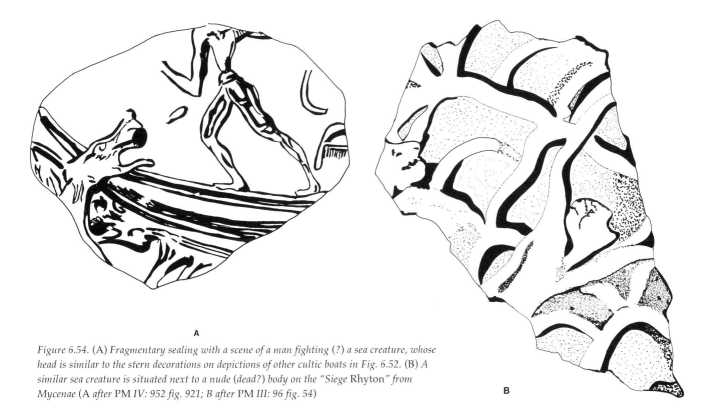

A

B

Figure 6.54. (A) Fragmentary sealing with a scene of a man fighting (?) a sea creature, whose head is similar to the stern decorations on depictions of other cultic boats in Fig. 6.52. (B) A similar sea creature is situated next to a nude (dead?) body on the "Siege Rhyton" from Mycenae (A after PM IV: 952 fig. 921; B after PM III: 96 fig. 54)

dess next to a man uprooting or shaking a sacred tree. An ivory inlay in the shape of a butterfly was found at Kato Zakro, and another butterfly is also engraved on a double ax.[134]

The vegetation cycle was a fundamental aspect of Minoan religion.[135] It appears that ships played a part in this cycle. Depictions of cultic boats and ships support this conclusion:[136] one boat has a cultic tree in it (Fig. 6.52: B). Boughs were a symbol of this cult. Perhaps this explains why they appear together with ships on the seals. At Thera, doves on the wing appear on the hull of the sailing ship accompanying the procession/race (Fig. 6.19). Interestingly, one scene relating to the tree cult portrays a flying dove in an identical manner (Fig. 6.53).[137]

HUMAN SACRIFICE AT THERA? A number of dead bodies float in the water on the north Miniature Frieze. The best known of these are the three discussed by Spyridon Marinatos (Fig. 6.7). Televantou notes the limbs of two additional bodies in the water on the north

Figure 6.55. Cult ship on Minoan seal from Makrygialos (Late Minoan IB) (after Basch 1987: 105: F–15)

Figure 6.56. A dead body floats in the water of the miniature frieze (after Doumas 1992: 29)

Miniature Frieze (Fig. 6.10).[138] A fresco fragment with a sixth body is displayed together with the south Miniature Frieze in the Athens Archaeological Museum (Fig. 6.56). Spyridon Marinatos identifies the dead men as "bad Libyans," more specifically a clan called *Makai* by Herodotus; these men were killed, in his view, because they bothered Aegean settlements.[139] Nanno Marinatos also considers the dead to have been enemies of the town who were killed by the detachment of soldiers.[140]

Morgan believes this a genre scene of coastal attack and equates it with other fragmentary scenes in Minoan and Mycenaean art.[141] Only one of the genre scenes brought by Morgan, the Mycenae "Siege *Rhyton*," actually shows hostilities and may, therefore, be reasonably interpreted as a coastal attack. And even here, the appearance of a sea monster among the nude figures in the lower portion of the vessel belies a purely military explanation for the entire scene (Fig. 6.54: B).

The explanations described above are all based on two assumptions:

• The bodies must have been killed in a military action.

• The soldiers marching on land are intent on military activities.

If we disassociate ourselves momentarily from these assumptions and examine the scene itself we find that, with the exception of the dead bodies and the soldiers, we are dealing with a pastoral setting that is uncomfortably incongruous with warlike activities. Spectators watch the paddled procession/race nearby (Fig. 6.7). Children herd their animals. Women carry jars on their heads. Nearby, worshipers gather at a peak sanctuary. *All these people are oblivious to the bodies in the water and the marching soldiers.* None of the actions of the nearby inhabitants makes any sense in relation to the warlike events—and life-threatening situations—presumed to be taking place at their metaphorical doorstep.

The bodies in the water and the marching soldiers are distinctly out of place in what appears to be a celebration complete with several different festivities. But if they are not the result of a battle, we must explain why soldiers are marching on shore and why dead bodies are floating in the water.

Perhaps the soldiers are on parade. Even today, religious festivities often include military pageantry, with the army taking the role of "guardian of the faith" (Fig. 6.57). This would be entirely consistent with all the other pageantry and cultic occurrences in the Miniature Frieze, particularly since identical boars' teeth helmets like those worn by the marching soldiers hang next to the men sitting in the ceremonial ships.[142] The sol-

Figure 6.57. Even today, the military often takes part in the religious pageantry of its culture. Here, Spanish Foreign Legion soldiers carry a life-size crucifix during an Easter pageant at Rhonda, Spain (photo by the author)

diers' warlike intent has been assumed because of the bodies in the water.

The death of these figures, however, may also have been the result of a cultic act: that of human sacrifice. Note the following considerations:

• All the bodies are naked. Morgan considers the nudity of the dead bodies to represent defeat in battle or at sea.[143] Nanno Marinatos notes, however, that in Minoan art males are normally depicted naked only when they are involved in specific cultic functions—as, for example, the two nude youths carrying fish in Room 5 of the West House at Thera.[144] Thus, the nakedness may have been a function of a cultic act.

• One of the bodies has an amorphous black "object" situated behind its back (Fig. 6.58). Spyridon Marinatos interprets this as a "ostrich wing," in the context of his theory of Libyan influence.[145] Were this really an object attached to the body, however, it would have needed a strap connected at *two* points. But this object is joined to the body with a single line that emanates in the region of the throat, beneath the body's outstretched arms. I believe that this "object" may be blood seeping into the water from a slit throat.

• In Minoan culture, sacrificial animals were, at least occasionally if not as a rule, slaughtered by cutting the victim's throat. The moment of sacrifice is not depicted in Minoan art.[146] The trussed bull portrayed on the Hagia Triada sarcophagus, however, has had its throat cut, and blood is pouring down from this mortal wound into a receptacle next to the table.[147] Furthermore, a seal from Mycenae depicts a similarly positioned bull with a dagger embedded in its throat.[148]

• The objects floating in the wa-

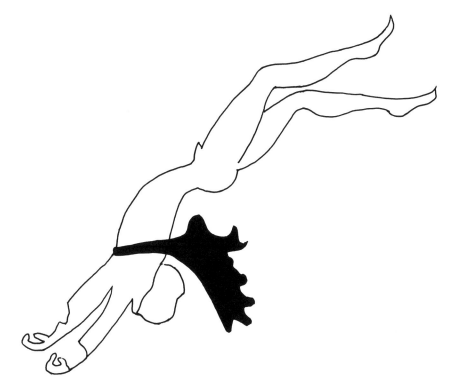

Figure 6.58. A black, amorphous blob issuing from the throat region of one of the dead bodies in the north Miniature Frieze may represent blood (after Marinatos 1974: pl. 93)

ter with the bodies at Thera also hint at a ritual significance. Morgan identifies the stick-like object with a curved top as a boat hook (Figs. 6.7, 59: A).[149] Although boat hooks may have existed in the Bronze Age Aegean, we do not know what they looked like, for there is not a single depiction of one. The staff in the water, however, bears a more than coincidental similarity to the winnowing rod carried by the (cultic) leader of the "Harvesters Vase" (Fig. 6.59: B). Furthermore, the rectangular (or cylindrical) objects, one with a strap at a narrow end and considered a shield by Morgan, also find an interesting parallel on a seal depicting a ship in cultic rig (Figs. 6.29: F, 59: C).[150]

• Depictions of cultic boats on Minoan seals may suggest the reason behind the cultic races and the human sacrifice. The figures in all the known depictions of cultic boats have ears of grain, or an elon-

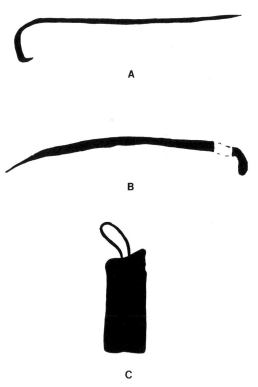

Figure 6.59. (A) Winnowing stick floating with the bodies on the north Miniature Frieze; (B) similar stick held by the leader in the "Harvesters Vase"; (C) rectangular object with strap floating in the water (A and C after Marinatos 1974: color pl. 7; B after Sakellarakis 1979: 65 fig. 184)

gated object (grain?) in place of a head, further connecting them to the vegetation cult (Figs. 6.52, 55).

A unique fragmentary sealing from Knossos depicts a figure (young god?) fighting a sea monster (Fig. 6.54: A). Four other representations of cultic boats have a zoomorphic head atop the stern that is identical to the sea monster in the sealing (Fig. 6.52). S. Hood interprets one of these scenes as depicting the journey of the goddess across the water in search of her consort (Fig. 6.52: B).[151]

In this regard, it is of interest to consider the traditions behind the dragon-boat festivals and the reasons given for the present-day dragon-boat races. Notes Bishop:

Aetiological myths explaining the ceremony appear in slightly variant forms according to the locality. They all agree however in ascribing its origin to popular distress over the fate of some upright statesman who was unjustly disgraced and who thereupon committed suicide by throwing himself into the water. The people, the tale goes on to say, instituted a search for his body, and the custom has been kept up ever since in commemoration.[152]

In reality the rite appears to be one of rainmaking, a link with agriculture. Not improbably, Bishop suggests that it once centered about human sacrifice by drowning and embodied the very widespread notion of a "dying god" and the return of the growing season.

Perhaps, in a similar manner, the Aegean boat races were meant to "save the god," and human sacrifice played a part in this ritual in the Bronze Age. If so, the waterborne procession may have reenacted the death at sea of a vegetation deity. This proposal finds support in another "dog-headed" monster. This

one swims among the dead bodies on the lower panel of the "Siege Rhyton," thus indicating a connection between this genre scene of nude bodies in the sea and the same frightening sea creature (Fig. 6.54: B).[153] Evans compares this creature to the one attacking the man on the Knossos sealing and identifies it as an early version of Scylla (Fig. 6.54: A).[154]

Concerning this hypothesis, Nanno Marinatos's comments are of interest regarding the possibility of burial at sea based on the appearance of marine motifs inside larnakes during the Post-Palatial period. Nanno Marinatos notes:

That the sea is meant to receive the dead is shown by the fact that fish are painted on the interior surfaces of the larnakes. Thus, the inside of the coffin imitates the sea. Perhaps this is a clue to understanding the paradox of the scarcity of Neopalatial burials. Could it be that the dead were at that time placed in boats and carried away by the waves? Burial at sea, suggested to me by E. Davis, is a tempting hypothesis. If that was the case, the custom was abandoned after the fall of the palaces, but the iconography of the larnakes is a symbolic reference to this practice.[155]

Human sacrifice may have been practiced by both the Minoans and the Mycenaeans. Possible evidence has been found in a Late Minoan IB building at Knossos.[156] Here, the skeletons of two young children reveal that the flesh had been carefully removed, perhaps in an act of ritual cannibalism. A pathological study indicates that the victims were in good health at the time of their death. This would have been required of sacrificial victims and suggests that they were killed in-

tentionally. There is no evidence of a battle and no reason to assume that the children had been prepared for secondary burial.

The bones were found together with *rhytons* and other pottery vessels of cultic use, which directly relate to rituals connected with a fertility cult in which the marine aspects of the goddess seem to have been emphasized.

Some of the children's bones bear delicate cut marks, regularly located away from the bones' extremities, suggesting that they were apparently not the victims of casual murder. Experts believe that this is instead indicative of flesh being removed from the bodies and not their dismemberment.

Furthermore, there is some evidence that suggests—although does not prove—that human flesh was consumed at the North House at Knossos. One of the large *pithoi* that had fallen and broken in the Cultic Room basement, near where the children's bones were exhumed, contained young human phalanges and vertebrae with signs of a knife-cut on it, together with shells and edible snails. Cooking was implied by scorched earth found in the vicinity of the *pithos*.

P. Warren connects the sacrifice of children with the Cretan Zeus, the young fertility god who dies and is reborn in a Dumuzi-like cycle. He interprets the psychological need for such enactments thus: "The quest for the fertility of the whole natural world would thus have been expressed both in ecstatic dancing rituals and in a ritual of child sacrifice and a possible sacramental meal, through which the Minoans may have identified themselves with the god reborn, and thus with the source of fertility, the Earth Mistress of whom he was consort."[157]

Human sacrifice also has been suggested in the case of a male skeleton found in a building at Anemospilia near Arkhanes.[158] The arguments put forward by the excavators in this case do not stand up to scrutiny, however.[159]

The Mycenaeans may also have practiced human sacrifice. A unique Linear B document from Pylos (Tn 316) refers to a special religious ceremony.[160] It was written in a month that has been interpreted as "the month of sailing," that is, the time when sailing was resumed each spring. Notes J. Chadwick:

> The formula continues with a reference to the carrying of gifts and the bringing of po-re-na. This too is a word missing from the later Greek vocabulary, but the verb translated "bring" implies that it means something which could walk. Then follows the entry: "(for) Potnia: one gold vessel, one woman." After this come four more names, presumably also deities, each receiving a gold vessel and in two cases a woman. This pattern is repeated in the other paragraphs with different names of deities; in two cases, where the deity is male, a man is substituted for a woman.
>
> It is impossible to resist the conclusion that the obscure word po-re-na in the introductory formula refers to the human beings, and, despite initial reluctance to accept the unpalatable fact, that these unfortunate people were to become sacrificial victims. The same word has now appeared again, in the dative plural, on a new tablet from Thebes (Of 26) indicating recipients of wool, but in a religious context. Since sacrificial victims in Greek ritual were frequently decked out with wool, this is some slight confirmation of the meaning of the word.[161]

Given the *possibility* of ritual human sacrifice in the Bronze Age Aegean, the incongruously pastoral atmosphere above the sea in which the nude bodies are floating in the north frieze, the religious significance of male nudity, and the ritualistic aspects of cultic ship races, human sacrifice becomes a reasonable interpretation for this scene.

If the proposed interpretation is correct, then human sacrifice was a more common aspect of Aegean religion than has previously been thought. R. J. Buck, in a review of the evidence concerning Tn 316, concludes that the *porenes* made up an "institutional" group within the palace.[162] Thus, this phenomenon was neither esoteric nor secretive; the *porenes* were, as Buck puts it, "part of the administrative machine." He concludes thus:

> All this makes it clear that human sacrifice was not something exceptional, but part of the administrative routine. This point does not mean that human sacrifice was practiced on the massive scale of, say, the Aztecs, but that it was something that was done from time to time, and that it was appropriate to have a pool of personnel available.
>
> We have as clear documentary evidence as we are likely to get, evidence that confirms what the Greek myths have long told us, and what archaeology has led us to suspect, that human sacrifice was a recognized, standard, fairly routine activity in the Mycenaean age; that small (probably) squads of *porenes* were kept on hand (like Theseus' group at Knossos), under the supervision of some palace official, at least at Pylos and probably at all Palace sites; that the *porenes* were fed and maintained by the Palace.[163]

Such an "institutional organization," such a "cultural normalcy" and acceptance of human sacrifice as that postulated by Buck in Mycenaean Greece—were it to have existed at Thera—would neatly account for the six bodies floating on the water. It would also explain why the physical sacrifice of human beings—so foreign and repugnant to the modern mind—could have been recorded in such a matter-of-fact manner on a wall painting at Thera.

The Continuation of Cultic Processions/Races in the Aegean

The ship procession or race depicted in the West House was, then, not a uniquely Theran festival. The custom continued in the Aegean long after Thera had sunk into the sea and after the autonomous Minoan culture had ceased to exist. This cultic race or procession was absorbed into various cultures and took place, presumably every spring, over millennia in the Aegean.

THE MYCENAEAN CULTURE. There are several clues suggesting that the Mycenaeans carried out similar ship processions/races:[164]
• A scene appearing on the thirteenth-century amphoroid krater

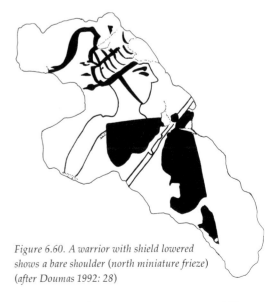

Figure 6.60. A warrior with shield lowered shows a bare shoulder (north miniature frieze) (after Doumas 1992: 28)

found at Enkomi may depict ships taking part in a cultic procession or race (Fig. 7.28).[165] Although at first glance there seems to be little similarity between these ships and those participating in the procession or race at Thera, a closer examination reveals that there are many parallels (Fig. 6.13).

Like the ships at Thera, the sails have been lowered on the Enkomi ships. They have decorations at both stem and stern, although the Minoan/Cycladic swallow adornment on the bowsprit has been re-placed with the Helladic water bird. The sternposts carry three or four curlicues. Warriors dressed in heavy robes, identical to those worn by the seated figures in the Theran ships, are portrayed above groups of men that, although painted black, are shown without clothes. This grouping is identical to the situation in the Miniature Frieze where the warriors sit in the center of the ships with paddlers on either side.

The figure to the right of the handle on the Enkomi krater wears a helmet, indicating that the paddlers were also soldiers. This was probably the case at Thera also. The apparel of the soldiers on shore in the Miniature Frieze is hidden behind their rectangular skin shields. However, they are definitely not wearing the robes of the seated figures in the ships: one warrior whose shield is held low shows a bare shoulder (Fig. 6.60). The soldiers were presumably the rowers of the ships beneath them (Fig. 6.7).

• The *ikria* was an important element of the cultic practice. It appears only on those ships at Thera taking part in the procession/race and is also a main element depicted on the talismanic seals. The large *ikria* painted on the walls of Room 4 of the West House further attests to its cultic significance.[166] Therefore, the possible appearance of *ikria* on a wall painting from Mycenae supports the conclusion that the *ikria*—and with it the procession/race—continued into the Mycenaean cult (Fig. 6.61).[167]

• A seal, discussed above, depicts a ship decorated in garlanded lines leading from the masthead to the ship's stem and stern in a manner identical to one of the Thera processional ships (Fig. 6.26).[168] Based on its material, shape, and style, J. Boardman dates the seal to the Late Minoan IIIB period—long

Figure 6.61. Panels perhaps representing ikria *from Mycenae (Late Helladic IIIB) (from* AJA *84 [1980]: 169 ills. 3–6 [Shaw])*

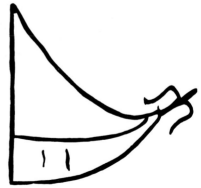

Figure 6.62. Linear B symbol depicting the bow of a ship with a swallow-shaped decoration (after Marinatos 1933: pl. 16: 69)

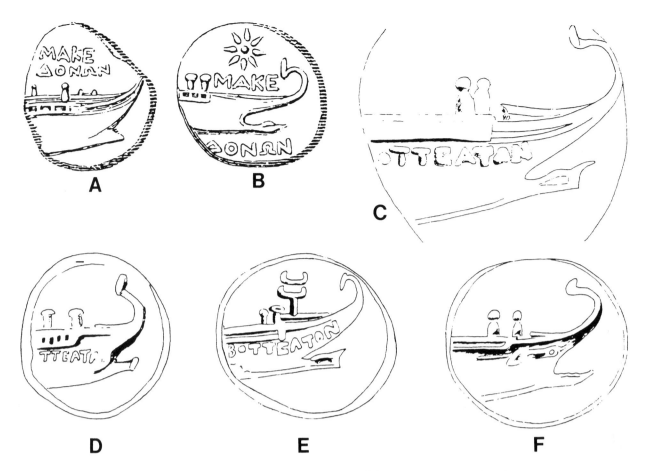

Figure 6.63. Ships' sterns with horizontal projections on coins (ca. 168–146 B.C.) (from Basch 1983B: 409 fig. 29)

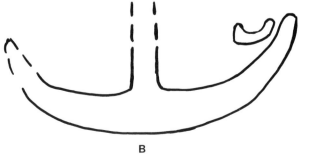

Figure 6.64. (A) Stone receptacle from the cave of Hermes Kranaios at Patsos with a ship engraved on it; (B) line drawing of the ship (from Warren 1966: pl. 43: a, 195 fig. 1; courtesy of the British School at Athens)

after the demise of the Minoan culture on Crete.[169] This ship is rendered without the stern device and *ikria*, however. Either on non- "talismanic" seals the seal makers did not need to include all the attributes of the ceremony, or the ship is garlanded for a different reason. As on the "talismanic" seals, one or two attributes were sufficient to indicate their religious significance. Alternately, the ship may be garlanded for a reason not associated with the ceremony.

Note also a Linear B sign depicting the forward part of a ship, from mast to bow, containing a swallow-shaped bowsprit device typical of ships taking part in the waterborne procession (Fig. 6.62).

THE CLASSICAL PERIOD. Basch cites horizontal devices on what he interprets as the sterns of ships portrayed on Macedonian coins from the second century B.C. (Fig. 6.63).[170] One ship's stern bears a double-crescent cultic object (Fig. 6.63: E): this is reminiscent of the lunates that appear in the bows of two Theran processional/race craft, on ships depicted on seals, and perhaps above a ship engraved on a stone cultic vessel (Figs. 6.13, 17, 18: B–C, 29: F, 64).[171] These coins may suggest a memory of the ceremony continuing into Classical times.

Additional Cultic Aspects in the Miniature Frieze

There can be little doubt today, after the detailed and exhaustive studies of the Miniature Frieze by Morgan, Nanno Marinatos, and others, of the cultic nature of the procession (race). As cult and seafaring seem to be inseparable at Thera, it is worth highlighting several additional aspects of cultic portent evident in the frieze.

SACRAL CLOTHING. Some of the figures in the Miniature Frieze wear garments of a sacral or cultic character.[172] The seated figures in the Theran ships wear heavy robes that envelop their arms. The same type of robe is worn by some of the spectators on the shore and by the figures taking part in the "Meeting on the Hill."[173] These are identical to the robe worn by the deceased/god on the Hagia Triada sarcophagus, on a wall painting from the same site, and from seals.[174] Both men and women wore this robe, the sacral nature of which was first identified by Evans.[175] M. P. Nilsson notes that this gar-ment was limited to deities and of-ficiates.[176]

Other figures on the shore wear knee-length hides (Fig. 6.65). Spyri-don Marinatos considers this evidence of a Libyan locale for the scene. However, animal-hide skirts were an integral part of Minoan sacral dress and are worn by the officiates on the Hagia Triada sarcophagus (Fig. 6.32).[177] A shoulder-length fur (?) robe is also worn by the leader on the "Harvesters Vase" from Hagia Triada.[178]

SACRAL KNOTS. Spyridon Marinatos, describing the clothing of the two figures in the "Scene on the Brook," writes, "The ribbons fastening the furs over the shoulders are so stiff that they suggest that they are the feet of the animal's

Figure 6.65. Sacral knots worn by men in the "Scene on the Brook" in the south Miniature Frieze (photo by the author; courtesy of the National Archaeological Museum, Athens)

Figure 6.66. Detail of men wearing sacral knots in one of the processional ships (after Marinatos 1974: color pl. 9)

A   B

Figure 6.68. (A) Sacral knot made of ivory (Knossos); (B) "La Parisienne" with sacral knot (after PM I: 430 fig. 308, 433 fig. 311)

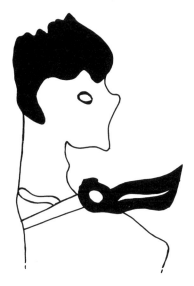

Figure 6.67. Sacral knot worn by a man in one of the processional ships (after Marinatos 1974: pl. 107)

skin"[179] (Fig. 6.65). The same item, however, appears on the chests of seated figures in the ships and on at least two of the figures in the "Meeting on the Hill," none of whom wear animal skins (Figs. 6.6, 66–67).

This object, which appears repeatedly in Minoan art, is a sacral knot (Figs. 6.68–69). A knotted cloth, somewhat like a tie, it had two extremities with fringes hanging down and a knot looped into the fabric.[180] A sacral knot is also worn by "La Parisienne," who may represent a goddess—thus confirming the knot's cultic importance (Fig. 6.68: B). Elsewhere, it appears in combination with a cultic double ax (Fig. 6.69: C–D).

CULTIC GESTURE. A crewman standing forward of the helmsman at the stern of one of the proces-

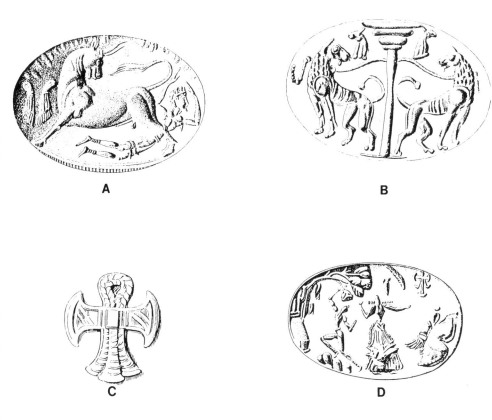

A   B

C   D

Figure 6.69. (A–B) Sacral knots in cult scenes; (C) small ivory relief of a combined sacral knot and double ax; (D) combined sacral knot and double-ax symbol in a cultic scene (from PM I: 432 fig. 310: a–b, d, c)

Figure 6.70. Man clapping his hands (?) on a fishing skiff. Tomb of Ipy (T. 217) at Thebes (Ramses II) (from Davies 1927: pl. 30; ©, the Metropolitan Museum of Art, New York)

A

A　　　　**B**

Figure 6.71. (A) Lead male statuette in worshipping pose (from Kambos in Messenia); (B) the model in profile (NTS) (A from Morgan 1988: 97 fig. 62 [The Miniature Wall Paintings of Thera: A Study in Aegean Culture and Iconography, Cambridge University Press]; B after photo by the author)

sional ships is shown with his hands in an unusual position (Fig. 6.14). Spyridon Marinatos identifies him as the *keleustés* who gave the rhythm to the rowers; two youths attending the "Meeting on the Hill" hold their hands in like manner (Fig. 6.6).[181]

Morgan considers this a cultic gesture.[182] She notes that the position is similar to those held by votive figurines found in peak sanctuaries and finds the closest parallel in a lead male statue from Kambos in Messenia (Fig. 6.71). A Minoan bronze figurine of a female worshipper strikes a similar pose, but with her right hand raised to her brow and her left hand touching her right shoulder (Fig. 6.72).[183] The cultic clothes, sacral knots, and votive postures further emphasize the cultic nature of the ship procession in the Miniature Frieze.

≈ ≈ ≈

The Minoans, as well as their Cycladic neighbors, seem to have viewed the sea and their ships with the religious awe in which they held the worldly powers. As we have seen, almost all their depictions of ships seem intertwined with their religious concepts of divinity, fertility, and the sea.

B

Figure 6.72. (A) Bronze female figurine in worshipping pose (provenance unknown); (B) the model in profile view (from Buchholz and Karageorghis 1973: 373 figs. 1224: c, a [Prehistoric Greece and Cyprus, Phaidon Press])

CHAPTER 7

Mycenaean/ Achaean Ships

Beginning in the sixteenth century B.C., the energetic Mycenaean culture made its appearance on mainland Greece. Mycenaean pottery, found throughout the eastern Mediterranean, is a valuable tool for comparative dating. At the same time, this vast spread of what is, archaeologically, a highly visible commodity has significantly confused our understanding of the Mycenaean role in Late Bronze Age trade. This is particularly true of the thirteenth century, when Late Helladic IIIB pottery flooded the East. On the other hand, more attention must be given to the role of Mycenaean and Achaean ships and seafarers in coastal raiding, mercenary activities, and colonization.

The Textual Evidence

Linear B

The Mycenaeans used a form of archaic Greek that they recorded in a script termed Linear B.[1] Clay tablets written in Linear B are known primarily from large caches at Knossos, Pylos, and, to a far lesser degree, from Mycenae and Thebes. The repertoire of Linear B documents consists mainly of inventories and receipts kept by the

palace bureaucracies. Linear B signs were also painted on jars. Although much about the world of the Linear B documents remains enigmatic, concentrated scholarly research in the decades since its decipherment has gleaned many insights into Mycenaean palace administration. But the documents are frustratingly telegraphic in nature.

Unlike other cultures in which clay tablets served as a principal form of documentation, most Linear B tablets were not intended for long-term recording; consequently, they were not kiln-baked. The tablets owe their survival to the same fires that hardened them while destroying the palaces in which they were stored. Thus, most Linear B documents appear to date to the last year, and possibly very near the time of destruction, of their find sites. Archival records meant for more permanent storage may have been recorded on materials that were more expensive, such as papyrus or animal skins, but unfortunately less durable than baked clay.[2]

There are many obstacles involved in defining the chronological and geographical distribution of the documents.[3] Differences

may have existed among the various Mycenaean centers: practices in one palace may not be assumed to apply to the entire Mycenaean world concerning subjects on which documentation is limited, as in the case of seafaring. Indeed, as we shall see, the reasons for preparing these documents may have varied from one site to the next. The Linear B script apparently went out of use with the destruction of the Mycenaean palaces at the end of the Late Helladic IIIB or the very beginning of the IIIC.

THE PYLOS ROWER TABLETS. Three texts of the Pylos An series refer to "rowers" (*e-re-ta*).[4] In An 610 *e-re-ta* appears in the damaged heading, indicating that the document deals with oarsmen allocated from various communities or supplied by officials. The text records 569 or possibly 578 men, but four entries are missing; J. Chadwick suggests that originally about 600 men were enumerated.[5] These would have been sufficient to man a fleet of some twenty triaconters or twelve penteconters.

The text is badly damaged, but its pattern is understandable. The men are identified by locations. In two cases, groups of forty and twenty men respectively are brought by two notables: *E-ke-ra₂-wo* and *We-da-ne-u*. *E-ke-ra₂-wo* clearly held a high rank within the kingdom and may have been the ruler of Pylos, while *We-da-ne-u* elsewhere appears as the owner of slaves and sheep and may also have owned lands on which flax was cultivated.[6] The rowers, for the most part, are classified as "settlers" (*ki-ti-ta*), "new settlers" (*me-ta-ki-ti-ta*), "immigrants" (*po-si-ke-te-re*), or by an unidentified term (*po-ku-ta*).[7]

The text contains fifteen lines of writing. After writing lines .1–.7 the scribe, apparently miscalculating the space needed to record all of his entries, began combining pairs of them on each line.[8] This limited the space available on each line, and therefore he omitted the term *ki-ti-ta* for the first entry on each subsequent line. The remaining lines contain only a place name together with a number and a man ideogram. On line .14 the scribe wrote three entries, causing a lack of space that resulted in the dropping of the man ideogram after *ko-ni-jo* 126. It is clear, however, that this entry also refers to men. Chadwick notes that in cases where the term *ki-ti-ta* is missing, the scribe would clearly have assumed that anyone reading the tablet would have understood that each main entry referred to *ki-ti-ta*; he would therefore have only felt it necessary to record men falling into other categories, such as *me-ta-ki-ti-ta* or *po-si-ke-te-re*.

Five of the entries refer to place names of coastal settlements, three of which also appear in An 1, discussed below. The remaining names also seem to be place names with nautical connections. Thus, the men are apparently being supplied by the kingdom's coastal towns. One group of rowers bears an ethnic term that may be restored as Zakynthos, the large

Figure 7.1. Linear B tablet PY An 724, recto (photo from the Archives of the Program in Aegean Scripts and Prehistory, courtesy of University of Cincinnati Archaeological Excavations)

island west of the Peloponnese.

Whereas An 610 deals with rowers that are available for service, An 724, on the other hand, focuses on rowers that are missing (Fig. 7.1). T. G. Palaima comments:

This tablet is difficult to interpret and none of the rival interpretations is thoroughly convincing. The surface of the tablet is damaged in places. There are several erasures at line ends which seem to be connected with inde-

Figure 7.2. Linear B tablet PY An 724, verso (photo from the Archives of the Program in Aegean Scripts and Prehistory, courtesy of University of Cincinnati Archaeological Excavations)

cision on the part of the scribe (Hand one = the normally reliable "master scribe" at Pylos) in regard to formatting and the actual information he was recording on the tablet. The meanings of several key lexical items are not apparent, and the syntax of the text is confusing or ambiguous. However, it shares vocabulary and place names with PY An 1, and most of its general purpose can be understood. The scribe has written clearly identifiable place names in the first position of lines .1 (*ro-o-wa*), .9 (*a-ke-re-wa*), and .14 (*ri-jo*). Notice that the first and last of these occur in the same order on consecutive lines of PY An 1. These place names divide the tablet into sections. Line .1 informs the reader that "rowers are absent" at the site of *ro-o-wa* and line .4 specifies that one of these men is a "settler" who is "obligated to row." The subsequent lines continue providing evidence about missing rowers:

lines .5–.6 record five men "obligated to row" and somehow associated with the important person *E-ke-ra₂-wo*; line .7 lists one man connected with the *ra-wa-ke-ta* or "military leader"; another man is described in line .8. The section pertaining to *a-ke-re-wa* lists individual men, at least one of whom is associated with the *e-qe-ta* or "followers," who seem to be high-level administrative officials. Line .14 might have listed the largest single group of missing rowers, ten or more, at the site of *ri-jo*.

On the reverse the scribe has drawn what appears to be a schematic image of a ship, comparable to a recently discovered ideogram on a tablet from Knossos.[9]

The ship incised on the back of An 724 is somewhat surprising (Figs. 7.2–3).[10] Abundant iconographical evidence indicates what Mycenaean oared ships looked like. This is not one of them. The

ship has a crescentic hull, identical to the many images of Minoan and Cycladic vessels discussed in the previous chapter. A semicircular construction is located amidships, and boughlike items extend from the ship's right side (bow?). The central structure finds its closest parallel in the seven vessels depicted on a jug from Argos, while the boughs are reminiscent of bow devices on some Minoan cultic boats (Figs. 5.26; 6.52: A–C). The Argos ships are shown under oar or paddle.

Similarly, Linear B ideogram *259 has a crescentic profile (Fig. 7.4). The mast has a curving line on either side of it, perhaps representing a mast partner, central structure, or rigging. The joining of several document fragments has this ideogram following the word [. . .]-*re-ta*, perhaps to be reconstructed as *e-re-ta*, although this is not certain.[11]

The third and final document of the Pylos rower texts is fairly

Figure 7.3. Detail of the boat incised on the verso of Linear B tablet PY An 724 (photo by the author; courtesy of University of Cincinnati Archaeological Excavations)

may indicate the complete roster of rowers required by the palace from each of the individual settlements mentioned.

This manner of "call-up" is in keeping with the methods used in taxation of other commodities. Killen compares it to the mustering of crews in an Ugaritic text, *KTU* 4.40. He notes that it is not clear if An 1 represents a call-up of men for a specific event or if this is a general form of recruitment. Whatever the purpose of the trip, the call-up was based on an already existent levy system that functioned in peacetime as well.

There are several reasons for large groups of rowers to be drafted for service on a fleet. Not

straightforward. An 1 is a list of thirty rowers raised from five settlements to man a ship bound for Pleuron (Fig. 7.5):

    .1 rowers to Pleuron / going
    .2 "from" *ro-o-wa*   MEN 8
    .3 "from" *ri-jo*   MEN 5
    .4 "from" *po-ra*   MEN 4
    .5 "from" *te-ta-ra-ne*   MEN 6
    .6 "from" *a-po-ne-we*   MEN 7

Palaima notes concerning this text: "The italicized words are

Figure 7.4. Linear B ideogram of a ship on a fragmentary tablet (KN U 7700 + X 8284 + FR IV–26 + FR VI–0 + FR VII–0) that may record rowers (after Bennett et al. 1989: 230 fig. 1)

place names in the palatial territory of Pylos. There is some evidence that *ro-o-wa* may have been the major port of Pylos. None of these sites has been positively identified with actual locations in Messenia. [The term] *ri-jo* is associated with Rhion, an older name for the Classical site of Asine, the equivalent of modern Koroni. The total number of men is thirty, perhaps the size of the crew of a particular single Mycenaean ship."

J. T. Killen has shown that this document is based on a system of dues.[12] Four sites (*ro-o-wa, ri-jo, te-ta-ra-ne,* and *a-po-ne-we*) mentioned in the same order in both An 610 and An 1 suggest a close connection between the two documents. The numbers of rowers taken from the settlements are proportional to those raised from the same towns in An 610 at an approximate ratio of 1:5. Thus, it appears that each settlement has contributed rowers based on a proportional evaluation of its tax requirements. If so, then An 610

Figure 7.5. Linear B tablet PY An 1 (photo from the Archives of the Program in Aegean Scripts and Prehistory, courtesy of University of Cincinnati Archaeological Excavations)

all have been given sufficient consideration in evaluating the happenings at Pylos reflected in the rower tablets (Fig. 7.6).[13]

In addition to the references to "rowers," the term *e-re-e-u*, interpreted by Palaima as "official in charge of rowers," appears in different forms on four other documents at Pylos.[14] One of these, An 723, was written by Hand One and found very near An 724. Under this heading, the text lists two men, *e-u-ka-ro* and *e-pa-re*, who are associated with the sites of *a-ri-qo* and *ra-wa-ra-ta* respectively.

A FLEET AND OFFICERS AT KNOSSOS. The term *po-ti-ro* appears in the heading of a number of documents and several fragments of the V(5) series at Knossos.[15] The texts consist of a title word in large characters, the word *po-ti-ro* followed by two personal names with the numeral one after each. Some of these personal names are common, appearing in other texts, but do not refer to the same persons.

Po-ti-ro, placed above the line, appears to define both names.[16] Chadwick likens the term to the Greek word *pontílos*, a synonym for *nautílos* (the paper nautilus),

while noting that the animal was so named because it was perceived to act like a sailboat. Thus, *pontílos*, like *nautílos*, can also mean "sailor." Chadwick concludes that the Mycenaean equivalent of this word may have a similar meaning and identifies the pairs of *po-ti-ro* in the documents as the ships' officers or navigators.[17]

The first word of the formula, which introduces each of the texts, is an adjective, apparently in the feminine form. Two of the six words preserved are place names recorded independently, and the rest can reasonably be recon-

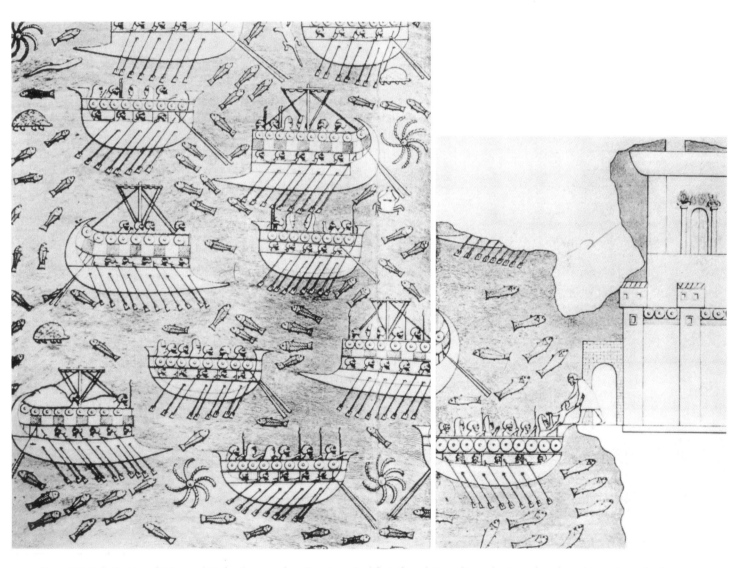

Figure 7.6. Luli, the king of Sidon, and his family escape from Tyre in a mixed fleet of oared, "round" merchant vessels and warships as Sennacherib advances on the city. All the ships are biremes and both types carry male and female passengers (from the palace of Sennacherib at Nineveh ca. 690 B.C.) (from Barnett 1969: pl. 1: 1; courtesy Israel Exploration Society)

structed similarly as place names, three of which recall the names of coastal sites in the Aegean. Chadwick offers two alternative interpretations for these opening terms: they may represent either the ships' names or the ports out of which the ships operated. He prefers the latter explanation because of the repetition of one name (*da-*22-*ti-ja*) on two texts with different pairs of *po-ti-ro*.[18]

A comparison with recorded names of Classical Greek ships, however, suggests that this may actually support their interpretation as names of ships. Names of *trieres* appearing in the Athenian naval lists during the late fifth and the fourth centuries B.C. are almost invariably feminine in gender.[19] Furthermore, about 10 percent of the ships in the lists are named after geographical sites, and many vessels bear the same name at the same time.

If Chadwick's interpretation of the Knossos V(5) series is correct, it further supports the conclusion, already indicated by the Pylos rower tablets that, when necessary, Mycenaean palaces were capable of organizing fleets of galleys.

PERSONAL NAMES AND ETHNIC ADJECTIVES. Some information concerning Mycenaean seafaring may be gleaned from different types of personal names that appear in the Linear B documents. These names are often of ambiguous significance. A number of personal names at Knossos and Pylos derive from roots related to seafaring activities and are suggestive of an involvement in seafaring.[20] These include "Fine-Harborer," "Fine-Sailing," "Fine-Ship," "Ship-Famous," "Ship-Starter," "Ship-man," and "Swift-Ship."

Place names from outside the Aegean occasionally appear as personal names. One shepherd at Knossos is named "the Egyp-

tian."[21] Other individuals are defined as "from Cyprus."[22] Some personal names suggest movement by sea within the realm of the Mycenaean world: it is likely that such transport took place in Mycenaean hulls. A tablet from Knossos mentions men of Nauplia, presumably the site in the Argolid; their arrival at Crete would have required a sea voyage from mainland Greece.[23] Similarly, a "Cretan" is mentioned at Pylos and a "Theban" at Knossos.

Groups of women in the Pylos Aa and Ab series are defined by ethnics derived from Aegean sites, primarily along the coast of Asia Minor: Knidos (*ki-ni-di-ja*), Miletos (*mi-ra-ti-ja*), Lemnos (*ra-mi-ni-ja*), Kythera (*ku-te-ra₃*), as well as the possible identifications of Lycia (*a-*64-*ja*), the Halikarnassos region (*ze-pu₂-ra₃*) and the more speculative identification of Khios (*ki-si-wi-ja*); others are known simply as "captives" (*ra-wi-ja-ja*).[24] Chadwick suggests that the ethnics probably pertain to the sites of the slave markets from which the women and children had been acquired. Presumably the women and children had been abducted in piratical sea (?) raids, which did not yield, however, similar quantities of adult males. These probably would have been dispatched. This practice is described by Homer: "From Ilios the wind bore me and brought me to the Cicones, to Ismarus. There I sacked the city and slew the men; and from the city we took their wives and great store of treasure, and divided them among us, that so far as lay in me no man might go defrauded of an equal share."[25] As we shall see, this accords well with the picture derived from other textual materials, discussed below, which also show a particular interest in *the taking of captives*.

Ahhiyawa

Valuable information concerning seafaring can be gleaned from Hittite documents pertaining to the Ahhiyawa. These chancellery documents, found in the Hittite capital at Boğhazköy, contain several names that bear a remarkable similarity to Greek names mentioned in the Homeric poems. These include the name *Ah-hi-ya-wa(-a)*, identified with Achaeans, as well as forms of the names *Miletos*, *Atreus*, and *Eteokles*. E. Forrer, who was first to note the similarity, argues that these names can be best explained if the Hittites, during their westward expansion in Anatolia, had encountered Mycenaean Greeks, who were based in the region of Miletos. Since that time, scholarly debate over the identity of the Ahhiyawa has been voluminous.

Considerable advances have been made since Forrer first proposed the connection between Ahhiyawa and the Mycenaean culture. Main among these are two:
• The realization, indicated by the decipherment of Linear B, that the contemporaneous Mycenaean culture did indeed speak an archaic form of Greek.
• The discovery of a significant number of Mycenaean sites in and along the coast of Asia Minor, where the Hittites and the Mycenaeans were likely to have met.

The Ahhiyawa are now generally identified as a part of, or the entire, Mycenaean *koine*.[26] The archaeological evidence of Mycenaean settlements in Asia Minor, particularly at Miletos and Iasos, fits comfortably into this interpretation of the written evidence.[27] Dissenting views to this identification are raised by scholars who identify the Ahhiyawa with other Aegean ethnic groups, placing them in Anatolia or its outlying islands.[28]

While the Ahhiyawa problem itself is outside the scope of the present study, several of the documents concern ships and their uses and have particular relevance to this work.

THE INDICTMENT OF MADDUWATAS. This document, long thought to be one of the latest documents of the Hittite correspondence, has been redated to the reigns of Tudkhaliya II and Arnuwadas I (ca. 1450–1430 B.C.), making it the earliest known Hittite document with a reference to Ahhiyawa.[29]

Madduwatas is charged with joining forces with his erstwhile enemy, Attarissiyas ("the man of Ahhiya"), in carrying out raids against Alashia (Cyprus), which Arnuwadas considers his own domain.[30] Madduwatas responds: "When Attarissiyas and the man of Piggaya made raids on Alašiya, I also made raids. Neither the father of Your Majesty nor Your Majesty, ever advised me (saying): 'Alašiya is mine! Recognize it as such! Now if Your Majesty wants captives of Alašiya to be returned, I shall return them to him.'"[31]

ANNALS OF MURSILIS II. Mursilis II (1330–1300 B.C.) describes how, when he attacked Arzawa and entered its capital, Apasa (Ephesos?), Uhhazitis, the king of Arzawa and apparently an ally of the Ahhiyawa, escaped by sea to a location where he was later joined by his two sons.[32] In Mursilis's fourth year, the badly damaged text mentions a son of Uhhazitis, the sea, the king of Ahhiyawa, and the returning of someone by ship.

TAWAGALAWAS LETTER. This document is now attributed to the Hittite king Hattusilis (1255–1230 B.C.).[33] In it, the king of Ahhiyawa is asked to hand over Piyamaradus, who has been raiding Hittite territory.

The king of Ahhiyawa responds

by ordering Atpas, apparently his representative at Millawanda (Miletus?), to hand Piyamaradus over.[34] When the Hittite king arrived there, however, Piyamaradus had escaped from Millawanda by ship, perhaps aided by Atpas himself, who was Piyamaradus's son-in-law. Piyamaradus continues to attack Hittite territory and take hostages while using Ahhiyawan areas as staging grounds. In the letter, the Hittite king entreats his Ahhiyawan counterpart to give Piyamaradus to him.[35]

AMURRU VASSAL TREATY. A treaty between Shaushgamuwa, the last king of the land of Amurru, and Tudkhaliya IV (ca. 1265–1235 B.C.) begins with the title "And the kings, who are of the same rank as myself, the king of Egypt, the king of Babylonia, the king of Assyria . . ."[36] Following this, the words *the king of Ahhiyawa* were written and then erased.

Since Assyria was hostile to the Hittites at the time, the king of Amurru is instructed to be unfriendly to Assyria. Merchants from Amurru are prohibited from trading with Assyria, and Assyrian traders are not to be allowed into Amurru. There then follow stipulations concerning preparations for war with Assyria, including the raising of an army and the preparation of a chariot corp. After this, on line 23, Tudkhaliya commands Shaushgamuwa that "no ship may sail to him from the land of Ahhiyawa."

This line has generally been interpreted as a reference to Ahhiyawan *merchant ships*, which are being circumscribed from trading through Amurru with Assyria.[37] For those scholars who equate the Ahhiyawa with the Achaeans or Mycenaeans, this is a powerful argument for the existence of Mycenaean merchant ships trading with the Syro-Canaanite coast.

Recently, G. Steiner has questioned the original translation of this line. He notes that the word translated by F. Somner as Ahhiyawa is partially missing and was restored by him on the basis of the erasure of the Ahhiyawan king in the document's title. He further emphasizes that this line is separated from the other stipulations concerning proscription of trade with Assyria by the instructions for military preparations. For these reasons, Steiner proposes to interpret line 23 as referring to "warships" belonging to Amurru. I am not able to judge the linguistic validity of Steiner's reconstruction.[38] However, it is difficult to understand, in the context of the treaty, why the Hittite king would in some way prohibit the use of warships by his own ally, Amurru.

On the other hand, Steiner's point concerning the positioning of this stipulation in the document in conjunction with military preparations is crucial, in my view, for understanding this document. If the text refers to Ahhiyawan ships, this would then make perfect sense. As we have seen in the previous documents, Ahhiyawan ships are consistently referred to as serving for coastal raids, the transport of captives taken in these raids, and, when necessary, for swift seaborne departures. In no other Hittite document concerning Ahhiyawa can trading intentions even be inferred in relation to ships. Given these considerations, I propose that Shaushgamuwa is being ordered to prevent Ahhiyawan (Mycenaean?) *ship-based mercenaries* from making common cause with Assyria through Amurru. Other textual evidence supports the existence of seaborne raiders from the Anatolian coast and points farther west who carried out mercenary activities and piratical raiding in the eastern

Mediterranean as early as the fourteenth century B.C.

In one of the Amarna tablets, the king of Alashia seems to be answering accusations previously made by the Egyptian pharaoh to the effect that Alashians had taken part in attacks on Egyptian territory, made by people of the land of Lukka. Denying these charges, the Alashian king complained that he also suffered from similar raids: "Indeed, men of Lukki, year by year, seize villages in my own country."[39]

This "seizing of villages" presumably refers to piratical attacks on Alashia for the express purpose of taking captives. *The king of Alashia's words echo the milieu of the Madduwatas text, with which, given its new dating to the late fourteenth century B.C., the Amarna document is now roughly contemporaneous.* They also better confirm theories as to the origins of foreign women at Pylos.[40]

Rib-Addi, the beleaguered king of Byblos during the Amarna period, refers repeatedly to the enigmatic *miši*-people who appear to be linked with ship-based warfare.[41] T. Säve-Söderbergh considers them early forerunners of the Sea Peoples.[42] In one Amarna tablet, of particular interest regarding the Shaushgamuwa Treaty, the Egyptian king is asked to prohibit *miši*-ships from going to the land of Amurru.[43]

From the reign of Ramses II onwards, Egypt and other eastern lands commonly used Aegean mercenaries.[44] However, an illustrated papyrus from Amarna in the British Museum may depict a scene of Mycenaean (?) mercenaries actively fighting alongside Egyptians.[45] Thus, it is not impossible from a historical viewpoint that the *miši*-ships mentioned in the Amarna tablets may refer to Aegean (Mycenaean?) ship-based mercenaries in the employ of the Egyptian court at Amarna.

The Archaeological Evidence

During the fourteenth and thirteenth centuries, Mycenaean influence in the Aegean replaces that of the Minoans.[46] What has been termed a seaborne "Mycenaean expansion" begins,[47] and it is no less profound—perhaps even more so—than that of the Minoans' influence during the previous period.[48] Some sites suggest actual settlement by Mycenaean colonizers. The homogeneity of the Mycenaean pottery at this time indicates considerable seaborne intercourse between the Greek mainland, Mycenaean Crete, and the outlying Aegean islands.

Later, with the destruction of the Mycenaean world at the end of the thirteenth century, fleeing Mycenaeans (or Achaeans, as they are called)—or at least groups making and using Late Helladic IIIC pottery—created settlements even farther afield, in Cyprus and along the Canaanite coast.[49] This waterborne emigration is one of the hallmarks of the Mycenaean culture. I consider this use of ships for the movement of populations a primary aspect of Mycenaean seafaring.

The Iconographic Evidence

A rich corpus of Mycenaean ship images exists consisting primarily of depictions painted on vases, incised in stone, or modeled in terracotta. Although of differing detail and accuracy, these depictions are almost invariably of oared ships, on the decks of which occasionally stride armed warriors.

The abundance of ship imagery bequeathed us by the Mycenaeans and their successors results, at least in part, from the interrelationship of ship iconography in the Mycenaean religion. In the Syro-Canaanite littoral and on Cyprus, indigenous ship depictions are rare, but anchors commonly appear in cultic contexts.[50] Anchors do not appear to have had cultic significance for Aegean Bronze Age seafarers, who seem, however, to have had a predilection to portray ships in circumstances suggesting that they had a religious significance.

Geographically, Helladic ship representations are found in mainland Greece, the Aegean, and on Cyprus. As the Mycenaeans and the Sea Peoples used basically the same type of ship and overlapped to a wide degree both chronologically and geographically, it is not always clear whether the portrayals discussed here represent Mycenaean—or Sea Peoples'—ships.[51]

In every ship style or rig there were certain characteristics that left a lasting impression on the ancient observer and that were most commonly emphasized in depictions of that particular ship type. For example, during the entire Bronze Age when the boom-footed rig was in use, it was invariably the multiple lifts supporting the yard and boom that seem to have caught the eye and attention of the artists.

Mycenaean ships were no different in this regard. Many of the Helladic ship depictions share similar elements. One such element is the device shaped like a water bird, or of a bird head, that often topped the ships' stems.[52] However, undoubtedly the single most characteristic element of Mycenaean ship architecture—the one attribute that most impressed the persons who portrayed them and that appears on most Helladic ship depictions—is a structure directly above the sheer that looks rather like a ladder lying horizontally on its side:

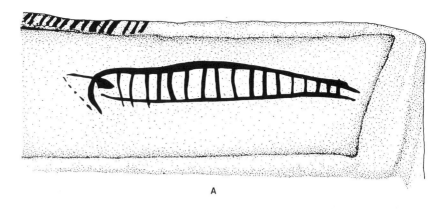

Indeed, at times, an abbreviated image of a ship is expressed in its entirety by a horizontal ladder design alone, with oars and rigging added, as for example in the cases of a schematic graffito of a ship painted upside down inside a Mycenaean *larnax,* or a ship painted on a sherd from Phylakopi on Melos (Fig. 7.7, 23).[53] Clearly, to understand the depictions of Mycenaean ships, our first imperative is to determine the ancient artists' intentions in creating this horizontal ladder design.

To do this, we must begin with the most detailed and clearest depiction of a Late Helladic ship. This was discovered by F. Dakaronia at the site of Pyrgos Livonaton in central Greece, which has been identified as Homeric Kynos.[54] Excavations at this Late Helladic IIIC site have revealed a wealth of ship iconography, including ships painted on sherds and fragments of terracotta ship models. Warriors, armed and armored, stand on their decks and in their forecastles. One galley, Kynos A, is depicted in particular detail (Fig. 7.8: A). The ship is nearly complete. The only parts missing are the device topping the stem, the lower part of the stern, the end of the sternpost together with the blades of the single quarter rudder, and the two sternmost oars.

The ship faces left and is divided longitudinally into three horizontal areas (Fig. 7.8: B: BC, XB, and AX). Area CB is the ship's hull, from the keel/keel-plank to the sheer. Above this is a reserved

Figure 7.8. (A) Kynos ship A. Late Helladic IIIC (B) Constructional details (photo A courtesy of F. Dakaronia; drawing B by the author.)

Figure 7.7. The element of the Mycenaean ship represented by the "horizontal ladder pattern" seems to have been so striking to the observer that, at times, sketches of Mycenaean ships consist of little else than this component, sometimes with oars and rigging added. One example of this is a ship painted upside-down inside a Late Minoan larnax *(A). Below, in (B), the ship is reversed (after Gray 1974: G47, Abb. 11)*

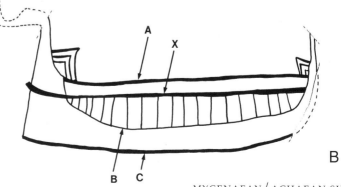

area (XB) intersected by nineteen vertical "lunates," which are curved on their right side (the side facing the ship's stern) but whose left edges are attached to vertical lines. This detail is particularly distinguishable in the fifth lunate from the bow, where the lunate is somewhat separated from the vertical line. The ship is being propelled by nineteen oars on its port side. Each oar begins at the bottom of a lunate (Fig. 7.9). Presumably, the artist intended to depict a penteconter but ran out of room.

The third area (AX) is decorated by two rows of semicircles, a common ornamental filler on Late Helladic IIIB and IIIC1 pottery.[55] Since this motif also decorates the bodies of bulls and the leather-covered sides of chariots on Late Helladic pottery, it may indicate that the Kynos ship carries a leather screen enclosing an open bulwark.[56] The fact that the mast can be seen through Area XA does not hinder this interpretation: this result would have been inevitable if the artist first drew the mast and only afterward added the superstructure.

Line X crosses the bow and continues beyond it, suggesting that this line represents a structurally significant element, perhaps a free-standing wale at the bottom of the screen (Fig. 7.8: B: X). Such reinforcement would be required to support the deck beams.

But where are the rowers? The oars begin at the lunates, so these clearly must be related to the rowers in some manner (Fig. 7.9). But how? Let us consider the following clues:
• The helmsman indicates how the artist perceived of the unarmored male body (Fig. 7.10).
• The oars are slanted toward the stern, suggesting that the rowers are at the end of their stroke. In that position the men are leaning backward on their benches with their oars drawn up near their bodies. In Late Geometric art, oarsmen depicted in this position are shown leaning backward on their benches with their left shoulder forward (Fig. 7.11).

Figure 7.10. Detail of the helmsman (drawing by the author)

The above considerations lead to the conclusion that the lunates represent the upper torsos of the rowers, while their heads are hidden behind the screen. For this to be possible, deck planking must not have been placed along the ships' sides.

The above interpretation is supported by several later parallels. A good illustration of this is seen on a fragment of a *dieres*, a two-banked Greek oared ship, painted on a Proto-Attic sherd from Phaleron (Fig. 7.12).[57] In this image, the lower-level oarsmen appear in the open rowers' gallery between *pairs* of wide stanchions while their heads are hidden behind the open bulwark above them.

Dated to about the same time (ca. 710–700 B.C.) but painted in Late Geometric style, two other sherds bear fragmentary images of *dieres*. In both cases the stanchions have been broadened into screens to protect the rowers. On one

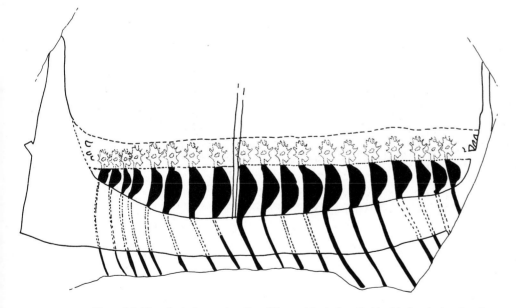

Figure 7.9. Hypothetical reconstruction of Kynos ship A. Oars that lead to the nineteen lunates indicate that they represent the schematic torsos of oarsmen as seen through an open rowers' gallery (Area XB in Figure 7.8). If Area AX is a screen at deck level, then the rowers' heads would be hidden from the viewer behind the screen. Similar "disappearing rowers' heads" are depicted on Greek warships from the late eighth century B.C. (see Figs. 7.12 and 14) (drawing by the author)

Figure 7.11. *An oarsman at the end of his stroke* (*Attic Late Geometric I*) (*after Basch 1987: 166 fig. 338*)

hatched screens (Fig. 7.13). In the second sherd, however, the men's torsos are hidden; only their arms and shoulders are visible peeking out from behind the screens (Fig. 7.14). From the height of their shoulders, however, we may deduce that their heads are hidden behind the superstructure.

Most writers who have discussed these three sherds from the late eighth century B.C. agree on their interpretation: they show two levels of rowers, one above the other, instead of a single level on either side of the ship. In the Proto-Attic ship the oars of the upper level are actually drawn across the side of the ship, while on the Late Geometric sherds the oars of the upper level reappear beneath the ships' hulls, indicating that both depictions represent two levels on the near (port) side of each ship.

It is generally accepted that the ships of the Geometric period are developed from Mycenaean ships. Since this "horizontal ladder" ele-

Figure 7.13. *Warship with two banks of oars depicted on a sherd from the Acropolis, Athens* (*ca. 710–700 B.C.*) (*after Morrison and Williams 1968: pl. 7: f*)

sherd, the artist has enlarged the height of the rowers' gallery so that the entire torso and head of the rowers in the lower level are depicted, and the rowers are visible in the openings between the

ment continues to appear prominently on Greek-oared ships of the Geometric period and later, it is reasonable to assume that it represents the same structural element in these later depictions.

From the above considerations we may conclude that the "horizontal ladder motif" on Mycenaean ship depictions, as on their Geometric descendants, represents an open rowers' gallery intersected by vertical stanchions.[58] Sometimes the stanchions have been omitted and, in one case, descussed below, the oars are attached at the height of the upper deck, indicating that these ships could be and were rowed from deck level, as were warships of the Late Geometric period. At Kynos, then, we have our first clear glimpse of the prototype ship that would eventually develop into the classical tradition of war galleys. As we shall see, ships of virtually identical appearance were also used by the Sea Peoples.[59]

Figure 7.12. *Warship with two banks of oars on a Proto-Attic sherd from Phaleron* (*after Williams 1959: 160 fig. 1*)

Figure 7.14. Warship with two banks of oars depicted on a sherd from the Acropolis, Athens (ca. 710–700 B.C.) (after Morrison and Williams 1968: pl. 7: e)

Returning to the Kynos A ship, note that the figure at the bow stands on a raised deck in the forecastle. The warrior standing behind the mast suggests that the ship was at least partially decked longitudinally. The helmsman, manning a single quarter rudder, is positioned in the sterncastle. He wears no armor, although he does seem to be wearing a (feather?) helmet similar to those worn by the two previous warriors. He holds the loom of the quarter rudder with both hands. No tiller is depicted, but two joining semicircles, perhaps indicating a control mechanism, are drawn on the fore side of the loom.

The ship has a single pole mast situated somewhat forward of amidships. This is probably traceable more to the artist's desire for sufficient room to display the warrior behind the mast than to any real structural meaning. All other Helladic ship portrayals show the sail planted squarely amidships. The sail and yard have been stowed. The circular mast-head indicates that the rig represented is of the newly introduced brailed design.[60] The only rigging shown is a single forestay and two slack lines that appear behind the mast, seemingly looped through one of the mast cap's sheaves.

The sharp manner in which the stem meets the keel but lacks a horizontal projection is identical in shape to the bows of the Sea Peoples' ship depicted repeatedly at Medinet Habu (Fig. 8.10). The keel is somewhat rockered and abuts an oblique stem. A model from Phylakopi shows how this type of fine bow may have appeared three-dimensionally (Fig. 7.42).

The castles are composed solely of groups of three inverted nestled angles, perhaps indicating that they were little more than an open framework, unenclosed by planking. The upper part of the stem bears numerous short lines extending from its inboard surface. These projections appear normally with bird-head stem devices, indicating that this stem was topped in the same manner (Figs. 7.15–17, 19, 28; 8.61: A–D).

Another depiction from Kynos consists solely of such a bird-head stem ornament, the torso of an armed warrior, and what may be the upper railing of the castle or open bulwark (Fig. 7.15). A row of projections runs along the upper end of the beak, over the head, and

Figure 7.15. Kynos ship B (Late Helladic IIIC) (courtesy F. Dakoronia)

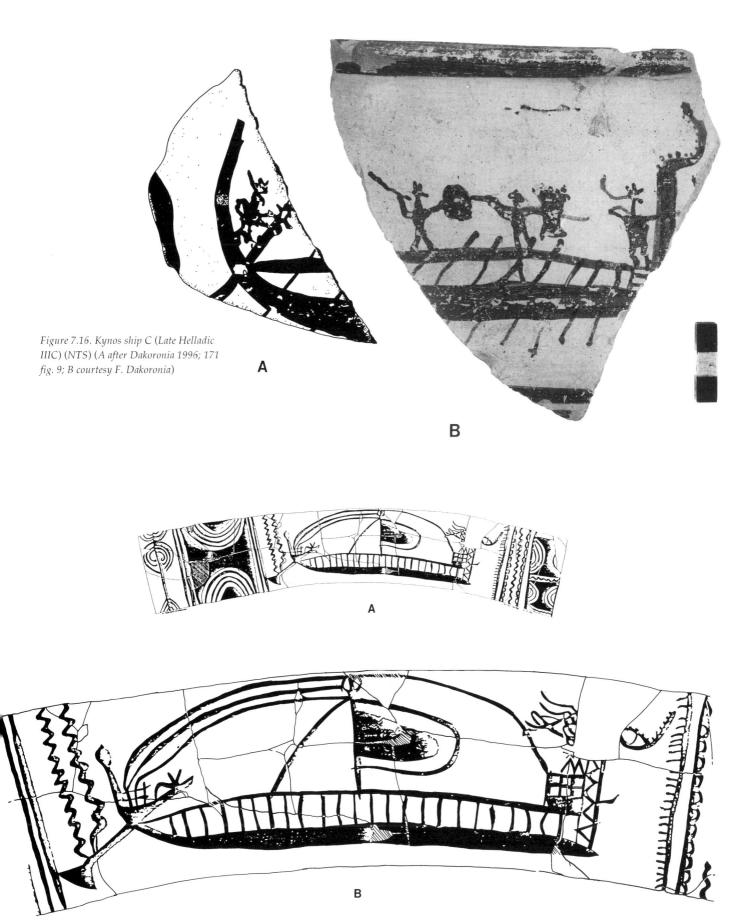

Figure 7.16. Kynos ship C (Late Helladic IIIC) (NTS) (A after Dakoronia 1996; 171 fig. 9; B courtesy F. Dakoronia)

A

B

A

B

Figure 7.17. (A) Decoration on a pyxis found in a tomb at Tragana, Pylos (Late Helladic IIIC); (B) detail of ship (from Korrés 1989: 200)

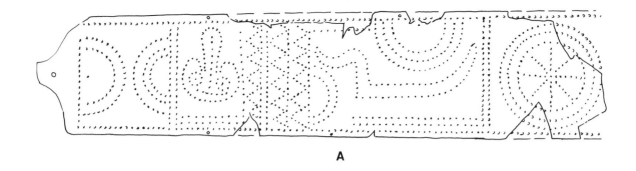

A

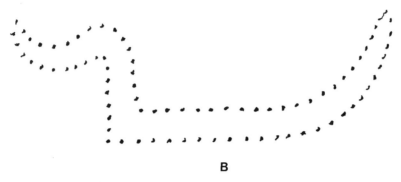

B

Figure 7.18. (A) *A reconstructed gold diadem found in Trench W–31 at Pylos bearing a ship with a bird-head stem ornament;* (B) *detail of the ship* (*after Blegen* et al. *1973: fig. 108:* d [*reconstructed by Piet de Jong*])

Figure 7.19. *Ship depicted on the side of a* larnax *from Gazi (Late Minoan IIIB)* (*photo by the author*)

down the bird's neck. The warrior carries a shield and throwing javelin. The stem's extremities are missing, but its central, remaining, part is either vertical or very nearly so. Similar stems appear on other Helladic ship depictions as well as the Sea Peoples' ships at Medinet Habu (Figs. 7.8: A, 16–19, 21, 29: A, 30: A).

A third ship drawing from Kynos portrays what appears to be the same ship type, sketched by a less-skilled hand (Fig. 7.16). It has a long, narrow hull and a stempost surmounted by a bird-head device with a strongly recurving beak. Twelve small projections protrude from the inner side of the bird's head and beak.

The hull is also divided lengthwise into three sections as on the first ship, although the open bulwark, perhaps with its screen lowered, is no more than a line. At the bow a warrior stands on three vertical lines, representing a structure at the bow, although its surface is level with the deck.[61] Here, as well as on other Bronze Age depictions, the stanchions have been omitted, perhaps to prevent confusion with the slanting oars. This is identical to the fashion in which warships are shown during the Late Geometric period: the stanchions are omitted when the ship is portrayed with the rowers working their oars from the lower level.[62]

To my knowledge, this illustration is unique to Mycenaean ship iconography in that it portrays oars continuing up to deck level, suggesting that the ship was being rowed from the upper deck. This development is significant because rowing these ships from the upper level was the first step toward creating a two-banked ship.[63]

Three warriors are arrayed on the forecastle and deck. The two on deck bear javelins and shields. The right arm of an archer standing on the forecastle is drawn back behind his head, a convention used in many cultures to depict the draw of a composite—but not a simple—bow (Fig. 8.1).[64] The upper tip of the bow is visible beneath the beak of the bird-head stem device.[65] More recently, a sherd bearing the stern portion of this ship depiction was found.[66] On it, a helmsman works a single quarter rudder, and the ship is shown to have a recurving sternpost, similar to that of the Skyros ship (Fig. 7.21). The galley's mast has been retracted.

A ship painted on a Late Helladic IIIC1 *pyxis* from Tholos Tomb 1 at Tragana near Pylos reveals striking similarities to the Kynos ships (Fig. 7.17: B).[67] The vessel from Tragana has a continuous, thick line representing the hull from the sternpost to the short horizontal spur at the bow.[68] Twenty-four vertical stanchions, placed at fixed intervals, connect the hull with a second narrow horizontal line. I take the latter to represent the line of the wale, beams, and central longitudinal deck, all of which are seen in profile. The stanchions form twenty-five rowers' stations, suggesting that the artist depicted a penteconter.

The bow consists of two vertical lines joined by a zigzag line and rising above the spur. Behind it is a forecastle that serves as the base of an emblem that has been previously identified as a fish.[69] The discovery of several additional sherds of the *pyxis* shows that this device is a water bird with a recurving beak.[70] A line jutting out midway up the stem is reminiscent of the bow projection in the same position on Kynos ship A (Fig. 7.8: A). In the Tragana ship, however, this bow projection does not continue the line of the possible wale as on the first Kynos ship.[71] Perhaps it represents a schematic duplication of a bird's head and upcurving beak or a primitive form of subsidiary spur (*proembolion*).[72]

The sternpost rises from the keel in a graceful curve, terminating in an acorn-shaped device. The castles have open balustrades, similar to those on the first Kynos ship. The Tragana ship carries a single quarter rudder, the tiller of which seems to be held in place by a linchpin connected to the loom.[73] The ability to remove the tiller from the loom would have been desirable when the mechanism was stored.

The mast cap has only two sheaves, indicating that the ship employed the newly introduced brailed sail. The sail billows out forward of the mast. A single forestay leads from the mast to the forecastle. Three lines, probably representing the backstay and the two halyards, lead from the top of the mast to the sterncastle. In this respect, the Tragana galley is similar to a depiction from Phylakopi (Fig. 7.25). A fourth line brought half astern, although seemingly attached to the mast, may indicate either bunched brails or a brace.

Two zigzag lines rise from the quarter rudder. A palm tree and three more zigzag lines—one vertical and two horizontal—are shown in the panel that separates the ship's bow from its stern (Fig. 7.17: A).[74]

Another ship portrayal with a prominent bird-head stem device was found at nearby Pylos (Fig. 7.18).[75] Embossed on a gold diadem, it finds its closest parallels in the Skyros ship and in the embossed bird-boat ornaments prevalent in Urnfield art (Figs. 7.21; 8.30).

The cutwater bow, or spur, seen on the Tragana ship appears earlier on a ship painted on a Late Minoan IIIB *larnax* excavated at

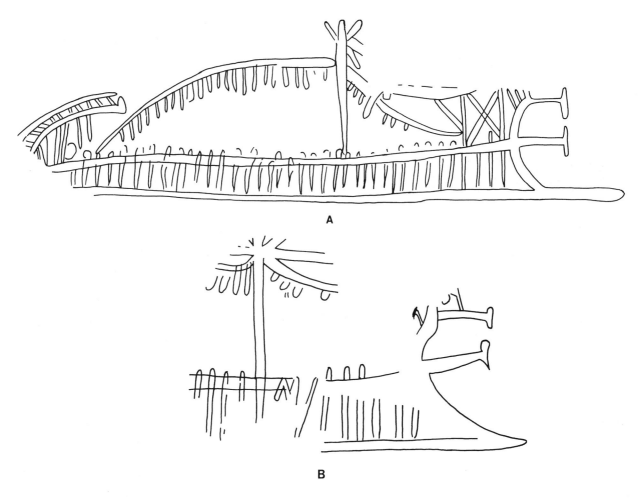

A

B

Figure 7.20. Two Late Geometric galleys depicted on sherds from Khaniale Tekke, near Knossos (after Boardman 1967: 73 fig. 6: 21)

Gazi, on Crete, and now exhibited in the Archaeological Museum at Iraklion (Fig. 7.19).[76] Although this is the largest known depiction of an Aegean Late Bronze Age craft extant today, several of its details are enigmatic.

The artist used three horizontal lines to compose the ship's hull and superstructure. The lowest of these represents the ship's hull up to the sheer. Twenty-seven vertical lines, one of which is the continuation of the mast, rise from it. The stanchions form twenty-eight rowers' stations; presumably, the artist intended to draw a penteconter.

A median horizontal line bisects the reserved area lengthwise, as if we are seeing two banks of rowers' stations, one above the other. There are several possible inter-

pretations or this, none of which I find entirely satisfactory:

• The rowers' galleries on both sides of the ship are depicted as if they were on one side, as in the Geometric ship on the British Museum bowl.[77]

• The lower area is the open rowers' gallery, while the upper area is the open bulwark with the screen removed but the stanchions supporting it still in place. Unfortunately rowers, who might have elucidated the ship's structure, are lacking.[78]

The Gazi artist seems to have had a liberal attitude with upright lines: an additional row of verticals connects the uppermost horizontal line with the lowest pair of diagonal lines, which run from the masthead to the ship's extremities. L. Basch identifies it as a screen to

protect the rowers at night, similar to those used on galleys from the seventeenth century A.D.[79] There are, however, no known contemporaneous parallels for this interpretation.

Alternately, this element may represent decorations hanging from the rigging similar to those borne on one of the Theran ships (Fig. 6.27). Similar decorative devices hang from the stays on two galleys depicted on Late Geometric sherds from Khaniale Tekke, near Knossos (Fig. 7.20).[80]

The bow of the Gazi ship continues past the stempost in an upcurving spur. The stempost rises at an angle from the keel and is topped by a stylized zoomorphic head with a number of short vertical lines rising from it. The figurehead is longer than the hori-

Figure 7.21. Ship painted on a stirrup jar from Skyros (Late Helladic IIIC) (after Hencken 1968A: 537 fig. 486)

zontal bow projection, precluding its use as a functional waterline ram. Basch identifies the stem device as a horse's head, a difficult interpretation because horse-head devices are otherwise unknown in Late Bronze Age Helladic ship iconography. Furthermore, the lines rising from the apparatus are paralleled on other bird-head devices (Fig. 8.61).[81]

The sternpost curves up and blends into the right side of the "frame" that surrounds the ship. A single steering oar stretches out horizontally behind the craft. Two horizontal lines at the top of the mast apparently represent the yard and the boom with the sail furled between them, while three sets of diagonal lines lead from the mast to the stem- and sternposts. This is similar to the rigging on

some ships depicted on Late Minoan seals (Fig. 6.21). On these ships a broad sail, hung between a yard and a boom, is placed high up on the mast with two or three diagonal lines descending from the mast to both of the ship's extremities. Perhaps this is the Cretan equivalent of an "exploded view" of the rigging, with the lifts depicted *beneath* the boom.

Two vertical wavy lines rise from the quarter rudder, with two additional sets of three wavy lines located beneath the yard on either side of the sail. Beneath the ship are two birds (of prey?) with down-curving beaks, placed antithetically.[82] Between them stand a schematic palm tree and a flower.[83] Spirals fill the space in front of the ship. All of these elements had a numinous significance within the

cultural milieu in which the scene was created. Taken together with the ship they form a statement, articulated in symbols and apparently addressing the theme of death and rebirth—a theme hardly surprising to find here, considering that the ship was painted on a *larnax*.[84] The Tragana ship, which appears on a tomb offering, bears an identical set of wavy lines rising from the quarter rudder, and a palm tree is painted in the metope on the *pyxis* (Fig. 7.17).

A ship painted on a Late Helladic IIIC stirrup jar found on Skyros has a long, narrow hull in profile (Fig. 7.21).[85] The stempost is elongated, raking forward and finishing in a bird-head device with a strongly recurving beak. This bow is closely paralleled by the posts of the Sea Peoples' galleys at Medinet Habu (Figs. 8.23, 35). A narrow, reserved line horizontally bisects the craft and continues up the stempost. A single quarter rudder, somewhat malformed, appears below the stern.

Although the ship is depicted without a sail, its mast cap consists of only two sheaves, indicating that its prototype carried the

Figure 7.22. Ship depicted on a vase from Asine (Late Helladic IIIC) (after Casson 1995A: fig. 29)

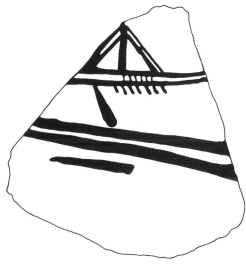

Figure 7.23. Oared galley painted on a sherd from Phylakopi (after Marinatos 1933: pl. 13: 13)

newly introduced loose-footed brailed sail. Rigging represented is limited to a single forestay and backstay.

An oared ship painted on a Late Helladic IIIC stirrup jar from Asine is so schematic that scholars even disagree as to which side of the ship represents the bow and which the stern (Fig. 7.22). G. S. Kirk and R. T. Williams consider the long, thick projection to the left to be a ram, with the ship subsequently to be facing left.[86] L. Casson, G. F. Bass, and Basch believe the ship to be facing right.[87] The following considerations support the latter view:

• In some ship graffiti the quarter rudders are occasionally strung out directly behind the ship as on the Asine ship (Fig. 7.19).[88]
• If the thick vertical line in the center of the hull is the mast, as Williams logically concludes, then the sail is billowing toward the right.
• The horizontal projections on the inboard side of the ship's

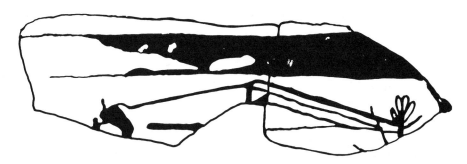

Figure 7.25. All that remains of one ship depiction from Phylakopi: its stem and stern devices and its rigging (Late Helladic IIIC) (after Marinatos 1933: pl. 13: 16)

stempost (if facing right) correspond to those painted on the stempost of a contemporaneous *askos* ship model from Cyprus (Fig. 7.48: A).

The ship has a cutwater bow. Eleven short vertical strokes that begin around the center of the hull and bisect the keel line probably represent oars. The sail is decorated with a net pattern, suggesting that the original was constructed from a number of small panels sewn together (compare Fig. 6.21).

A schematic—almost telegraphic—depiction of an oared galley comes from Phylakopi, on the island of Melos (Fig. 7.23).[89] The ship's bow and stern sections are missing. The hull and superstruc-

ture consist of two parallel lines joined by six narrower vertical lines. In this much-abbreviated form, the artist has captured the salient aspect of a Helladic galley: an open rowers' gallery intersected by stanchions. Beneath the hull are seven oars, shown at the beginning of the stroke, and a single large quarter rudder, depicted in an unusual manner, with its blade angled toward the bow. The ship has stowed its sail and has two lines (presumably stays) running fore and aft from the mast.

Parts of two other ships, of Late Helladic IIIC date, are painted on several sherds from Phylakopi. Of one galley only part of the hull, with five oars and a quarter rudder, remains (Fig. 7.24). A vertical

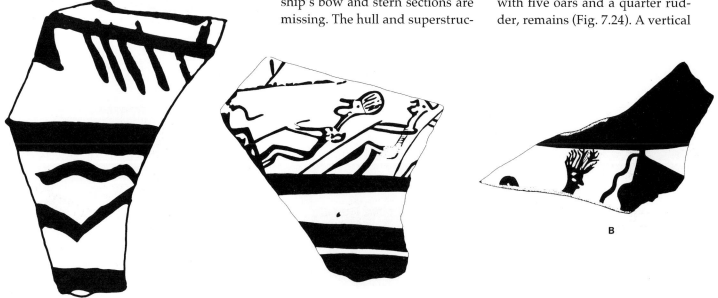

Figure 7.24. Hull of an oared ship depicted on a sherd from Phylakopi (Late Helladic IIIC) (after Marinatos 1933: pl. 13: 16)

Figure 7.26. Parts of ships and their crews painted on Late Helladic IIIC sherds from the Seraglio, Cos. Note the (feather?) helmets worn by the figures (after Morricone 1975: 360 fig. 358, 359 fig. 356)

line above the hull may represent the ship's mast. Here also the oars are angled toward the bow.

Of a third ship, only the posts, mast, and rigging remain (Fig. 7.25). The stem ends in a zoomorphic device, perhaps a bird head (Fig. 8.36).[90] A palmette-shaped apparatus surmounts the sternpost. The rigging includes one forestay and three lines running from the tip of the mast to the sternpost. As on the Tragana ship, these are best identified as a single backstay and two halyards tied to cleats located in the stern.

Some of the Helladic ships discussed are portrayed under oar. Representations of oarsmen, however, are rare. A Late Helladic IIIC sherd from the Italian excavations at the Seraglio in Cos depicts two rowers and the oar, as well as the lower arms and left (?) leg of a third as they strain at their oars

(Fig. 7.26: A).[91] The rowers face left, suggesting that the galley faces right. The hull is drawn as a single broad horizontal band. The two bands beneath it, according to L. Morricone, encircle the jar and are therefore not related to the ship.

An angular structure, with a vertical line rising from it, is located to the left of the rowers. Perhaps these are the decorated sternpost and sterncastle. To the right of this vertical is a line in the form of a compound curve. The sterncastle, if it is indeed such, seems to be an open frame covered with hides. It bears similarities to castles appearing on the ship depictions from Tragana and Kynos as well as to the castles on the ships of the Sea Peoples from Medinet Habu.

Remnants of a second ship, together with the head of a figure, appear on another Late Helladic IIIC sherd from the same excava-

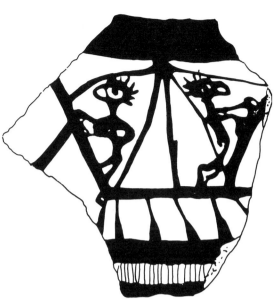

Figure 7.27. *Ship portrayed on a sherd from Phaistos (Late Minoan IIIC) (after Laviosa 1972: 9 fig. 1b)*

tion (Fig. 7.26: B). The sail seems to be billowing toward the crewman, suggesting that the ship is facing left. A wavy line runs diagonally down from the masthead. The man-

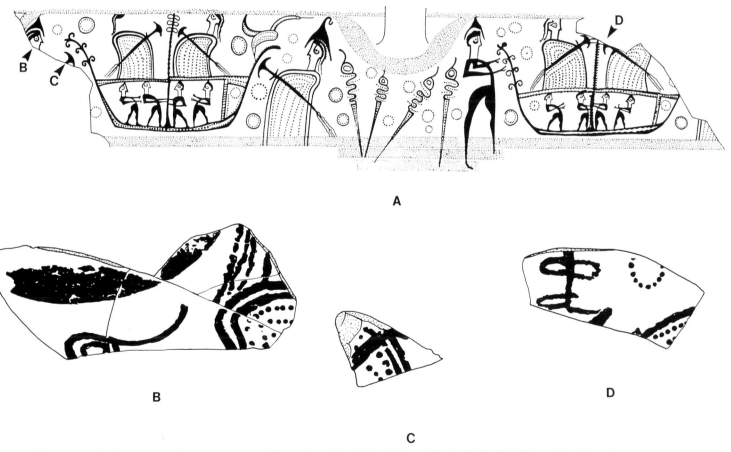

Figure 7.28. (A) *Ship scene on a Mycenaean amphoroid krater from Enkomi, Tomb 3. Late Helladic IIIB (B–D) Additional sherds from the same krater (A from Sjöqvist 1940: fig. 20: 3. B–D after Karageorghis 1960: pl. 10: 7)*

ner in which this cable is drawn finds an exact parallel in the hawser used to raise a stone anchor on a ship portrayed on a later Cypriot jug (Fig. 8.41: A). At left is a semicircular element with a reserved dot at its center: this may represent the top of a bird-head device, the reserved dot being its eye.

On both of the Cos sherds, the figures are wearing helmets that have been interpreted as feather helmets like those worn by some of the Sea Peoples on the Medinet Habu reliefs. This raises the question of the ethnic identity of the men (and of the ships) depicted at Cos.[92]

A Late Minoan IIIC sherd from Phaistos bears a graffito of an oared ship (Fig. 7.27).[93] The hull consists of a single thick horizontal line with a curving stempost and a raking sternpost; the vessel's extremities are missing. The line of the hull continues past the junction with the stem, creating a horizontal spur. A quarter rudder, held by a helmsman facing aft, descends diagonally abaft the sternpost.

The ship is being rowed: six oars appear beneath the hull. Four lines lead off from the mast. The upper two appear to be a yard with downcurving ends, and the lower pair seem to be stays (compare Fig. 8.41: B). A small, pointed projection at the junction of the sternpost and hull is reminiscent of the miniature stern spur on two of the Sea Peoples' ships (Figs. 8.11: E, 12: A).

Two ships appear on a Late Helladic IIIB krater from Enkomi (Fig. 7.28: A).[94] Additional sherds belonging to this krater bear portions of the figure standing to the left of the scene and the top of a whorl-shell (Fig. 7.28: B–C), while the top of the mast and part of the figure standing to the right on the ship at right appear on another sherd (Fig. 7.28: D).[95]

The vessels are at least partially decked, and there is a structure in the bow, although its top does not protrude above deck level. The stem of the left ship is curved and fitted with a water-bird device; that of the ship at the right is missing, but presumably it ended in the same manner.

The curving sternposts are decorated with sets of volutes somewhat reminiscent of the stern device on a ship depiction from Phylakopi (Fig. 7.25). The masts rise amidships and are drawn as "bumpy" lines that may indicate decorations or wooldings. The masts are stepped in small triangles, perhaps representing maststeps or tabernacles (compare Fig. 8.41: A–B). Although no rigging is depicted, the artist has supplied us with evidence to suggest that these ships from the thirteenth century B.C. continued to use the boom-footed rig for the mast cap. It consisted of pairs of sheaves, like those on the Theran ships, which served to hold the multiple lifts and the halyards (Fig. 6.13). The hulls, however, have apparently been altered considerably by the artist.

All four men "below" the deck stand in the same manner, facing each other in pairs. On the deck above them are two antithetical warriors wearing helmets and mantles. They carry swords in scabbards that end in wavy lines. In all these elements, down to the fringes on the scabbards, they are identical to the warriors on shore in the miniature frieze from Thera (Fig. 6.7). On either side of the ship on the left, a warrior dressed in the same manner faces the ship. The helmeted head and sword pommel are all that remain of the figure on the left. The men standing in, on,

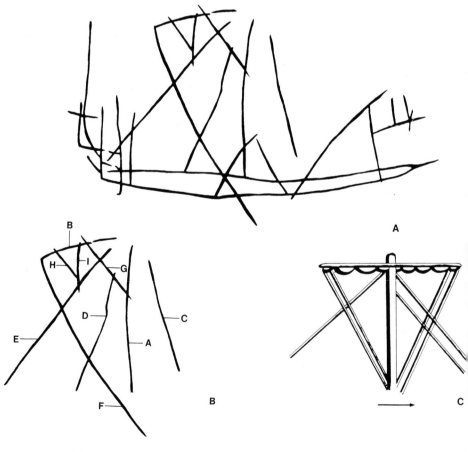

Figure 7.29. (A) Ship graffito on a stele from Enkomi (Late Cypriot III); (B) detail of the ship's rigging; (C) detail of the rigging on Phoenician ships ca. 700 B.C. (A after Schaeffer 1952: 102 fig. 38; C after Casson 1995A: fig. 78)

and next to the ships all face each other in heraldic patterns. Thus, the men below deck are positioned in that manner owing to artistic considerations and not because the action in which they are involved requires them to be arranged thus. The figures' posture is conventionalized and therefore does not elucidate what they are doing.[96]

The ship at right, apart from its missing stem, is identical in all respects to the better-preserved vessel on the left. Its hull is slightly narrower, and the sternpost has an additional pair of volutes. The figure to the left of the ship is portrayed in the same manner as the men below deck but wears a helmet, implying that all these figures also had a military function. The preponderance of fighting personnel, lack of any cargo in the hull, and the similarity of certain elements of these ships (such as the bird insignia and stern decoration) to those appearing on other representations of Late Helladic IIIB–C galleys all suggest that these craft depict galleys with a more military than mercantile purpose and that they are taking part in a waterborne procession of the sort depicted at Thera.[97]

A schematic ship graffito of Late Cypriot III date is carved on a stele at Enkomi (Fig. 7.29: A).[98] Assuming that the ship faces right, then the graffito makes perfect sense as a warship in the Helladic tradition. But is the ship facing right? The ship seems to be under sail—and the sail appears to be billowing to the left. If this is correct, then the ship itself must also face left, resulting in a rather odd-looking craft somewhat reminiscent of Aegean longships, a type of vessel never depicted with a mast and not otherwise recorded in the eastern Mediterranean since the end of the third millennium (Figs. 5.1–4).[99]

The graffito is damaged, result-

Figure 7.30. Ship graffiti incised on a rectangular pillar from a tomb at Hyria (end of Middle Helladic–Late Helladic periods) (from Blegen 1949: pl. 7: 6; courtesy of the American School of Classical Studies at Athens)

ing in several incomplete and missing lines to the right of the mast.[100] Since this depiction dates to the twelfth century or later, it would have carried a brailed sail. With this in mind, I suggest that the ship is indeed facing right and that it carries a brailed rig with a furled sail. Thus, in Figure 7.29: B, line A represents the vessel's mast; B, the yard; C, a single forestay; D, the halyard or brails; E, a backstay; and F, a brace. Triangles BHI and BGA are portions of the furled sail. The resultant rigging is identical to that appearing on ships of later

Figure 7.31. Ship graffiti incised on a rectangular pillar from a tomb at Hyria now at the Museum of Schiamatari (end of Middle Helladic–Late Helladic periods) (from Blegen 1949: pl. 7: 6; courtesy of the American School of Classical Studies at Athens)

yond it is a horizontal line, crossed by a second line and with two others rising vertically from it. This device is reminiscent of the bow projection located midway down the stempost on the Tragana ship (Fig. 7.17: B). Later parallels include the two bow projections on both of the Late Geometric ship depictions from Khaniale Tekke as well as a forked object projecting from the bow of a ship depicted on a sherd from the Heraion at Argos (Fig. 7.20).[101]

The graffito's stern was first finished with a vertical post that was later altered into a curving sternpost by the addition of several lines. Both angular (Figs. 7.22, 27) and curving (Figs. 7.16–19, 21, 28: A) sternposts appear on Helladic ship representations. Several lines in the stern may indicate a castle. The mast is stepped in a massive triangular tabernacle.

Five rough graffiti of ships are incised on two parts of a broken rectangular pillar from a pillaged tomb near the village of Drámasi, a site identified with Homeric Hyria (Figs. 7.30–31).[102] The tomb dates to the end of the Middle Helladic or the very beginning of the Late Helladic period. The hulls of all five ships are crossed by a series of vertical lines. Here the open rowers' galleries have been enlarged by the "artist" at the expense of the ships' hulls.[103]

Even the most detailed ship is crudely made (Fig. 7.30: A). The ship appears to be facing to the right. The hull from the keel to the sheer, as well as the open bulwark, are little more than two deeply engraved lines joined by a row of verticals. The hull is rectangular. Although the exact number is difficult to determine, it appears to have about twenty-two "windows" in what appears to be the open rowers' gallery. Given the crudeness of the depiction, this may suggest that

date shown with their sails furled (Figs. 7.29: C; 8.41: B). Furthermore, the furled sails of the Egyptian and Sea Peoples' ships at Medinet Habu show that the central portion of the sail was not as

tightly furled as at the yardarms (Figs. 2.35–42; 8.3–4, 6–8, 10–12).

The hull continues into a spur. A large forecastle nestles in the bow. Midway down the castle's forward side and extending be-

the prototype for this graffiti was a penteconter, as in the case of the Tragana—and probably the Gazi—representations.

The graffito's hull has been narrowed to little more than a line. There is a vertical stem and a slightly angled but straight sternpost. A spur appears to jut out at the keel line, forward of the stem. The stem is topped by a horizontal zoomorphic (?) device carved deeply into the pillar. The ship has castles in its bow and stern, depicted as horizontal rectangles placed over the stanchions at either end but that do not rise above deck level (compare Figs. 7.16, 28). A line descending from the sternpost suggests a single quarter rudder, its blade angled toward the bow, like the quarter rudders on the Phylakopi ships (Figs. 7.23–24). The ship carries a mast and a sail, which billows toward the bow in a manner reminiscent of the Tragana ship (Fig. 7.17).

Three vertical lines are engraved above the deck. Basch identifies these as stanchions with lunate tops, used to support the rig when the sail is in its lowered position. Although such stanchions appear on the Minoan/Cycladic Theran ships, they are absent on other *Mycenaean* ship imagery. These schematic lines may represent humans, which are commonly included in portrayals of Helladic ships (Figs. 7.8: A, 15–16, 26–28).

Just below this ship is a second vessel that has a rockered keel, identified by Basch as a "round" merchant ship (Fig. 7.30: B). It should be remembered, however, that a profile view of a ship with such a keel, or a crescentic-shaped hull seen in profile, need not necessarily indicate a round ship.

The sternpost, at left, is curved. In this respect the graffito is almost identical to the Tragana ship (Fig. 7.17). The rockered keel rises at the

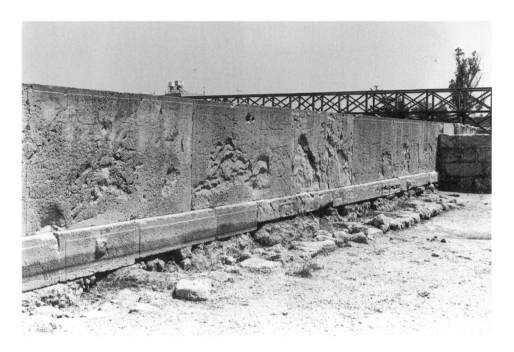

A

B

Figure 7.32. (A) *The southern wall of Temple 1 at Kition with ship graffiti engraved in it, looking east;* (B) *the wall, looking west (photos by the author)*

bow in a steeper curve than at the stern, similar to the stem of the Skyros ship (Fig. 7.21). The open rowers' gallery has been emphasized at the expense of the hull, which has shrunken to little more

than a line. Castles nestle in the bow and stern.

Three other elongated horizontal objects appear on the other (upper?) half of the broken pillar (Fig. 7.31: A–C). These items are so sche-

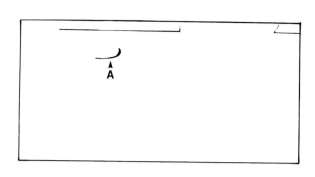
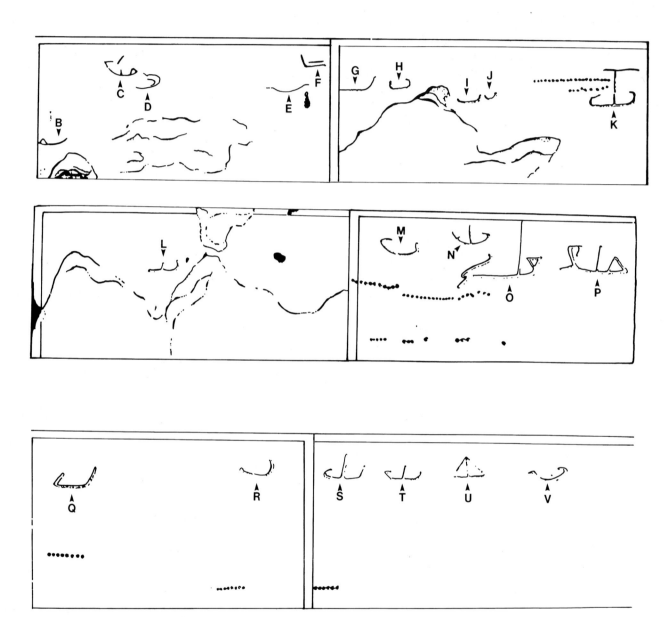

Figure 7.33. Map of ship graffiti on southern wall of Temple 1 at Kition (after Basch and Artzy 1985: 330 fig. 3)

Figure 7.34. Detail of the wall showing the section with ships M–Q (photo by the author)

badly weathered, making multiple interpretations possible.

Basch and Artzy consider graffito "P" to be facing left with a large ram at the bow (Fig. 7.36). Such a massive ram is unparalleled in the period to which the graffito is dated. A triangular light shelter, according to this interpretation, nestles in the stern.

But perhaps the ship is facing right. The triangle at right then becomes a forecastle similar to that on the contemporaneous Enkomi graffito (Fig. 7.29: A). And the line at lower left may be interpreted as a quarter rudder, similar to those depicted on other Helladic ship representations (Figs. 7.16–17, 19, 21–22, 27).[108]

Basch and Artzy identify some of the Kition ships as belonging to the "round ship" type but do not explain the reasoning behind their conclusion.[109] Emphasizing that it is premature to give the Kition graffiti an ethnic identity, they do

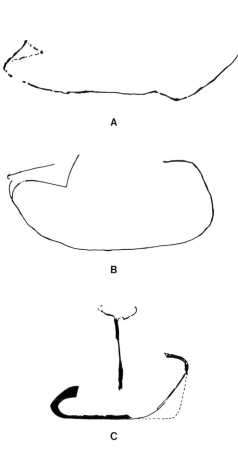

Figure 7.35. Ship graffiti from the southern wall of Temple 1 at Kition: (A) ship no. 5; (B) ship no. 2; (C) ship no. 16 (after Basch and Artzy 1985: 331 figs. 4–6)

matic that even their identity as ships would be questionable were it not for the two previous ship graffiti that they somewhat resemble. Two graffiti have a "castle" at one end (Fig. 7.31: A, C). The middle graffito lacks its right (bow?) extremity (Fig. 7.31: B).

Ship graffiti were also found in Area II at Kition incised on a wall of Temple 1 and on the altar of Temple 4.[104] Basch and M. Artzy suggest that the graffiti and anchors at Kition may indicate a mariners' cult at the site and that the temple may have been dedicated to a deity who protected seafarers.[105]

Nineteen ship graffiti have been identified on the southern wall of Temple 1 (Figs. 7.32–34). The *terminus post quem* for the construction of the wall is ca. 1200 B.C.; the wall was visible, however, until the destruction of Kition. Since the site is inundated with Late Helladic IIIC pottery at this time, these depictions *may* represent Achaean ships.[106] Of these graffiti, only four have been published in enlarged line drawing and one as a photo (Figs. 7.35–36).[107] The graffiti are

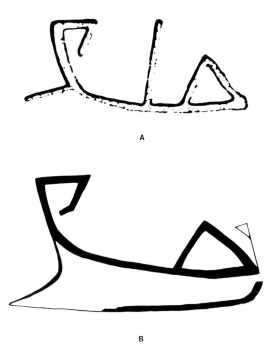

Figure 7.36. (A) Drawing of ship graffito "P" from the southern wall of Temple 1 at Kition; (B) Basch and Artzy's alternate interpretation of ship graffito "P" (after Basch and Artzy 1985: 332 figs. 8B and 8C)

Figure 7.37. Ship graffiti on the altar of Temple 4 at Kition (photo by the author)

propose linking the ships to the Acco graffiti that Artzy considers of Sea Peoples' origin.

An altar in Temple 4 dating to the eleventh century bears two additional ship graffiti (Fig. 7.37). The right termination of one ship is interpreted by Basch and Artzy as a "fan" similar to those described on the Acco graffiti. This finial, however, bears more than a passing resemblance to an inward-facing bird head (Fig. 7.38: A). The second graffito bears a vertical termination at one extremity and a recurving post at the other (Fig. 7.38: B).

In my view, it is necessary to reserve conclusions concerning the existence of a fanlike device attributed to the Acco and Kition ships by Basch and Artzy until a more unambiguous illustration of this device is found.

Models, the majority of which apparently represents oared ships, are a valuable addition to our knowledge of Helladic naval architecture. They confirm and elucidate several of the structural details already noted on the linear depictions of these ships.

A terra-cotta model from a tomb at Tanagra, dating to the Late Helladic IIIB period, has a crescentic hull, reminiscent of Minoan and Cycladic ships (Fig. 7.39).[110] Inside the hull, a central longitudinal painted line may represent a keel jutting into the hull, above the garboards.[111] Fifteen lines painted across the model's breadth symbolize frames or beams. The model's most interesting detail, however, is painted on its exterior.

Here, the central area of the hull is taken up by a horizontal ladder design with twenty-six vertical lines. This might indicate an open bulwark were it not for the number of compartments. The twenty-seven stations fall between those of the ship depictions from Tragana (twenty-four verticals for twenty-five rowers' stations) and Gazi (twenty-seven verticals for twenty-eight stations), suggesting that these numbers are not coincidental. All three images approximate the number of rowers' sta-

A

B

Figure 7.38. Details of ship graffiti A and B on the altar of Temple 4 (photo A by the author; B after Basch and Artzy 1985: 329 fig. 2B)

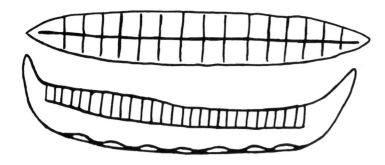

Figure 7.39. Terra-cotta ship model from Tanagra in the Museum of Thebes (Late Helladic IIIB) (after Basch 1987: 141 fig. 293: 1)

tions of a penteconter. Thus, the artist has painted here the open rowers' galleries with its vertical intersecting stanchions. This detail of the Tanagra model is paralleled on a Proto-Geometric terra-cotta ship model now in the Nicosia museum (Fig. 7.40).[112] Later models of more developed ships occasionally illustrate this in plastic detail.[113]

A second model from a Tanagran tomb depicts the keel and three frames painted on the inside of the hull, while the hull's exterior is shown with eight vertical stripes (Fig. 7.41).[114] A bird-head device caps the stem.

The meaning of the external

stripes is unclear. The lines clearly do not suggest the frames seen in "X-ray" view for, were this to be the case, the artist would have depicted the same number of verticals both on the interior and the exterior of the model. I consider the phenomenon of vertical lines painted on the exterior of Mycenaean terra-cotta ship models as possibly representing, in an abstract manner, either the stanchions of the rowers' gallery or the oars (Figs. 7.42, 46).

A small Helladic model from Phylakopi suggests the manner in which the hull planking might have been brought in to meet the blade of the stem structure at the

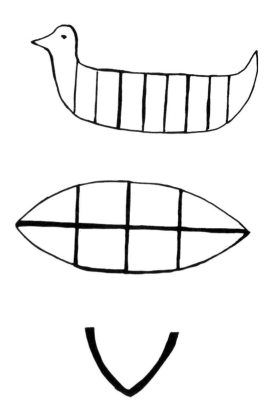

Figure 7.41. Terra-cotta ship model from Tanagra in the Museum of Thebes (Late Helladic IIIB) (after Basch 1987: 141 fig. 293: 2)

bow (Fig. 7.42). The nearly vertical stem protrudes well forward of the fine bow; the upper portion of the stempost is missing. On either side of it are painted *oculi*; these are the forerunners of the bow patches, mentioned by Homer, that appear on Geometric ships (Fig. 8.17: A).[115] Bands perpendicular to the keel are prominent on the interior and exterior of the model just as on the second model from Tanagra.[116] Details of a molded post and keel that protrude outward and beneath the hull appear on a fragment of a ship model from Mycenae made of terra-cotta (Fig. 7.43).[117]

Another terra-cotta ship model, found at Oropos in Beotia and possibly of Late Helladic date, bears some similarities to the ships under discussion (Fig. 7.44).[118] It has a vertical stem and recurving stern. A pronounced forecastle rakes for-

Figure 7.40. Proto-Geometric model in the Cyprus Archaeological Museum, Nicosia (from Westerberg 1983: 91 fig. 19)

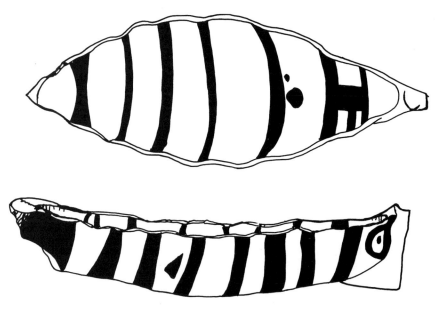

Figure 7.42. Terra-cotta ship model from Phylakopi (Late Helladic) (after Marinatos 1933: pl. 15: 26)

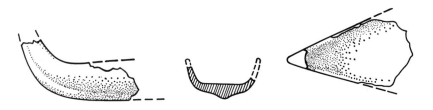

Figure 7.43. Fragment of a terra-cotta boat model from Mycenae (Late Helladic IIIC) (drawing by V. Amato; courtesy of Paul F. Johnston)

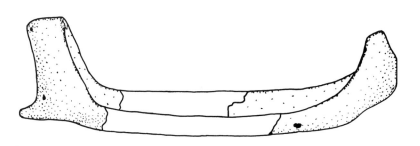

Figure 7.44. Fragmentary terra-cotta ship model from Oropos, Attica (Late Helladic [?]) (after van Doorninck 1982B: 281 fig. 6: B)

with a forward-facing bird-head (?) device decorated with a row of bands.[119] Beneath it is a horizontal line, perhaps representing a wale. The keel ends at the bow in an upcurving waterline spur. And, as on the Gazi ship, the stem ornament extends beyond the spur. Here also, the spur was clearly not intended as an offensive weapon.

The bow is decorated with two vertical zigzag lines on its port side and one horizontal zigzag line on its starboard side. The interior of the hull has two painted longitudinal stripes, perhaps indicating wales. Four lines, perpendicular to the keel, presumably are intended as frames or beams.

Other fragments of terra-cotta ship models of contemporaneous date from Tiryns have sections varying from V–shaped to rounded (Figs. 7.46–47). One has slanting lines painted on either side, perhaps depicting oars (compare Fig. 7.16).

Askoi made in Proto-White

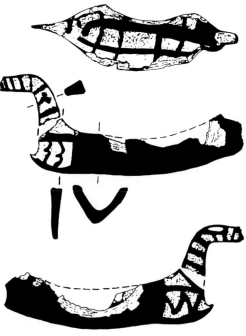

Figure 7.45. Terra-cotta ship model from Tiryns (Late Helladic IIIB) (after Kilian 1988: 140 fig. 37: 8)

ward over the spur at the junction of the keel and stem, precluding its use as a waterline ram. Holes at bow and quarters probably were used for hanging the model.

A Late Helladic IIIB (developed) model found at Tiryns bears a striking resemblance to the ship depiction from Gazi (Figs. 7.45, 19). It has a rockered keel, a wide, V–shaped midships section, and a fine bow.

The keel line continues into an upcurving spur. The stem is capped

Figure 7.46. Ship model fragment from Tiryns (Late Helladic IIIB) (after Kilian 1988: 140 fig. 37: 5)

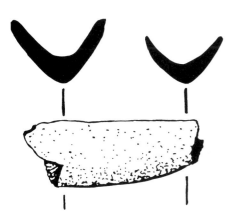

Figure 7.47. Ship model fragment from Tiryns (Late Helladic IIIB [?]) (after Kilian 1988: 140 fig. 37: 7)

Painted or White Painted I fabric in the shape of Mycenaean galleys, both with and without a bow projection, have been found on Cyprus. This pottery, although of local Cypriot creation, is derived from Mycenaean prototypes.[120] *Askoi* are a popular shape in Proto-White Painted Ware, although they usually portray birds or other zoomorphic shapes.[121]

One *askos*, of unknown provenance, depicts a warship with a keel ending in a spur or cutwater bow that bears several similarities to the Tragana ship (Fig. 7.48: A): a cutwater bow or spur, a vertical zigzag design on the bow that continues down to the spur, and an open rowers' gallery with stanchions. Additionally, the unpainted aft side of the stem is crossed by six horizontal lines as on the Asine ship (Fig. 7.22). Similar lines appear on the aft side of the stem or on the upper surface of the head and beak of bird-head

devices on the ships from Kynos and Gazi (Figs. 7.8: A, 16 B, 19; 8.61).[122]

Although these are familiar decorations on Proto-White Painted Ware, in this specific case they may be plausibly interpreted as representing actual ship elements. The manner in which the "horizontal ladder" decoration continues up the sternpost is paralleled on later Greek war galleys. The vertical zigzag line is identical to that on the Tragana ship (Fig. 7.17).

A second *askos* ship model of this series, from Lapithos, is similar to the first, but in place of the waterline spur it has a cutwater bow similar to those on the Kynos and Asine ships.[123] The *askos* has a vertical lattice bow decoration, although all the other painted elements seem to be purely ornamental.

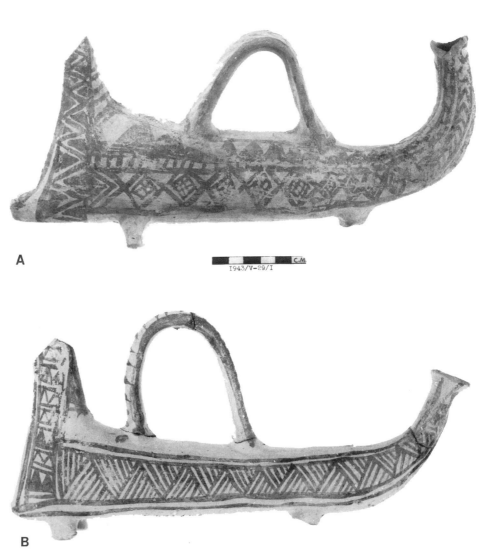

Figure 7.48. Askoi *in the form of ship models from Cyprus dating to the Late Cypriot III period: (A) provenance unknown; (B) from Lapithos (published by permission of the director of antiquities and the Cyprus Museum)*

Figure 7.49. Bow of a terra-cotta ship model from the Acropolis, Athens (Late Helladic IIIC) (courtesy of the Agora Excavations, American School of Classical Studies, Athens)

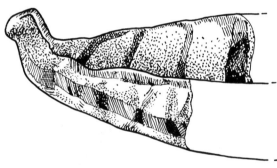

Figure 7.50. Terra-cotta ship model fragment from Asine (Late Helladic III) (after Göttlicher 1978: Taf. 25: 332)

The stems of both of the previous models are missing. A third *askos* model from Lapithos indicates, however, that the stem finished with an inboard-curving bird-head device (Fig. 8: 47).[124] As we shall see below, this reversal in the direction of the ubiquitous bird-head decoration is a key clue to understanding the relationship of Aegean oared galleys (from the end of the Late Bronze Age) and the ships of the Sea Peoples to Greek Geometric ships.

Although made of different ma-

terial, the forefoot of a terra-cotta ship model found in a Mycenaean fill at the Athenian Acropolis is strikingly similar to the Cypriot *askoi* models (Fig. 7.49).[125] The bow is decorated with straight (and now familiar) zigzag lines. A model fragment from Asine supplies details of internal hull construction (Fig. 7.50).[126] The model is much reconstructed; only the bow section is original. The zoomorphic device capping the stem is comparable to those on the following two models.

Two models, said to have originated in Cyprus, have a crescentic hull with a zoomorphic head at the stem and an inward-curving sternpost.[127] Although dated to the Late Cypriot I–III, they bear a remarkable resemblance to one of the later Phoenician models from Achziv.[128] However, they also bear comparison to earlier ship graffiti from Kition (Fig. 7.33).

The first of these models is now exhibited in the Israel National Maritime Museum, Haifa (Fig. 7.51).[129] Dated to the mid-eleventh century on the basis of the ware and decoration, its exact provenance in Cyprus is unknown. The model has a narrow, crescentic hull with a vertical stempost ending in a zoomorphic head. The second model is similar in shape but lacks the painted decoration (Fig. 7.52).

A Late Helladic terra-cotta ship model from Argos lacks its stem- and sternposts (Figs. 7.53–54).[130] The gripe rises at an acute angle from the keel. At the stern, the post rises at a steep angle from the keel and then angles out to form a spacious stern area. A small ledge at the stern is comparable to one molded on a terra-cotta model from Maroni *Zarukas* (Fig. 4.7: A). An amorphous broken object attached to the floor of the Argos model in the stern may perhaps be

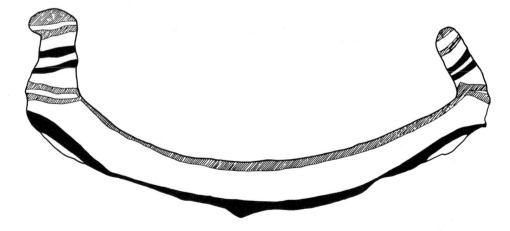

Figure 7.51. Terra-cotta ship model from Cyprus now in the Israel National Maritime Museum, Haifa: provenance within Cyprus unknown (eleventh century [?] B.C.) (after Göttlicher 1978: Taf. 7: 107)

Figure 7.52. *Terra-cotta ship model, provenance unknown* (Late Cypriot I–II) *(from Westerberg 1983: fig. 10)*

accentuated with plastic detail on the interior of the hull. The model has a cutwater bow and an upright stem.

About half of the second model is preserved. This model is decorated with painted lines that help to emphasize the details. The keel is accentuated by paint both inside and outside the hull. Lines perpendicular to the keel assembly may indicate either frames or beams. There is a row of vertical lines delineated by horizontal stripes. Although the model is broken, the excavator reconstructs it as having about twenty-five stations, indicating a penteconter. A third model fragment consists solely of a bird-head device.[132]

Figure 7.53. *Terra-cotta ship model from Argos* (Late Helladic period) *(after Palaiologou 1989: 227)*

all that remains of a helmsman. The base of a mast is located in the center of the vessel, with a single floor to either side of it. It is unclear if the two floors indicate that this model is patterned after a small vessel or whether they are simply representative of those used in the model's prototype. The 1:3 beam/length ratio and the differences between this and the other models raise the distinct possibility that this model may depict a merchantman. If so, it is the only portrayal of a "round" Mycenaean merchant ship of which I am aware.

Additional information is derived from model fragments found with Late Helladic IIIC pottery at Kynos.[131] One model fragment belongs to a ship's bow. Painted lines indicate the sheerstrake, keel, and stem. The painted keel is further

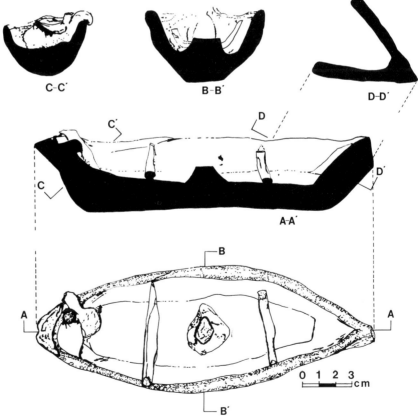

Figure 7.54. *Terra-cotta ship model from Argos, internal details* (Late Helladic) *(after Palaiologou 1989: 228)*

Discussion

Trade

INTERREGIONAL TRADE. Some artifacts inscribed with Linear B inscriptions point to interregional trade within Mycenaean Greece. Vases bearing inscriptions containing Cretan place names have been found on mainland Greece, indicating sea contact between mainland Greece and Crete.[133] Neutron activation analysis of these vessels confirms that, for the most part, they were made in central and western Crete. Fifty-six inscribed sealings suggest the transfer of livestock or their products from sites in Euboea to Boeotian Thebes.[134] Bronze tripods at Pylos are identified as "of Cretan workmanship" and were presumably made on that island.[135] Thus, either the items or the artisans who made them had been transported by ship over the sea.

Thirty-two pairs of chariot wheels at Pylos are defined as of "Zakynthian" type.[136] An 610 lists seven rowers with the same ethnic identity, and a "Zakynthian" is mentioned in a text from Mycenae. Assuming that Zakynthos is to be identified with the Ionian island of that name (which is probable but not certain), this suggests close contacts between Zakynthos and Pylos.

Trade items identified in Linear B by Semitic or Anatolian terms, or by words of unknown origin, imply that the materials themselves were derived from afar. These goods, however, cannot identify the principal carriers who brought them to the Aegean world. The items include spices (cumin and sesame), ivory, blue glass paste, gold, and garments, as well as words of unknown origin such as bronze, purple dye, boxwood and false ebony, alum, and terebinth resin.[137] Note that this list includes many of the trade items on board the Uluburun ship.[138]

The Cypro-Minoan marks made on Mycenaean pottery in the Argolid may indicate the presence of Cypriot traders who organized at least some of the trade between their homeland and the Mycenaean city-states.[139]

INTERNATIONAL TRADE. Documentation of international trade is conspicuously absent in the Linear B documents. Even Amnisos, the main port—presumably the primary maritime entrance for foreign goods to reach Knossos and which appears repeatedly in the Knossos documents—is never mentioned in relation to maritime activities.[140]

The reasons for this phenomenon are unclear.[141] A palace like Pylos, which was capable of raising the fleet(s) mentioned in An 610 and An 724, clearly had the technical, economic, and administrative ability to carry out significant overseas trading ventures had it wished to do so. The question is whether it, and other Mycenaean palaces, did.

International trade may have been in the hands of independent traders who were not responsible to the palace; they would therefore have been invisible in the myopic view of the Linear B administrative texts, which were concerned solely with aspects of palace management. Such an economic scenario seems implausible, however, given the degree of palace control exhibited in the texts.

Trade was obviously taking place: whether international trade was carried out entirely by independent Mycenaean merchants, non-Mycenaean sea merchants, or a combination of both (and was thus completely outside the control of the palace), we could legitimately expect at least echoes of the arrival of foreign goods to be reflected in the texts. One might be tempted to consider the 1,046 kilograms of metal (bronze or copper) mentioned in PY Ja 749 as the arriving cargo of a seagoing trader, were it not for the consideration that this document is believed to represent the total of all metals listed in the Jn series (with the exception of PY Jn 829).[142]

Indeed, it is this "deafening silence" concerning international trade that argues against any simplistic conclusions based on the evidence—or, more correctly, the lack thereof—from the Linear B tablets. At Ugarit, texts dealing with international affairs and trade were stored in separate archives from those containing administrative texts.[143] A. Uchitel notes that other Near Eastern archives sometimes employed separate languages and different materials for recording "economic" versus "chancellery" materials.[144] At the Hittite capital of Boğhazköy, for example, literary texts and documents treating international relations were written on clay tablets that were later baked and thus preserved. The economic texts, however, were probably written on wooden tablets (perhaps similar to the diptych found at Uluburun) in the Luwian hieroglyphic script and have not survived.[145] Similarly, at Nineveh the chancellery materials were recorded in cuneiform script on baked clay tablets and thus have been preserved, while documents dealing with economic matters were probably written in Aramaic on perishable materials that have long since disappeared. If a similar situation existed in Mycenaean palaces, it would go a long way toward explaining the lack of references to international and mercantile affairs in the Linear B tablets. If this scenario is correct, then it is impossible to determine (based on the Linear B evidence) whether Mycenaean palaces carried out international trade.

Because absolutes are an unlikely condition when dealing with human behavior, it seems a reasonable assumption that Mycenaean ships (galleys?) on trading missions probably did, at least on occasion, voyage past Cyprus and visit the Syro-Canaanite mainland. Even if so, however, this seems to have had minimal impact on trade. Indeed, the Uluburun ship strongly suggests that international trade was remarkably complex and diversified. Bass and C. M. Pulak note a Mycenaean presence on board when the ship went down.[146] This presence may perhaps be indicative of one form of Mycenaean trading beyond the Aegean and Cyprus. As Late Bronze Age ships at times are known to have carried foreign nationals, perhaps Mycenaean merchants/representatives were sailing—and trading—on Cypriot or Syro-Canaanite ships.[147]

Characteristics of Mycenaean Oared Warships

Iconography supplies an important view of the general appearance of Mycenaean war galleys. We remain woefully ill-informed, however, concerning the manner in which these ships were constructed. We do not even know whether they employed mortise-and-tenon joinery or whether they were sewn.

At first glance, the Mycenaean/Achaean oared ships do seem to form a cohesive group. Although there is a general conformity of specific elements, the ships themselves exhibit considerable variety. This is in marked contrast to the seeming conformity of galleys depicted during the Late Geometric period. However, it is important to emphasize that much of the Late Geometric warship imagery was made by a single group of painters (the

Dipylon school) at one location (Athens) over a period that is not likely to have lasted longer than six decades.[148] Thus, there is inherent here a conformity of both artistic convention and specific regional ship types (Athenian cataphracts and aphracts), which were being depicted during a relatively short period. Geometric ships of other regions of Greece also show a distinct cohesion, as noted in the vessels appearing on Boeotian fibula.[149]

In contrast, the situation is reversed concerning depictions of Mycenaean ships of the Late Helladic IIIB–IIIC. Images of these ships are spread out across the eastern Mediterranean from Pylos in the west to Enkomi in the east. Furthermore, they range chronologically over three centuries, and the "artists" who created these images in many cases seem to have been under few "conventions" other than their own artistic ability (or lack thereof).

In only a few cases can one reasonably argue that a single artist created more than one ship depiction: perhaps two of the Kynos ships (Figs. 7.8: A, 15); two ships from Phylakopi with the blade of the quarter rudder slanted toward the bow (Figs. 7.23–24 [?]); two ships depicted on the same krater from Enkomi (Fig. 7.28); and the five Hyria ships (Figs. 7.30–31). Indeed, the most noteworthy aspect of our catalogue of Mycenaean ships is the independence of styles in which they were created. To this must be added the consideration that the majority of these images were created during the tumultuous times of the Late Helladic IIIC, which was filled with upheavals that promoted insularity.

One can reasonably assume a certain amount of experimentation, innovation, and development in the ships of this period. All these variables, however, make it difficult to determine whether differences observed on these ships result from actual regional, or temporal, distinctions in ship construction or whether they are traceable simply to the artistic attitudes and capabilities of their creators.

Given the above considerations limiting the likelihood of commonality of depiction, the Mycenaean ship representations are actually remarkably similar to each other. As a group there emerges a cohesive picture of Mycenaean galley types. In general, the following observations may be noted concerning Mycenaean/Achaean oared ships:

• The most characteristic element shown is an open rowers' gallery intersected by vertical stanchions at regular intervals. This element sets Mycenaean ship portrayals apart from the ships of the other Late Bronze Age cultures, with the notable exception of the Sea Peoples' ships. The latter were either adapted from the Mycenaean war galley or actually belonged to bands of fleeing Mycenaeans/Achaeans who may have constituted a significant portion of the Sea People coalition.[150] Indeed, the depiction of an oared ship could be reduced to two horizontal lines connected by vertical stanchions and oars (Fig. 7.7, 23). Despite the abbreviated manner in which the artists painted the ships, their intentions are clear.

• Since the rowers' gallery was open, the oarsmen could be seen here at their oars, as in the case with Late Geometric ships. Thus, for example, the rowers' torsos are visible in a ship from Kynos (Fig. 7.8: A). As is clear from the manner in which the oars are arranged on another of the Kynos ships, by the twelfth century these ships could be rowed from the upper deck level (Fig. 7.16). This is significant because this manner of rowing, depicted also in Late Geometric paintings, was an important step in the development of the *dieres*.[151] This detail may also be revealed on a model fragment from Tiryns (Fig. 7.46).

• Often, to emphasize the rowers' gallery so peculiar in the Late Bronze Age to Mycenaean/Achaean/Sea Peoples' galleys, this element takes up the entire height of the ship. The hull from the sheer to the keel is relegated to a narrow line, a peculiarity that has caused considerable confusion in interpretation.

• With few exceptions, the models portray hulls that were long and narrow. Of the linear depictions, some hulls are shown with straight keels (Figs. 7.16–19, 23–24, 26: A, 27, 30: A, 33: A, F–L, O–Q, T–U). Other ships have rockered keels (Figs. 7.8: A, 21–22, 28, 29: A, 30: B, 31, 33: B–C, E (?), M–N, R–S, V). The models, however, illustrate ships primarily with rockered keels (Figs. 7.39, 41–42, 44–45, and particularly 50–52). Only in three models—the Cypriot *askoi*—are the ships' bottoms rendered as straight lines (Figs. 7.48: A–B; 8.47). This may result more from the conventions of the *askoi* than from an accurate reflection of their prototypes.

• In a few models, the keel is more pronounced on the interior of the hull than on its exterior (Figs. 7.39, 41, 46 [?]). The best example of this phenomenon is on a model from Kynos. This detail may be indicative of a keel that protruded upward and inside the central part of the hull instead of downward below the garboards.[152] Some ships have a pronounced gripe (Figs. 7.8: A, 22, 42, 48: B). Other depictions show the keel extending into a short spur (Figs. 7.17, 19, 27, 29: A, 30: A, 36: A, 44–45, 48: A).

• The stem is usually angular, but

the angle varies: it may be vertical (Figs. 7.16–18, 30: A, 45, 48: A, 49); rake forward (Figs. 7.19, 21, 27–28, 30: B, 44); or slope aft (Figs. 7.8: A, 22, 29: A, 48: B, 51–52). A few ship models have a curving bow (Figs. 7.39, 41, 43, 50); several indicate a fine bow (Figs. 7.43–45, 50–52). Several models and at least one painted depiction suggest that in those ships lacking a spur at the bow, the stem formed a pronounced gripe to which the hooding ends of the strakes were joined (Figs. 7.8: A, 42–43, 49, 51–52, 54 [?]).

• On the stems of some ships, the post bears a lattice design (Figs. 7.17, 48: A–B, 49). It is not clear what the artists intended to represent in this manner, for it makes the stempost assembly appear exceptionally flimsy. Perhaps they are implying that the bow construction contained ligatures, a phenomenon known from both Egyptian Nile boat models as well as from the construction of the fifth-century B.C. Maagan Michael shipwreck.[153] Arguing against this interpretation is the consideration that these parallels are distant in both time and space from the ships under discussion. The stems, when not missing, are normally topped with a water bird or, more commonly, with a bird-head device (Figs. 7.15–19, 21, 25, 26 [?], 28, 41, 45, 50–52 [?]).[154]

• The ships normally end in a curving stern, which presumes a scarf connection between the keel and the sternpost (Figs. 7.16–19, 21, 28, 30: B, 39, 41, 44, 48: A–B, 51–52; 8.47). In the Asine ship the stern is partially hidden by the trailing quarter rudder, but the sternpost does appear to curve (Fig. 7.22).

• There are several exceptions to this rule, however. The Phaistos ship has an angular sternpost/keel joint (Fig. 7.27). The Enkomi graffito originally ended in a vertical sternpost, but additional lines

were then added to form a curving stern (Fig. 7.29). At Hyria a vertical and a curved sternpost are depicted on two ships, presumably created by the same artist (Fig. 7.30: A–B). This may indicate that the two types of stern existed contemporaneously.

• Kynos ship A bears the clearest depiction of an open bulwark covered with a screen at deck level (Figs. 7.8: A, 7.8: B: Area AX). The screen was apparently removable, however: the "area" above the stanchions of the open rowers' gallery is often portrayed as no more than a narrow line, and at times warriors are seen standing on it (Figs. 7.16–17, 28).

• Raised castles nestled in the bow and stern were a standard feature (Figs. 7.8: A, 17, 22 [?], 26 [?], 29: A, 30: A, 31: B–C, 42 [?], 44, 49). They are consistently depicted as frameworks of light construction. In some cases forecastles (?) end at deck height (Figs. 7.16, 28: A, 30: A). The significance of this is unclear, but this detail is repeated with sufficient frequency to suggest that it is not traceable to artists' error.

• A deck is shown on several ships (Figs. 7.8: A, 16, 28). It is likely that this was a central deck that ran the length of the vessel but was omitted along the sides, as was apparently the case with the ships of the Sea Peoples depicted at Medinet Habu as well as with Late Geometric warships.

• Ships dating to the thirteenth century on which the rigging can be determined or inferred use the boom-footed rig with its attendant multisheaved mast cap (Figs. 7.19, 28). Those dating to the Late Helladic IIIC consistently depict the double-sheaved mast cap indicative of a brailed rig (Figs. 7.8: A, 17, 21, 29). This change from boom-footed to brailed rig is also confirmed at Medinet Habu, where both the Sea Peoples' and Egyptian ships are outfitted with brailed rigs. It seems that the brailed rig made its appearance in the Aegean ca. 1200 B.C.

• Most linear ship depictions show the ships with their masts stepped; masts are missing in nearly all of the Mycenaean models, however. It is likely that masts were retractable on Mycenaean ships as was the case on Late Geometric ships. Indeed, one of the Kynos ships is now shown to be without a mast (Fig. 7.16).

• Mycenaean ships were steered with a single quarter rudder (Figs. 7.8: A, 17, 19, 21–24, 27, 30: A–B, 33: O–P, 36: A). This may hark back to third millennium longships. This is an interesting characteristic, because contemporaneous (as well as earlier) Mediterranean ships used two steering oars placed over the quarters (Figs. 2.26; 3.3; 8.10, 12). By the Late Geometric period the use of a pair of rudders became common, although not exclusively so.[155]

• There is evidence for several types of oared ships, primarily penteconters and triaconters, but ships of ten and twenty oars also probably existed. The repeated appearance of approximately twenty-five rower stations in the open rowers' galleys on the ship depictions from Kynos, Gazi, and Tragana suggests that these ships represented penteconters. The thirty men listed on PY An 1 were probably the complement of a single triaconter that was being sent to Pleuron. Homer mentions twenty-oared ships, fifty-oared penteconters, and larger craft; he does not include triaconters, but Herodotus mentions that they were used in the early colonization of Thera.[156]

• Little evidence exists for Mycenaean round-hulled merchant ships driven solely by wind. Sail-ing merchantmen may have existed but have not been considered as suitable, or worthy, for depiction. Alternately, the Mycenaeans may have relied solely on sailing galleys, like those portrayed in their ship imagery, for transport.[157]

In summary, although there is a tendency to interchange the various elements of these oared warships, when studied together they form a cohesive class of craft. As they appear in the thirteenth through eleventh centuries B.C., these galleys are in a stage of experimentation that will stabilize into Greek Geometric war galleys.

The Horizontal Bow Projection

A number of the ship depictions have at the bow a projecting horizontal or upcurving spur that continues the line of the keel forward of the stem (Figs. 7.17, 19, 22, 27, 29–30, 33: P, 36: A, 44–45, 48: A, 49). The appearance of this projection raises the question of whether this feature represents a nautical weapon: a true waterline ram. If it is not a true ram, then what was its function? And what relationship does it have to the rams appearing on Late Geometric war galleys?

There are several reasons to conclude that the horizontal bow projection does not represent an actual ram on Late Bronze Age ships:

• With only one possible exception, discussed below, the depictions of ships' bows on which the spur appears show no hint of the hull-strengthening necessary to permit a ramming ship to be able to withstand the shock of impact.

• The Tragana and Gazi ships, as well as the Enkomi ship graffito and a terra-cotta ship model from Tiryns, carry stem decorations that jut out over the horizontal projec-tion (Figs. 7.17, 19, 29, 45). These ornaments would be damaged if the projection was intended as an effective ram.

• Finally, during the thirteenth through eleventh centuries, some galleys have a projection while others do not. As Casson notes, the ram "was a weapon like the naval gun—once one fleet had it, all had to have it."[158]

The spur's function must be sought in terms of the ships' architecture. The horizontal bow projection appears at this time on galleys. Furthermore, there is contemporaneous historical evidence to suggest that such galleys saw use by both the Mycenaeans and the Sea Peoples in acts of war and piratical attacks.

It is likely that when attacking coastal settlements, these ships were rowed bow-first, straight up on to the beach, in order to conserve time and to sustain the element of surprise. This form of beaching is illustrated in the miniature frieze at Thera and is described by Homer (Fig. 6.7).[159] With these considerations in mind, Kirk proposes the following scenario for the gradual invention of the ram:

When the Bronze Age ship-builder first turned from the construction of the merchant-ship type, with its curved stem and stern formed by a direct prolongation of a curving keel, to the building of narrow, shallow-draught vessels which, to reduce water-resistance, had to have a narrow upright cutwater, he must have found that a simple joint between the ends of two timbers set more or less at right angles—keel and stem—was too weak to stand the shock of a head sea or of beaching at speed. To protect this joint from horizontal shocks, and to prevent damage to the base of the stem, the keel and sometimes other longitudinal timbers were continued ahead of the stem, and slightly pointed to reduce water resistance. The underside of the ram so formed was given a pronounced upward curve . . . so that even on the steeply shelving beaches common in the Aegean there would be no jarring impact, but a gradual sliding up on to the sand, with the main longitudinal timbers taking any strain. Thus the ram, far from preventing stem-first beaching, actually aided it, according to this theory of its origin. Doubtless its use as a method of holing an enemy ship in a head-on attack was discovered very early, and this additional use ensured the preservation of what was from the constructional point of view perhaps a rather clumsy device.[160]

In Kirk's reconstruction the ram seems to have developed on ships that were already being used for functions of war; however, the origins of the projecting forefoot may have been considerably more diverse. It may have been a standard manner for handling the bow-keel join on ships of all types and sizes. Most of the evidence for this phenomenon is much later in date. In Classical times such projections are not limited to war galleys: they are a prominent feature on craft of all sizes and purposes, from tiny rowboats to enormous seagoing merchantmen.[161] The pointed bows

of these craft clearly lacked any military function.

Evidence for the existence of horizontal bow projections on non-military craft is scanty during the Bronze Age. However, the third-millennium terra-cotta model from Mochlos, generally assumed to represent a small craft, carries horizontal projections at both stem and stern (Fig. 5.16). J. Hornell, discussing double-ended Oceanic craft with horizontal projections, suggests that these resulted from the inability of the early shipwrights to curve up the ends of the keel into stem- and sternposts.[162] Because of this, the keel was continued in a long, ramlike projection at either extremity.

Ship reconstructionist J. R. Steffy believes that by lengthening the keel, the spur gave the ship more longitudinal control.[163] In the Athlit Ram the shock of ramming was transferred to a ramming timber, which was locked into place forward of the keel and which transferred the shock via a pair of massive wales that curved downward toward the keel/stem junction. The only hint for such a construction in Mycenaean iconography is on the model fragment of a ship's bow from the Acropolis at Athens on which a painted line on either side of the bow slants downward, perhaps depicting wales (Fig. 7.49).

Whatever the reason for its origin, the bow projections on Late Bronze Age oared ships may be considered "proto-rams" since

they were the immediate predecessors of the true ram. As this shipwright's feature was found useful *ad hoc* for the ramming of enemy ships, gradual changes and additions would have been made in the projection and the ships' architecture in order to enable the galley to sustain the shock of impact when ramming. At first, no doubt, when the ramming ships still lacked additional strengthening, it was anybody's guess which of the two ships—the one doing the ramming or the one being rammed—was more likely to sink first.

When did the transition from "proto-ram" to full-fledged ram take place? It must have happened over an extended period of time, based in large measure on trial and error. Up to the beginning of the Iron Age, after which time there is an iconographic gap, there is no indication of this change. By the ninth century B.C., when ship depictions reappear, they do so with bow fittings that may be considered waterline rams.[164]

The transition appears to have taken place during the intervening hiatus after the disintegration of the Late Bronze Age cultures. Casson notes that the economic aspects of the ram's introduction may be connected with the widespread piracy of the "Dark Ages" and may have been aided and abetted by the taking over, on the part of the *poleis,* of the expenses of outfitting ships.[165]

APPENDIX:
The Pylos Rower Tablets

Unless we accept that raising a fleet requiring six hundred rowers was a normal occurrence at Pylos, the rower tablets strongly suggest that something out of the ordinary—something exceptional—was taking place at Pylos just before its demise.[1] This impression is further strengthened by textual references to the collection (and scarcity) of metal to make weapons, the possibility of human sacrifice, and particularly the *o-ka* tablets, which refer to "watchers" who are guarding the coast.[2] To these considerations must be added one final and obvious one: soon after these tablets were written, the palace of Pylos was indeed destroyed.

Assuming for the moment that the rower tablets do indicate a state of crisis at Pylos in anticipation of a danger approaching from the sea—a view that is held by some but not all Linear B scholars—what purpose might the fleet of galleys have served?

The large numbers of men mentioned in An 610 and An 724 have been interpreted by some scholars as evidence of the mustering of a Pylian war fleet. Fleets of oared ships bring to mind thoughts of Troy, Salamis, and Actium, of

battles and piracy. This equation of "oared ships" with "warships" seems so obvious that little consideration has been given to alternative reasons for the massing of oared ships.

There are other, nonmilitary, contexts where we might expect to find records of numerous rowers. For example, Hatshepsut seems to have required about a thousand rowers just for the towboats pulling her obelisk barge from Aswan to Karnak.[3] Many paddlers, or rowers, would have been required for flotillas taking part in pageants or races during cultic festivals, as at Thera (Figs. 6.46–47). And since trading was also done on merchant galleys, fleets of oared ships would have also required enlisting many rowers (Figs. 2.2, 11).[4]

Herodotus relates that the Phocaeans used penteconters in their voyages of exploration and trade.[5] In doing so, he emphasizes the commercial aspects of this extended navigation by his reference to Tartessus, the Biblical Tarshish, a site noted by Ezekiel for its metals.[6] Assyrian reliefs frequently depict Phoenician trading galleys (Fig. 7.6).[7] An Iron Age Cypriot terra-cotta model depicts a deep and round merchant galley with a

row of oar-ports on either side of the hull.[8]

Oared ships could also be used in expeditions of colonization or for mass forced migrations when insurmountable forces threatened. In Classical times, penteconters were used to transport entire populations and their movables when danger threatened. Miltiades escaped from Tenedos before the approaching Phoenicians in five galleys (*trieres*) laden with his possessions.[9]

Undoubtedly, the most informative example of this phenomenon is Herodotus's description of the Phocaean escape from Ionia before the advancing Persian army: "The Phocaeans launched their fifty-oared ships, placed in them their children and women and all movable goods, besides the statues from the temples and all things therein dedicated save bronze or stonework or painting, and then themselves embarked and set sail for Chios; and the Persians took Phocaea, thus left uninhabited."[10]

Sennacherib describes a similar waterborne flight, this time from the viewpoint of the invader: "And Lulî, king of Sidon, was afraid to fight me (*lit.* feared my battle) and fled to Iadnana (Cyprus), which is in the midst of the sea, and (there) sought a refuge. In that land, in terror of the weapons of Assur, my lord, he died. Tuba'lu I placed on the throne of his kingdom, and imposed upon him my royal tribute."[11]

In his palace at Nineveh, Sennacherib's artists recorded Luli, together with his retinue, escaping Tyre by ship from Sennacherib's superior forces (Fig. 7.6).[12] Luli's fleet consists of warships with waterline rams as well as round merchant galleys. The heads of men and women passengers peeking out from above the bulwarks suggest that both types of ships were used in this waterborne migration.

The prophet Ezekiel, in the lamentation for Tyre in which he compares that city to a merchant ship rich in cargo that has sunk to the bottom of the sea, includes both oarsmen and soldiers among the ship's crew.[13] The prophet may be speaking here of either—or both—types of ships in Sennacherib's reliefs, for both fit the bill, being oared biremes that carried soldiers.

Which of these explanations best fits the evidence of the rower tablets at Pylos? Do they refer to a military fleet, a cult ceremony, a massive trading venture, or perhaps an act of flight and migration?

PY An 610 and An 724 may record preparations for a shipborne emigration—at least of the upper levels of Pylos's stratified society—to escape an expected overwhelming attack. Most of the oarsmen of PY An 610 are classified as "settlers," "new settlers" or "immigrants," while one of the men absented in PY An 724 is defined as a "settler who is obligated to row."[14] Such terms could also

make sense if these documents record an act of overseas migration, in which the rowers are among those migrating to the new location. If so, such a situation would parallel that of the Phocaeans as described by Herodotus.

This explanation also fits well into what we know of the Mycenaean world at the end of the thirteenth century B.C. In the Late Helladic IIIC period, as their world fragmented, Mycenaeans fled their cities, establishing numerous colonies and settlements abroad.

The fact that the oarsmen in An 610 and An 724 are differentiated into "new settlers" and "settlers" seems to presume the previous establishment of a site. Perhaps the documents refer to the enlargement of a preexisting Pylian settlement or region, already organized and controlled by the palace at Pylos.

In archaeological terms, what might we expect to find at Pylos if it had been abandoned and destroyed by its inhabitants instead of attacked and pillaged by invaders?

• It is reasonable to assume that the migrants would have attempted to take their most valuable possessions with them, together with those items and livestock most needed to begin life in a new location. Items of lesser importance would have been left behind because of the lack of space on board the transports. Furthermore, fleeing inhabitants, realizing there was no return, might themselves destroy as much as possible of what they had to leave behind to prevent it from falling into enemy hands.

A study of the artifacts found on the acropolis indicates that all the valuable metal vessels listed in the Linear B documents had been removed from the palace before it

was burned: *not a single metal vessel of value was discovered in the palace.*[15] Explaining this "housecleaning" as the work of invading pillagers is possible, but I believe it does not account for the fact that strata that have been destroyed and, presumably, pillaged in the process will normally still contain some valuables. Pillagers are not infallible. And although metal hoards—at least some of which must have been interred for safekeeping with the intention of later recovery—are a particularly common feature of Mycenaean sites in the thirteenth century B.C., *no hoards were found at Pylos.*[16]

The vast majority of artifacts recovered consists of large quantities of pottery, abandoned in the palace pantries in mint condition.[17] The vases, which had been stacked neatly according to type, collapsed in groups as the fire that swept the palace burned away the wooden shelves on which they were stored. Pottery, easily made from local clay at any given destination, is unlikely to have been allotted valuable (and limited) shipboard space.

• No struggle would have taken place. The invaders, if and when they arrived, would find the palace abandoned, empty of valuables, and perhaps even burned to the ground. Despite the massive excavations at Pylos and the many skeletal remains retrieved there, *not a single bone can be identified as human,* leading the excavators to conclude that the inhabitants had escaped Pylos before the burning of the palace.[18]

Thus, the archaeological evidence fits well with the interpretation of Pylos having been abandoned instead of destroyed by external enemies. The ease with which the later Phocaeans took to their ships to leave their homeland when threatened by superior military forces suggests that they were not the first in the Aegean world to choose this option in times of crisis. This interpretation of events at Pylos might aid in explaining the psychological and organizational mechanisms at work behind the phenomenon of mass seaborne Aegean migrations to the eastern Mediterranean at the end of the Late Bronze Age, of which Pylos may be a microcosm.

Indeed, the "northwesterners" who settled in Cyprus, Syria, and Israel (whether for the short term or for the long) during the upheavals of the twelfth century B.C. *must have originally left somewhere.* To do so, therefore, required at least some form of bureaucratic organization and preparation. The Pylos rower tablets may reflect one—palace-oriented and therefore highly organized—form of preparation for a seaborne migration. Given the size of the estimated population of the kingdom of Pylos, the expedition registered on An 710 and An 724 probably would have been only one (and perhaps the last) of many such expeditions required to transport even a small portion of the people of Pylos, together with their servants, belongings, and livestock, to the new location.[19]

If the above working hypothesis for the meaning of the rower tablets—and with them, for the last days of Pylos—is correct, it would have a profound effect on our understanding of the other Linear B documents found there. But perhaps the most intriguing question that would arise if the people of Pylos abandoned and perhaps torched their own palace before sailing off into the horizon is this: where did they go?[20]

CHAPTER 8

The Ships
of the Sea Peoples

The Late Bronze Age ended in cataclysmic upheavals caused by mass migrations, at least some of which were seaborne. A variety of ethnic groups emerged that were collectively termed "Sea Peoples" by the literate cultures upon whom they preyed. Appearing first as sea raiders in the fourteenth century B.C., these groups were the Late Bronze Age equivalent of the Huns and the Vikings combined. By the late thirteenth century, their raids had been replaced by full-scale land and sea migrations. The Mycenaeans, the Hittites, and many of the Syro-Canaanite city-states fell before this onslaught, never to recover.

Only Egypt, protected by its peculiar geography and located at the southern end of the advance, was able to repulse the invaders—but at a terrible cost to itself. Ramses III managed to stop the approaching Sea Peoples in two major battles: one on land, the other on water. He claims to have later resettled them as mercenaries on Egypt's borders. More likely, after being repulsed by Egypt, they took advantage of her weakened position to resettle areas that they themselves had previously ravaged.[1] Ramses commemorated

these battles graphically on his mortuary temple at Medinet Habu, near modern-day Luxor. His carved relief of the naval battle is an invaluable source of information on a type of vessel used by the Sea Peoples.

Other iconographic sources, mainly rough graffiti and terracotta models, supply additional information about these vessels and suggest that the Sea Peoples' vessel-type represented at Medinet Habu follows an Aegean tradition. Furthermore, the bird-head finials capping the ships' ends imply a distinct connection with religious beliefs prevalent in central Europe at the end of the Late Bronze Age and during the Iron Age.

The Textual Evidence

From their first appearance the Sea Peoples, like the Ahhiyawa, were described as raiders or mercenaries.[2] In this they followed an age-old Aegean tradition.[3]

After their settlement on the southern coast of Palestine in the twelfth century, the Sea Peoples appear to have become traders. Nowhere is there absolute proof for this view, but it may be inferred

from the following considerations:
• On his outgoing voyage from Egypt, Wenamun's ship put in at Dor, which belonged to the Sekel/Sikila. Had this Sea Peoples' group been engaged in brigandage at that time, it is unlikely that the ship would have stopped there.
• In fact, Dor of the Sekel/Sikila appears to have been a "safe haven." Wenamun had no trouble in presenting his case before Beder, the Sikila prince.[4] Indeed, when Wenamun later "liberated" thirty *deben* of silver from a ship off Tyre, apparently belonging to the Sikila, he was clearly acting outside the law.[5]

Important information concerning the tactics used by the Sea Peoples in their seagoing ships and the organization of their fleets has been uncovered at Ugarit. There, texts dating to the very last days of Ugarit were found. These documents include maritime aspects of the deteriorating political situation caused by the advance of the Sea Peoples.[6] Two of the tablets are of particular interest.

One document is a copy of a dispatch sent by the king of Ugarit to the king of Alashia. In it, the Alashian ruler is informed that cities belonging to Ugarit have been destroyed by a flotilla of seven enemy ships, presumably belonging to a marauding group of Sea Peoples.[7] The king of Ugarit includes a request to update him on the enemy's naval movement. This appeal was acted upon: a dispatch, sent by the chief prefect of Alashia to the king of Ugarit, contains information of enemy movements.[8]

In another text Ibnadušu, a man of Ugarit, was required to appear before the Hittite king to report on the Sikila (Šikala) from whom he had escaped.[9] These Sikila are apparently the same group of Sea Peoples referred to in Egyptian texts as the Tjeker (*tkrw*), as in the Tale of Wenamun, in which they inhabit the coastal site of Dor.[10] The Hittite king wishes to interview Ibnadušu concerning the foreign invaders who "live on ships." This is certainly a fitting description for an ethnic group belonging to the "Sea Peoples." Also of interest is the abduction of an Ugaritian by the invaders, an event reminiscent of the taking of prisoners that appears in other contemporaneous texts.[11]

These texts allow several relevant conclusions:
• The number of enemy ships in any given group is relatively small (seven and twenty), particularly when compared to the 150 ships that Ugarit is requested to provide in another text.[12]
• On occasion, Syro-Canaanite ships were pressed into service in the Sea Peoples' naval complement. This suggests that the fleets of the Sea Peoples were more polyglot than one would assume from the Medinet Habu relief.
• The tactics used by the Sea Peoples take the form of piratical coastal raids by small flotillas of ships.[13] They arrive at a seaside settlement, pillage it, and set it to the torch, disappearing without a trace usually (but not always) be-

fore the local military can engage them in a pitched battle.
• Finally, ships used in these raids must have been able to move when necessary under their own propulsion: that means they must have been swift galleys. As the method of attack was based on hit-and-run tactics, these ships could not depend for locomotion solely on the vagaries of the wind.

Questions remain. Where does this event fit into the "micro"-history of Ugarit's last days as seen through the kiln texts? What relationship, if any, did the Sikila who captured Ibnadušu have to the seven enemy ships that terrorized Ugarit's coastal cities in *RS* 20.238? How did Ibnadušu escape from the Sikila? In the general picture that emerges from the encounters of the Sea Peoples with the major, literate Late Bronze Age cultures, there is much that is reminiscent of the emergence and expansion of the Vikings in the ninth to twelfth centuries A.D. The mechanics of the two expansions have similarities. For example, A. E. Christensen notes:

> The background of Scandinavian expansion in the Viking Age is complex and not fully explained. Pressure of population at home was considerable, and it is widely accepted that it was chiefly on this account that the Vikings set out on their voyages. A fact that is often overlooked is that a large percentage of the Vikings were peaceful settlers in search of land. The reason for the tactical superiority of those who preferred plunder to tillage, however, is still not clear. Most of the bands were small and often loosely organized. When they met regular Frankish or Anglo-Saxon troops in battle they frequently lost the contest. Nevertheless, the Vikings managed to harass the

coasts of Europe profitably for two centuries. Their main assets were the ships and the "commando" tactics these enabled them to use. Appearing "out of the blue," the shallow-draft vessels would land their crews on any suitable beach to carry out a quick raid and be away before any proper defence could be organized.[14]

Change only the names, and this same text accurately describes what we know of the Sea Peoples at the close of the Late Bronze Age in the eastern Mediterranean. There can be no doubt that their swift-oared ships were a major asset in the commando-style tactics used by the Sea Peoples, as were the ships of the Vikings. Probably, like the later Vikings, the Sea Peoples used a variety of ships for different purposes.

The warlike, almost barbarian character of the Sea Peoples as they appear in the textual evidence may be somewhat misleading. N. K. Sandars notes that "there is a sense in which literacy actually distorts the archaeological record, for while it illuminates the centers of civilization, it makes the darkness surrounding even darker."[15] The material culture of the groups of Sea Peoples that settled on the present-day Mediterranean coast of Israel at the end of the Late Bronze Age reveals a very high cultural level that is not apparent from the written record.[16] This is hardly surprising, considering the records were written by inhabitants victimized by the Sea Peoples. Again, this is akin to our understanding of the Vikings, who until recently were considered rough barbarians—mainly on the basis of the literary records of the people upon whom they preyed. Now, however, other less warlike aspects of their culture are being re-

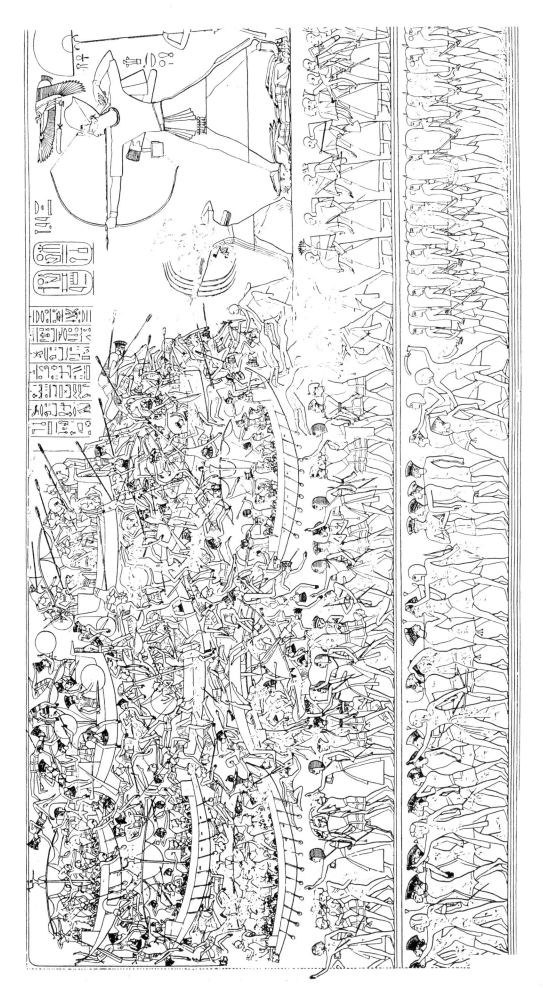

Figure 8.1. The naval battle depicted at Medinet Habu (from Nelson et al. 1930: pl. 37 [H. H. Nelson et al., Medinet Habu I: Earlier Historical Records of Ramses III, University of Chicago. Introduction © 1930 by the University of Chicago, all rights reserved. Published June, 1930])

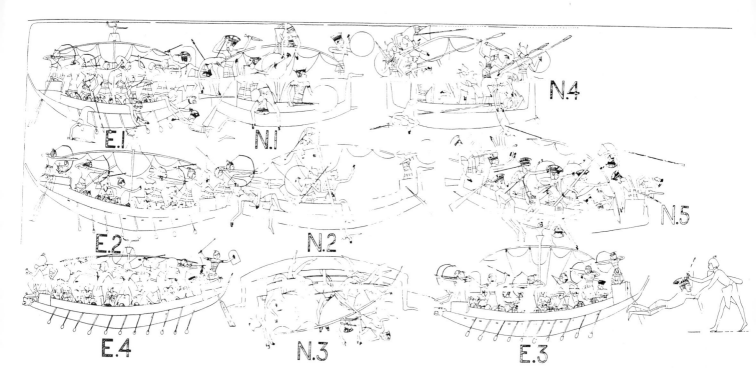

Figure 8.2. The scene of the naval battle with the floating bodies removed (*from Nelson 1943: fig. 4*)

vealed, mainly through the archaeological record.

The Archaeological Evidence

The introduction, clearly by sea, of a foreign culture with strong Aegean affinities in Cyprus, along the Israeli coastal plain, as well as at Hama in Syria indicates a major use of ships within the mechanism of this mass migration.[17]

The Iconographic Evidence

Medinet Habu: The Ships of the Sea Peoples

The most important iconographic evidence for the ships used by the Sea Peoples is Ramses III's relief depicting the naval battle in which he defeated a coalition of Sea Peoples including the Peleshet, Sikila, Denyen, and Sheklesh in his eighth regnal year (ca. 1176 B.C.). The relief appears on the outer wall of his mortuary temple at Medinet Habu (Fig. 8.1).

Figure 8.3. Ship N. 1 (*photo by B. Brandle*)

This scene is instructive concerning ship-based warfare before the introduction of the ram as a nautical weapon.[18] The Sea Peoples' ships are stationary in the water: their oars are stowed and their sails furled. Apparently the invaders were caught at anchor. Indeed, the accompanying text alludes to an

ambush that took place in a closed body of water: "The countries which came from their isles in the midst of the sea, they advanced to Egypt, their hearts relying upon their arms. The net was made ready for them, to ensnare them. Entering stealthily into the harbor-mouth, they fell into it. Caught in their

Figure 8.4. Ship N. 2 (photo by B. Brandle)

Figure 8.5. Ship N. 3 (photo by B. Brandle)

Figure 8.6. Ship N. 4 (photo by B. Brandle)

Figure 8.7. Ship N. 5 (photo by B. Brandle)

place, they were dispatched and their bodies stripped."[19]

H. H. Nelson has noted that the scene is organized around three conceptual elements: spatial, ideological, and temporal.[20] It gives a feeling of a vigorous water battle, almost as if it is a snapshot taken during the battle. Within the framework of this scene, however, the artists have skillfully intertwined various phases of the battle (Fig. 8.2).[21] The beginning of the battle is portrayed by Egyptian ship E. 1 and Sea Peoples' ship N. 1. The middle phase is represented by ships E. 2 and N. 2, while E. 3 and N. 3 signify the end of the battle. A final time element is indicated by ship E. 4, which is loaded with shackled prisoners and is heading for the victory celebration.

It is to be expected that the artists stereotyped the Sea Peoples' ships into only one form, in keeping with their generalizing portrayal of the naval battle (Figs. 8.3–8, 10–12, 14). We need not assume that this was the only kind of ship in their service.

The same holds true of the Egyptian ships. An inscription on the Second Pylon at Medinet Habu indicates that on the Egyptian side, at least three classes of ships took part in the battle.[22] Only one Egyptian ship type, depicted four times, appears in the relief, however. Evidently, the relief contains five representations of the *same* Sea Peoples' ship instead of depictions of five *different* ships.

Nelson emphasizes the vivid nature and uniqueness of the Medinet Habu reliefs, which depart to a degree from conventional Egyptian art:

The artist has indicated not merely the accessory elements of dress and weapons incident to this or that foreign nation, but the

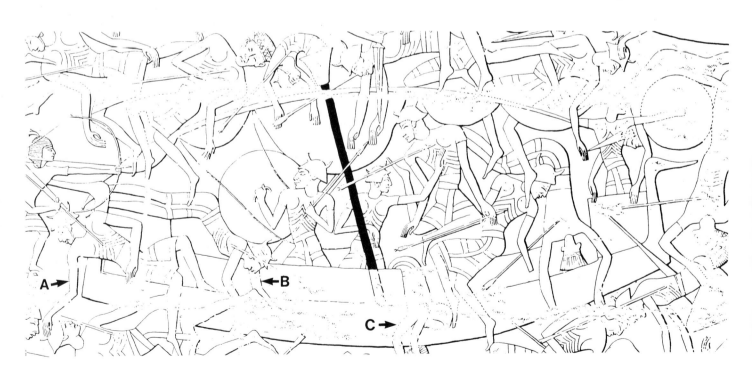

Figure 8.8. Ship N. 2 (detail from Nelson et al. 1930: pl. 39 [H. H. Nelson et al., Medinet Habu I: Earlier Historical Records of Ramses III, University of Chicago. Introduction © 1930 by the University of Chicago, all rights reserved. Published June, 1930])

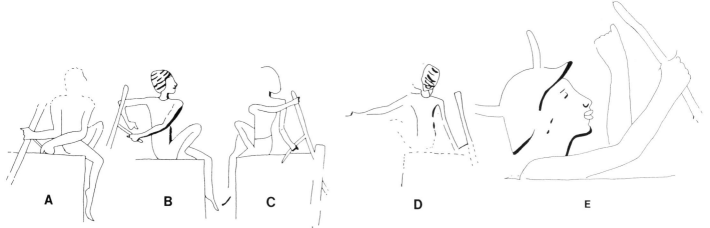

Figure 8.9. The helmsmen of ships E. 1–E. 4 (A–D) and N. 4 (E) (after Nelson et al. 1930: pl. 39)

variations in features, expression, profile, and other physical characteristics are clearly marked. The facial renderings are in some cases unprecedented in the history of art. They not only discriminate between the living and the dead, but there is an unmistakable effort to make the features express fear, anguish, or distress. Another unprecedented psychological element is to be recognized in the upthrown arm of a drowning man [Fig. 2.36: A: B]. Older Egyptian art always showed the entire human figure in such a case; but the ancient artist at Medinet Habu has understood the horror suggested by the despairing gesture of a drowning enemy engulfed by the sea and invisible except for his upthrown arm.[23]

What was the artist's source for this depiction? We know that artists took part in Egyptian campaigns and trading expeditions outside the borders of Egypt.[24] Perhaps a field artist could have recorded one of the invading ships that had been washed ashore or taken prize. Such a drawing could have later served as a master copy for the artists portraying the Sea Peoples' ships on the Medinet Habu relief.

To understand the ships, we must first understand the art form in which they were created. Origi-

Figure 8.10. Ship N. 1 (detail from Nelson et al. 1930: pl. 39 [H. H. Nelson et al., Medinet Habu I: Earlier Historical Records of Ramses III, *University of Chicago. Introduction © 1930 by the University of Chicago, all rights reserved. Published June, 1930])*

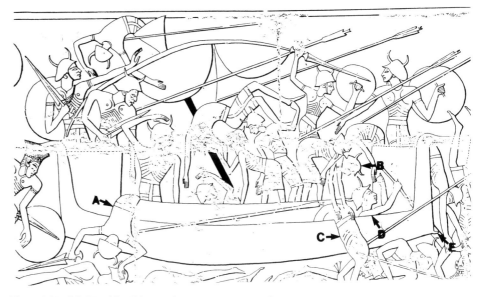

Figure 8.11. Ship N. 4 (detail from Nelson et al. 1930: pl. 39 [H. H. Nelson et al., Medinet Habu I: Earlier Historical Records of Ramses III, *University of Chicago. Introduction © 1930 by the University of Chicago, all rights reserved. Published June, 1930])*

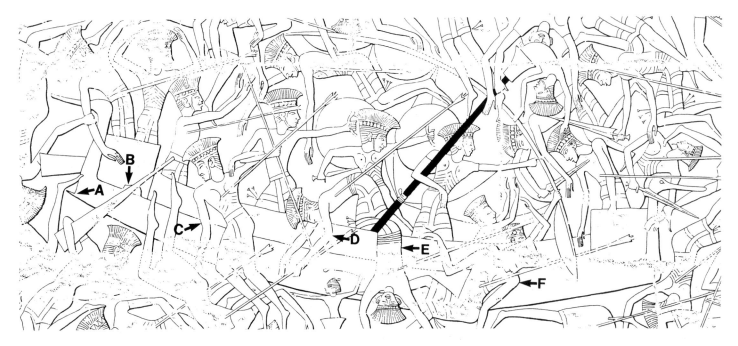

Figure 8.12. Ship N. 5 (detail from Nelson et al. 1930: pl. 39 [H. H. Nelson et al., Medinet Habu I: Earlier Historical Records of Ramses III, University of Chicago. Introduction © 1930 by the University of Chicago, all rights reserved. Published June, 1930])

nally, the relief was painted. In Egyptian painted relief, the artist did not necessarily differentiate between the relief and the painting. Indeed, the plastic representation appears to have been subordinated to the painting. Nelson's description of another war scene at Medinet Habu, where the paint had been preserved, is illuminating in this regard:

Here, in the upper portions of the relief, even the water-color paint is unusually well preserved, and we find that the bare sculpture has been extensively supplemented by painted details distinctly enriching the composition. The colors of the garments worn by the Libyans stand out clearly. Between the bodies of the slain as they lie upon the battlefield appear pools of blood. The painter has suggested the presence of the open country by painting in wild flowers which spring up among the dead. Moreover, it is apparent that the action takes place in a hilly region, for streams of blood run down between the bodies as the enemy attempt to escape across the hills from the Pharaoh's pursuing shafts. The details of the monarch's accoutrements are indicated in color, relieving him of the almost naked appearance often presented by his sculptured figure when divested of its paint. It is not infrequent to find such details as bow strings or lance shafts partly carved and partly represented in paint. The characteristic tattoo marks on the bodies of the Libyans are also painted in pigment only. When all these painted details have disappeared, though the sculptured design may remain in fairly good condition, much of the life of the original scene is gone and many aids to its interpretation are lost.[25]

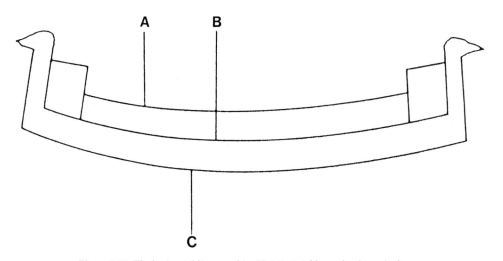

Figure 8.13. The horizontal lines on ships N. 1–2, 4–5 (drawn by the author)

This is one way to explain why some elements on the Sea Peoples'

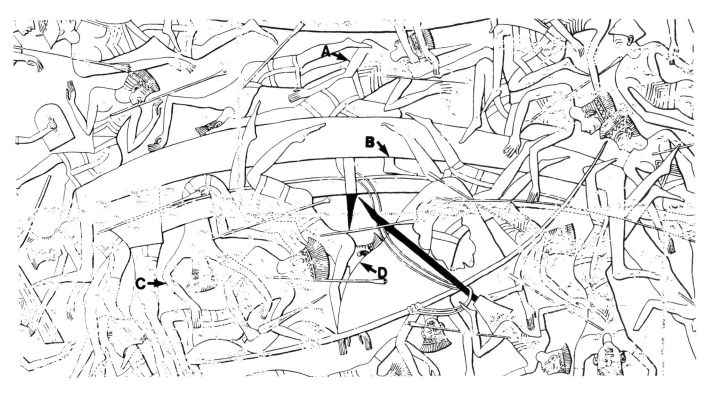

Figure 8.14. Ship N. 3 (detail from Nelson et al. 1930: pl. 39 [H. H. Nelson et al., Medinet Habu *I:* Earlier Historical Records of Ramses III, *University of Chicago. Introduction © 1930 by the University of Chicago, all rights reserved. Published June, 1930])*

ships are not represented consistently. Presumably, the same detail may have been applied in paint in some cases and carved (and painted) in others.

Sadly, many details of the ships have been lost, along with the paint. The relief that remains is only the skeleton of the original work. Furthermore, plaster was used extensively to cover up defects in the masonry and to make corrections (Fig. 2.36: B–D).[26] In some cases, only the original draft of the design is left. The final draft had been carved into plaster that has long since disappeared.

There are numerous "disappearing" elements. Note, for example, that on ship N. 2 the brails appear on the left side of the mast only and that the bird head at the stern of ship N. 5 is eyeless while the head capping the stem has a carved eye (Figs. 8.8, 12).[27]

The quarter rudders on the invaders' ships now lack tillers;

originally they did have tillers, which were represented in paint only and have long since vanished. This is evident from the manner in which the helmsman of ship N. 4 grasps the loom of his quarter rudder in his right hand while his left hand is clenched around a now nonexistent tiller (Fig. 8.9). Compare this to the two-handed manner in which the helmsmen on the Egyptian craft are maneuvering their steering oars. All four hold the tiller with their left hand; two also hold the loom with their right hand.

The Sea Peoples' craft have gently curving hulls ending in nearly

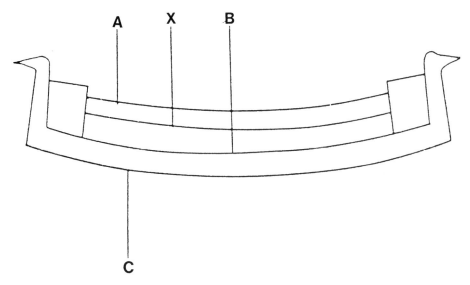

Figure 8.15. The horizontal lines on ship N. 3 (drawn by the author)

perpendicular posts capped with bird-head devices facing outboard. Raised castles are situated at both bow and stern. The actual structure of these ships may be derived from a careful study of the horizontal parallel lines that appear on the ships and the manner in which the live warriors and dead bodies are positioned relative to them. Care must be taken when interpreting this evidence, however.

The hulls of four of the Sea Peoples' ships—N. 1, N. 2, N. 4, and N. 5—are defined by three horizontal lines that we shall term, from top to bottom, A, B, and C (Fig. 8.13). At first glance, these seem to correspond to the three horizontal parallel lines on the

Figure 8.16. Ship construction scene from the Tomb of Tí. A plank with mortise-and-tenon joints is being aligned on the hull. Note the worker's leg visible between the plank and the hull (Fifth Dynasty) (from Steindorff 1913: Taf. 120)

Egyptian ships that represent, from top to bottom, the border of a light bulwark protecting the rowers, the caprail, and ship's bottom (Figs. 2.35–42).[28] A closer study, however, indicates that this is not the case. The following observations clarify this matter:

• Warriors standing in the center of the ship are covered by line A at varying heights from shin to thigh level; dead bodies bent over line A cross lines B and C (Figs. 8.8: C, 10: A, 11: A, 12: E [note also 12: C, F]). These figures reveal that the areas between lines A, B, and C all represent the ship's sheer view. They do not denote the deck area in plan view.

• Line B appears as a baseline with bodies appearing directly above it. In ship N. 2, the warrior being skewered at the bow is resting on line B (Fig. 8.8: A). This is not accidental since his left foot is placed on the same line. To the right of A, his companion, B, is falling headfirst. His body crosses line A, but his left arm seems to disappear behind line B. Similarly, in ship N. 4 the helmsman and a dead warrior appear directly above line B (Fig. 8.11: C–D). The dead man is being held by his companion, B, who is standing above him and behind line A. This indicates that, in addition to the raised decks in the castles, the craft must have been at least partially decked.[29]

• Ship N. 3 differs from the other Sea Peoples' ships by having an additional horizontal line between lines A and B (Fig. 8.14). We shall term this line X (Fig. 8.15). The key to understanding the three horizontal areas (AX, XB, and BC) formed by these four lines is to study the manner in which the dead and dying bodies of the fallen warriors are arranged in relation to them.

The ship has capsized. One warrior lies on keel line C (Fig. 8.14:

A).[30] His left leg disappears behind the hull in area BC, but his foot, B, reappears in area XB. Similarly, body C is "folded over" area AX; its abdomen is visible in area XB while the torso emerges below line A. The leg of another body, D, disappears behind area AX and reappears in area XB, passing outside the ship's hull over lines B and C.

These three independent clues indicate that area XB must represent an open space. The only explanation for this space is that it served as an open rowers' gallery through which oars were worked, located between the caprail and the light bulwark. If line X is added to ships N. 2 and N. 4, the positioning of the figures in relation to them becomes immediately clear. Originally, line X may have been painted on ships N. 1, 2, 4, and 5, as perhaps were the stanchions that would have been required to support the light bulwark.

These ships find their closest contemporaneous parallels in the Late Helladic galleys discussed in the previous chapter. In particular, they are virtually identical in nearly all surviving details to Kynos A (Fig. 7.8: A).

Artists' errors appear on the representations of Sea Peoples' ships at Medinet Habu. Note that the mast mistakenly crosses area AB in ship N. 2 and area AX in ship N. 3 (Figs. 8.8, 14), although it is depicted correctly in ships N. 1, N. 4, and N. 5.

Although the hand of a master artist appears to have guided the wall relief, the work was evidently carried out by artists of varying capabilities.[31] Some of the artists made errors in depicting the ships' construction. Note, for example, the figure in ship E. 1 bending over to grasp a sword from the floating body of an enemy warrior (Fig. 2.36: A: A). Unlike the two other soldiers plausibly portrayed leaning over the screen, the upper body of the former is placed in an impossible manner, leaning over the line that represents the sheer-line and the screen. To best understand correctly what the Egyptian artist(s) had in mind when portraying a ship, therefore, it is important to have several independent clues corroborating the same details. Happily, such is the case in N.3. The bodies disappear behind the screen and then reappear on the other side in proper perspective. The method used here by the artist to display the three bodies woven around elements of the vessel's structure on ship N. 3 is not unique in Egyptian art, although it is exceedingly rare.

Another example of a human figure disappearing behind an object and then reappearing, as do the bodies in ship N. 3, exists in the Fifth Dynasty mastaba of Tí at Saqqara, where a plank is being

Figure 8.17. The deck structure of Greek Geometric galleys: (A) figures stand on the rowers' benches in an area that is not covered by a deck; (B) the legs of a figure sitting at deck level appear through a "window" of the open rowers' gallery (A after Morrison and Williams 1968: pl. 1e [Geom. 2] and Casson 1995A: fig. 68; B after Morrison and Williams 1968: pl. 7b [Geom. 38])

Figure 8.18. (below) (A) Tentative isometric reconstruction of a Sea Peoples' ship depicting the main elements of the ship's architecture as indicated by the bodies of the dead warriors (B) Tentative sheer view of a Sea Peoples' ship with the three bodies of warriors in ship N.3 added to better illustrate constructional details (drawings by F. M. Hocker. Courtesy of the Institute of Nautical Archaeology.)

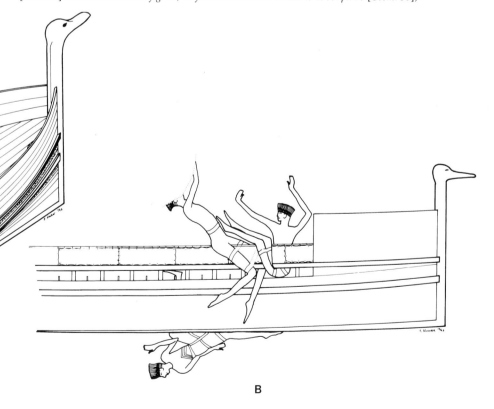

fitted to a hull in a scene of ship construction (Figs. 8.16; 10.16–17).[32] One worker is supporting the hull with a short rope. Next to him another man kneels behind the plank and hammers it down with a small cylindrical weight. The man's right leg disappears behind the plank, but his foot reappears in the space between the plank and the hull. The foot could be mistaken for a tenon were it not for its red skin color that is still visible.[33]

The men depicted in the ships suggest that the deck on the Sea Peoples' ships ran the full length of the hull, from the forecastle to the sterncastle. The intertwining of bodies in the manner shown in ship N. 3, however, would be impossible if the deck had extended the entire width of the ship. This means that planking must have been left out along the sides.

This feature connects the Sea Peoples' vessels to the Aegean tradition of galleys as it appears on Mycenaean and Greek Geometric warships. Planking must have been missing along the sides of the Kynos A ship to allow the rowers' heads to disappear behind the screen (Figs. 7.8: A, 9); L. Casson notes that in some fighting scenes, warriors are shown standing on the rowers' benches at a point that was not covered by the raised deck and that the part left undecked must have been along the sides where the rowers sat (Fig. 8.17).[34] Figure 8.18: A is a tentative isometric reconstruction of a Sea Peoples' ship illustrating the basic elements discussed above. Figure 8.18: B is a tentative sheer view of a Sea Peoples' ship with the three warriors' bodies added to better illustrate the constructional details.

Note that the bodies are depicted to a scale larger than that of the ship.

The Sea Peoples, it appears, brought with them to the eastern Mediterranean the concept of the oared warship with an open rowers' gallery supported by vertical stanchions. From the twelfth century B.C. onward, the development of warships in the Aegean and along the Phoenician coast followed separate lines of development from a common ancestor, resulting ultimately in the Greek *dieres* and the Phoenician bireme. This explains the appearance of bird-head devices on later Phoenician warships (Fig. 8.53).

Perhaps the prototype of the Sea Peoples' ships depicted at Medinet Habu was a penteconter. While in the water battle relief we see their ships solely in their fighting mode; these same ships may also have been used at times to transport the families of combatants, as well as their movables, during the waterborne migrations. Indeed, this may explain why, as we have seen above, the Hittite king defines one group of Sea Peoples, the Sıkıla, as those "who live on ships."

The Sea Peoples' ships carry two (Figs. 8.10, 12), one (Figs. 8.8, 11), or no (Fig. 8.14) quarter rudders. Of the ships with two quarter rudders, N. 1 has both placed on its

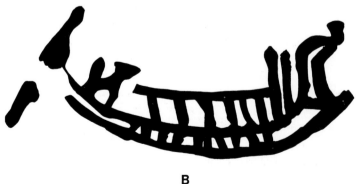

Figure 8.19. (A) *Painted decoration, including a ship, depicted on a funerary urn found at Hama (ca. 1200–1075 B.C.); (B) detail of the ship. Note the bird-head device capping the stem (A from, B after Ingholt 1940: pl. 22: 2 [© 1940, Munksgaard International Publishers Ltd., Copenhagen, Denmark])*

starboard quarter, which is the side of the ship facing the viewer; ship N. 5 appears to have a rudder on either quarter. The quarter rudder on the near (starboard) side is held in what seems to be a wooden bracket (Fig. 8.12: B).[35]

Presumably, the normal complement was two steering oars, and those missing are attributable to loss during battle. In this matter they differ from contemporaneous representations of craft from the Aegean but seem to herald the use of the double steering oars that were to become common equipment on Geometric craft.[36] Alternately, the Sea Peoples may have adopted the use of a pair of quarter rudders after encountering—and capturing—Syro-Canaanite and Egyptian seagoing ships that normally used two steering oars, one placed on either quarter (Figs. 2.17–18, 26; 3.2–3, 10, 12–13). On two ships a small, pointed projection appears at the junction of sternpost and keel (Figs. 8.11: E, 12: A). The position and form of these elements invite comparison with the stern device that appears earlier (apparently with cultic connotations) on Aegean craft.[37]

The rigging of the Sea Peoples' ships is identical to that carried by the Egyptian craft with which they are engaged. Both carry the newly introduced brailed rig. Indeed, this is one of the earliest appearances of this type of loose-footed sail.[38] The masts are topped by crow's nests.[39] The yard curves downward at its extremities and is raised by twin halyards; these appear only on ship N. 3 (Fig. 8.14). The block through which they must have worked is not represented, nor (with the exception of the brails) are other details of the rigging.

The Hama Ship

A Sea Peoples' ship was probably the inspiration for a vessel de-

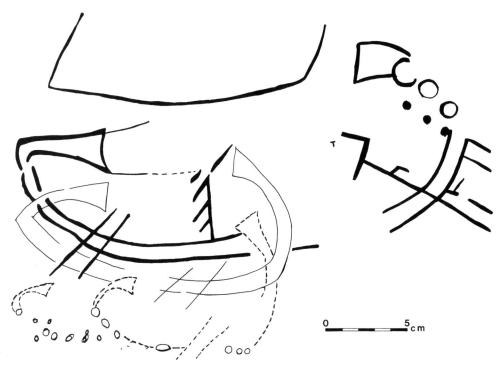

Figure 8.20. Ship graffiti on a stone receptacle from Acco as reconstructed by Artzy and Basch (after Artzy 1987: 77 fig. 2)

picted on a burial urn uncovered at Hama in Syria (Fig. 8.19).[40] The urn was found in Period I of the cremation cemeteries there (Hama F, early phase), which contained nearly 1100 cremation-burial related urns and which dates to ca. 1200–1075 B.C.[41] This form of burial is clearly intrusive as it diverges completely from known local traditions. The material culture of this new group is of European tradition and includes fibulae, flanghilted swords, and the urnfield burials themselves.[42] These clearly indicate the arrival of an intrusive element at Hama. The Danish excavators of Hama associated Hama's urnfield level to the migrations that took place at the end of the Late Bronze Age.[43]

The keel line of the Hama ship is rockered; the stem is vertical, capped by a bird-head device with an upcurving beak (Fig. 7.21; compare 8.61: B–D). The horizontal line that crosses the stem may represent the free-standing wale that can be clearly seen on one of the

Kynos ships (Fig. 7.7). The Hama ship has a pronounced, upcurving cutwater bow that continues the line of the keel and extends slightly forward of the bird-head device capping the stem.

Two vertical lines abaft the stem and a structure at the stern may indicate castles. The ship is formed from three painted, curving horizontal lines. The two horizontal bare spaces between the lines are

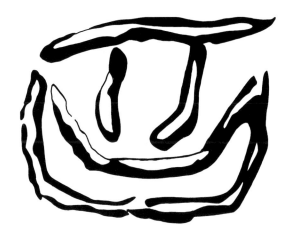

Figure 8.21. Ship engraved on a stone seal from T. 6 at Enkomi (Late Cypriot) (after Schaeffer 1952: 71 fig. 22)

segmented by rows of vertical lines. If one of the sets of vertical lines represents the open rowers' gallery with stanchions, then the upper set may represent the supports for the open bulwark.

Acco
Several ship graffiti were found incised on a small altar dated ca. 1200 B.C. that was uncovered at

A

B

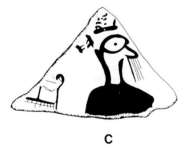

C

Figure 8.22. Figures wearing (feather?) helmets reminiscent of those worn by contingents of the Sea Peoples in the Medinet Habu reliefs (from Morricone 1975: 360 fig. 357: a–c)

Acco in 1980 (Fig. 8.20).[44] This appearance of ship representations on a cultic receptacle is paralleled in the Aegean (Fig. 6.64). The largest ship is the most deeply incised. In profile it has a long, narrow hull recurving at stem and stern. Two quarter rudders, one bearing a tiller, indicate that the vessel is facing left. The port rudder has a tiller. A mast is stepped amidships; above it is a square sail. M. Artzy interprets several slanting lines attached to it as shrouds. This identification is dubious, in my view. The remains of two or three additional hulls of similar shape have been identified below the bow of the largest ship.[45]

Artzy considers the graffiti to represent "round ships" but does not explain the basis for this conclusion. She places emphasis on the finials of the stem and stern, which she terms "fans." These she compares to the papyrus umbels of Hatshepsut's Punt ships and to the *aphlaston*. Neither comparison is convincing. The papyrus umbel was not flat like a fan: it was discoid.[46] A probable source for the *aphlaston* is discussed below. Artzy suggests that the graffiti represent a type of Sea Peoples' ship that at present might find its only possible parallels in the ship graffiti from Kition.[47]

Enkomi
A ship, perhaps of Sea Peoples' origin, may be engraved on a stone seal of Late Cypriot III date found in T. 6 at Enkomi (Fig. 8.21). C. F. A. Schaeffer defined it as "un sujet difficile à interpréter (bateau)."[48] The object represented appears to be an extremely schematic attempt to portray a double-ended ship under sail. The hull is narrow and curved. Schaeffer compares it to the Sea Peoples' galleys at Medinet Habu.[49]

Discussion

Differentiating Mycenaean Ships from Those of the Sea Peoples
Although the ships of the Sea Peoples are undoubtedly related to the mainstream of Aegean galley development, it is important to emphasize that no conclusions concerning the ethnic identity of the Sea Peoples as a whole may be deduced from this. Ship varieties can be and were adopted and adapted by peoples having no ethnic connection with the traditional users of the craft. The remarkable similarity of the Sea Peoples' ship depictions at Medinet Habu to representations of Aegean warships in the fourteenth through twelfth centuries—and now particularly to Kynos ship A—necessitates several key questions. When is a ship portrayed on Late Helladic pottery to be identified as a Sea Peoples' ship, and when is it a Mycenaean ship? Is it at all possible to differentiate between them?

Indeed, the division of depictions of oared galleys in the twelfth century B.C. into Mycenaean and Sea Peoples ships is largely arbitrary. The problem is compounded because these ships appear, for the most part, at a time (Late Helladic/Late Minoan IIIB–C) and in regions (Greece, Crete, the Aegean, Cyprus, the Levant) where both fleeing Mycenaeans and bands of marauding Sea Peoples are believed to have roamed. Our lack of knowledge as to the ethnic composition of the Sea Peoples following the decline of the Mycenaean world further complicates an already difficult problem that, for the most part, cannot be resolved.

One manner to deal with these questions is to identify the crews depicted on the ships. If we assume that the nationality of a ship's crew reveals the vessel's

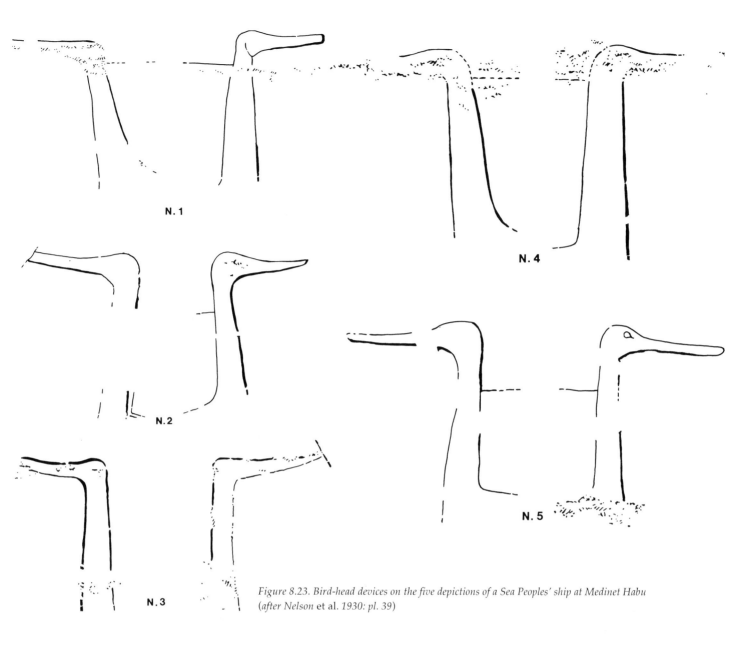

N. 1

N. 4

N. 2

N. 5

N. 3

Figure 8.23. Bird-head devices on the five depictions of a Sea Peoples' ship at Medinet Habu (after Nelson et al. 1930: pl. 39)

nationality (and even this assumption is open to argument), by defining the crew, we can identify the ship. The Mycenaean/Cycladic warriors connected with the ships depicted on the Late Helladic IIIB krater from Enkomi suggest that these craft are Aegean (Mycenaean) (Fig. 7.28). The vessels of the northern invaders shown at Medinet Habu belong, of course, to the Sea Peoples.

Sandars has identified as feather helmets the headgear of rowers and other figures portrayed on sherds from Cos (Figs. 7.26; 8.22).[50] The slightly earlier "northern

bronzes" found in the Laganda tomb at Cos certainly suggest the presence of northerners.[51] Similar helmets with multiple protrusions (feathers?) are worn by warriors on the Kynos ships (Figs. 7.8: B, 15, 16).[52] Are the crews and the ships depicted at Cos and Kynos Sea Peoples' galleys?

*Bird-head Devices
on Mediterranean Ships*
One of the most striking elements of the five depictions of a Sea Peoples' craft at Medinet Habu is the water bird-head devices capping the stem- and sternposts of

the invaders' ships (Fig. 8.23). Bird-head finials in a myriad of forms served as symbolic and prophylactic devices on Mediterranean ships, beginning no later than the second millennium.

In later times bird-head devices were the hallmark of Roman cargo ships. These were depicted as a long-necked bird-head stern mechanism, usually facing aft (Figs. 8.24–25: D). On occasion, however, this stern device could face forward (Fig. 8.25: G). Together with these naturalistic representations, an abstract form of a horizontal stern bird-head device facing for-

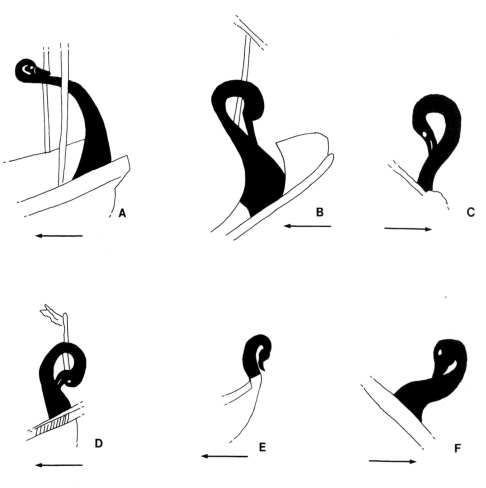

Figure 8.24. Bird-head stern ornaments on merchant craft (ca. first and second centuries A.D.) (*after Casson 1995A: figs. 139, 151, 150, 156, 181, and 146*)

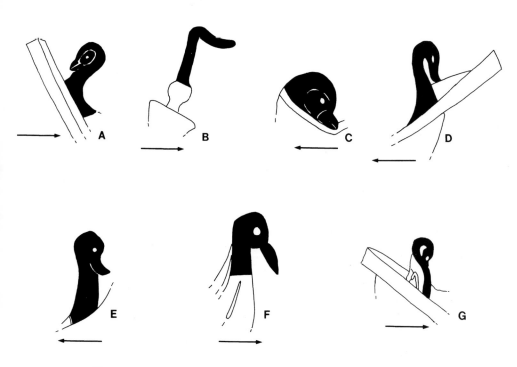

Figure 8.25. Bird-head ornaments on merchant craft (ca. third century A.D.) (after Casson 1995A: figs. 147, 179, 147, 147, 149, 148, and 191)

ward also appears (Fig. 8.25: B).[53] In the Roman Imperial period, a variety of birds make their appearance as stern ornaments on merchant ships (Fig. 8.25: A, C, E–F).

A lesser-known fact is that bird-head devices were also standard on warships of the Late Bronze Age, Iron Age, and the Classical period. Furthermore, a strong argument may be presented for identifying these bird-head ornaments as the immediate precursors of two specific devices that appear on Greek and Roman warships: the volute and the *aphlaston.*

One of the greatest enigmas concerning the Sea Peoples pertains to their origins. The bird-head symbols may be of help in this regard. A connection, though difficult to define, appears to exist between the Sea Peoples and the Urnfield cultures of central and eastern Europe. The possible Sea Peoples' ship (complete with a bird-head stem device with an upcurving beak) that is depicted on a crematory urn from Hama in Syria seems to support this connection (Fig. 8.19). The manner in which the bird-head ornaments are positioned on the Sea Peoples' ships at Medinet Habu—facing outboard at stem and stern—invites comparison with the "bird boats" (Vogelbarke) of central Europe, a connection first noted by H. Hencken.[54]

J. Bouzek dates the earliest central European bird boats to the early Bronze D period (ca. 1250–1200 B.C.).[55] These are ornaments from the Somes River at Satu Mare in northern Rumania and from Velem St. Vid in Hungary (Figs. 8.26–27). An ornament from Grave 1 at Grünwald, Bavaria, dates to the Halstatt A1 period (ca. twelfth century B.C.) (Fig. 8.28: A). The motif continues to appear on Urnfield and Villanovan art (Figs. 8.28: B–E, 29–31). Bouzek suggests that a double bird-headed decoration

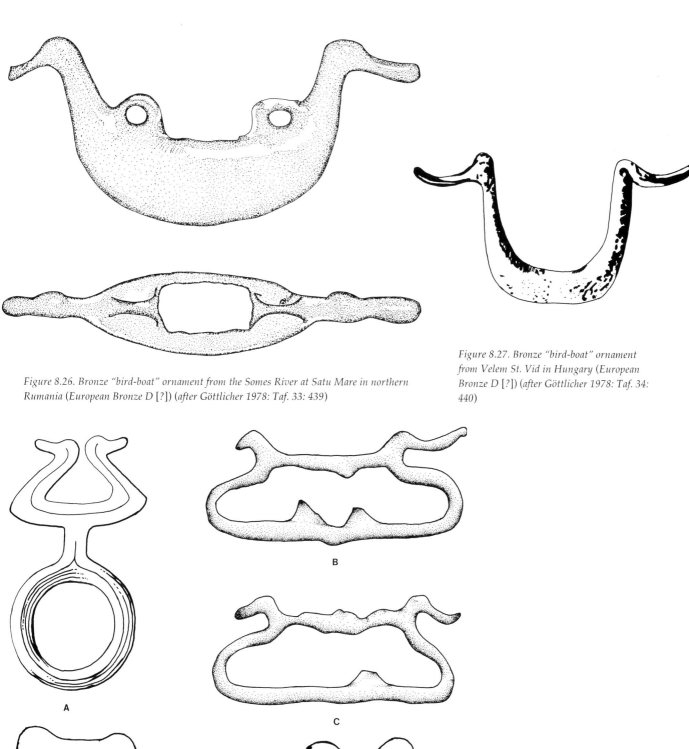

Figure 8.26. Bronze "bird-boat" ornament from the Somes River at Satu Mare in northern Rumania (European Bronze D [?]) (after Göttlicher 1978: Taf. 33: 439)

Figure 8.27. Bronze "bird-boat" ornament from Velem St. Vid in Hungary (European Bronze D [?]) (after Göttlicher 1978: Taf. 34: 440)

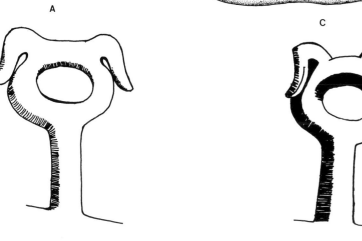

Figure 8.28. Double-headed "bird boats" in the round: (A) on an ornament from Grünwald, Bavaria (Halstatt A1); (B–C) cheekpieces from Impiccato, Grave 39 (probably Villanovan I); (D) lunate razor-blade handle from Selciatello Sopra, Grave 147 (Villanovan IC); (E) lunate razor-blade handle from Selciatello Sopra, Grave 38 (probably Villanovan II) (after Hencken 1968A: 516 fig. 478: f [after Kossack], 236 fig. 214: b, 105 fig. 92: b, 247 fig. 226 [after Pernier])

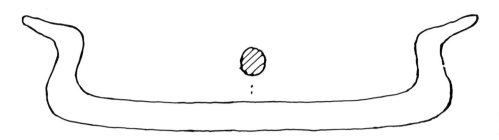

Figure 8.29. Bronze ornament from near Beograd (after Bouzek 1985: 177 fig. 88: 5)

A

B

C

D

Figure 8.30. Single and double "bird boats" represented in embossed Urnfield ornament: (A) from Lavindsgaard, Denmark (Halstatt A2); (B) from "Lucky," Slovakia (Halstatt A2); (C) from Rossin, Pomerania (Halstatt B); (D) from Este, Italy (Este II [= Villanovan II]) (after Hencken 1968A: 516 fig. 478: a, b, e, and g [after Kossack])

Figure 8.31. Terra-cotta ship models of the Villanovan culture bearing bird's-head insignia facing outward at stem and stern (A) or at stem alone (B and C) (first half of first millennium B.C.) (from Göttlicher 1978: Taf. 35: 460 [after Montelius], 461 and 469)

Figure 8.33. Duck-headed papyrus raft. Tomb of Ipy (T. 217), Ramses II (from Davies 1927: 30; ©, the Metropolitan Museum of Art, New York)

Figure 8.32. "Bird boat" painted on a krater sherd from Tiryns (Late Helladic IIIC) (after Bouzek 1985: 177 fig. 88: 6)

A

B

Figure 8.34. (A) Seal with a deity in a boat with bird-head ornaments (Irbid); (B) seal of Elishama, son of Gedalyahu, with motif similar to A (A after Culican 1970: 29 fig. 1: d; B after Tushingham 1971: 23)

Figure 8.35. Crested or horned bird-head device on the stem of the Skyros ship depiction (Late Helladic IIIC) (after Sandars 1985: 130)

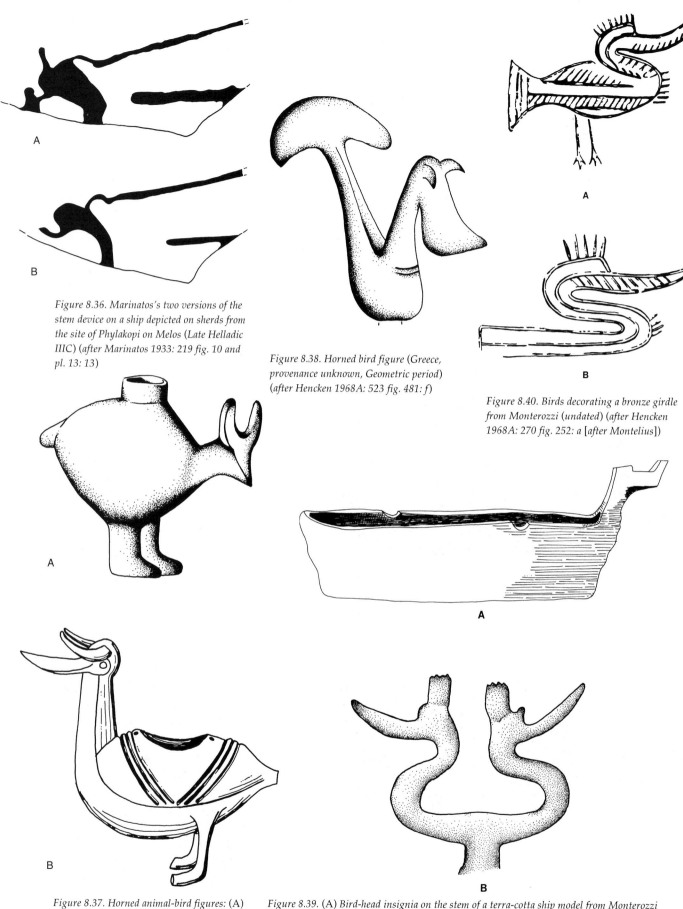

Figure 8.36. Marinatos's two versions of the stem device on a ship depicted on sherds from the site of Phylakopi on Melos (Late Helladic IIIC) (after Marinatos 1933: 219 fig. 10 and pl. 13: 13)

Figure 8.38. Horned bird figure (Greece, provenance unknown, Geometric period) (after Hencken 1968A: 523 fig. 481: f)

Figure 8.40. Birds decorating a bronze girdle from Monterozzi (undated) (after Hencken 1968A: 270 fig. 252: a [after Montelius])

Figure 8.37. Horned animal-bird figures: (A) from Vienna-Vösendorf (Halstatt A); (B) from Vrhovce, Slovakia (Halstatt B or C) (after Hencken 1968A: 521 fig. 480: c, f)

Figure 8.39. (A) Bird-head insignia on the stem of a terra-cotta ship model from Monterozzi (Villanovan I–II); (B) crested bird heads on a double-headed bird-boat ornament on a bronze vessel from Impiccato, Grave I (Villanovan IC) (A after Göttlicher 1978: Taf. 34: 447; B after Hencken 1968A: 119 fig. 108: c)

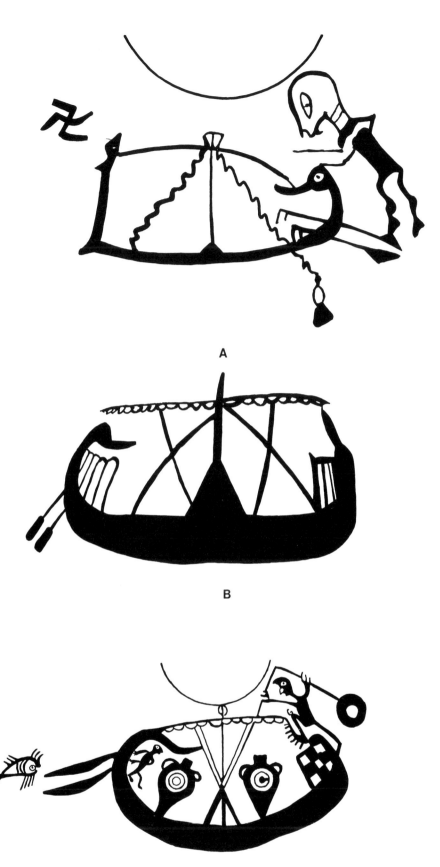

A

B

C

Figure 8.41. Ships depicted on three Cypriot jugs from the seventh century B.C. illustrate the progressive transformation of a naturalistic bird head (A) to a stylized (B) and then abstract (C) sternpost device (after Karageorghis and des Gagniers 1974: 122–23 nos. 11: 2, 3, 1)

on a Late Helladic IIIC krater fragment from Tiryns may portray a bird boat, although the painter may not have been aware of what he was depicting (Fig. 8.32).

Finally, a possible indication of the influence that the beliefs of the newly arrived Sea Peoples' mercenaries had on the Egyptians during the Ramesside period is found in the tomb of Ipy. Here he is depicted hunting birds from a papyrus raft with a bird-head stem decoration (Fig. 8.33). Craft similar to bird boats that appear on two Syro-Palestinian seals of Iron Age date portray a god in a boat (Fig. 8.34).[56]

Several Late Helladic IIIC ship depictions have another element that may be related to European cult iconography. The Skyros ship's bird-head device has a vertical projection rising from the back of its head (Fig. 8.35).[57] A similar projection exists on one of the two drawings given by S. Marinatos for a stem ornament on a ship depiction from Phylakopi, on the island of Melos (Fig. 8.36: A). In the second portrayal, the stem ends in a bird head with an extremely upturned beak identical to the beak of the Skyros ship's stem device (Fig. 8.36: B).[58] This "projection" may represent either horns or a crest on the bird's head. Horned birds and "animal-birds" are known from later European art (Figs. 8.37–38); bird heads with crests appear in Villanovan art (Figs. 8.39–40).[59]

The key to understanding the different forms—varying from naturalistic to abstract—in which bird-head devices may be depicted in the Mediterranean itself is to be found on ships portrayed on three Cypriot jugs dating to the seventh century B.C. (Fig. 8.41). On the first ship, A, a naturalistically depicted bird-head ornament, complete with eye, caps the stern and faces inboard. In ship B, the bird's eye

Figure 8.42. Ship devices in the form of birds: (A) bird-stem ornament on a ship krater from Enkomi (Late Helladic IIIB); (B) ship's bird-stem ornament on a pyxis from Tragana (Late Helladic IIIC); (C) bird ornament on the stem of a ship depicted on a Geometric Attic skyphos (ca. 735–710 B.C.); (D) bird ornament portrayed twice on the sternpost of the same ship shown on a Geometric Attic krater (ca. 735–710 B.C.) (A after Sjöqvist 1940: fig. 20: 3; B after Korrés 1989: 200; C–D after Casson 1995A: 30, 65–66)

Figure 8.43. Birds on the stem- and sternposts of an Archaic galley. Note how the shape of the stem device imitates the bird's head and neck (ca. 700–650 B.C.) (after Morrison and Williams 1968: pl. 8: d)

has disappeared, and the head has become stylized. The final, abstract phase appears on ship C, where the sternpost has become little more than a complex curve. Even if this progression is the result of nothing more than the abstraction of the bird head by the artist(s) who created these three ships, the bird-head devices on these vessels show a clear and obvious connection.

This cyclic development of the bird-head ornaments was repeated constantly on ships in antiquity, judging from the iconographic evidence. Natural depictions gave way to stylized representations. These evolved into totally abstract forms that are little more than a complex curve.[60] The forms are repeatedly followed by a "rejuvenating" trend to return to the natural rendering of an actual bird's head.

If only the final, abstract phase of this constantly evolving bird-head form is studied outside of the context of the entire cycle, the curved beak of these Mediterranean vessels may be—and has been—misinterpreted as representing an animal's horn or other symbolic figure.[61] Each phase of this cycle blends into the next, and at times we find two different stages of development on the same ship representation. These bird-head devices may point inboard, outboard, up, or down. On the same ship they can appear at both extremities, as on the Sea Peoples' ships, or at only one end. The permutations are virtually unlimited.

The evidence for bird-head devices decorating the stem- and sternposts of Mediterranean craft suggests that they originated in the Aegean. The earliest known example of a bird-head ornament is of Middle Helladic date (Fig. 5.25). Ornaments representing entire birds also appear on the stems of ships, beginning in the thirteenth century and continuing down into

Geometric times. One such device appears on the stem of a Late Helladic IIIB ship depiction from Enkomi (Fig. 7.28; 8.42: A). The discovery of additional sherds of the *pyxis* on which it is painted enables G. S. Korrés to demonstrate that the bow device on the Tragana ship—long thought to be a fish—is actually a bird with an upturned beak (Fig. 7.17; 8.42: B).[62] These birds and bird-head devices clearly represent the same type(s) of water bird commonly found on contemporaneous Mycenaean and Philistine pottery.[63]

During the Geometric period, devices in the form of a bird are occasionally affixed to the stem- and sternposts of warships (Figs. 8.42: C–D, 50: C). Slightly later, in the Archaic period, birds appear at the bow and stern of a galley (Fig. 8.43). Ornaments in the form of bona fide birds are known both from antiquity (for example, the Minoan swallow device) and from modern ethnographic parallels (Figs. 8.44–46).[64] During the Aegean Late Bronze Age the bird/bird-head device was normally stationed on the stem and faced outboard, as, for example, did the devices on the Gazi and the Late Helladic IIIB terra-cotta ship model from Tiryns (Figs. 7.19, 45).

By the twelfth century the number, the direction, and the position of the bird-head devices began to vary on ships. At Medinet Habu they appear for the first time, on a depiction of a seagoing ship, at the stern facing outboard (Figs. 8.8, 10–12, 14, 23). The earliest known bird-head device facing *inboard* appears on a Late Cypriot III *askos*/ship model (Fig. 8.47). Two additional and virtually identical *askoi* in the form of ships also originally had devices topping their stems, but these had been broken off in antiquity (Fig. 7.48). Several of the Kition graffiti have what

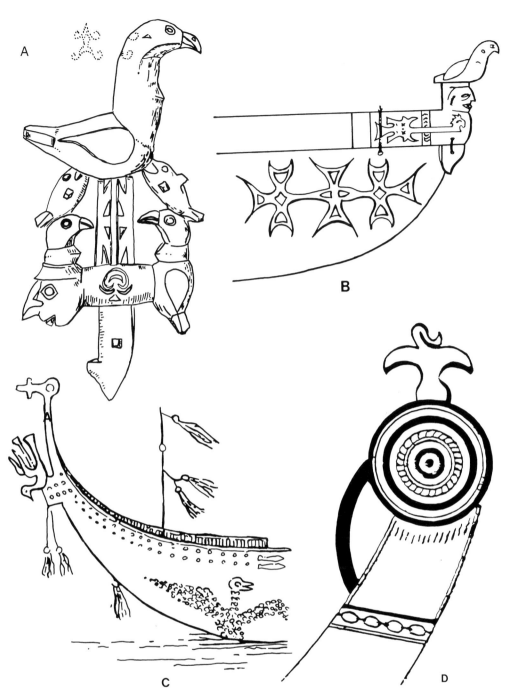

Figure 8.44. (A) *Stem decoration from Walckenaer Bay, Netherlands Papua;* (B) *side view of a small canoe with bird device from Papua;* (C) *ornaments on an Ora canoe from the Solomon Islands;* (D) *figurehead of an Arab ganja* (A–C *after Haddon 1937: 317 fig. 180: a, 316 fig. 179: c, 88 fig. 59: a;* D *after Hornell 1970: 236 fig. 46*)

appear to be abstract bird-head devices (Fig. 7.33: K, M–O, T, V).

Similar bird-head ornaments are known on other terra-cotta ship models as well. A Late Helladic IIIA2 bird-head device topping a post was found at Maroni in Cyprus; it is unclear, however, if

this faced inboard or outboard (Fig. 8.48). Another head, of Late Helladic IIIC date, was found at Kynos.[65] The latter device has eyes and vertical lines, three of which continue into hanging loops.

During the Proto-Geometric period, the bird's long, upcurving

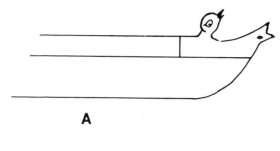

A

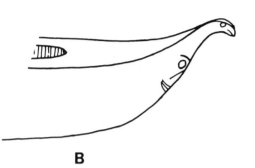

B

Figure 8.45. (A) *Bird-head decorations on a small canoe from Papua;* (B) *bow of a seagoing outrigger canoe* (nimbembew) (*southwestern Maleluka, New Hebrides*) (*after Haddon 1937: 316 fig. 179: a, 22 fig. 12*)

beak becomes the center of attention. The bird's head itself virtually disappears, as, for example, on the Fortetsa ships, as well as on a ship painted on a krater from Dirmil, Turkey (Fig. 8.49: A–B).[66] This continues a propensity to recurve the device's beak, a feature that had already become visible in the twelfth century B.C. The Fortetsa devices find their closest parallels on a ship depiction from Kynos (Fig. 7.16; 8.61: C). In Figure 8.49: A, the Kynos devices are placed on either side of the Fortetsa ship for comparison.[67]

Homer, in describing his warships, uses the adjective κορωνίς, which most probably means "having curved extremities." There is a very similar word, however, which is the name of a seabird: κορώνη. It is quite possible that this is a deliberate play on the two similar words and that κορωνίς is intended to im-

ply "having curved extremities that are bird-shaped."[68]

This term accurately describes the stylized/abstract bird-head devices, facing inboard from both the stem- and sternposts, that were popular in the Geometric period. In these ornaments, emphasis was placed on the bird's beak. The devices on the warship-shaped firedogs from Argos are indeed sufficiently naturalistic that the birds' heads and beaks may be differentiated (Fig. 8.50: A). In other Geometric ship representations, the head-beak has become one continuous curve (Fig. 8.50: B–C). Compare these to the abstract bird-head device capping the stern of the ship in Figure 8.41: C. A naturalistic, regenerating phase of a bird-head stem ornament appears on depictions of galleys dated to the last quarter of the eighth century B.C. (Fig. 8.51).

The stem device on these ships is usually portrayed horizontally and faces backward, toward the stern. A slight angle may differentiate the "head" from the beak (Fig. 8.52: D). More often, the device appears as one continuous compound curve. At times the stem ornament is shown in outline and filled with a hatched decoration (Figs. 8.50: B, 52: C).[69] Earlier, this motif appeared on a device from Kynos (Fig. 8.61: D). The stem device on one Geometric galley is interesting in that it begins in an inward-facing abstract bird head but then recurves, copying the neck and head of the long-necked bird that stands in front of it (Fig. 8.52: C). This phenomenon is repeated later on an Archaic bronze fibula (Fig. 8.43).

By the eighth century, the water bird-head device had ceased to be solely a Helladic tradition. A Phoenician warship, portrayed in a relief from Karatepe, has an inboard-facing bird head as a stern

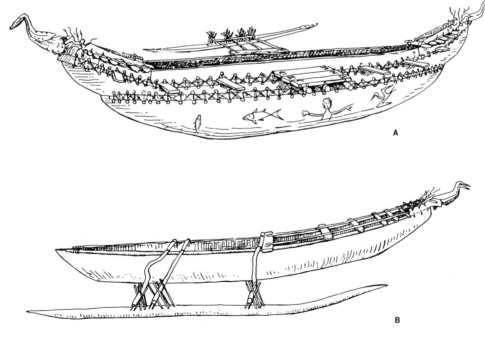

A

B

Figure 8.46. *Canoes of Atchin, New Hebrides:* (A) *large seagoing canoe with ordinary, single-beaked* solub e res *figurehead;* (B) *coastal canoe with double bird-head* solub wok wak *figurehead* (*after Haddon 1937: 27 fig. 15: b, a*)

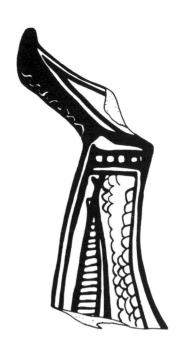

Figure 8.47. Askos in the form of a ship, from Lapithos. A bird-head ornament tops the stem and faces inward, toward the stern (Late Cypriot III) (after Göttlicher 1978: Taf. 9: 149)

Figure 8.48. Bird-head stem (?) or sternpost ornament of a ship model. From Maroni, Tomb 17, Cyprus (Late Helladic III A2) (from Johnson 1980: pl. 63: 132)

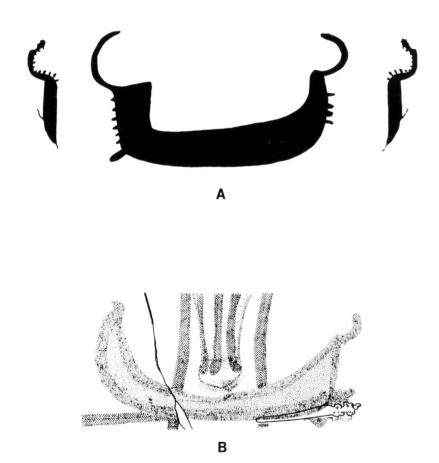

A

B

Figure 8.49. (A) One of two ships depicted on a Proto-Geometric krater from Fortetsa, Crete. The bird-head devices capping the stem- and sternpost are compared to the device on one of the Kynos ships. (B) Ship painted on a Proto-Geometric krater from Dirmil, Turkey (A from Kirk 1949: 119 fig. 6; B from van Doorninck 1982B: 279 fig. 3)

device (Fig. 8.53).[70] Here, the naturally depicted head, complete with eye, is differentiated from the beak by a vertical line. Approximately contemporaneous with this is an early seventh-century Archaic ship whose stern terminates in a naturalistic inboard-facing bird-head device (Fig. 8.54).[71] The beak is spoon-shaped, as if seen from above.

During the late sixth through fourth centuries, the bird-head stem device is less common on Greek galleys. When it does appear it faces inboard with the beak positioned vertically (Fig. 8.55: A–C). At times the beak is recurved over the bow, replicating a bird-head ornament like that on the Skyros ship placed on its back (Fig. 8.55: B). The devices vary from smooth (Fig. 8.55: A–B) to angular (Fig. 8.55: C). In the latter case, the head is differentiated from the beak. This vertical bird head is rare in later times, although its appearance on a small craft from the second century B.C. re-

Figure 8.50. Abstract bird-head ornaments in the form of a compound curve topping the stem- and sternposts of representations of Geometric warships (eighth century B.C.) (A after Göttlicher 1978: Taf. 25: 338–39; B–C after Casson 1995A: figs. 72 and 65)

veals that the form is latent but not forgotten (Fig. 8.55: D).

During the seventh through fifth centuries B.C., the stern device on Greek warships also undergoes a metamorphosis. The vertical, abstract bird head appears rarely (Fig. 8.56: B). The bird head is now more often portrayed in a naturalistic manner, the eye and beak often differentiated. The heads face inboard and downward but are shortened and recurve strongly,

forming the outline of a volute (Fig. 8.56: A, C–D). A progression of Archaic bird-head stern devices illustrates how the volute may have developed from this particular form of bird-head device (Fig. 8.57). In other ships of this time, the bird-head sternpost device adopts a more angular shape and points downwards (Fig. 8.58).

Appearing first in its developed form in the fifth century B.C., the *aphlaston* became the hallmark of

Figure 8.51. Bird-head stem ornament on a Geometric aphract galley (ca. 725–700 B.C.) (after Casson 1995A: fig. 64)

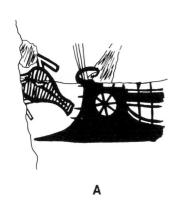

A

C

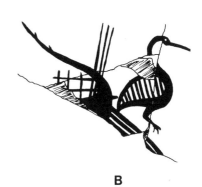

B

Figure 8.52. (A) Bird in front of Geometric galley on an Attic krater (ca. 760–735 B.C.); (B) bird behind a Geometric galley on the same krater; (C) long-necked bird before the bow of a Geometric galley. The ship's stem device copies the shape of the bird's head and neck (ca. 735–710 B.C.); (D) galley with stem and stern decorations in the shape of abstract bird's heads (ca. 760–735 B.C.) (A and B after Morrison and Williams 1968: pl. 2: c–d; C and D after Casson 1995A: 74 and 62)

D

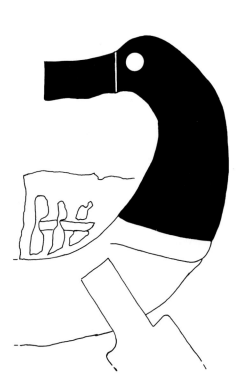

Figure 8.53. Bird-head stern device on a ship depicted on an orthostat from Karatepe, Turkey (ca. 700 B.C.) (after de Vries and Katzev 1972: 55 fig. 6)

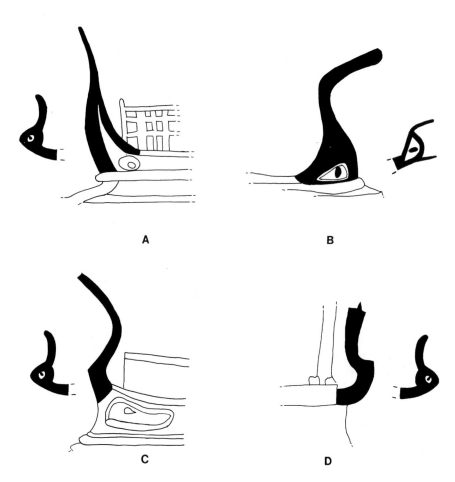

A

B

C

D

Figure 8.55. (A–C) Abstract bird-head stem decorations on Greek warships: A ca. 510 B.C.; B ca. 520–480 B.C.; C ca. 400–322 B.C. The device on ship B is compared to the bird-head device on the stem of the Skyros ship (see Figure 8.42). (D) Abstract bird-head stem decoration ca. second century B.C. (A and C after Morrison and Williams 1968: pls. 20: e, 27: a; B and D after Casson 1995A: figs. 84, 176)

Figure 8.54. Bird-head decoration on an Archaic galley (ca. 700–650 B.C.) (after Morrison and Williams 1968: pl. 8: b)

warships in the Classical, Hellenistic, and Roman periods. The *aphlaston* did not leap into existence from a void as Athena came forth from the head of Zeus, however. The *aphlaston* is best understood as *a developed form of an abstract bird head with multiple beaks facing inward from the stern.* In the *aphlaston*, the bird's eye was enlarged and became the "shield" that normally appears at the base of the *aphlaston* (Fig. 8.59: B–C). A remarkable ethnological parallel to this phenomenon is seen on a stem device in the form of an abstract frigate bird head used on the *Solima* canoes of the Solomon Islands (Fig. 8.60).

On Geometric galleys, several strake ends sometimes project from the curving stem- and stern-posts (Figs. 8.42: D, 50: B–C, 52: B).[72] Since this does not result from a technical problem, the planks were evidently left to spring free for a reason. Similarly, in the sixth century, a second, abstract bird head is sometimes shown above the naturalistically depicted one (Figs. 8.56: A, C, 57: B–C, D). Either or both of these phenomena may have led to the introduction of a multiple-beaked bird-head device.

Alternatively, the *aphlaston* may have derived from the protuberances jutting from the upper or

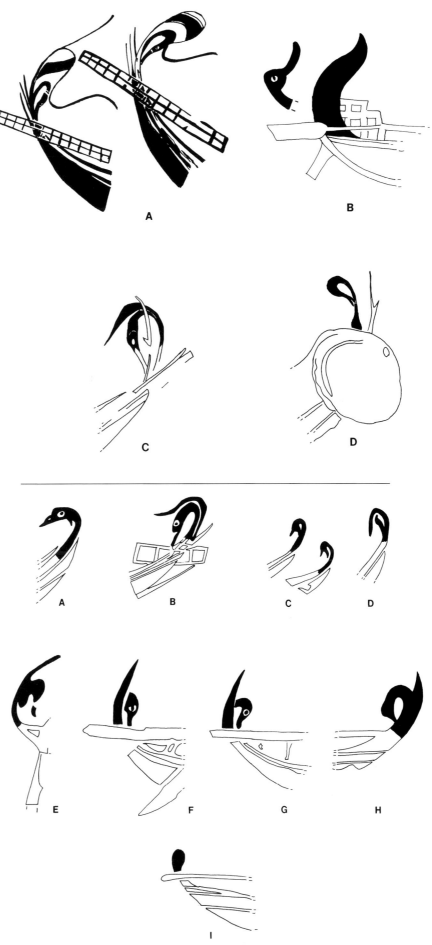

Figure 8.56. (right) (A) *Bird-head stern decorations on Greek warships (ca. 530–480 B.C.); (B) stern of an Archaic galley on an ivory plaque from the Temple of Artemis Orthia in Sparta (ca. 650–600 B.C.); (C–D) stern decoration on archaic Attic black-figure (C) volute krater and (D) hydria (ca. 600–550 B.C.) (A after Casson 1995A: fig. 90; B–D after Morrison and Williams 1968: pls. 10: d, 11: a, d)*

lower edges of the beak and head of the bird-head devices. These items appear first in the thirteenth century on the Gazi ship (Fig. 8.61: A). In the twelfth century they appear on the ship depictions from Tragana and Kynos (Fig. 8.61: B–E). Similarly, in the Enkomi ship the protuberances are found on the inner face of the stem (Fig. 8.42: A). Horizontal lines, apparently representative of the same items, are painted on the stems of terra-cotta models portraying Helladic galleys (Figs. 7.22, 45, 48). In the seventh century B.C., an identical set of protuberances appears on the lower edge of an inboard-facing bird-head device with a highly recurved, vertical beak (Figs. 8.41: C, 62).

Because of the small size of the depictions, the protuberances comprise little more than lines or dots. Thus, their identity remains uncertain. Perhaps they represent rows of tiny bird-head ornaments affixed to the decorative devices surmounting the posts similar to the one nestling in the crook of a stern ornament on a Greek fifth-century galley (Fig. 8.59: A).

Why multiply the bird's beak? This is best understood as a strengthening of the device's protective

Figure 8.57. (right) *Sixth-century B.C. stern decorations on Archaic galleys in the form of a bird's head develop into an inward-curving stern volute (A–D ca. 550–530 B.C.; E–H ca. 530–510 B.C.; I ca. 510 B.C.) (after Morrison and Williams 1968: pls. 14: g, 13, 14: b, a; 17: d, c, a, e; 18: d)*

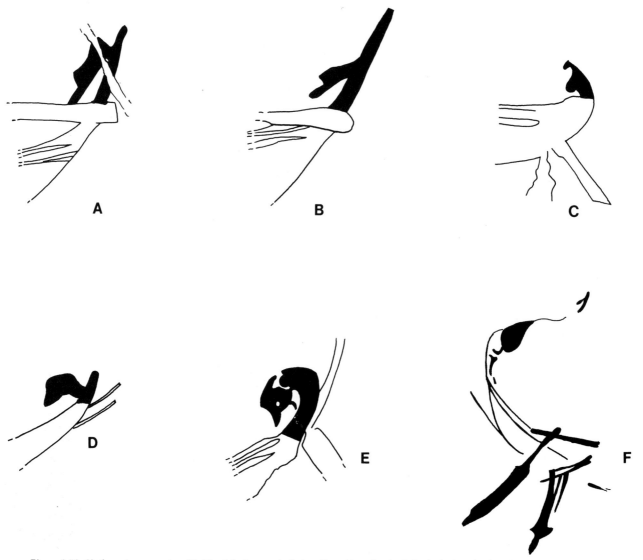

Figure 8.58. Sixth-century B.C. stern bird-head devices on Archaic galleys. Note that in C the device has developed into an inward-curving volute (A–B ca. 510 B.C.; C–D ca. 520–480 B.C.; E ca. 530–480 B.C.; F ca. 600–550 B.C.) (A to E after Morrison and Williams 1968: pls. 18: a, b; 21: b, d; 16: c; F after Casson 1995A: fig. 83)

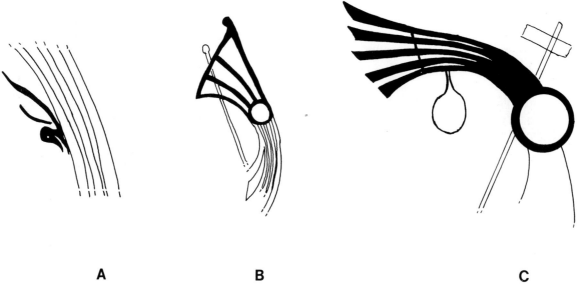

A

B

C

Figure 8.59. Aphlasta on Greek and Roman warships: A ca. 480–400 B.C.; B ca. 200 B.C.; C ca. second century A.D. (A after Morrison and Williams 1968: pl. 26: a; B–C after Casson 1995A: figs. 108, 114)

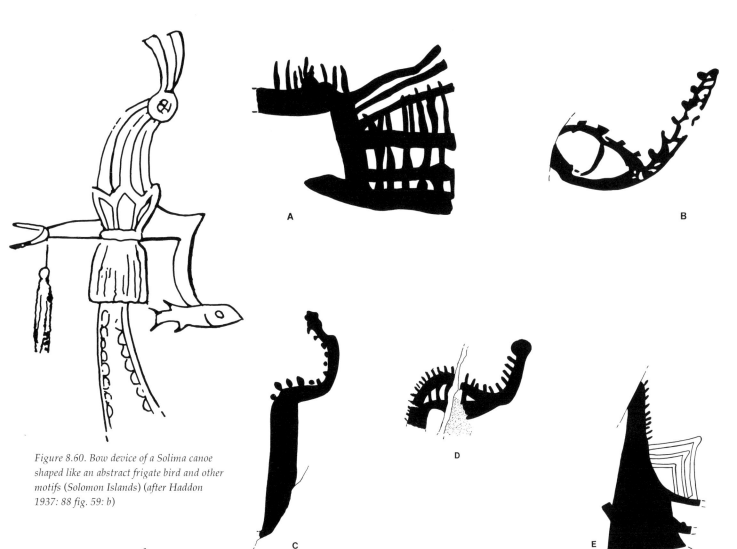

Figure 8.61. Bird, or bird-head, devices with many projections, lacking any structural purpose, extending out from the upper or lower surface of the beak. (A) Bird-head on ship painted on the Gazi larnax (Late Minoan IIIB); (B) head of bird device on the bow of a warship depicted on a pyxis from Tragana (Late Helladic IIIC); (C–D) bird-head stem devices on ship depictions from Kynos (Late Helladic IIIC); (E) stem of ship from Kynos. The stem's upper part has been broken off, but the beginning of a curve and the protuberances on the stem's inboard side reveal that it was originally capped by a bird head (Late Helladic IIIC) (A after photo by the author; B after Korrés 1989: 200; C–E after photos courtesy F. Dakoronia)

Figure 8.60. Bow device of a Solima canoe shaped like an abstract frigate bird and other motifs (Solomon Islands) (after Haddon 1937: 88 fig. 59: b)

Figure 8.62. A row of protuberances appear on the lower (inboard) part of the beak of a bird-head stem ornament of a seventh-century B.C. ship depiction on a jug from Cyprus (after Frost 1963: monochrome pl. 7 (opp. p. 54)

power. C. Broodbank, in his study of ships on Cycladic "frying pans," notes that in primitive societies, the doubling of motifs must be read not as a numerical duplication but as a doubling of the power and attribute of the image.[73]

Ethnological parallels from the recent past are useful when trying to understand this phenomenon. Bird-head ornaments were used on the New Hebrides island of

Atchin. The large seagoing canoes have devices at both stem and stern (Fig. 8.46: A); the smaller coastal canoes carry the device at the stem only (Fig. 8.46: B). These devices appear in two forms: with a single head or with a double head. A. C. Haddon notes:[74]

The figurehead (*solub*) is lashed on the fore end of the hull of the smaller canoes. In the ordinary

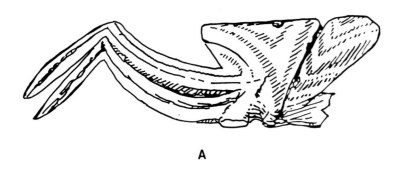

A

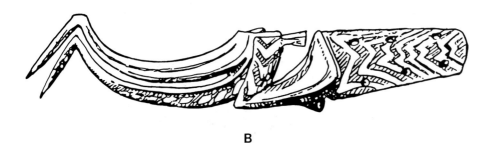

B

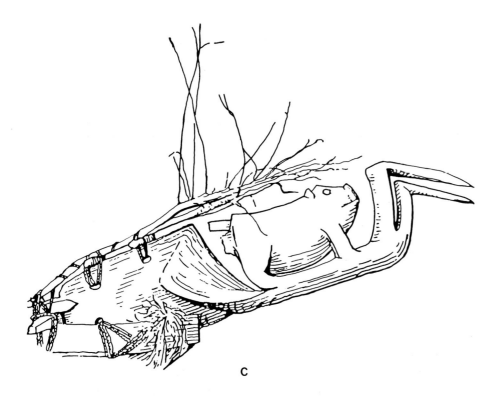

C

Figure 8.63. (A) Single-beaked solub e res *figurehead; (B) double bird-head* solub wok-wak *figurehead; (C)* Solub wok-wak *figurehead with a pig (after Haddon 1937: 28 fig. 16: a–c)*

bird figurehead (*solub e res*), to which anyone has the right without payment, the slit, representing the mouth of the beak, ends at the first bend [Fig. 8.63: A]. A figurehead in which the slit is continued down the neck is called *solub wok-wak* [Fig. 8.63: B–C] and the right to this has to be bought from someone already possessing one. When a man gets on in years he feels the need of something superior to a plain *solub wok-wak* on his everyday canoe. He then goes to one whose figurehead is decorated with a pig or other figure and after having arranged a price one of the parties to the negotiation will make a copy of it. There is a third type (*solub war*) which resembles the *solub wok-wak* except that the tip of the under beak is reflected over the upper beak, doubtless to represent a deformed boar's tusk, hence its name.

In the *solub wok-wak* the single bird head of the *solub e res* has evolved into two separate bird heads. The multiplication of the beak enhances the value of the *solub wok-wak.* A similar phenomenon may have taken place in the ancient Mediterranean.

Clearly, these bird-head images were not attached to ships because they were considered aesthetically beautiful but instead for the magical properties with which they were thought to invest the craft.[75] The multiplication of the bird's beak may have been perceived as strengthening the protective magic of the device's deity.

What significance did the ubiquitous bird-head device, in its many forms, have for the ancient mariner? J. Hornell, in discussing the tutelary deity of Indian ships, describes most clearly the basic need that primitive man felt for a protective presence to guard his craft:

Among Hindu fishermen and seafaring folk in India and the north of Ceylon numerous instances occur indicative of a belief in the expediency of creating an intimate association between a protective deity and the craft which they use, be it catamaran, canoe or sailing coaster. The strength of this belief varies within wide limits; occasionally it is articulate and definite; more often it is vague and ill-defined, often degenerating to a level where the implications of the old ceremonies are largely or even entirely forgotten. In the last category the boat folk continue to practice some fragmentary feature of the old ritual for no better reason than the belief that by so doing they will ensure good luck for their ventures and voyages, a belief usually linked with a dread of being overlooked by the "evil eye."

Outside of India similar beliefs were probably widespread in ancient times; today shadowy vestiges remain here and there, their survival due mainly to a traditional belief, sometimes strong, sometimes weak, in their efficacy to ensure good fortune or to counteract the baleful glance of the mischief minded.[76]

Ethnological parallels suggest that devices mounted at the stem and stern were intended to endow the ship with a life of its own. C. W. Bishop, in describing the dragon boats of southeastern Asia, notes that the practice of attaching the carved head (and sometimes the tail) of a dragon to these craft before ceremonial races originates in the belief that the devices magically transformed the boats into the creatures they represent.[77]

This concept of the ship having a life of its own is illustrated by a ceremony reported by Hornell.[78]

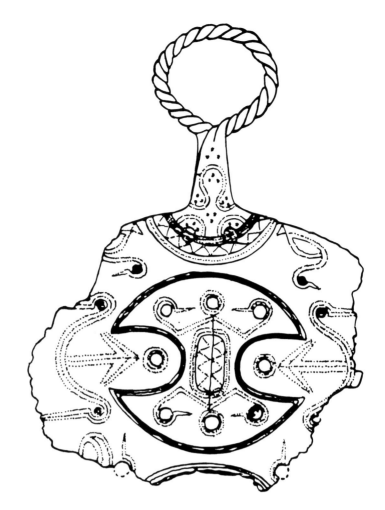

Figure 8.64. Bronze razor in the abstract form of a female idol. The head is formed by the razor's handle; the neck is decorated. Embellishments include a double-ax decoration, water birds, and anthropomorphic figures with arms and legs formed from "bird boats" (from Italy, provenance unknown) (after Bouzek 1985: 216 fig. 103: 11)

The Hindu ships that traded between the Coromandel Coast and the north of Sri Lanka had *oculi* carved on either side of the prow. The final rite before launching a new ship was termed "the opening of the eye." This was meant to endow the boat with sentient life and constituted it the vehicle of the protective goddess. The goddess would then live in and protect the ship during sea voyages. The protective entity was thus installed in the craft, her individuality being merged with it. In India the shielding deity is nearly always feminine. Hornell writes, "By this association of the boat with a female deity, the identity and sex of the protectress are merged with those

of the boat itself; as we may infer that many other peoples have reasoned and acted similarly, this may explain the fact that ships are generally considered as feminine."[79]

Of particular interest in this regard is a Proto-Villanovan Type O European bronze razor from Italy, dated to about the ninth century B.C. (Fig. 8.64). The razor, of unknown provenance, is in the abstract form of a female idol. Its head is formed by the handle of the razor; the neck is decorated. A double ax (?), serving as a central motif, is decorated by a mirror-image figure with arms formed of bird boats with inward-facing bird heads.[80] Additional figures are positioned within the two cavities of the double ax. These have legs made of bird boats with outboard and downward-facing bird heads. Four additional water birds nestle at the corners of the figure.[81] In this case the symbolism strongly suggests that the bird boat is symbolic of a goddess.

It seems likely, therefore, that the duck represents a female deity.[82] It may be argued, however, that this motif embodies an even greater symbolic realm. M. Yon notes:

The duck (this is of course the wild duck, not the farmyard animal) contains in itself a multiplicity of symbols: it is at the same times terrestrial, aerial, aquatic, as it walks, flies and swims. . . .

F. Poplin has shown the tight relationship in our imagination of ‹‹the horse, the duck, and the ship››, as more or less conscious variations of means of transport; equines, palmipeds and boats come together and replace each

other in languages (Homeric expressions or modern slang) as well as fantastic narrative (the swan of Lohengrin, or the geese of Nils Holgersson) and in plastic representations (fountain of Bartholdi at Lyon, or arm-rests on Hellenistic and Roman beds). The symbolic equivalence thus appears ancient; that which interests us here is its presence in the European world at the end of the Bronze Age, when it passed to the eastern Mediterranean with the population movements which marked the end of the second millennium.

Moreover, the duck is a migratory bird, appearing and disappearing each year. As such it is a symbol of renaissance and fertility, reinforced by the connection with water, from which life comes forth. . . .

It becomes part of an ensemble of beliefs and of a symbolism which links cultural groups apparently as diverse as the peoples of central Europe where palmi-

peds live in misty marshes, the ‹‹Sea Peoples›› who came from the north as do the wild ducks, and the islands of the eastern Mediterranean such as Cyprus or Crete where the new population of this period placed in their tombs representations of the animal which symbolized their voyage and their vital force.[83]

Bird-head devices continued in use into the latter part of the sixth century A.D., when a Nile vessel is described as "wild-goose-sterned."[84] Presumably they did not cease at that time, however. Indeed, decorative devices reminiscent of bird heads and bird boats are still found on present-day craft.

In Greece, devices capping the sternposts of some fishing boats are sometimes shaped like a bird head (Fig. 8.65: A). On occasion, the "beaks" of these ornaments are multiplied in a manner reminiscent of the *aphlaston* (Fig. 8.65: B). Similarly, "bird boat"–like ornaments have been recorded in this

A

B

Figure 8.65. Stern devices on modern Greek boats at Ayia Galini, Crete (photos taken in 1980 by the author)

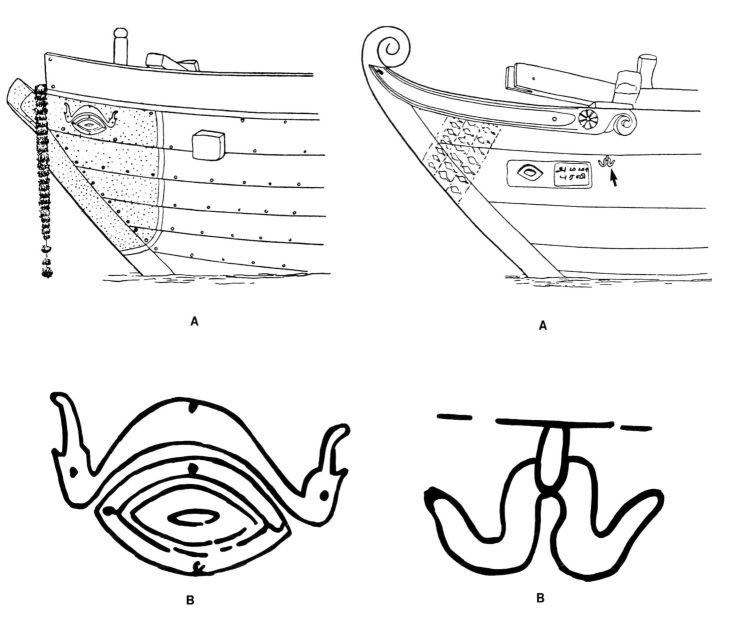

Figure 8.66. (A) Decorated bow of Ganges River cargo boats, Benares; (B) detail of inverted bird boat-like ornament (from Hornell 1970: 279 fig. 68 [J. Hornell, Water Transport, Cambridge University Press, 1946])

Figure 8.67. (A) Bow of a kalla dhoni with an abstract bird boat-like ornament (Point Calimere, South India); (B) detail of the ornament (from Hornell 1970: 272 fig. 67 [J. Hornell, Water Transport, Cambridge University Press, 1946])

century on Indian craft, as witnessed by Hornell's drawing of the decorated bow of a Ganges River cargo boat at Benares (Fig. 8.66). The same design in a degenerated form is found on the bow of a *kalla dhoni* recorded at Point Calimere, South India (Fig. 8.67). The relationship, if any, of these modern decorative motifs to the bird-head devices of antiquity remains to be determined.

Finally, what are we to make of this curious ship, sighted and described by W. J. Childes in this century?

A sight of this kind I watched one summer evening on the coast of the Black Sea, when a long boat, whose bow was shaped like a swan's breast, put off from the shore. Her stern projected above the hull and was curved into a

form resembling roughly the head and neck of a bird preparing to strike. Upon the mast, hanging from a horizontal yard, was set a single broad square-sail, and under the arching foot could be seen the black heads of rowers, five or six men on either side, and a bare-legged steersman placed high above them in the stern.[85]

APPENDIX:
Homer's νηυσὶ κορωνίσιν

BY JOHN R. LENZ

Shelley Wachsmann makes the interesting suggestion that Homer's phrase "beaked (?)" ships describes the abstract bird-head devices he himself has detected at the stems and sterns of ships of the Bronze Age, the Geometric, and other periods. This depends on the meaning of the adjective κορωνίς used of ships in formulae such as παρα νηυσὶ κορωνίσι(ν). A standard etymology derives this adjective from the noun κορώνη, a seabird, perhaps a shearwater, with reference to its curved beak.[1]

Homer applies the adjective κορωνίς only to ships.[2] The noun κορώνη, from which it probably derives, has two distinct meanings: either (A) a seabird or a crow,[3] or (B) a curved extremity of various types. Both senses occur in Homer. Of type B, Homer has a door handle and the golden tip of a bow.[4] Other, later usages of this type include the tip of a plow-pole, any tip, a crown, or a culmination of a festival.[5] Aratus once uses κορώνη to describe a ship's stern.[6]

The Greek lexicon considers the latter-named (type B) uses of κορώνη as secondary, derived from the similarity of each of these objects to a bird's curved beak.[7] If Homer's κορωνίς likewise derives independently from κορώνη (A), this would support Wachsmann's idea that the ships' curved devices themselves originated as birds' beaks.

However, κορώνη (A) and (B) must be dissociated etymologically. Both Latin and Greek show two distinct roots, kor/cor, one (A) meaning "crow" and another (B) "curved." Words for "horn" often exhibit a root kor/cor, as well.[8] I classify related Greek and Latin words as in Table 1.

Since a crow's beak is not markedly curved, Indo-European words for "crow" probably reflect the onomatopoeic root kor. The English "crowbar" preserves the sense of "bent" and has no connection with the bird.

Where does Homer's adjective κορωνίς, used of ships, fit in? If derived from the noun κορώνη (B), it should mean curved—but how? The objects called κορώνη (B) always represent curved extremities, added onto something that

TABLE 1

A	B	C
"crow"	"curved"	"horn"
κόραξ	κυρτός ("convex")	κέρας, κεραΐς
κορώνη (A)	κορώνη (B)	κορωνίς [9]
corvus	κορωνίς	κορωνός [10]
cornix	curvus	κόρυμβα(?) [11]
	corona	κορώνιος [12]
		cornu
		cervus.

they cap or "crown."[13] Thus, the adjective κορωνίς implies something more than the natural prolongation of a ship's stem- and sternposts. The epithet probably refers to curved elements crowning the ships' stems and sterns. That is, besides meaning "curved," it seems to embody a sense of a crowning element such as a head or horn, which have virtually homonymous Indo-European roots.[14]

Homer also calls ships "straight-horned"[15] and uses κόρυμβα, a word derived from "horn," for the "projecting terminal elements at the stem and/or stern of a ship."[16] As noted, Theocritus uses κορωνίς for (probably) "horned."[17] Homer's word, too, might imply "horned."

The lexicographer Hesychius once equates κεραΐς (apparently a "horned" bird) with κορώνη ("crow").[18] If there is no strict etymological connection between "horn" and "crow" (columns C and A of Table 1), the semantic connection he draws shows that the two may be conflated, or confused, in ordinary usage. Similarly, our example of κορωνίς may exhibit some overlapping between types A and B ("crow" and "curved") in the above table, besides (as already discussed) B and C ("curved" and "horn").

Thus, there is some room for ambiguity. Homer loved word-play, and poetically κορωνίς may still evoke κορώνη (A), a "seabird."[19] But etymologically, its closest connection is with κορώνη (B), which we must consider further. After Homer, we find κορωνίς used as a noun to indicate various curved extremities.[20]

The Greek and Latin words listed above under "curved" have sometimes been taken to mean "bent" but must originally have meant "circular." It is easier to derive a sense of "curved" or "bent" from "rounded" or "circular" than vice versa.[21] The meaning "bent" has resulted from an improper derivation of κορώνη (B) from a supposedly curved beak implied in κορώνη (A). Its Latin cognate, corona, or "crown," always designates a circular crowning ornament,[22] and the Greek noun κορωνίς, when first attested, means "garland" or "wreath."[23] Later Greek uses, as noted above, maintain the sense of "crowning" but without requiring a circle.

Homer's uses of κορώνη (B), a bow-tip and a door handle, are best seen as secondary usages from an original meaning of "a round crowning element," instead of from κορώνη (A), "crow." The κορώνη by which (in Homer) a door is pulled closed,[24] which has been imperfectly understood, may indeed be a circular ring. But equally, it may already reflect the sense of "bent." In both Greek and Latin, other words for door handles, κόραξ and cornix, are the same as those for "raven."[25] This shows some semantic overlapping between the two roots I have differentiated as (A) "crow" and (B) "curved," as in the English "crow-bar." This would provide indirect support for Wachsmann's connection of Homer's κορωνίς with—as commonly assumed—κορώνη (A), or "seabird," "crow."

The basic meaning of κορωνίς may be "with curved or rounded extremities," so it probably refers to curved ornamental devices such as those Wachsmann has identified.[26] The exact derivation of the word itself from κορώνη (a bird) is, as indicated, difficult or ambiguous with respect to Indo-European etymology. The word κορώνη (A), "shearwater" or "crow," is homonymous with κορώνη (B), "a rounded or curved projecting element." The Greeks, like modern readers, sometimes conflated words with similar roots, either by imagining a common etymology or by semantically assimilating words of similar roots. Even when we distinguish the etymologies (as above) they sometimes blur, and we cannot always tell what resonances a word held for Greek ears or for a great poet such as Homer.[27]

APPENDIX:
Additional Evidence

In recent years, additional depictions of ships of Aegean Bronze Age tradition have come to the attention of scholars. These are valuable contributions to our corpus of ship representations.

Ashkelon, Israel

A sherd uncovered at Ashkelon bears a ship's post ending in a bird-head device (Fig. 8A.1).[1] Although found in a fill, the sherd's fabric is typical of Late Helladic IIIC 1b ware found at Ashkelon and is believed to have been made at the site. The painting on the sherd is a fragment of a larger scene that originally must have contained at least one ship.

The post—it is not possible to determine whether this is a stem or sternpost, or whether it faces inboard or outboard—essentially is horizontal at its extremity. The bird-head device capping the sternpost is formed by a simple circle, with the eye represented by a central dot. The beak continues the curving lower line of the post. Theoretically at least, this could also represent the head and neck of a device in the shape of a bird, as on the ship depictions from Tragana and Enkomi as well as on

Geometric period ships (Figs. 7.17, 28: A; 8.42–43). The latter possibility seems unlikely, however, judging from its size relative to the preserved legs of a man standing upon it.

The post is decorated with single zigzag lines along its upper and lower edges. Similar ornamentation appears on the vertical bow of the Tragana ship (wavy and zigzag lines are also shown rising skyward from this ship's steering oar), on a terra-cotta ship model from Tiryns, on three Cypriot ship *askoi*, as well as on a fourth *askos* from the Athenian Acropolis, and on the bird-head device from Maroni (Figs. 7.17, 45, 48: A–B, 49; 8.48).

The muscular legs of a man standing on the post have been preserved up to thigh level. The figure's legs are slightly bent at the knees and, assuming a frontal view, the heel of his left foot is planted forward, on top of the bird-head device, while his right foot is placed behind it, on the post. The left foot has a line rising vertically from it near the toe. If the artist's intention was to depict footwear curving at the toe— known from the Aegean as well as Asia Minor—that attempt was unsuccessful.[2] Behind the figure's

legs is another curving line, which may perhaps represent either the curving profile of a shield (compare Figs. 7.8: A, 15) or the arm of a bow (compare Fig. 7.16).[3]

Warriors are often depicted on Aegean ships standing in the fore and sterncastles adjacent to the posts. Such is the case at Medinet Habu on ships N.1–2, 4 and 5 (Figs.

Figure 8A.1. Late Helladic IIIC 1b sherd from Ashkelon depicting a bird-head post ornament with the lower portions of the legs of a man who is standing on it (drawing by P. Sibella. Courtesy of L. E. Stager and the Leon Levy Expedition to Ashkelon)

8.3–4, 6–8, 10–12). Warriors are situated at the bow on all three of the ships from Kynos described above (Figs. 7.8: A, 15–16). Additionally, men facing outboard at the bow and the stern appear on a ship from Phaistos (Fig. 7.27). The closest parallels for figures actually standing *on* post ornaments come from a depiction of an Attic Geometric galley dating to the middle eighth century B.C. and a seventh-century B.C. Beotian bronze fibula found in Crete.[4]

The appearance of a ship with a bird-head device on a Late Helladic IIIC 1b sherd from Ashkelon is dramatic evidence that the ships used in the waterborne invasion of Egypt continued to be used by the Sea Peoples/Philistines after their settlement along the Canaanite coast.[5]

Nahal ha-Me'arot, Carmel Coast, Israel

In 1967 E. Wreschner and M. W. Prausnitz discovered a number of rock graffiti at Nahal ha-Me'arot, next to the Carmel Caves.[6] Among these, they noted a graffito of a ship near the top of the valley's northern bluff.[7] More recently, during a regional survey carried out to complement her excavations at Tel Nami, M. Artzy and her team located numerous other boat representations there, and another near the entrance to Nahal Oren, a large valley situated five kilometers north of Nahal ha-Me'arot.[8]

Preservation varies among the graffiti. Some are badly eroded, while others are clearly visible. Artzy defines three types of vessels. Based on what appear to be bird-head devices on their stems (?), Artzy compares one group of these ship graffiti to the Sea Peoples' ships portrayed at Medinet Habu (Fig. 8A.2: A; compare also Fig.

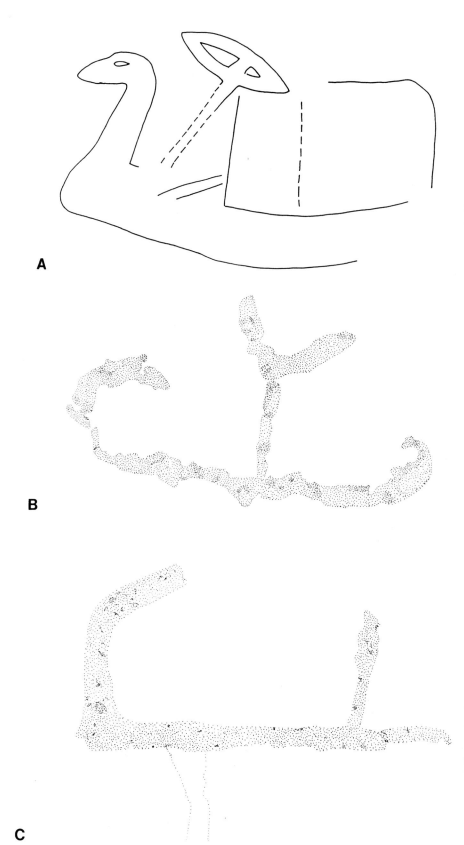

A

B

C

Figure 8A.2. Ship graffiti from Nahal ha-Me'arot (NTS) (after Artzy 1994: 2–3)

Figure 8A.3. Grafitto of an Aegean-style (Mycenaean/Sea Peoples?) ship carved on a rock at Teneida, in the Oasis of Dakhla, Egypt (after Basch 1994A: 24 fig. 14)

7.41). She notes that all the known ship graffiti of this type have a bird head at only one extremity, and that in all cases the bird-head faces the Mediterranean in the west.

A second group she parallels to the Aegean ship representations on the altar from Acco, as well as at Kition (Fig. 8A.2: B; compare Figs. 7.33–35, 8.20). A third group bears more than a passing resemblance to an Aegean ship type with a straight hull, stem projection, vertical stem post and recurving stern (Fig. 8A.2: C). Compare these elements to similar ones on the ship representations appearing, for example, in Figs. 7.7: B, 17, 19, 21, 27, 29, 30: A, 36: A.

The documentation and future thorough publication of the Nahal ha-Me'arot ship graffiti will be a valuable contribution to our growing corpus of Aegean ship representations.

Egypt

During his survey of rock graffiti undertaken in 1937–38, H. A. Winkler photographed a ship graffito carved on a rock at Teneida, on the eastern border of the Oasis of Dakhla.[9] Winkler's photograph

of this ship remained unpublished until recently, when L. Basch, in a penetrating study, pointed out the distinct similarities this vessel has with the Aegean ship tradition (Fig. 8A.3).[10]

The ship faces right and is portrayed with a straight keel/keel plank, a vertical stem and a diagonal sternpost. The line of the keel/hull continues past the stem as a ram-like cutwater. It has a mast in the center of the hull. A two-level forecastle is nestled behind the stem (compare Fig. 7.28: A). A diagonal line from the sternpost to the mast top may represent a halyard. Unfortunately, the top of the

stem, where we might expect to find a bird-head device, is broken. At left, a large quarter-rudder descends from the sternpost in a manner reminiscent of that found in a ship depiction from Phaistos (Fig. 7.27).

On and around the ship, however, are at least nine figures. Next to four of these are what Basch has reasonably identified as model boats (Fig. 8A.4). The models have a straight hull, with vertical stem and sternposts. A single vertical line rising from each of the hulls presumably represents the model ships' masts. Each of the models' stems is crossed by a single hori-

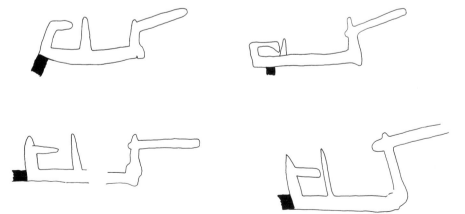

Figure 8A.4. Ship models(?) held by four of the figures in the Teneida ship graffito (after Basch 1994A: 25 fig. 15)

zontal or slightly rising line, which Basch interprets as representing a bird head with an exaggerated, long beak. Similar but smaller decorations face inward from the sternposts.

The figures are decidedly un-Aegean, with long appendages (hats or masks?) on their heads and exaggerated genitals. Basch connects the appearance of an Aegean ship in the oasis with the bands of Libyans, including the Meshwesh, that participated in the Sea Peoples' alliance in their battles against Ramses III.

There is evidence for contact between the Oasis of Dakhla and the Nile Valley during the New Kingdom.[11] The earliest historical reference to the oasis dates to the ascension of Amenhotep II.[12]

CHAPTER 9

Shipwrecks

The development of SCUBA following World War II introduced a new dimension into the study of ancient seafaring. For the first time, archaeologists were able to go underwater and study the remains of ancient shipwrecks, their cargoes, and their accoutrements on the seabed. Even though Bronze Age shipwrecks remain rare, nautical archaeology has revealed and clarified aspects of ancient ships and their purposes to an astounding degree. Two articulated shipwrecks in particular, found off the southern coast of Turkey at Cape Gelidonya and Uluburun, have contributed immensely to our understanding. At the same time, they have raised many new questions. The known Bronze Age Mediterranean sites are summarized below by country and in chronological order.[1]

Shipwreck Sites

Greece

DOKOS. In 1975 P. Throckmorton discovered quantities of Early Helladic pottery adjacent to the southern side of Cape Myti Komeni at the northeast corner of the Bay of Skindos on the island of Dokos.[2] During a 1977 survey, three distinct concentrations of pottery dating to a late phase of the Early Helladic II period were found at depths ranging from eight to twenty-six meters.

Vessel shapes found at Dokos include jugs, bowls, amphoras, cups, jars, *askoi,* and *pithoi,* along with supports for household clay spits, braziers, and clay hearths. Cycladic elements have been noted in the pottery. The site also contained grinding stones and fragments of a lead bar (ingot?) that may also be related to this complex. Bowls, amphoras, and spouted sauceboats in a variety of shapes and sizes predominate at the site. Apparently cultic in nature, these terra-cotta vessels are believed to have originated in Attica. Interestingly, Dokos is located on the presumed sea route between south Euboea and the Saronic and Argolid gulfs, one end of which is at Lerna.

To date, no timber has been reported from this site, raising the question of whether this is indeed a shipwreck. Furthermore, additional Early Helladic pottery was recovered from offshore on the *northern* side of Cape Myti Komeni. It is difficult to interpret the concentrations of pottery on both sides of the cape as resulting from a single shipwreck. Complete excavation and publication of the Dokos site will hopefully supply answers to this and other questions.

CAPE IRIA. A collection of pottery, primarily of Cypriot origin and dating to the end of the thirteenth century B.C., was located at Cape Iria, south of Asine, in the Argolid Gulf.[3] First surveyed in 1974 by Throckmorton and a team of Greek divers, the site, which is located at a depth of seventeen to twenty-five meters and over a length of thirty meters, contained three *pithoi* and many pottery sherds. Most of the sherds belong to coarse-ware domestic types: *pithoi,* amphoras, deep basins, a pitcher, and a Mycenaean stirrup jar. The Cypriot ceramics raised from the Cape Iria site may constitute one of the largest assemblages of Late Cypriot transport containers found to date in the Aegean region. A stone anchor was discovered near the site at a depth of six meters.[4]

Turkey

SHEYTAN DERESI. In 1973 a Bronze Age wreck site was found at a depth of thirty-three meters off

Sheytan Deresi on the southwestern coast of Turkey.[5] The site was excavated in its entirety, but no remains of a ships timbers were found, although the sand was sufficiently deep to preserve hull fragments had the cargo covered it. This led G. F. Bass to conclude that the craft may have capsized or perhaps that it was made of skins. The close proximity of the jars and the presence of stones that could have been ballast may indicate that the cargo was not jettisoned. A study of pottery distribution suggests that a number of artifacts had drifted away from the surface intact, perhaps meaning that they had been empty when the ship sank.

The Sheytan Deresi pottery, which has been dated to ca. 1600 B.C., has a mixture of Aegean and Anatolian characteristics. The modest amount of cargo and the total lack of personal items suggest that the craft may have been a small vessel that transported pottery between neighboring villages. There are no known contemporary habitation sites in the cargo's vicinity.

ULUBURUN. Uluburun is a cape several kilometers east of the Turkish town of Kaş.[6] A wreck was first sighted there by Turkish sponge diver Mehmet Çakir, who described the piles of copper "oxhide" ingots on the seabed to the authorities as "metal biscuits with ears."[7]

In 1983 C. M. Pulak surveyed the site, which begins at a depth of forty-three meters. Excavation began the next year. The site originally was thought to end at fifty-one meters, but it soon became apparent that spillage from the shipwreck continues farther down-slope.[8] The lower end of the shipwreck is the bow, the higher end is the stern.[9] The deepest part of the wreck excavated is located between fifty-three and sixty

meters, a depth far beyond that of normal sport diving. This factor made the excavation a protracted and potentially dangerous project. The eleventh and final season of excavation took place during the summer of 1994 (Fig. 9.1).[10]

The Uluburun ship was a merchantman with a valuable cargo. Detailed site plans help to reconstruct the manner in which the cargo and other items were stored in the hull (Fig. 14.1). The hull is of pegged mortise-and-tenon joinery, pushing back by a millennium our knowledge of the use of this ship construction technique on seagoing Mediterranean ships.[11]

Concerning the date of the ship's demise, Bass and Pulak note a Late Helladic IIIA: 2e *kylix* found on the wreck. They emphasize, however, that it may have been in use for some time before the ship sank. The Mycenaean pottery found on the wreck dates to the Late Helladic IIIA2 period, about the time of Akhenaton's reign—but no later than that of Tutankhamen.[12] The excavators originally suggested a date around the end of (or just after) the Amarna period. On the basis of a gold scarab of Nefertiti and a cut gold ring found on the wreck, J. Weinstein argues that the ship sank *after* the Amarna era.[13] He prefers a date in the last quarter of the fourteenth century or the opening years of the thirteenth century.[14] Most recently, a date of 1315 B.C. has been assigned to the shipwreck on the basis of dendrochronological analyses of a branch carried on board, perhaps intended as firewood.[15]

Concerning the origins of the vessel, Pulak notes that a Near Eastern origin for the ship is quite likely.[16]

Of particular interest in regard to the identity of the Uluburun shipwreck is the cast-bronze fe-

male figurine found during the 1992 expedition.[17] Her extremities are covered with gold foil. She wears a fillet in her hair, and a multistranded necklace adorns her neck. Although no exact parallels to this figurine are known, Pulak notes the similarities that it shares with other bronze artifacts from the Syro-Canaanite littoral, as well as to a unique gold plaque from Lachish.[18] He tentatively concludes that the Uluburun figurine originated from that region and that she may be one of a pair of a divine couple. Alternately, she may have been a "traveling god," similar to the "Amun-of-the-Road" that accompanied Wenamun on his journey.[19] In this case, the figurine may have belonged to a passenger.

A third possibility is that the statuette may have been the ship's tutelary goddess. In pre-Classical times, the protective deities of ships appear to have been primarily (if not exclusively) feminine.[20] The figurine was found in Square G24, near a stone ceremonial ax head that had originated in the Black Sea region (Fig. 14.1).

Among many cultures throughout history the bow was the abode of the guardian goddess, protectress of the ship.[21] J. Hornell notes that in Gerzean ships, the bow was the location of the deity.[22] Later Egyptian depictions of ships showing offerings at the bow suggest that it remained the site of the deity (Fig. 2.9). Such was apparently also the case on Syro-Canaanite ships during the Late Bronze Age. Men offer incense while standing before the mast and facing the bow on two of the ships depicted in the

Figure 9.1. (Facing page) The Uluburun shipwreck (photo by R. Piercy; courtesy Institute of Nautical Archaeology)

tomb of Kenamun, presumably in thanks for the completion of a safe journey (Figs. 3.3, 5).

In the religious texts of Ugarit, *Asherat-of-the-Sea* was the name of the great goddess, wife of El and mother of Baal (Resheph).[23] As her name implies, she played a significant role as sea-goddess. Interestingly, the Uluburun ship also carried several varieties of gold pendants bearing symbols that are identified in Ugaritic texts with El and his consort.[24] Might the little Uluburun statuette be a depiction of *Asherat-of-the-Sea*?

CAPE GELIDONYA. Another important shipwreck had been found earlier by a sponge diver off Cape Gelidonya, on the southern coast of Turkey.[25] In a landmark excavation that marked the beginning of true scientific archaeological research on the seabed, the site was explored in 1960 by an expedition from the University Museum of the University of Pennsylvania under Bass's direction (Fig. 9.2).

The ship apparently sank after hitting the nearby cliff. The extant cargo consisted mainly of copper oxhide and bun ingots (Figs. 9.3–4). The lay of the cargo on the seabed suggests that the craft had not capsized before coming to rest on the seabed. Because of a lack of sedimentation in the area little, if any, of the vessel itself was found.[26]

Bass considered artifacts not related to the cargo, most of which were located in one area, the crew's personal possessions. He proposed that these defined the crew's living quarters. As cabins are normally located in the stern on seagoing ships, it followed that the find area was the craft's stern. The goods on board the Gelidonya wreck indicated that the vessel had voyaged from the Levant and in the direction of the Aegean when she sank. Identifying the ship's

ethnic origins proved more problematic, however. Was she built and used by Syro-Canaanites, Cypriots, Mycenaeans, or people of some other nationality? Bass notes that the ship's origin was directly related to that of the crew.[27] Based on a study of the personal finds, he suggests that the Gelidonya wreck was North Syrian.

This opinion did not go unchallenged. The personal gear found on the wreck, it was argued, was common throughout the Near East; the artifacts could have come from Cyprus or from farther south along the Syro-Canaanite littoral.[28] Bass later acknowledged the possibility that the ship may have been Cypriot.[29] G. Cadogan and J. D. Muhly identify the wreck as Mycenaean.[30]

Radiocarbon tests of twigs from the dunnage gave a dating of 1200 B.C. ±50.[31] Was the shipwreck from the thirteenth century (Late Bronze Age) or the twelfth century (Iron Age)? Bass, concluding that the manufacture of oxhide ingots had ceased at the end of the Late Bronze Age (ca. 1200 B.C.), suggests that the ship sank in the thirteenth century.[32] H. W. Catling dates the bronzes, and the ship along with them, to the twelfth century.[33]

On visits to the site in 1987, 1988, 1989, and 1994, Bass and a team from the Institute of Nautical Archaeology found a number of artifacts that had been overlooked during the 1960 excavation: two stone balance-pan weights, a zoomorphic head, metallic tin (the first such find on the site), several bronze knives, fragments of copper ingots, and a bronze plowshare. A bronze sword was found in a crevice on top of a boxcar-like boulder located in the center of the site, implying that the boulder had rested on the sea floor when the ship sank.[34]

Pottery found during the 1960

campaign was fragmentary at best.[35] Perhaps the pieces raised then were broken fragments of earlier cargoes that had been left in the ship's bilge, while the intact items may either have been moved from the site by the strong local current or tumbled out when the ship sank. Two large Late Helladic IIIB stirrup jars found about fifty meters to the southeast of the wreck site during the 1988 survey seem to have suffered this fate.[36] These jars, along with the scarabs found on the wreck, appear to confirm a thirteenth-century date for it.[37] A single stone anchor was found near the site in 1994(Fig. 12.48: C).[38]

Israel

The Israeli coast has yielded evidence of Late Bronze Age wrecks and cargoes. Because of the shallow coastal profile and the primarily open coastline, however, most ships that sank in this area exist only as scattered cargo sites, making their interpretation difficult.

CARMEL COAST. In 1981 a group of metal artifacts was discovered on the seabed off Kibbutz Hahotrim, south of Haifa. The artifacts were scattered around two large stone anchors to which they may or may not be related (Fig. 12.54).[39] These consist primarily of scrap metal intended for remelting: a plowshare of a type common at Cape Gelidonya, pieces of broken horse bits, chisel(s?) and small fragments of oxhide, and other ingot types.[40] A lead bun ingot and pieces of several others were found. Two of these bear signs, possibly of Cypro-Minoan origin; a third lead ingot fragment from Hahotrim is of a variety previously known solely from Eighteenth Dynasty Theban tomb paintings.[41] Subsequently, additional lead ingots with holes at their apexes were found opposite Kfar Samir.[42]

A well-preserved oxhide ingot was found together with five amorphous tin ingots opposite Hishulei Carmel, north of Hahotrim.[43] The excavators believe that the ingots, as well as a group of four stone anchors that were found fifty meters away, belong to a single ship that sank in the vicinity.[44] The Carmel Coast abounds in stone anchors found in groups and singly, however, making the relationship of the anchors to the ingots tenuous at best. I find no compelling reason to assume that the anchors are related to the metal artifacts. There is also nothing to suggest that the four anchors were tied to a ship and were thus carried closer to shore. At Uluburun, about half of the ship's anchors were carried in the hull as spares.[45]

A third group of metal ingots was discovered opposite Kfar Samir.[46] This is the northernmost of the three sites and is about three kilometers from the Hahotrim site, which marks the southern border of the locations containing holed lead ingots. The metal artifacts of both sites may have come from the cargo of a single ship that, for whatever reason, left her cargo spread out along the Carmel Coast. Since Hishulei Carmel is located between these two sites and contains compatible material, it may also belong to the same context. The reason for this spread into the sea is unclear. Lightening a ship's load was normal procedure in storms, but this was certainly not the only reason for "deep-sixing" merchandise.[47]

Other Bronze Age Wrecks?
Solitary finds on the Mediterranean seabed hint at the possible existence of additional Bronze Age wrecks that have as yet eluded discovery. A wreck site containing pottery of the Capo Graziano culture, ca. eighteenth century B.C.,

Figure 9.2. Recording artifacts at Cape Gelidonya (photo by H. Greer; courtesy University Museum, Philadelphia)

has been reported off Lipari at a depth of forty meters.[48] Oxhide ingots found off Euboea, and in Turkey in the Bay of Antalya and at Deveboynu Burnu (Cape Krio), also suggest the existence of additional wrecks (Fig. 13.1: d and g).[49] Middle Bronze Age II pottery found in Tantura Lagoon, the ancient harbor of Tel Dor, raises the tantalizing possibility of a shipwreck buried in the cove's sand, while a Late

Bronze Age dagger and a Canaanite sickle sword found in the sea near Beit Yannai, north of Netanya on Israel's Mediterranean coast, may indicate a Late Bronze Age wreck site there.[50]

In 1983 a group of fifteen stone anchors, most of which are of H. Frost's Byblian type, was discovered and excavated opposite Kibbutz Naveh Yam, three kilometers south of Athlit.[51] The excava-

Figure 9.3. A diver loosens a concreted mass of the cargo of copper ingots found resting on brushwood dunnage during the Cape Gelidonya excavation (photo by H. Greer; courtesy University Museum, Philadelphia)

tor, E. Galili, interprets this anchor group on the seabed as the result of a shipwreck.[52] The anchor site was located between eighty and one hundred meters from the shore at a depth of three to three and one-half meters. During the excavation of the anchors, two hematite weights, a bronze chisel, and an adze were found at a distance of fifty to sixty meters from the anchor site.

Discussion

On Problems of Shipwreck Ethnic Identification

Identifying a wrecked ship's home port is particularly difficult.[53] The nautical excavator can date the craft and chart its final voyage, based on the ship's cargo, but the freight gives no indication of the craft's origin. Only if the ship's ownership is validated, however, can the craft and its cargo of information be placed in the correct economic-historical background.[54]

Documents found on a wreck are of particular value in this regard. Writing on the now-missing wax of a wooden diptych found at Uluburun, for example, could have answered a number of questions still pending on that wreck.[55] Just the identity alone of the script used on the wax could have helped to identify the traders.

Ideally, one might hope for a name-device, like the *epismon* or *parasemon* of the Classical period.[56] Alternatively, shipwright marks, like those on the Cheops ship and the Punic wreck at Marsala, could help pinpoint the ethnic identity of the carpenters who built the craft.[57] On a wreck found in the Mediterranean, however, even this has limited value, for shipwrights could work in foreign dockyards.

Assuming a lack of written evidence, how can a vessel's final

Figure 9.4. Divers fill lifting bag to raise artifacts to the surface during the Cape Gelidonya excavation (photo by P. Throckmorton; courtesy University Museum, Philadelphia)

home port be determined? The emphasis here is on the word *final*. The original construction site may not have been the ship's home port. Ships were bought and sold, captured and waylaid in the Bronze Age. A ship could have been built at Byblos, sold to Ugarit, and then prized by Egyptian forces. All these actions were possible in the Late Bronze Age. How would the excavators of such a wreck identify its home port?

On the remains of a small ship in which all of the personal items are of a more or less homogeneous nature (as at Cape Gelidonya), it seems valid to accept Bass's identification via personal items found. This approach cannot be applied to a wreck that contains personal goods of numerous cultures, as at Uluburun.

The Mycenaean seals, the globed pin, and pottery articles of everyday use suggest the presence of two Mycenaeans on board.[58] This raises an important question: what constitutes "evidence beyond reasonable doubt" that a person or persons of a given nationality were on board a ship at the time of sinking? Can this be determined solely on the basis of nontextual artifacts found on the wreck? On a shipwreck, this question is crucial. The Uluburun ship carried personal memorabilia of at least five different cultures when it went down: Assyrian (Mesopotamian), Egyptian, Kassite, Mycenaean, and Syro-Canaanite. How are these to be interpreted?

There are several reasons that persons of varied ethnic origins might have sailed on the same ship:

• Egyptian tomb paintings give the impression that the crews of foreign ships were monolithically ethnic—as if Egyptian ships had only Egyptian crew members and Syro-Canaanite ships had only Syrian or Canaanite mariners. This is probably misleading, resulting more from a tendency toward artistic stereotyping than from a reflection of contemporaneous realities. Then, as now, sailors of various nationalities could join, or be conscripted, onto a single ship. This fact of seafaring life is admirably illustrated in the story of Jonah, when the sailors in their desperation pray to *different* gods: "But the Lord hurled a great wind upon the sea, and there was a mighty tempest on the sea, so that the ship threatened to break up. Then the mariners were afraid, *and*

each cried to his god; and they threw the wares that were in the ship into the sea, to lighten it for them. But Jonah had gone down into the inner part of the ship and had lain down, and was fast asleep. So the captain came and said to him, `What do you mean, you sleeper? Arise, call upon your god! Perhaps the god will give a thought to us, that we do not perish.'"[59]

The personal memorabilia found at Uluburun may represent the archaeological expression of this phenomenon. Apart from the different cultural identities represented by these artifacts, they had *numinous* significance for their owners. That is, they represent faith in different gods and beliefs and may, in general terms, be indicative of persons of varying ethnic and religious backgrounds on board the ship during its final voyage.

It would be unwise, however, to equate any specific object with an owner of like ethnic identity: objects having prophylactic significance could have been acquired by anyone. Furthermore, these objects may simply have been collected by crew members during their travels and have no significance at all vis-à-vis the ethnic identity of the persons on the ship when it sank.

• Throughout history, merchant ships carried paying foreign passengers: "But Jonah rose to flee to Tarshish from the presence of the Lord. He went down to Yaffo and found a ship going to Tarshish; *so he paid the fare, and went on board,*

to go with them to Tarshish, away from the presence of the Lord."[60] The king of Alashia refers three times to his messenger and an Egyptian messenger traveling together between the two countries, presumably by ship.[61] Whatever the nationality of their ships, at least one of the messengers would always have been a "foreign passenger." Similarly, Amanmasha sailed to Egypt, presumably on a Byblian ship, and Wenamun used a Syro-Canaanite ship (home port not stated) on his outgoing trip and a Byblian craft on the first part of his return voyage.[62]

• Kidnapping and slaving were additional reasons for foreign ethnics to have been on board a ship.[63]

⚯   ⚯   ⚯

The problem of defining a seagoing ship's ownership remains perplexing. One form of evidence that may reveal a Bronze Age ship's final home port is her anchors. This is because, in the Bronze Age, the various countries and states used diagnostic forms of stone anchors. Regardless of where along the ship's route the anchors were made, they would have been cut to the same characteristic shape. The Karnak anchor is a good example of this phenomenon.[64] Unfortunately, it is not always possible to correlate anchors found in the sea with those found in stratified land sites.[65]

Aspects of
Maritime Activity

CHAPTER 10

Ship Construction

The single most important aspect of seafaring is the ability to build vessels capable of withstanding the rigors of sea travel, with its waves, storms, and other dangers. The little we know about the actual construction of Bronze Age seagoing ships comes from the meager remains of fragmentary seagoing hulls—little more than bits and pieces of timber—found on the Mediterranean's seabed as well as on land in Egypt.

There is, however, much ancillary information: Nile ships found interred in various forms of burial, or reuse of their dismembered timbers; documents dealing with the construction and repair of ships and records of dockyards; and wall reliefs depicting scenes of ship construction.

Although this information is valuable, it is important to emphasize that most of it comes from Egypt and relates primarily to craft that plied the quiet waters of the Nile rather than to seagoing ships. Thus, the data can teach us about local Egyptian traditions but are of lesser value in interpreting deep-water vessels.

Primary Materials

Hull Remains
of Seagoing Ships

WADI GAWASIS. Several wood fragments with mortise scars were found at the Middle Kingdom Red Sea port of Wadi Gawasis.[1] One of the timbers is cedar (*Cedrus* sp.) and has been radiocarbon dated to ca. 1975 B.C.[2] These fragments may be remnants of a ship-assembly operation that were subsequently used as firewood since some pieces are charred. The largest fragment is 38 centimeters long, 14 centimeters wide, and 12 centimeters thick. It has three rectangular mortises along one edge that measure 6 centimeters long, 2.5 centimeters wide, and 4 centimeters deep (Fig. 10.1).

Assuming the plank edge has not been abraded, these mortises are exceptionally shallow for ships built using the Egyptian unpegged mortise-and-tenon technique. The normal depth of mortises on the Dashur boats, for example, is 12–13 centimeters.[3] Tenons of the Cheops ship were 10 centimeters long by 7 centimeters wide and 1.5 centimeters thick.[4] This suggests a mortise depth of 5–6 centimeters. Therefore, the mortises in these fragments were probably used to

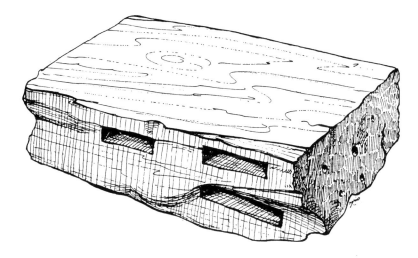

Figure 10.1. Mortised block of cedarwood, apparently a leftover from ship construction at Mersa Gawasis (Twelfth Dynasty) (from Sayed 1980: 157 fig. 3)

seat planks in *lashed* construction, as in Cheops I and the Lisht timbers. The manner in which the three mortises on the Wadi Gawasis timber fragment are staggered finds its closest parallels in the Lisht timbers.[5]

ULUBURUN. The Uluburun shipwreck is the only Late Bronze Age wreck found in the Mediterranean that has supplied definite information on hull construction.[6] A section of the ship's hull discovered beneath a large stone anchor included portions of the keel-plank, the garboards, and fragments of additional strakes (Fig. 10.2).[7] During the 1986 campaign, additional unidentified timbers

were found beneath the rows of copper ingots north of the rock outcrop.[8] The 1990 campaign revealed that planking on the ship's port side is well-preserved as it continues beneath the oxhide ingot pile but is poorly preserved on the starboard side.[9] The keel-plank is 28 centimeters sided (wide); the garboard is 17 centimeters wide, while the second strake is 26 centimeters wide and 6 centimeters thick. The strakes are connected with pegged mortise-and-tenon joinery, with tenons placed at 21-centimeter intervals. One collapsed mortise measures 7 centimeters wide by 17 centimeters deep. The pegs locking the mor-

tise-and-tenon joints are about 2.2 centimeters in diameter on the hull's inner surface.

The hull section in Grid Squares M15–O15 and M16–O16 was documented during the 1993 season (Fig. 14.1). Probe excavations in this area had indicated the existence of a keel-plank, as well as the port side of the garboard strake, a second strake, and fragments of a third. A section about 1.8 meters along the line of the keel-plank and 1 meter in width was well-preserved. No frames were found here, or in the other surviving sections of hull. C. M. Pulak suggests that the preserved portion was too limited to contain frames, particularly if they had not been attached to the keel.[10]

The keel is larger in its sided dimension (28 centimeters) than in its molded dimension (22 centimeters), making it a keel-plank, or a rudimentary keel, rather than a true keel. Of particular interest is the discovery that the keel-plank protruded only slightly beneath the outer surface of the hull planking. This is analogous to the evidence derived from contemporaneous ship models, as well as from Hatshepsut's Punt ships depicted at Deir el Bahri.

A starboard section of the hull was also preserved beneath the third and fourth rows of ingots in Grid Squares N17–O17 and N18–O18. This part had been badly damaged by the crushing weight of the cargo as it settled on the steep seabed, making interpretation difficult. Despite the damage, Pulak was able to identify a planking scarf as either a flat scarf or a drop strake. The scarf still bore one well-preserved mortise-and-tenon joint, and remnants of a second. As a result of the poor state of preservation, not all mortise-and-tenon joint peg pairs could be located; however, spacing between pegs

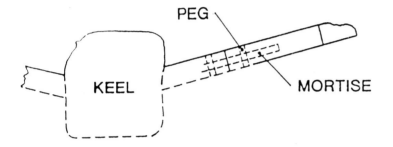

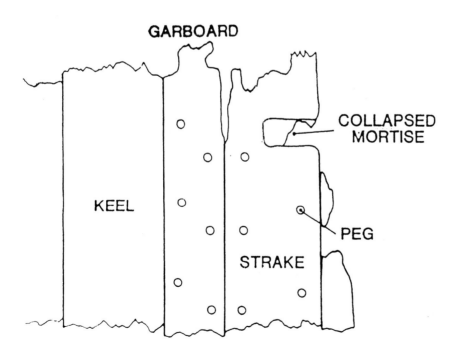

Figure 10.2. Hull remains from Uluburun (late fourteenth century B.C.*) (from Pulak 1987: 130 ill. 73)*

was, on average, 23 centimeters. In this area, the garboard narrows towards the bow (downslope), a detail particularly noticeable at the lower extremity.

The forward-most section of hull had been preserved beneath the fourth row of ingots in Grid Squares N18–O18. This portion, which is about 1 square meter in area, includes part of the keel-plank, as well as portions of the first six strakes on the ship's starboard side. These planks had a pattern of varying width similar to the more centrally located section found in Grid Squares M15–O15, with alternating narrow (15–16 centimeter) and wide (25 centimeter) planking. As this feature is exhibited on all three sections found, Pulak concludes that it is probably a typical feature of the hull.

This section of the keel-plank is not in alignment with the one higher up the slope. This is probably a result of this hull section sliding southward as it settled against a rock outcrop on the seafloor. Pulak notes that the third through sixth strakes here seem to conform roughly to four of the surviving five strakes that had been preserved under the third row of copper ingots. Determining the exact relationship is, however, difficult due to the fragmentary preservation of the hull in this area.

The wood of the keel-plank, and possibly that of the second strake, is identified as cedar (Cedrus sp.); the tenons and pegs are thought to be oak (Quercus sp.). At present, this is the earliest known example of pegged mortise-and-tenon joinery used in the construction of a watercraft.[11] Pegged mortise-and-tenon joinery seems to have been a requirement for seagoing ships. Already at Uluburun the joinery appears well developed, and we must assume, therefore, a consid-

erable period of evolution leading up to it.

Several large timbers have framelike shapes. At first these were considered to be part of the ship's structure, but they are now thought to have been spare parts for repairs.[12] The purpose of one adjacent timber and others found nearby, on which the knobs of branches or roots are still visible, remains unverified but thought to be firewood. These timbers also have been identified as cedar. Fragments of wood, at least some of which belong to the vessel's hull, were found in several areas of the site. Additional information on the ship's hull is derived from careful recording of sectional profiles of all ingot rows and by plotting the tips of each oxhide ingot.[13] This will allow the excavators to determine the hull's curvature in areas where the hull itself has long since disappeared.

Beneath one stone anchor, the excavators uncovered a row of five rounded stakes.[14] The longest of these is 1.7 meters long. One (lower?) extremity of each stake has been shaped to a point by means of several blows of an adze or ax. Between the stakes excavators found closely spaced withies, more or less perpendicular to the stakes. The withies seem to have formed matting independent of the stakes. Pulak notes the similarity in form this construction has with the fencing depicted on the Syro-Canaanite ships painted in the tombs of Kenamun, Nebamun, and the mnš-ship determinative (Figs. 3.2–10). The upper end of the longest stake is worked and, therefore, reminiscent in this respect to those in the Kenamun tomb.

The excavators believe the ship was about fifteen meters long.[15] Interestingly, this approximates the proposed calculated length for the ship type of eighteen oars postu-

lated from the Ugaritic evidence.[16] It will take considerable additional research to determine whether the Uluburun ship had been strictly a sailing vessel or whether it might have been a merchant galley. The latter possibility should not be ruled out at this stage, however. In the lower part of the wreck, where the ship's bow was confined by huge rocks, it will be possible to reconstruct this area of the ship based on the manner in which the oxhide ingots came to rest.[17]

CAPE GELIDONYA. The wood recovered from the shipwreck at Cape Gelidonya was in such fragmentary condition that doubt remains as to whether any of the pieces actually belonged to the ship's hull (Fig. 10.3).[18] Some of the published wood pieces appear to be pegs. Other wooden fragments have holes, perhaps for wooden pegs.[19] Fragment Wd 2 may be a broken tenon fragment. This suggests that the Cape Gelidonya ship, like the Uluburun vessel, was built of pegged mortise-and-tenon joinery. The worked timbers were identified as cypress (Cupressus sp.) and oak (Quercus sp.). No metal fasteners were found at either Uluburun or Cape Gelidonya.

In summary, at present there is evidence for at least two separate traditions of construction used in seagoing ships in the Bronze Age: pegged mortise-and-tenon joinery (Uluburun and probably Cape Gelidonya) and some form of internal lashed construction in which unpegged mortise-and-tenon joints were used to seat the planking (Wadi Gawasis).

Ancillary Materials

Hull Remains of Nile Ships
Numerous remains of Nile craft have been found in Egyptian excavations. Although it is imperative to emphasize that seagoing

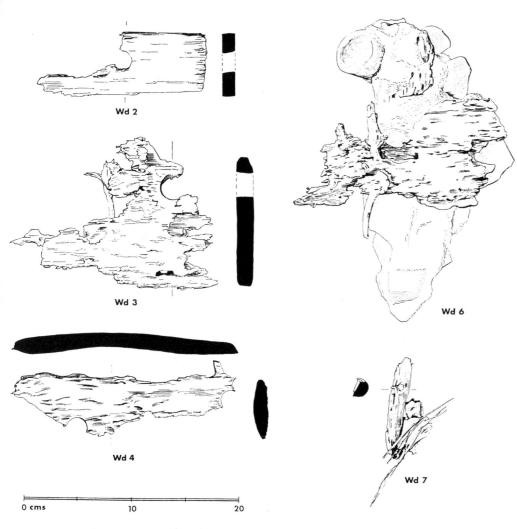

Wd 2

Wd 3

Wd 4

Wd 6

Wd 7

0 cms   10   20

Figure 10.3. Wood (hull?) remains from Cape Gelidonya (late thirteenth century B.C.) (from CG 1967: 50 fig. 51)

vessels may have differed radically from ships that plied the Nile, these vessels nevertheless do shed valuable light on the types of ship construction that existed contemporaneously in ancient Egypt. For this reason, a short review of this evidence is in order here.

In antiquity the Egyptians were notorious for doing things differently from other peoples. This was certainly true of the techniques they used in shipbuilding.[20] While many cultures built "sewn" or "lashed" ships with their planks held together with ligatures, only the Egyptians used transverse lashings that did not penetrate the hull. Furthermore, while the shipwrights of other nations were care-

ful to create straight planking seams, the ancient Egyptian shipwrights intentionally "joggled" their planking edges into jigsaw-like patterns that prevented longitudinal sliding. These features, together with a liberal use of unpegged mortise-and-tenon joints, endowed Egyptian hulls with considerable structural strength.

Egyptian shipbuilders seem to have taken pains to avoid piercing the exterior of their hulls in any manner.[21] Indeed, C. W. Haldane suggests that this may explain why *pegged* mortise-and-tenon joinery, which had been used in Egyptian carpentry from early times, was utterly foreign to all of the forms of indigenous Egyptian shipbuild-

ing known to date. That pharaonic shipwrights did at times pierce the hull is evident from the iconographic record, however. Sahure's ships have ligatures that clearly pass through holes in the hull (Fig. 2.3).

ABYDOS. In 1991 twelve planked boats dating to the end of the Predynastic period or the beginning of the Dynastic period were discovered at the Northern Cemetery at Abydos.[22] The boats are about fifteen to eighteen meters long. They were buried in mud-brick coffins and contained pottery offerings. Following their interment, the vessels were entombed under a layer of mud-brick and plaster. The future excavation of this "fleet" will contribute considerably to our understanding of ship construction in early Egypt.

THE TARKHAN PLANKS. W. M. F. Petrie uncovered a group of planks at Tarkhan in tombs dated to the First Dynasty.[23] The timbers bear V-shaped and L-shaped lashing mortises as well as mortise-and-tenon joinery; both of these elements exist on the later Cheops ship and the Lisht timbers. Petrie interprets these timbers as having been parts of wooden buildings: he believes that the timbers had been assembled to form a "niched wall." He sees this wooden construction as a prototype of the niched brick architecture common in the Early Dynastic period. H. Frankfort opposes this view, suggesting that the timbers had actually come from Nile watercraft.[24]

S. M. Vinson concludes that although evidence is lacking to definitively prove that the Tarkhan planks are derived from ships, it would be curious if they did not because of the similarities they share with other hull remains known from Egypt.[25] More recently, however, Haldane expresses reservations as to whether these timbers had been used in shipbuilding.[26]

FIRST DYNASTY BOAT GRAVES. Some twenty-five boat graves dating to the First Dynasty are known from Lower Egypt. Nineteen of these were uncovered at Helwan by Z. Y. Saad.[27] Others were excavated by W. Emery at Saqqara.[28] All of these originally contained boats. Because of a combination of lack of remains and the inadequate manner of publication of those remnants that did survive, it is difficult (if not impossible) to learn anything about the construction of the vessels originally interred in these tombs.[29]

CHEOPS I AND II. There are six known royal ship graves around the Great Pyramid of Cheops at Giza.[30] In 1952, during the removal of sand from the southern side of the pyramid, two additional boat pits were discovered. The ship in one of the pits, Cheops I, was excavated in 1955.[31] The vessel was found disassembled, rather like a model kit, with all the parts in place. After many trials and five reconstructions, the ship was restored by Ahmed Youssef Mous-

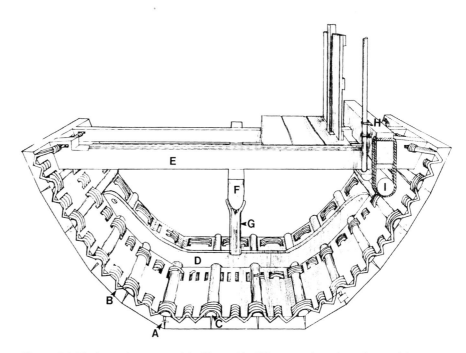

Figure 10.4. The internal structure of the Cheops ship: (A) *unpegged mortise-and-tenon joint;* (B) *V-shaped mortise for transverse lashing;* (C) *batten;* (D) *floor timber;* (E) *beam;* (F) *carling;* (G) *stanchion;* (H) *stringer;* (I) *stringer hold-down (from Lipke 1984: 75 fig. 48)*

tafa and is now exhibited in a museum constructed over the pit from whence it came.[32]

Cheops I is one of the most outstandingly elegant and aesthetically beautiful artifacts to have reached us from the past.[33] The ship is built of Lebanese cedar; her tenons are made of sycamore and sidder.[34] The vessel is 43.4 meters long and has a beam of 5.9 meters. The planks are 13 to 14 centimeters thick. They are edge-joined with mortise-and-tenon joints serving to seat the planks, which are held together with lashings woven through V-shaped mortises in the planks (Fig. 10.4: A–B). The rope used in the lashing, which was also deposited in the pit, was

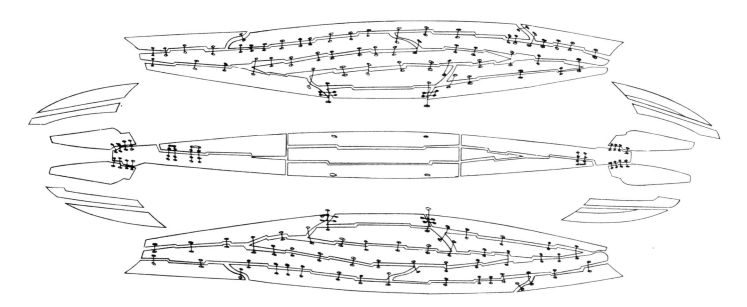

Figure 10.5. *Rough planking diagram of the Cheops ship showing lashing holes and scarfs (from Lipke 1984: 66 fig. 42)*

made of halfa grass.[35] The lashings are placed over wooden battens (Fig. 10.4: C). The ship is constructed of twelve bottom planks; twenty-two planks make up her sides, with an additional eight timbers finishing off her ends (Fig. 10.5). For structural strength, the hull has both floor timbers and beams (Fig. 10.4: D–E). The beams are supported on a thick central carling that rests on stanchions supported by frames (Fig. 10.4: F–G). Two stringers lie over the beams, and each is attached to them by being bound to a narrow stringer hold-down that passes beneath each beam (Fig. 10.4: H–I).

In 1987 a hole was drilled through one of the cover stones over the second boat pit, and the interred hull of the remains was studied using a specially designed camera.[36] Various elements of structure identified inside the tomb suggest that this boat was built in the same manner as the first one. Cheops II has not been excavated.

THE LISHT TIMBERS. Timbers derived from one or more ships found at Lisht represent an otherwise unknown third type of Egyptian naval construction.[37] About ninety dislocated timbers were found in the immediate vicinity of the pyramid of Sesostris I and are thus contemporaneous to Papyrus Reisner II, discussed below. These timbers are of particular interest since they are derived from functional, rather than cultic, craft. Haldane emphasizes that the shipbuilding techniques exhibited by the Lisht timbers to combat the strains of heavy cargoes may have been similar to technologies used to solve similar stresses on seagoing vessels. The purpose for the timbers' deposition at the site is unclear: a few other pyramids are also known to have had emplace-

ments of timber. These have been described as "quarry roads" or "construction ramps."

Similar to the Cheops ship, lashing is used; but, as at Dashur, deep mortise-and-tenon joinery is the principal form of fastening. The thickness of the planks suggests that the vessel (or vessels) from which they came must have been substantial. The thick timbers have fastenings on three of their surfaces. The timbers used, either *Acacia* sp. or *Tamarix* sp., are both native to Egypt. Joggled edges, used to maintain hull integrity, are a common feature of the Lisht planking.[38]

Mortise-and-tenon joints are visible on the timbers: they are 9 to 9.5 centimeters wide and 12 centimeters deep. The tenons are elongated polygons and have been further strengthened by the insertion of wooden slips at either side of the tenon.[39]

In addition to this, a form of lashing, at present known only from these timbers at Lisht, was also used to fasten the timbers together. The lashing-holes were L-shaped and contained webbing or straps of fibrous material that has been tentatively identified as halfa grass. Most timbers had no less than four webbing fastenings consisting of two mortises, each about 6.5 to 9.5 centimeters wide, 5 centimeters deep, and slightly over 1 centimeter thick.[40] The mortises met at right angles, but, as in the Cheops ship, these never passed through to the exterior of the hull.[41]

On one plank, a trapezoidal peg was driven from inside the hull into a mortise-and-tenon joint to strengthen it.[42] The tenon did not penetrate the plank's exterior. This is the only known case of a *pegged* mortise-and-tenon joint in Egyptian Bronze Age ship construction.

An unusual tripartite frame,

excavated at the beginning of the century, is of particular interest (Fig. 10.6).[43] It consists of a curved floor having two timbers connected with mortise-and-tenon joints and webbing to its upper extremities. The inner edges of the two upper timbers are separated by a cavity of about fifty centimeters: this coincides with a notch one centimeter deep on the upper side of the floor timber. Twelve triangular notches are cut into its bottom surface.

Into these are cut three circular openings that might have facilitated seating the frame inside the hull on small pegs that did not penetrate it. The manner in which the frame is constructed suggests that it was meant to support some structural element in its center. Furthermore, mortise-and-tenon scars are visible on its side surface, indicating that it was attached to another, adjacent, frame, which would have created a massive support system. Haldane believes that the timber's upper surface was prepared to receive a longitudinal strengthening timber or carling, a type of construction that she favorably compares to several Eleventh Dynasty boat models from Meir.[44]

In addition to ships' timbers, two large models were discovered at Lisht near the mastaba of Imhotep.[45] The smaller of these is the only ancient Egyptian model yet known that was built out of planks. This model, 1.95 meters long, is constructed with mortise-and-tenon joinery and has a planking pattern similar to that of the Dashur boats. Because of the thin planking used—no timber is thicker than one centimeter—the model was so damaged when found that it was reburied.

DASHUR BOATS. Five or six interred boats were uncovered by J. de Morgan at Dashur in 1894–95.[46] Of these, two are now in the

A

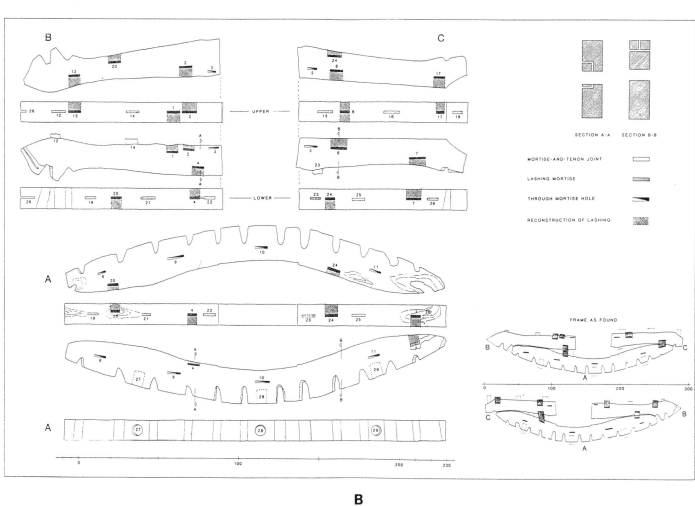

B

Figure 10.6. Three-piece boat frame found at Lisht (Sesostris I) (A from an Egyptian Expedition photo, courtesy Metropolitan Museum of Art, New York; B from Haldane 1992A: pl. 132; Lisht frame © C. Haldane, after a Metropolitan Museum of Art drawing)

Cairo Museum, one is in the Chicago Museum of Natural History, and a fourth is in the Carnegie Museum (Figs. 10.7–8). Two other boats have disappeared from the historical record.

The boats were buried to the southwest of Senusret III's pyramid complex and, therefore, are generally believed to have been interred with that pharaoh. B. Landström notes, however, that at least the two in the Cairo Museum were built largely of reused wood and that their construction lacks the finesse of the Cheops ship.[47] This being the case, he questions whether such poor craft would be suitable for interment with the greatest king of the Twelfth Dynasty and suggests that the boats may have belonged to the burial of a person of lesser rank. Haldane remarks, however, that although all four of the curated Dashur boats underwent repairs after they were discovered, only one hull shows evidence of ancient repairs.[48] The hulls are about ten meters long; their planks are attached to each other primarily with deep mortise-and-tenon joints. Dovetail joints found on these hulls appear to be later additions, cut into existing lashing mortises and made after the boats were discovered in the nineteenth century.[49]

The Dashur boats have no frames: they are supported by beams that pierce the hull and are fastened to it by a single peg driven through each beam into the strake beneath it. Some of the deck beams on the Carnegie boat exhibit V-shaped lashings, like those found on the Cheops ship. Haldane hypothesizes that these may have served to attach deck furniture or are perhaps the remnants of reuse of these timbers: she notes that at least one through-beam was in secondary use, reused from an earlier hull.[50]

No keel is present. In its place is a tripartite, thick central keel plank, comparable to that on the Cheops ship and the Lisht planked model. The similarity of planking patterns on these various vessels argues for a strong shipbuilding tradition that continued through the First Intermediate Period.[51] Furthermore, the fact that the Dashur boats and the Lisht model were built to the same specifications suggests that Egyptians may have had distinct requirements for the manner in which certain ships and boats were to be constructed.

THE MATARIA WRECK. In 1987 a Nile working boat was uncovered in Mataria, a suburb of Cairo located on the ancient site of Heliopolis.[52] It dates to the Late Graeco-Roman period and has been radiocarbon dated to about 2450 ± 50 B.P. It is 11 meters long, 4 meters in breadth, and 1.2 meters deep. The planks were made of sycamore (*Ficus sycomorus*). They are short, thick, and edge-joined with mortise-and-tenon joints. Some of these were secured with wooden pegs.[53] The tenons are a minimum of 17 centimeters in length by 10 centimeters wide and 2 centimeters thick. Peg heads measure 2 centimeters in diameter. This is the only known hull from Egypt constructed with pegged mortise-and-tenon joinery. No frames were found in the hull. These were apparently removed in antiquity, since impressions of frames are still visible. Haldane notes how

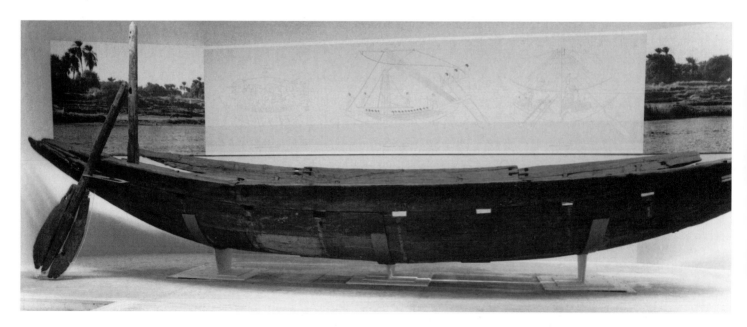

Figure 10.7. The Carnegie Dashur boat, sheer view (Sesostris III) (from Patch and Haldane 1990: 2 fig. 1 [Accession 1842–1]; photo by M. O. McNaugher, used by permission)

Figure 10.8. The Carnegie Dashur boat, view from the bow (Sesostris III) (from Patch and Haldane 1990: 33 fig. 18 [Accession 1842–1]; photo by M. O. Naugher, used by permission)

closely the construction of this hull resembles the description of Egyptian shipbuilding given by Herodotus, with which the Mataria hull was roughly contemporaneous.

The Textual Evidence

The following documents pertain to the construction and repair of ships. They present numerous problems in interpretation, particularly in the many technical terms, the exact meaning of which continues to elude us.

Egypt

PAPYRUS REISNER II. This papyrus, which dates to a period of three and a half years during the reign of Sesostris I, deals mainly with details of carpentry and the recasting of metal tools for use in the royal dockyard of This.[54]

B.M. 10056. Timber issued to several superintendent craftsmen over a period of eight months in the royal dockyard of *Prw nfr* is recorded in this document.[55] *Prw nfr* was apparently the chief port and naval shipyard under Thut-

mose III.[56] S. R. K. Glanville suggests that *Prw nfr* was located near Memphis or at el Badreshein. It may have owed its origins to the urgent need for sea transports for Thutmose's many Syro-Canaanite campaigns.[57] The text refers to timber being delivered "from a lake near the magazine."[58] C. D. Jarrett-Bell notes that this passage may mean that the Egyptians kept their logs in water to season until they were required.[59] The text often records the purposes for which the timber is issued.

In his conclusions, Glanville turns to G. S. Laird Clowes to make sense of the various entries in the text vis-à-vis their contribution to our understanding of ancient shipbuilding.[60] Clowes gathers all references to one particular ship, an *ı̓mu*, named *Payeh*. He includes all entries referring to timber supplied to Tity, the workman who is building the boat, as well as to "the boat of Tity." Clowes notes:

> It seems to me that the only items on which we can build with security are the three big issues:
>
> 12 pieces of *wnḫ* of 161 cubits run and 13.5 cubits average length, before the 13th day of the first month of Inundation.
>
> 12 pieces of *ḫst.t* of 258 cubits run and 21.5 cubits average length, on the 13th day of the first month of Inundation.
>
> 60 pieces of *ı̓swt* of 848 1/2 cubits run and about 14 cubits average length on the 17th day of the first month of winter, i.e. more than 4 months later.
>
> Considering the large quantities of *ı̓swt* issued and *the late date of this issue* it seems highly probable that *ı̓swt* represents the outer skin planking of the vessel *which is of necessity put on last* and which involves great superficies.[61]

Clowes concludes that the twelve pieces of *wnḫ* were deck beams; the *ḥst.t* was used to build the two "gunwales" and the "keel or central bottom member." In other words, Clowes, writing in the early 1930s, assumes that the ship was being constructed "skeleton-first."[62] We now know, however, that ships were built "shell-first" in the Late Bronze Age and for at least two millennia later.[63] Perhaps the *wnḫ* planks had been used for the hull's bottom planking and backing timbers. It is interesting to note in this regard that the bottom planking and backing timbers of the Cheops ship consist of twelve timbers (Fig. 10.5).

The word *wnḫ* derives from the common root for "clothe" but may also mean "bind" (as a fillet of hair). Another substantive of this word is "dislocation," particularly of the vertebrae. Glanville suggests that these were the outer planking that "clothed" the hull.[64] Clowes considers them beams.[65] The planks were used over the whole length of the ship in the first stage of construction/renovation. This word is known also in the fuller form of *Ḥt-n-wnḫ*, literally "wood of clothing."[66] A similar term appears at Ugarit. When Byblos sold ships to Ugarit, the *lbš.anyt* (literally, "garment of the ships") was sold separately.[67] Virolleaud considers this "couverture, revêtement (du navire)" or perhaps derived from a ship class termed *mašku la-bi-šu*.[68]

PAPYRUS ANASTASI IV. Another text discussing the refitting of a ship appears in the Ramesside period Papyrus Anastasi IV. It contains a description of the inspection of an old Nile ship and the steps required for its repair:

The scribe of the treasury Kageb speaks to the scribe Inena and the shipwright Amennakhte.

Further, as regards the cast-off *skty*-bark of acacia wood which has not been in the water for many years, the fact is they failed to put onto it high gunnels; those things which were put onto it as gunnel(s) were (but) a few thole-boards of acacia wood which failed to uphold the *ḳ3s*'s of the boat, and it went to pieces very rapidly before it had been in the water many days. It is that a few high gunnel-pieces of acacia wood were not put onto it, nor a few high gunnel-pieces of (even) *im*-wood were put onto it either so that they might grip the boat. When my letter reaches you you shall go in one party and shall look at the deal planks which happened to be left over from the bark of the gods which is there in the store-house at Resynu, and you shall choose from amongst them four planks very high, very good and very broad, and you shall use them for gunnels of the *skty*-bark of acacia wood which you have at the ship-yard, two of those planks on (either) side, and you shall see whether there is there any good lining-wood left over, and you shall distribute (it) from bow to stern. *F*.[69]

The use of planks "left over from the bark of the gods" may refer to surplus timber from previous construction or the salvaging of usable materials from older craft.[70] The repeated use of ships' timbers is hardly surprising considering Egypt's difficulties in acquiring foreign timber suitable for shipbuilding.[71] The guesswork involved in interpreting the many technical terms again hampers our understanding of this and the following text.

HERODOTUS ON EGYPTIAN SHIP CONSTRUCTION. Herodotus, writing in the fifth century B.C., describes a traditional form of ship construction in Egyptian ships: "From this acacia tree they cut planks 3 feet long, which they put together like courses of brick, building up the hull as follows: they join these 3-foot lengths together with long, close-set dowels; when they have built up a hull in this fashion [out of the planks], they stretch crossbeams over them. They use no ribs, and they caulk seams from the inside, using papyrus fibers."[72] Herodotus is referring here to the use of short timbers of acacia wood held together with unpegged mortise-and-tenon joinery: this bricklike construction is portrayed in several Egyptian illustrations (Figs. 6.70; 10.22).[73]

It has been suggested that Herodotus is not referring to caulking the seams but is actually describing the internal transverse lashing of a hull built in the same manner as the Cheops ship.[74] A review of the uses of πα+ κτόω, the word Herodotus uses to describe this action, indicates that he seems to mean caulking and not lashing.[75] On the other hand, there is no evidence to date for the use of caulking in any of the ancient hulls uncovered in Egypt.

ELEPHANTINE PAPYRUS COWLEY NO. 26. This fascinating letter, written in Aramaic, dates to 412 B.C. It is addressed to Waḥpremakhi, an Egyptian bureaucrat, by Anani, who served as the chancellor and scribe to Arsames, the Persian satrap of Egypt.[76] The letter meticulously catalogs all the furnishings needed for the repairs of a Nile boat—down to the last nail. Indeed, in comparing this document to those discussed above, note that for the first time metal nails are required for the repairs. This suggests that this boat was built (or at least was going to be repaired) in a manner other than the traditional Egyptian ones. The text reads:[77]

RECTO
From Arsames to Waḥpremakhi.

And now, . . . [. . .] to us, saying: Mithradates the boatholder thus says: Psamsinei[t . . . *and PN . . . all* (*told*) *two, the boatholders of*] the Carians, thus said: "The boat which we hold-in-hereditary-lease—time has come its NEEDS to d[o]."
[. . .] let it be drawn up onto the dry land and let (word) be sent to the accountants of the treasury. Let them with [the] foreme[n . . . *that boat*] see and its RECKONING make. And let (word) be sent to whomever was (in charge). The MATERIAL, its COATING and other (things) which [. . .] let them give and immediately let its NEEDS be done, and other (things) about which from me (word) is sent to them.
About this they sent (word) and [*said*] thus: "[. . . *on*] the sand which is in front of the fortress [. . .]. Mithradates the boatholder showed us the boat (that) we may see (it. The boat) which is in the hands of Psamsineit and PN, all (told) two, the boatholders of the Carians, is drawn up on the dry land and we showed (it) to Shamashshillech and his colleagues the foremen (and) Shamou so[n] of Konufe, chief of the carpenters, WHITENER, and thus they said: "Time has come its NEED[s] to do. This is the MATERIAL which is necessary its NEEDS to do:

new wood of cedar and   ᵓr:

ṭp			ten cubits;
šym	[for] *bṭq*		eighty cubits by three hand-breadths
including *sgnn*			twelve cubits;
šp		fifteen,	each one twenty cubits;
sᶜbl			seventy cubits;
ḥnn	for the belly	three;	
qlᶜs	for the MAST/BOW	one;	
wood	of the DECK		sixty cubits;
mooring post	for *pᶜrᶜr*	one,	two cubits;
stanchion(s)	under the DECK	five;	
bronze and iron nails		two hundred.	

strong old cedar wood:

PANELLING	twenty cubits.

(For) all (of this) he shall bring (as) their replacement old and broken (wood) to the treasury.

Thick linen CLOTH	one hundred and eighty karsh;[78]
SHEETING	two hundred and fifty karsh;

new cedar wood:

ḥnn		two,	each five cubits (and) three handbreadths by three handbreadths;
bronze nails	for the DECK	one hundred and fifty,	each three handbreadths,
		two hundred and seventy-five,	each ten fingerbreadths,
all (told) nails:		four hundred and twenty-five;	
bronze plates			twenty cubits;
their nails		two hundred;	

VERSO

wood of old *ršwt* cedar:

mṣn   one talent, ten
                                                                      mina.

(To) all (of these) add:
sulphur   ten karsh;
and arsenic   for COATING   one hundred karsh.

And let them add onto the wood which will be given:

onto *tp* in the length, to each, three handbreadths OVERCUT and onto the width and the thickness two fingerbreadths;

and onto *šym* in the length, to each, three handbreadths OVERCUT and onto the width two fingerbreadths;

and onto *šp* and the *ḥnn* in the length, to each, one handbreadth;

and onto *s'bl*, the wood for the DECK, (and the) PANEL SECTIONS, in the length, to each (of these), three handbreadths OVERCUT and onto the width one fingerbreadth.

The linen CLOTH, the PLATING, the arsenic, the sulphur—in Persian weight are to be given.'

Let (word) be sent, saying: 'This MATERIAL is to be given into the hand of Shamou son of Konufe, chief of the carpenters, WHITENER, before our eyes (to do the) NEEDS on that boat and immediately let him do (them) as order has been issued.'"

Now, Arsames thus says: "You, do according to this which the accountants say, as order has been issued."

Anani the Scribe is Chancellor. Nabuakab wrote.

Waḥpremakhi . . . to be given . . . according to it . . . as order has been issued [. . .] wrote. (DEMOTIC:) Sasobek wrote.

(DEMOTIC) The boat [. . .]

From (*sealing*) Arsames who is in Eg[ypt to Waḥpremakhi].

Nabuakab the scribe. On the 13th [of] Tebeth, year 12 of Dari[us the king].

The most striking difference between the Anastasi IV and the Elephantine papyri is the requisition of bronze and iron nails: in the latter, a total of 825 nails of various types is ordered. Wood is referred to as "new" or "broken." Perhaps both fresh and used timber was to be utilized in the boat's repairs. Alternatively, this might refer to unseasoned and seasoned wood.

GRAECO-ROMAN SHIPBUILDING IN EGYPT. Papyrus Flor. I 69 records the salaries of shipwrights and sawyers for a period of three weeks in the mid-third century A.D.[79] The vessel referred to must have been a fair-sized craft, for it required scaffolding. The number of shipwrights working on it varied from four to eleven along with a pair of sawyers. L. Casson notes that this ship must have been built "shell-first," based on the order in which the timbers were prepared. First the planks, made of persea wood, were cut and then frames were prepared from acacia wood.

The Syro-Canaanite Coast

SYRO-CANAANITE SHIPBUILDING. At present, very little is known about Syro-Canaanite ship construction. This situation could change dramatically, however, if the Uluburun shipwreck proves to be of Syro-Canaanite origin.[80] Byblos and Tyre were centers for shipbuilding on the Syro-Canaanite coast: Ugarit purchased ships from Byblos, although it also had its own shipbuilders.[81] Ezekiel refers to expert shipbuilders from Byblos, and Diodorus Siculus mentions a dockyard (*ta neōria*) at Tyre.[82]

Later writers repeatedly relate traditions connecting the introduction of shipbuilding to the Phoenician (Syro-Canaanite) coast. Eusebius, in quoting Philo of Byblos's claim that Tyre invented the science of ship construction, seems to be describing a monoxylon: "Then Usoos (Οὔσωος = Ushu) took a trunk of a tree, stripped it of its branches and was the first man to dare sail in it on the sea."[83] Pliny ascribes to Hippus of Tyre the invention of the cargo ship and to the Phoenicians the invention of the skiff.[84]

Interestingly, in the description of the manner in which the Children of Israel were to build the

Holy Tabernacle, its planks were to be made of acacia wood: each of the boards was to have two tenons (*yadot*), which were to fit into forty sockets made of silver.[85] These are unpegged mortise-and-tenon joints.[86]

The excavation of the Marsala wreck has shown that the Phoenician word *wāw* means "nail."[87] This raises the likelihood that the Hebrew cognate, which appears in Exodus thirteen times in the plural form concerning the tabernacle, refers also to "nails" instead of "hooks."

EZEKIEL. The prophet's famous lament for Tyre contains information on the kinds of timber considered ideal for various ship's parts.[88] Strakes (?) (*luḥotaim*) were made of *brošim* from Snir. Doubt remains as to identity of this wood, but it is generally considered juniper.[89] The mast was made of Lebanese cedar, the oars of oak. The deck planking (?) (*kerašim*) was built of *bat-ašurim*—usually identified as cypress—from the "Isles of the Kittim" (i.e., Kition = Cyprus).[90]

In likening Tyre to a merchant ship, Ezekiel writes, "The elders of Byblos and her skilled men were in you, "caulking your seams" (*maḥazikai bidkeh*)."[91] There is another possible translation for this term, however: *maḥazikai* derives from the Hebrew root *ḥizek*, which means "to gird," "to strengthen," "to make fast," or "to tie";[92] *bidkeh* comes from *bedek*, which means "breach," "gap," "rent," "repair," or "overhaul."[93] Thus, the prophet may be describing shipwrights with expertise in lashed-ship construction, or he may be communicating the same action described by Herodotus in his portrayal of Egyptian Nile shipbuilding.

The Aegean

LINEAR B TEXTS. The term "shipbuilders" (*na-u-do-mo*) ap-pears in several Linear B texts.[94] This term heads PY Vn 865, which contains a list of twelve male names. In Na 568, a group of ship-builders is exempted from contrib-uting fifty units of flax. This is the most generous release from pay-ment in the entire series and may indicate a pressing need for ships experienced by the palace at Pylos. The term appears a third time on a fragmentary tablet from Knossos (KN U 736) in connection with 181 "oar straps" and ninety-three units of another item, the name of which is lost.[95]

PY Vn 46 and Vn 879 contain lists of construction materials in specific quantities. These were originally interpreted as timbers for use in the building of a Myce-naean structure.[96] H. Van Effen-terre suggests that these materials were actually destined for the con-struction of a ship.[97] The V series of texts from Pylos lack deter-minatives that would allow defi-nition of their contents and, thus, are open to multiple interpreta-tions. Van Effenterre's point of departure is the word *ka-pi-ni-ja*, which he relates to the later Greek σκάφος/σκάφη, meaning ship. He suggests that the word refers to a ship, or part of the ship, such as the hull (coque).[98] He then studies the numbers of each type of tim-ber listed and tries to make sense of them in comparison to elements of ship construction.

More recently, T. G. Palaima, together with ship reconstructors J. R. Steffy and F. M. Hocker, re-studied these texts and concluded that van Effenterre's interpretation is viable, although by no means proven.[99] They assume that the text refers to an average Mycenaean ship from the end of the Late Helladic IIIB period and approxi-mate its length to be in the ten-to-fifteen-meter range.

HOMER. The poet refers to oak, poplar, pine, and fir used in ship construction; masts and oars were made of fir.[100] The boat Odysseus built when he left Calypso was constructed with pegged mortise-and-tenon joinery.[101] In classical times, the Greek ships that amassed for the attack on Troy were believed to have been made of lashed construction.[102]

In relating Odysseus's blinding of Polyphémus, Homer gives this figurative description of the drill-ing of holes in a ship's hull: "They took the stake of olive-wood, sharp at the point, and thrust it into his eye, while I, throwing my weight upon it from above, whirled it round, as when a man bores a ship's timber with a drill, while those below keep it spinning with the thong, which they lay hold of by either end, and the drill runs around unceasingly."[103]

The Iconographic Evidence

In 1923 H. Lallemand dealt with the technical sense of the Egyptian word *mnḥ* in carpentry. Using P. Lacau's study of New Kingdom wooden sarcophagi, Lallemand brings examples of the various methods employed by the ancient Egyptians to connect pieces of wood:[104] lashing, pegs used to re-tain a carved tenon to a mortise, a freestanding wooden tenon used to connect two mortised pieces of wood and then held with pegs, and the assembly of small pieces of wood by means of pegs. He notes the use of mortise-and-tenon joints on the Dashur boats and rec-ognizes the same methods in the ship construction scene in the tomb of Tí.

The determinative of the word *mnḥ* is a mortising chisel:[105]

This tool, together with a wooden mallet, is repeatedly put in the hands of workers cutting mortises in shipbuilding scenes with the word *mnḫ* appearing next to them (Figs. 10.11, 13, 15–20, 22–23). Because the cutting of mortises was one of the main tasks in ships built with mortise-and-tenon joinery, it is hardly surprising that this is the most popular motif in scenes of shipbuilding in Egyptian art. Other tools are also depicted: adze, ax, ferule and lead, one- and two-handed saws, and a stick used to tighten lashings. Although men dubbing with adzes are more commonly depicted than sawing, recorded hull timbers indicate that the saw was a principal tool for Egyptian shipbuilders.[106]

Vessels constructed of wood joinery appear to have survived into this century in Africa. W. F. Edgerton quotes J. H. Breasted's description of descending the rapids at the Fourth Cataract in 1907 in a vessel that was built entirely with "wooden pegs."[107] The boat's hull contained no metal at all.[108]

Two forms of planked-ship construction are commonly illustrated in Egyptian iconography: internal lashing and *unpegged* mortise-and-tenon joinery. A single scene depicts a third type of construction: either *pegged* mortise-and-tenon joinery or, alternatively, the use of hull-penetrating treenails. The vast majority of ship construction scenes illustrates *unpegged* mortise-and-tenon joinery. A few of the most significant of these scenes are discussed below.[109]

Lashed Construction

TOMB OF NEFER. The most complete scene of a planked ship being lashed appears in the tomb of Nefer (probably Fifth Dynasty) (Fig. 10.9).[110] A hogging truss is used to keep the hull's planks at the proper tension while the ship is being launched.[111] One worker is shown tightening a rope in a manner familiar from scenes of papyrus raft-lashed construction (Fig. 10.10). Next to him, another pounds with a maul inside the hull. A similar action is depicted in a scene from the Fifth Dynasty tomb of Ptahhotep at Saqqara (Fig. 10.32).[112] These men are apparently pounding on a *rope* batten in order to compress it as they tighten the transverse lashings that go over it. This is evident when their actions are compared to T. Severin's description of the lashing of the *Sohar*, the ship he built to replicate the voyages of Sinbad.

Having connected the garboards to the keel, a thick rope batten (Severin calls it a "python") fabricated of coconut husks wrapped with string was inserted at the chine between the two timbers. Thick coir was then strung across the batten, and pairs of workers—one standing inside the hull, the other outside of it—lashed the hull: "Each pair worked at passing a strand of the finest-quality coir cord out through a hole in the plank, back through the opposite hole in the keel, round the python, and out again. There the outside man took a turn of the cord around his lever of stout wood, put his feet against the hull, leaned back and hauled the string as tight as he could. *On the inside, his partner tapped on the string to help it tighten, and pounded on the python with a mallet to compress the coconut fibers.*"[113]

There are differences between the methods of lashing used in an-

Figure 10.9. *A hogging truss is employed in a scene depicting the launching of a lashed-ship. In the stern, one worker tightens a lashing while a second man apparently pounds on a rope batten. From the tomb of Nefer at Saqqara. Probably Fifth Dynasty (from Moussa and Altenmüller 1971: pl. 19. © by the German Institute of Archaeology)*

Figure 10.10. Construction of papyrus rafts in the mastaba of Achethetep at Saqqara (Fifth Dynasty) (detail from Davies 1901: 13)

cient Egypt and those employed in the building of the *Sohar*. The latter used ligatures that penetrated the hull and followed the planking seams, a form of lashing unknown at present from ancient Egypt. The Cheops ship also had wooden battens in place of *Sohar's* coir "python" (Fig. 10.4: C). Nefer's scene must mean, however, that rope battens were employed in ancient Egypt. This scene reappears in another Old Kingdom tomb at Zawiet el Meitin.[114]

CHAMBER OF RAHOTEP. A planked ship in the shape of a papyrus raft is being lashed in the Fourth Dynasty chamber of Rahotep at Medum (Fig. 10.11).[115] To the right, a worker is chiseling mortises. In his left hand he holds a mortising chisel: his raised right hand is missing in a lacuna but presumably held a mallet. Next to him appears the term *mnḫ*. At left a worker dubs the hull with an adze. In the center of the craft two men lash the hull. The head and raised arm of the worker on the right are missing in the lacuna. Presumably, as in Nefer's scene, he was holding a maul or mallet and banging on a rope batten.

CHAMBER OF ATET. An almost identical, although badly mutilated, scene appears in the nearby chamber of Atet at Medum (Fig.

10.12).[116] In this wall painting, two ships are under construction. All that remains of the upper ship is the left part of the hull. A worker at left with a raised mallet in one hand is presumably intent on chiseling mortises. A laborer amidships holds a rope, while to his right a man's raised hand holding a mallet is all that is left of his coworker. Since the direction of the action is the rope lashing, presumably he is pounding the rope batten during the lashing process.

The bottom vessel is entirely obliterated. There remains only one worker dubbing the left extremity of the hull with his adze and the raised hand of a second worker holding coils of rope—identical to those held by the man lashing the ship in Rahotep's chamber.

Unpegged Mortise-and-Tenon Construction

TOMB OF TÍ. The Fifth Dynasty mastaba of Tí at Saqqara contains a painted relief that is the most detailed extant depiction of unpegged mortise-and-tenon ship construction from antiquity (Fig. 10.13).[117] Five ships are being built in three registers. In the following discussion, the hulls are referred to in this order:

Register I: Hull 4   Hull 5
Register II: Hull 3   Hull 2
Register III: Hull 1

Three additional phases of ship construction appear in the lowest register; three types of hulls are portrayed. J. Hornell believes the craft were expanded dugouts be-

Figure 10.11. Scene of lashed-ship construction from the chamber of Rahotep at Medum (Fourth Dynasty) (detail from Petrie 1892: pl. 11; courtesy of the Committee of the Egypt Exploration Society)

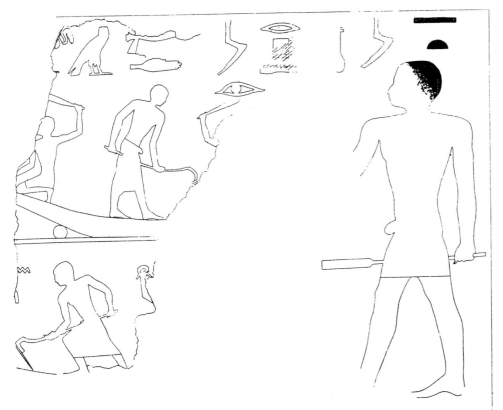

cause they are being dubbed with adzes.[118] Landström, more reasonably, considers them planked ships.[119] The sequence of ship construction is from the bottom register up. All the hulls are supported on blocks.

Dressing a log (Register III, left). A log is being dressed by two workers wielding axes; a third shipwright works the log with an adze (Fig. 10.14). Three bases of branches are visible.

Sawing a log or plank (Register III, right). A worker saws a log or plank in a vise (Fig. 10.15).[120] The height of the timber may have been shortened to fit it vertically into the register.

Mortising a plank (Register III, far right). Two workers, using mallets and mortising chisels, cut mortises into the top surface of a plank supported on two Y-shaped

Figure 10.12. Scene of lashed-ship construction from the chamber of Atet at Medum (Fourth Dynasty) (detail from Petrie 1892: pl. 25; courtesy of the Committee of the Egypt Exploration Society)

Figure 10.13. Ship construction scene from the tomb of Tí at Saqqara (Fifth Dynasty) (from Steindorff 1913: Taf. 119)

crutches (Fig. 10.15).[121] The mortises appear as small rectangles on the plank's upper side. Above the workers is the term *mnḫ*.

Hulls 1 and 2 show stages in the actual laying of a strake onto the hull:

Hull 1 (Register III, center). At center, a new strake is being installed onto the hull (Figs. 10.16–17). The workers are carefully aligning the mortise-and-tenon joints as a first step in attaching the plank. Under the orders of a (master?) shipwright, two men hammer the strake down with small cylindrical (stone?) weights. Two other men align the plank using a stick and a short length of rope. Four other workers are dubbing the hull with adzes. Tenons are visible in the space between the hull and the freshly laid plank.

Hull 2 (Register II, right). Having aligned the strake and made the necessary adjustments, two workers vigorously pound it into place with large, two-handled, biconical (wooden?) mauls (Fig. 10.18). A third figure standing outside the hull aligns the fit with a mortising chisel. Diagonals visible on this hull apparently represent scarfs.

Ferule and lead (Register II, center). These tools are held by a figure facing Hull 3 (Fig. 10.18). In a construction scene from the tomb of Mereruka, these are being used in the boat's construction process.[122]

Hull 3 (Register II, left). At left, two men with adzes dub the upper edge of the top strake while three men cut mortises in the upper planking (Fig. 10.19). Other workers dub the outside of the hull with adzes.

Hulls 4 and 5 are shown in the same stage in ship construction:

Hull 4 (Register I, left). This hull is papyriform (Fig. 10.20). Three workers cut mortises on the upper surface of the hull while an

Figure 10.14. Dressing a log in the ship construction scene from the tomb of Tí at Saqqara (Fifth Dynasty) (detail from Wilde 1953: pl. 129, © IFAO)

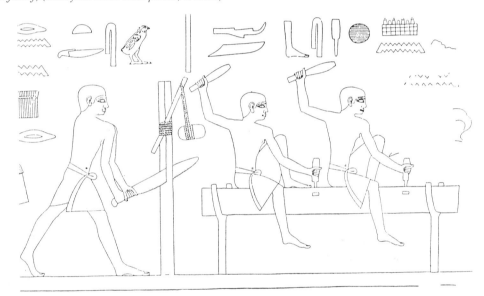

Figure 10.15. Sawing a log or plank and mortising a plank (detail from Wild 1953: pl. 129, © IFAO)

other works on a strake with an adze. Two laborers prepare poles: one cuts a straight pole with a saw while the other dubs a long bifurcated stanchion (?) with an adze. Beneath the hull, one worker uses a handsaw on the hull while two other men dub the hull with adzes.[123]

Hull 5 (Register I, right). The upper left and central parts of the ship have been destroyed (Fig. 10.21). Two men cut mortises in the

planking. Two men dub the outside of the hull with adzes.

TOMB OF KHNUMHOTEP. The short timbers of a ship under construction in the Twelfth Dynasty tomb of Khnumhotep at Beni Hassan match the "brick-like" manner of Egyptian shipbuilding described by Herodotus (Fig. 10.22).[124] This craft has been interpreted as being lashed because of the worker who is holding two ends of a rope.[125] This vessel too,

Figure 10.16. Hull 1: beginning the installation of a plank on the hull (detail from Wild 1953: pl. 129, © IFAO)

Figure 10.17. Hull 1: detail (from Steindorff 1913: Taf. 120)

however, is being built of wood joinery. Khnumhotep's worker is not lashing the ship: he is carrying out the same task as the man holding a rope in Tí's Hull 1, steadying a plank as it is laid onto the hull (Figs. 10.16–17). Note that the postures of men tying papyrus rafts are quite different (Fig. 10.10).

TOMBS OF ABBA (*Deir el Gebrawi and Thebes*). Perhaps the most unusual shipbuilding scene is one in the tomb of Abba, "Royal Chancellor" to Psammetichus I. This worthy decorated his tomb at Thebes with scenes that he had copied directly from the tomb of an earlier official, also named Abba, at Deir

el Gebrawi.[126] The earlier tomb dates to the Sixth Dynasty, the later to the seventh century B.C.; thus, the two tombs are separated by a span of almost two millennia. The inscriptions above the later scene are also derived from the earlier tomb with minor differences of wording and spelling.

Figure 10.18. Hull 2: final phase of installing a plank on the hull (detail from Wild 1953: pl. 129, © IFAO)

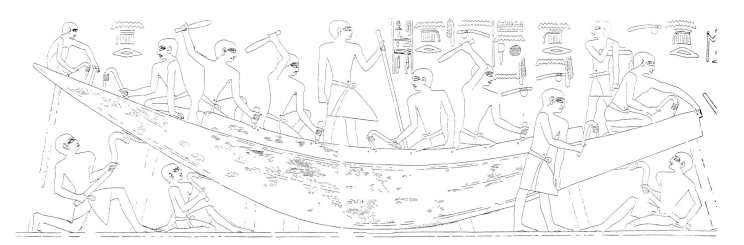

Figure 10.19. Hull 3 (detail from Wild 1953: pl. 129, © IFAO)

Figure 10.20. Hull 4 (detail from Wild 1953: pl. 128, © IFAO)

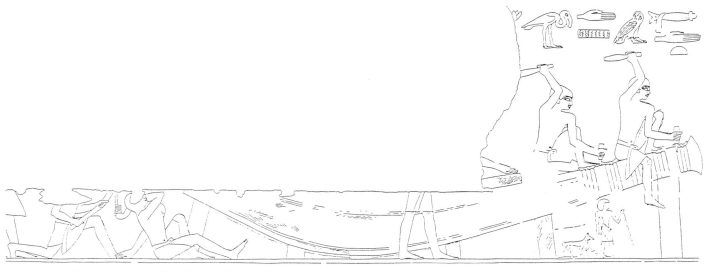

Figure 10.21. Hull 5 (detail from Wild 1953: pl. 128, © IFAO)

Figure 10.22. Ship-construction scene from the tomb of Khnumhotep at Beni Hassan (Twelfth Dynasty) (after Newberry 1893: pl. 29)

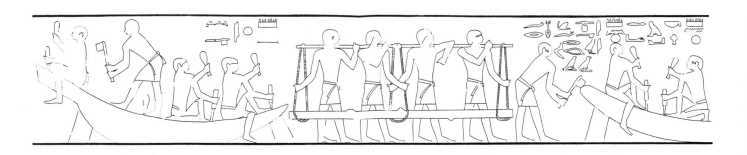

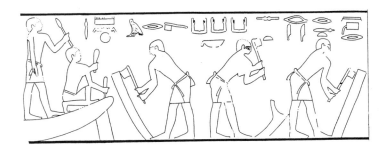

Figure 10.23. Register depicting shipbuilding in the tomb of Abba at Deir el Gebrawi (Sixth Dynasty) (from Davies 1902 (I): pls. 15–16)

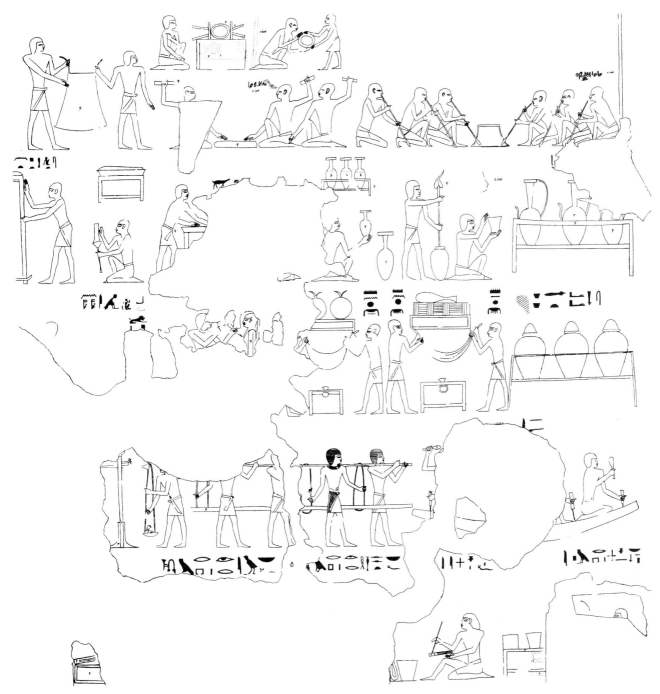

Figure 10.24. Workshop scene from the tomb of Abba (T. 36) at Thebes (Psammetichus I) (from Davies 1902 (I): pl. 24)

In the earlier scene, from Deir el Gebrawi, two ships are under construction (Fig. 10.23). Six workers cut mortises with mallets and chisels, while two others work on the hulls with axes. Between the two hulls, four workers carry a log supported by ropes looped around a pole that they shoulder. At right, three shipwrights wield axes. The worker at left seems to be fashion-

ing a curving frame; the central worker may be forming a knee from a tree trunk with a basal branch; the man at right works on a straight timber.

The later scene, from Thebes, is abbreviated (Fig. 10.24). On the left side of the fourth register, four workmen carry a log to a construction site.[127] At right, a ship is being worked by three shipwrights, all

of whom are cutting mortises into the upper planking with mallets and mortising chisels. Additional workers may have been situated in the now missing central portion of the vessel.

Pegged Mortise-and-Tenon or Treenail Construction?
TOMB OF QAHA. The Late Period Mataria wreck is the first—

and, for the present, the only—hull found in Egypt in which the hull was edge-joined with *pegged* mortise-and-tenon joinery. When was this variety of joinery first used on Egyptian hulls? Perhaps the answer is to be found in a wall painting depicting a shipbuilding scene from the tomb of Qaha (T. 360; Ramses II) at Deir el Medinah that contains three details of ship construction that are at present unique to it (Fig. 10.25):[128] amidships two men are using a bow-drill, to the left another man works with a two-handed mallet, and thirteen dots pock the hull. As noted above, the Egyptians seem to have avoided penetrating the hull in their normative forms of construction, both lashing and unpegged mortise-and-tenon joinery. Therefore, Qaha's scene must represent something quite foreign to usual Egyptian shipbuilding tradition.

The men drilling the holes and driving in the pegs are represented above the ship. With respect to Egyptian art conventions, they are to be understood as drilling the holes and driving the pegs *from inside the hull*. The drill is represented vertically. Again, this may

be only an artistic convention. It is similar, however, to the manner in which bowyers are depicted sawing the sides of ibex horns attached to primitive vises when in fact they are cutting the lateral and dorsal surfaces of the horn and would have stood at a ninety-degree angle to it.[129] Thus, the workmen may actually be drilling holes horizontally into the strakes.

The novel juxtaposition in the Qaha scene of a bow-drill, together with the two-handed mallet and the dots on the hull's exterior, suggests a new process or activity not previously connected in Egypt with ship construction (or at least not recorded graphically as such). But what sort of construction has the artist depicted for us?

One way to cut a mortise is to drill holes at either side and then chip away the intervening wood with a chisel and mallet. This explanation for the appearance of the bow-drill here seems unlikely, however, for the act of mortising was always shown in Egyptian shipbuilding scenes as being accomplished with only a mortising chisel and a mallet—never with a bow-drill (Figs. 10.11–13, 15–24).

There are two other possible explanations, though. The bow-drill could have been used to bore holes for treenails, which were then used to fasten the frames to the planking.[130] If this is what the artist is depicting, then the two-handled mallet is being used to drive in the treenails, the heads of which are represented by the dots. Alternatively, the men may be drilling holes for pegs that are being hammered into place with the mallet, locking the mortise-and-tenon joints into place. In this case, the dots portray the heads of pegs.

The dots are not aligned in opposing pairs across strake seams as one would expect of pegs used to lock mortise-and-tenon joinery, but neither do they conform to a pattern of framing treenails. The artist seems to be depicting the "impression" of multiple small heads piercing the hull, without aiming for accuracy. Thus, both interpretations are possible, although the fact that a two-handed mallet is better suited for hammering treenails than pegs favors the former interpretation.[131] Qaha's scene of pegged joinery is unique and appears late in the Pharaonic

Figure 10.25. Ship-construction scene from the tomb of Qaha at Deir el Medinah (Ramses II) (after Bruyère 1933: pl. 26, © IFAO, all rights reserved)

A

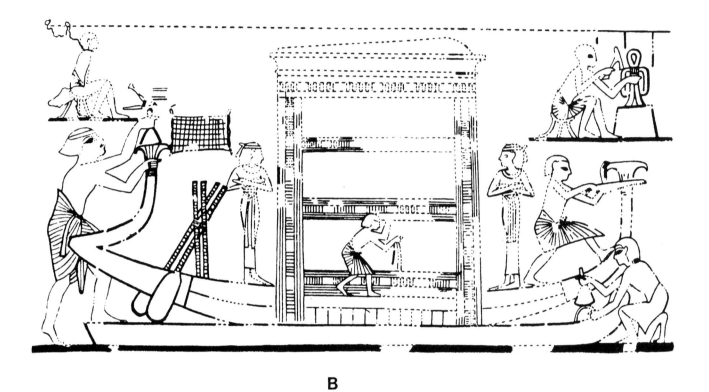

B

Figure 10.26. (A) Preparing the funerary accoutrements in the tomb of Ipy (T. 217) at Thebes (Ramses II); (B) detail of Ipy's funerary boat under construction (A from Wreszinski I: 369; B from Davies 1927: pl. 34; © , the Metropolitan Museum of Art, New York)

Figure 10.27. Ipy's funerary ship under construction (detail from Wreszinski I: 369)

period. It strongly suggests that the technique depicted there was foreign and only introduced into Egypt late in Pharaonic times.

Undefined Construction

TOMB OF IPY. Ipy's funerary boat, resting on its sled, receives its finishing touches from four workmen (T. 217, Ramses II) (Figs. 10.26–27).[132] It is possible that these are artisans instead of shipwrights and that Ipy's funerary boat was actually a large model, like those found at Lisht. The workman at left is pounding the papyrus umbel into place on top of the stern-post with a wide-headed mallet held upside down. The hands of the man at center are missing in a lacuna. A third workman pounds a staple into the front of the sled with a wide-headed mallet, again held upside down. A fourth artisan saws the lower part of the papyrus umbel with a handsaw. One-handed saws are uncommon in ship construction scenes (Fig. 10.20).

Discussion

Lashed Construction and the Transportation of Ships Overland

The ships used by the Egyptians on the Punt and Sinai runs were almost certainly of lashed construction, even in New Kingdom times. The Egyptian Red Sea coast is an extremely harsh, treeless area. R. O. Faulkner assumes that the ships on the Punt run in the New Kingdom were built at Thebes and then reached the Red Sea via a canal that was excavated in Wadi Tumilat.[133] P. E. Newberry, noting that there is no evidence for such a canal, was the first to suggest that ships on the Punt run were lashed.[134] As they were termed *Kbn* ships, he thought that they were built at Byblos and transported in

sections overland to the Red Sea port where they were rebuilt. However, the Wadi Gawasis inscriptions indicate that the vessels were constructed on the Nile.[135]

On Antefoker's stele at Wadi Gawasis, the ships he had built for the Punt run were termed "ships of (?) the dockyards of Koptos"; concerning their construction, however, Antefoker notes: "Lo, the herald Ameni son of Menthotpe was on the shore of the Great Green building these ships."[136] This must mean that the ships had been built originally on the Nile before being hauled overland and reassembled on the shores of the Red Sea.[137] Several other Egyptian sources refer to the overland route from Koptos through the Wadi Hammamat to the Red Sea, over which all nautical voyages to Punt or southern Sinai had to pass.[138] Presumably, these were also transversely lashed ships that could be taken apart for transport across the Eastern Desert.

Henu, an official who served Mentuhotep Sankhekere (Eleventh Dynasty), describes the building of a ship destined for Punt on the shore of the Red Sea:[139]

[My lord, life, prosperity], health! sent me to dispatch a ship to Punt to bring for him fresh myrrh from the sheiks over the Red Land, by reason of the fear of him in the highlands. Then I went forth from Koptos upon the road, which his majesty commanded me. . . .

I went forth with an army of 3,000 men. I made the road a river, and the Red Land (desert) a stretch of field, for I gave a leathern bottle, a carrying pole (*sts*), 2 jars of water and 20 loaves to each one among them every day. The asses were laden with sandals ⌈___ ___ ___ ___⌉.

Now I made 12 wells in the

bush, and two wells in Idehet (*Ydʒht*), 20 ⌈square⌉ cubits in one, and 31 ⌈square⌉ cubits in the other. I made another in Iheteb (*Yʒhtb*), 20 by 20 cubits on each side ⌈___ ___ ___ ___⌉.

Then I reached the (Red) Sea; then I made this ship, and I dispatched it with everything, when I had made for it a great oblation of cattle, bulls and ibexes.[140]

Now, after my return from the (Red) Sea, I executed the command of his majesty, and I brought for him all the gifts, which I had found in the regions of God's-Land. I returned through the ⌈valley⌉ of Hammamat, I brought for him august blocks for statues belonging to the temple. Never was brought down the like thereof for the king's court; never was done the like of this by any king's-confidant sent out since the time of the god.

Henu's three-thousand–man expedition can only be explained if they were needed as porters to transport the ship's precut timbers from Koptos to the Red Sea shore.

Khenty-khety-wer, an official under Amenemhet II, raised a stele in Wadi Gasus, in commemoration of a nautical expedition to Punt. The stele depicts Amenemhet II drinking to Min of Koptos, while below Khenty-khety-wer raises his arms in worship. An accompanying inscription states:

Giving divine praise and laudation to Horus ⌈_____⌉, to Min of Coptos, by the hereditary prince, count, wearer of the royal seal, the master of the judgement-hall Khentkhetwer (*Ḥnt-ḥt-wr*) after his arrival in safety from Punt; his army being with him, prosperous and healthy; and his ships having landed at Sewew (*Śʒww*). Year 28.[141]

Ramses III also describes a nautical expedition to Punt:[142]

I hewed great galleys with barges before them, manned with numerous crews, and attendants in great number; their captains of marines were with them, with inspectors and petty officers, to command them. They were laden with the products of Egypt without number, being in every number like ten-thousands. They were sent forth into the great sea of the inverted water,[143] they arrived at the countries of Punt, no mishap overtook them, safe and bearing terror. The galleys and the barges were laden with the products of God's-Land, consisting of all the strange marvels of their country: plentiful myrrh of Punt, laden by ten-thousands, without number. Their chief's children of God's-Land went before their tribute advancing to Egypt. They arrived in safety at the highland of Coptos; they landed in safety, bearing the things which they brought. They were loaded, on the land-journey, upon asses and upon men; and loaded into vessels upon the Nile, (at) the haven of Coptos. They were sent forward down-stream and arrived amid festivity, and brought (some) of the tribute into the (royal) presence like marvels.

There are a number of references in antiquity to ships being taken apart for transport overland.[144] Diodorus Siculus reports that Semiramis sent for shipwrights from Phoenicia, Syria, Cyprus, and other places and ordered them to "build vessels that might be taken asunder and conveyed from place to place wherever she pleased." Alexander's ships on the Euphrates were brought in sections from the Mediterranean and rebuilt on that river.

Thutmose III's Barkal Stele records entire boats being carried overland. During his eighth campaign (thirty-third year), Thutmose transported vessels to enable him to ford the Euphrates to engage Naharin: "When my majesty crossed over to the marshes of Asia, I had many ships of cedar built on the mountains of God's Land near the Lady of Byblos. They were placed on chariots, with cattle drawing (them). They journeyed in [front of] my majesty, in order to cross that great river which lies between this foreign country and Naharin."[145]

Craft constructed of unpegged mortise-and-tenon joinery could conceivably have been taken apart, although with great difficulty. It is unlikely, however, that the Egyptians ever used ships built in this manner for open-sea voyaging. With nothing to hold the tenons securely in place, the incessant movement of waves and storms would soon have loosened the joinery, opening the ship's seams.[146]

This leaves open the possibility of using "slips" inserted into the mortise on either side of the tenon (as in the Lisht timbers) for a ship that was meant to be taken apart. It is doubtful that this form of construction would have been efficient enough to hold the planking together in sea conditions. Therefore, to allow the ships to be assembled and disassembled repeatedly, the vessels used by the Egyptians in the Red Sea were almost certainly transversely lashed. Since Hatshepsut's ships show no evidence of external sewing, they must have been internally transversely lashed, like the Cheops ships and the Lisht timbers (Fig. 10.4). The mortised wood fragments found at Wadi Gawasis also suggest the use of *unpegged* mortise-and-tenon joinery used to seat the planking for lashing, as in the

Cheops boat. The manner in which the two funerary ships of Cheops were found, stripped apart for interment, may reveal the procedure used when transporting the ships to and from the Red Sea coast.[147]

On the Evolution of Pegged Mortise-and-Tenon Construction

How and where did pegged mortise-and-tenon joinery on Mediterranean seagoing vessels originate? Although this subject must remain conjectural, there are several possible clues.

All ancient ships built using mortise-and-tenon joinery were constructed "shell first." *And yet, "shell first" construction is not a requirement of the mortise-and-tenon method.* As L. Basch notes, the Nemi ship's deck was built "skeleton first" using edge joinery.[148] This may hint at a possible direction of inquiry. Edgerton points out that whenever joinery and lashing exist together, lashing must have evolved first.[149] "Shell-first," or "shell-based," construction is a requirement in the assembling of sewn and lashed ships, however, for frames cannot be inserted before the hull is lashed. Severin's comments on the construction of the *Sohar* are again illuminating in this regard: "The ship had to be constructed like an eggshell; that is, we would have to put the planks in place and form the complex curves of the hull before we were able to fit the inside supporting ribs. The reason for this apparently roundabout technique was simple—*we could not stitch the planks on the inside if there were ribs in the way.*"[150]

Fastenings are sometimes translated into different materials as a form of ship construction evolves. For example, Hornell notes that in Sudanese Nilotic craft, iron nails had replaced wooden mortise-

and-tenon joinery but continued to carry out the same function.[151] Is it possible that pegged mortise-and-tenon joinery evolved from a specific type of lashed construction?

In one form of lashing the strakes are edge-joined with wooden pegs, while the rope holes themselves penetrate the hull. After the lashing has been completed, the holes are plugged with short wooden pegs driven into them *from inside the hull*, and the rope on the outside of the hull is then cut off.[152] This form of construction is found in the Mediterranean Sea on the Bon Porté, Giglio, and Gela wrecks, all of which date to the sixth century B.C.[153] The *mtepe* of the Lamu Archipelago of East Africa was

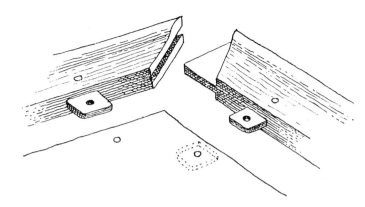

Figure 10.29. Detail of pegged *mortise-and-tenon joints connecting frame to table* (from *Ricketts 1960: 530 fig. 229: 1; courtesy British School of Archaeology, Jerusalem*)

also built in this manner. Writes Hornell: "When the sewing was completed, pegs were driven into the holes from within to secure the stitches and to prevent leakage; this had the added advantage that it permitted those parts of the stitching which appeared on the outside to be cut away in order to reduce surface friction."[154]

Such wedged stitches have several points in their favor, as J. F. Coates points out:

> By clamping ligatures in their holes, not only can the stretched parts of stitches be loaded to breaking point, but the loosening of those parts which are UN-loaded (i.e. diagonals that are NOT stretched by the sheer load on the seam) is prevented from spreading to parts carrying load, causing the stitching as a whole to slip. Sufficient clamping can easily be achieved by pegs driven into stitch holes, as has been widely practised. It can be calculated that a peg or wedge driven in until its grain is crushed by pressure in the hole, can generate a clamping force sufficient when the ligature is pulled round a right angled bend (the end of a hole), to sustain its breaking stress. Similarly, a ligature of uncrushed diameter one fifth of the plank thickness can be effectively locked by a peg if it reaches 0.8 or more through the plank thickness and, again, is crushed across its grain. Thinner ligatures can be thus effectively locked by shorter pegs.

Locking pegs enable symmetrical zig-zag, or helical stitching to resist shearing forces be-

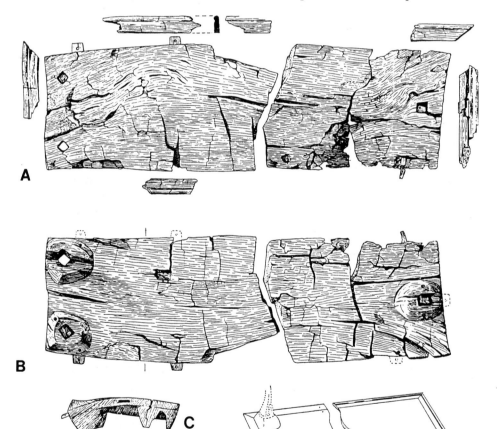

Figure 10.28. Wood table constructed with pegged mortise-and-tenon joinery found in Tomb H at Jericho (Middle Bronze IIB): (A) top; (B) underside; (C) elevation of end; (D) section; (E) reconstruction of underside (from Kenyon 1960: 462 fig. 198; courtesy British School of Archaeology, Jerusalem)

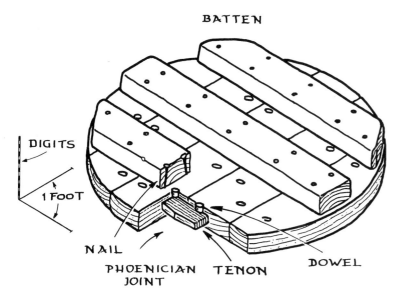

BATTEN

DIGITS

1 FOOT

NAIL

PHOENICIAN JOINT   TENON   DOWEL

Figure 10.30. Schematic reconstruction of Cato's oil-press disk (orbis olearium) *with "Phoenician joints" (courtesy A. W. Sleeswyk)*

tween planks. Such stitching has been found in the sixth Century ships at Bon Porté, with a peg in every stitch hole. This type of stitching cannot be effective without pegs.[155]

Note that the structural concept of this form of sewn construction is identical to that of pegged mortise-and-tenon joinery. In the former, the internal side of the rope stitching acts as a tenon held in place by pegs. At times, wooden dowels in mortises are used to hold the planks in position.[156]

In classical antiquity sewn, or lashed, vessels were considered ancient. Perhaps this type of "pegged-sewn construction with tenons" considerably predates the sixth century B.C. in the Mediterranean, and perhaps pegged mortise-and-tenon joinery evolved from it when someone pegged the tenons and did away with the ligatures.

Pegged mortise-and-tenon joinery is preferable to pegged sewing because sewn ships must be oiled and repaired repeatedly. Thus, by doing basically the same amount of cutting and drilling, the shipwright created a much more eco-

nomical craft. This reconstruction of events might also explain the Mediterranean tradition of driving the locking pegs *from inside the hull* (Fig. 10.25).[157] Alternatively, this phenomenon may have occurred because by driving the pegs from inside the hull, the smaller grain-end is presented to the water.[158]

Where, then, might pegged mortise-and-tenon joinery on seagoing ships have originated? As we have seen, it does not seem to have been an Egyptian innovation. The evolution of ship construction was a slow process. The knowledge of a type of joinery in a culture's carpentry repertoire does not imply *a priori* that it was used for shipbuilding in that country. Indeed, in Egypt there is no correlation between the knowledge of pegged mortise-and-tenon joinery in carpentry and its use in shipbuilding. If Qaha's artist depicted *pegged* mortise-and-tenon joinery, then this form of fabrication appears in Egypt at a time when there is evidence for strong Syro-Canaanite influence on Egyptian ship construction.[159] Might the Egyptians have inherited this tradition from Syro-Canaanite shipwrights?

The earliest recorded evidence for pegged mortise-and-tenon joinery on the Syro-Canaanite littoral is a Middle Bronze II table found in Tomb H–6 at Jericho (Figs. 10.28–29).[160] If the ships Thutmose III built near Byblos were made of pegged mortise-and-tenon joinery instead of lashed, it would explain why they were not taken apart for the difficult haul overland.

There is another clue that points in this direction. The Romans termed pegged mortise-and-tenon joinery "Phoenician joints," perhaps because they adopted this form of construction from their Punic (West Phoenician) foes (Fig. 10.30).[161]

These considerations, although admittedly far from conclusive, suggest an early Syro-Canaanite connection with pegged mortise-and-tenon joinery construction on seagoing ships.

Keels on Seagoing Ships in the Late Bronze Age
As we have seen, Hatshepsut's Punt ships strongly resemble a type of hull commonly known from Eighteenth Dynasty models of Nile traveling ships.[162] Was this latter class of boat used for deepwater seafaring during the Eighteenth Dynasty and later? Indeed, Landström has suggested that these ships had actual keels.[163]

A model patterned after this ship variety found at Byblos raises the interesting possibility that such vessels were frequenting that port (Figs. 3.16–17).[164] It may be argued that this model could have been a local copy of an Egyptian wooden model that somehow found its way to Byblos.[165] This, however, is unlikely since all the wooden Egyptian models of this ship type known to date have hulls made out of solid blocks of wood. *The artisan who created this model must have seen an actual ship of this sort at Byblos.* Otherwise, it is difficult to explain his knowledge of the ship's internal construction.

The Byblos model clearly shows a massive keel-like structure inside its hull. This element projects outward at bow and stern but becomes flush with the hull toward the center of the ship in the same manner as do the ship models from the tombs of Amenhotep II and Tutankhamen (Figs. 2.19–23). Landström attributes this to a desire to have the models stand upright on a flat surface.[166] I think not, for the same element is depicted on Hatshepsut's Punt ships in painted relief, where this reasoning does not apply.

This raises some fascinating questions concerning the construction of these ships: did they have keels? And what, then, constitutes a keel? If Hatshepsut's ships were built with keels, then why did the Egyptians apparently take the added precaution of using a hogging truss? It appears that Hatshepsut's ships did have a "developing" form of keel, notwithstanding the hogging truss.[167] This form of keel, or "proto-keel," which projects primarily inside the hull, might be considered strictly an Egyptian development were it not for clues suggesting that this same type of primarily internal spine may have been used on the ships of other countries as well during the Late Bronze Age.[168]

The detailed Cypriot ship model from Tomb 2B at Kazaphani shows no evidence of a keel on its exterior surface. But a narrow molded strip along the model's centerline may represent the internal projection of the keel above the level of the garboards (Fig. 4.5: C: A).[169] Several models found in the Aegean region also exhibit this characteristic. The most illustrative of these is a Late Helladic IIIC

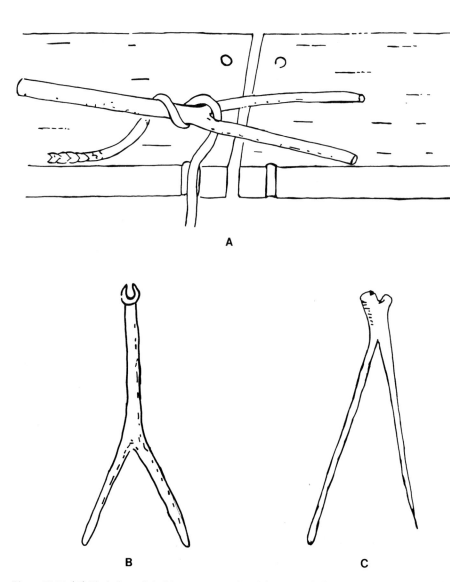

A

B   C

Figure 10.31. (A) *The* keke, *a forked instrument used to tighten seam lashings on sewn canoes in the Cook Islands;* (B) keke *from Taumotu Archipelago;* (C) *device for tightening lashings of sewn canoes in the Society Islands (after Hornell 1975: 175 fig. 112, 58 fig. 39: b2, 143 fig. 92: a3)*

Figure 10.32. *A wooden stick is being used by a shipwright while building a papyrus raft in the tomb of Ptahhotep at Saqqara (Fifth Dynasty) (from Servin 1948: 65 fig. 9,* © *IFAO, all rights reserved)*

terra-cotta model recently discovered at Kynos.[170] On its exterior, dark brown painted lines accentuate the keel, the sheer, and the stempost. Inside the hull, however, the keel is further stressed by the addition of a molded strip. Similarly, a model fragment from Tiryns dated to the Late Helladic IIIB period embellishes the keel with a molded strip (Fig. 7.46). The two small models from Tanagra have frames and a keel painted inside the hull (Figs. 7.39, 41).[171] No mention is made of whether the keel is shown on the exterior of the hulls. At Uluburun, the keel-plank juts primarily up inside the hull, projecting only minimally beneath the hull. This confirms what the iconographic evidence suggests: that on at least some Late Bronze Age seagoing ships, keels/keel-planks jutted primarily up, inside the hull.

Sticks for Tightening Lashings
A device for tightening lashings is a necessary tool in all sewn or lashed forms of ship construction. This may take the form of a stout piece of wood like those used in the building of the *Sohar*.[172] Often, however, they are forked sticks, like those recorded by Hornell in the Pacific Ocean (Fig. 10.31). One such device appears in a scene in which a wooden platform is being lashed to a papyrus raft in the tomb of Ptahhotep (Fig. 10.32).[173] Another is used by a worker in the tomb of Puimre (T. 39, Thutmose III) to tighten the floor lashings of a chariot (Fig. 10.33). Presumably, they were also used in the construction of contemporary Egyptian transversely lashed seagoing ships.

Mortise-and-Tenon Construction in the Aegean
L. Morgan notes that the extensive use of timber in Minoan and Cycladic ashlar masonry teaches

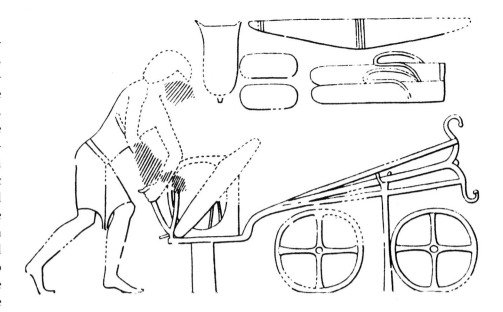

Figure 10.33. Detail of a chariot under construction in the tomb of Puimre (T. 39) at Thebes (Thutmose III) (from Davies 1922: pl. 23; ©, the Metropolitan Museum of Art, New York)

us about Aegean woodworking techniques that may have been used in shipbuilding.[174] Wooden clamps and dowels were employed.[175] Mortises for dovetail-shaped clamps appear almost exclusively at Knossos and came into use toward the end of the Middle Minoan period. Square or round mortises, cut or drilled into the upper surfaces of ashlar blocks, were meant for wooden tenons. These were used primarily to join stone to wood, particularly to seat wooden window frames on sills of ashlar blocks. The earliest date for their use is also Middle Minoan IB.

In the "West House" at Thera, plaster casts of holes revealed the use of planks and long wooden pegs in the building's construction.[176] The transverse pegs were 50 to 60 centimeters long and 3 to 5 centimeters in diameter. The planks were about 3 centimeters thick. One plank measured 45 by 28 centimeters; another, of trapezoidal shape, was 28 centimeters wide with long sides measuring 46 and 50 centimeters respectively. Wooden rods, 3 to 7 centimeters thick, were also placed transversely between floor beams in the construction of build-

ings at Thera.[177] The plaster cast of a bed found at Thera has at least one unpegged tenoned joint.[178]

I am not aware of any evidence for a knowledge of *pegged* mortise-and-tenon joinery in the Aegean. From the above considerations, we may conclude that the Minoan culture was acquainted with mortise-and-tenon joinery. Evidence for the use of this form of joinery in Aegean ship construction, however, is lacking at present.[179]

Finally, no discussion of Aegean Bronze Age woodworking would be complete without a reference to the impressive two-handled saws known from Minoan Crete. Saws up to 1.7 meters long with widths between 20 to 30 centimeters were discovered in the palaces of Knossos and Kato Zakro as well as at Hagia Triada.[180]

APPENDIX:
Did Hatshepsut's Punt Ships Have Keels?

BY FREDERICK M. HOCKER

The question has been raised of whether several representations of watercraft from the New Kingdom depict vessels with keels. If so, these are the earliest indications of a major advance in ship construction. Earlier Egyptian vessels seem to have relied on a keel plank, central strake, or, as the Cheops barge shows, a broad, heavy bottom made up of three relatively wide, thick strakes. Evidence for the development of the keel in the rest of the eastern Mediterranean basin is lacking until the late fourteenth century B.C. and the Uluburun wreck. This site provides archaeological evidence of a keel, or keel-like member, in an isolated bit of hull remains thought to lie at the original centerline of the ship (Fig. 10.2).[1] This keel is a heavy beam of substantial molded depth, part of which projects upward, above the inboard face of the garboards, as do the central strakes of the Dashur boats. The difference in thickness between the Dashur central strake and garboards is in some places negligible, however.[2]

In order to determine whether the structure represented on the relief of Hatshepsut's Punt ships at Deir el Bahri, on models from the tombs of Amenhotep II and Tut-

ankhamen, and on the Byblos model are in fact keels, two questions must be answered:

- What defines a keel?
- Can the represented structures function in this way?

I would define a keel as a centerline timber, outboard of the frames, of sufficient cross-sectional area and attachment to the rest of the hull to offer significant longitudinal strength and stiffness to the vessel. Normally, this means a beam at least as deep as it is wide, fastened to either the garboards, the frames, or both. Timbers of substantially greater breadth than depth are generally called keel planks, since they may offer a point of attachment for other timbers (such as posts and frames) but do not possess enough rigidity on their own to qualify as keels. Between keels and keel planks is a gray area, where breadth exceeds depth but depth is still considerably greater than planking thickness. Keels normally project below the exterior surface of the planking and provide resistance to lateral motion (leeway) in addition to strength, but this is not always the case.

In the case of the Hatshepsut ships, the artist has shown a line

that apparently delineates the join between the round, planked portion of the hull and the flat blade of the stem- sternpost. This line, similar to a rabbet line or bearding line, continues down to the waterline in many cases but gradually approaches the line representing the exterior limit of the hull. The impression is of a keel projecting below the planking at the ends but disappearing toward amidships. This interpretation is more or less confirmed by carved models from the tombs of Amenhotep II and Tutankhamen, in which the blade of the stem- sternpost continues to protrude below the planking near the ends but gradually disappears amidships. A similar effect can be seen in medieval cogs, in which the hooks, the backbone timbers at the ends, extend below the planking but the keel plank projects very little.

It would be hard to deny that the Punt ships of Hatshepsut have some sort of backbone structure that includes a centerline member of substantial depth, at least at the ends. I suspect that this timber is also quite robust amidships but that it projects inboard, like the upper portion of the Uluburun keel and the keel-like timber seen in the Byblos model. The question that remains is how thoroughly this member is attached to the rest of the structure. Although no direct evidence exists, common sense and the general traditions of Egyptian shipbuilding argue for mortise-and-tenon joints (probably unpegged, but there is no way of knowing) between the keel and garboards.

One argument against the use of keels in these ships is the hogging truss, which is also depicted. If a keel offers longitudinal strength, why should a hogging truss be necessary? This is not a major problem, in my view. A keel may provide substantial longitudinal strength and stiffness, but it is not sufficient by itself: there must be other timbers, working together, to form a perfectly rigid structure. In the case of Egyptian ships, there is reason to believe that one aspect of hull structure—framing—was relatively poorly developed (even in this century, frameless vessels of moderate size were used on the Nile). Perhaps also the keel (or proto-keel) was a recent development in Hatshepsut's time, and so its use and advantages were not yet fully appreciated. The history of technology is full of examples of older technology used alongside innovations until the new ideas had won the confidence of the user. Another maritime example is the introduction of the sternpost rudder into the Mediterranean in the Middle Ages. For nearly a century, many ships were equipped with both quarter rudders (the old technology) and sternpost rudders (the new).

If a short answer is needed, then yes, most of Hatshepsut's ships had keels, but they were not yet fully developed.

CHAPTER 11

Propulsion

Before the introduction of motorized water transport in the nineteenth century, seagoing ships were propelled by manpower or by using the inherent energy of the weather. Once man learned to harness the wind, it became a significant form of ship propulsion. Even with today's modern technology, "turbo sails" are being considered to harness wind power and to cut fuel costs on motorized transport.[1] The ability—or lack thereof—to utilize wind power had a profound influence on sea routes and navigation in antiquity.

Paddles and Oars

The earliest seagoing vessels were paddled: rowing was a later development. The first evidence for the rowing of seagoing ships appears on those of Sahure and Unas (Figs. 2.2–3, 5, 7). Paddling, however, continued into the latter part of the Bronze Age on small craft and in cultic use (Figs. 6.13, 23: A, 24, 42).[2]

The rowing of Hatshepsut's Punt ships has attracted scholarly attention. G. A. Ballard argues that Hatshepsut's vessels were rowed with long sweeps because the oarsmen are standing up to pull on their oars (Figs. 2.15, 18).[3] He theo-

rizes that the men stood near the ships' longitudinal median line but were foreshortened by the Egyptian artist.

C. D. Jarrett-Bell used the four positions depicted at Deir el Bahri in the scenes of the voyage to Punt, a procession on the Nile, and the moving of the obelisk barge to reconstruct a single entire stroke.[4] At the beginning of the stroke the oarsmen sit leaning forward, with their oars at a forty-degree angle from the vertical (Fig. 11.1: A). In the next stage they are still sitting and leaning forward, but with their oars now at an angle of twenty-

eight degrees (Fig. 11.1: B). They then stand up and lean backward with the oars at a fifteen-degree angle (Figs. 2.25; 11.1: C). In the final phase the oarsmen stand erect, with the inboard arm pressed across the chest and the oar at a nine-degree angle (Fig. 11.1: D). Jarrett-Bell concludes that the oars were turned sideways on the return stroke and never left the water, resulting in a short, choppy stroke.[5]

One advantage of this kind of stroke is that it gives additional room inboard, which is an important consideration if the cargo was

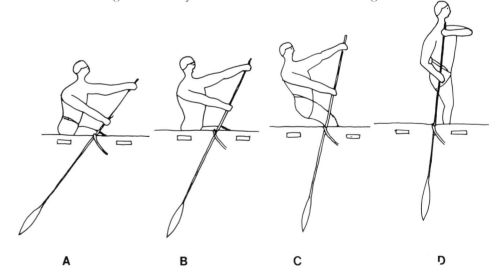

A   B   C   D

Figure 11.1. The four positions of oarsmen in the Deir el Bahri reliefs (after Jarrett-Bell 1930: 12 fig. 1)

carried on deck.[6] B. Landström, however, points out that Egyptian models complete with oarsmen show the oars lifted high from the water, suggesting that rowing was done in the normal manner: he therefore considers these postures to be the result of artistic convention.[7]

Rowlocks were used in Egypt by the end of the Old Kingdom.[8] The oars on Hatshepsut's Punt ships, however, were worked against grommets (Fig. 2.24). These are also seen on ships taking part in a cultic procession at Deir el Bahri.[9]

Sails

During the entire Bronze Age the sail used by the Mediterranean cultures, with some variations, was one that was stretched between a yard and a boom. The yard in its lowered position (and the boom at all times) were held in place by lifts connected to the mast cap. The lifts were one of the most conspicuous elements of this rig and almost always appeared in iconographic depictions of ships carrying this type of rig. The boom was generally lashed to the mast in a fixed position. The sail was furled by lowering the yard to the boom. This sort of rig is reproduced in the greatest detail on Hatshepsut's Punt ships (Figs. 2.11, 15–18).

The concept of a sail used to move a vessel may have originated on the Nile in Predynastic times when people noticed, perhaps for the first time, the propulsive power of wind on shields placed in Gerzean ships.[10] R. Le Baron Bowen suggests that the boom was a carryover from those times, representing the shield's lower frame. The earliest known representation of an actual sail dates to the Late Gerzean period (Fig. 11.2).[11] Square sails still exist, or existed in the recent past, on primitive craft throughout the world.[12]

Kenamun's depiction of Syro-Canaanite ships shows small lines hanging down from the boom, which may be toggles (Figs. 3.3–6). Toggles found on post-Bronze Age wrecks are thought to have been used as part of an antiluffing device permanently attached to the leeches of sails for the quick attachment and removal of lines.[13] If these objects on the Kenamun ships are indeed toggles, then they must have had another purpose since they are connected to the boom: perhaps they were used to wrap the sail when it was in the furled position. Alternatively, they may represent tassels similar to those seen on Herihor's royal galley (Fig. 11.7).

The sail could not be taken in on this type of rig: like the later lateen rig, in order to reduce sail it was necessary to remove the sail and replace it with a smaller one.[14] This is illustrated in the Middle Kingdom tomb of Amenemhet at Beni Hassan, where two ships towing a funerary barge are virtually identical in every detail—with the notable exception of the sail (Fig. 11.3). The forward ship (A) has a square sail twice the height of the short, rectangular sail carried by the ship (B) that follows it.

On Hatshepsut's Punt ships cables, tightened with staves, are wound around either side of the mast's base where it intersects the hogging truss (Figs. 2.15–18, 33–34; 11.4). Because no staves to tighten the hogging trusses are shown on these ships, R. O. Faulkner suggests that the cables served to tighten the hogging truss.[15] This conclusion is unlikely for the following reasons:
• Similar arrangements appear on Old Kingdom seagoing *and* river craft. The latter do not have hogging trusses (Figs. 2.5, 7, 10).[16] These cables were used for lateral strengthening on Old Kingdom craft and were tightened by staves thrust through them and lashed

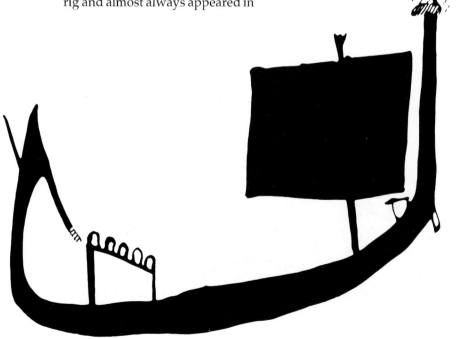

Figure 11.2. The earliest known depiction of a sail, painted on a Gerzean jar (after Frankfort 1924: pl. 13)

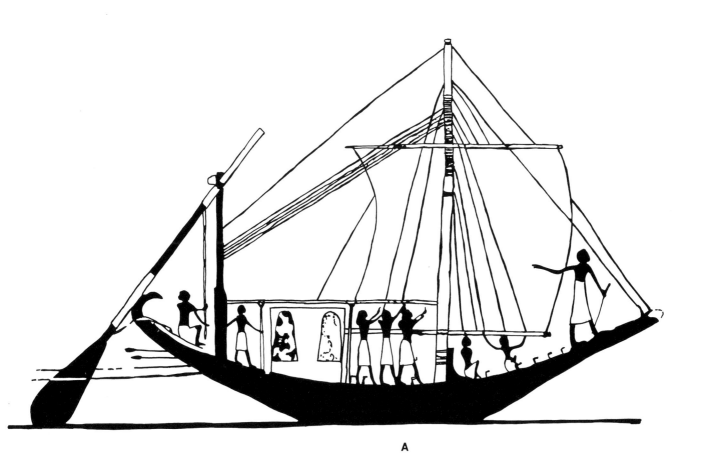

A

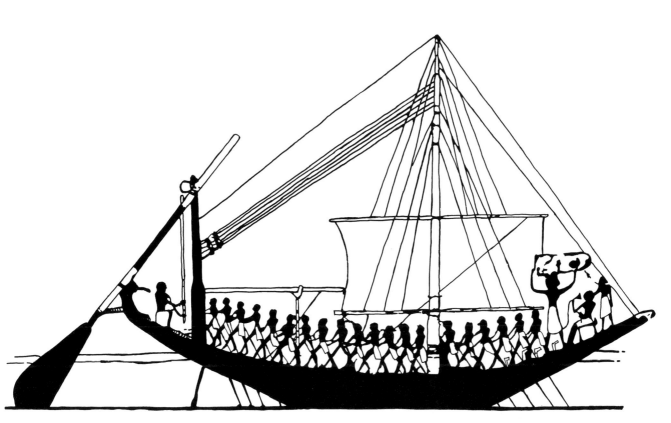

B

Figure 11.3. The sail could not be taken in on the boom-footed rig. In order to reduce sail, it was necessary to replace the entire sail with a smaller one. This is demonstrated in the tomb of Amenemhet at Beni Hassan, where two virtually identical ships towing a funerary barge carry sails of different sizes (Twelfth Dynasty) (after Newberry 1893: pl. 14)

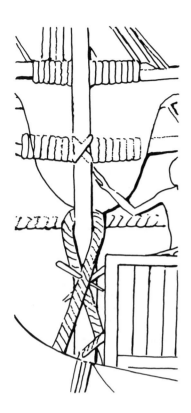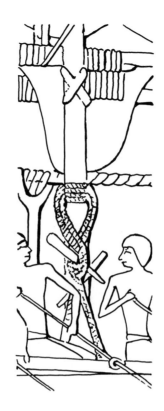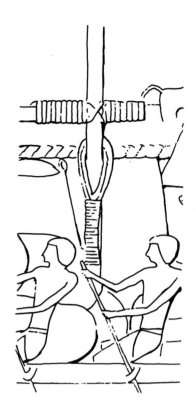

Figure 11.4. Detail of massive cables wrapped around the masts of three of Hatshepsut's Punt ships (after Naville 1898: pls. 72, 75)

down. There is a natural progression from these lateral cables to those appearing on various depictions of Late Bronze Age seagoing ships.

• Fragments of a painted relief from the Eleventh Dynasty temple at Deir el Bahri bear ships' parts on which cables are held in place with thick belaying pins and connected to the hull. This is accomplished by means of a U-shaped apparatus that is identical to ones used to hold down the lateral lashings on the ships of Unas (Figs. 2.5, 7; 11.5).[17] Since the cables on the Eleventh Dynasty ships are not tensed by twisting, they may represent an experimental method of tightening the cable, perhaps something akin to a Spanish windlass. This experiment apparently was not successful, for the device does not appear again.

• If Faulkner's theory was correct, as the truss was tightened it would have moved down the mast, taking on a characteristic V-shape with its center at the mast and its high ends at the two nearest crutches: ⌐‾‾ ∨ ‾‾¬. The Egyptian artists would have shown this as the normal shape of the truss, but they invariably portrayed the hogging truss as a horizontal line from stem to stern: ⌐‾‾‾‾‾‾¬. Either the artists did not include the tightening staves in the relief (although they existed on the actual ships) or the hogging truss was being tightened in another way.

• Similar lashings appear on the mast of Kenamun's Syro-Canaanite ships, which do not carry hogging trusses (Fig. 3.4).

What purpose, then, did these cables serve? Normally, a mast requires shrouds to support it laterally. Shrouds are not depicted at Deir el Bahri or on Kenamun's ships.[18] This is apparently neither accidental nor due to artistic conventions. Indeed, shrouds would have been extremely difficult to use with a boom-footed rig. Perhaps the massive cables supported the mast laterally, in place of shrouds.

Cypriot models give additional evidence for lateral cables. The Kazaphani model is perforated amidships by a circular maststep (Fig. 4.5: C: B); on either side of this is a molded hook-shaped object (Fig. 4.5: C: D–E). Model A50 from Maroni *Zarukas* has horizontal convex ledges with vertical piercing located amidships on either side of the hull's interior (Fig. 4.7: B–C). These may have served the same function as the hooks in the Kazaphani model. These hooks and lateral-pierced projections perhaps represent some form of internal structure used to attach such lateral cables to the ship's hull. The lateral cables were better suited to the bipod and tripod masts on which they originally evolved. But with the introduction of the pole mast, this solution continued in use. Although far from ideal, it may have been enough if the sail was used only when running before the wind.

The boom-footed sail was superseded by an innovative system from which the boom had disappeared. Lines, called "brails," are attached at intervals to the foot of the sail and brought vertically up it through "brailing rings" or "brail fairleads" sewn to the sail. The lines are carried up over the yard and then brought astern in a bunch. This type of sail, which works on the same principle as Venetian blinds, is furled by pulling on the brails—resulting in a considerable saving of time, effort, and manpower.

This rig appears in the Mediterranean at the end of the Late Bronze Age. At Medinet Habu, the Egyptian (as well as the Sea Peoples') ships are outfitted with brailed rigs (Figs. 2.35–42; 8.3–8, 10–12, 14). The Aegean evidence is particularly interesting. Ship depictions from the Late Helladic/Late Minoan IIIB (thirteenth century B.C.) on which it is possible to determine the type of rig used (based either on sail shape or the mast cap) invariably show boom-footed rigs, or a mast cap with multiple rings for supporting such a rig (Figs. 6.26, 7.19, 28: A, D). All decipherable known ship portrayals from the Late Helladic IIIC suggest the use of a brailed rig (Figs. 7.8: A, 17, 21, 25, 29).

Experimentation with brails, however, began at least a century before they became common in the Mediterranean. A transitional phase between the two varieties of rig is preserved in several Egyptian depictions. In the tomb of Neferhotep (T. 50) at Thebes, which dates to the reign of Horemheb (ca. 1323–1295 B.C.), one ship has a yard and a boom. Its sail, however, is

A

B

Figure 11.5. Part of ships' rigging (lateral strengthening cables [?]) depicted on relief fragments from the Eleventh Dynasty temple at Deir el Bahri (from Naville and Hall 1913: pl. 13: 7; courtesy of the Committee of the Egypt Exploration Society)

furled to the yard in the manner typical of the brailed rig (Fig. 11.6).

Similarly, in a scene from the temple of Khonsu at Karnak, the royal galley of Herihor, which is taking part in the Opet ceremony, has a rig sporting a yard and boom. The sail is shown in the act of being furled to the yard by members of the crew (Fig. 11.7). The yard has been lowered to half-mast. Ten crewmen stand on the boom or climb on the lifts as they furl the sail in a manner reminiscent of that used on square-riggers during the Age of Sail. In the center, two men work lifts that continue vertically up the mast behind the yard (Fig. 11.7: A–B). These are probably the same lifts that held the tips of the yard in tension and which had to be released as the yard was lowered with the halyards.

Figure 11.6. This funerary barque bears a yard and boom, but the sail has been raised to the yard in a manner normal for the boomless brailed rig (tomb of Neferhotep [T. 50] at Thebes; Horemheb) (after Vandier 1969: 946 fig. 355)

Other men haul on lines that cross over the yard (Fig. 11.7: C–D). These may be brails, or perhaps hand-holds meant for the crew as they furled the sail. Another crew member, who holds a rope in his right hand, seems to be securing the furled sail (Fig. 11.7: E). Herihor's scene dates to ca. 1076–1074 B.C., long after the brailed rig was commonly used.[19] It is thus an example of a tradi-

tional ship element continuing in cultic use long after it disappeared from working ships.

This evidence for a state of experimentation with sails in Egypt does not necessarily mean that the brailed rig was invented there. Indeed, it seems that the Egyptians followed, instead of led, in this development. L. Casson notes that the brailed rig does not seem to have developed in Egypt, nor does

it appear to have originated in the Aegean.[20] It seems that both Egypt and the Aegean adopted this rig from outside their borders. But from where?

R. D. Barnett suggests that the Sea Peoples may have been influenced in their shipbuilding by the Syro-Canaanites.[21] It is likely that the brailed rig also originated on the Syro-Canaanite littoral. This possibility gains support from two considerations. On both the Egyptian and Sea Peoples' galleys at Medinet Habu (along with the brailed rig), there are two additional elements that may hint at its source. First, the yards curve down at their tips; and second, the masts are surmounted by crow's nests. Although both of these factors are foreign to Egypt and the Aegean, they are characteristic of earlier Syro-Canaanite craft from the Late Bronze Age with which these peoples had maritime interconnections.

Yards depicted with down-curving tips are exceptionally rare on Egyptian vessels portrayed in Egyptian art. They do, however, appear on several river boats from the fifteenth-century Theban tombs

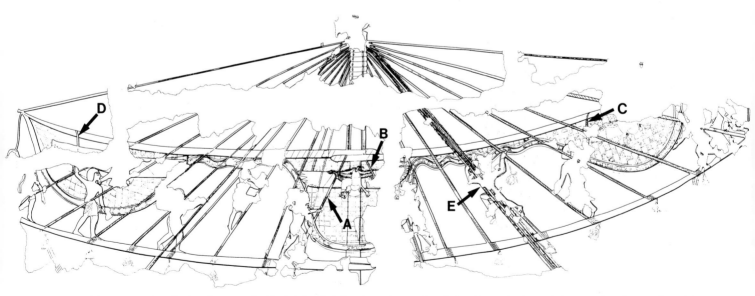

Figure 11.7. The sail of Herihor's royal galley is being furled to the yard, even though the ship carries the typical Bronze Age rig, complete with boom and multiple lifts (detail from SKHC: pl. 20 [Scenes of King Herihor in the Court: The Temple of Khonsu I: Plates 1–110, the University of Chicago, Oriental Institute Publications, 1979. © The University of Chicago. All rights reserved])

of Rechmire (T. 100), Menna (T. 69), Amenemhet (T. 82), and Sennefer (T. 96B).[22] These, however, are the exceptions and not the rule. Furthermore, these representations may be artists' variations on a single drawing taken from a common source, or copybook, used in the preparation of Theban tomb decorations.[23] If so, their number is misleading.

This rarity of illustrations of yards with downward-curving tips in portrayals of indigenous Egyptian ships—the country with by far the most comprehensive record of ship development in the Bronze Age—argues against them being in common use there. Downcurving yards, however, do appear on representations of Syro-Canaanite ships from the tomb of Nebamun, on the thirteenth-century scaraboid from Ugarit, and on the schematic graffito of a ship from Tell Abu Hawam (Figs. 3.7–9, 12–13).

Kamose (the founder of the Eighteenth Dynasty), during his struggle to expel the Hyksos, was forced to place his lookouts on the cabins of his ships because they were not equipped with crow's nests. No other Egyptian ships before the rule of Ramses III are depicted with one.[24] A crow's nest is carried by a Syro-Canaanite ship in the tomb of Kenamun, and in other ships of that scene lookouts appear, although the crow's nests are hidden in the rigging (Figs. 3.3–6). The mast of the Syro-Canaanite ship painted in the tomb of Nebamun is surmounted by a rectangle that may also represent a crow's nest; alternately, it can be interpreted as a mast cap (Fig. 3.8–9).[25]

But if the brailed rig originated in the Syro-Canaanite littoral, why do we not have any evidence for it? The fact that there are no known representations of Syro-Canaanite ships postdating Amenhotep III may explain why this type of yard

appears first in depictions of Egyptian ships. As described above, there are only two detailed depictions of Syro-Canaanite vessels in the Late Bronze Age. The later of these, in the tomb of Kenamun, dates to the reign of Amenhotep III, from a quarter- to a half-century before the painting in the tomb of Neferhotep:

Reign	Dates	Syro-Canaanite	Egypt	Sea Peoples
Amenhotep II	1427–1400 B.C.	Nebamun		
Amenhotep III	1390–1352 B.C.	Kenamun		
Horemheb	1323–1295 B.C.		Neferhotep	
Ramses III	1184–1153 B.C.		Medinet Habu	Medinet Habu

Another consideration is that the ships depicted in the tomb of Nebamun and Kenamun may have been based on an illustration from a copybook that considerably predated the reign of Amenhotep III, and perhaps even that of Amenhotep II.

Sails were made primarily of linen, perhaps sewn together in patches (Figs. 6.21, 7.22).[26] Linen is made from flax, particularly from the parts of the plant that transport water.[27] This results in a fiber that is strong when wet and stands up well in damp conditions.[28] No remnants of sails have been found on the many shipwrecks excavated in the Mediterranean to date. This may result from the small percentage of waxes and lignin contained in processed linen.[29] A sail with a wooden brail fairlead still attached, which has been carbon dated to circa 150 B.C. ± 50, is the oldest known sail to date. Its final use in antiquity had been to wrap a mummy.[30]

In Classical times, brail fairleads were usually made of lead or wood and often had a protrusion with one or two piercings to allow them to be sewn to the sail.[31] Three

bronze rings, each with an additional external loop attached to its outer surface, were found at Enkomi and identified as pieces of horse accoutrement. They may, however, represent an early form of brail fairlead (Fig. 11.8).[32] Two of the rings were found in the *Trésor de bronzes* and date to the twelfth century B.C.; the third comes from an unknown context.

Like modern-day spinnakers, the square sail was designed primarily for traveling before the wind. When winds were contrary, crews either bided their time at anchor or took to their oars. The ability of a ship to sail to windward is influenced by numerous factors: the type of rigging used, the hull design, and the ability of the hull to prevent drift to leeward, to name just a few. Scholars speculate as to how far into the wind (if at all) a ship could sail with a square rig. Ballard and C. V. Sølver theorize that the sail was not capable of using a wind much more than four points off the stern.[33] A wind any farther abeam, in their opinion, would cause the craft to move too far to leeward. Le Baron Bowen and Casson consider the square sail capable of sailing as close as seven points into the wind.[34] That means against a northerly wind, a ship headed north could do no better than west by north on one leg and east by north on the other.

The best data on sailing capabilities come from the *Kyrenia II* replica. Using a brailed sail, with-

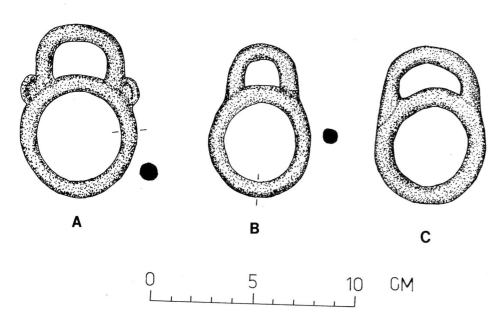

0   5   10   CM

Figure 11.8. Bronze rings—perhaps brail fairleads—from Enkomi: A and C are from the Trésor de bronzes *and may date to the latter half of the twelfth century* B.C.; *the context of B is unknown (after Catling 1964: fig. 23: 5–6 and pl. 48: h)*

out a boom, the ship was capable of sailing fifty to sixty degrees (that is, four to five points) off the direction of the wind.[35] A boom would have severely hampered her ability to sail to windward, however.

There is little information on the speed at which the different types of ships in the Late Bronze Age might have sailed. As in all periods, this depended on the sort of ship and sail used.[36] Two Amarna texts may contain evidence of ships' speed. Rib-Addi, the beleaguered king of Byblos, repeatedly requests that archers arrive at Byblos within the space of two months.[37] He considered this a reasonable time for his message to reach Egypt and for the archers to be organized, dispatched, and transported to Byblos, perhaps by ship.

Knots and Rope

Rope and knots were an integral part of seafaring throughout the ages. Yet today, little research has been done on the types and uses of knots in antiquity.[38] Perhaps the earliest known ones are the simple overhand knots in cordage dating to the seventh millennium from the Prepottery Neolithic B deposit in the Naḥal Ḥemar Cave in the Judean Desert.[39]

The most detailed portrayals of seagoing craft, such as Hatshepsut's Punt ships, show loops where the lifts are tied to the yards. This suggests that the knots were tied for a quick release (Figs. 2.30, 31, 33–34).[40] Rope was made from a variety of fibers in antiquity:[41] date palm,[42] Doum (Dum) palm,[43] esparto grass,[44] flax,[45] grass or reed (?),[46] halfa grass,[47] hemp,[48] and papyrus.[49]

Middle and New Kingdom models of Nile ships with their rigging preserved demonstrate a number of recognizable knots, primarily hitches and lashings.[50] The use of a specific knot on a ship model does not necessarily mean that it was used on actual ships;

however, the knots on models do indicate, at the very least, that such knots were known.

❧   ❧   ❧

The boom-footed square sail had a profound effect on the seafaring capabilities and sea routes used in the Bronze Age. For example, the oft-stated ties between the Minoan (and now the Cycladic) culture and Libya assume direct two-way traffic between the Aegean and Africa. This is an illusion, for ships could not normally sail across the Mediterranean directly from south to north against the predominantly northwest wind. Unable to sail effectively into the wind, the circuit of the Mediterranean was necessarily counterclockwise.

The unwieldiness of the boom-footed rig precluded the use of shrouds. In their place in the Late Bronze Age—at least on the seagoing ships of Egypt, the Syro-Canaanite littoral, and Cyprus—a lateral cable system stabilized the lower part of the mast. How successful this system was in countering lateral forces on ships' masts requires additional study.

It is not clear how these cables were fastened inside the hull. Were there internal constructions for this purpose as suggested by the Cypriot evidence? This lack of shrouds, coupled with the apparent preference for having the keel rise upward into the interior of the hull instead of protrude below the hull (where it would have served to prevent leeward drift), suggest that in the Bronze Age, seafarers were not overly concerned with winds from far off the stern. It also appears that the boom-footed rig was used only, or at least primarily, with following winds.[51]

CHAPTER 12

Anchors

Anchors are to a ship what brakes are to a car; and just as a car needs brakes, a seagoing ship must carry some form of anchoring device. In the eastern Mediterranean during the Bronze Age, these consisted of pierced stones. Through the ages, anchors were left on the sea bottom where, as a result of modern underwater archaeological exploration and sport diving, they are now being discovered in large numbers in some parts of the Mediterranean.

The British researcher Honor Frost first brought attention to the significance of the pierced stones that litter the Mediterranean seabed and are also found on Levantine land sites.[1] She pointed out that by studying anchors on stratified land sites, anchors of diagnostic shape—found out of archaeological context on the sea floor—can be dated and their nationality defined.

The study of anchors is important to nautical archaeology for several reasons. An anchor on the seabed assumes the passing of a ship.[2] Thus, if the anchor type belonging to a specific nationality can be defined, then finding a trail of that kind of anchor in the sea must signify a route used by ships of that nation.

Similarly, anchors of definable origins found in foreign precincts are a valuable indication of direct sea contact. Perhaps the most important contribution of the study of anchors is the theoretical possibility of identifying the home port of a wreck based on the typology of its stone anchors.[3] Finally, since anchors are the main security for a storm-tossed ship, they have always had a cultic significance. Stone anchors found in cultic contexts can teach us about ancient religious practices.

Numerous anchor sites exist under the Mediterranean in areas that modern shipping would normally avoid.[4] Apparently, these anchorages were necessary for ships that could not sail into the wind and, therefore, were forced to wait for following winds.

Frost defines three varieties of pierced stone anchors:[5]
• "Sand-anchors" are small, flat stones with additional holes for taking wooden pieces that function like the arms of the later wooden and metal anchors. The stone's weight is minimal and is not an anchoring factor. These anchors are particularly suited for grasping a sandy bottom.
• "Weight-anchors" have a single hole for the hawser; they anchor a craft solely by their weight. These anchors may tend to drag on a flat and sandy bottom.
• "Composite-anchors" are heavier than sand-anchors but like them have additional piercings for one or two wooden "arms." These anchors hold the bottom with their weight and arms.

All datable Early Bronze Age anchors are weight-anchors.[6] Composite- and weight-anchors are found together in Middle Bronze and Late Bronze Age contexts at Ugarit and Kition. Thus, the weight-anchor preceded the composite-anchor but continued in use alongside it. G. Käpitan suggests a progression of stone anchors originating from amorphous stones lashed to a rope and developing into pierced stones (Fig. 12.1).

In this chapter the various kinds of evidence (textual, iconographic, and archaeological) for stone anchors and their facsimiles will be discussed. The archaeological evidence is organized in geographical order. This is followed by an overview of stone anchors found on Mediterranean wrecks. Finally, several aspects of anchor study are discussed.

The Textual Evidence

The Gilgamesh epic mentions "Things of Stone" that were used in some way by Urshanabi, the boatman of Utnapishtim (the Mesopotamian Noah), for crossing the "Waters of Death."[7] Urshanabi claims that Gilgamesh has broken these objects. Frost suggests that the "Things of Stone" are stone anchors.[8]

KTU 4.689 is an Ugaritic text that lists a ship's equipment. Among the gear is a *mšlḥ ḥdṯ,* a term that M. Heltzer has tentatively identified as "a new anchor," as well as a rope (*ḥbl*).[9]

Herodotus describes the use of stone anchor-like "braking devices" used by Nile ships in his day:

These boats cannot move upstream unless a brisk breeze continue; they are towed from the bank; but downstream they are thus managed: they have a raft made of tamarisk wood, fastened together with matting of reeds, and a pierced stone of about two talents weight; the raft is let go to float down ahead of the boat, made fast to it by a rope, and the stone is made fast also by a rope to the after part of the boat. So, driven by the current, the raft floats swiftly and tows the "baris" (which is the name of these boats), and the stone dragging behind on the river bottom keeps the boat's course straight.[10]

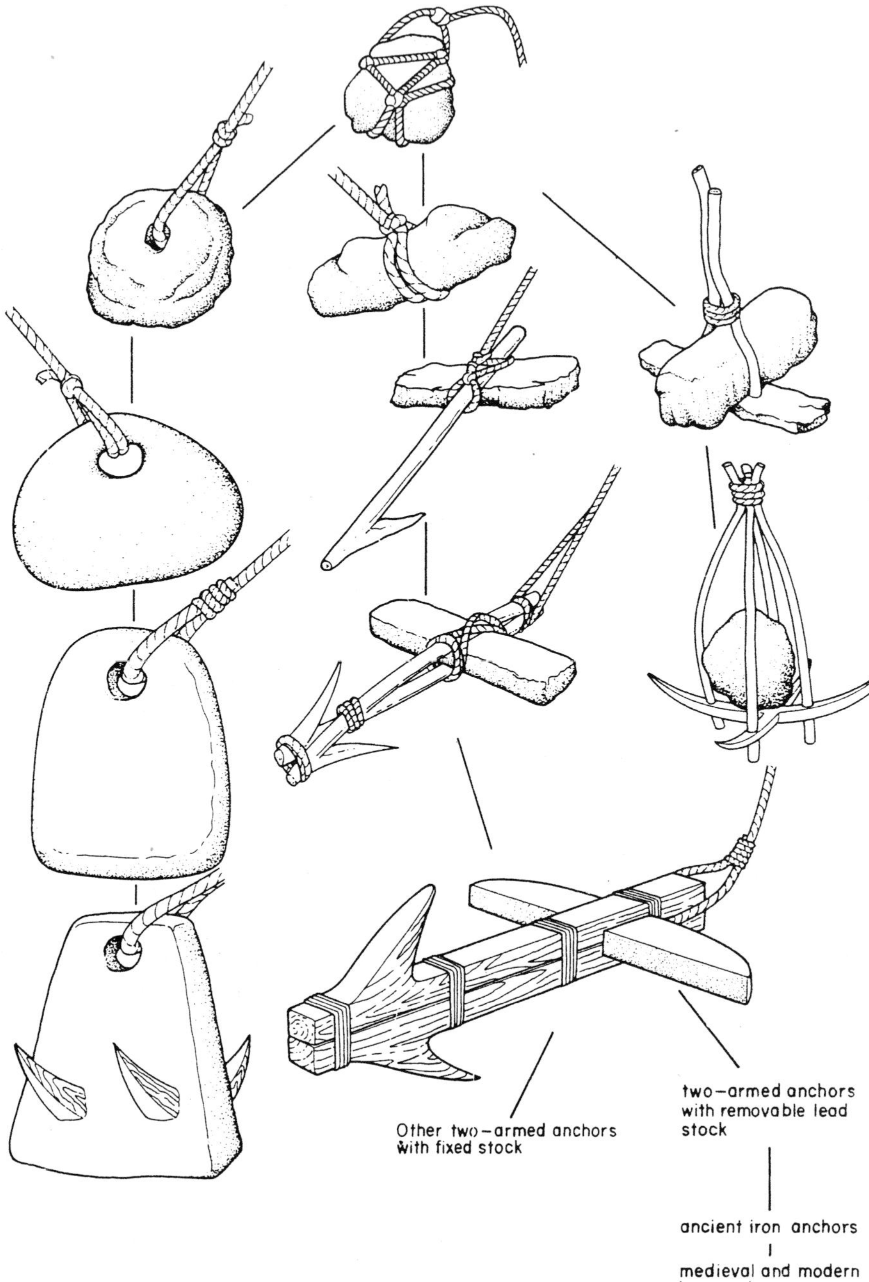

The Iconographic Evidence

Stone anchors appear on representations of the seagoing ships of Sahure and Unas (Figs. 2.5; 12.2: A–B).[11] The anchors have a markedly triangular shape. This has caused some confusion, and, on occasion, they have been mistakenly identified as Byblian anchors.[12] They have domed tops, however, a feature typical of Egyptian anchors. Apical rope grooves, another feature common to Egyptian anchors as well as to those of other lands, are not portrayed. Perhaps this is the result of a lack of artistic detail.

The anchors of Sahure and Unas are shown standing upright. This may be attributable to artistic license; anchors stationed in the bows were (at least on occasion) placed upright, however. The better-made large stone anchors often have flat bottoms. Even in mild seas, however, such anchors must have been locked firmly into place against the ship's sheerstrakes to prevent them from coming loose and causing damage.

Otherwise well-made anchors

two-armed anchors
with removable lead
stock

Other two-armed anchors
with fixed stock

ancient iron anchors

medieval and modern
iron anchors

Figure 12.1. Diagram illustrating the probable development of ancient anchors (from Kapitän 1984: 34 fig. 2)

A

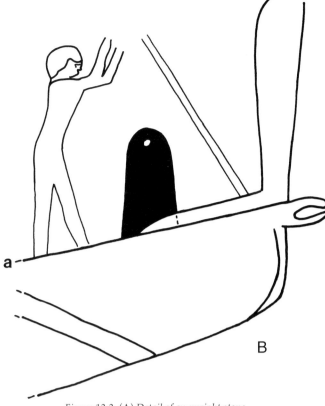

B

Figure 12.2. (A) *Detail of an upright stone anchor, with hawser-hole indicated, in the bow of a seagoing ship depicted in the causeway of Unas at Saqqara (Fifth Dynasty);* (B) *line drawing of* A *with anchor emphasized in black. The anchor is assumed to be standing on a deck parallel to line* a (photo and drawing by the author)

have an asymmetrical shape, as do the Wadi Gawasis anchors (Figs. 12.10, 11: A). They seem to "lean" to one side. This feature was apparently traceable to a desire for the anchor to stand vertically on a slanting bow or stern deck. This phenomenon is evident from studying an anchor in the bow of one of Unas's ships. It is assumed to stand on a baseline (Fig. 12.2: B: a). When the anchor is placed on a horizontal line, it takes on the asymmetrical appearance exhibited by the Wadi Gawasis anchors (Fig. 12.3: A–B). This tendency is not solely an Egyptian idiosyncrasy: it also appears on a number of Syro-Canaanite (?) anchors found in Israeli waters (Figs. 12.3: C, 54).[13]

One manner in which stone anchors were raised and lowered is graphically demonstrated on two Cypriot jugs (Figs. 8.41: A, C; 12.4). In one case, the hawser is passed

through a sheave in the mast cap. The second depiction is more complicated and was interpreted by Frost as a boom.[14] More recently, Frost suggests that Bronze Age ships had derrick-arms or "cargo-derricks" attached to the mast for maneuvering anchors.[15] Alternatively, the artist may have intended an "exploded view" of the operation and, for reasons of composition, preferred to depict the angle where the hawser went through a sheave in the masthead, above and to the right of it.

Egyptian hieroglyphics have no word for anchor: the Book of the Dead refers only to mooring posts.[16] Stone anchor-shaped objects appearing on Egyptian river craft are usually interpreted as offerings of bread.[17] Indeed, if these objects were used as "braking stones" like those described by Herodotus, then they should have

been positioned on the stern deck. The objects, however, are consistently displayed at the bow.

Frost and L. Basch believe that stone anchors were not used in antiquity on the Nile.[18] The discovery of a group of stone anchors (including one of a distinctly Egyptian type) at Mirgissa at the Second Cataract and at Tell Basta indicates that, at least occasionally, stone anchors were indeed used on the Nile in pharaonic times. A scene from the Sixth Dynasty tomb of Zau at Deir el Gebrawi may hint at the use of an anchor (Fig. 12.5).[19] In it, a crew member is coiling a rope depicted in the vertical plane to show its characteristic form. The rope goes over the bow and vertically straight into the water. N. de

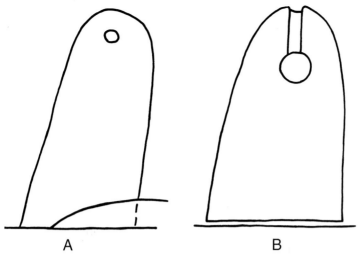

Figure 12.3. Asymmetrical stone anchors: (A) the anchor depicted at the bow of one of Unas's seagoing ships is asymmetrical when placed on a horizontal line; (B) asymmetrical anchor from Mersa Gawasis (Twelfth Dynasty); (C) asymmetrical anchor found underwater in the ancient harbor of Dor (A after photo by the author; B after Sayed 1977: 164 fig. 6; C, photo by the author; courtesy Israel Antiquities Authority)

G. Davies identifies this as an anchor cable.[20] The use of stone anchors on the Nile might explain the function of enigmatic objects, usually called "bowsprits," that appear on Middle Kingdom ship models; these may have been fairleads for an anchor rope.[21]

C. Boreux interprets another Old Kingdom scene from the mastaba of Akhihotep-heri as depicting a man raising a stone anchor at the stern of a Nile boat.[22] Basch suggests that this scene portrays a water pitcher being lowered into the river to be filled.[23] It is difficult to determine which of these two interpretations is correct. In New Kingdom images, crew members are normally shown dipping their containers into the river while bending over the caprails.[24] No ropes are used.

Iron anchors are recorded on the Nile by the third century A.D., and on the Nile today, ships carry iron anchors.[25]

The Archaeological Evidence

Egypt

The earliest datable Egyptian anchors belong to the Fifth Dynasty.[26] An anchor in the mastaba of Kehotep at Abusir acted as the lintel of the false door (Fig. 12.6: A).[27] The anchor's base carries the following inscription: "The sole friend, the beloved in the presence of [pharaoh's name erased], Kehotep." Other stone anchors have been reported from the mastabas of Mereruka and Ptahhotep as well as in

Figure 12.4. The raising of a round stone anchor is depicted on a seventh-century B.C. jug from Cyprus (from Frost 1963B: monochrome pl. 7 [opp. p. 54])

Figure 12.5. Ship scene from the tomb of Zau at Deir el Gabrawi (Sixth Dynasty) (from Davies 1902: pl. 7)

the funerary temple of the Fifth Dynasty pharaoh Userkaf (Fig. 12.6: B–C).[28]

Egyptian anchors have two diagnostic characteristics: an apical rope groove near the hawser hole and an L-shaped basal hole for a second rope. Although the rope groove is found on stone anchors of other Bronze Age nationalities, the basal hole remains unique to Egypt.

The shape of the typical Egyptian stone anchor was first defined by Frost on the basis of a single anchor from the "Sacred Enclosure" at Byblos with a *nfr* hieroglyph incised on it (Figs. 12.7, 28: 21).[29] The rope groove is particularly deep. Frost notes that the chisel marks are so well preserved that the anchor was probably

never used at sea. It weighs 188.5 kilograms. Another Egyptian anchor was found in the Temple of Baal at Ugarit (Fig. 12.33: 11).[30]

Anchors of Middle Kingdom date found at the Red Sea site of Wadi Gawasis are important because they conclusively establish the standard Egyptian anchor shape. The shrine-stele of Ankhow was constructed of seven anchors (Figs. 12.8–11).[31] Four anchors, with oval tops and tubular rope holes, form the base of the shrine; the three truncated anchors constituting the shrine's sides still bear the L-shaped basal holes. One of these is a blind hole (Fig. 12.9: B [upper left]). The anchors weigh about 250 kilograms each.

Frost suggests that the seven anchors in Ankhow's shrine rep-

resented seven ships used in the expedition.[32] She argues that the anchors' total weight of 1,750 kilograms would be prohibitively heavy for a single ship. The anchors from Naveh Yam and Uluburun, however, indicate that large ships normally did carry many heavy anchors.

Two hundred meters west of Ankhow's shrine, another anchor served as the pedestal for the contemporaneous stele of Antefoker (Fig. 12.12).[33] This anchor lacks the typical L-shaped hole and apical

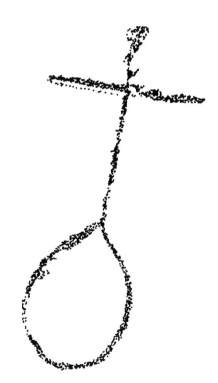

Figure 12.7. Nfr pictograph carved on the Egyptian anchor found at Byblos (after Frost 1969B: pl. 5)

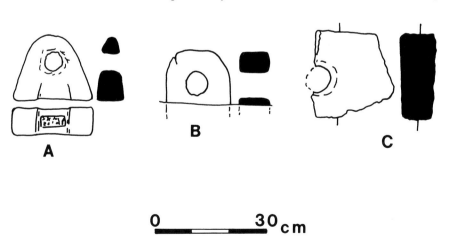

0   30 cm

Figure 12.6. (A) Anchor fragment that served as the lintel of the false door in the tomb of Kehotep at Abusir (Fifth Dynasty); (B) anchor implanted in the floor of the ceremonial chapel in the tomb of Mereruka at Saqqara (Sixth Dynasty); (C) probable anchor fragment from the tomb of Ptahhotep at Saqqara (Fifth Dynasty) (after Frost 1979: 141 fig. 1, 143 figs. 2, 2c)

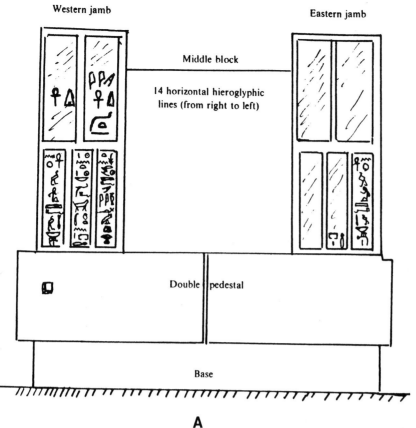

A

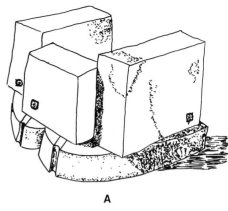

A

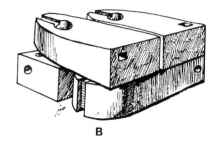

B

Figure 12.9. The stele of Ankhow from Wadi Gawasis on the shore of the Red Sea (Sesostris I) (NTS): (A) rear view; (B) diagram of the four anchors forming the stele's pedestal (A after Sayed 1977: 157 fig. 2; B from Sayed 1980: 155 fig. 1)

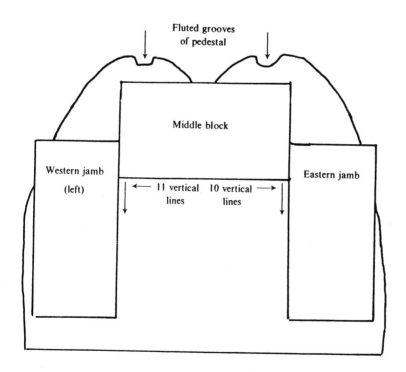

B

Figure 12.8. The stele of Ankhow from Wadi Gawasis on the shore of the Red Sea (Sesostris I): (A) front view; (B) plan view (from Sayed 1977: 158 fig. 3, 159 fig. 4 [A. M. A. H. Sayad, "Discovery of the Site of the Twelfth Dynasty Port at Wadi Gawasis on the Red Sea Shore (Preliminary Report on the Excavations of the Faculty of Arts, University of Alexandria, in the Eastern Desert of Egypt—March, 1976)," Rd'É 29: 140–78])

groove but has eight notches on its four vertical edges. The channel cut into the top surface was a later addition to secure the standing stele.

Two unfinished anchors and a third, smaller, anchor were found on the northern slope of the entrance to Wadi Gawasis.[34] The hawser-hole of one anchor was blind, suggesting that at least some of the anchors were prepared at the site. A twelfth anchor, broken and slightly smaller than the others, was found at the port proper of Mersa Gawasis.[35]

Seven stone anchors were discovered at the Egyptian fortress of Mirgissa on the Second Cataract of the Nile.[36] The site dates to the Middle Kingdom through the end of the Second Intermediate period. At least four of the anchors (which

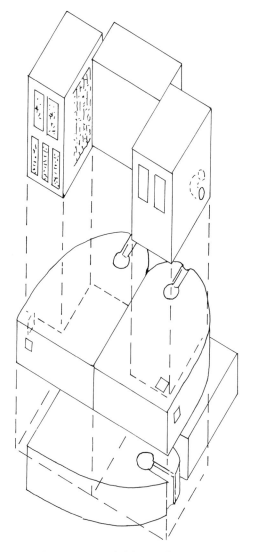

Figure 12.10. Exploded view of the seven anchors comprising Ankhow's stele (after Frost 1979: 148 fig. 3e)

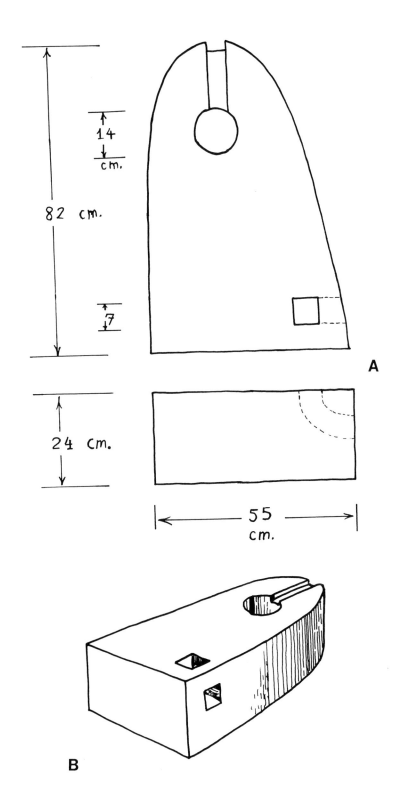

A

B

Figure 12.11. The easternmost of the top pair of anchors forming the pedestal of Ahkhow's stele, Wadi Gawasis (Sesostris I) (after Sayed 1977: 164 fig. 6, 163 fig. 5 [A. M. A. H. Sayad, "Discovery of the Site of the Twelfth Dynasty Port at Wadi Gawasis on the Red Sea Shore (Preliminary Report on the Excavations of the Faculty of Arts, University of Alexandria, in the Eastern Desert of Egypt—March 1976)," Rd'È 29: 140–78])

are made of limestone and sandstone) have apical rope grooves, but only one has the typical Egyptian shape with a basal L-shaped hole and an apical rope groove. Three additional stone anchors were recovered from New Kingdom levels at Tell Basta.[37] None of the three has basal holes: one has a long and narrow profile.

The mixture of anchors with and without basal holes or apical rope grooves at Mersa Gawasis and Mirgissa—sites that are clearly Egyptian—as well as the lack of diagnostically Egyptian anchors at Tell Basta indicate that all of these anchor types were in use in pharaonic Egypt. It would, however, be

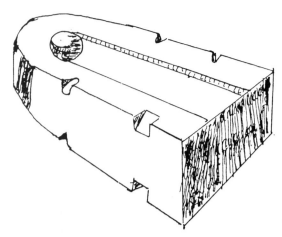

Figure 12.12. Anchor that formed the pedestal of Antefoker's stele from Wadi Gawasis (Sesostris I). The groove on the anchor's upper surface was cut to position the stele more firmly. The anchor lacks the typically Egyptian basal rope-hole but has four notches cut on its sides (from Sayed 1980: 155 fig. 2)

virtually impossible to identify a stone anchor as specifically Egyptian unless it came from a clearly Egyptian context or had a basal hole. Without a basal hole these anchors are indistinguishable from many found along the Levantine coast, most of which are presumably of local origin.

Of much later date are five distinctive stone anchors from the region of Alexandria: these are shaped like isosceles triangles with one or two holes at their bottom side.[38] At the apex of each of the anchors is a thin, rectangular piercing cut through the narrow side of the anchors, placing them at a ninety-degree angle to the lower holes. The upper slots appear to be better fitted for the insertion of a wooden stock than for directly attaching the hawser. The unbroken anchors vary from 51 to 161 kilograms. The largest anchor, which is broken, has a calculated weight of 185 kilograms. Three of the anchors are from Ras el Soda, where a small temple to Isis existed during the Roman period. Apparently

the anchor group is to be dated to that period.

Although controlled at times by Egypt in the Bronze Age, the region of Mersa Matruh was within the cultural realm of Libya.[39] A. Nibbi reports about three hundred pierced stones found along a short stretch of coast at Mersa Matruh.[40] At present, it is not clear what connection, if any, these stones have with Bates' Island. Most of the stones weigh under 12 kilograms, suggesting that they were used as fishnet weights instead of anchors. One rectangular limestone block illustrated by Nibbi has a median groove and wear at its two narrow ends; it may have served as the stone sinker of a killick, or perhaps the stock of a wooden anchor.[41]

Israel

SHFIFONIM. The earliest anchor-shaped artifacts in Israel are found at land sites around the Sea of Galilee (in Hebrew, Yam Kinneret). In the excavations of Tel Beit Yerah (Khirbet Kerak), two phases of an Early Bronze Age gate were uncovered. A large basalt monolith belonging to the earlier phase was found standing upright on a stone plinth outside the gate (Fig. 12.13: A).[42] The monolith was unusual in that it had a large biconical piercing in its upper extremity (Fig. 12.13: B–C). Bar Adon termed it in Hebrew a *shfifon* (pl. *shfifonim*).[43] The *shfifon* found by Bar Adon was interesting in another respect. Although it was well cut in its upper area, its lower extremity was left unfinished, suggesting that it was meant to be placed in the ground.

Since Bar Adon's discovery, many more *shfifonim* have been found around the Sea of Galilee. The majority come from fields and were discovered singly or in groups, out of archaeological context. They now grace the gardens

and museums of the local kibbutzes.

Shfifonim may be divided into several types:

• Some of them have the upper area well prepared, usually in the shape of a trapezoid, while the lower extremity is left unworked (Fig. 12.14). On occasion, the natural shape of the stone is used; the base, however, is differentiated from the upper part.

• Other *shfifonim* reveal no significant difference between their top and bottom parts (Fig. 12.15). They come in varying, generally amorphous, shapes: some tend toward a pointed apex.

• A third subtype of particular interest includes *shfifonim* that were abandoned before their holes were completed. Examples of this phenomenon are rare; only three having blind holes have been recorded. One of these was found in situ in secondary use in an Early Bronze Age II stratum at Tel Beit Yerah (Fig. 12.14: A [lower left]).[44] A second example is now located in Kibbutz Beit Zera (Fig. 12.16). A third specimen, with cup marks on its surface, lies outside the local museum at Kibbutz Shaar ha-Golan.[45] There is also a single example of a *shfifon* with a second hole drilled into it, beneath its original, broken hole (Fig. 12.17).

The *shfifonim* are perhaps best understood as "dummy" anchors: they appear to have been intended to represent anchors and had some at present, unknown, cultic significance.[46] That they were meant to represent stone anchors is implied from their limited topographical range (adjacent to the shores of the Kinneret) and their general stone-anchor shape (particularly the biconical hole).

That they may have had a cultic significance is suggested by the following considerations:

• Although the *shfifonim* seem to

A

B

C

Figure 12.13. Shfifon found next to Early Bronze Age gate, Beit Yerah: (A–B) the shfifon *standing on a stone plinth before the city gate; (C) the* shfifon *as it appears today (photos A–B by P. Bar Adon; photo C by the author; courtesy Israel Antiquities Authority)*

A

B

C

Figure 12.14. Shfifonim with upper areas well prepared, while their lower extremities are left unfinished (photos A and C by the author; photo B by D. Boss; courtesy Israel Antiquities Authority)

A
B
C

Figure 12.15. Shfifonim *of amorphous shape, with no significant differences between the top and bottom parts* (*photos by the author; courtesy Israel Antiquities Authority*)

A
B

Figure 12.16. Shfifon *with a biconical blind hole* (*photos by D. Boss; courtesy Israel Antiquities Authority*)

imitate stone anchors, they were created with the clear intention of placing them in the ground. The *shfifon* found in situ by Bar Adon indicates that they were not functional. The use of anchors and dummy anchors for cultic purposes is known from a number of land sites, both in temples and in tombs.

• The largest boats on the Kinneret in historical times before this century measured about seven to nine meters.[47] It is unlikely that craft on the lake in the Early Bronze Age were any larger. Even the majority of smaller *shfifonim* would be too heavy for use in these craft.

• No usable anchors in the well-cut *shfifon* shape have been reported from Yam Kinneret. The lake has not been extensively surveyed by divers because of its poor visibility. A long-term drought that drastically lowered the level of the lake during the late 1980s, however, did not result in the discovery of any *shfifon*-type anchors. Thus we have the facsimile—but not the prototype. Two *shfifonim* found in the water at the foot of Tel Beit Yerah probably fell from the land site as it eroded over time. The stone anchors discovered in and around the Sea of Galilee are invariably small and have narrow rope holes.[48]

B

Figure 12.17. (A) Shfifon *with the remains of a hole that was broken in antiquity; subsequently, another hole was cut beneath it.* (B) Detail of the *upper portion of the* shfifon (*photos by the author; courtesy Israel Antiquities Authority*)

A

• The walls and ceiling of a tomb built in the Middle Bronze Age I at Degania "A" are constructed from two *shfifonim* and four other monoliths:[49] the floor of the tomb is a cultic basin (Figs. 12.14: A [center], 18).[50] All seven pieces may have originally belonged to a single Early Bronze Age cultic installation that existed in the immediate area, perhaps at Tel Beit Yerah.[51]

• The cup marks on one unfinished *shfifon* may imply cultic connotations.

The *shfifonim* found in two stratigraphic excavations at Tel Beit Yerah indicate that the group cannot be dated later than the Early Bronze II period (ca. 3050–2650 B.C.).[52] By the Middle Bronze I, judging from the cavalier manner in which these stones were reused in the Degania "A" tomb, they were no longer serving their original purpose. Thus, the *shfif-*

onim are at present the earliest datable anchorlike stones known from the Near East.

Interestingly, one *shfifon* was recently discovered serving as a reliquary underneath the altar in the central apse of a church on Mount Berenice, above the ancient site of Tiberias and overlooking the Sea of Galilee (Fig. 12.19).[53] The unhewn bottom of the *shfifon* had been hacked away. The church on Mount Berenice was built in the sixth century A.D. and continued in use until the end of the Crusades in the thirteenth century. The excavator connects the placement of the *shfifon* in the church to the use of the anchor as a symbol for hope and security in early Christianity.[54]

This is the latest example known to me of a stone-anchorlike object used in a cultic manner. Thus, the Sea of Galilee seems to have the notable distinction of being the lo-

cation of the earliest—and latest—evidence for stone anchors or their facsimiles.

ANCHORS. Israel's Mediterranean coast abounds in stone anchors.[55] Rare indeed is the dive in which at least one stone anchor is not sighted. Scores of anchors of varying shape and size have been recorded underwater at Dor alone (Fig. 12.20).[56] As opposed to the situation in Bronze Age coastal sites in Lebanon, Syria, and Cyprus, however, very few anchors have been found on land in Israel. This makes dating and identifying the sea anchors difficult. The following is a brief summary of the most significant published finds.

A pair of anchors, each bearing the incised drawing of a quarter rudder, was recovered at Megadim (Fig. 12.21).[57] The tillers point respectively to the right and left, perhaps indicating that they were

A

B

the ship's (stern?) starboard and port anchors. R. R. Stieglitz identifies the quarter-rudder pictographs as the Egyptian hieroglyph *ym* and the anchors as Egyptian. This classification has been generally accepted.[58]

The identification of these anchors as Egyptian is questionable, in my view. Many stone anchors found in Israeli waters, presumably of Syro-Canaanite origin, are rectangular with a rounded top, similar to the two Megadim anchors discussed here. The Megadim anchors lack the attributes that define Egyptian anchors—particularly the L-shaped notch. The only reason to claim that they are Egyptian is the quarter-rudder pictograph on each. This is, however, only a single symbol, not a hieroglyphic inscription: anyone could have made the signs of a ship's quarter rudder without being Egyptian, or without even intending to represent an Egyptian hieroglyph.[59]

The same ship that left the "quarter-rudder" anchors may have left behind an additional pair of inscribed anchors at Megadim.[60] One anchor bears an hourglass-like symbol (Fig. 12.22: B). The companion anchor, which is identical in shape to the "quarter-rudder" anchors, is an ashlar block doing secondary duty as an anchor. It bears part of an Egyptian relief on one of its narrow sides (Fig. 12.22: A, C). Presumably the stone had been removed from a building in Egypt, although even this is not definite.[61] The relief does not make the anchor itself Egyptian; it lacks the L-shaped notch and apical groove, and its shape is compatible with a Syro-Canaanite origin.

Several other stone anchors from the Mediterranean coast of Israel bear signs. One anchor, found in the sea near Dor, has an

Figure 12.18. (A) *A* shfifon *in secondary use serves as a monolithic cover on the Middle Bronze Age I built tomb excavated at Kibbutz Degania "A" in 1971. The hole had been plugged with a stone in antiquity.* (B) *The same tomb after removal of the* shfifon *and monolithic stele that formed the tomb's roof. A second* shfifon *served as the tomb's southern wall* (*photos courtesy of M. Kochavi*)

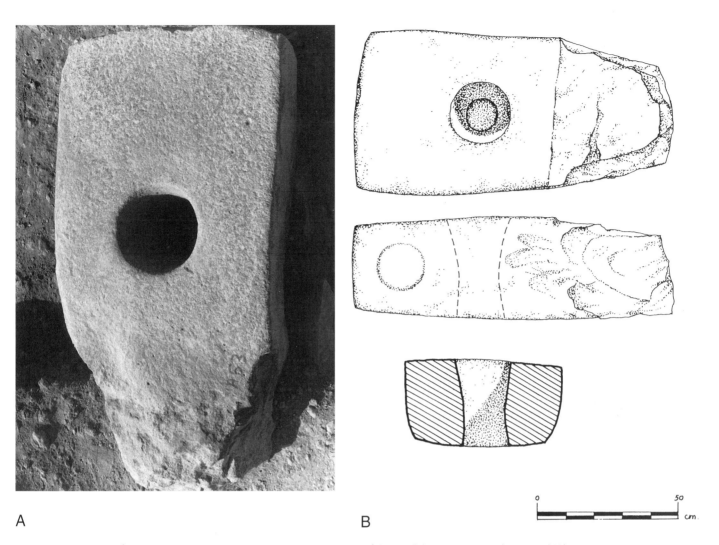

A   B

Figure 12.19. The shfifon *from the Byzantine-period church on Mt. Berenice (photo and drawing courtesy of Y. Hirschfeld.)*

H-shaped design incised into one of its narrow sides (Fig. 12.23). Another anchor, bearing a turtle-like design, was found opposite Kfar Samir, south of Haifa.[62]

In his description of Stratum V at Tell Abu Hawam, R. W. Hamilton notes (Figs. 12.24–25): "The pavement at the north-west corner of 53 contains a large perforated stone—perhaps a door socket, or more probably a drain, since the hole penetrates to the sand and there are no signs of the attrition that would be caused by a door on the surface of the stone. Similar pierced stones were inserted in a pavement at 57 in F 5."[63]

These pierced stones are, of course, anchors (Figs. 12.26–27).[64] They are now lost to the archaeo-

Figure 12.20. A stone anchor found in the ancient harbor of Dor (photo by the author; courtesy Israel Antiquities Authority)

Figure 12.21. Two limestone anchors with quarter rudder pictographs having tillers facing right and left respectively. Found together on the Carmel coast (photo by the author)

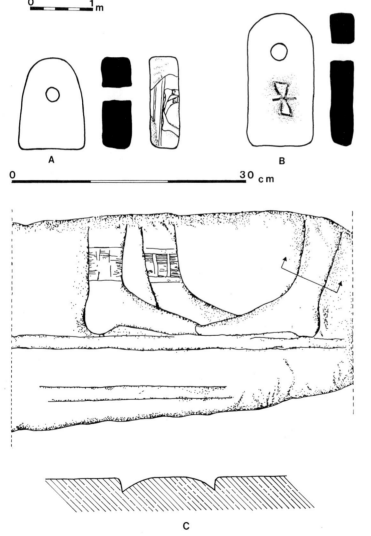

Figure 12.22. Two anchors found together at Megadim: (A) anchor with remnants of an Egyptian relief on one of its narrow sides; (B) anchor with an "hourglass" design; (C) detail of the Egyptian relief fragment on anchor A and a schematic cross-section of a leg (after Galili and Raveh 1988: 43 fig. 3, 44 figs. 5–6; courtesy Israel Antiquities Authority)

Figure 12.23. The stone anchor seen in situ in fig. 12.20 has a sign on one of its narrow sides (from the ancient harbor of Dor) (photo by the author; courtesy Israel Antiquities Authority)

Figure 12.24. (Opposite page) Tell Abu Hawam Stratum V, showing find spots of stone anchors at loci 53 and 57 (from Hamilton 1935: pl. 11; courtesy Israel Antiquities Authority)

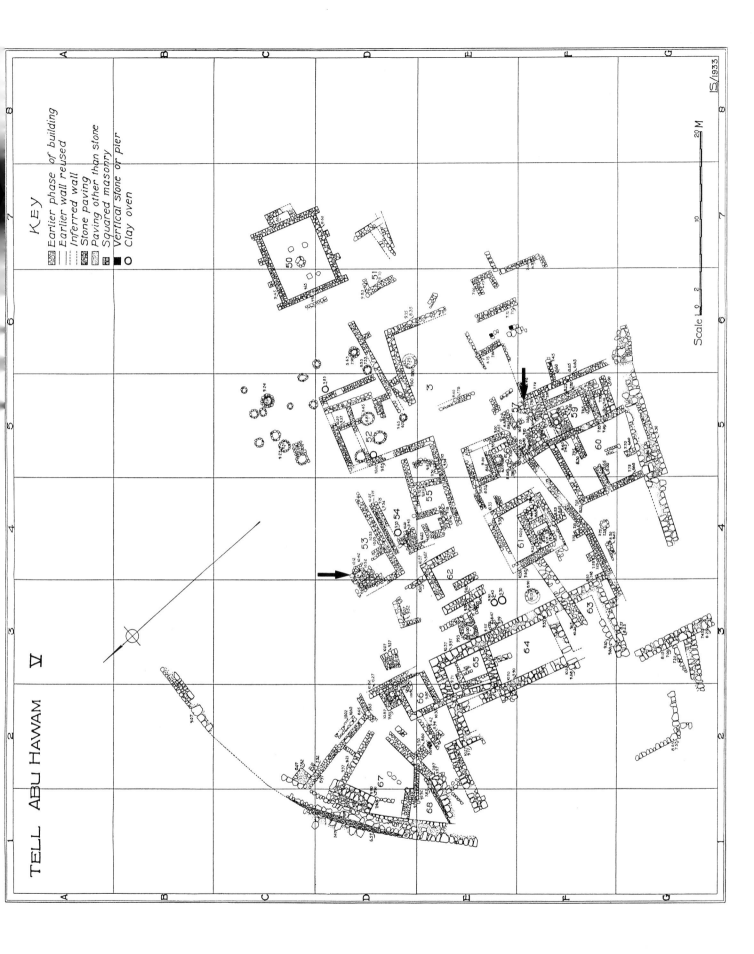

TELL ABU HAWAM

V

KEY

Earlier phase of building
Earlier wall reused
Inferred wall
Stone paving
Paving other than stone
Squared masonry
Vertical stone or pier
Clay oven

Scale 1 0 2   10   20 M

IS/1933

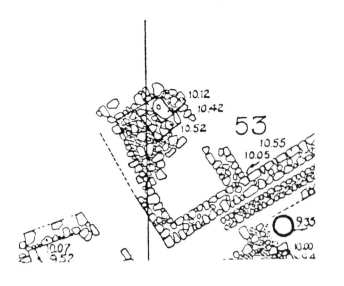

A

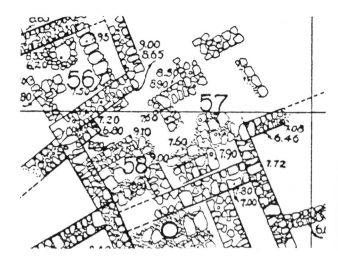

B

Figure 12.25. Details of locations of stone anchors found in Tell Abu Hawam Stratum V at loci 53 and 57 (from Hamilton 1935: pl. 11; courtesy Israel Antiquities Authority)

logical record, and it is difficult to describe a typology from Hamilton's stratum plan and the photos discussed by J. Balensi. Recent excavations at Tell Abu Hawam have revealed six additional stone anchors.[65] Three anchors were found in secondary use in strata dating

from the Late Bronze Age to the fourth century B.C.; the remaining three lacked archaeological context.[66] Anchors also have been found in the Bronze Age strata of Tel Acco.[67] Another stone anchor was discovered in secondary use at Tel Shiqmona near Haifa in a

stratum dating to the sixth and fifth centuries B.C.[68]

ANCHORS IN INLAND WATERS. A number of stone anchors have been reported from the Sea of Galilee, but most of them lack an archaeological context. Two stone anchors were found in the Iron Age strata at Tel Ein Gev.[69] One anchor, made of limestone, is rectangular with a rounded top and weighs 41 kilograms. The second stone is probably a net weight: it is made of local basalt and weighs 7.5 kilograms. Two stone anchors, the first to be discovered and identified as such in the Sea of Galilee, were found together with twenty-nine cooking pots by the Link Expedition near Migdal: this complex probably represents a boat's cargo and equipment. The pottery dates from the mid-first century B.C. to the mid-second century A.D.[70] Two stone anchors were discovered out of stratigraphic context, in the vicinity of the Kinneret boat.[71]

Figure 12.26. Stone anchor at Tell Abu Hawam Stratum V, locus 53 (courtesy Israel Antiquities Authority)

Two other pierced stones, probably anchors, were found in secondary use during the excavation of Khan Minya (Mamaluke-Ottoman periods) on the northwest shore of the lake.[72] J. MacGregor described a stone at Capernaum that may be the stone stock of a wooden anchor.[73]

Several stone anchors are known from the shores of the Dead Sea. A single stone anchor, apparently of Roman date, was reported from Rujm el Baḥr.[74] Four more were found near Ein Gedi.[75] Two of these anchors still had remains of rope hawsers, the longest being 1.6 meters long. Radiocarbon dating of the rope suggests a date around the fourth to third centuries B.C. The rope was found to be double-stranded. This is the only rope reported from nonmodern stone anchors.

In general, it appears that stone anchors continued to be used on both the Sea of Galilee and the Dead Sea well into Classical times and probably later.

Lebanon

BYBLOS. Twenty-eight stone anchors were located in the excavations of Byblos.[76] Seven were found in and around the Temple of the Obelisks (Fig. 12.28: 1–4, 7–9). They date from the nineteenth to the sixteenth centuries B.C. Two anchors, both triangular, are definitely in a sacred context: standing upright on a bench-shelf against the wall of the "Amorite" chapel next to the Temple of the Obelisks. This chapel had votive obelisks, one of which was dedicated to Herchef or Reshef. Frost assumes that the two anchors served the same purpose. Another triangular anchor was found resting on the northern side of the temenos wall that surrounded the cella.

The lowest step of the stairs leading up to the Tower Temple is constructed of six chalk "dummy" anchors set in a row (Fig. 12.28: 23–28).[77] This temple dates to the twenty-third century B.C. Only the top face of the anchors has been

Figure 12.27. Stone anchors at Tell Abu Hawam Stratum V, locus 57 (courtesy Israel Antiquities Authority)

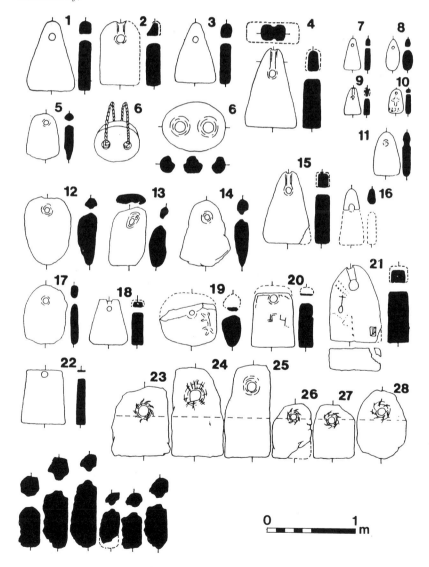

Figure 12.28. The stone anchors of Byblos (from Frost 1969B: 426)

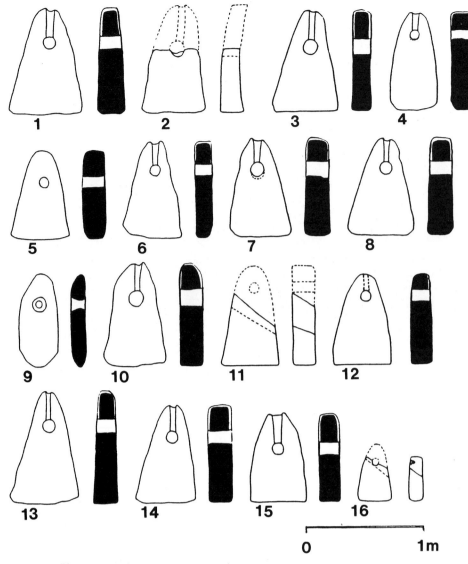

Figure 12.29. The Naveh Yam anchors (after Galili 1987: 16/ fig. 1)

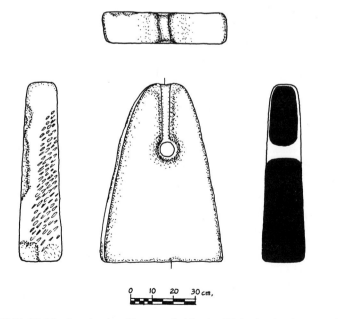

Figure 12.30. "Byblian" anchor found between the islands of Ḥofami and Tafat at Dor (drawing by E. T. Perry; courtesy Israel Antiquities Authority)

worked: this, along with their find spot, indicates to Frost that these were in themselves offerings. She suggests that the number of anchors may reveal the complement of anchors carried by a single ship.

Three more anchors, dated to the twenty-third through twenty-first centuries B.C., were also found in the enclosure (Fig. 12.28: 17–18, 22). Nine other anchors were discovered in secondary use in later strata (Fig. 12.28: 10–16, 19–20).

With the exception of one undated anchor, all those found at Byblos are weight-anchors. Frost defines the typical Byblos anchor shape as a tall, equilateral stone slab with one apical hole; above the hole is a well-defined rope groove. The hawser hole is round and biconical: the latter attribute is best illustrated in an unfinished anchor with a blind hole (Fig. 12.28: 11). The anchors are of medium size at Byblos; here, the gigantism of the Ugarit and Kition anchors is lacking.[78] The largest anchors at Byblos are calculated to weigh about 250 kilograms. The similarity between Byblian and Egyptian anchors may result from Egyptian influence at Byblos.[79]

Interestingly, at Byblos itself the "Byblian" anchor is not in the majority. Only six of the large-size anchors have the characteristic triangular shape (Fig. 12.28: 1, 3–4, 15–16, 18). Perhaps anchors were normally contributed to the temple by nonlocal seafarers, as, for example, must be the case of the Egyptian anchor found at Byblos (Fig. 12.28: 21).

Most "Byblian" anchors known to date come from off the Israeli Mediterranean coast.[80] A group of fifteen stone anchors of Frost's Byblian type was found at Naveh Yam (Fig. 12.29); another was found south of Dor, between the islands of Ḥofami and Tafat at the entrance to Tantura Lagoon (Figs.

12.30–31). Another "Byblian" anchor was located two kilometers north of the Megadim anchors, between Megadim and Hahotrim (Fig. 12.32).[81] The same site contained a Canaanite jar: the relationship between the anchor and the amphora, however, is unclear. A Byblian anchor is also reported from Cape Lara, on the southeast tip of Cyprus.[82]

Syria

UGARIT. Frost describes forty-three stone anchors found at Ugarit and its main port, Minet el Beida.[83] Of these, twenty-two are located in or around the Temple of Baal (Figs. 12.33: 1–17).[84] The Ugaritic anchors have three main shapes: an elongated rectangle, a squat rectangle, and a triangle. Four of the anchors weigh about half a ton each (Fig. 12.33: 2–3, 5–6).

C. F. A. Schaeffer dates the level of the temple in which the anchors were found to the reigns of Sesostris II through Amenemhet IV. Interestingly, the nearby Temple of Dagon lacked any anchors whatsoever. It appears that anchors were dedicated to *specific* gods, most probably those (like Baal) in charge of the weather. Two anchors, for which Frost proposes a fifteenth- or fourteenth-century date, were found flanking the entrance to a tomb (Fig. 12.33: 27–28).[85] These anchors find a close parallel in one discovered underwater at Dor.[86]

Cyprus

Cypriot Late Bronze Age harbor sites are rich in stone anchors. Many others have been found in underwater surveys. The earliest published pierced stone from Cyprus dates to the sixth millennium and was found in Stratum III at Khirokitia (Fig. 12.34).[87] The stone is roughly triangular with a small biconical piercing and an

Figure 12.31. A "Byblian" anchor from Dor (courtesy Israel Antiquities Authority)

apical rope groove. It weighs 10.4 kilograms and is probably a net weight. In Israel to this day, stones still serve as net weights for some fishermen (Fig. 12.35).

HALA SULTAN TEKE. A number of anchors have been found in the land excavations at Hala Sultan Teke and in the neighboring underwater site of Cape Kiti (Figs. 12.36–39).[88] Numerous stone anchors were also discovered off Cape Andreas (Figs. 12.40–42).[89]

KITION. The largest single group of anchors from an excavated land site comes from Kition, where some 147 stone anchors have been recorded in the temple complexes (Fig. 12.43).[90] Frost notes a "family resemblance" between the anchors from Ugarit and those from Kition.[91]

At Kition anchors were classified by lithological thin sections.[92] Three anchors were found to be of stone foreign to the site.[93] The stone of one anchor was identified

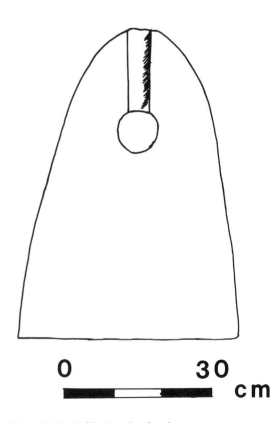

Figure 12.32. "Byblian" anchor found between Megadim and Hahotrim (after Ronen and Olami 1978: 10 no. 21: 1; courtesy Israel Antiquities Authority)

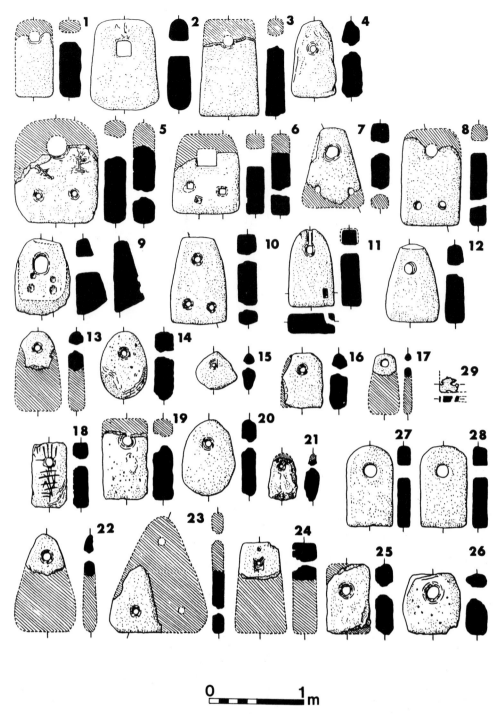

Figure 12.33. The stone anchors of Ugarit (from Frost 1969A: 245)

0 _____ 1 m

as originating in Turkey or Egypt. This, however, does not necessarily indicate a foreign ship, for vessels could have picked up stone blanks for their anchors anywhere and prepared them on board while under sail.

The Kition anchors are squat with rounded corners and range in shape from rectangular to triangular.[94] They resemble Ugaritic anchors but contrast markedly with the triangular Byblian shape. A style of anchor that Frost defines as regional to Kition is composite and has a rounded, triangular shape. This kind of anchor seems to be far-ranging. Frost mentions examples found off the island of Ustica and also discovered together with a metal ingot off Cape Kaliakri, in the Black Sea. Several of this variety were also found underwater at Cape Andreas, Hala Sultan Teke, and Cape Kiti (Figs. 12.36: A [1–2], 37: C, E, 38: L–M, 41: A–D). Three such anchors bear the three-line Cypro-Minoan arrow sign (Fig. 12.36: A [1, 3]).[95] The Karnak anchor has this typical Cypriot shape but is made of local limestone (Fig. 12.44).[96]

Fifteen of the Kition anchors have a rectangular shape first noted on an embedded anchor (?) in the tomb of Mereruka (Fig. 12.6: B). Since the Mereruka anchor predates those at Kition by nearly a millennium, this only establishes that the shape was a common one.[97]

Turkey

A number of unpublished stone composite- and weight-anchors are exhibited in the courtyard of the Bodrum Museum of Underwater Archaeology.[98] We know nothing of stone anchors used by Late Bronze Age Anatolian seafarers.

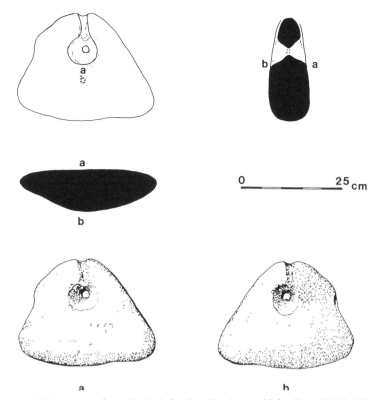

The Aegean

Very few stone anchors are known from the Aegean. Since Aegean Bronze Age seafarers needed some form of anchoring device as much as others of their day, it is not clear why stone anchors appear to be so rare on the Aegean seabed. Perhaps this is because of the steep nature of the sea floor there, compounded by the nearly total lack of sport diving in Greece.

Alternatively, perhaps Aegean seafarers used killicks, devices that utilize stones as weights for a wooden anchoring structure.[99] Since fieldstones of a desired shape can be used in killicks, these would leave no archaeological trace once the artifact's organic structure had decomposed. Furthermore, few stone anchors have

Figure 12.34. Pierced stone from Khirokitia (sixth millennium B.C.)(after Frost 1984A: 146 fig. 77)

Figure 12.35. Fishing boat with net that employs stone weights (Acco, Israel). Inset: detail of one of the stones (photos by the author; courtesy Israel Antiquities Authority)

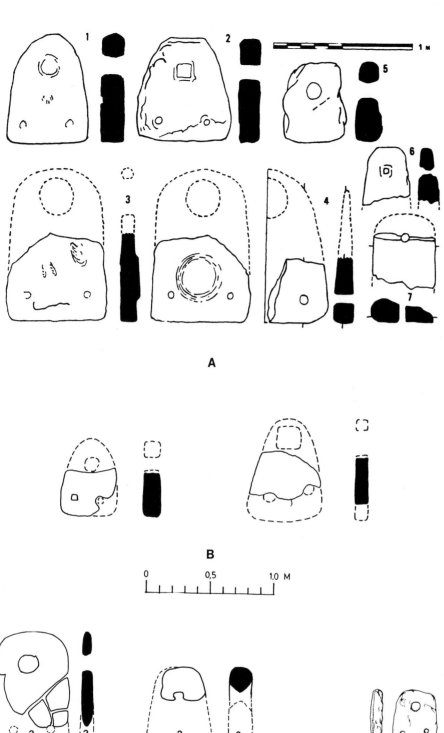

Figure 12.36. Stone anchors from Hala Sultan Teke (A from Frost 1970A: 14 fig. I; B from Öbrink 1979: 72 figs. 102A–102)

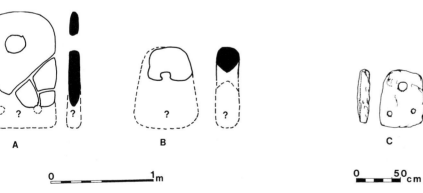

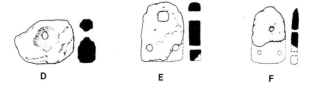

Figure 12.37. Stone anchors from Hala Sultan Teke (A–C from Hult 1977: 149 figs. 170–71; 1981: 89 fig. 140; D–F from McCaslin 1978: 119 fig. 215, nos. N4000, F4004, N9040)

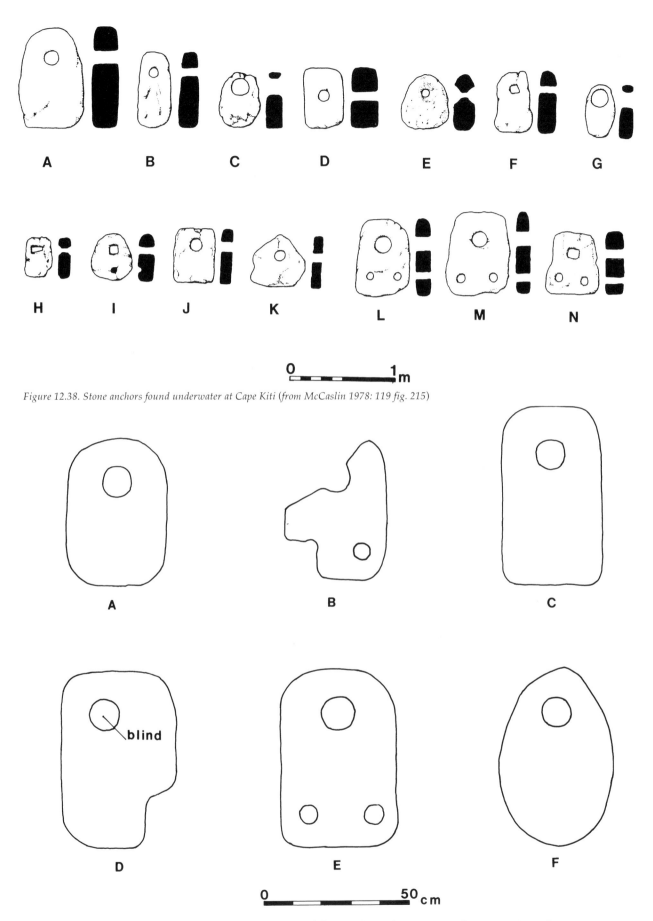

Figure 12.38. Stone anchors found underwater at Cape Kiti (from McCaslin 1978: 119 fig. 215)

blind

Figure 12.39. Stone anchors sighted near the lighthouse at Cape Kiti (after Herscher and Nyquist 1975: figs. 48: 2–5, 49: 7, 9)

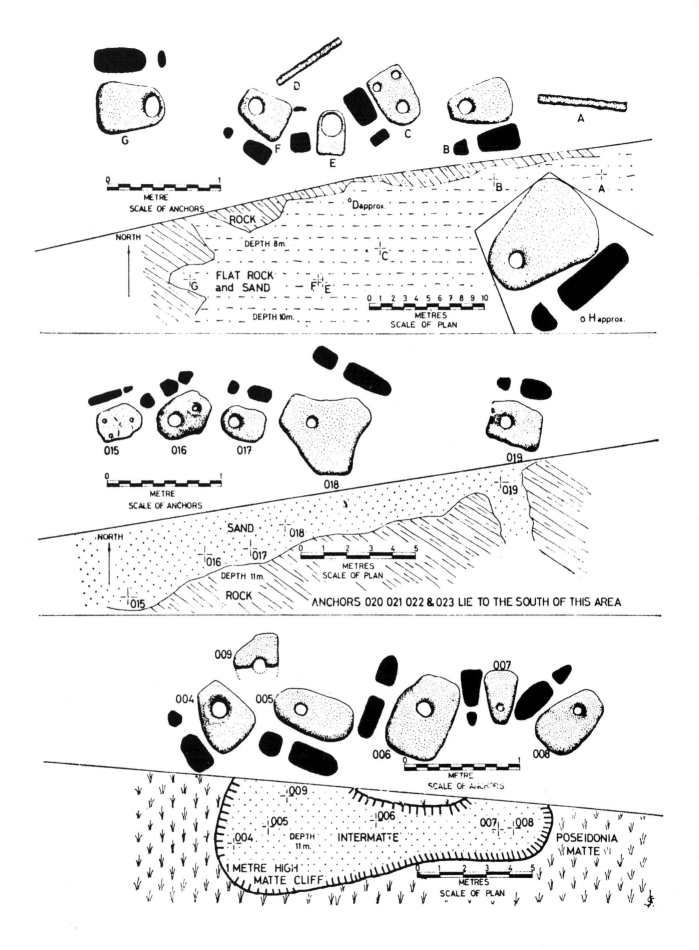

Figure 12.40. Stone anchors from three anchor sites near Cape Andreas, Cyprus (from Green 1973: 170 fig. 30)

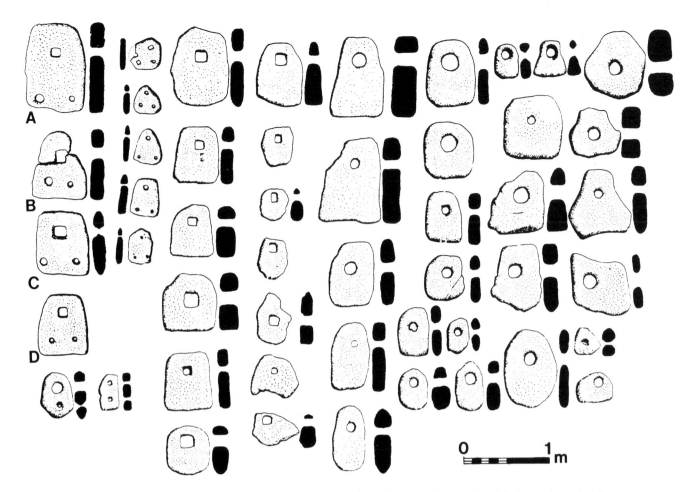

Figure 12.41. Stone anchors from anchor sites at Cape Andreas, Ayios Philos (Philon), Ayios Photios, Aphrendrika (Ourania), and Khelones, Cyprus (from Green 1973: 173 fig. 31A)

been found on land, apparently because anchors were not normally dedicated in cultic contexts in the Minoan and Mycenaean religions.[100]

MAINLAND GREECE. At present, the typology of Mycenaean anchors remains unknown. Two stone anchors—one round, the other somewhat rectangular— were recovered off Cape Stomi at Marathon Bay.[101] A three-holed composite anchor was discovered off Point Iria near a concentration of Late Helladic pottery.[102]

DOKOS. Two stone anchors were recovered from the Dokos site.[103] The anchors weigh about twenty kilograms each and are of nondescript shape, with small rope holes. The excavators have

tentatively dated these to the Early Helladic period, suggesting that they are derived from a ship from that period that had wrecked at the site. Since these anchors are of a size, type, and style that continued in common use throughout the Mediterranean into modern times, this conclusion seems to overstep the available evidence.

CRETE. Three Middle Minoan stone anchors were found at Mallia (Fig. 12.45: A–C).[104] The area where two of the anchors were found was originally thought to be a stonemason's workshop but has more recently been identified as a sanctuary.[105] All three of the anchors have a triangular shape with a rounded top; one has a square rope hole. The stones were freshly cut,

suggesting that they had never seen service in the sea.

A beautifully carved pierced porphyry stone, decorated with a Minoan-style octopus, was found by A. Evans at Knossos (Fig. 12.45: D).[106] The stone weighs twenty-nine kilograms: Evans believed it was a weight for weighing oxhide ingots. This artifact is so elaborate, however, that it may have been intended for cultic use.[107]

Five pierced stones, originally identified as anchors, were found in a Late Minoan III context at Kommos (Fig. 12.46: D).[108] H. Blitzer later thought that some of these stones were weights used in olive presses instead of anchors.[109] During the summer of 1993, two Bronze Age stone anchors were

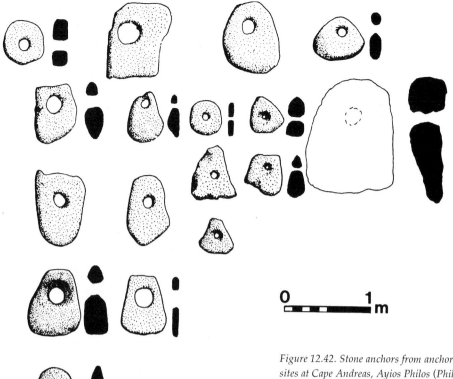

Figure 12.42. *Stone anchors from anchor sites at Cape Andreas, Ayios Philos (Philon), Ayios Photios, Aphrendrika (Ourania), and Khelones, Cyprus (from Green 1973: 173 fig. 31B)*

0   1 m

Figure 12.43. (below) *Stone anchors in situ at Kition (photos by the author)*

discovered within the Minoan civic buildings at Kommos (Fig. 12.46: A–C).[110] The anchors are composite, with one large hole at the apex and two smaller holes near the bottom. The larger of the two anchors is 74 centimeters high, 60 centimeters wide at the bottom, and 15 centimeters thick. It weighs 75 kilograms. This is the first recorded discovery of three-holed composite-anchors reported from a land site in the Aegean. The latter two anchors were reused as bases for wooden supports. They date to the Late Minoan IIIA1–A2 and were found together with Canaanite, Cypriot, and Egyptian as well as local Minoan sherds.

Another broken anchor, perhaps of Late Minoan IB date, was found at Makrygialos.[111]

THERA. S. Marinatos identifies a pierced stone found at Thera as an anchor (Fig. 12.47). The rope hole is exceptionally small (about 4 centimeters) for the stone's 65-kilogram weight, and it is difficult to understand how the stone could have served as an anchor without having some additional form of binding. The stone is described by Marinatos as being "roughly oval, black trachyte stone, about 60 cm long." He mentions two additional

Figure 12.44. The Karnak anchor. This anchor, although made from local limestone has a diagnostic Cypriot shape. The anchor was found in the Temple of Amun at Karnak (photo by L. Basch. Courtesy of L. Basch)

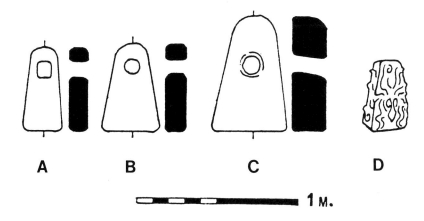

A   B   C   D

1 M.

Figure 12.45. (A–B) Stone anchors excavated at Mallia, ca. nineteenth century B.C. Estimated weight: about twenty-five and forty kilograms. (C) Stone anchor from Mallia, ca. 1750 B.C. Estimated weight: sixty kilograms. (D) Porphyry anchor-shaped weight (?). The stone is decorated in relief with an octopus (A–D after Frost 1973: 400 fig. 1: 6)

pierced stones, found in Sector Δ, but gives no further details.[112]

MYKONOS. A three-holed composite anchor is exhibited at the Aegean Maritime Museum on the island of Mykonos.[113]

RHODES. An anchor was found in Tomb 27 at Ialysos.[114]

Anchors on Shipwrecks

ULUBURUN. Twenty-four stone anchors have been found on the Uluburun wreck (Figs. 9.1; 12.48: A–B; 14.1).[115] Most are made of sandstone; two small anchors consist of hard, white, marblelike limestone. Eight anchors, including the two smaller ones, had been carried in the center of the hull between two stacks of copper oxhide ingots. Sixteen other anchors are located at the bow, in the

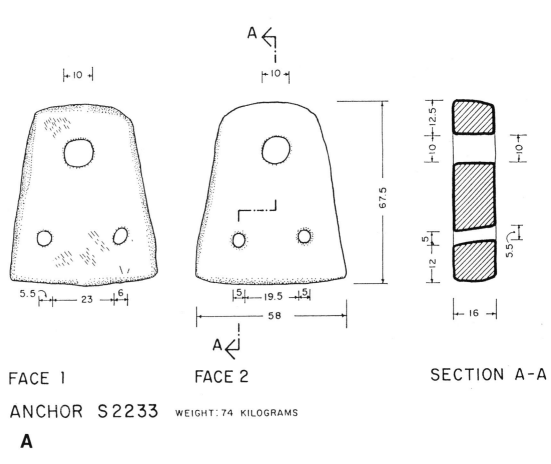

FACE 1   FACE 2   SECTION A-A

ANCHOR S2233   WEIGHT: 74 KILOGRAMS

A

B

FACE 2   SECTION B-B

ANCHOR S2234   WEIGHT: 75 KILOGRAMS

KOMMOS

0 10 20 30 40 50 CM.

GIULIANA BIANCO 1993

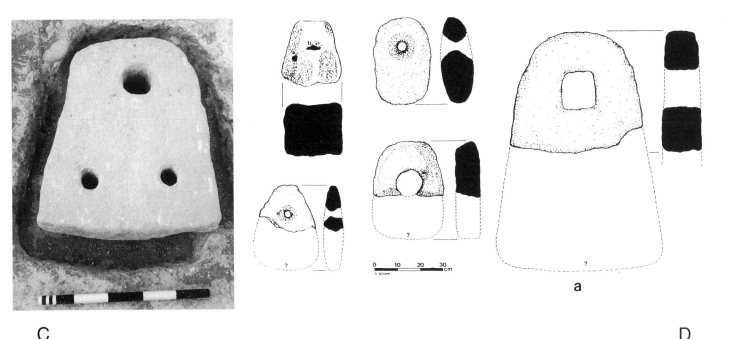

C

D

Figure 12.46. Anchors from Kommos: (A and B facing page) (A) *anchor S2233 (Late Minoan IIIA1–2);* (B) *anchor S2234 (Late Minoan IIIA1–2);* (C) *anchor S2233 in situ;* (D) *pierced stones (anchors?) at Kommos (Late Minoan III)* (A–C *courtesy Drs. J. and M. Shaw; D from Shaw and Blitzer 1983: 94–95 fig. 2)*

lower perimeter of the wreck.[116] A study of the site plans and photos published to date suggests several distinctions:[117]

• All are weight-anchors, each with a single hole.

• The anchor shapes vary from trapezoidal with truncated top to roughly triangular with rounded top.

• At least six of the anchors have square rope holes.

• No rope grooves are visible on the plans or in the published photos of the anchors.

Because anchors in use were carried primarily at a ship's bow, the fact that so many anchors were found at the lower end of the wreck supports the conclusion that this is the craft's bow. The ship may have lost some of her anchors attempting to avoid the coast. The large number of stone anchors carried by the Uluburun ship seems indicative of both the anchors' *expendability* as well as their *unreliability*. Presumably, the ship also carried quantities of rope for use with the anchors, although no rope has been reported from the excavation. At present the closest parallels on land sites to the Uluburun anchors, as a group, seem to come from Ugarit, Kition, and Byblos.[118] Six of the anchors that have been weighed varied between 121 and 208 kilograms.[119] Based on their average weight, the twenty-four anchors on the Uluburun ship weigh over four tons!

CAPE GELIDONYA. During the 1960 excavation of the Cape Gelidonya shipwreck, no stone anchors were found. Their absence at the site remained an enigma that became even more remarkable when seen in contrast to the twenty-four anchors recovered at Uluburun. During the 1994 Institute of Nautical Archaeology underwater survey off Turkey, the team located and raised a single stone anchor at Cape Gelidonya (Fig. 12.48: C).[120] This is a large weight anchor that weighs 219 kilograms and is made

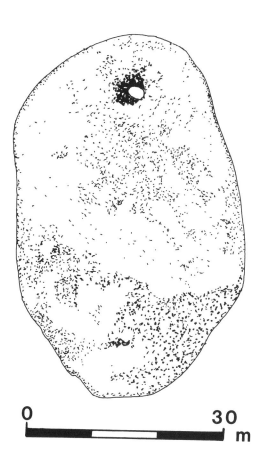

Figure 12.47. Pierced stone from Thera. Weight: sixty-five kilograms (after Marinatos 1974: pl. 29)

A

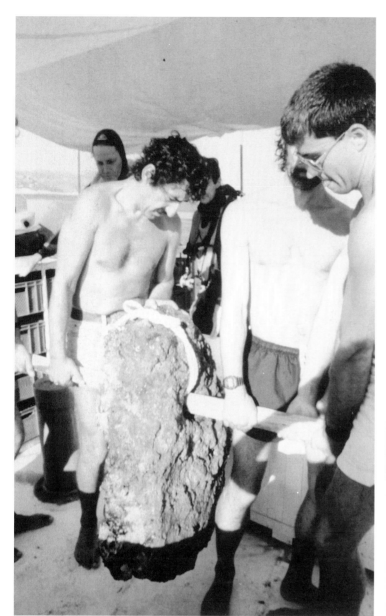

B

C

Figure 12.48. (A) (opposite page) Stone weight anchors spill down from the lower part (bow) of the Uluburun shipwreck (B) The difficulty in deploying heavy stone anchors at sea is demonstrated in this photo, which shows members of the Uluburun excavation moving one (C) The stone anchor recently discovered at Cape Gelidonya, in the process of being weighed by Cemal Pulak (photos by D. Frey; courtesy of the Institute of Nautical Archaeology)

of sandstone of a type somewhat more coarse than the Uluburun anchors.

The Gelidonya ship undoubtedly carried additional anchors. Where are they? Perhaps some had been lowered by the crew in a desperate attempt to prevent the ship from crashing into the rocks.[121] If so, they would now be located in deeper waters. Another possibility is that a significant portion of the shipwreck is still missing.

NAVEH YAM. The Naveh Yam anchors must have come from a single ship (Fig. 12.29).[122] The majority of the anchors are triangular, have apical rope grooves on both of their flat sides, and range in weight from 60 to 155 kilograms; their original weight, not including three broken anchors, totals 1,187 kilograms.[123]

E. Galili divides the anchors into the following groups: anchors with rope grooves on both sides (Fig. 12.29: 1, 3–4, 6–8, 10, 13–15); an anchor without rope grooves (Fig. 12.29: 5); an anchor with a rope groove on only one side (Fig.

12.29: 12); broken anchors (Fig. 12.29: 2, 11, 16); and an elliptical anchor of non-Byblian shape (Fig. 12.29: 9). Five of the anchors have bases flat enough to allow them to stand independently on a flat surface. They are all made of soft limestone, exposures of which are known from Egypt, Israel, Lebanon, and Syria. Two hematite weights, a bronze chisel, and a bronze adze were also found near the anchors.

At Naveh Yam, anchors having rope grooves on both sides, on only one side, and without any grooves at all were found side by side, indicating that a single ship could carry a variety of anchors types. Most of the Naveh Yam anchors were found in an area of seven-by-seven meters on the seabed.[124] Two of the anchors, among the largest in the group, were discovered at some distance from the rest (Fig. 12.29: 1, 4).

The tops of the broken anchors were missing. Galili suggests that some of the anchors—at least the broken ones—served as the ship's ballast. He believes that the anchor site is the result of a shipwreck caused by the vessel hitting an underwater reef located directly southwest of the site.[125]

Discussion

Small Anchors

At Wadi Gawasis, at Naveh Yam, as well as at Uluburun, groups of large stone anchors have been found in situ, together with smaller anchors that could not have been functional for the same craft in the same manner as the larger anchors.[126] What purpose did these small anchors serve? There are three possible explanations for this phenomenon: they may represent hawser weights, sacred anchors, or the anchors for ships' boats. Let us examine the evidence for each of these possibilities.

HAWSER WEIGHTS. A modern anchor chain serves as a "shock absorber" in rough seas. For a ship rocked by waves while standing on a stone anchor with a rope hawser, however, the situation is quite different. Notes H. Wallace:

Indeed if the seas approach the height of his bows, A's situation [Fig. 12.49] could be desperate, since it is certain that one or more of three unpleasant things must happen: the anchor is lifted clear of the bottom with every wave, or if so much weight is placed on it or it wedges in a cleft, and so cannot lift, either the rope will break or the waves will break over the bows of the ship which cannot rise to them. Even if the height of the waves is much less, they will still give A a most uncomfortable ride, the rope going slack when the ship descends into the trough and then tightening with a jerk as it rises. Even the heaviest anchor with rope can't stand this treatment for very long.

Contrast now the cases of B and C which can rise with the waves to B_1 and C_1 respectively before they are faced with the troubles we have described for A. And all the time there is a tension on the rope or chain so that there is no jerk till all is off the bottom and the ship attempts to lift the anchor. This point, of course, should never be reached if chain of sufficient length and weight in relation to the size of the ship and the waves is used.[127]

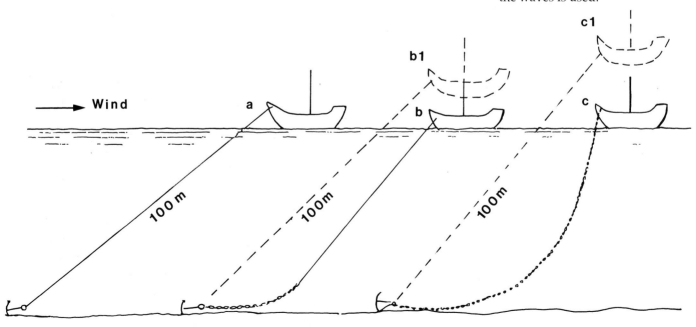

Figure 12.49. The difference between rope and chain when anchoring in waves (after Wallace 1964: 15 fig. 1)

Wallace suggests that auxiliary stone anchors were attached to the primary hawser to act in the same manner as a chain.[128] He notes that this method was still being used on Spanish fishing boats in recent times:

However, in this case the weights were not attached directly to the anchor cable, but were strung along an auxiliary line which was only attached to the main cable at intervals and hung down in loops in between. Though at first sight puzzling, this method of attachment would appear to have advantages for larger boats when it came to hauling in the anchor, as if the weights were attached direct to the main cable [as in Fig. 12.50], it would be necessary to lift the whole cable whenever a weight came up to the gunwale—not an easy thing to do while still maintaining the tension on it. But with the weights on an auxiliary line a separate detachment of the crew could bring the weights inboard, without interrupting the main party hauling on the main cable.[129]

Another possible reason for the anchors' being attached on a separate line is that they would have been likely to foul anchor lines in a crowded harbor. Wallace notes that similar weights were used on the tidal reaches of the Thames. Frost opposes this interpretation:

I have a file of letters telling me that in order to counteract the potential dragging of a stone weight attached to a boat by rope, the ancients must also have weighted the rope itself with smaller pierced stones so that it would lie along the bottom like a chain, thus preventing surface movement from being transmitted to the anchor.

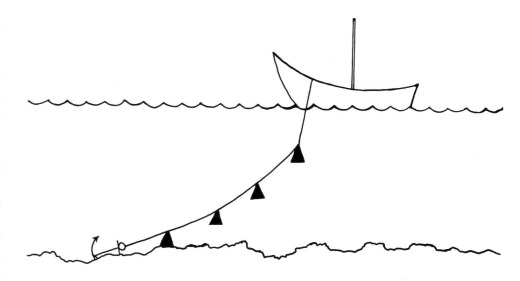

Figure 12.50. Theoretical reconstruction of subsidiary anchors used to weigh down an anchor's rope hawser (after Wallace 1964: 16 fig. 3)

This is logical but again it runs counter to the evidence, because had the weighting of ropes been common practise, then sets of smaller pierced stones each weighing a few kilos would be found beside the larger stone anchors on all the groups of lost anchors that have been examined and surveyed during the past thirty years and this is never the case.[130]

The evidence is not quite so clear-cut. First, anchor sites often contain large and small anchors jumbled together haphazardly, making it possible that two or more had been combined on a single hawser. It is virtually impossible to prove this because of the jumble of stone anchors on the seabed. Second, sets of weights need not be postulated: a single subsidiary anchor placed up the hawser from the primary anchor would have been sufficient in most weather to function as a brake on the main anchor.

Perhaps the strongest argument *against* small weight-anchors having been used as hawser weights is the consideration that so few of them are found with the large an-

chor groups. Had the small anchors been used as hawser weights, one would have expected to find more of them at Wadi Gawasis, Naveh Yam, and Uluburun.

SACRED ANCHOR. Seagoing ships normally have an additional anchor to be used as a last resort should the bower anchors fail to hold. This is now termed a sheet anchor.[131] In antiquity, this anchor had cultic connotations and was considered sacred. Perhaps the small anchors at these sites are "sacred" anchors.

Appolonius of Rhodes (third century B.C.) gives a detailed account of the dedication by the Argonauts of an anchor at a spring sacred to Artacie.[132] The helmsman, Typhis, suggests that they dedicate their small stone anchor and replace it on the *Argo* with a heavier anchor. Presumably, if there was a small anchor, it was small in relation to other, larger, anchors. But why dedicate the *small* anchor? Was this perhaps the holy anchor?

Frost suggests that the anchor being raised by a ship on a Cypriot jug represents that ship's holy anchor (Fig. 8.41: A).[133] The large figure above the anchor, in her opinion, is a deity, his hands held in benediction, who, hearing the distress call signified by the dropping of the holy anchor, has come to save the ship.[134]

SHIP'S BOAT'S ANCHOR. Bass and C. M. Pulak suggest that the small anchor found at Uluburun was either a hawser weight or a spare for the ship's boat.[135] Similarly, A. M. A. H. Sayed notes that the small anchor found at Mersa Gawasis was possibly used for a small "rescue" boat.[136]

It is probable that a ship like the one that wrecked at Uluburun—which was capable of carrying four tons of anchors—would have had a tender. Indeed, in the Deir el Bahri relief, a launch is depicted transporting Egyptian trade items to the shore at Punt (Fig. 12.51). The Egyptians must have brought such launches with them, even though none is portrayed on board the ships.[137] In conclusion, at present it seems preferable to explain the small anchors as belonging on ships' boats.

Brobdingnagian Anchors

The heaviest anchors yet recorded come from Kition (Fig. 12.52: D–E).[138] The largest of these has a calculated weight of about 1,350 kilograms. Frost assumes that all the largest anchors found at Kition were functional; that is, they were actually used on ships. It seems prudent, however, to restrict the upper weight limit of stone anchors that were used at sea during the Bronze Age to the weight of the largest specimens actually found on the seabed.

Two half-ton anchors found on the Mediterranean seabed have been published.[139] One of these comes from the harbor of Tabarja in Lebanon and is presumably of Middle or Late Bronze Age date (Fig. 12.53).[140] The other is one of two anchors found together with Late Bronze Age scrap metal off Hahotrim, south of Haifa on the Israeli Mediterranean coast (Fig. 12.54). Two other large anchors, made of basalt, have been recorded by divers off Tartous and

Cape Greco.[141] Even these half-ton anchors must have been difficult to manage in the primitive manner depicted on the Cypriot jugs.

Later wooden anchors reached unusually large proportions. The largest recorded lead stock from the Mediterranean is 4.2 meters long and weighs 1,869 kilograms.[142] Anchors of this size must have been handled with capstans, for which there is ample evidence in the Classical period.[143] However, there is nothing to indicate that pulleys and capstans were known in the Bronze Age—or during most of the Iron Age, for that matter, to judge from the Cypriot vases.

Square Hawser Holes

The rope situated between the hawser hole and the anchor's apex will chafe as a stone anchor is dragged on the seabed or as it rises and falls with the waves on the ship. This part of the hawser would have worn out most often. The rope grooves observed on Egyptian and Byblian anchors were ap-

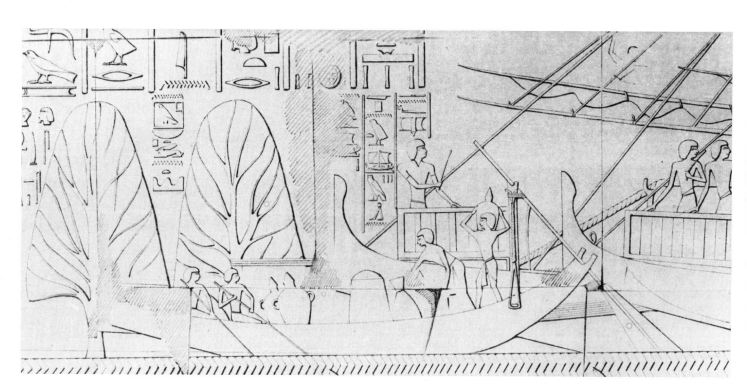

Figure 12.51. Detail of a ship's boat ferrying trade goods to the coast at Punt (Deir el Bahri) (from Naville 1898: pl. 72)

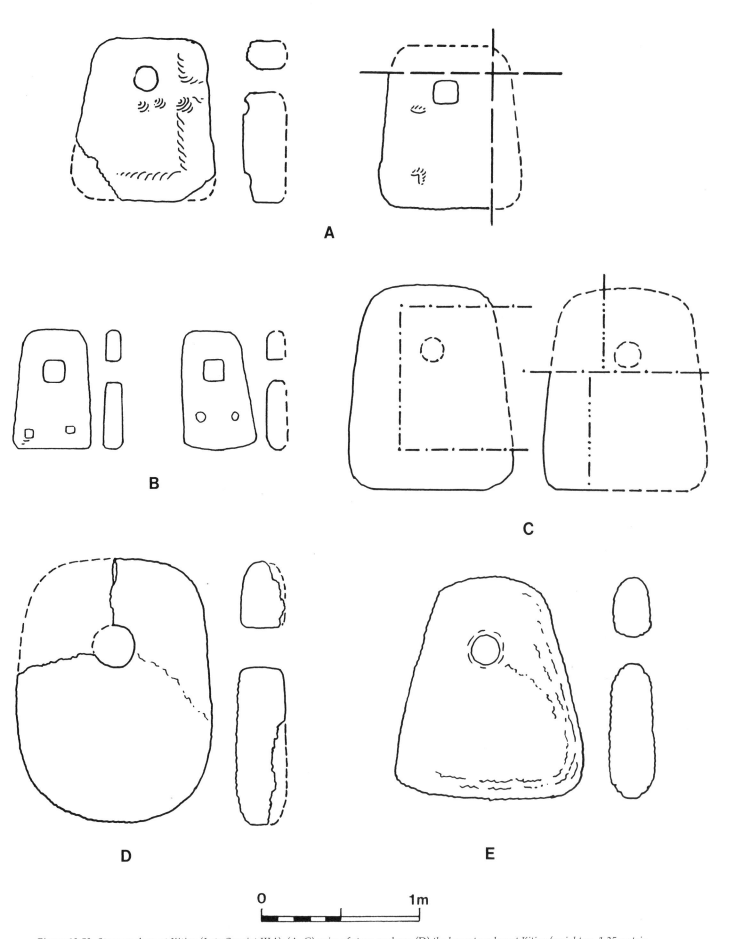

Figure 12.52. Stone anchors at Kition (Late Cypriot IIIA): (A–C) pairs of stone anchors; (D) the largest anchor at Kition (weight ca. 1.35 metric tons); (E) large anchor (weight ca. 700 kilograms) (from Frost 1986C: 297 fig. 4: 1–4, 302 fig. 7: 4–7)

0   1m

parently an attempt to avoid the inevitable damage done to this part of the rope, as well as to seat the eye.

In antiquity, a short piece of rope may have been passed through the hawser hole and spliced, forming an eye, or ring. The hawser would then be attached to the eye. When the eye wore out, it would have been easily replaced without doing any damage to the hawser. Such an eye is visible on the triangular stone anchor on a Cypriot jug (Fig. 8.41: A).[144] Composite stone anchors called *sinn* (Arabic for "tooth"), used by Arab craft in the Persian Gulf, are still attached in this manner.[145]

There is another reason for having such a rope eye on heavy stone anchors. The eye would enable a wooden staff to be inserted, allowing the anchor to be manhandled by two or more men once it broke the water and was brought on deck.

Frost rightly notes that, functionally, square rope holes are difficult to explain (Fig. 12.55).[146] It is indeed patently illogical to cut a square hole for a rope that is round

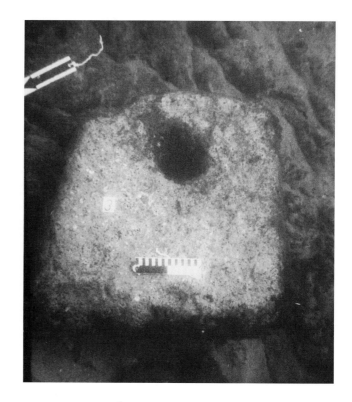

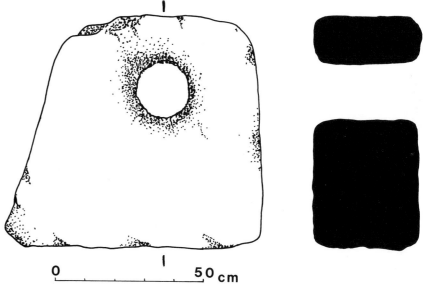

Figure 12.54. Brobdingnagian stone anchor found near Late Bronze Age metal artifacts around Kibbutz Hahotrim. In fig. A, the anchor, with an estimated weight of about half a ton, is seen in situ on the seabed (photo by the author; courtesy Israel Antiquities Authority)

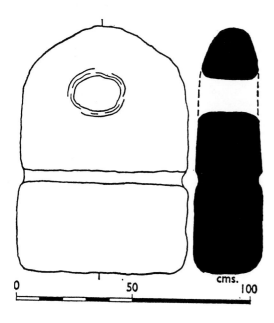

Figure 12.53. Half-ton stone anchor found in the harbor of Tabarja, Lebanon (from Frost 1963B: 43 fig. 5)

in section. The square holes noted on anchors from Ugarit, Kition, and Uluburun must therefore have had a technological *raison d'être*.

These square holes may have resulted from a preference to pass four or five smaller eyes, instead of one big eye, through the hole (Fig. 12.56). If one or two of the

eyes parted, the anchor would still not be lost. Perhaps anchors with square holes were used when anchoring on a rocky bottom when the eye was more likely to chafe, while anchors with round holes were reserved for sandy bottoms. In later times, chafing was avoided by placing the hawser hole on the

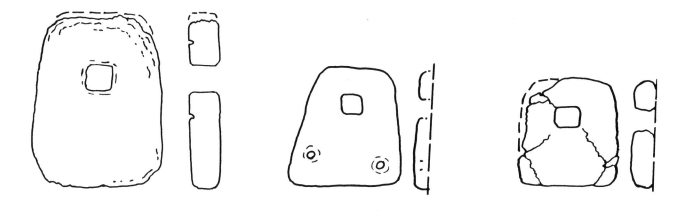

Figure 12.55. Stone anchors from Kition with square hawser-holes (from Frost 1986C: 312 fig. 12: 15, 317 fig. 14: 2, 310 fig. 4)

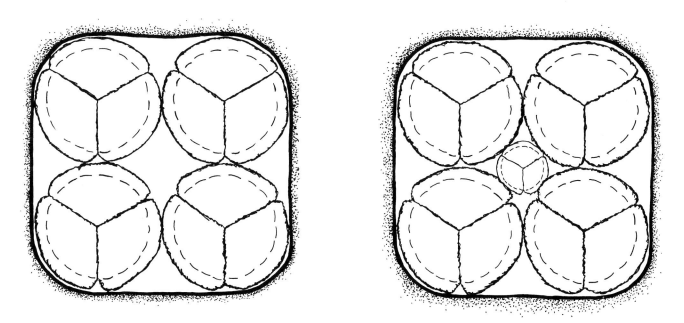

Figure 12.56. A square rope-hole suggests that it was intended for four (A) or even five (B) smaller cables instead of one large cable (drawn by the author)

narrow side of the anchor.[147] In support of this explanation, note that the rope hawser of the stone anchor from the Hellenistic period found near Ein Gedi—the only hawser yet found in connection with an ancient stone anchor—was made of two separate ropes.[148]

One type of Cypriot stone anchor has an exceptionally large anchor hole that seems nonfunctional (Figs. 12.38: C, G, 40: G, E, 57).[149] Specimens found on the seabed signify that this anchor type was indeed used at sea, however.

An anchor found underwater near the lighthouse at Cape Kiti has a blind hole (Fig. 12.39: B). I have seen another unfinished anchor on the seabed at Dor. These two artifacts suggest that stone blanks were, at least on occasion, taken aboard ship and prepared while the craft was at sea.

Anchors Found in Cultic Connotations

Anchors found in temples at Byblos, Ugarit, and Kition share common features in their positioning.[150] These features include their use as *betyls* standing over *bothroi*, anchors standing upright among other votive offerings, as well as the inclusion of groups of anchors as part of the temple architecture

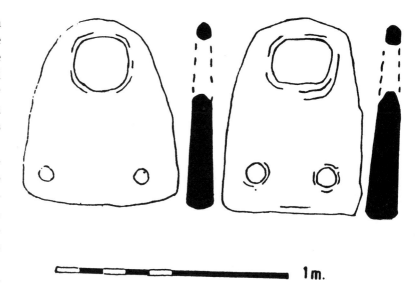

Figure 12.57. Two "basket-shaped" anchors from the sea off Cyprus (from Frost 1970A: 21 fig. 4: 7, 11)

but serving no structural purpose.[151] They also appear in tombs, near or in wells, and aligned in thresholds and walls, normally in sets of two, three, four, and six (Figs. 12.28: 23–28, 58).

Cup marks, presumably indicative of cultic practices, are occasionally found on stone anchors uncovered in temple precincts. Frost suggests that at Kition, the anchors were made in and for the temples. Unfinished anchors were found at Byblos, Kition, and among the *shfifonim*.

Many anchors at Kition were found in pairs (Fig. 12.52: A–C).[152]

In Byblos, a pair of anchors was found in the dromos of a tomb (Fig. 12.33: 27–28). This apparent cultic connection to a *pair* of anchors may be traceable to the manner in which pairs of anchors were used in the sea. At Dor, two large, virtually identical anchors were found lying *in situ* on the seabed in a manner that suggests the ship had lowered the two anchors from one end and had moored between them.[153] Six of the Kition anchors and eight of the Ugaritic ones exhibit signs of burning, also apparently caused by cultic operations.[154]

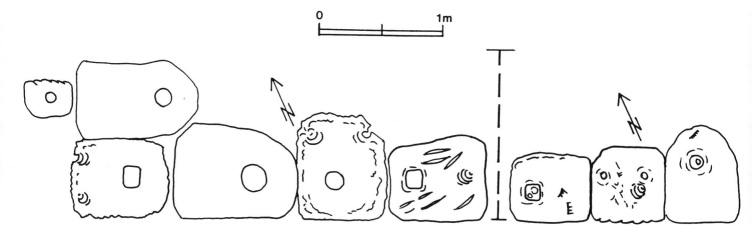

Figure 12.58. Anchors in groups in the walls of Temple 4 at Kition (Late Cypriot IIIA) (from Frost 1986C: 301 fig. 6)

Anchors on the Seabed

Why are so many anchors found in certain areas of the Mediterranean seabed? Some were no doubt left behind when the hawser parted. Also, anchors must have been considered expendable: some may have had their hawsers cut to allow a hasty retreat when it was necessary to escape danger. Raising an anchor in the manner portrayed on the Cypriot jugs would have been extremely dangerous in any kind of sea. Just manhandling an anchor weighing 150 to 200 kilograms aboard a ship in quiet waters is difficult enough, as the staff of the Uluburun excavation came to realize (Fig. 12.48: B). No doubt a Bronze Age captain would have preferred to cut his hawser rather than have a quarter-ton (or more) stone anchor swinging wildly over his fragile wooden hull as it was lifted on board.

Sedimentation may be another cause for leaving anchors behind on the seabed. On shallow, sandy shores, storms can displace enormous amounts of sand in a relatively short time. At the end of a storm, a ship anchored in a "proto-harbor" may have found its anchors buried so deeply in the sand that they could not be raised.

Some stone anchor groups found in the breaker zone may have been left behind because it is impossible to kedge with stone anchors. Thus, in order to float free, a ship stuck on a sandbank could only resort to lightening herself. In all likelihood the first items to go overboard were the anchors, as these could be most readily replaced.

❧ ❧ ❧

Anchors are a major element for the study of Bronze Age seafaring, but anchor research is still in a formative stage. Although important strides have been made in the study of Bronze Age anchors, much remains unknown, and a definitive corpus of all known anchors is urgently needed. There remain entire regions that are *terra incognita* vis-à-vis stone anchors. We know almost nothing of the anchors of Mycenaean Greece or the Anatolian coast, for example. What kind of anchors was used by the seafaring merchants of Ura? We do not know. Similarly, the typology of Canaanite anchors has yet to be defined.

CHAPTER 13

Navigation

The sailing season in antiquity was normally limited to the summer months, between March and November, when northwesterly winds prevail in the eastern Mediterranean.[1] This had a profound effect on the sailing routes plied during the Bronze Age, for the boom-footed square rig then in use was intended primarily for sailing with a following wind. Although it was possible to travel a direct path from Europe to Africa, the return voyage had to be made following the Levantine coastline.

Sea Routes

The following Mediterranean sea routes are documented in the Bronze Age:

Egypt/Syro-Canaanite Coast (Fig. 13.1: A)
Evidence, discussed above, indicates the intense use of the sea route along the Syro-Canaanite coast between Ugarit and Egypt as early as the Late Uruk period.[2] These include voyages to and from Egypt and intercity contacts, particularly by Syro-Canaanite and Egyptian ships.

Cilicia/North Syrian Coast (Fig. 13.1: B)
Ugarit carried on an active maritime trade with Ura (c), which was the main Mediterranean port for the Hittite kingdom. Ura was probably located in Cilicia, perhaps near modern Silifke, or about sixty kilometers to the west in the region of Aydincik.[3]

Syro-Canaanite Coast/Cyprus/Egypt (Fig. 13.1: C–D)
In *EA* 114, Rib-Addi, the embattled king of Byblos, reports that he is under land and coastal siege by his enemy, Aziru, who has taken control of the sea routes.[4] Toward the end of the letter, Rib-Addi emphasizes his isolation by bringing the following action to the pharaoh's attention:

> *Under the circumstances*
> *it goes very badly with me.*
> *Here is the other,*
> *Amanmasha.*
> *Ask him if I did not send him*
> *(via) Alashia to thee.*[5]

W. L. Moran, in his commentary to this text, notes that the order of the words emphasizes the place name, Alashia.[6] Amanmasha is presumably the same Egyptian official who had been previously stationed at Byblos.[7] Y. L. Holmes notes that Rib-Addi is saying that because of the difficult situation, he considered it necessary to send Amanmasha to Egypt by a route other than the normal coastal route between Byblos and Egypt.[8]

Now if Alashia is located north of Byblos on the North Syrian coast or in Cilicia as some scholars contend, then Rib-Addi's actions are incomprehensible. Not only would Amanmasha be sailing in the wrong direction, but this would also require him to sail along the Syrian coast—precisely the area that was under Aziru's control and which Rib-Addi would have wished Amanmasha to avoid at all costs.

If Alashia is located in Cyprus, however, then Rib-Addi's actions are clear and make perfect sense. To avoid Aziru's ships that lurked along the coast, Amanmasha's vessel would have sailed across the open sea from Byblos to Cyprus (Fig. 13.1: C). From there, with the aid of the predominantly northwestern wind, Amanmasha would have then sailed safely across the

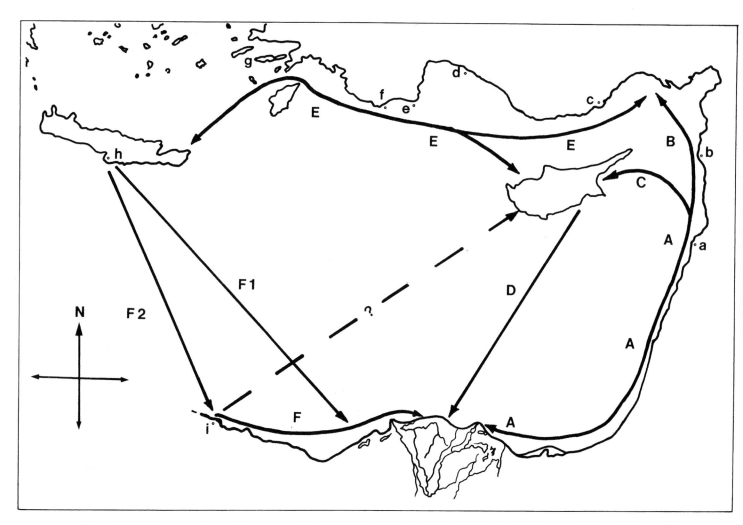

Figure 13.1. *Mediterranean Bronze Age sea routes. Sites:* (a) *Byblos,* (b) *Ugarit,* (c) *Ura (?),* (d) *the Side shipwreck,* (e) *Cape Gelidonya,* (f) *Uluburun,* (g) *Deveboynu Burnu,* (h) *Kommos,* (i) *Mersa Matruh (drawn by the author)*

open sea to Egypt (Fig. 13.1: D).[9] Both legs of the "Alashia route" (Syrian coast-Cyprus, Cyprus-Egypt) must have been familiar to Rib-Addi for him to send Amanmasha that way. This text is also notable in that it is the earliest *recorded* open-sea voyage in the Mediterranean.

There are numerous references to Alashians located in Ugarit and in Egypt.[10] One Ugaritic text is a (partial?) lading of the cargo of an Alashian ship docked at Atallig, one of Ugarit's ports.[11] Anchors add to this evidence. Ugaritic and Byblian anchors found underwater off Cyprus, and what appears to be a Cypriot "basket-handle" anchor uncovered at Ugarit, indi-

cate the movement of ships between these two lands.[12]

Aegean/Syro-Canaanite Coast (*Fig. 13.1: E*)

The earliest evidence for this route is the appearance of a Caphtorite (Minoan) at Mari in the early eighteenth century B.C.[13] On their way to the Levant, the Minoans evidently influenced the indigenous Cypriot culture, for the Cypro-Minoan script derives from Linear A.[14] The "Admonitions of Ipuwer" also may allude to the early use of this route.[15]

A royal dispensation given to Sinaranu, an Ugaritic merchant, reveals that Syro-Canaanites were voyaging to the Aegean by the lat-

ter part of the Late Bronze Age and that this run was apparently considered especially lucrative.[16] A Hittite vassal treaty with Amurru dating to the end of the Late Bronze Age also indicates sea contact between Ahhiyawa and the Syro-Canaanite coast.[17]

This route had a number of variations. One of these is mentioned much later in the itinerary of Abbot Nikolás, an Icelander who made a pilgrimage to the Holy Land in the twelfth century A.D. (Fig. 13.2). After crossing the Aegean, his ship appears to have stopped at Kos, Patara, Kastellorizon and/or Kaş (Myra), and Cape Gelidonya.[18] From there the ship headed southeast to Paphos in Cyprus and then on to Acco.

G. F. Bass notes that the east to west transit of this route is evidenced by the shipwrecks and find-sites of single oxhide ingots at Side in the Bay of Antalya (Fig. 13.1: d), Cape Gelidonya (e), Uluburun (f), and Deveboynu Burnu (Cape Krio) (g).[19] He suggests that these sites mean that the route hugged the coast. Another possibility is that they represent craft that had been blown off course from a route that kept farther away from the coast to avoid its dangers.[20]

There was the ever-present problem of shore-based pirates. And with primitive and unreliable anchors, a lack of good rope-hauling machinery, and a rig of limited maneuverability that made being caught against a lee shore in any kind of weather a very dangerous experience, the Bronze Age seafarer probably deemed the coast something to be avoided. This consideration is emphasized by the quantities of ancient ships that wrecked on the Mediterranean's shores.

The Aegean (Fig. 13.3)

A topographical list on the base of a statue in the forecourt of Amenhotep III's mortuary temple at Kom el Hetan contains a list of Aegean place names.[21] Amenhotep's name appears in the center of the base's front side above a sm3 sign with two Syro-Canaanites bound to it. To its right are two place names:

1) Keftiu   2) Tinay

To the left of the sm3 sign are three additional names. Nine more names, and part of a tenth, appear on the base's left side. They are:

1) Amnisos   4) Mycenae
2) Phaistos   5) Tegai
3) Kydonia   6) Messenia

7) Nauplia   10) Knossos
8) Kythera   11) Amnisos
9) Ilios   12) Lyktos

R. S. Merrillees theorizes that the lack of any apparent geographical order in the list makes it of limited historical significance.[22] When the sites are plotted on a map, however, a different picture emerges. The list begins with a cruise around Crete (1–3) and then describes a trip along mainland Greece (4–7). It then visits Kythera (8) and perhaps describes a visit to the Asiatic coast (9).[23] The list finally returns to Crete (10–12), repeating Amnisos (1 and 11).

Although somewhat confused, these names appear to be based on an itinerary of a clockwise circuit of the Aegean.[24] Only in this manner is the double appearance of Amnisos understandable. The list is not derived from a pilot, as several of the sites are inland.

The earliest sea routes in the Aegean may have followed seasonal fish migrations.[25]

Aegean/Egypt (Fig. 13.1: F [1])

The appearance of Minoans in the Theban tomb wall paintings requires *at the very least* two separate visits to Egypt by Minoan envoys during the combined reigns of Hatshepsut and Thutmose III.[26] There may have been more visits by Minoans, perhaps many more —but for these, evidence is lacking.

More recently, the discovery of fragments of Minoan-style wall paintings (some of a religious na-

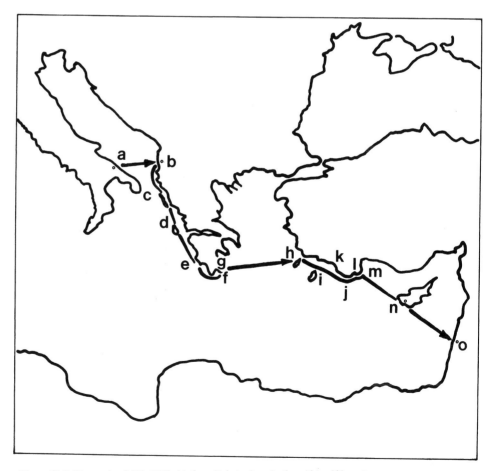

Figure 13.2. The route of Abbot Nikolás from Italy to Acco in the mid-twelfth century A.D. included the following sites: (a) Bari, (b) Durazzo, (c) Corfu, (d) Cephalonia, (e) Sapienza, (f) Cape Malea, (g) Martin Carabo, (h) Kos, (i) Rhodes, (j) Kastellorizon, (k) Patara, (l) Myra, (m) Cape Gelidonya, (n) Paphos, (o) Acco (after Gelsinger 1972: 158 fig. 1)

Figure 13.3. Map illustrating the sites mentioned in the topographic list of Aegean names from Amenhotep III's mortuary temple at Kom el Hetan: (a and k) *Amnisos,* (b) *Phaistos,* (c) *Kydonia,* (d) *Mycenae,* (e) *Tegai,* (f) *Messenia,* (g) *Nauplia,* (h) *Kythera,* (i) *Troy (Ilios),* (j) *Knossos,* (l) *Lyktos (drawn by the author)*

juniper are conifers.[31] *Meru* wood was imported from the Syrian coast. Since it is highly unlikely that conifers grew and were harvested in the western delta, Vercoutter logically assumes that the timber was imported. Because there is no reason for wood imported from the Syro-Canaanite coast to arrive via the *western* delta, Vercoutter suggests that Merikare is alluding to goods arriving from the Aegean via the direct sea route.

Vercoutter raises a second point, which I believe to be the strongest evidence available in support of the Minoans using a blue-water route on their way to Egypt. It is this: the Egyptians always considered Keftiu a *western* country.[32] Had they known the Minoans only as arriving by way of the Syro-Canaanite coast, they would have thought that Keftiu was located northeast of Syria.

Minoans may have first reached Egypt via the Syro-Canaanite coast. Eventually, however, they must have realized the advisability of sailing straight across the Mediterranean. The appearance of Minoans in Egypt at Tell el-Dab^ca at the time of the Thirteenth Dynasty suggests that they were the first navigators to open this route.[33] In charting this course, the Minoans may have followed bird migration routes; alternately, the discovery of a direct route from Crete to Egypt may have occurred from an involuntary drift voyage.[34] A Minoan ship blown off-course by the Etesian winds while on the southern coast of Crete would have been carried to Egypt.

Presumed direct contact back and forth between the Minoan culture and Libya is difficult to sustain because the return journey from Libya to Crete would have nearly always required a trip along the Syro-Canaanite coast. Predynastic artifacts found in Crete do

ture) at Tell el Dab^ca strongly suggests that Minoans actually lived there during the latter part of the Second Intermediate period and that they were in close contact with the ruling class.[27]

By which route did the Minoans reach Egypt? Did they follow the Anatolian and Syro-Canaanite coasts in a clockwise route, or did they venture south in blue-water voyages across the Mediterranean? Writing in 1950, A. Furumark assumes that in the Late Bronze Age, ships never left sight of land. He believes that all traffic between Crete and Egypt went via the Syro-Canaanite coast.[28] Minoan ships, in

his opinion, never got farther than the Syro-Canaanite coast, and all Minoan contacts with Egypt were therefore indirect.

The obvious sea route from the Aegean to Egypt, however, is directly across the Mediterranean with the predominant northwest winds.[29] A western open-water route from Crete to Egypt may be indicated in "The Teachings of Merikare," dated to the end of the twenty-second century: "I pacified the entire west, as far as the coast of the sea. It works for itself, as it gives *meru*-wood, and one may see juniper. They give it to us."[30] J. Vercoutter notes that both *meru* and

not necessarily indicate early trade contacts: a strong argument can be made for them being brought as "antique" trinkets that arrived in the Aegean during the Middle Minoan III–Late III periods.[35]

Homer supplies us with the earlier literary reference to the open-sea route from Crete to Egypt. Odysseus relates:

> We embarked and set sail from broad Crete, with the North Wind blowing fresh and fair, and ran on easily as if down stream. No harm came to any of my ships, but free from scathe and from disease we sat, and the helmsman guided the ships.
>
> On the fifth day we came to fair-flowing Aegyptus, and in the river Aegyptus I moored my curved ships.[36]

Elsewhere, Odysseus calls this route "a far voyage."[37] Classical references describe a three- to four-day crossing from Crete to Egypt.[38]

Although such goods were rare in the Aegean, the Uluburun ship was laden with Cypriot pottery when she went down.[39] Bass and C. M. Pulak suggest that this cargo was not meant for the Aegean region but that the ship may have been on a counterclockwise circuit of the eastern Mediterranean, a trade route previously proposed by Vercoutter.[40]

After dropping off its main cargo in the Aegean, the ship would have continued across the Mediterranean, possibly reaching land at the Libyan port of Mersa Matruh, the only natural harbor between Alexandria and Tobruk, before continuing on to Egypt (Fig. 13.1: F [2]).[41] Excavations at the Late Bronze Age site on Bates' Island near Mersa Matruh revealed Egyptian, Palestinian, Minoan, and Mycenaean sherds—but primarily Cypriot pottery.[42] This pottery dates to the Eighteenth Dynasty. The excavator suggests that Bates' Island served primarily as a way-station for ships to take on supplies arriving from the Aegean.

A Late Bronze Age ship wishing to return to Cyprus from Egypt without following the Syro-Canaanite coast could, theoretically, sail from the Nile Delta to Mersa Matruh and from there directly to Cyprus (Fig. 13.1?). The sailing direction from Mersa Matruh to the western end of Cyprus is northeast by east; thus, this route lies nine points off the predominant northwest wind. Although feasible in theory, there is no evidence that ships plied this course in the Bronze Age. The return voyage from Egypt across the Mediterranean to Cyprus was possible using a (brailed) square rig, as is illustrated by the later voyage of the *Isis*.[43]

Navigational Techniques

"They looked at the sky . . . they looked at the land," wrote the Shipwrecked Sailor of his drowned companions.[44] Seafarers in antiquity must have had a working knowledge of navigational techniques and meteorology. Lacking it could prove fatal. When King Solomon built ships for the run to Ophir, he wisely manned them with Tyrian seafarers who "were familiar with the sea."[45] Interestingly, when Jehoshaphat later built "ships of Tarshish" to repeat Solomon's feat (without Phoenician experts), the ships were wrecked at Etzion Gever.[46]

Information on seafaring navigational techniques of the Bronze Age is limited. With the notable exception of sounding weights, I am unaware of nautical navigational instruments surviving in the archaeological record of any of the Bronze Age cultures that peopled the eastern Mediterranean. This does not necessarily imply a lack of navigational knowledge, however: highly developed navigational systems may have existed without leaving any archaeological trace, beyond evidence for the open-sea voyages themselves.

Ancient navigation was an art—not a science. It depended on a vast and intimate knowledge of position-finding factors that were entirely committed to memory.[47] This is admirably illustrated by Pacific navigation. Despite the impressive results of native Oceanic navigation, no position-finding instruments were ever taken aboard ship.[48] The only navigational aids were stick charts, and these were used only as mnemonic devices that were not taken to sea.[49] Theoretically, a similar situation may have existed in the Bronze Age Mediterranean.

Navigational knowledge is usually a well-guarded secret, shared only by a select cadre of navigators. In Oceania, for example, navigational lore was restricted to a privileged few.[50] This may result in the loss of navigational techniques, as was almost the case in Oceania until the work of modern investigators.[51]

It is possible that during the Late Bronze Age, also, navigational techniques were kept secret and may have been lost during times of unrest and turbulence. The Minoans had the navigational knowledge required to use the open-sea route to Egypt. Perhaps the ability to navigate southward across the Mediterranean was lost for a time when the autonomous Minoan culture fell and was never acquired by the Mycenaeans. This is one possible reason for the apparent cessation of direct trade links between the Aegean and Egypt at the end of the Late Minoan IB period.[52]

Sounding Weights

Kenamun's artist depicted lookouts in the bows of two ships measuring the river's depth with sounding poles, but these would have been useless in coastal navigation (Figs. 3.3, 6). Middle Kingdom models sometimes portray the lookout holding a sounding weight.[53] A large lead weight found at Uluburun may have been the ship's sounding lead.[54] The small pierced stones commonly found underwater along the coasts of the Mediterranean are generally taken to be fishnet weights (Fig. 12.35): some of these may have been used as simple sounding weights.

Birds

It is likely that birds were used as a land-finding method in the Bronze Age Mediterranean.[55] This land-finding technique, described in the stories of Noah and Utnapishtim, is of great antiquity.[56] There are two basic manners of using birds in nautical navigation. In the first, ships sail carrying caged land birds—such as doves, ravens, or swallows—which are incapable of landing on water. When the direction of land beyond the horizon is desired, a bird is released. After gaining height, it will invariably make a beeline for the nearest land—if such is sighted. If it finds no land, the bird has no choice but to return to the ship.

The second manner in which birds can be used depends on knowing the range of seabirds that feed far out at sea but return to their rookeries every evening. Noting the direction that the flocks take in the early morning when they leave their nesting grounds, or in the late afternoon when they return home, indicates land.

Wind Roses

It is generally assumed that before the introduction of the magnetic compass, Mediterranean navigators took their bearings from the winds.[57] The invention of the Mediterranean wind rose is associated with the Phoenicians.[58] The reasoning behind this kind of "compass" is that each wind had a different "signature" with respect to temperature, moisture, and other characteristics.[59]

Homer knew four winds: Boreas (the north wind), Euros (the east wind), Notos (the south wind), and Zephuros (the west wind). The Greeks later developed this into an eight-wind system, as depicted on the first-century B.C. Athenian "Tower of the Winds" (Horologium).[60] The four additional winds more or less bisect the angles between the original four. The Italians adopted the Greek wind system, giving the winds Italian names. This was later expanded to twelve, then to sixteen, and finally to thirty-two winds.

Wind roses are very real tools in the "art" of navigation, as is evident from their use by Oceanic navigators.[61] However, winds can be only secondary directional indicators; they must often be compared with more reliable phenomena. For travel in sight of land, landmarks are sufficient.

In the Mediterranean, navigators no doubt learned visible landmarks that were given names, like the "Antelope's Nose" mentioned by Uni.[62] There are no known Bronze Age parallels, however, to the *periploi* that were used in Classical times.[63] This may be attributable in part to a lack of general literacy in the nonalphabetic scripts in use at that time. Theoretically at least, this should not have been a problem for an Ugaritic navigator

using that city's alphabetic script. The diptych found on the Uluburun shipwreck raises the possibility that at least one person on board that vessel may have been literate.[64] I am not aware of any Bronze Age nautical charts.

Other navigational systems depended on the sun. The points where the sun rises and sets fluctuate considerably with the seasons, however. Fixed points were needed, and these could only be supplied by the stars. The original Mediterranean wind rose may have been based on a sidereal compass. Since Mediterranean seafaring was largely in sight of land, however, the need for this may not have arisen.

Stellar Navigation

The later Greeks are said to have learned stellar navigation from the Phoenicians. The Greek poet Aratus (ca. 315–240 B.C.) notes that the Phoenicians used the *Ursa minor* (Little Bear) constellation, which contains Polaris (the Pole star) for navigation.[65] Clearly, Aratus had only a hazy concept of stellar navigation, for noninstrumental stellar navigation must be based on the knowledge of many stars, as has been demonstrated by D. Lewis.[66] If stellar navigation existed in the Mediterranean Bronze Age, it was probably not unlike that practiced in Oceania.[67]

Weather Lore

Bronze Age seafarers must have developed their own weather lore: to quote the Shipwrecked Sailor, "They could foretell a stormwind before it came and a downpour before it happened."[68] Both the Psalmist and Ezekiel seem to consider the east wind the most dangerous.[69] Presumably, it was also an east wind that wrecked Wenamun's ship on Alashia's shore.[70] Josephus describes gale-force winds called the "Black Norther" that destroyed the Jewish rebel fleet at Jaffa in A.D. 67.[71] Elsewhere, he notes the destructive southwest wind.[72]

Perhaps the best-known ancient weather lore appears in the New Testament. When asked to perform a miracle, Jesus—who must have had considerable experience sailing on the Sea of Galilee—answers: "When it is evening, you say, 'It will be fair weather; for the sky is red.' And in the morning, 'It will be stormy today, for the sky is red and threatening.' You know how to interpret the appearance of the sky, but you cannot interpret the signs of the times."[73]

Here Jesus is referring to the well-known sailor's rhyme:

Red sky in the morning,
Sailors take warning.
Red sky at night,
Sailors delight.

This weather lore has meteorological wisdom. The weather flow in the northern horse latitudes is generally westerly. A red sunset indicates that the next day's weather in the west is dust-laden and, therefore, dry.

Land and Sea Breezes
Land and sea breezes were essential for coastal sailing, particularly with a boom-footed square sail. Wenamun twice refers to the time of his ships' departure from harbor: he left Tyre for Byblos "at crack of dawn," and the ship on which he was to sail back to Egypt from Byblos was to leave at night.[74] This timing may have resulted from a

desire to utilize land breezes, which follow the cooling of the land after sunset. These winds are normally of low velocity and are restricted to the immediate coastline, but for a ship using a square rig, land breezes would have been invaluable in allowing the craft to clear the coast to catch the offshore winds.

≈ ≈ ≈

There is ample evidence for Late Bronze Age sea routes in the eastern Mediterranean. The mariners may have had a developed navigational system that left virtually no archaeological trace. The seafaring capabilities of the Late Bronze Age would seem to support this conclusion, although, with the data presently at our disposal, it cannot be proven.

CHAPTER 14

Sea Trade

Although the mechanics of Bronze Age sea trade are beyond the scope of this study, this chapter will focus primarily on Late Bronze Age cargoes as typified by the Uluburun and Cape Gelidonya shipwrecks. These supply us with an extraordinarily intimate view of the diversity of the commodities traded. This information is complemented by documentary and iconographic evidence of "invisible" materials that are unlikely to survive long periods under the sea.

Ships, as well as timber for shipbuilding, were in themselves significant items of trade. Indeed, the importation of ready-made timber from the Syro-Canaanite coast to Egypt may have had a profound influence on Egyptian shipbuilding.

Shipwrecks

Uluburun
Since final publication of the Uluburun wreck is being completed at the time of writing, any description of its cargo must remain preliminary, based on the detailed field reports published to date.[1] Nevertheless, these allow an intimate and fascinating view of the cargo of what is presumably a

relatively large class of Late Bronze Age merchantman (Fig. 14.1).[2] Other finds hint at aspects of shipboard life for the crew—and perhaps the passengers.

The ship is believed to have carried at least fifteen tons of cargo.[3] This calculation does not include the additional weight of the stone ballast, the long-perished organic cargo, and the approximately four tons of stone anchors.[4]

Raw materials. The Uluburun wreck carried a main cargo of raw materials. The heaviest portion of the cargo consisted of copper and *tin* ingots in a variety of oxhide, bun, and other forms, some of which at present are unique to Uluburun.[5] This is the earliest appearance of tin ingots of oxhide shape. G. F. Bass had previously identified white, oxhide-shaped ingots portrayed in Theban tombs as tin.[6]

The ship carried a total of 317 copper oxhide ingots. This is more oxhide ingots than are presently known from the entire Near East![7] The weight of these ingots alone is calculated at a stunning ten tons.[8]

Lead isotope analysis has been carried out on four of the Uluburun oxhide ingots, five bun ingots, and one slab ingot.[9] With the

exception of one of the bun ingots, all were made of Cypriot copper. Interestingly, similar analysis of Late Minoan/Late Helladic III bronzes suggests Lavrion as a primary source of copper in mainland Greece and Crete.[10] Although too few objects have been examined to date to reach any definite conclusions, this research does raise the question of where the Uluburun ship was to deliver its copper cargo.

The oxhide ingots were stacked in overlapping rows, in a manner reminiscent of roof shingles.[11] Each stack contained from eight to eleven ingots, all of which were placed with the mold (smooth) side facing downward. This may have facilitated a better grip and left the marks on the ingots visible.

Interestingly, to date no lead ingots have been uncovered at Uluburun, nor were any found at Gelidonya. Apparently, during the Late Bronze Age the Aegean was not importing its lead from the East.[12]

Some, if not all, of the gold jewelry was being carried as scrap, intended for remelting. This included a lump of molten gold, an entire gold ring and a fragment of a second ring, and part of a gold

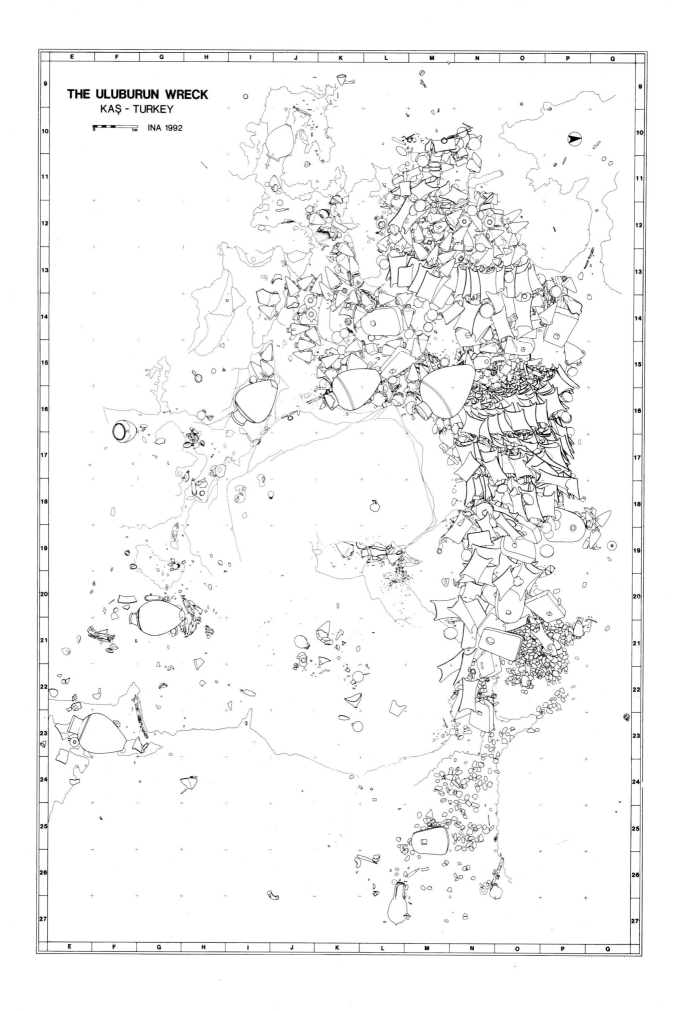

THE ULUBURUN WRECK
KAŞ - TURKEY
INA 1992

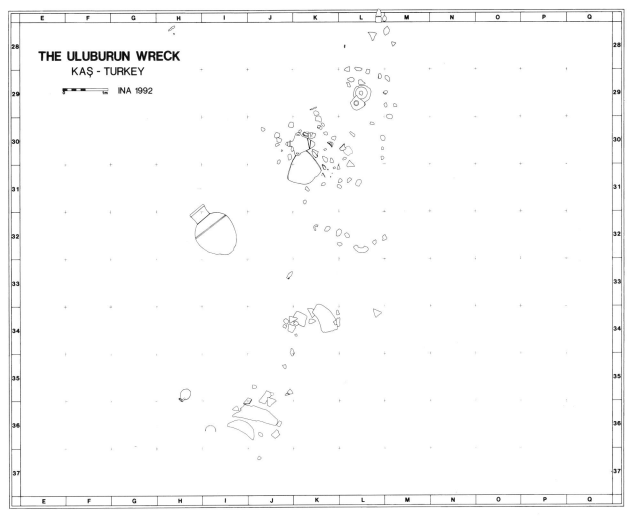

THE ULUBURUN WRECK
KAŞ - TURKEY

INA 1992

Figure 14.1. Site plan of the Uluburun wreck (courtesy Institute of Nautical Archaeology)

bar or disk that had its edges removed with a chisel.[13] The ship also carried about 175 round glass ingots, primarily of a cobalt-blue hue.[14] Other raw materials dispersed in the wreck included ivory and precious woods: a section of unworked elephant tusk, the complete tusk of a small elephant, hippopotamus teeth, logs and a worked section of African blackwood (the ancient Egyptian *hbny*), and other as yet unidentified woods.[15] At least one jar was filled with orpiment (yellow arsenic).[16]

ORGANIC MATERIALS. Thanks to meticulous excavation techniques, including the sieving of all closed pottery containers, archaeologists have retrieved a wide variety of organic materials at Ulu-

burun.[17] This information promises a new understanding of the wealth of organic commodities that constituted a significant element of Late Bronze Age trade—of which we know so little.

Canaanite jars contained about 1.5 tons of terebinth resin, making it the second most abundant substance in the ship's cargo.[18] Later Classical authors describe the collection of resin from the *Pistachia terebinthus* in the Levant's coastal region.[19] Incense was also used on board at least some Late Bronze Age ships; in the tomb of Kenamun, Syro-Canaanite seamen burn incense (Fig. 3.4–5).

A list of the organic materials recovered at Uluburun includes the following: acorns, almonds,

bits of matting, blades of grass, capers, charred wheat and barley grains, rachis and fragments from barley chaff and other grains and grass, coriander, fig seeds and fruit fragments, residues of two types of grape seeds, a few kinds of small grass seeds, nigella (black cumin), oak and beech leaves, olives and olive stones, pine cone fragments, pine nuts, wild pistachio nutlets, pomegranate seeds, at least three types of pulses, safflower, sumac seeds, twigs, and some twenty species of weed seeds.[20] Thorny burnet shrubs were used as dunnage to prevent the heavy cargo from harming the hull.[21]

Additional archaeobotanical remains included fragments of

basketry, rope, matting, and wood chips, as well as leaves of conifers, oaks, and pistachio trees.[22] Eight different varieties of shrubs and trees were represented in the numerous charcoal fragments. Many insects were also found among the organic remains.

One *pithos* contained remains of whole pomegranates.[23] Fig seeds, which were found throughout the site as well as in pilgrim flasks and a *pithos,* may have originated as dried-fig stoppers on closed containers.[24] A dark stain in the sand seems to be the result of a liquid, as yet unidentified, seeping from a *pithos.*[25] Purple, crimson, and blue animal hairs and cloth fibers are all that remain of an unknown quantity of woven materials carried by the ship.[26] Bolts of cloth are shown being brought to Egypt by foreigners depicted in the Theban tombs.[27]

The ship also carried ostrich eggshells—some of which actually managed to survive the shipwreck intact!—and fossilized shell.[28] One of the most unusual cargoes discovered on the wreck contained thousands of murex *opercula,* or "doors."[29] C. M. Pulak notes that these may be a by-product of the purple-dye industry and speculates that *opercula* may have been employed for medicinal purposes and as an ingredient for incense.

MANUFACTURED MATERIALS. Some bronze (or copper) bowls were found in sets, nestled inside each other.[30] Additional cauldron straps and the handle of a bronze jug or cup hint at a variety of bronze vessels carried aboard.[31]

Ten *pithoi* of three different sizes had tumbled down the slope.[32] These are reminiscent of the large jars portrayed in the bows of Syro-Canaanite seagoing ships (Figs. 3.2–6). One *pithos* contained twenty-one lead fishnet sinkers, a lamp, and a Syrian pil-

grim flask.[33] Another contained eighteen pieces of Near Eastern pottery, most of them of Cypriot origin.[34] Open pottery shapes of like type had been packed inside each other, as in a modern china barrel. Additional Cypriot pottery, pilgrim flasks, lamps, and wall brackets were found strewn throughout the wreck.[35] Many of these are believed to have spilled from the *pithoi* as they rolled down the slope. The quantities of Cypriot pottery are enigmatic if the vessel's final destination had been the Aegean: the Uluburun ship carried more Cypriot pottery than is presently known from the entire Aegean.[36]

The wreck contained many Canaanite jars in three basic shapes.[37] Potsherds found inside these jars may have prevented the clay stoppers from touching the jars' liquid contents.[38] Containers of leather, or some other perishable materials, had also probably been on board.[39]

Musical instruments included an artifact that may be a tin whistle, a pair of bronze cymbals, and at least five tortoise carapaces, used in antiquity for the sound boxes of lyres and lutes.[40] Beads were scattered throughout the wreck. These are made of a variety of materials: agate, amber, bone, faience, glass, ostrich-eggshell, quartz, rock crystal, shell, and an undefined stone; at least some of these beads may have come on board ship decorating textiles that disintegrated over time.[41] One Canaanite jar was filled with glass beads that had concreted solidly together.[42] Rings carved from seashells, probably Mediterranean top shells, were also found.[43]

Prestige items. Some items on board ship may have had a particular prestige value. A unique gold cup is reminiscent of the one given to Odysseus by Alcinous,

king of the Phaeacians.[44] The date and provenance of the Uluburun cup remain elusive.[45]

Metal vessels made of tin included a mug, a plate, and a pilgrim flask.[46] Lead isotope ratio analysis of the pilgrim flask suggests that it was made of metal mined in Turkey's Taurus Mountains.[47]

The ship carried gold and silver jewelry of Syro-Canaanite design.[48] Interestingly, gold roundels like those found on the ship are worn by seven Syro-Canaanite seamen in the Kenamun tomb painting (Figs. 3.4–6, 29; 14.6).[49] It is not clear if any of the Uluburun roundels were meant for shipboard use.

In addition to the raw ivory on board, the ship carried several luxury items made of ivory: parts of at least two duck-shaped ivory cosmetic containers, probably from the Syro-Canaanite coast or Egypt;[50] ivory scepters and ivory (or bone) finials;[51] and, of particular interest, a hippopotamus incisor carved in the shape of a ram's horn or *shofar.*[52] Other prestige items at Uluburun were made of faience. At least five faience *rhyta* in the form of rams' heads and one shaped like a woman's head closely parallel artifacts uncovered in Enkomi and Tell Abu Hawam.[53]

PERSONAL ITEMS AND SHIP'S EQUIPMENT. Some items may represent personal belongings of the crew and passengers. Other artifacts were for shipboard use.

Seals found on the wreck included the following: part of an Egyptian inscribed gold signet ring that had been intentionally cut for scrap; a gold scarab bearing the name of Queen Nefertiti; a faience scarab with the name of Thutmose I; several scarabs with decorative designs; a stone scarab with a baboon decoration; a small rectangular stone plaque with a hieroglyphic inscription to "Ptah, Lord of Truth and Perfect in Favors"; a quartz cylinder seal with gold caps (similar to Kassite seals from Babylonia dated ca. 1350 B.C.); an Old Babylonian cylinder seal of hematite cut ca. 1750 B.C. with additional elements added four centuries later by an Assyrian artisan; a faience—or sintered quartz—cylinder seal of a type common across Mitannian lands but that probably originated near Ugarit ca. 1450–1350 B.C.; and two other cylinder seals: one of Kassite origin made of rock-crystal, the other of faience.[54]

Of particular interest are Mycenaean objects of a personal nature on a ship that was heading to the Aegean. These include two lentoid seals, blue glass relief beads of probable Mycenaean origin, Minoan or Mycenaean green stone (steatite?) seal blanks, and a globed pin, as well as several types of Mycenaean pottery: a *kylix*, stirrup jars, a pitcher, a dipper, a one-handled cup, a beaked jug, and fragments of other vessels.[55] Taken together, these artifacts suggest the presence of Mycenaean ethnics on board the ship when it sank.

A bronze female figurine with gold foil covering her head, hands, and feet may have been the ship's tutelary deity.[56] It was found together with a stone ceremonial ax head that apparently originated in the Black Sea region.[57] Utensils for cooking, grinding, and pounding must have been used in the preparation of meals on board the ship.[58] Lead fishnet sinkers, fish hooks, a harpoon, a trident, and fish remains suggest that the crew supplemented its diet from the sea.[59] Lead isotope analysis of four of the fishnet sinkers suggests that they were made of lead from the Taurus Mountains and the Laurion mines.[60]

Trade was carried out by means of pan balance weights, of which

the ship carried a variety, in geometric and zoomorphic shapes.[61] Pierced lead disks may have been weights of Aegean origin.[62] A diptych, made of boxwood with ivory hinges, was discovered in a *pithos*.[63] This is the earliest known "book."[64] Two additional hinge parts may have belonged to additional diptychs that did not survive.[65] The diptych raises the interesting possibility that at least one person on the ship may have been literate.

A variety of weapon types was carried on board: swords, daggers, knives, spearheads, arrowheads, mace heads, and a collared ax head.[66] A single scale of bronze armor is of a type common throughout the Near East.[67] The diverse kinds and origins of the weapons seem to support the interpretation that these were carried for defense, not as items of trade.[68]

The tools included ax blades, a bow drill, a saw, adze blades, chisels, drill bits (awls), razors, a hoe, sickle blades, knives, and a pair of tongs.[69] It is not clear if all of these were for shipboard use or if some tools were being carried as cargo. Abrasive stones and an antler tine, which had probably been originally stored in a bag made of leather or some other perishable material, were used to hone utensils.[70] Astragals could have been used for divination or for whiling away the time with games of chance.[71]

The quantities of raw materials and luxury items on board at Uluburun suggest that the main part—if not the entire cargo—may have been a royal gift, similar to those mentioned in the Amarna tablets.[72] Culture and diplomacy sailed hand-in-hand with merchandise in the Late Bronze Age. The king of Alashia asks repeatedly that his messengers be returned quickly.[73] In one text, the

reason for this haste becomes clear: *"These men are my merchants. My brother, let them go safely and prom[pt]ly. No one making a claim in your name is to approach my merchants or my ship."*[74] Evidently maritime traders, in addition to their commercial activities, also served as international diplomats.

The Uluburun ship may be indicative of the mechanism of indirect trade during the fourteenth century. Several clues suggest an eastern origin for the ship.[75] If so, and if, as suggested by Bass and Pulak, the ship was sailing a counterclockwise course throughout the waters of the eastern Mediterranean, this would then explain how Mycenaean pottery—and even an intimate knowledge of the Aegean—might have been carried to Egypt, and how Egyptian objects reached the Aegean, without the two contributing cultures actually coming into direct contact.[76]

Cape Gelidonya
The Gelidonya wreck was a small craft, apparently a tramp that collected metal junk for reuse. Its cargo consisted primarily of copper oxhide ingots, bun ingots, and bronze tools.[77] Smaller artifacts were found scattered nearby. Most of the oxhide ingots had been stacked in three piles.[78] Fragments of matting found between the ingots suggest that they were either wrapped together or separated from each other by layers of matting: twigs uncovered in the wreck were apparently dunnage used to cushion the hull from the heavy metal ingots.[79]

Personal effects belonging to the ship's crew included scarabs, a lamp, mace heads, whetstones, an astragal, a cylinder seal, weights, and traces of food.[80] There are similarities between the cargo at Gelidonya and the lading of an Alashian ship recorded at Ugarit.[81]

Discussion

Terebinth Resin

In a monograph dealing with the meaning of *sntr*, V. Loret concludes that this is the Egyptian term for terebinth resin, commonly used in Egypt as incense.[82] Terebinth resin was also employed in antiquity as an astringent in aromatic ointments.[83]

Although a species of *sntr* tree grew indigenously in Egypt (and the resin was also imported into Egypt from Punt and Nubia), the primary source for *sntr* resin was the Syro-Canaanite coast. In the tomb of Rechmire, six jars labeled *sntr* are depicted, together with jars of olive oil and salve (*sft*) and a basket of lapis lazuli, in the bottom row of the display of Syro-Canaanite tribute/trade (Fig. 14.2: A).[84]

Large quantities of *sntr* are recorded in Thutmose III's annals.[85] The total liquid volume of *sntr* received by Thutmose is recorded for five of the years covered by his annals: year twenty-four, 12,345 liters; year thirty-three, 12,420 liters; year thirty-four, 10,395 liters; year thirty-five, (only) 1,260 liters; year thirty-eight, 9,840 liters. These imports average 9,250 liters per year. If this average held true for all twenty of the years that Thutmose was active in Asia, then Egypt would have imported some 185,000 liters of *sntr* during that time.

J. L. Melena tentatively identifies *ki-ta-no* recorded in Linear B inventories as pistachio nuts (*Pistachia terebinthus*).[86] The word is written, however, with a symbol suggesting that it was an aromatic or a condiment; Bass, in consideration of the resin found on the Uluburun shipwreck, equates *ki-ta-no* with terebinth resin.[87] Over 18,400 liters of *ki-ta-no* are recorded at Knossos.[88]

These quantities of *sntr* in the Egyptian, and *ki-ta-no* in the Lin-ear B, documents place into historical perspective the 1.5 tons of resin carried by the Uluburun ship. Indeed, Thutmose III's annals for year thirty-five may refer to a single shipment of resin, of approximately the amount on board the Uluburun ship.

If intended for off-loading in an Aegean port, however, the terebinth resin may have been destined, at least in part, for a purpose other than incense or perfume. In this regard, the "Admonitions of Ipu-wer" contains a fascinating comment: "No one really sails north to [Byb]los today. What shall we do for cedar for our mummies? Priests were buried *with* their produce, and [nobles] were embalmed with the oil therof as far away as Keftiu, (but) they come no (longer)."[89] Ipu-wer seems to be saying that resins that had previously been imported from Byblos on the Syro-Canaanite coast to Egypt for use in the mummification process were used for embalming in Keftiu (i.e., Crete and/or the Aegean world).

Although there is no evidence for mummification in the Late Bronze Age Aegean, the following points suggest that some form of embalming (that is, the immersing of a cadaver in preservative liquids) may have been practiced:[90]

• Resin is one of the main ingredients required in mummification as practiced by the ancient Egyptians. Herodotus and Diodorus describe "cedar oil" used in the mummification process.[91] This was either injected into the body or used to anoint it.[92] However, this oil was almost certainly derived from the juniper tree and not from the true cedar.[93] Terebinth resin was not normally used for mummification in New Kingdom Egypt.[94]

• There are a number of striking similarities between the Cult of the Dead in Egypt and in Crete.[95] These suggest that the Minoan culture, and through it perhaps the Mycenaean also, was profoundly influenced in its religious beliefs and practices by its contact with Egypt. M. P. Nilsson, in discussing the Greek concept of the "Land of the Blessed," notes, "Its varying features are derived from the Minoan Age and agree so closely with Egyptian conceptions that it seems probable that an intimate connexion may be supposed with Egyptian belief in this case."[96] Thus, embalming—a considerably simplified form of the complex Egyptian practice for preserving the bodies of the dead—may have been included among the burial beliefs and customs adopted or adapted from the Egyptians by the Minoans and transmitted through them to the Mycenaeans also.[97]

• *Pithos* burials became widespread throughout the Aegean world during the Middle Bronze Age: these would have been suitable for immersing a body in a preservative liquid.[98] Clay coffins began to replace storage jars at Knossos toward the end of the Middle Minoan period. Some containers were lined with plaster, perhaps to render them less porous.

• Minoan signet rings depicting cult scenes sometimes show large *pithoi* like those used in the burials (Figs. 6.53, 69: D).[99] A. W. Persson suggests that these represent some rite of mourning for the dead god before his joyful resurrection.[100] This may be related to the Greek myth in which Glaukos, the son of Minos, dies by falling into a jar of honey—but is revived by means of an herb revealed by a snake.[101] Persson proposes that this myth, along with many other later references, may be reminiscent of a time when the dead were embalmed in Crete, although he assumes that the embalming was done in honey.

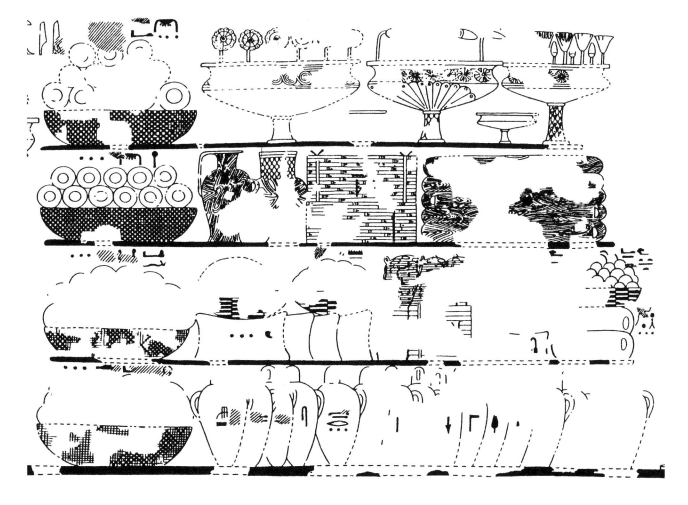

A

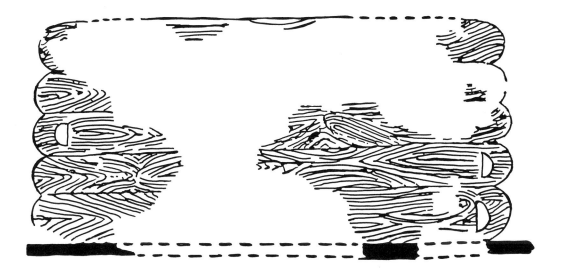

B

Figure 14.2. (A) *Syro-Canaanite display in a scene of foreign tribute from the tomb of Rechmire (T. 100) at Thebes. Note the timber at the right side of the second row (Late Thutmose III–early Amenhotep II).* (B) *Detail of timber (from Davies 1943 [II]: pl. 21; ©, the Metropolitan Museum of Art, New York)*

• Finally, H. Schliemann describes the remarkably preserved remains of a man whom he found in Grave 4 in Grave Circle A at Mycenae:

But of the third body, which lay at the north end of the tomb, the round face, with all its flesh, had been wonderfully preserved under its ponderous golden mask; there was no vestige of hair, but both eyes were perfectly visible, also the mouth, which, owing to the enormous weight that had pressed upon it, was wide open, and showed thirty-two beautiful teeth. From these, all the physicians who came to see the body were led to believe that the man must have died at the early age of thirty-five. The nose was entirely gone. . . . The colour of the body resembled very much that of an Egyptian mummy.[102]

Unless Schliemann is exaggerating, which is always a possibility, it would seem that this body may have undergone some form of embalming.[103]

Hippopotamus Ivory in Egyptian Tomb Paintings

The appearance of hippopotamus ivory at Uluburun emphasizes another trade commodity that has been given only limited attention until recently.

Foreigners bringing hippopotamus tusks are depicted twice in Egyptian tomb art. In one, dating to the Old or Middle Kingdom, a porter carries two tusklike objects on his shoulder.[104] These are similar in appearance to the ibex horns that were imported into Egypt during the New Kingdom as a raw material in the construction of composite bows.[105] In this case, however, they are definitely not ibex horns; the composite bow was introduced into Egypt only later, during the Second Intermediate period.

In the tomb of Menkheper-resonb (T. 86) at Thebes, a porter carries over his shoulder two tusk-like objects that can be identified as hippopotamus teeth.[106] These might be mistaken for elephant tusks, like those carried singly or in pairs by Syro—Canaanite, Minoan, or Nubian porters in the scenes of foreign tribute from the tombs of Rechmire (T. 100) and Sebekhotep (T. 63).[107] The ivory carried by Menkheperresonb's porter is quite unlike the other depictions of elephant tusks, however: the former are narrower and more hook-shaped, appearing to point upward instead of curving down over the shoulder. They *are*, however, identical to teeth portrayed in the mouth of a hippopotamus in a contemporary tomb painting.[108]

Trade in Timber and Ships

Egypt has indigenous trees that are suitable, although not ideal, for shipbuilding: acacia, Doum palm, persea, sycamore, and tamarisk.[109] However, timber for use in shipbuilding as well as for other purposes was a most important Syro-Canaanite export to Egypt throughout pharaonic times.[110]

Considerable evidence exists for the exportation of cedar (and other woods) from Lebanon to Egypt.[111] The earliest-recorded appearance of wood identified as cedar in Egypt dates to the Predynastic (Badarian) period.[112] Two ancient Egyptian depictions of Lebanese forests have come down to us. The earliest, from the tomb of Amenmose at Thebes (T. 42; Thutmose III—Amenhotep II), shows a fortified Syro-Canaanite city with crenelated walls in a forest setting (Fig. 14.3). Norman de Garis Davies identifies the trees as pine because they reach a considerable height before beginning to branch out. Another scene, from

the Temple of Amun at Karnak, depicts Lebanese princes felling trees (identified as Lebanese cedar) for Seti I (Fig. 14.4).[113] As two men with axes cut the base of one tree, two others grasp ropes attached to the upper portion of the tree and wound around neighboring trees. Perhaps Tjekkerbaal had this purpose in mind when he told Wenamun, "Give me the ropes [that] you have brought [to lash the pine log]s which I am to fell in order to supply them to you."[114]

After they were felled, the cedar logs were left to season in the mountains before being brought down to the coast.[115] The Old Kingdom ax head found in the Adonis River, near Byblos, suggested to A. Rowe that the timber may have been floated down the stream from inside the country to the river's mouth (Fig. 2.1).[116] If this was carried out in the spring, when the river was swollen with water, it may explain Tjekkerbaal's boast to Wenamun: "I have but to let out a cry unto the Lebanon so that as soon as the heavens open up, the logs are (already) lying here on the seashore."[117] Once the logs reached the coast, they were transported as cargo in ships or towed behind them in makeshift rafts.[118]

Senufer, an official during Thutmose III's reign, describes in his tomb (T. 99) at Thebes a mission to Lebanon to acquire cedarwood: "I entered the forest-[preserve]. . . . [I caused] that there be presented to her [the goddess of Byblos] offerings of millions of things on behalf of [*the life, prosperity and health of thy majesty*] . . . *in* Byblos, that I might give them to her lord for her [heart's] satisfaction . . . gave . . . of the choicest thereof. I brought away (timbers of) 60 cubits in [their] length. . . . They were sharper than the beard of grain, the middle thereof *as thick*. . . . I [brought] them [*down*] from the

Figure 14.3. Lebanese forest depicted in a scene of foreign tribute in the tomb of Amenmose (T. 42) (Thutmose III–Amenhotep II) (from Davies and Davies 1933: pl. 36; courtesy of the Committee of the Egypt Exploration Society)

highland of God's Land. They reached as far as the forest-preserve."[119]

The "gifts" that Senufer brought for the goddess of Byblos, whom the Egyptians equated with Hathor, were actually a polite statement for payment of the timber.[120] Indeed, even during the Late Bronze Age when Asia was under Egyptian dominance, Egypt apparently paid dearly for its timber. This is evident from the following exchange between Tjekkerbaal and Wenamun:

> He [Tjekkerbaal] responded saying to me: On what sort of business have you come? And I told him: It is in quest of lumber for the great and noble barge of Amon-Re, King of the Gods, that I have come. What your father did and / what your father's father did, you will also do. So I said to him. And he said to me: They did in fact supply it. You have but to pay me for supplying it, and I will supply it. Actu-

Figure 14.4. Lebanese princes cut down trees for the pharaoh. Karnak: exterior of the north wall of the grand hall (Seti I) (after Wreszinski II: 35)

ally, it was only after Pharaoh, l.p.h., had sent six freighters loaded with Egyptian products which were unloaded into their warehouses that my (people) carried out this commission. But you, what is it that you have brought me in my turn?

He had a journal roll belonging to his ancestors brought and had it read out in my presence. It was verified that a thousand *deben* of silver and miscellaneous items (had been entered) in his journal roll. / And he said to me: As for the Ruler of Egypt, he has been the lord of what is mine, and I have been his servant as well. It was not with the words, "Carry out the commission from Amon!" that he used to send silver and gold. Was it not a delivery of royal gifts that used to be made unto my father?[121]

Many of the timbers used in BM 10056 are of imported ꜥš wood.[122] This term originally specified a species of fir (*Abies cilicia*) that grows in Lebanon.[123] S. R. K. Glanville, however, concludes that this was not so much a particular wood as the general term for ready-for-use imported timber:

...ꜥš is precisely connoted by the English word "deal," in its sense of timber derived from pine or fir. It is tempting to see still another, fortuitous, resemblance between the two words. "Deal" originally means a plank or board, a piece of sawn wood. The extension of meaning to define the nature of the wood is due to the fact that the commonest kind of wood imported in plank form for general purposes, was the North European pine and fir. Now both common sense and the nature of the determinative demand that ꜥš was imported into Egypt, if not actually in planks, at all events as

logs which had already been trimmed, which in the case of conifers involves a fair amount of lopping. To the Egyptian joiner or shipwright, acquainted with the names and differentiation between the three or four local trees of any use to him, whose short, twisted branches he was used to cutting for himself, the outstanding feature of the timber he called ꜥš would be its "ready-for-use" appearance. In very few cases would he have seen the trees, from which the wood came, in their natural state. It is possible that the word ꜥš was a local Syrian name for a species of fir or pine, or for certain conifers in general, and that the Egyptian expeditions which were sent to get the wood learned the native name from the source of supply. It is also possible, however, and very tempting in view of the modern analogy of deal, that ꜥš, like "deal" originally meant "cut wood," and only later came to be applied to the type of tree which produced it. . . . To sum up, may not the determinative of šꜥ "to cut" in the Pyramid Texts suggest that ꜥš originally signified "cut wood" and that the wood derived its name from the verb?[124]

Glanville's suggestion is supported by two additional considerations. First, there are textual references to prepared timbers arriving in Egypt. Kamose mentions "wooden planks" among the ships' cargoes he captured from the Hyksos when he conquered Avaris.[125] A half-millennium later, when Tjekkerbaal sent seven timbers as gifts to Egypt, Wenamun notes that he sent not logs but preshaped ship's timbers: a stempost, a sternpost, an item identified as a keel (?), and four hewn timbers.[126] Second, in the tombs of Useramun (T. 131; Thut-

mose III) and Rechmire (T. 100; Thutmose III—Amenhotep II), cut timbers appear in the display of Syro-Canaanites' trade items (Figs. 14.2, 5). The timbers are straight with rounded ends and with semicircular mortises cut into one of their extremities. They are painted light brown, with red lines indicating the wood's grain (cedar?). This importation of prepared ship parts may have influenced ship construction in Egypt, as did Syro-Canaanite shipbuilders who were employed there.

This in no way detracts from the massive importation of timber in the form of logs into Egypt, as we have seen in the documents of Sahure, Senufer, and Wenamun. Just the construction of the Dashur boats alone would have required an estimated ten or more tons of imported cedarwood.[127] Timber in the form of long, straight logs (cedar?) is also portrayed in tomb depictions of ship construction (Figs. 10.14, 23–24).[128]

The wood fragments from Wadi Gawasis reveal that the Egyptians built *seagoing* ships of cedarwood.[129] The ship of Cheops is also made of cedar, as are the Dashur boats, and a stele of Tutankhamen mentions the construction of a cultic ship made of cedarwood brought from Lebanon.[130]

Economic texts suggest that ships' timber was expensive in Ramesside times in Egypt.[131] A mast could cost twice as much as the most expensive bull. The high cost of the ꜥš wood, which came from the Syro-Canaanite coast, may have resulted from political circumstances during the Twentieth Dynasty.

Apart from the importation of wood for shipbuilding, seagoing ships themselves were an item of trade. In the Amarna texts, Aziru promises to supply eight ships that the pharaoh has requested.[132]

Figure 14.5. The Syro-Canaanite display in a scene of foreign tribute from the tomb of Useramun (T. 131) includes imported timber (Thutmose III) (drawing courtesy of E. Dziobek)

Egypt appears to have imported ships from Cyprus also. The ruler of Alashia writes to the pharaoh: "[All th]at thou desirest, I [wi]ll bring up to thee. . . . [S]hips in quantity I will build."[133] E. Lipinski suggests that the ships mentioned in one Ugaritic text were built in Egypt to be exported to Alashia; this is most unlikely.[134]

"Invisible" Trade Items

Some forms of merchandise will not normally be conserved on wrecks. For evidence of their existence, we must turn to textual and iconographic sources. One Ugaritic text refers to milk, fish, wool, and clothing brought from Ashdod to Ugarit.[135] Similarly papyrus, for the trade in which the city of Byblos received its Greek

name, would probably not be preserved on a wreck.

Mammals, such as horses and bulls, were also traded by ship. Two bulls are being off-loaded from the Syro-Canaanite ships in the tomb of Kenamun (Fig. 14.6),[136] but skeletal remains are rare on ancient shipwrecks. A single mammalian bone found at Uluburun may be physical evidence of a trade item but was more likely intended for the crew's cooking pot.[137]

Slaves, apparently a particularly lucrative trade commodity, were often transported by sea. The two Syro-Canaanite ships captured by Thutmose III carried "male and female slaves," and in the Kenamun scene a group of men, perhaps slaves, is being brought forward by a Syro-Cana-

anite trader (Fig. 14.6, center left).[138] The later Phoenicians were particularly notorious as slavers.[139]

Port Scenes and Recreation Ashore

The hustle and bustle of active port trade is dynamically depicted in the tomb of Kenamun (Fig. 14.6). In a parallel and very vibrant scene from another Theban tomb, crew members of a Nile ship are, in the immortal words of N. de G. Davies, "spending their wages with female hucksters on the bank" (Fig. 14.7).[140] The scented cones and lotus blossoms on the women's heads are usually depicted only in scenes of banquets or on women at their toilet.[141] This suggests that the women are prostitutes receiving their pay "in kind" from their clients.[142]

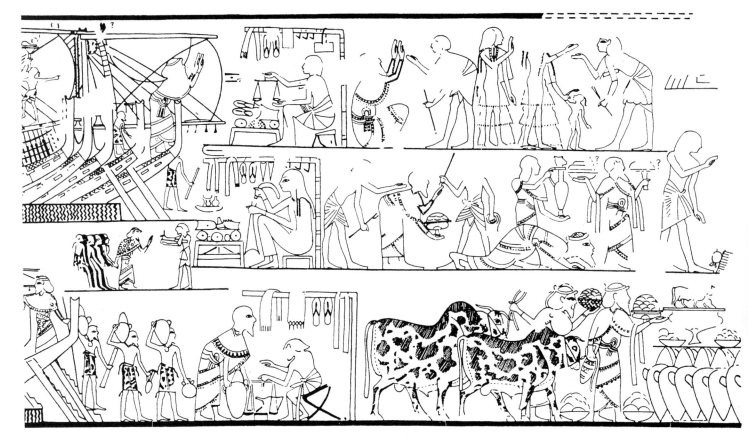

Figure 14.6. Harbor scene from the tomb of Kenamun (T. 162) at Thebes (Amenhotep III) (from Davies and Faulkner 1947: pl. 8)

Convoys of Trading Ships

Merchant ships on occasion traveled in convoys for protection. The two Syro-Canaanite ships captured by Thutmose III mentioned previously may have been together when taken. Similarly, Rib-Addi complains that Iapa Addi has robbed two of his ships; Abimilki, the king of Tyre, writes that the "man of Sidon" has abandoned that city in a convoy of two Egyptian (?) ships.[143] Elsewhere we hear of three Byblian ships that have succeeded in running the blockade imposed on that city by Arwad.[144] Tjekkerbaal tells Wenamun of a convoy consisting of six Egyptian (?) ships.[145]

Iconographic representations are less trustworthy in this regard. Do the five ships represented at Deir el Bahri shown on the outgoing and return voyages from Punt indicate the actual number of craft taking part in the voyage, or are they simply an artistic convenience showing various stages in a trip that was undertaken by a single craft?[146] Similarly, all the ships in Kenamun's painting are presumably based on a single master source from a copybook.

The number of ships portrayed, therefore, lacks significance.[147]

✍   ✍   ✍

Apart from the major sea powers, there must have been a variety of smaller peoples involved in maritime affairs. One such group that has been virtually ignored but is visible in the texts is the Carians.[148] The occasional appearance of Grey Minyan Ware in Crete, Cyprus, and Syria may reveal some (as yet undefined) maritime contact with this ethnic group.[149]

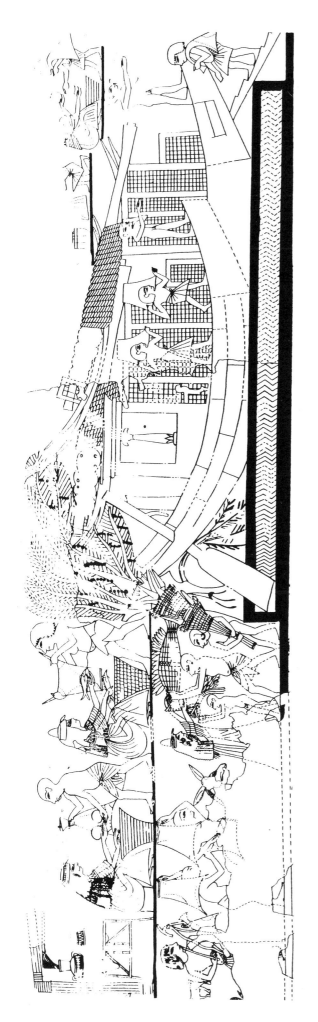

Figure 14.7. The crewomen of a Nile ship rush to spend their wages on shore. Tomb of Ipy (T. 217). (Ramses II) (from Davies 1927: pl. 30; ©, the Metropolitan Museum of Art, New York)

CHAPTER 15

War and Piracy at Sea

War and piracy in antiquity are so closely linked that it is not always clear when an enemy action denotes an act of war or one of piracy. Although classical tradition held that Minos was the first to fight a battle with a fleet, there is evidence for several nautical battles that took place in the latter part of the Late Bronze Age.[1]

War

A poorly preserved reference on a stele of Ramses II from Tanis refers to a successful battle against Shardanu ships in the open sea.[2] Shuppiluliuma II, the last Hittite king, mentions *three* sea battles in which he bested an Alashian fleet: "My father [. . .] I mobilized and I, Shuppiluliuma II, the Great King, immediately [crossed / reached (?)] the sea. The ships of Alašiya met me in the sea three times for battle, and I smote them; and I seized the ships and set fire to them in the sea."[3]

The land-locked Hittite empire lacked a fleet; Shuppiluliuma may have pressed into service ships of the North Syrian and Cilician maritime cities.[4] The kiln texts from Ugarit indicate that Alashia was its ally, and hence a friend of

the Hittites; this seems to be at variance with Shuppiluliuma's sea battles.[5] Apparently, either the Alashian fleet did not belong to the indigenous population but to the enemies in the Ugaritic texts, or Alashia had switched allegiance.[6]

Ramses III's relief at Medinet Habu is the only complete Late Bronze Age iconographic representation of a sea battle. Early in the battle, the Egyptians took advantage of the superiority of their long-range composite bows and slings over the Sea Peoples' medium-range throwing spears.[7] In this way, the Egyptians could disable the crews of the enemy craft while staying out of range of their opponents' weapons. Once the enemy had been neutralized, the Egyptian ships closed the distance. The only specifically nautical weapon portrayed is a four-armed grapnel.[8]

How was the grapnel used in the battle? To understand this, we must remember that Egyptian art is "aspective."[9] This permits—in fact, often requires—parts of the same subject to be represented as seen from different directions. The Egyptian artist wished to draw the subject in its clearest, most universal manner. Thus a human face is

always depicted in profile, but the eye is drawn frontally; a table may be portrayed in profile while the necklaces that are actually *on* it are drawn as seen from *above* it; bovines are portrayed in profile, but their horns are almost always shown frontally.[10]

In like manner, the Medinet Habu artists depicted the ships from two different viewpoints. The ships are always drawn in profile, but the mast in each case is portrayed frontally.[11] Thus, the Sea Peoples' ships seem to be upright in the water, when in fact the angles of their masts prove that they are listing at varying degrees. Indeed, the ships are in the process of capsizing.[12] The following phases of this capsizing operation are depicted:

• Ships E. 1 and N. 1, signifying the beginning of the battle, are portrayed facing each other (Figs. 2.35–36: A; 8.3, 10). The mast of N. 1 is upright, ninety degrees from the horizontal. An Egyptian, standing amidships before the mast, has thrown a grapnel into the rigging of the enemy mast (Figs. 8.10: B; 15.1). It would have been illogical and quite impossible for him to have thrown the grappling hook from amidships, if the

Figure 15.1. An Egyptian sailor, standing amidships in ship E. 1, throws a four-hooked grapnel into the rigging of Sea Peoples' ship N. 1 (detail from Nelson et al. 1930: pl. 39 [H. H. Nelson et al., Medinet Habu I: Earlier Historical Records of Ramses III, University of Chicago. Introduction © 1930 by the University of Chicago, all rights reserved. Published June, 1930])

Figure 15.2. Sea Peoples' ship N. 3 is capsized by means of the grapnel, attached to the bow of Egyptian ship E. 3 (detail from Nelson et al. 1930: pl. 39 [H. H. Nelson et al., Medinet Habu I: Earlier Historical Records of Ramses III, University of Chicago. Introduction © 1930 by the University of Chicago, all rights reserved. Published June, 1930])

ships had been facing each other as portrayed. The ships must have been *parallel* in the water. Presumably, once the archers had incapacitated the enemy, the Egyptian ships came alongside the Sea Peoples' craft, allowing the grapnels to be thrown into the enemy rigging.

• There then follow three renditions of the Sea Peoples' ship with the masts placed at varying angles. These represent the increasing angle of the hull's list (Figs. 8.4, 6–8, 11–12 [ships N. 2, N. 4, and N. 5]). To emphasize the slant of the deck, the fighters in the ships are shown in unusual poses: falling forward and backward, hanging onto the mast, and lying on the side of the hull. To add to the impression of confusion, ships N. 2 and N. 5 are shown listing *lengthwise* also.

• In the final phase, the invaders' ship has capsized (Figs. 8.5, 14; 15.2). Ship N. 3's mast is broken and is floating away at an angle. Although the mast is probably meant to be floating on the water (zero degrees), interestingly, this angle (forty to forty-two degrees) is the most acute of the series. Here again the grapnel's rope, although not the grapnel itself, appears. In this case, however, the rope is connected to the bow of the opposing Egyptian ship. This suggests that once the grapnel had caught in the enemy rigging, the Egyptians maneuvered their ships perpendicular to the enemy and then backwatered—causing the rival craft to capsize.

The following table and figures 15.3–4 illustrate the ships' varying lists based on the angle of the mast to the horizon. Since some of the ships are listing lengthwise, the angles of the masts to the hulls' profiles are also supplied. They are virtually identical.

Angle of List of the Sea Peoples' Ships					
	N. 1	N. 2	N. 4	N. 5	N. 3
°/horizon	90	73.5	64.5	47	40
°/profile	90	78.5	65	56	42

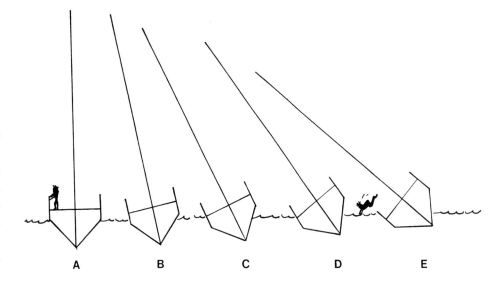

Figure 15.3. Progressive list of Sea Peoples' ships based on the angle of the mast to the profiles of these ships. The mast of N. 4 is reversed left to right. The angle of N. 3 is based on the upper part of the broken mast: (A) N. 1 (90°), (B) N. 2 (78.5°), (C) N. 4 (65°), (D) N. 5 (56°), (E) N. 3 (42°) (drawn by the author)

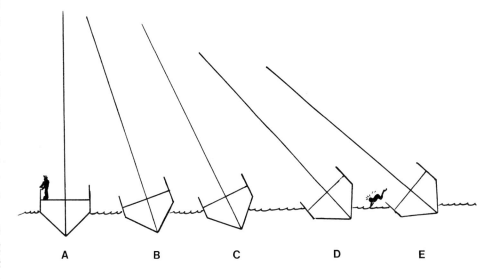

Figure 15.4. Progressive list of Sea Peoples' ships based on the angle of the mast to the horizon. The mast of N. 4 is reversed left to right. The angle of N. 3 is based on the upper part of the broken mast: (A) N. 1 (90°), (B) N. 2 (73.5°), (C) N. 4 (64.5°), (D) N. 5 (47°), (E) N. 3 (42°) (drawn by the author)

Piracy

Piracy has been a constant companion of mercantile ventures in the Mediterranean. As H. Ormerod notes:

> Throughout its history the Mediterranean has witnessed a constant struggle between the civilised peoples dwelling on its coasts and the barbarians, between the peaceful trader using its highways and the pirate who infested the routes that he must follow. At different stages of their history most of the maritime peoples have belonged now to one class and now to the other. From the time when men first went down to the sea in ships, piracy and robbery have been regarded only as one of the means of livelihood that the sea offered. The earliest literature of Greece shows us the Homeric pirate pursuing a mode of life at sea almost identical with that of the Frankish corsairs.[13]

Thucydides, describing the state of affairs of Aegean seafaring before Minos's thalassocracy, observes that piracy was considered an honorable pursuit: "For in early times the Hellenes and the barbarians of the coast and islands, as communication by sea became more common, were tempted to turn pirates, under the conduct of their most powerful men; the motives being to serve their own cupidity and to support the needy. They would fall upon a town unprotected by walls, and consisting of a mere collection of villages, and would plunder it; indeed, this came to be the main source of their livelihood, no disgrace being yet attached to such an achievement, even some glory."[14]

As with normal shipping, piracy was a seasonal occupation.[15] Throughout history, individual groups carrying out small-scale raids almost always relegated them to particular seasons. A good example of this is the following description of Svein Asleifarson, an Orkney Viking chieftain from the twelfth century A.D.: "Every spring Svein was very busy and had a huge amount of seed sown and took a big part in this work himself. But when the work was done he would go out Viking and would raid the Hebrides and Ireland and come home at midsummer. He called this his 'spring Viking.' Then he would stay at home till the fields had been reaped and the grain stored away. After this he would go out Viking and not come back till one month of the winter was over, and he called this his 'autumn Viking.'"[16]

This same situation is illustrated in an Amarna text in which the king of Alashia complains to the Egyptian pharaoh that the Lukki attack his lands each year, an obvious allusion to seasonal piratical raids.[17]

Piracy wore many identities. One form was shipwreck salvage. Nauplius represents in Greek mythology the professional wreckers who used false flares to lure the ships to their destruction.[18] A fascinating example of this is the undated "Pirate's Walls" between the islands of Paros and Antiparos in the Aegean.[19] This is a barely submerged wall, invisible to ships, constructed to trap them by grounding. Later Roman law required provincial officials to prevent coastal peoples from looting shipwrecked craft and from wrecking.[20]

Another aspect of piracy was the plundering of seashore settlements by groups of ships that slipped into a settlement, wreaked havoc, and then disappeared before the local military could attack them.[21] Texts dating to the last days of Ugarit refer to just such raids, apparently carried out by marauding groups of Sea Peoples.[22] Although corsairs were able to overcome unprotected settlements, they were likely to lose when cornered into fighting military units. This was true of the later Vikings: the nautical battle in which Ramses III beat the Sea Peoples suggests that it was also true for them.[23]

Another preventive measure against pirate attacks was the use of "early warning systems" in which lookouts were stationed at watchtowers. A structure that may be a lookout tower is situated between the central and right cities on the Miniature Fresco at Thera.[24] At the approach of an enemy craft, signal fires were lit. This practice, which may explain the lights seen by Odysseus on his return to Ithaca, is well recorded in the later Mediterranean.[25] Ormerod describes the use of such a system in more recent times:

> The signal would naturally be given by the smoke of beacons or by their flames at night. This was a common warning in later days. While Thévenot was sailing from Acre to Jaffa, his ship was suddenly fired on from a fort on shore, and flares were lit all along the coast. As he approached Jaffa, the ship was fired on, and when admitted to harbour, he found the inhabitants under arms and the women and children fled. The reason was that the boat had been mistaken for an Italian corsair operating off the coast, which had recently made a descent at Castle Pelegrino (Atlit), between Acre and Jaffa.[26]

Coastal sieges consisted of attempting to prevent all communication by water from the besieged city and capture of all ships.[27] Thus, for example, Rib-Addi complains that Iappa-Addi had already seized one of his ships and planned to confiscate his other vessels.[28]

In times of war, ships were taken as "prizes." Thutmose III's capture of two Canaanite ships is best understood in this manner.[29] The text does not indicate if they were captured at sea or in harbor. Similarly, the weapons found at Cape Gelidonya and Uluburun may have served as protection against piracy and to prevent these vessels being taken as prizes.[30]

ॐ ॐ ॐ

Clearly, as in later periods, warfare and piracy played an integral role in Late Bronze Age seafaring. The earliest recorded nautical battles took place during this period. Since the waterline ram was not introduced as a nautical weapon until the ninth century B.C., ships in the Late Bronze Age were used for two main military purposes: as rapid troop transports and, when doing battle, as mobile firing platforms. The only truly nautical weapon in use was the grapnel.[31]

Piracy consisted primarily of raids against coastal settlements and the taking of prizes on the high seas. Preventive measures against the depredations of marine marauders included "early warning systems" and intelligence reports.

CHAPTER 16

Sea Laws

Maritime mercantile endeavors cannot flourish without a code of law. Although evidence for nautical laws in the Late Bronze Age is limited, a code of maritime conduct apparently existed, at least along the Syro-Canaanite coast and Cyprus.

Shipwreck

One Ugaritic text implies a law dealing with shipwrecks. Here the king of Tyre informs the king of Ugarit that while en route to Egypt, one of the latter's ships had been partially wrecked in a storm. Its cargo was seized by an enigmatic figure termed the *rb-tmtt*—literally, "lord of killing."[1] The Tyrian assures his peer that all is in hand. He had taken the cargo back from the *rb-tmtt,* and the ship is now anchored at Tyre.[2]

The conduct of the king of Tyre is best understood in light of a treaty from the seventh century B.C. between the Assyrian king Esarhaddon and Baal I, a later ruler of Tyre.[3] One condition of the treaty states: "If a ship of Baal or of the people of Tyre is shipwrecked off (the coast of) the land of the Philistines or anywhere on the borders of Assyrian territory,

everything that is on the ship belongs to Esarhaddon, king of Assyria, but one must not do any harm to any person on board ship, they should *li*[*st*] their names and inform the king of Assyria."[4]

The Bronze Age Tyrian king appears to have been following a similar ruling. The later treaty must have drawn the clause from an accepted maritime law that was already ancient when the treaty was written.

Willful Shipwreck

A fascinating text from Ugarit discusses a court case that was judged by Pudehepa, the mother dowager of the Hittite king, Tudkhaliya IV.[5] The case was between an Ugaritian and a person named Shukku. From the terminology of the text, it is clear that the ship and the cargo belonged to the man of Ugarit. Thus, Shukku was charged with willfully wrecking the ship after the harbor master swore to this.

Two interpretations have been given for this case. F. C. Fensham likens it to a law in the Code of Hammurabi that deals with the responsibility of the ship's captain to the merchant who hires the

ship.[6] The law requires the captain to compensate the merchant for the ship and the cargo if the ship is wrecked because of negligence.[7] This same principle appears in the earlier Law of Eshnunna, where a stipulation protects both the ship's owner and merchants for cargoes carried by a negligent ship captain.

In relating these earlier laws to the Ugaritic case, Fensham notes that it can only be understood in the light of Mesopotamian law. The "man of Ugarit" was probably the owner of the ship and perhaps also of its cargo. Shukku was apparently the ship's captain. This is interesting because the name is Hittite, and Hittites are not generally thought to have engaged in seafaring. This may also explain why the case was judged before the Hittite king instead of the Ugaritic ruler. Perhaps Shukku was one of the merchants of Ura mentioned in other Ugaritic texts.[8]

Lacking maritime laws of their own, the Hittites apparently depended on legal practices that were used throughout the Near East. Fensham emphasizes that the decision was seemingly made on the basis of a legal principle from the Mesopotamian Middle Bronze Age generally accepted in Late

Bronze Age Ugarit. This example of basing a maritime code of laws on the earlier legal principles of other nations is hardly unique. It is comparable to the Rhodian Sea Law, which later served as the foundation for maritime laws over considerable space and time.[9]

Another explanation for this text is offered by J. R. Ziskind, who argues that the case was judged on the principles pertaining to sea or bottomry loans. Known as *faenus nauticum* or *traiectito pecunia* in Latin, this law was unique for two reasons: the creditor assumed liability in the case of a loss of ship or cargo, and the creditor's right to demand repayment was linked to the safe arrival of the merchantman with its cargo.[10] If the security was lost at sea and there was no evidence of fraud on the part of the borrower, then the payment to the lender, both principal and interest, was canceled. Ziskind writes:

> In this Akkadian text, the defendant Shukku (citizenship unstated), claimed that the Ugaritian plaintiff's ship was destroyed accidentally when it struck a wharf. The plaintiff claimed that Shukku intentionally wrecked the ship. The captain of the ship was ordered to swear an oath, and Shukku had to make good the worth of the ship and its cargo. Shukku had either borrowed money from the king of Ugarit or was in the employ of someone who did in order to undertake a maritime enterprise in Asia Minor, and when it became apparent to Shukku that the obligation would not be met, he tried to sink the ship and falsely claim that an accident took place. In this way, Shukku or his employer would be free of the obligation to repay the loan, and they would also avoid possible enslavement for defaulting on a debt. Evidently, the captain of the ship caught Shukku in the act.[11]

Ziskind suggests that fluctuating prices may have been a cause for Shukku's actions. If prices had dropped on the return of the ship, the borrower would not have been able to repay his loan. He also interprets *KTU* 4.338 in light of bottomry loans.[12] Ziskind translates *lbš. anyt* as "the cargo of ships" and assumes that the text is a memorandum of a sea loan given to the king of Byblos with ships and cargo hypothecated to the lender, the king of Ugarit. Alternatively, D. Pardee interprets the same text as describing a loan of ships to Ugarit by the king of Byblos.[13]

Law of Reprisal

The existence of a "law of reprisal" is evident from Wenamun's reception on being shipwrecked in Alashia. From his words to the princess Heteb, Wenamun makes it clear that by killing him and his Byblian crew the Alashians would be acting contrary to normal conduct and would be liable, therefore, to reprisal by the king of Byblos. As Wenamun puts it: "If the sea rages and the winds waft me to the land where you are, you should not let them take charge over me to kill me seeing that I am an envoy of Amon. Now look here, as for me, I shall be searched for until whatevery day (shall come). Regarding this crew of the Prince of Byblos whom they are seeking to kill, surely its lord will find ten crews belonging to you and kill them in return."[14]

The Sekel ships that Wenamun found waiting for him at Byblos were also acting under this law;[15] this may have been Wenamun's assumed "legal" basis for "liberating" the silver from the Sekels:

> ". . . a freighter. I found their *deben* of silver in it, and I seized possession of it. [I said to the ship owners: I have seized possession of] your money. It shall remain in my possession [un]til you have found [my money or the thief] who stole it. I have not ⌜robbed you⌝, but am (only) going to ⌜confiscate⌝ it."[16]

The "law of reprisal" was accepted conduct in Classical times and later.[17] Writes H. Ormerod:

> Not less dangerous to the peace of the seas was the ancient law concerning reprisals, and here again the legal terminology differed little from that which described the pirate's doings. In the fourth century, Demosthenes states that owing to the reprisals undertaken by the Athenian captains it was impossible for an Athenian to go anywhere without a flag of truce. Reprisals could be undertaken by the state, that is to say, a general permission granted to all and sundry to plunder the inhabitants and commerce of another state, just as the Lacedaemonians in 416 B.C., in reply to continued Athenian depredations carried out from Pylos, issued a general permission to their subjects to plunder Athenians, without yet declaring war. There are numerous examples of similar practises in Hellenistic times, which greatly embarrassed the Romans in their endeavours to secure peace and quiet in Greece.[18]

Theft in Harbor

Wenamun's problems with the Sekels began in the harbor of Dor when a crewman from his ship absconded with Wenamun's gold and silver. Following the theft, Wenamun went to Beder, the ruler of Dor, and demanded that he investigate the case: "I got up on that very morning and went to where the prince was, and I said to him: I have been robbed in your harbor. Now it is you who are the prince of this land, and it is you who are its investigator. Search for my money!"[19]

Beder's response to this allegation is illuminating: "And he said to me, 'Are you serious, or are you ⌐fabricating⌐? Look here, I cannot comprehend this protestation that you have made to me. If it were a thief belonging to my land who boarded your freighter and stole your money, I would repay it to you from my own storehouse until / your thief, whatever his name, has been found. Actually, as for the thief who has robbed you, he belongs to you and he belongs to your freighter. Spend a few days here visiting me that I may search for him.'"[20]

As Beder's reply indicates, custom required that if the theft had been perpetrated by one of a visiting ship's crew members, then the case fell under the jurisdiction of the ship's captain, not the port authorities.[21] Beder was gracious in offering to look for the culprit, even though this was not his responsibility.

Indeed, it is curious that Wenamun had not asked for intervention from Mengebet, the Syrian captain of the ship on which he was traveling.[22] Perhaps he did so, but to no avail. The Rhodian Sea Law that came much later contains the following stipulation that may clarify the situation: "If a passenger comes on board and has gold or something else, let him deposit it with the captain. If he does not deposit it and says 'I have lost gold or silver,' no effect is to be given to what he says. But the captain and the sailors, all those on board together are to take an oath."[23]

The existence of a similar stipulation in effect along the Levantine coast in the eleventh century B.C. would explain the behavior of both Wenamun and Beder. Given Wenamun's later actions in trying to hide his "travelling idol" from others, it is not unreasonable to assume that instead of entrusting his gold and silver to the ship's captain during the voyage to Dor, Wenamun had guarded his valuables himself.[24] If so, and if a form of the above condition did apply, then Mengebet would have borne no responsibility for a theft that took place on board his ship. In that case, Wenamun would have had no recourse but to try his luck with the local port authority, Beder, who correctly rebuffed him.

❧ ❧ ❧

The evidence for maritime laws in the Late Bronze Age along the Levant is admittedly limited. However, the actions of the seafarers discussed above make sense only if we assume that some form of maritime law did exist. Since no text of a written code has been found to date, it is possible that the laws were not codified but instead formed an oral doctrine of accepted conduct.

CHAPTER 17

Conclusions

In the eastern Mediterranean during the Bronze Age, international maritime ventures were undertaken by a variety of peoples who had developed or absorbed to varying degrees the knowledge required to build and use seagoing ships. However, based on its own specific needs and capabilities, each culture seems to have developed its own—perhaps unique—relationship with the sea.

Egypt's interests in the Mediterranean were concentrated on the political and economic subjugation of the Syro-Canaanite coast. The Egyptians do not appear to have been explorers. They were content to ply three main routes: in the Mediterranean to the Syro-Canaanite coast and in the Red Sea to Punt and to the southwest coast of Sinai. There is no concrete evidence at present to indicate that Egyptian ships sailed any farther during the Bronze Age.

Egypt's Mediterranean seafaring ended with the demise of its domination in Asia. Already evident in the tale of Wenamun, this trend was to continue into later times, when the Egyptians hired Phoenicians to do their seafaring for them. A main incentive for the Egyptians to venture out into the

Mediterranean was the need for high-quality wood for ship construction and other purposes. Such wood was unavailable in the Nile valley during the Pharaonic period but common in Lebanon. This was apparently the primary, although certainly not the only, reason for Egypt's early trade connections with Byblos.

Egypt entered the New Kingdom period using a developed version of a seagoing ship that had been evolving for over a millennium, and perhaps much longer. These vessels appear in a state of change at Deir el Bahri. They probably had a protean, evolving keel and were likely to have been one of the types of ships on which the Egyptians voyaged into the Mediterranean. The adoption of foreign construction techniques seems to have received a strong impetus under Thutmose III, a result of his need for reliable transports to support Egypt's Asiatic conquests.

Egypt's ventures into the Red Sea required an incredible amount of effort even before the sea voyage itself began. The ships were built on the Nile, dismantled, hauled overland through the Eastern Desert, and rebuilt on the shores of the Red Sea. The near

"assembly kit" organization of the Cheops ships illustrates how this might have been accomplished. This process emphasizes the incredible (to our modern minds) value placed by the ancient Egyptians on the commodities available in Sinai and Punt. This effort expended in mercantile contacts in the Red Sea with Punt is paralleled in the later trading practices of Solomon and Hiram with the equally elusive land of Ophir.

The excavations at Wadi Gawasis have made a valuable contribution to understanding Egyptian seafaring practices in the Red Sea. Yet much still remains unclear. Of particular interest would be the future investigation of the pharaonic port identified by W. F. Albright near Abu Zneima on the southwest coast of in Sinai.

The Syro-Canaanite littoral supplies the clearest picture of a corporate trading power that played a significant—perhaps primary—part in Late Bronze Age maritime shipping, particularly during the fourteenth to thirteenth centuries. There are repeated references to ships with valuable cargoes. Syro-Canaanite ships sailed to Egypt, Cyprus, Cilicia, and the Aegean. The smattering of evidence for a code of maritime conduct along this coast further enhances this view. So, also, do the clearly merchant nature of the ships depicted in Egyptian tomb paintings and the repeated connection in the texts to Syro-Canaanite ships bearing valuable cargoes of trade goods.

The Kenamun wall painting is the most detailed extant depiction of a Late Bronze Age Syro-Canaanite seagoing ship; yet, it leaves much to be desired. We can guess at—but never be quite sure of—the Egyptianizing elements with which the artists have saturated these vessels.

Probably, the artists of Kenamun and Nebamun worked from copybooks. They sought to create a wall painting based on accepted art forms and were not making an ethnological study of contemporary seacraft. Created under strict art canons, the depictions of the Egyptian artists were pleasing to their contemporaries but lack the accuracy that the modern student might wish. Furthermore, the artists seem to have lacked a technical knowledge of the ships themselves. Keftiu ships were apparently Syro-Canaanite craft on the run to the Aegean: perhaps the Uluburun shipwreck, if future research reveals it to be from the Levantine coast, is a vessel of this sort.

The ship models found at Byblos are copies of Egyptian ships or ship models. Previous identifications in which the Byblian models were considered to represent Syro-Canaanite ships emphasize the dangers of labeling iconographic representations based on their find locations. The Iniwia ships are imaginative creations made up of an amalgamation of elements derived from different sources that never existed on their own.

Ships and traders of Cyprus may have played a crucial role as middlemen between Egypt, the Syro-Canaanite coast, and the Aegean world during the Late Bronze Age. The Amarna tablets strongly support this conclusion if Alashia equates with Cyprus, as seems to be indicated by *EA* 114. Even without this document, however, there is a strong argument for considerable sea trade by Cypriots at that time.

The Karnak anchor indicates that Cypriot seafarers were reaching Egypt in pharaonic times; Cypro-Minoan texts found at Ugarit suggest a Cypriot presence there. Furthermore, Cypro-Minoan signs incised on Mycenaean pottery on the Greek mainland may indicate Cypriot merchants, located in Greece, controlling at least some of the trade with their homeland. The large quantities of anchors found on Cypriot land sites, many of which are dedicated in temples, further emphasize the importance of seafaring in Late Bronze Age Cyprus.

The three ship models from Kazaphani and Maroni, if my reading of them is correct, represent an indigenous type of beamy, planked, seagoing merchant ship. Most of the ship images from Cyprus, however, represent foreign ships, mainly of Achaean (Sea Peoples?) origin.

The primary class of craft depicted in iconography during the Aegean Early Bronze Age was a narrow longship with a high stem and a low stern. Lacking a sail and propelled by rows of paddlers, this craft first appears after it had already evolved considerably. Of the vessels used to bring Melian obsidian to the mainland in the Upper Paleolithic and Mesolithic periods and of the ships used to colonize Crete in the Neolithic period—the record is a blank.

In the Early Minoan III period, a new type of ship came into use in the Aegean. And although never shown with the sail raised during the Early Minoan III–Middle Minoan periods, these vessels did use a sail. Little can be said of this class beyond noting that to carry a sail without an outrigger, it must have been greater in beam than the earlier longships. Presumably these craft are the ancestral prototypes for the large Minoan/Cycladic ship type depicted at Thera.

The Minoans were, it seems, the marine explorers *par excellence* of the Late Bronze Age. Although their first contact with Egypt probably took place along the Syro-Canaanite coast, the Minoans likely deserve credit for opening the trade routes between the Aegean and both the Syro-Canaanite coast and Egypt. If so, they may have been the earliest seafarers to intentionally cross the Mediterranean on an open sea route (from Crete to Egypt) on a regular basis.

The Theran material is unusually rich and clarifies other representations of Minoan ships. The waterborne procession at Thera must be studied in the context of its Minoan/Cycladic milieu. The Theran scenes, and with them virtually all iconographic materials depicting Minoan ships (or ships' parts), are directly connected to Minoan cult practices in combination with cultic ship races/processions. These are the same kinds of ships, it is reasonable to presume, that played a crucial role in the relationships between Minoan Crete and its neighbors, whatever the political and economic reality reflected in the archaeological record. There may have been (and probably were) some differences between Cycladic ships and Minoan ships, but at the present level of information it is not possible to pinpoint specific differences.

Thera was abandoned before the final cataclysm. What became of its people? To where did the inhabitants of Thera emigrate? And is there any connection between this event and the sudden appearance of Minoan-style frescoes from Middle Bronze Age contexts in Syria, Israel, and Egypt? These questions remain to be answered.

Of prime importance in understanding the waterborne procession at Thera is a seal from Thebes that proves conclusively that the procession/race was linked with the vegetation/fertility cult. The miniature frieze apparently depicts a yearly Aegean springtime festival connected with this cult. The procession must have held a tremendous fascination for the inhabitants of the Aegean. Apparently a race carried out over a short course, it began at a time when paddled longboats were used and may well predate the Bronze Age. The annual procession continued at least to the end of the Bronze Age, and memories of it may have lingered on as late as the Hellenistic period.

Mycenaean maritime *trading* outside the Aegean has been highly overrated in the past by Hellenocentric scholars. The sudden disappearance of Aegeans representing the west in the Egyptian cosmology at the time of Amenhotep II's accession may point to the end of direct Aegeo-Egyptian contact following the fall of the autonomous Minoan culture at the end of the Late Minoan IB period. Other evidence is consistent with this conclusion. This direct communication does not seem to have been reopened by the Mycenaeans. The fact that no names from the Linear B onomasticon can be identified at Ugarit further supports this judgment.

The evidence cited for the presumed involvement of Myce-naeans in trade with the eastern Mediterranean is based primarily on quantities of fourteenth- and thirteenth-century Mycenaean ceramics found on foreign shores. However, pottery alone cannot establish the ethnic identity of the hull in which it was transported.

Apart from the handful of exceptions discussed above, artifacts lacking inscriptions can only give a positive or tentatively negative answer to the existence of trade. Furthermore, the kind of trade involved—whether direct or indirect—cannot be deduced from the finds alone. Thus, the onus of proof for extensive direct Mycenaean *trade* contacts with the Syro-Canaanite coast and Egypt must fall on those scholars who argue for its existence. For the present at least, this evidence is lacking.

On the other hand, the role played by ships and seafaring in the expansion of the Mycenaean culture overseas has, I believe, been decidedly underemphasized in the past. This phenomenon, a Mycenaean hallmark, could only have evolved in a culture that had highly developed its seafaring capabilities. If the Pylos "Rower Tablets" refer to preparations for the abandonment of Pylos and the emigration to another site by certain echelons of the population, then the other Pylos tablets may also portray the same event. They could, therefore, greatly help in clarifying bureaucratic aspects of the organization for Mycenaean seaborne migrations and colonization in the Late Helladic IIIA–IIIB.

Pylos would then also represent a microcosm of the great seaborne ethnic movement that was soon to follow, in which masses of people migrated eastward. It might better allow us to understand the structure behind the establishment of sites like Maa-*Palaeokastro* and Sinda in Cyprus as well as Ashdod and Ashkelon in Israel, in which Late Helladic IIIC 1b pottery has been found.

In the Hittite texts, Ahhiyawan ships are recorded in use by raiders who seem to have had a predilection for coastal depredations, primarily aimed at capturing living cargoes of the two-legged type. This also fits well with the Egyptian evidence for waterborne raiding. The ships were also used for rapid disengagements. All of this suggests that the vessels and their crews would have been well suited as shipborne mercenaries, and it may be in this role that Tudkhalia IV denies them access to Amurru.

The single most important iconographic document for the ships of the Sea Peoples is the Medinet Habu tableau. Unfortunately, because of the ravages of time, much evidence, along with the paint and plaster, has disappeared from the wall. My reading of the ship that served as the prototype for the five depictions at Medinet Habu is that (with the exception of the *manner* in which the bird head is affixed at stem and stern, which suggests influences from farther north) it is identical to portrayals of Late Helladic IIIB and IIIC oared vessels. This means that the carriers of the Late Helladic IIIC 1b pottery are either to be identified as fleeing Mycenaeans known by another name to the cultures confronted by them or that they included a considerable number of Mycenaean refugees within them.

The bird-head devices on the Sea Peoples' ships at Medinet Habu are a link in a long chain of tradition that spans at least four millennia. This symbol—perhaps originating as an epiphany of the Old European Great Goddess—appears on the stems and sterns of ships from the Middle Helladic period down to the present day. For most of this time, mariners were probably not even aware of why they used this symbol in its myriad forms or what it originally represented. Certainly a modern Greek Orthodox boat owner would be horrified to learn that his vessel carries the symbol of a pre-Christian earth deity!

The multiplicity of the bird's beak may have strengthened the magic inherent in the stem and stern devices. This would explain why the *aphlaston* developed from a multiple-beaked bird head.

That some connection existed between the Sea Peoples and the Urnfield cultures is self-evident, but the nature of this relationship requires additional elucidation. One important avenue of research would be a serious review of the Urnfield level at Hama.

The ability to reach shipwrecks on the seabed has opened up a new dimension in the research of seafaring. The significant contribution of the Uluburun wreck is an expression of this. Already it has given us a hitherto undreamed-of view of the lading and workings of a large open-water Late Bronze Age merchant vessel.

The problem of the Uluburun ship's ethnic identity, and for that matter of all Bronze Age wrecks, remains the single most difficult question to solve in shipwreck archaeology. The interpretation of personal objects vis-à-vis ethnic character is particularly problematic. The Uluburun wreck, which is maddeningly eclectic in personal finds, raises the question of what evidence is acceptable in identifying its home port.

Concerning the general outlines of the various facets of the art and functions of seafaring in the Late Bronze Age, several considerations are worthy of mention. One particular Egyptian term, *wnḫ*, may mean planks used for hull

strakes. Because of problems of interpretation, however, many of the other technical terms in the ancient texts treating ship construction remain obscure. There is much room here for future cooperation between nautical archaeologists and linguists in interpreting these texts.

Egyptian ships traveling on the Red Sea were of necessity transversely lashed. Although we cannot be entirely sure, it is very likely that Egyptians also sailed the Mediterranean in lashed ships, at least until the reign of Thutmose III. The facts that Hatshepsut's ships were lashed and that they continue a class of ships used during the Old Kingdom *on the Mediterranean* strongly support this conclusion.

If this were not true, then what form of construction might the Egyptians have used in their Mediterranean vessels? They employed mortise-and-tenon joinery in their Nilotic ship construction, yet only adopted the system of locking the mortise-and-tenon joinery with wooden pegs very late. Without locking the tenons, this form of joinery could not be used on open-water craft. It seems that, at least before Thutmose III, the Egyptians did not need to use pegged joinery. Unpegged joinery sufficed for their Nilotic craft, and lashed craft *could* be used in the Mediterranean, as they were in the Red Sea.

Perhaps pegged joinery evolved in Syro-Canaanite ship construction. If so, this technique, along with other elements of Mediterranean construction, may have arrived in Egypt as early as the reign of Thutmose III. The appearance of pegged mortise-and-tenon joinery at Uluburun suggests that by the Late Bronze Age, this technique had been introduced for use on deep-water ships. Pegged mortise-and-tenon joinery may have devel-

oped from a type of pegged sewn construction. Alternatively, it may have developed directly from unpegged mortise-and-tenon joinery—although judging from the Egyptian evidence, this seems unlikely.

The boom-footed rig used during the Bronze Age may have developed on the Nile in Predynastic times. The rig used by seagoing ships in Egypt and the Syro-Canaanite littoral seems to have been virtually identical. The sail was spread by raising the yard to the masthead with a pair of halyards. The yard and boom were supported on a system of lifts; the boom was lashed to the mast. It was an awkward rig at best that only worked well with the wind nearly astern. The Aegean rig, while also boom-footed, seems to have been a variant with several peculiarities. The use of this square rig had a profound effect on the capabilities of ship movement and defined the use of sea routes.

Perhaps the most interesting aspect of the Late Bronze Age rig is the lack of shrouds for lateral support on seagoing ships. In their place, there evolved a system of cables that secured the lower part of the mast and which were anchored in some manner laterally inside the hull. A form of this rigging existed on Old Kingdom seagoing and river craft. In the Late Bronze Age, evidence for these cables is found on the seagoing ships of Egypt (Deir el Bahri), the Syro-Canaanite littoral (Kenamun), and Cyprus (the Kazaphani and Maroni models). Lateral support and leeward drift are most pronounced when the wind is abeam a vessel. The lateral cables used in place of shrouds, along with the possible introversion of the keel on seagoing ships, may indicate that Bronze Age sailors, with their clumsy boom-footed rig, did not use the sail unless the wind was directly (or nearly directly) astern.

M. Liverani, in his usual insightful manner, makes an interesting comment concerning the restructuring of the regional economy of the East after the cataclysms that ended the Late Bronze Age: "As for sailing techniques, I personally am not aware of precise innovative elements introduced about 1200 B.C. which could be said to characterize Iron Age I shipping in contrast to Late Bronze Age navigation. However, I am strongly inclined to postulate some such innovation, since we get the impression of a sudden widening of sea routes and of a technical and operative freedom."[1]

The nautical innovation that Liverani intuitively postulates is, of course, the brailed rig, which makes its appearance—after a gestation period—in the eastern Mediterranean ca. 1200 B.C. This new rig allowed for better usage of the wind and propelled the Iron Age cultures into new vistas in seafaring, opening up the entire Mediterranean and beyond to intense seaborne traffic.

Stone anchors are one of the most important threads of evidence for Late Bronze Age Mediterranean seafaring. Still, much about them remains enigmatic. If *shfifonim* do actually represent stone anchors, then they assume a well-cut stone anchor prototype that has yet to be found in the Sea of Galilee. Perhaps *shfifonim* were patterned after anchors used by seagoing ships in the Early Bronze Age on the Mediterranean. Interestingly, no Early Bronze Age remains are known from Israel's shores despite the large number of wrecks and cargo sites that litter her Mediterranean coast. This may result from several factors: seafaring in the Early Bronze Age may

have been an extremely rare phenomenon, the coastal profile may have changed significantly in the past five thousand years so that wrecks are buried in areas not currently surveyed, or Early Bronze Age seafaring practices were in some way different from those of later periods.

Ships carried quantities of anchors. At least some of them stationed in the bow could, and were, carried upright, no doubt locked securely into the vessel's superstructure. This would have prevented clutter in the bow and also perhaps facilitated their rapid deployment when necessary. Spare anchors were carried in the hold, where they also served as ballast. Stone blanks for anchors could have been picked up en route and prepared either at the quarry site or on board ship.

Not all anchors on a single ship were necessarily identical. Thus, at Uluburun some anchors have square holes, others are biconical. At Naveh Yam, some anchors have apical rope grooves while others lack this characteristic. At Wadi Gawasis, the anchor-stele-base of Ankhow's stele lacks the normal L-shaped basal hole. Small anchors found together with groups of large ones may be interpreted in several ways. At Naveh Yam, Uluburun, and Wadi Gawasis, they are best explained as spares for the ship's boat.

A typical "Canaanite" anchor remains to be defined and requires study. Based on the many anchors on the Israeli seacoast, one might tentatively suggest a shape with a flat base, rounded top, and asymmetrical sides.

A variety of routes interlaced the Mediterranean in the Late Bronze Age. Most routes followed —but probably did not hug—the coastline: the only truly open-water routes were the direct runs

from the Aegean and Cyprus to Egypt. Under favorable conditions, the longest open-water route could be crossed in three to five days. Thus, during this period and in this region, the division of seagoing ships into coasters and open-water craft has little meaning.

No artifactual evidence for navigational instruments during the Late Bronze Age is known. And yet it is possible, and indeed quite probable, that systems of navigation, which would have left no trace in the archaeological record, had evolved by that time.

All legs of the counterclockwise Mediterranean circuit proposed by the excavators of the Uluburun wreck are documented in textual and archaeological evidence. However, not all ships sailing from the Levant to the Aegean necessarily continued in a circuit. Sinaranu's ships, for example, are described as returning from Caphtor. Presumably, these are Ugaritic ships that sailed on the run directly to and from the Aegean.

The cargo on board the Uluburun wreck is perhaps most expressive of the many facets of Late Bronze Age sea trade. Whatever the identity of the traders on board when she came to grief, this shipwreck represents a large—but perhaps not the largest—type of Late Bronze Age merchant ship. The preliminary picture received from Uluburun is that trade was infinitely more complex than was previously thought: the ship's cargo was exceptionally varied. The wreck also illustrates the mechanics of indirect trade, in which two cultures can trade commodities without ever meeting.

The identification of the contents of the closed containers on board through sieving has created a new dimension of the understanding of trade. Particularly striking is the large quantity of terebinth resin, valued as incense or perhaps for use in embalming. Wood was a major trade item, particularly for timber-starved Egypt. Much of this wood was ready for use, a fact that may have been an influence (although perhaps not a primary one) on Egyptian shipwrights in adopting Syro-Canaanite shipbuilding techniques.

Besides the cultures discussed above, many smaller ethnic groups were probably active in trade, although they are now undefinable in the archaeological/historical record.

The waterline ram had not been introduced as a nautical weapon during the Bronze Age. Thus, ships used for military or piratical purposes served primarily as rapid transports for deploying land troops. In marine battles, vessels served mainly as mobile firing platforms, not unlike chariots in contemporaneous land-based warfare. The only specifically nautical weapon was the grapnel, used in capsizing enemy craft after the defenders had been incapacitated by long- or medium-range weapons. Ships were also used successfully during sieges against coastal cities. Techniques for combating various forms of piracy and coastal marauding included "early warning systems" and intelligence reports traded among allies.

It appears that marine affairs were circumscribed by a recognized code of laws that existed at least along the coast of the Levant. This was a prerequisite of maritime trading, since only with a set of laws could the nautical merchant travel with a reasonable amount of safety.

Although trade in luxury items, easily identifiable in the archaeological record, stops at the beginning of the Iron Age, it is unlikely that trade, travel, or transport by ships on the sea lanes ceased during that time. Ugarit was destroyed ca. 1187 B.C. Wenamun, visiting the Levantine coast a scant century later, found a vibrant panoply of trading communities there. These consisted of a lively mixture of newly arrived immigrants and descendants of Syro-Canaanite traders who were, as Wenamun walked among them, evolving into the Phoenician culture.

Much has been written concerning the overlordship of the seas during the Late Bronze Age: of Minoan thalassocracies and Egyptian hegemonies, of Mycenaean and Syro-Canaanite trading empires. But these are viewpoints imported into the past instead of perceptions of actual past realities. The seafaring world of the Bronze Age was far richer, more diversified, and more complex than that. Its main attribute was a multiplicity of interactions by a panoply of peoples.

Of this world, and of the ships that made it possible, in truth, we know very little.

APPENDIX:
Texts from Ugarit Pertaining to Seafaring

BY J. HOFTIJZER AND W. H. VAN SOLDT

This appendix contains revised translations of the most significant documents pertaining to nautical matters found at Ugarit. This city-state, located slightly north of Latakia on the Syrian coast, was a major entrepôt during the Late Bronze Age (Fig. 13.1: b). Until the end of that period, Ugarit belonged to the Egyptian sphere of influence, as demonstrated by the diplomatic correspondence from Amarna (*EA* 1: 39; 45: 35; 89: 51; 98: 9; 126: 6; 151: 55). About 1330 B.C., Ugarit came under Hittite suzerainty.

Political stability in Syria guaranteed Ugarit's prosperity through trade after the reign of its king, Niqmaddu II, and particularly after the brief rule of his son Arkhalba (on the absolute chronology for reigns of the kings of Ugarit, see van Soldt 1991: 44–46). Following the peace treaty between Egypt and Hatti, quantities of Egyptian goods once more found their way to the city.

This relatively peaceful period lasted for over a century but came to an abrupt end at the beginning of the twelfth century B.C. with the invasion of the Sea Peoples. This attack spelled sudden annihilation for most of the Syro-Canaanite coastal cities, including Ugarit (Liverani 1995). Several letters, which must date to the last tumultuous days of Ugarit, give a vivid account of these times (see below, *RS* 34.129, *RS* 20.18, *RS* L.1, and *RS* 20.238). The tablets reveal that the threat that ultimately destroyed Ugarit came from the sea.

Ugarit's palace had five archives. Three were administrative, containing mostly lists of landowners, persons who received rations or paid taxes, and so on. These documents had titles—such as "balance," "list," "food rations," or "provisions"—followed by the persons' names to whom they applied. The lists are laconic: often, even the type of administrative action intended is unclear. In the "central archive" and the "southern archive" were kept, respectively, the tablets regulating the transfer of land inside Ugarit and those pertaining to Ugarit's foreign relations.

The documents were written in the Ugaritic and Akkadian languages. Ugaritic, a cognate to Hebrew, is a branch of West Semitic that was written with an alphabetic script of thirty cuneiform signs. Normally, as with Akkadian, Ugaritic was inscribed on moist clay tablets that were baked afterwards. The prefect (*Sākinu* in Ugaritic) was the most important person after the king and was responsible for the city-state's day-to-day management (see below, *RS* 34.129). Directly under the prefect, various overseers, including an "overseer of the harbor" and an "overseer of the seamen," were responsible for administration (see below, *RS* 17.133).

To judge from the texts, Ugarit seems to have had a simple social structure. Two groups are distinguished: "people of the king," employed by the palace; and free citizens, called "sons of Ugarit." This two-part division is apparent everywhere in the palace administration, which always distinguishes between the guilds on the one hand and the towns and villages on the other. Mainly concentrated in the city of Ugarit itself, the guilds consisted of specialized craftsmen who were gold- and silversmiths, scribes, soldiers, priests, house builders, shipbuilders, cartwrights, and bowmakers, among others.

The population in the towns and villages apparently represented the nonspecialized segment of society: the farmers and the

333

herders. While the "people of the king" were economically dependent on the palace, which provided them with rations and land, the free citizens were independent in this respect.

Ugarit's importance on the international political level during its heyday is evident from numerous documents concerning international relations. Ugarit's strength lay in its trade; its military capacity was negligible.

The comprehensive terminology that existed in Ugarit for different types of ships, as well as the numerous references to nautical matters, indicate the importance of its maritime connections. Ships sailed to and from Egypt, to the other city-states along the Syro-Canaanite coast, to Cyprus, Cilicia, and to the Aegean.

Texts in Ugaritic Alphabetic Script

The following texts are translated in the order in which they are published in *KTU*. Some of them were found still in the kiln in which they were being baked when Ugarit was overrun (against the idea they were found in a kiln, cf. Millard 1995: 119). These texts must therefore date to immediately before Ugarit's downfall, ca. 1185 B.C. Not every text concerning ships, shipment, and related matters in Ugaritic alphabetic script has been translated here (for a description of Ugarit as a naval power, see Linder 1981; Artzy 1987).

KTU 2.38
Your ship was damaged
Virolleaud 1965: 81–83; Sasson 1966: 137; Lipiński 1967: 283; Hoftijzer 1979: 383–88; Dietrich and Loretz 1985: 507; Cunchillos 1986; 1989: 349–57; Aboud 1994: 101–102. Found in the kiln.

1–3 To the king of Ugarit, my brother, speak: Message of the king of Tyre your brother.[1]

4–9 May you be well. May the gods guard and preserve you. Here with me it goes well. Is everything going well with you there? Answer me, please.

10–25 As to a ship of yours that you sent to Egypt, that (ship) is in Tyre. Serious damage happened to it in a torrential rainstorm. They were found, and the *rb tmtt*[2] took all their *grain* from them.[3] But I took all their grain (and) the crew, all that belonged to them,[4] from the *rb tmtt*, and I gave it back to them. And *another* ship of yours is unloaded[5] in Acco. Let my brother not be troubled about anything.

Notes

1. This is an Ugaritic translation of an original letter sent by the king of Tyre (cf. however Millard 1995: 120) that deals with two ships, not two parts of a fleet, as Cunchillos (1986; 1989: 351–52 n.9.; cf. also Tropper 1994A: 467) suggests, nor does it deal with *one* ship (against e.g. Dietrich and Loretz 1985: 507; Renfroe 1992: 68; Aboud 1994: 102). The text makes it probable that there was a kind of international entente whereby ships of various nations and their cargoes were respected in time of peace (Sasson 1966: 137).

2. The *rb tmtt* is probably a high Tyrian official in charge of salvage operations (Sasson 1966: 137) against Dietrich and Loretz (1966: 132) and Cunchillos (1986: 138; 1989: 354), who consider him the head of the ship's crew, and against Virolleaud (1965: 82), who suggests that he was a pirate.

3. The *drc* in ll. 17 and 19 is translated as "grain"; a translation of "crew" is possible but seems less probable (Hoftijzer 1979: 387–88; Aboud 1994: 102).

4. Instead of *kl klhm* (all that belonged to them) in l. 21, one could possibly read *w.]aklhm* (= and their food; cf. *KTU*).

5. For the translation of *cryt* with "is unloaded," see Lipiński (1967: 283 n. 5). Cunchillos's (1986: 135, 141; 1989: 356–57) translation "has returned" is less probable. Lines 24–25 (*w.anyk.tt by.cky.cryt*) can also be translated, "A second ship of yours is in Acco, naked, i.e. having lost its sails" (Pardee with Cunchillos 1989: 357; cf. also Dietrich and Loretz 1985: 507; Aboud 1994: 102).

KTU 2.39
Send copper
Virolleaud 1965: 84-86; Sasson 1966: 133; Dijkstra 1976; de Moor 1979: 651; Pardee 1981; Hoftijzer 1982. From the kiln.

1–2 Message of the Sun to Ammurapi, speak:[1]

3–4 With the Sun[2] everything is extremely well.

5–10[3] At the fe[et of the lo]rd, the Sun, his lord your servant truly resides, verily he is his se[rvant], his *sglt*,[4] and the [. . . of his lord] he protects [or: through the { . . . of his lord} he is protected?] and my lord will lack no [. . .],[5] I really acknowledge him [sc. as my overlord].[6]

11–16[7] Now, [if you are] his servant, his *sglt* for the Sun your lord, now if you verily acknowledge the Sun your lord, why didn't you come with the Sun your lord for already one, two years?[8]

17–30 As to the tablets concerning food [/ grain] that[9] you sent to the Sun your lord, because there was no food anymore in your realm,[10] the sun[11] may perish, if I will come . . . [rest too damaged to be translated].

31–35 The enemy is over us [. . . and] there is no copper[12] [. . .] purify copper, . . .[13] search [for it], wherever[14] you can get it and send it to me.

Notes

1. This is probably the translation of an original letter sent by the Hittite king to Ammurapi, the last king of Ugarit (cf. however Millard 1995: 120).

2. "The Sun" is the epithet with which the Hittite king refers to himself.

3. Lines 5–10 are probably a quotation from a letter king Ammurapi sent to the Hittite king (Hoftijzer 1982: 383). In ll. 5–10, King Ammurapi underlines his faithfulness. These lines are damaged and are difficult to restore.

4. The *sglt* indicates the vassal of whom the overlord may expect complete dedication, but also the vassal who because of this may expect the complete protection of his overlord (Hoftijzer 1982: 381–82).

5. Of what there is no shortage remains unclear. The restoration *d̠[rᶜ* (cf. *KTU*) (grain) remains completely uncertain.

6. *Ydᶜ* indicates here a vassal's loyalty to his overlord (Huffmon 1966; Huffmon and Parker 1966).

7. Lines 11–16 are the Hittite king's response. The tone of the latter is extremely rude (contrast *KTU* 2.46, below). There are no pleasantries; note the stress laid on the fact that it is very good with the addresser (ll. 3f. and elsewhere).

8. The visit mentioned in ll. 15f is an official one that the king of Ugarit ought to pay to his overlord to indicate his allegiance. This is not necessarily a visit he had to pay after his accession to the throne (Hoftijzer 1982: 379–80; Cunchillos 1989: 400).

9. See Parker (1967: 75) for *ky* used as the introduction of a relative clause (l. 17) against Pardee (1977: 7), Verreet (1988: 197–98).

10. For *ḥwt* indicating "realm" or "country," see Herdner (1969: 132).

11. It is improbable that *špš*, "sun," in l. 21 indicates the sun as an epithet of the Hittite king, because it is the subject of a feminine form of the verb. The addresser is instead saying that he prefers the perishing of the sun to his going to . . . (the rest is lost) (Hoftijzer 1982: 385; against Tropper 1994A: 467).

12. For *spr* in l. 32 meaning "bronze," see Hoftijzer 1982: 386–87; Dietrich and Loretz 1986. For the translation with "copper" in this text, see Zaccagnini 1970: 322–24. On the use of "bronze," see Zaccagnini (1990).

13. I know of no convincing interpretation for *adm* in l. 33. The interpretation with "a man," "anyone" (cf. Pardee 1981: 152, 156; Verreet 1988: 123: "the man") seems less convincing.

14. On *a̠tr*, see Rainey (1978: 65); Dietrich and Loretz (1984: 62); Israel (1995: 260).

KTU 2.42
The king may seek ships

Virolleaud 1965: 14–15; Sasson 1966: 134; Lipiński 1977; Pardee 1987: 204–209. For the archaeological context of the room in which the text was found, see van Soldt (1991: 88).

1–3 To the king [my] lo[rd] speak: Message of the chief of . . . [. . . your servant]:[1]

4–9 At the feet of my lord from afar seven times and seven times [I bow down]. I declare to Baal [. . .],[2] to the eternal Sun, to Astarte, to Anat, to all the gods of Alashia[3]: Nimmuriya is king forever.[4]

10–13 The king my lord, the land [. . .] he will get in arrears [??][5] and to my lord [. . .] ten times I have sent [. . .] and my lord . . . [. . .]

14–19 [. . .] ten [or twen{ty}] . . . he may put [. . .] the city of the k[ing] [. . .] in them and [. . .]

20–28 I will give [or you may give?][6] si[lver . . .] I will send [. . .]

Now he has sent [or [I] have sent] [. . .] and the king may make inquiry into these [. . .] them and their ships [. . .] this merchant and I say [. . .] the king may seek ships and I [?, . . .] and I [?] will carry out the transaction and the king may send [?] to [. . .].[7]

Notes

1. Amenhotep III (Nimmuriya) is mentioned in l. 9 (see Virolleaud 1965: 15), making this text one of the oldest found in Ugarit (contra Rainey 1974: 188). Thus, the tablet must date to the first half of the fourteenth century B.C. It was sent from an Ugaritic official to the king of Ugarit. It is unnecessary to presume, as does Lipiński (1977: 214), that this is a copy of a letter sent by a high Egyptian official at Ugarit to the pharaoh.

The writer's name is not included. This absence of the name is understandable if there was only one functionary of this stature at any given time. The suggestion to read it as *rb mi(ḫd)* is attractive (Heltzer 1976: 82 n. 28; Liverani 1979B: 499), particularly if it referred to Maḫadu, Ugarit's main port. Concerning Maḫadu, see Astour 1970: 113–22; Guzzo Amadasi 1982; Saadé 1995. This would also fit the context of the letter that speaks of merchants and vessels. Pardee (1987: 206), preparing his new edition of the text, could not find the fragment of l. 3 that reads (ᶜ)*bdk*, "your servant." Concerning this fragment, see Virolleaud 1965: 14; Pardee 1987: 206.

2. The first deity mentioned in l. 6 probably was Baal-Sapon (Liverani 1979A: 1303; Pardee 1987: 206–207).

3. It is not unusual to find "all the Gods of Alashia (Cyprus)" mentioned in l. 8, for Ugarit had important trade relations with Cyprus, and this text is clearly concerned with trade. Concerning Alashia, see above, pp. 61–62, 295–96.

4. The words *mlk ʿlm* (l. 9) are often considered as the translation of a title of the god Osiris, with whom Amenhotep III was identified (Gaál 1974; Pardee 1988: 89–90 n. 48). The corresponding Egyptian title, however, was only applied to Amenhotep III after his death (Radwan 1973). One would not expect a reference to the identification of the deceased king with Osiris in a letter that is concerned with matters of trade and shipping. At that time the pharaoh was the overlord of the Ugaritic king, so it is possible to explain the words *nmry mlk ʿlm* as an acknowledgment of the pharaoh's overlordship. In the Hebrew Bible, a comparable formula is used to express the power of the Lord (Jeremiah 10:10, Psalms 10:16). Furthermore, *mlk ʿlm* was used in Ugarit as an epithet of the god Rapi'u (*KTU* 1.108: 1, 19, 20), who is identified with Baal. In *KTU* 1.2 iv 10, *mlk ʿlm* indicates the everlasting kingship of Baal. Comparable formulae are also used in the Bible to acknowledge the power of the Judean king (Psalm 45:7, see also Psalms 21:5, 61:8; I Chronicles 17:14).

5. The reading *yšiḫr* in l. 11 (Pardee 1987: 205) seems preferable. For the interpretation, cf. Tropper 1990: 23–24.

6. In l. 20 the reading *atn* is accepted, although the reading *ttn* is also possible (Pardee 1987: 209).

7. The rest of the tablet is too damaged to allow any certain restoration. The addresser is clearly writing concerning trade and ships. Concerning the problems of reading the beginning of the last line, see Pardee's (1987: 209) commentary.

KTU 2.46
Supply seagoing vessels
Virolleaud 1965: 87–88; Astour 1965: 255; Sasson 1966: 134; Hoftijzer 1983: 97. Found in the kiln.

1–3 The message of *Pgn:*[1] To the king of Ugarit speak:

4–5 May you be well. May the gods protect [and] preserve you.

6–9 Here with me it is well. Is it well there with my son in every respect? Answer me, please.

9–25 Whereas my son has sent to me tablets about food[2] often and over and over again,[3] let my son supply [send] here[4] seagoing vessels[5] . . . [. . .].

[The rest is too uncertain to be translated.]

Notes

1. This is probably a translation of a letter (however, cf. Millard 1995: 120) addressed to the king of Ugarit from a foreign ruler on the Mediterranean coast, perhaps the king of Alashia (= Cyprus), with whom the last king of Ugarit had friendly relations (Astour 1965: 255). Concerning these relations, see e.g. Astour 1981: 28.

2. The "tablets about food" refer to a letter in which the king of Ugarit asked for food supplies, see *KTU* 2.39 above.

3. The interpretation of l. 11 (*midy wġbny*) remains uncertain. I follow here the clause division proposed by Pardee (1975B: 354; 1976: 248). It is possible to translate ll. 9–11, "Whereas my son has sent tablets about food, with me there is plenty and abundance" (Dietrich, Loretz, and Sanmartín 1973: 96; Tropper 1994B: 479).

4. For the interpretation of *hnkt* in l. 12 as "here," see Hartmann and Hoftijzer 1971; Renfroe 1992: 116 (contra Gordon 1965: no. 787: *hnk* = "levy," *hnkt* = plural; Rainey 1966: 261; 1971: 160; Cunchillos 1983: 161–62, *hnk* and *hnkt* are demonstrative pronouns; see also Dijkstra and de Moor 1975: 207 n. 294); Tropper 1990: 35: *hnkt* = "really."

At the time that this letter to send ships was written, Ugarit was experiencing a shortage of vessels (Hoftijzer 1979: 384–85; see below,

KTU 2.47 and *RS* 20. 238), which gives the addresser's kind offer a sardonic twist.

5. I leave the difficult *yšrn* in l. 14 untranslated. Dijkstra and de Moor's (1975: 207) proposed translation, "to despatch" or "to stow," is less probable, for it assumes that the food was to be sent from Ugarit to Alashia.

KTU 2.47
A request for 150 ships
Virolleaud 1965: 88–89; Sasson 1966: 133; Heltzer 1979: 252; Hoftijzer 1983: 97–98. Found in the kiln.

1–11 The message of Yadinu to the king, his lord.[1] Protect your country.[2] Will, please, supply ships, will supply 150 ships . . .[3] and 400 Apiru[4] and the king [rest too damaged to be translated].

12–21 And the king who governs in his homeland[5] to Yadinu the servant of the king, whom he has made commander of his army.[6] Let the dynasty not go to ruin.[7] The border patrol[8] has taken *kwsʿt*,[9] let your army . . . border.

Notes

1. This tablet contains summaries of two letters: one from Yadinu to the king of Ugarit, and the other from the king to Yadinu. All the obligatory polite formulae are absent in Yadinu's "letter." Also, note the "and" at the beginning of l. 12. On the peculiar style of this document, see Kaiser 1970: 14.

The addresser is a military commander serving the Ugaritic king (cf. l. 15). Against Lambrou-Phillipson 1993: 165, who sees him as a minor official placed in charge of the king's children who knew nothing about naval matters.

2. The use of an imperative in l. 2 is not indicative of a rude or impolite style. The translation "guardian of your house / country" is less probable (contra Lambrou-Phillipson 1993: 164).

3. The manner in which the re-

quest for ships is formulated (ll. 3ff.) gives a sense of great urgency. The fact that Yadinu asks for ships means that he must have been situated somewhere along the Mediterranean coast. For the translation "supply," see Tropper 1990: 35.

4. Apiru refers to socially uprooted communities from which many people were recruited for military service.

5. The *šph* (ll. 12 and 16) probably means "dynasty."

6. *Ḫrd* (ll. 15, 17, 19) probably means "army" (Heltzer 1979: 245–53); less likely are the translations "guard" or "watchman" (Dietrich, Loretz, and Sanmartín 1974A: 27–28; Dietrich and Loretz 1987: 29). The manner in which the king describes Yadinu underlines Yadinu's subordinate position: he must do as the king commands. The insistence that he go on with his task becomes understandable if one realizes that the king is not able to meet Yadinu's request for the 150 ships. On the shortage of ships at that time, see above, *KTU* 2.46. That Ugarit has been a great naval power is shown by the very fact that Yadinu asks for such a high number of ships (contra Lambrou-Phillipson 1993).

7. For the root *ḫbṭ*, see Dijkstra 1975; Tropper 1990: 151; Renfroe 1992: 114–15.

8. For the meaning of *ᶜps* in l. 17 see van Soldt 1989: 385: boundary (stone). Whether this border patrol was inimical to Ugarit remains uncertain, but the gloomy tone of l. 15 could suggest that it was.

9. I have translated *kwsᶜt* in ll. 17f. as the name of a town, but this remains uncertain. Less probable is Dietrich and Loretz's (1987: 29) interpretation of "a jar with grain."

KTU 4.40
Ships' crews
Virolleaud 1937: 167–68; Gaster 1938; Herdner 1963: 167–68; Heltzer 1976: 21–23; Dietrich and Loretz 1977.

1–2 Heavily damaged, untranslatable.
3–6 [Men from] Ṭibaqu [. . .], men from Maqa[bu][1] 1[?]9 [men], in total . . .[2]
7–9 The crew of the ship of *Bin Kṯan*, in total [1]9 [m]en.
10–18 The crew of the ship of Abdichor,[3] men from Pidu 5 men, men from Sinaru 9 me[n], men from Gibala 4 men, men from Ṭibaqu [. . .]

Notes
1. The place names mentioned in this text—Gibala, Maqabu, Pidi, Sinaru, and Ṭibaqu—are localities within the realm of Ugarit (for the topography, see van Soldt 1994: 366–67, 377; Astour 1995: 63–66). The text mentions the numbers of men from these places who were called up for service on the king's ships. Whether this is a military call-up for service on warships (Gaster 1938: 105; Heltzer 1976: 21–23) or for service on the king's merchant fleet remains uncertain.

2. The translation "total" for *ǵr* as proposed by Dietrich and Loretz (1977) is contextually the most probable one. The translation "crew" for *ǵr* (de Moor 1971: 134) seems less likely, for this idea is already represented by the term *ṣbu*.

3. Adan, *Bin Kṯan*, and Abdichor are names of the ships' captains.

KTU 4.81
Ships from Maḫadu
Virolleaud 1941: 34; Herdner 1963: 173–74.

1 The ships from Maḫad[u][1]
2–19 The *br*-vessel[2] of Ṭipatbaa[l], the *br*-vessel of *dmty*, the *ṯkt*-vessel[3] of Yadlinu, the *ṯkt*-vessel of Ṭarriyanu, the *br*-vessel of Abdimilku . . .

[The rest of the text is heavily damaged; it contained at least two other *ṯkt*-vessels and ten other *br*-vessels.][4]

Notes
1. This is a list of ships from Maḫadu, Ugarit's main harbor (see above, the commentary for *KTU* 2.42).

2. A *br*-vessel is a big ship, used for international trade or as a war vessel. See also n. 3.

3. A *ṯkt*-vessel is apparently one of smaller dimensions. Concerning these ship types, see Alt 1951: 69–71, Sasson 1966: 131–32. There is a reference to *ṯkt*-vessels in Isaiah 2: 16 (Lipiński 1971: 87).

4. It is not certain whether the personal names are those of the ships' owners (Heltzer 1976: 23) or their captains.

KTU 4.338
Silver for the ships
Virolleaud 1965: 129–30; Sasson 1966: 133; Dietrich, Loretz, and Sanmartín 1974B; Ziskind 1974; Pardee 1975A; Freedman 1977: 56-57; Heltzer 1978: 143; Miller 1980: 335–37; Dietrich and Loretz 1990; Aboud 1994: 99–100 (only ll. 1–18). Found in the kiln.

1–3 List of people who have entered the palace of the king [that is, who have entered into the king's service] and who have not been put in a document [that is, who have not been listed] before:
4–9 Yarimᶜal the Tyrian, Irseyu, Yaᶜziraddu, Ayachu, Bin Ayaltu.
10–18[1] 540 [shekel] is the silver for the ships [or a ship] that has entered into[2] a ship [or ships] for the king of Byblos [that is, it has been loaded in this ship / these ships], and the king of Byblos has taken 50 [shekel of] silver for the outfitting [?][3] of his ships in ᶜrm[4] as the silver due for its payment.[5]

Notes
1. The tablet contains two texts on entirely different subjects, ll.

1–9 and 10–18, respectively, separated by two strokes.

2. The ʿrb b on l. 12 has been interpreted in a completely different manner. It is then considered as referring to the giving of a guarantee or pledge (Virolleaud 1965: 129; Dietrich, Loretz, and Sanmartín 1974B; Ziskind 1974: 135–36; Pardee 1975A: 612–16; Heltzer 1978: 143; Hoftijzer 1979: 384; Miller 1980: 346). This interpretation is less probable, however (Freedman 1977: 56–57; Pardee 1980: 34–35 n. 47). The meaning given by both authors for ʿrb b as "to be paid" is less likely. Against the original interpretation, see also Dietrich and Loretz 1990: 94. Lines 10–13 probably deal with the rental due for ships that the king of Ugarit had hired or purchased from the king of Byblos (Cunchillos 1989: 352). For kbd in l. 11, see Liverani 1970: 106–108; Wesselius 1980: 450.

3. Lines 14–19 are concerned with the payment for the outfitting (?) of the ship(s).

There is no need to emend lbš in l. 16 to lbnš as proposed by Dietrich, Loretz, and Sanmartín (1974B; 1975A: 556; Dietrich and Loretz 1990: 95). Instead, it seems preferable to consider it a nominal form of the root lbš (Hoftijzer and van Soldt 1991: 206 n. 55). An l may be missing before lbš because of haplography (Miller 1980: 347 n. 39).

4. It seems unnecessary to amend b ʿrm in l. 17 to arb ʿm (contra Dietrich, Loretz, and Sanmartín 1973: 86, 1974B; Dietrich and Loretz 1990: 95).

ʿrm is best understood as the name of a locality within the realm of Ugarit.

5. As we have seen in KTU 2.46, there was a shortage of ships at Ugarit. KTU 4.338 may represent an attempt by Ugarit to alleviate the situation by either buying or hiring

ships from Byblos. On this situation, see Hoftijzer 1979: 384–85; Dietrich and Loretz 1990: 95–96.

KTU 4.352
Jars of oil
Virolleaud 1965: 117–18; Liverani 1970: 96; Aboud 1994: 94 (only ll. 1–4). Found in the kiln.

1–2[1] 660 [jars of] oil for Abiramu the Alashian [the Cypriot].
3–4 130 [jars of] oil for Abiramu the Egyptian.
5–6 248 [jars of oil][2] for the srbdnm.[3]
7–12 100 [jars of oil] for Bin Azmat the man from Reshu.[4] 100 [jars of oil] for Talmiyanu the son of Adaya. [. . .] for adddy. [. . .] for Kukulan [. . .].

Notes

1. The contents of this document (like those of the preceding text) give some idea of the riches that Ugarit still possessed at the moment of its downfall.

2. Although the word "oil" is not mentioned anymore in ll. 5ff., it seems probable that the whole text refers to jars of oil. Lines 1–4 refer to the export of oil to foreign countries (through foreign merchants?).

3. It is uncertain which group of men is indicated by the word srbdnm (l. 6). The men have been considered bronze smiths (Zaccagnini 1970: 315–17; Heltzer 1982: 41). Van Soldt (1989: 379 n. 27) thinks the word might indicate a special group of merchants. The fact that the meaning of srbdnm is uncertain makes it the more difficult to define the function of the people mentioned in ll. 7ff. Were they merchants in service of the king?

4. Reshu is a locality belonging to Ugarit (van Soldt 1994: 368; Astour 1995: 60).

KTU 4.366
A list of tkt-ships
Virolleaud 1965: 109–10. Found in the kiln.

2–15[1] Kunammu the son of A[. . . , a tkt-vessel];[2] Pulsibaʾal the son of N[. . . , a tkt-vessel]; Chaya the son of Dananu, a tkt-vessel; etc.[3]

Notes

1. This is a list containing the names of persons together with the names of their fathers. More than one line is lost before l. 2 and after l. 15.

2. Concerning the tkt-vessel, see note 3 for KTU 4.81.

3. This text was found in a royal archive, suggesting that it is a list of captains in the king's service, each of whom had responsibility for one of the king's tkt-ships, instead of independent ship-owners.

KTU 4.370
A possible list of cargoes
Virolleaud 1965: 95. Found in the kiln.

1–2 List of the king's men who solicit an ʿmsn [?].[1]
3 bṣr, Abnu, Shapshiyanu.[2]
4–5 Diqnu, Achalmeni, etc. [l. 14], the house-builders; Rashap-abu, Risana, etc. [. . . , {l. 35} the makers of] fine objects [??];[3] . . . , Yaʾbadu, Kilatu, etc. [l. 45], the stonecutters . . . [. . .].[4]

Notes

1. This text is concerned with ships and trade only if the difficult term ʿmsn means "shipload" (Gordon 1965: no. 1872). In view of the contents of ll. 3ff., and particularly ll. 14, 35, and 45, however, this interpretation seems highly uncertain. Perhaps it is best to interpret ʿmsn as a personal name, as suggested by Sivan (1990: 315 n. 28), and to understand the preceding verbal form taršn not as an active but as a passive one (N). The translation of ll. 1–2 would then be "List of the king's men who have to be summoned: ʿmsn." In that case ʿmsn is a personal name, perhaps related to the biblical name Amos.

If so, this text has nothing to do with ships or cargoes.

2. There is a stroke between ll. 3 and 4, indicating that there is no connection between the persons mentioned in the two lines.

3. The translation of *qtn* in l. 35 as "fine objects" (Heltzer 1982: 88) remains highly uncertain.

4. The difficult *ṣnr* at the end of l. 45 (which I left untranslated) is perhaps a personal name added to the list (Virolleaud 1965: 95). Gordon's (1965: no. 2177) suggestion to translate this as "pipe" is less reasonable. Moreover, the reading of the *r* is uncertain, and after it there originally existed one or more additional signs (Dietrich, Loretz, and Sanmartín 1974A: 35).

KTU 4.390
A ship from Alashia
Virolleaud 1965: 74.

1–13 A ship from Alas[hia . . . .][1] which is in Atallig[2] . . . 15 . . ., a talent of c[opper],[3] 6 shields,[4] 2 . . ., a trowel of bronze, a shovel . . . [. . .], 5 . . [. . .], 6 . . [. . .], 1[1] [. . . of] purpl[e . . .],[5] shovel . . .[6]

Notes
1. This text lists the cargo of a ship from Alashia.

2. Atallig is a coastal locality belonging to Ugarit. See van Soldt 1994: 367, 377; Astour 1995: 63–64.

3. For *tlt* in l. 4 (= copper), see Zaccagnini 1970: 317–24; Sanmartín 1988A: 176–77.

4. For the possible translation of *hrt* in l. 5 as "shield," see Dietrich, Loretz, and Sanmartín 1973: 87.

5. I have translated *irgm(n)* in l. 12 as "purple," because translating it as "tribute" seems less probable in this context (contra Pardee 1974: 277; see, however, Pardee's comments there in n. 14).

6. Most of the terms denoting objects are damaged, and their identification remains highly uncertain. For the *ult* in l. 7 trans-

lated here as "trowel," see Renfroe 1992: 79.

KTU 4.394
A ship with copper is lost
Virolleaud 1965: 132. Found in the kiln.

1–4 hundred ten / twenty . . . copper is lost in a ship.[1]
5 20 for the people from *Umd*.
6 10 for Kutilana.[2]

Notes
1. One must see the loss of this ship against the background of shortage of ships mentioned in *KTU* 2.39 and *KTU* 2.46. Line 4 is destroyed.

2. Lines 5 and 6 are also probably concerned with copper.

KTU 4.421
Another list of ships
Virolleaud 1965: 75.

1[1] [too damaged to translate]
2–5 ships [or a ship?] of the king . . . and 3 *br*-vessels,[2] which . . . and 4 *ʿtk*-vessels[3] . . ., an *ʿtk*-vessel . . . [. . .].

Notes
1. The purpose of this badly damaged list of ships is unclear. There were originally one or more lines in front of l. 1. The "ship[s] of the king" probably belonged to the royal fleet since the text was found in a royal archive.

2. On the *br*-ship, see the commentary to *KTU* 4.81 note 2.

3. It is unclear what a *ʿtk*-vessel is. Dietrich, Loretz, and Sanmartín (1974A: 34) have suggested "moored ship."

KTU 4.647
A list of br-ships
Virolleaud 1965: 146.

1–7 . . . . . [. . . . .] and a *br*-vessel[1] of Bin I[. . .] and [. . . . .] in the hand of Yachmenu . . . . [. . .] a *br*-vessel of Yadinu [. . . . .] the Carian[2] the son of

Yadudanu, . . . a *br*-vessel of Purikallu the shipowner which is in the hand of Abira[mu].[3]

Notes
1. Concerning the *br*-vessel, see *KTU* 4.81 note 2.

2. The presence of a Carian emphasizes Ugarit's international contacts.

3. This text indicates that, besides the royal fleet, there were also private shipowners in Ugarit.

The significance of one man's ship being "in the hands of" another man is unclear. The latter is evidently not the lawful owner, but whether the vessel in question was entrusted to him by the owner as the ship's captain or whether it came into his possession in some other way cannot be determined. It is also unclear why this text was stored in a royal archive.

KTU 4.689
A ship's equipment
Heltzer 1982: 189–190; Xella 1982.

1 Document describing the equipment[1] of a ship.
2 Nine oars[2]
3 A new piece of cloth[3]
4 and a hatch [?][4]
5 and a mast and ropes
6 and a mast cap.[5]

Notes
1. For the interpretation of *npṣ* as "equipment," see Ribichini and Xella 1985: 54–55; Xella 1990: 472–73. See also Stieglitz 1981; Heltzer 1982: 189 n. 7; contra Baldacci 1989: 120. For the interpretational problems of this word, cf. Renfroe 1992: 135–36.

2. For this interpretation see Heltzer 1982: 189 n. 8; Xella 1982: 33; Sanmartín 1988B: 273 n. 37. Heltzer's suggestion to translate this as "pairs of oars" seems less likely, as is the interpretation of this being "cloth of combed wool"

(Dietrich, Loretz, and Sanmartín 1975B: 164). Huehnergard's (1987: 186) emendation of *mṯṯm* to *mt‹ḫ›ṯm* "ship's cloths" is unnecessary.

3. For this interpretation see Huehnergard 1987: 181. The other interpretations seem less convincing: ("anchor") Heltzer 1982: 189 n. 9; ("supply" or "shipment") Xella 1982: 33; ("beak") Sanmartín 1988B: 272–73.

4. The literal meaning of the term *mṣpt ḥrk* is possibly "covering of the opening." *ṣpt* is derived from the root *ṣpy* "to lay over." Other interpretations seem less likely: (*mṣpt* = cloth) Dietrich, Loretz, and Sanmartín 1975B: 164; (*mṣpt* to be derived from the root *ṣpy* "to look out" = "crow's-nest," *ḥrk* = grill) Xella 1982: 33; (*mṣpt* derived from root *ṣpy* "to look out, to watch," and *ḥrk* = starting?, setting in motion?) Sivan 1984: 245, 223; (*mṣpt ḥrk* = top consisting of bars) Sanmartín 1988B: 272 n. 34. See also Heltzer's (1982: 189 n. 10) remarks.

5. For this interpretation see Huehnergard 1987: 139–40. Xella's (1982: 34) equation of this term with a "gang-plank" seems less likely. See also Heltzer's (1982: 189 n. 13) remarks. The word apparently refers to the mast cap, to which the rigging is attached.

The Akkadian Texts (Miscellaneous Texts)

RS 16.238 + 254
If his ship comes back from Crete . . .

Published as *PRU* 3: 107. See Linder 1970: 50–54; Miller 1980: 291–92. From the central archive of the palace.

(dynastic seal)

1–6 From this day on, Ammishtamru, son of Niqmepa, king of Ugarit, has exempted[1] Sinarānu son of Siginu; he is clear as the Sun is clear.[2]

7–9 Neither his grain, nor his beer, nor his oil will enter the palace (as tax). His ship is free (from claims).

10–15 If his ship comes (back) from Crete,[3] he will bring his present to the king and the herald[4] will not come near his house.

15–17 Sinarā(nu) is dedicated to the king, ...[5] (ruling)

18–20 May Baʿlu, lord of Mount Ḥazi,[6] destroy whoever contests any of these words.[7]

21–22 The . . . s[8] belong to his sons' sons forever.

Notes

1. It is difficult to translate the verb *zakû*, "to be clean, free," in such a way that the literal meaning is preserved in every instance. The wordplay with the "bright Sun" is especially hard to reproduce. I have therefore translated the occurrences of *zakû* according to their contexts.

2. See note 1. I take *za-ka-at* as a stative and not as an adjective. Support comes from the alphabetic text *RS* 15.125 (*KTU* 2.19): 2'-3': *km.špš d brt*, "like the Sun who is clear," and the syllabic text *RS* 16.267: 5 (*PRU* 3: 110). See Huehnergard 1989: 188 n. 366; van Soldt 1991: 460 n. 200.

3. The text has kur DUGUD-*ri*, to be read *māt Kapturi*. The sign DUGUD stands for the Akkadian *kabtu*, "heavy" or "important," but is used here as a kind of rebus writing for *kaptu-*. For similar spellings, see van Soldt 1991: 244 n. 9; 1990: 324–25. The interpretation of Kapturu as Crete follows the traditional view.

4. I follow the CAD s.v. *nāgiru* 1b–2'. The passage has been discussed by Kestemont (1977: 195).

5. The last line is broken at both beginning and end. I venture no translation. See provisionally Nougayrol, *PRU* 3: 108. According to my collation, his readings and translations are possible.

6. Mount Ḥazi corresponds to Ṣapānu of the alphabetic texts and classical Mons Casius. It is identified with modern Jebel el-ʿAqra.

7. For a discussion of this line, see Huehnergard 1989: 137 n. 61; van Soldt 1991: 408 n. 18.

8. The first word of this line probably refers to the rights acquired by Sinarānu. It is intended to ensure that these rights will be transferred to his sons after his demise. For this type of clause, see Kienast, *RlA* 5, 535, §20.

RS 17.133
A court case

Verdict by letter from the Hittite king (probably Tudkhaliya IV).[1] Published as *PRU* 4: 118. For the seal of Queen Pudukhepa, see *Ugaritica* 3: 13 fig. 16, 18 fig. 23. See Linder 1970: 47–50. From the southern archive of the palace.

(bilingual seal of Pudukhepa)

1–3 Thus says His Majesty.[2] Speak to Ammishtamru:[3] (ruling)

4–8 When the man from Ugarit and Shukku appeared for a legal decision before His Majesty,[2] Shukku spoke as follows:

8–9 "His ship has been wrecked in the harbor."[4]

9–11 And the man from Ugarit spoke as follows:

11–12 "Shukku has wrecked my ship *intentionally*."[5]

13–15 His Majesty has rendered them the following verdict:

15–22 "Let the overseer of the seamen of Ugarit take an oath,[6] and let Shukku (thereupon) pay an indemnity for his ship (and) any belongings of his that were in his ship." (ruling)

Notes

1. Nougayrol, *PRU* 4: 118. Otten (1975: 26) leaves the matter of the identity of the king undecided.

2. Literally, "My Sun."

3. King of Ugarit.

4. Probably the harbor of Ugarit, ancient Maʾḥadu, modern Minet el Beida. See, in general, Astour 1970.

5. The text has *a-na da-a-ni*. CAD s.v. *danānu* s. 2 takes this as an or-

thographic variant of *da-na-ni* and translates it "maliciously." The context requires such a meaning. The translation chosen here takes into account that the statement is intended to put the blame on Shukku.

6. Apparently to vindicate the claim of the man from Ugarit.

RS 20.162
Do not withhold information
Letter from Parṣu of Amurru to the king of Ugarit. Published as *Ugaritica* 5: no. 37, fig. 27. See Linder 1970: 66–69; Steiner 1989: 407; Izre'el 1991 (2): 98–100. From the house of Rap'ānu.

1–3 Speak to the king of the land of Ugarit: thus says Parṣu, your servant.

4–5 I fall at the feet of my lord. May you be well.

6–8 My lord, has the king of Amurru not spoken[1] to you in the following terms:

8–11 "As soon as you hear a report about the enemies,[2] write to my country."[3]

11–16 But now, why has my lord not written to us as soon as you had learned about the enemies?[4] (ruling)

17–19 Furthermore, my lord, the land[3] of Amurru and the land[3] of Ugarit are one!

20–23 If you, my lord, hear a report about the enemies, then my lord should write to me.

23–24 My lord, herewith *I am writing to you*:

25–27 I will surely send the ships which are with us, for your inspection. My lord should know (this)! (ruling)

Notes
1. A number of verbal forms in this text (lines 8, 13, and 23) have to be interpreted as third person, although they are actually first-person forms.

2. The exact reading of ˡⁿ́kúr.KU.meš is not clear. According to Berger 1970: 288 (followed by Izre'el 1991 [2]: 100), we have

to read ˡⁿ́kúr.dúr.meš = *nakrūtu aḫûtu*, "alien enemies" (Izre'el's translation). One could also think of a phonetic indicator (KU to ensure the reading kúr). In that case, however, one would expect KU in front of PAP instead of after it.

3. MEŠ after KUR could be an ideogram marker (for which phenomenon see Izre'el 1991 [1]: 30) or a plural marker. A plural, however, can hardly be translated into English.

4. The change of person (third to second) is unexpected.

RS 20.212
A large shipment of grain
Letter from the king of Carchemish(?) to the king of Ugarit. Letter concerning the shipment of barley to Urâ. Published as *Ugaritica* 5: no. 33, fig. 42. See Berger 1969: 287; Linder 1970: 32–37; Heltzer 1977: 209. From the house of Rap'ānu.

1–4 Thus says (. . . [1]). Speak (to . . .), king of Ugarit: (ruling)

5–6 With His Majesty[2] everything is very well.

7–11 The king has exempted you from service obligations and, when he sealed and gave you the documents, did he not say because of that, "He will obey and carry out whatever they write him (to do)"? (ruling)

12–18 But now, why have you not carried out what they write you [to do]? Just as I have carried out[3] all the things that the king, your lord, has ordered me (to do) (and) he has exempted [me],[4] you must also do whatever the king, your lord, writes you (to do).

19–22 Now, the people from Urâ[5] have requested food from His Majesty (and) His Majesty has assigned to them two thousand (measures[6] of) barley from Mukish.

23–28 And you, give them one big ship and (its) sailors in order to transport this barley to their country; they will bring (it) in one or two turns. You must not deny them the ship!

29–32 In connection with this matter, His Majesty has sent Aliziti, the king's attendant,[7] and Kunni. (It is a matter of) life and death! Send them quickly on (their) way.[8]

1'–3' Bring [. . .] and give (it) to their elders,[9] be it in [Mukish] or in another country. . . . Give, (it is a matter of) life and death!

Notes
1. Since the writer appears to be a mediator between the Hittite king and the king of Ugarit, one expects him to be the king of Carchemish.

2. Literally, "The Sun"; see line 21, ᵈutu-*šu*.

3. The form ⸢e⸣-*te-pu-uš* can hardly be anything but a first-person singular.

4. Or this part belongs with what follows: "(Remember:) he has exempted you."

5. Probably nothing after ᵘʳᵘ*ú-ra-a-a*-⸢*ú*⸣. I prefer Nougayrol's reading over Berger's *a-k*[*à*-(*an*-)*na*].

6. See above, p. 41; Heltzer 1977: 209–10.

7. The exact sphere of activities of the *ša rēš šarri* is not clear. See Oppenheim 1973; Heltzer 1974.

8. Berger 1969: 287. The same expression is attested in *RS* 34.133: 14, 20; *RSO* 7: no. 36.

9. Literally, "fathers."

RS 20.255A
A complaint
The names of sender and addressee are broken off. Published as *Ugaritica* 5: no. 30, fig. 44. See Linder 1970: 73–76. From the house of Rap'ānu.

1'–3' May you be well. May the gods keep you in good health. (ruling)

4'–8' Have I not written about the ʾ*algabaṯu*[1] and the *kabdu*[2] (which are to be sent) to me, my son? But you have not sent me (anything)!

9'–12' Now, my son should send me the ʾ*algabaṯu* and the *kabdu*. (ruling)

13'–16' Furthermore, come with

your ships[3] to His Majesty,[4] your lord.

16'–18' Now, His Majesty has spoken to me in the following terms: "..." (break, what remains of the text is too fragmentary for translation).

Notes

1. The text gives this (Ugaritic) word as a gloss to the ideogram na₄.meš ge₆, "black (dark?) stones." Nougayrol (*Ugaritica* 5: 101 n. 1), followed by Stieglitz (1979: 18), therefore regards ʾalgabaṭu as basalt and connects it with Hebrew ʾelgābīš (Nougayrol: "lava"). I would like to connect it with Akkadian algamešu despite the different ideograms. Concerning this interpretation, see most recently Heimpel 1987: 50 and text *RS* 34.135, below. For the use of different ideograms for the same material, see van Soldt 1990: 340: síg.sag.gil.mud and síg.za.gìn sa₅ for ḫašmānu, síg.ḫé.me.da/ta and síg sa₅ for tabarru. Note that in these instances, just like in the case of ʾalgabaṭu, the compound ideogram is replaced with a simple color indication. The exact identity of the dark stone called ʾalgabaṭu remains obscure.

2. See previous note. Gloss to the ideogram na₄.meš babbar, "white stones." The Ugaritic word has the literal meaning "heavy." See Nougayrol, *Ugaritica* 5: 101 n. 1.

3. Literally, "Your ships and you on them."

4. Literally, "(My) Sun."

RS 26.158
More about grain

This tablet seems to deal with the same topic as *RS* 20.212. Unfortunately, the text is too broken for a coherent translation. See *Ugaritica* 5: no. 171; Linder 1970: 37–41. What remains reads:

3' barley [. . .]
4' to Urâ [. . .]
5' this barley [. . .]
6' and you [. . .]

7' all the ships
8'–12' [. . .] [five lines too fragmentary for translation]
13' this barley [. . .]
14' to Urâ [. . .]
15' may it be entrusted [. . .]
16' of the king of Hatti
17' and of the queen of [Ḫatti]
18' to go . . .
(rest broken).

RS 34.135
A demand for stones

Letter from Rabbu-kēn[1] (written at Ugarit?) to the king of Ugarit concerning the release of algamiššu[2]-stones for the king of Amurru. Published as *RSO* 7: no. 17; see also pl. 21 (photo).

1–3 To the king of Ugarit, my lord, speak: thus says Rabbu-kēn, your servant. (ruling)

4 I fall twice seven times at the feet of my lord.

5–12 My lord, now, the king of Amurru, my lord, has written to me as follows: "Write to the king of Ugarit in the following terms: 'Why have you withheld the algamiššu-stones from Baʿlu-maʿdir?[3] Your people will have to carry (them); neither my servants nor my ship will bring[4] them!'" (ruling)

13–23 Now then, the king, my lord, should let Baʿlu-maʿdir go,[5] so that he can take the algamiššu-stones and that the houses of the king be constructed. Now, the houses are standing there without algamiššu-stones. May the king, my lord, do[6] no such thing![7] Release the algamiššu-stones to Baʿlu-maʿdir. (ruling)

24–26 Whatever stones will come out of Amurru, I will keep them; are we not one country?

Notes

1. The reading of gal–gi.na is not certain.

2. For algamiššu, see above text: *RS* 20.255A, note 1.

3. Alphabetic bʿlmḏr: see *KTU* 4.172: 3, 4.266: 3, and 6.16: 1. Compare possibly ᵖᵈiškur–ma-zi-ri in *RS*

16.136: 8 (*PRU* 3: 142).

4. Reading i-na-ši-ši-[na-ti]; see Malbran-Labat in *RSO*.

5. Literally, "send!"

6. Second person.

7. I read ⌈a-ma-ta an⌉-ni-ta.

RS 34.145
Keep the ships nearby

Letter from the king (of Carchemish) to the queen of Ugarit concerning various topics. Published as *RSO* 7: no. 9; pl. 20 (photo).

1–3 Thus says the king. Speak to the queen of Ugarit:

4 May you be well.

5–8 (not related to lines 9–14)

9–14 As for the ships you wrote me about: let them go to Byblos and Sidon, but they should not go on a long journey.

RS 34.147
A list of old ships

List of ships belonging to the king of Carchemish that have been taken out of use. Published as *RSO* 7: no. 5; pl. 20 (photo).

(Seal of Kumma-walwi)

1–3 Ships belonging to the king of Carchemish that have become very old[1] and are no longer able[2] to go anywhere: (ruling)

4–17 The ship of Yamūt-šarru, the ship of Pululunu, the ship of Tuppiršu, the ship of Aburu,[3] the ship of Ṣidanayu,[4] through Zuʾabu,[5] the ship of Abimānu, the ship of ʿAbdi-ilima, the ship of Kurwasu,[6] the ship of Makuya, the ship of Matēnu, the ship of Akkuya, the ship of ʿAbdi-Ṣapāni, the ship of Šamu-Addu. (ruling)

18–20 Kumma-walwi has collected the equipment of Šamu-Addu's ship. (ruling)

21–22 Seal of Kumma-walwi, son of Uwani.

Notes

1. Note that the verbal form is in the singular.

2. See note 1.

3. The reading of the name is not certain.

4. Interpreted as "The Sidonian" by Malbran-Labat. Note, however, that the name of the city of Sidon is always spelled Ṣidunu at Ugarit.

5. Unless the person comes from outside Ugarit (as, for example, from Emar), the name cannot be read Ḏū-abi. Zu'abu was probably responsible either for all the aforementioned ships or just for the ship of Ṣidanayu.

6. For the spelling, see *KTU* 4.655:2, *krws*.

Correspondence Concerning a Seaborne Invasion

RS 34.129
Report of an abduction
Letter from the Hittite king to the prefect of Ugarit. Published as *RSO* 7, no. 12. Photo: *Ugaritica* 7: pl. 11. See Dietrich and Loretz 1978; 1982–85: 508; Lehmann 1979; Rainey in Wachsmann 1982: 304 n. 1. See above, pp. 128–30, 164. Unstratified.

1–4 Thus says His Majesty,[1] the Great King. Speak to the prefect: (ruling)

5–14 Now, (there) with you, the king your lord is (still too) young. He knows nothing. And I, His Majesty, had issued him an order concerning Ibnadušu, whom the people from Šikala[2]—who live on ships—had abducted. (ruling)

15–30 Herewith I send Nirga'ili, who is *kartappu* with me, to you. And you, send Ibnadušu, whom the people from Šikala had abducted, to me. I will question him about the land Šikala,[3] and afterwards he may leave for Ugarit again. (ruling)

Notes
1. Literally, "(My) Sun."

2. See, in general, Lehmann 1979.

3. Note the difference in spelling.

RS 20.18
A report on enemy movement
Letter from Eshuwara, chief prefect of Alashia, to the king of Ugarit. Published as *Ugaritica* 5: no. 22 and fig. 31. Berger 1969: 217; Linder 1970: 63–66; Dietrich and Loretz 1982–85: 509; Steiner 1989: 408–409. From the house of Rapᵓānu.

1–4 Thus says Eshuwara, the chief prefect of Alashiya. Speak to the king of Ugarit: (ruling)

5–6 May you and your country be well. (ruling)

7–13 As for the matter concerning those enemies: (it was) the people from your country (and) your own ships (who) did this![1] And (it was) the people from your country (who) committed these transgression(s).[2] (ruling)

14–15 So do not *be angry* with me![3] (ruling)

16–24 But now, (the) twenty enemy ships—even before they would reach the mountain (shore)[4]—have not stayed around but have quickly moved on, and where they have *pitched camp* we do not know.[5]

25–28 I am writing you to inform and protect you. Be aware! (ruling)

Notes
1. This translation is more or less prompted by lines 12-13. The sender of the letter seems to refer to a previous confrontation during which the people from Ugarit may have suffered damage. The *-ma* in line 9 points to a contrast with the enemies in line 7.

2. The word *iteqtu* is not known from other sources.

3. I tentatively take the form *te-ze-em-me* as a mistake for *tezenne* (from *zenû*). The same interpretation was followed by von Soden, *AHw* s.v. *zemû*.

4. The translation is tentative. Read perhaps in line 19: *it-ta[l-k]a-ni-me*. See *Ugaritica* 5: photo, fig. 31.

5. The reading of the verb in line 23 is difficult. I follow Nougayrol, who read *it-ta-dú-ú*. The sign TU can be defended on the basis of the copy and the photo. However, unless the form refers to the enemies in general, the masculine plural would remain unexplained. Therefore, one could also consider a reading *it-ta-la-ka¹*, "(And where) they are heading." For LA with two horizontals at the beginning, see line 20. Only one horizontal is found in lines 3, 15, 18, 24.

RS L.1
Make preparations
Letter from the king (of Alashia) to Ammurapi, king of Ugarit. Published as *Ugaritica* 5: no. 23 and fig. 29. See Berger 1969: 219; Linder 1970: 69–72; Dietrich and Loretz 1982–85: 510; Yamada 1992. From the house of Rapᵓānu (?).

1–4 Thus says the king.[1] Speak to Ammurapi, king of Ugarit: (ruling)

5–7 May you be well! May the gods keep you in good health! (ruling)

8–14 Concerning what you wrote to me: "They have spotted enemy ships at sea"; if they have indeed spotted ships, make yourself as strong as possible.

14–21 Now, where are your own troops (and) chariotry stationed? Are they not stationed with you? If not, who will deliver you from the enemy *forces*?[2]

22–28 Surround your towns with walls; bring troops and chariotry inside. (Then) wait at full strength for the enemy. (ruling)

Notes
1. *RS* 20.238 is an answer to this letter. Yamada 1992: 437–39 claims that the king of Carchemish is the sender of the letter. However, the subject matters in *RS* L.1 and *RS* 20.238 are very similar, despite Yamada's reservations. I therefore follow Nougayrol, who identified the "king" with the king of Alashiya.

2. The translation is based on a

reading *i-na gi?1-re-et* ˡᵘkúr. Collation shows that what is visible before ḪI might be the beginning of GI, although there seem to be too many wedges. A reading *i-na šà?ḫi-ri-it* does not give better sense. Berger's reading *e-ḫi-re-et* is not borne out by a collation of the text.

RS 20.238
An attack from the sea
Letter from the king of Ugarit to the king of Alashia in answer to *RS* L.1. Published as *Ugaritica* 5: no. 24; see also fig. 30. See Berger 1969: 220; Linder 1970: 58–62; Dietrich and Loretz 1982–85: 510. From the house of Rapᵓānu.

1–4 Speak to the king of Alashia, my father:[1] Thus says the king of Ugarit, your son. (ruling)

5–11 I fall at the feet of my father. May my father be well! May your estates, your consorts, your troops, everything that belongs to the king of Alashia, my father, be very, very well! (ruling)

12–18 My father, now enemy ships are coming (and) they burn down my towns with fire. They have done unseemly things in the land!

19–27 My father is not aware of the fact that all the troops of my father's overlord[2] are stationed in Ḫatti and that all my ships are stationed in Lukkā.[3] They still have not arrived, and the country is lying like that! My father should know these things.

27–31 Now, the seven enemy ships that are approaching have done evil things to us.

32–36 Now then, if there are any other enemy ships[4] send me a report somehow, so that I will know. (ruling)

Notes
1. The kinship terminology used by the king of Ugarit does not necessarily imply a family relationship.
2. The (collated) text reads: érin.meš en ⌈a-bi-ia⌉. See van Soldt 1991: 466.
3. Probably Lycia.
4. Huehnergard 1986: 191.

Text *RS* 17.465 only mentions Rašapᵓabu as overseer of the harbor. Texts *RS* 20.141B and *RS* 34.180,13 are too broken for translation.

NOTES

Chapter 1: Introduction

1. See below, pp. 177–97.
2. I follow the chronology outlined in Kitchen 1987.
3. Davies 1930: 29.
4. Tzalas's (1990) delightful description of the many changes introduced by a church artist who "faithfully" depicted the *Kyrenia II* replica during a voyage to Cyprus is a warning to those who would take ship iconography at face value.

Chapter 2: Egyptian Ships

1. Faulkner 1964: 126, 261; Jones 1988: 216 no. 40, 226 no. 101 (*nᶜ i* and *š3s*).
2. Boreux 1925: 3; Casson 1995A: 3–4; Clarke and Engelbach 1990: fig. 41. Basch (1987: 51–52) notes the existence of coracles in the delta region and assumes them to be of high antiquity. On evidence for Predynastic vessels, see Vinson 1987. Recently a fleet of twelve Predynastic vessels has been discovered at Abydos (see below, p. 218).
3. Hornell 1970: 49.
4. Breasted 1917. Clarke (1920: 51, 42 fig. 13) describes a reed raft called *ramus*. On ancient Egyptian reed rafts, see Boreux 1925: 175–234; Servin 1948; Casson 1995A: 11–13.
5. Edgerton 1922–23: 133.
6. Säve-Söderbergh 1946: 31–70.
7. Nibbi 1975A, 1975B, 1979, 1984, and other publications. This is not the place to discuss Nibbi's theories beyond noting that the evidence is overwhelmingly against her. Concerning the meaning of the term the *Great Green Sea*, see Kitchen 1978: 170–71; 1983: 78. The appearance of this term on the Antefoker stele at Wadi Gawasis on the shores of the Red Sea definitively confirms that the term means "sea" (Sayed 1977: 170 and n. 18; 1983: 29).
8. *ANET*³: 227.
9. Montet 1928: 271. Frankfort (1926: 83–84) suggests that a Protodynastic temple may have existed at Byblos. On the earlier contacts between Egypt and Mesopotamian colonies established in North Syria during the Late Uruk period, see below, p. 41.
10. *ANET*³: 228. Uni was sent five times to quell insurrections in the "Land of the Sand-Dwellers." On the geopolitical background to these events, see Redford 1992: 48–55.
11. *BAR* I: §315: d; *ANET*³: 228 nos. 10–11; Aharoni 1979: 135–37.
12. *BAR* I: §465.
13. Redford 1992: 78–80.
14. *LAE*: 50–56. For a recent discussion of this text, see Baines 1990 and the additional bibliography there.
15. Faulkner 1940: 4.
16. The regular cubit was .45 meter long (thus the ship would be 54 meters long and 18 meters in beam). The royal cubit was slightly longer (.525 meter). This would give the ship a length of 63 meters and a beam of 21 meters. See Gardiner 1969: 199: § 266: 2; *EM*, s.v. measurements (*midot*).
17. Janssen 1961: 7.
18. Säve-Söderbergh 1946: 78.
19. Redford 1992: 66.
20. See below, p. 308,
21. *BAR* I: §464: d; Säve-Söderbergh 1946: 34.
22. *BAR* II: §454, 460: c.
23. Säve-Söderbergh 1946: 35.
24. *ANET*³: 239.
25. Säve-Söderbergh 1946: 36; *BAR* II: §472, 483, 492, 510, 519, and 535. See below, pp. 51–52.
26. *ANET*³: 243.
27. *EA* 155: 69–70. Säve-Söderbergh 1946: 68; Katzenstein 1973: 43.
28. *EA* 153: 9–14.
29. *EA* 129: 50, 132: 53–55.
30. Byblos: *EA* 105: 83–84, 127: 17–19; Ṣumur: *EA* 67: 10–13; Ugarit: Rainey 1967: 88–89.

31. KN Db 1105 + X1446: Ventris and Chadwick 1973: 136; Palmer 1963: 178–79 (Doc. 56); Chadwick 1976: 66; Killen and Olivier 1989: 74; Palaima 1991A: 280.
32. *ANET³*: 260.
33. *BAR* IV: §408. Concerning expeditions to Punt, see below, pp. 18–19.
34. *BAR* IV: §408: a.
35. Rothenberg 1972: 201.
36. Ibid.; Rothenberg et al. 1988; Lipschitz 1972.
37. *BAR* II: §888, IV: §209, 331; Foucart 1924; Davies 1948: pl. 12. A much-degenerated form of this procession still takes place at Luxor each year (Hornell 1938A; Desroches-Noblecourt 1963: 190 fig. 110). See Canney (1936) for a general discussion on ships and boats in temples.
38. See below, pp. 311–12.
39. Rowe 1936.
40. Montet 1928: 73–74 no. 58, 271 pl. 40.
41. See below, pp. 256–62.
42. Edgerton 1922–23: 133.
43. Ibid.: 123–26.
44. *BAR* IV: §65; Nelson 1943: 44; Casson 1995A: 38; Wachsmann 1981: 191.
45. Gaballa 1976: 5.
46. Ibid.: 23–24.
47. Bietak 1988.
48. *LAE*: 147–48.
49. Redford 1992: 51–55.
50. Hornell 1970: 26.
51. Sølver 1961: 26.
52. For discussions on the development of keels on seagoing ships, see below, pp. 241–46.
53. Kennedy 1976: 159–60.
54. Greenhill 1976: 62 fig. 20.
55. Hogging trusses in the form of steel rods were used in recent times on river steamers of shallow draught, particularly on stern-wheelers (Ballard 1920: 155; Kennedy 1976: 161). These craft had a tendency to hog because their boilers and engines were kept at their extremities. Occasionally, hogging trusses were used on Far Eastern dragon boats (Fig. 5.15: B; Bishop 1938: 416). Similarly, the *hypozomata* of Greek *trieres* were used to reinforce the hull (Casson 1995A: 91–92; Kennedy 1976).
56. See below, pp. 238–39.
57. See below, pp.219–20.
58. Edgerton 1922–23: 131–32. Italics added.
59. Sølver 1961: 26.
60. Hornell 1970: 225.
61. Hassan 1954: 138–39 fig. 2.
62. Tripod masts also appear on Old Kingdom Nile ships (Borchardt 1913: 159 fig. 20).
63. See below, pp. 248, 250–51.
64. Landström 1970: 68, 42 fig. 109. See also Borchardt 1913: 159 fig. 20; Vandier 1969: 814 fig. 313.
65. Faulkner's (1941: pl. 3) model of this ship type incorrectly lacks a boom.
66. Landström 1970: 65 fig. 194. There he also identifies three vertical stems as those of three individual *seagoing* ships. Only one ship is preserved, however, and it lacks a hogging truss (Landström 1970: 43 fig. 116; Goedicke 1971: 110–11).
67. Concerning contacts with Punt and Egyptian seafaring in the Red Sea, see below, pp. 32–38, 238–39.
68. Redford 1992: 149–53.
69. Säve-Söderbergh 1946: 8–30.
70. *BAR* I: §161. On the location of Punt, see particularly Kitchen 1971. The identity of Punt remains problematic: see most recently Sayed 1977: 176–77; Sleeswyk 1983. On meteorological conditions and navigation in the Red Sea, see Sølver 1936: 437–46.
71. *BAR* I: §360; Säve-Söderbergh 1946: 11.
72. *BAR* I: §351.
73. *BAR* I: §361; Newberry 1938.
74. See below, p. 238.
75. See below, p. 238.
76. Faulkner 1941: 3. In later times the term was used to describe funerary barques, and in the Twenty-sixth Dynasty it defined warships. Both Amasis and Psammetichus III had fleets of warships termed Byblos ships (Newberry 1942: 65).
77. Newberry 1942. See below, pp. 238–39.
78. Naville 1898: pl. 69; Peck 1978: 115 fig. 45.
79. Danelius and Steinitz 1967.
80. On the problems of source material for scenes in Egyptian tomb paintings, see below, pp. 54–60.
81. Fishing tackle was found on the Uluburun wreck. See below, p. 307.
82. Similarly, Thutmose III's "botanical garden" at Karnak suggests to Davies (1930: 35) that artists accompanied his expeditions.
83. On loss of painted detail in relief art, see below, pp. 169–71.
84. Gaballa 1976: 53.
85. *BAR* II: §252.
86. Ibid.: §253.
87. For possible evidence of ship's boats on large seagoing merchantmen from the Late Bronze Age, see below, pp. 288.
88. *BAR* II: §252.
89. Ibid.: §265. The identity of "cinnamon" is uncertain (Lucas 1962: 308–309).
90. *BAR* II: §257.
91. Ibid.: §266.
92. Naville 1908: pl. 174.
93. Gaballa 1976: 24, 52–53.
94. Clarke 1920: 45.
95. Sayed 1977: 170.
96. Landström 1970: 107–109; Jones 1990: 4, 16 (Type B), 28–37 pls. 16–33—Objects 273, 284, 287, 306, 309–10, 314, 597.
97. Concerning keels on Late Bronze Age ships, see below, pp. 241–43.
98. Faulkner 1941: 8.

99. Reisner 1913: 98 no. 4946 (hull), 113–14 no. 5034, 116 no. 5049 (stem and stern ornaments); Carter 1933: pl. 61: B; Davies 1933: pl. 22; Davies 1948: pl. 34; Mekhitarian 1978: 130.

100. Casson 1995A: 21.

101. Davies 1908: pl. 5; Reisner 1913: 96–99 nos. 4944 and 4946 (floors of castles), 138–39, no. 5164; Carter 1933: pl. 63; Davies 1943: pl. 69; *Treasures*: 2.

102. Naville 1908: pl. 154; Vandier 1969: 88 fig. 60.

103. Ballard 1920: 167; Sølver 1936: 461.

104. Sølver 1936: 457, 459 figs. 11–12.

105. Nelson et al. 1930: pl. 37. See also Hornell 1937.

106. Faulkner 1941: 8.

107. Reisner 1913: 2 fig. 7, pl. 28 (no. 4869).

108. Crew members are occasionally seen standing or sitting on the booms of Syro-Canaanite craft and New Kingdom Nile vessels (Figs. 3.2–3.5); Davies 1933: pls. 42–43; Mekhitarian 1978: 80.

109. Ballard 1920: 169.

110. On possible origins of the boom, see below, p. 248.

111. On the implications of the sailing capabilities of the boom-footed rig, see below, pp. 295–99.

112. Faulkner 1941: 8.

113. Davies and Gardiner 1915: pl. 12. This was first noted by Landström (1970: 99).

114. On knots, see below, pp. 254.

115. Ballard 1920: 171; Sølver 1936: 459.

116. Le Baron Bowen 1962: 54.

117. Landström 1970: 105.

118. This detail is also portrayed on Nile ships (Davies and Gardiner 1915: pl. 12; Davies 1933: pl. 42).

119. Faulkner 1941: 8.

120. See below, pp. 247–48.

121. Edgerton 1926–27: 256–60.

122. Reisner 1913: 7–8.

123. Sølver 1936: 434; Faulkner 1941: 8.

124. Hornell 1970: 214–15.

125. Hornell 1940: 142 fig. 7.

126. Jarrett-Bell 1933.

127. Abercrombie 1977: 338–39.

128. Hornell 1970: 217–18.

129. On the nature of the battle and the artistic problems in understanding this scene, see below, pp. 165–71, 317–19.

130. Nelson 1943: 42–44.

131. See below, p. 171.

132. Schäfer 1974: 134–37.

133. Ibid.: 137 fig. 117.

134. Faulkner 1941: 9; Casson 1995A: 37–38.

135. Landström's (1970: 113 fig. 351) reconstruction of an Egyptian ship from the Medinet Habu relief is misleading in this regard.

136. Ibid.: 99 fig. 313; Jones 1990: 16–28 pls. 10–13, 30–32 (Types A1, A2, and A3).

137. Faulkner 1941: 9.

138. Edgerton 1926–27: 257–62.

139. See below, p. 171.

140. On the brailed rig, see below, pp. 251–54.

141. Basch 1978: 115–18.

142. Davies 1935; Säve-Söderbergh 1946: 22–25; Vandier 1969: 933–34.

143. Davies 1935: 46.

144. Landström 1970: 35 fig. 95, 36 fig. 97, 48 figs. 131–32.

145. Casson 1989: 9, 19, 21, 55, 67, 117–18, 162–63.

146. Gardiner and Peet 1952: pl. 91; 1955: 13.

147. Gardiner and Peet 1955: 12, 60–64 nos. 13, 16–17; 77–78 nos. 47–48; 89 no. 77; 100 no. 92; and perhaps 92–93 no. 85; 123 no. 120; 209 no. 412.

148. Sayed 1983: 30–32.

149. Albright 1948: 10 fig. 2, 13–15.

150. Gardiner and Peet 1955: 218 no. 503.

151. On the development of the stanchion and loom on Egyptian ships, see Edgerton 1926–27.

152. Compare Reisner 1913: 1 fig. 1 (no. 4798), 4 fig. 15 (no. 4799), 6 fig. 21 (no. 4801), 33 fig. 126 (no. 4845), 49 fig. 173 (no. 4872).

153. Gardiner and Peet 1955: 219 no. 506.

154. Compare Quibell 1908: pl. 26: 9; Garstang 1907: 97 figs. 88–89; Schäfer 1908: 71 fig. 111, 72 figs. 112–13, 75 figs. 118–19, 76 fig. 120; Reisner 1913: 65 figs. 233–34 and pl. 16 (no. 4910).

155. Gardiner and Peet 1955: 219 no. 507.

156. Newberry 1893: pl. 16.

157. Gardiner and Peet 1955: 220 no. 517.

158. Ibid.: 222 no. 524.

159. Newberry 1893: pl. 16 (right).

160. Gardiner and Peet 1955: 220–21 no. 518.

161. Newberry 1893: pl. 16; 1894: pl. 18; Davies 1920: pl. 18; Petrie and Brunton 1924: pl. 20: 2106 and 2111; Winlock 1955: 70, 72–76.

162. Compare Fig. 2.21.

163. Gardiner and Peet 1955: 220 no. 516.

164. Ibid.: 221 no. 520.

165. Yadin 1963: 77–78, 184–85; Davies 1987: 43–47, 49–50, and pls. 18–24 (nos. 101–36).

166. Gardiner and Peet 1955: 221 no. 521.

167. Compare Winlock 1955: pl. 82; Vandier 1969: 918 fig. 344: 2; Landström 1970: 89 fig. 272.

168. Gardiner and Peet 1955: 218 no. 501.

169. Davies 1908: pl. 5; 1943: pls. 68–69.

170. Landström 1970: 99 (reconstruction), 103 fig. 325.

171. Ibid.: 102 figs. 322 and 324.

Chapter 3:
The Ships of the Syro-Canaanite Littoral

1. "Syro-Canaanite" is used here as a general term to define all the cultural entities along the length of the Levant's littoral region, from the Bay of Iskenderun to the coast of Sinai. It is preferable to the term *Canaanite*, for Canaanites were considered foreigners at Ugarit (Rainey 1963), and to *Phoenician*, for although this Iron Age culture descended directly from the Syro-Canaanites, it developed its own unique mate-

rial culture that was quite different from its Bronze Age ancestors (Mazar 1990: 355–57; 1992: 296–97).

2. See above, chap. 2 n. 6; Muhly 1970.

3. Sasson 1966; Rainey 1967: 87–90; Astour 1970; Heltzer 1977; 1978: 12, 150–56; Linder 1970; 1981. The texts deal with various aspects of maritime activity and are discussed in the appropriate chapters and in an appendix; see below, pp. 333–44. On the various Ugaritic terms for ships and their equipment, see Stieglitz in press.

4. *CG*: 74–78, 164–67; Bass 1973; 1991; in press; Sasson 1966. Bernal (1987) in *Black Athena* I notes that racial prejudices may have caused Classical scholars of the last century to deemphasize Semitic and Egyptian influences on early Greek civilization.

5. Gonen 1984; 1992: 216–19.

6. For the historical background, see Astour 1981; Redford 1992: 125–229; Singer 1991.

7. Harden 1962: 157; Linder 1981. See below, pp. 333–34.

8. Concerning a ship depiction from Tell el Dabᶜa, the site of ancient Avaris, see below, p. 42.

9. *ANET*³: 554–55.

10. Ibid.: 239.

11. *EA* 101: 16–18, 105: 20–21; Rainey 1967: 89 n. 144.

12. *EA* 168: 7–10.

13. *EA* 245: 28–30. The term for ship used here is *a-na-yi* (in Ugaritic, *any*).

14. Rainey 1967: 87–88; Linder 1970: 114–16. Astour (1970: 117–18) suggests that the Ashdodians had settled in *Maʾḫadu*, the main harbor of Ugarit (Minet el Beida).

15. *KTU* 2.38 and *KTU* 4.394; see below, pp. 334, 339.

16. *ANET*³: 557; Rainey 1995: 483–84.

17. *KTU* 2.47; see below, pp. 336–37.

18. Heltzer 1977: 210 (text Bo 2810); Tammuz 1985: 61–65.

19. Heltzer 1988. See below, *RS* 16.238 + 254, p. 340. For a general overview of Ugarit's connections with the Aegean, see Astour 1973.

20. Chadwick 1976: 66.

21. Ventris and Chadwick 1973: 135–36, 225–31; Chadwick 1973A: 441; 1976: 119–20, 144; Palaima 1991A: 278–79. Traces of cumin have been found on the Uluburun shipwreck. See below, p. 305. Kupairos and the "Phoenician" spice were used in the Mycenaean world in the manufacture of perfume (Shelmerdine 1984: 82; 1985: 17–18, 20–23, 25, 99).

22. Ventris and Chadwick 1973: 221–22 texts 99, 100; Chadwick 1973: 441; 1976: 121. The amounts of "Phoenician" spice mentioned in the two texts total eight kilograms.

23. Ventris and Chadwick 1973: 319–20, 345–46, 558, 580; Chadwick 1976: 144; Palaima 1991A: 278 n. 24, 279.

24. Van Soldt 1991: 96 fig. 9, 110–14. See below, *KTU* 2.38, 2.39, 2.46, 2.47, 4.338, 4.352, 4.366, 4.370, 4.394, pp. 334–39.

25. On the conditions for change, see Liverani 1987.

26. See above, p. 12.

27. *LAE*: 145–46.

28. Ibid.: 150.

29. Goedicke 1975: 51.

30. See below, p. 337.

31. Linder 1970: 16–19, 98. See below, p. 126.

32. Heltzer 1982: 188–90.

33. Professor J. R. Steffy, personal communication.

34. See below, *RS* 20.212, p. 341. On the location of Ura, see below, p. 295. An Akkadian letter from Ugarit found at Tel Aphek mentions a shipment of 250–1/3 *kor* of wheat sent to Jaffa (Owen 1981: 8, 12). It is not clear whether the wheat had been shipped from Ugarit or was transferred locally.

35. Nougayrol 1960: 165; Astour 1965: 255; Linder 1970: 36, 98; Casson 1995A: 36 n. 17.

36. The ship went down in the northern Aegean off the island of Alonisos carrying a load of wine amphoras (Rose 1993; Hadjidaki 1993; 1995).

37. Frost 1991: 369. See below, pp. 288–89.

38. Frankfort 1924: 118–42; 1941.

39. Frankfort 1941; Kantor 1992: 14–17; Redford 1992: 17–24; Mark 1993; in press. Concerning these colonies, see most recently Oates 1993 and the additional bibliography there.

40. Yannai 1983: 68–70. Concerning figurines of smiting gods found outside of the Syro-Canaanite littoral, see *PM* III: 477–80; Harden 1962: 314 fig. 93; Vermeule 1964: 302, 406 pl. 48: D; Negbi 1976: 37–40, 168–69; Rutkowski 1986: 59 fig. 60, 182 figs. 264–65, 184, 185 fig. 268, 199.

41. Porada 1984: 486 ill. 1, pl. 65 fig. 1. Concerning the Uluburun figurine, see below, pp. 206, 208.

42. Porada 1984.

43. Bietak 1984; Redford 1992: 102, 114–15.

44. Daressy 1895; Basch 1987: 63 figs. 111–12, 65 fig. 115.

45. Davies and Faulkner 1947.

46. Wachsmann 1987: 12–25.

47. This Egyptian tendency to exaggerate ships' sheerlines perhaps stemmed from a desire to show as much of the craft as possible above the waterline.

48. Davies and Faulkner 1947: 41. Similar lacing appears on a hull in the Iniwia relief (Figs. 3.24, 3.30: A).

49. Glanville 1972: frontispiece, 1 fig. 1, 14 fig. 13, pls. 1: a, 3: b.

50. Basch (1987: 63, 65 fig. 115) notes a widening stempost top on one of the ships in Daressy's publication. He compares it to those on Phoenician ships portrayed in Assyrian reliefs.

51. The concave tops are somewhat reminiscent of the bifurcated posts on Micronesian canoes from the recent past (Dodd 1972: 69).

52. Landström 1970: 114 figs. 352–53, 138 fig. 405.

53. See below, p. 217.

54. Tillers are lacking on the large ships at left.

55. Säve-Söderbergh 1946: 56–57; Davies and Faulkner 1947: 41.

56. Casson 1995A: 35. See below, pp. 54–60.
57. Casson 1995A: 36; Basch 1987: 63.
58. The Syro-Canaanites are identified by their coiffures, beards, and clothing. See Pritchard 1951; *ANEP*: figs. 2, 5, 8, 43–56; Wachsmann 1987: 44–48.
59. See above, p. 14.
60. Casson 1995A: 69, 231.
61. See below, p. 248.
62. Davies and Faulkner 1947: 43.
63. See below, pp. 248, 250–51.
64. Davies and Faulkner 1947: 42; Basch 1987: 130 n. 113.
65. Säve-Söderbergh 1946: 54–56; 1957: 25–27; Casson 1995A: 35; Gaballa 1976: 66–67.
66. Février (1935: 115) incorrectly dates the painting to the earlier part of Thutmose III's reign (Säve-Söderbergh 1946: 54).
67. Müller 1904: Taf. 3.
68. Downward-curving yards on boom-footed rigs on Egyptian craft are rare, but a few examples do exist. See Davies 1923: pls. 24–25; Casson 1995A: 35 n. 15; Wachsmann 1982: 302.
69. Davies and Gardiner 1915: pl. 12; Edgerton 1922–23: 125 fig. 9; Davies 1943: pls. 63–69; *Treasures*: 2.
70. Säve-Söderbergh 1946: 57–58.
71. Basch 1978: 99–109; 1987: 65.
72. *BAR* III: §274. See also above, pp. 10–11.
73. Wachsmann and Raveh 1984B: 224, 228.
74. See below, p. 251.
75. Note particularly the broad horizontal band with vertical lines (stanchions?) situated atop the sheerstrake, which reasonably may be interpreted as a fence, similar to those depicted on the ships of Kenamun and Nebamun, the *mnš* determinative, as well as on the Uluburun shipwreck. Concerning the Uluburun evidence, see below, p. 217.
76. Hamilton 1935: 38 no. 233, pl. 23: C; Wachsmann 1981: 214–15 fig. 29. For a recent summary on the excavations at Tell Abu Hawam, see *NEAEHL* 1: 7–14 (s.v. Abu Hawam, Tell), and the additional bibliography there.
77. Schaeffer 1962: 147, 134 figs. 114–15.
78. Casson 1995A: 19.
79. Öbrink 1979: (Artifact N4007) 16–17, 70 fig. 86b, 67 fig. 69, 73 fig. 104.
80. Merrillees 1968: 188–89. See below, pp. 63–66.
81. Casson 1995A: fig. 78; Göttlicher 1978: 30 and Taf. 7 nos. 102 and 103.
82. Dikaios 1969: 434–37; 1971: 536.
83. Davies and Gardiner 1915: pl. 12; Edgerton 1922–23: 125 fig. 9; Carter 1933: pl. 63: A; Davies 1943: pls. 68–69.
84. See above, n. 63.
85. Davies and Faulkner 1947: 43; Wachsmann 1981: 214, 216 fig. 30. On the additional "masts" at the stem and stern of the *mnš* determinative, see Basch 1978: 106–109; 1987: 65–66.
86. Casson 1995A: figs. 110, 140–41.
87. *BAR* II: §492.
88. Jones 1988: 149 no. 80.
89. Glanville 1931: 116, 121. See below, pp. 223–24.
90. Glanville 1932: 22 n. 56.
91. Säve-Söderbergh 1946: 43–45, 47; Vermeule 1972: 114.
92. Herodotus (II: 112), in describing the large Tyrian population dwelling in Memphis in his day, notes that their compound, known as "the Camp of the Tyrians," surrounded a temple dedicated to "Aphrodite the Stranger." He may be describing a later continuation of the Bronze Age Astarte cult mentioned in B.M. 10056. See below, pp. 223–24.
93. Säve-Söderbergh 1946: 53–54.
94. Casson 1995A: 141–42.
95. Glanville 1932: 31 n. 2.
96. Hayes 1980: 387. In a similar vein, see Stieglitz (1984: 136); Basch (1987: 126); and Redford (1992: 242).
97. See above, p. 40.
98. Dunand 1939: 223–25 no. 3306; Février 1949–50: 135 figs. 2–3.
99. Glanville 1972: 41 fig. 40, 44 fig. 43, pl. 8: a–b.
100. On the development of keels in the Late Bronze Age, see below, pp. 241–43, 245–46.
101. The protruding ends of the beams at the model's extremities are missing in a line drawing reproduced by Basch (1969: 146 fig. 2: 2) and Göttlicher (1978: Taf. 7 no. 105).
102. Février 1949–50: 136–39.
103. Basch 1987: 67–68 figs. 124–26.
104. See below, p. 175. A similar stern projection appears on a ship representation painted on a Late Minoan IIIC sherd from Phaistos (Fig. 7.27). The position and form suggest a vestigial style of the stern device that appears earlier, apparently in cultic connotations, on Aegean craft. See below, p. 106.
105. See above, pp. 23–24. Note particularly the similarity in shape to a wooden model from the tomb of Tutankhamen (Jones 1990: pl. 21: Obj. 597).
106. The longitudinal internal member in this model is probably not a keelson. Note, however, that some Egyptian Eleventh Dynasty models of river craft have a construction that has been interpreted as such. The ship type on which these occur, however, is considerably earlier and has a significantly different hull shape than the one discussed here. Among other things, it lacks any evidence of a keel, having presumably had a keel plank in its place. See below, p. 220. Note also that no evidence for a keelson was found above the remnants of the Uluburun ship's keel/keel-plank.
107. Dunand 1939: 434 no. 6681; Février 1949–50: 134 fig. 1.
108. Février 1949–50: 135–36; Sasson 1966: 127.
109. Reisner 1913: 75 fig. 280, pl. 18 (no. 4918).
110. Dunand 1954: 337–38 nos. 10089–92.
111. Negbi and Moskowitz 1966: 23–26.
112. Newberry 1894: pl. 18; Reisner 1913: 4 fig. 15, pl. 1 (no. 4799); Landström 1970: 83 fig. 251; Glanville 1972: 52–53 fig. 24 (no. 35293).

113. Landström 1970: 138–39.

114. Wachsmann 1987: 4–11.

115. Davies 1930: 35.

116. Bodenheimer 1949: 257–59 fig. 32. The imaginary difficulties of the unfortunate artist whose responsibility it was to gather the plants during Thutmose's Syro-Canaanite campaigns are humorously described by Davies (1930: 35). On Thutmose III's botanical garden, see Beaux 1990.

117. Wreszinski I: 273; Davies and Davies 1933: pls. 4–5; Furumark 1950: 228 fig. 25.

118. Davies 1943: pls. 18–20.

119. On the recently rediscovered tomb of Iniwia, also known as Nia or Iniuia, see Porter and Moss 1979: 707; Martin 1991: 200; Schneider 1993. On the ships of Iniwia, see Landström 1970: 138 fig. 403, 139.

120. Landström 1970: 139 fig. 407.

Chapter 4: Cypriot Ships

1. Cherry 1981: 43; 1990: 148–57; Todd 1987; Simmons 1988; 1991; Simmons and Reese 1993; Reese 1992; 1993.

2. For a summary of scholarly opinions, see Merrillees 1987 and the additional bibliography there.

3. See below, pp. 295–96.

4. *EA* 33–40; Holmes 1973: 96–98; 1975: 94–96, 98.

5. *EA* 35: 30–34.

6. *EA* 39: 17–20.

7. See below: *KTU* 2.46, *RS* L.1, *RS* 20.238, pp. 336, 343–44.

8. See below: *KTU* 4.352, p. 338.

9. *KTU* 4.102.

10. Rainey 1967: 90.

11. Masson (1974: 29–55) interprets *RS* 20.25, written in Cypro-Minoan script, as a list of Hurrian names.

12. See below: *KTU* 4.390, p. 339. Linder 1972. It is not clear if the lading is incoming or outgoing.

13. Masson 1956; 1969; 1974; Merrillees 1973: 182.

14. PY Cn 121, Cn 719, Jn 320, and Un 443. See Himmelhoch 1990–91: 94–96 and the additional bibliography there.

15. Bennett et al. 1989: 204–205; Palaima 1991A: 281, 291–95.

16. Himmelhoch 1990–91: 96–104. She also discusses (91–94, 104) the possibly parallel term *a-ra-si-jo* ("Alashian"), which appears on three tablets from Knossos, but concludes that this term must remain enigmatic based on the evidence presently available.

17. Hirschfeld 1990A; 1990B.

18. *LAE:* 154–55. Concerning the identity of the Alashian fleets with which Shupiluliuma did battle, see below, p. 317.

19. Basch 1978: 118–21; Frost 1979: 155–57; Wachsmann 1985B: 483. On Cypriot anchors, see below, pp. 273–81.

20. See pp. 49–51, 141–42, 145–49, 151–53, 175, 184, 187.

21. Basch 1987: 72 fig. 137.

22. Buchholz and Karageorghis 1973: 161, 471 no. 1718; Westerberg 1983: 9–10 fig. 1; Basch 1987: 70–71 figs. 132–35.

23. Dussaud 1914: 419–20 fig. 310.

24. Sasson 1966: 127.

25. Basch 1987: 70 n. 39.

26. Frankel 1974; Westerberg 1983: 10 and fig. 2.

27. Hornell 1970: pls. 16: A–B, 17: A, 19: A–B, 20.

28. Westerberg 1983: 10 no. 3 and fig. 3.

29. Ibid. 1983: 11 no. 4 and fig. 4.

30. Merrillees 1968: 188; Göttlicher 1978: 37 and Taf. 12 (no. 167); Westerberg 1983: 11–12 no. 5, fig. 5.

31. See below, pp. 241–43, 245–46.

32. Walters 1903: 6 no. A–50; Göttlicher 1978: 34 and Taf. 9 (no. 147); Merrillees 1968: 188 pl. 37: 2 (right); Westerberg 1983: 13–14 no. 7, fig. 7; Johnson 1980: 18 and pl. 16 (no. 60); Basch 1987: 73–74 figs. 143, 145.

33. On the possible purpose of these features, see below, pp. 248, 250–51.

34. Walters 1903: 6 no. A–49; Merrillees 1968: 188 pl. 37: 2 (left); Göttlicher 1978: 34 and Taf. 9 (no. 146); Johnson 1980: 15 and pl. 9 (no. 15); Westerberg 1983: 12–13 no. 6, fig. 6; Basch 1987: 73–74 figs. 143–44. See discussion on dating in Westerberg.

35. Vandier 1969: 888 fig. 335, 889 fig. 336, 890 fig. 337, 892 fig. 338, 950 fig. 357: 1, 966 fig. 369, 976 fig. 372, 977 fig. 373, 986 fig. 379, 987 fig. 380, 1004 fig. 384, 1011 fig. 385.

36. Hornell 1936: 385 fig. 275, 393 fig. 282, 410 fig. 296; Haddon 1937: 168 fig. 103: a–b; Dodd 1972: 69.

37. Merrillees 1968: 189.

38. One is reminded of the multiple shrouds/stays—up to eleven per side—used on the large *nuggars* of the upper Nile. These shrouds counter longitudinal weakness, preventing the ships' sides from spreading as a buttress prevents a masonry arch from spreading. It thus takes the place of the hogging truss of antiquity (Hornell 1939: 428 pl. 4: 1–2; 1970: 218 pl. 36: A).

39. Barnett 1973: 5. See below, p. 217.

40. Basch 1987: 71–73.

41. Compare Casson 1995A: fig. 94.

42. Kenna 1967: 573 fig. 31; Westerberg 1983: 18 no. 16, fig. 16. The seal bears only one ship, not two as stated by Westerberg.

43. Basch 1987: 73–74 figs. 147–48.

44. Westerberg 1983: 16–17 no. 12, fig. 12.

45. Westerberg 1983: 14–15 no. 8, fig. 8.

46. Casson 1995A: 65–66 figs. 86–87.

47. Westerberg 1983: 16 no. 11; Basch 1987: 254.

Chapter 5: Early Ships of the Aegean

1. This chapter includes Aegean materials from earliest times till the seventeenth century B.C. See below, Chap. 6, n. 1.

2. Johnstone 1973: 3–4; Johnston 1982: 1; Diamant 1979: 217. Concerning early seafaring exploration and settlement in the Aegean, see Cherry 1990: 158–71; Davis 1992; Jacobsen 1993. For a comprehensive bibliography of Franchthi Cave, see Tzalas 1995: 459–62. Broodbank (1992; 1993) believes that the development of settlement on the Cyclades was a result of definable patterns of colonization. He proposes the existence of specialized trading colonies in the Cyclades during the Bronze Age, arguing that their choice of location was based primarily on control of the local sea lanes.

3. Tzamtzis (1987) suggests that these early craft may have resembled *papirella,* primitive reed rafts still constructed on Corfu. In the summer of 1988, an experimental *papirella* six meters long was successfully paddled by a crew of five from Lavrion, on the southwest point of Attica, to the island of Melos (Tzalas 1989; 1995; Troev 1989; see also Johnstone 1973: 4–6). Basch (1987: 76–77) notes that Paleolithic craft may have been made of skins or were rafts supported by leather bags. Hutchinson (1962: 91) presumes that the Neolithic colonization of Crete was carried out in monoxylons and notes that such craft still existed in this century on Lake Prespa in Macedonia.

4. Recent research seems to prefer an interpretation that the agriculture arrived in Greece from the Near East as part of the cultural baggage of a migration (Cherry 1981; Hansen 1992; Davis 1992: 702 n. 8 and the additional bibliography there). Such a migration could have been seaborne.

5. Broodbank and Strasser 1991.

6. Renfrew 1967: 5; 1972: 318, 356–57, fig. 17: 7 and pl. 28: 3–4; Casson 1995A: 41–42.

7. Casson 1995A: 41; Basch 1987: 78–79.

8. Renfrew 1967: 5, pl. 3: 15–16.

9. Coleman 1985.

10. Casson 1995A: 30–31. For photos of all twelve ships, see Basch 1987: 80–81 figs. 159–67.

11. Coleman 1985: 203–204.

12. Coleman (1985: 196) argues that these are only of secondary importance. Nevertheless, their appearance cannot simply be dismissed.

13. See also Basch 1987: 88–91 figs. 183–88.

14. Petrie 1896: pls. 66: 3, 6, 10, 67: 13–14; 1921: pl. 34: 46, 45S; Bishop 1938: pl. 4 fig. 8; Raphael 1947: pl. 31: 3; Hornell 1970: 279 fig. 68.

15. Wachsmann 1980: 288–89; 1995B: 14; Basch 1987: 84.

16. Doumas 1967: 118–19 figs. 49–50, 121–23 figs. 54–55; 1970.

17. *PM* II: 240 fig. 137; Basch 1987: 83 figs. 170–71.

18. Marinatos 1933: 184 fig. 1.

19. This does not necessarily require the blunt end to be the bow, as some scholars have assumed. See Casson 1975: 9 n. 17. The much-later Kinneret boat also reaches its widest beam abaft amidships (Steffy 1987: 328 fig. 3; 1990: 40, foldout 2).

20. Bass 1972: 17.

21. Woolner 1957; Casson 1995A: 36.

22. Johnston 1982: 2; Basch 1987: 85.

23. Broodbank 1989: 329.

24. For summaries of the argument, see Johnstone 1973: 6–11; Johnston 1982; Basch 1987: 84–85.

25. Casson 1975: 9.

26. Casson 1995A: 31. When did the monoxylon develop in the Aegean? Basch (1987: 77) notes that the earliest known European dugout dates to ca. 6000 B.C. and suggests that the coniferous forests that once covered Crete make it a prime candidate for the site of the dugout's Aegean origin.

27. Higgins 1967: 54. Coleman (1985: 204) believes the frying pans to have had no cultic significance.

28. Basch 1987: 86 fig. 177.

29. See below, pp. 108–11.

30. Bishop 1938: 415–24.

31. Broodbank 1989: 326–32.

32. Ibid.: 332–34.

33. Bishop 1938: pl. 4, fig. 8; Hornell 1936: 211 fig. 141; Dodd 1972: 71, 104.

34. Broodbank 1989; 1993: 327.

35. Broodbank 1989: 333–34 fig. 6.

36. Casson 1995A: 34–35; Bass 1972: 28 n. 14; Basch 1975: 201; 1987: 132.

37. Marinatos 1933: 175 and pl. 15: 27; Göttlicher 1978: 318 and Taf. 25 (no. 321); Basch 1987: 147 fig. 308.

38. Casson 1995A: 35.

39. Hornell 1950: pl. 24: 2; 1970: 210; Basch 1975: 202–203 fig. 4.

40. Haddon 1937: 177–78.

41. Hornell 1936: 295 figs. 212–13.

42. Casson 1995A: 85, 331, figs. 137, 145, 147, 176–77, 182, 191–92. The Kinneret boat probably had a cutwater bow, like that on a boat in a mosaic from the nearby site of Migdal (Steffy 1987: 328 fig. 3; Steffy and Wachsmann 1990; Wachsmann 1988: 31; 1995B: 156–58).

43. Buchholz and Karageorghis 1973: 118, 119 fig. 40, 121, 393 pl. 1409d, and the additional bibliography there.

44. Chadwick 1987B: 57–61.

45. Olivier 1975; Sakellarakis 1979: 30–31; Basch 1987: 136–37 fig. 285.

46. Haddon 1937: 88.

47. Basch 1986; 1987A; Coates 1987.

48. Deilaki 1987: 123.

49. Theocares 1958: 18.

50. Vermeule 1964: 259 fig. 43a; Morrison and Williams 1968: 7, 9, pl. 1a.

51. Casson 1995A: 42 n. 4.

52. Bass 1972: 20.

Chapter 6: Minoan/Cycladic Ships

1. The arguments in support of raising the date of the abandonment of Thera, and with it the latter part of

the Late Minoan IA, to ca. 1628 B.C., are compelling (Kuniholm 1990). If this high date is accepted, it would have profound significance for Aegean chronology.

Paradoxically, Egyptian chronology, to which Aegean chronology is inescapably linked, has moved in the opposite direction. Thutmose III's reign must now be placed at 1479–1425 B.C., a full quarter-century later than previously thought (Kitchen 1987). Chronological links indicate that the transition from Late Minoan IB to Late Minoan II took place in the latter part of Thutmose III's reign (Wachsmann 1987: 127–29). Consequently, the end of Late Minoan IB must have occurred during the third quarter of the fifteenth century B.C. This is problematic, as it results in the "stretching" of Late Minoan IB—previously allotted a mere half-century—to a period of from 160 to 185 years.

Several solutions have been proposed to resolve this dilemma. One is to ignore the Egyptian evidence and to raise the Late Minoan IB/II transition to the sixteenth century, as S. W. Manning (1988A) has done. Alternately, one may place inordinate weight on the Egyptian links and argue that they require the total abandonment of a seventeenth-century date for Thera's destruction, as J. D. Muhly (1991) has proposed.

Neither of these scenarios is satisfactory in my view. One solution that merits further investigation is that Late Minoan IB, together with the final portion of the Late Minoan IA that postdates the abandonment of Thera, did indeed last longer than previously thought (Manning 1991: 249 and the additional bibliography there). M. Popham (1990), on the basis of an analysis of pottery styles, allots a mere twenty-five years (one generation) for Late Minoan IB, with an additional fifteen years for the end of the Late Minoan IA after the destruction of Thera, resulting in a total of only forty years. In the accompanying discussion, however, W. D. Niemeier emphasizes that, since Late Minoan IB pottery is known only from the destruction level and not from tombs, it is possible that earlier pottery within this period is missing.

2. Malamat 1971.

3. The Middle Bronze Age date of this text precludes the Caphtorite being a Mycenaean. The name *Keftiu/ Caphtor* continued to refer to the Aegean after the fall of the autonomous Minoan culture at the end of the Late Minoan IB. See below, pp. 297, 340.

4. Rainey 1967: 89 n. 168.

5. Chadwick 1973A: 394–95; 1987B: 50–52; Palaima 1989A: 40–41; 1989B. See also Hooker 1985.

6. See below, pp. 297–98.

7. *KTU* 1.6.52; Caquot, Sznycer, and Herdner 1974: 97, 99, 270.

8. Thucydides 1: 4, 8; Herodotus 1: 171; 3: 122.

9. See particularly articles in *Thera; Thera* I; *Thera* II; *MT*; Barber 1981; Doumas 1982; Wiener 1987; 1990: 145–50; Davis 1992.

10. Branigan 1981.

11. Furumark 1950: 150–83; Mee 1982: 81.

12. Wiener 1984, 1990.

13. Wooley 1953: 76–77; 1955: 228–32 pls. 36–39.

14. Niemeier 1991: 196 n. 67.

15. Ibid. and the additional bibliography there. Also, note the appearance of conical cups and pumice in a cultic context later, at thirteenth-century B.C. Tel Nami, on Israel's Carmel coast (Artzy 1991A).

16. Niemeier 1991: 198–99.

17. Wooley 1953: 157–58 pl. 17: b; 1955: 191, 294–95 pl. 79. The lamp was found discarded in a pit in Level II (thirteenth century B.C.) but is believed to have come from an earlier level.

18. Wooley 1955: 295. Interestingly, a variant of Nuzi pottery found in Level II at Alalakh and termed "Atchana Ware" exhibits Minoan motifs such as a tree that incorporates double axes and stylized papyrus plants (Wooley 1955: 350, 397 pls. 102–103, 105, 107; Evans 1936). Wooley (1953: 156) proposes that the motifs were derived from a single Minoan vessel that had been preserved as an heirloom.

19. Niemeier 1991: 199 n. 91 for additional bibliography; Gordon 1954: 126–27.

20. Dussaud 1937: 234; Parrot 1937: 354; 1958: 109; Kantor 1947: 31, 77; Dossin 1939: 111–12; Smith 1965: 18, 96–106.

21. Parrot 1953: figs. 112–13; Smith 1965: 99–100 fig. 128.

22. Lloyd and Mellaart 1965: 33, 62; Lloyd 1967: 81.

23. *DD*: 13; Bietak 1992; 1995; Hammond 1993; Hankey 1993; Dickinson 1994: 244, 246–47 pl. 7.1; Morgan 1995. Bietak notes two distinct periods of contact, one during the early Thirteenth Dynasty (early eighteenth century B.C.) and a second that spans the end of the Second Intermediate period, as well as the beginning of the Eighteenth Dynasty (latter part of the sixteenth century B.C.). He proposes that the earlier group of frescoes may have resulted from a royal marriage between the Hyksos and Minoans.

24. Vercoutter 1956; Wachsmann 1987 and the additional bibliography there. Most recently, concerning the clothing worn by Aegeans depicted in the Eighteenth Dynasty tombs, see Rehak 1996. On evidence for the importation of decorated cloth from the Aegean to Egypt, see Barber 1991: 311–57.

25. Wachsmann 1987: 127–29. This synchronism does not require the abandonment of a seventeenth-century date for the destruction of Thera as Muhly (1991) has argued. See above, note 1.

26. Marinatos 1974: 19–31 color pl. 2.

27. Ibid.: 19–32; Televantou 1990: 309.

28. Marinatos 1974: cover, 34–38 fig. 4, pl. 85, color pl. 6; Marinatos 1984: 35–38 fig. 18; Doumas 1992: 52–55.

29. Marinatos 1984: 45–46 fig. 26. Televantou (1990: 313)

concludes that this figure decorated the east jamb of the connecting opening between Rooms 4 and 5 (Fig. 6.3: F).

30. Morgan 1990: 253–58 and the additional bibliography there.
31. Abramovitz 1980: 62, 66 pls. 5: C, 6: a–b (fragments 90, 96–99).
32. Morgan 1990: 255.
33. Abramovitz 1980: 62, 66 pl. 6: a–b.
34. Marinatos 1974: 29 pls. 62: B, 63: A.
35. Ibid. 1974: color pl. 8; Marinatos 1984: foldout A, fig. 17, 44–45, fig. 25; Morgan 1988: 146–50; Doumas 1992: 64–67.
36. Televantou 1990: 313–14.
37. Marinatos 1974: 40 pl. 101, color pl. 7; Rutkowski 1978: 662–63; Morgan 1988: 156–58; Doumas 1992: 58–59.
38. Compare the Theran corpses to the manner in which the dead and dying are portrayed floating in the water in the Medinet Habu relief (Figs. 2.35–42; 8.3–8, 10–12, 14, 15.1–2).
39. Smith 1965: figs. 84–86.
40. Televantou 1990: 315–21.
41. One of these is a stern section originally placed by Marinatos behind the best-preserved ship at upper left in Fig. 6.7. See Doumas 1992: 62.
42. On the *stylis* used on Classical ships, see Svoronos 1914: 81–120; Casson 1995A: 86, 116, 346.
43. Morgan 1988: 130.
44. Marinatos 1974: 49–50. Morgan (1988: 123) accepts this interpretation.
45. On talismanic seals, see below, pp. 98–99, 101.
46. Marinatos 1974: 49; Tilley and Johnstone 1976: 286; Brown 1979: 629, 639; Morgan 1988: 123, 138.
47. Basch 1986: 423–24.
48. Kirk 1949: 132; Marinatos 1974: 40, 49; Prytulak 1982; Basch 1987: 131–32.
49. Laffineur 1983A: 42–46; 1983B: 115–16; 1984: 136–37. See also Immerwahr 1977; Negbi 1979.
50. Niemeier 1990.
51. See below, Chap. 7.
52. Compare Marinatos 1974: pl. 104 and color pl. 9.
53. Basch 1987: 131 fig. 270.
54. Morgan 1988: pl. 171.
55. Ibid.: 123, 126.
56. Casson 1975: 5, 9; Basch 1987: 121 figs. 236–37.
57. Marinatos 1974: pl. 104, color pl. 9.
58. Emanuele 1977.
59. Morgan 1988: 124–25.
60. Ibid. 1988: 132.
61. See also Basch 1987: 130–31.
62. Reisner 1913: 29 figs. 116–17, pl. 7 (no. 4841); Winlock 1955: pls. 33–34, 42, 71.
63. Reisner 1913: pls. 27 (no. 4956), 28 (no. 4869), 29 (nos. 4839 and 4894); Landström 1970: 80 figs. 240–42. This is perhaps an additional, if indirect, consideration in support of a high date for the destruction of Thera.

64. Casson 1975: 5 n. 7; Brown 1979: 630.
65. Morgan 1988: 128.
66. Betts 1973. For a comprehensive illustrated catalogue of Minoan seals and sealings bearing ship depictions, see Basch 1987: 95–106 figs. A1–H6.
67. As, for example, has been done by Basch (1987: 94 A–E, 107–17).
68. Onassoglou 1985: pls. 12–13.
69. Marinatos 1933: 200–208 figs. 5–7 and the additional bibliography there; Hutchinson 1962: 95; Basch 1987: 107–12.
70. Van Effenterre 1979: 595–96.
71. Basch 1987: 107 fig. 192.
72. *PM* I: 672–74, IV: 445–50; Betts 1968; Kenna 1969.
73. Betts 1973: 330–31.
74. Italics added.
75. Brown 1979: 639.
76. Betts 1973: 327; Hutchinson 1962: 94.
77. Basch 1987: 101 no. C–12.
78. Concerning the lack of shrouds on Bronze Age sea-going ships, see below, pp. 250–51.
79. Wachsmann 1977; Basch 1987: 114.
80. Eccles 1939–40: 45 fig. 12; Demargne 1964: 113 figs. 142–43.
81. This combination of a ship and a pair of fish is not unique. See Eccles 1939–40: 44 no. 4, 45 fig. 1: a–b.
82. Note particularly Fig. 6.33.
83. Basch 1976A; 1987: 106 nos. H1–H6, 138–40.
84. Basch 1987: 98–100 nos. B1–B11, 114, 115 fig. 221: A.
85. Betts 1973: 334.
86. Italics added.
87. Long 1974: 46, 48–49 pl. 19, fig. 52.
88. Johnston 1985: 23–24 (BA 9–13).
89. Ibid.: 26–27 (BA 17), 30–31 (BA 23).
90. Ibid.: 27–28 (BA 18). See Johnston for complete bibliography of this and the following models.
91. Ibid.: 24 (BA 14).
92. Ibid.: 25–26 (BA 15).
93. Ibid.: 34 (BA 27).
94. Ibid.: 29 (BA 20); Basch 1987: 141 fig. 292.
95. Basch 1987: 115–16 fig. 225.
96. According to my own travel notes, the model comes from the cult cave of Eileithyia, the goddess of fertility, at Inatos, in southern Crete. It is exhibited in the Iraklion Archaeological Museum in the hall devoted to the Proto-Geometric and Early Geometric periods (ca. 1100–300 B.C.) (Gallery 11, case 149 no. 13320). See Sakellarakis 1979: 96. Caves may bear graffiti of ships. Petrocheilou (1984: 155) mentions "ships shown with their sails" in the Cave of Asphendou, Crete.
97. Marinatos 1984; Morgan 1988.
98. Marinatos 1974: 55.
99. Basch 1987: 119, 125–26.
100. Morgan 1988: 88–92. Concerning possible locations for the procession within the Aegean, see Laffineur 1983B.
101. Basch 1987: 121, 123 fig. 245.
102. Alexiou n.d.: 70 figs. 24–25, 71 fig. 26, 72 fig. 27, 73

fig. 28. On the lion motif in Minoan cult scenes, see Morgan 1988: 44–49; Marinatos 1993: 154–55, 167–71.

103. *PM* II: 240.

104. Hutchinson 1962: 94.

105. Marinatos 1974: 50; Morgan 1988: 135–36.

106. Casson 1975: 8–9.

107. De Cervin 1977; Casson 1978.

108. Gillmer 1975: 323.

109. Reynolds 1978.

110. Kennedy 1978.

111. Basch 1983: 406; 1986: 426; 1987: 128.

112. Morgan 1988: 135–37.

113. I intend to discuss the identity and cultic significance of the Aegean horizontal stern device in a future monograph.

114. Brown 1979: 631; Morgan 1988: 127; Wachsmann 1995B: 10.

115. Marinatos 1974: 51.

116. Tilley and Johnstone 1976: 288.

117. Gillmer 1975: 324.

118. Betts (1973: 330) suggests that the horse was a later addition to the seal that made this sealing and that it was cut *over* the ship.

119. Basch 1987: 105 no. F–16.

120. Casson 1975: 7. For references to nautical festivals in antiquity, see Brown 1979: 641 n. 5.

121. Marinatos 1933: 192 n. 3.

122. See above, p. 69.

123. Bishop 1938; Worcester 1956; 1971: 256–57, 404, 459–61, 531–35; Spencer 1976: 74, pl. 18; Smith 1992A. On boat races in Classical times, see Gardner 1891A; 1891B; Harris 1972: 126–32.

124. Smith 1992B.

125. Bishop 1938: 420.

126. See above, p. 74.

127. See above, p. 75.

128. Basch 1983: 406–407; 1987: 104 no. F7, 135.

129. Basch (1987: 135 no. F7) considers this a *gréement à perches* placed at the stern but does not explain how it could function in that position.

130. Compare, for example, Nilsson 1950: 267 figs. 131–32, 268 fig. 134, 269 fig. 135; Kenna 1960: pls. 11: 282–84, 14: 351, 375; Demargne 1964: 138 fig. 181, 140 fig. 188, 180 fig. 248; Higgins 1967: 186–87 figs. 238–40; Doumas 1992: 137–38, 154, 156, 160; Marinatos 1993: 127–46.

131. Amiran 1972; *NEAEHL* 1: 82 (s.v. Arad).

132. Sakellariou (1980: 150–52) compares it to the *Isidis Navigium* in which a sacrificial vessel heavily laden with gifts was launched at sea. Morgan 1988: 143–45.

133. Sakellarakis and Sapouna-Sakellaraki 1981: 216.

134. Evans 1925A: 53–64, 65 fig. 55, pl. 5; Nilsson 1950: 195 fig. 90; Platon 1971: 145, 148; Alexiou n.d.: 121.

135. Alexiou n.d.: 70–78.

136. Marinatos 1933: 223–35; Alexiou n.d.: 113–14. On the authenticity of the Ring of Minos, from which the cult vessel in Fig. 6.52:A derives, see Platon 1984; Pini 1987; Warren 1987; Wedde 1990.

137. On birds as epiphanies in Minoan cult, see Nilsson 1950: 330–40.

138. Televantou 1990: 318.

139. Marinatos 1974: 45, 54.

140. Marinatos 1984: 40.

141. Morgan 1988: 150–54.

142. Ibid.: 109–15.

143. Ibid.: 90, 97–98, 152–53.

144. Marinatos 1984: 35–36; 1993: 216–17.

145. Marinatos 1974: 45.

146. Marinatos 1988: 15.

147. *PM* IV: 43 fig. 27; Long 1974: pls. 30–31, figs. 86–87.

148. *PM* IV: 41 fig. 24, 568 fig. 542: b; Long 1974: 62, pl. 90. See also Nilsson 1950: 229–30 fig. 113. Concerning human sacrifice in the Greek world, see Hughes 1991.

149. Morgan 1988: 154.

150. Ibid.: 153.

151. Hood 1971: 139.

152. Bishop 1938: 417.

153. Morgan (1988: 150–54), who identifies the bodies as symbolic defeat, ignores the existence of the sea monster on the Siege Rhyton. On sea monsters in later Greek art and culture, see Vermeule 1981: 186–96.

154. *PM* I: 697–98; III: 96; IV: 952.

155. Marinatos 1993: 231.

156. Warren 1980; 1984; Wall, Musgrave, and Warren 1986: 386–88.

157. Warren 1984: 55. Warren (1988B: 28–29, fig. 17) also interprets a scene on a ring impression from Khania as indicative of human sacrifice. See also Dickinson 1994: 266.

158. Sakellarakis and Sapouna-Sakellaraki 1981; 1991: 146–56 and the additional bibliography there.

159. Physical anthropologist J. Zias of the Israel Antiquities Authority notes that citing the crematory practices as proof of human sacrifice at Anemospilia—that the bones were blackened because of loss of blood from the carotid artery—is inaccurate. He emphasizes that color of skeletal material is determined by the heat of the fire: material cremated in a fire in which the pyre is fired well results in the substance turning white. If it is poorly fired, the material is blackened or charred black. It is common for the center of the body, where the pyre is the hottest, to be white and the extremities, where the heat is less intense, to be black. J. Zias, personal communication.

160. Ventris and Chadwick 1973: 284–89; Palmer 1963: 261–68; Bennett and Olivier 1973: 233–36; Chadwick 1973A: 458–64; 1976: 89–92, 179, 192.

161. Chadwick 1976: 91–92.

162. Buck 1989.

163. Ibid.: 136–37.

164. On the differentiation and mixing of the Minoan and Mycenaean religions, see Chadwick 1976: 85.

165. Morgan 1988: 95.

166. Marinatos 1974: 25–26 pls. 52, 54, 55: a, color pls. 2, 4; Doumas 1992: 86–95.
167. Shaw 1980; 1982.
168. Morgan (1988: 166, 31 fig. 16) notes that these dress lines appear twice on Late Minoan IB marine-style pottery, although they are missing on Late Minoan IA or earlier pottery.
169. Boardman 1970: 106 pl. 196; Betts 1973: 328.
170. Basch 1987: 129–30 figs. 264–65.
171. The stone receptacle dates to the Late Minoan I and comes from the cave of Hermes Kranaios at Patsos (Warren 1966). These objects are thought to be libation tables or lamp holders. The ship is crescentic and lacks rigging. It has a thick mast in the center and a lunate (or horns of consecration) at one extremity.
172. See also Morgan 1988: 93–101.
173. Marinatos 1974: pl. 101, color pl. 7; Morgan 1988: 93–96.
174. Long 1974: pl. 19 fig. 52; Sakellarakis 1979: 113.
175. Evans 1900–1901: 20.
176. Nilsson 1950: 158–60.
177. Marinatos 1993: 135–37.
178. Demargne 1964: 173 fig. 234; Hood 1978: 145 fig. 138. A similar dress is worn by a figure on a seal (Nilsson 1950: 156 fig. 62, 160–62 fig. 66).
179. Marinatos 1974: 46.
180. Nilsson 1950: 162–64; Alexiou n.d.: 92–93.
181. Marinatos 1974: 49; Iakovides 1981. Note that a man in the stern of a fishing boat in the tomb of Ipy at Thebes (perhaps depicted in the act of clapping) holds his hands in a somewhat similar manner, but in this case the right hand is outstretched (Fig. 6.70). This similarity is probably fortuitous.
182. Morgan 1988: 97 fig. 62, 117–82.
183. Buchholz and Karageorghis 1973: 101 n. 1224, 373 fig. 1224: a–d.

Chapter 7: Mycenaean / Achaean Ships

1. Ventris and Chadwick 1973; Chadwick 1976. On the decipherment of Linear B, see Chadwick 1958; 1987B: 12–21. For a thoughtful historical study of the Mycenaeans and their world, see Thomas 1993.
2. The Minoan seals found at Kato Zakro by Hogarth were apparently used to seal parchment documents (Weingarten 1982).
3. See Palaima 1991A for a comprehensive commentary of references to seafaring in the Linear B tablets.
4. Ventris and Chadwick 1973: 183–88; Chadwick 1973A: 430–32; 1976: 173; Palmer 1963: 129–32; Bennett and Olivier 1973: 43, 50, 54; Lindgren 1973 (I): 163–64; (II): 49–50.
5. Chadwick 1987A: 77.
6. *E-ke-ra$_2$-wo*: Ventris and Chadwick 1973: 265; Chadwick 1976: 71; Lindgren 1973 (I): 46; (II): 50, 84, 135, 150, 153–55, 187, 197, 209. *We-da-ne-u*: Ventris

and Chadwick 1973: 186–87, 200, 279; Lindgren 1973 (I): 127–28; (II): 37–38, 50–51, 84, 134–36, 152, 154, 161–62, 179, 185–88, 197, 210.
7. Chadwick 1973: 431; Palmer 1963: 90–91, 131, 136–37; Palaima 1991: 286. See Lindgren 1973 on: *ki-ti-ta* (I): 170–71; (II): 82–83; *me-ta-ki-ti-ta* (I): 174; (II): 82, 97; *po-si-ke-te-re* (I): 180; (II): 124; *po-ku-ta* (I): 179; (II): 118–19.
8. Chadwick 1987A: 76.
9. Professor T. G. Palaima, personal communication (May 20, 1991). I thank Professor Palaima for his comments on An 724 and An 1 and for his translation of An 1 quoted on p. 126.
10. Bennett et al. 1989: 230–31; Palaima 1991A: 286–87.
11. Palaima 1991A: 286 pl. 63: a.
12. Killen 1983.
13. On a possible explanation for the reality reflected in the rower tablets, see below, pp. 159–61.
14. Palaima 1991A: 301–304.
15. Chadwick 1973B; Killen and Olivier 1989: 340—V(5) 756 + 7806; 342—V(5) 1002 + 5766 + 7650, V(5) 1003 + 5958, V(5) 1004, V(5) 1005 + 7530 + 7567 + fr., V(5) 1043, 7709 + fr.; 344—V(5) 1583 + 7747 + 7887 + frr.; 346—V(5) 7577 + 7734, V(5) 7670 + 7746; 347—V(5) 7964; Palaima 1991A: 286, 304–308.
16. Ventris and Chadwick 1973: 574; Palmer 1963: 448.
17. See Casson 1995A: 300.
18. *KN* V 756 and V 1002. Palaima (1991: 286, 304–308) presents a revised listing of the V(5) series and reviews their interpretation. He concludes that they may refer to nautical affairs if Chadwick's interpretation of the word *po-ti-ro* is correct.
19. Casson 1995A: 346 n. 10, 350–54.
20. Palaima 1991A: 284.
21. See above, p. 10.
22. See above, p. 11.
23. Palaima 1991A: 280–84.
24. Chadwick 1988: 79–84, 91–93. See also Ventris and Chadwick 1973: 156, 159; Chadwick 1973A: 417; 1976: 80–81; Vermeule 1983: 142; Palaima 1991A: 279–80.
25. *Odyssey* IX: 39–43.
26. Wainwright 1939: 151; Gurney 1990: 38–45; Garstang and Gurney 1959: 81; Immerwahr 1960: 4; Vermeule 1964: 272; 1983; Desborough 1964: 218–20; 1972; Smith 1965: 33; Huxley 1968: 15–25; Page 1976: 1–40; Iakovides 1973: 189–90; Güterbock 1983; 1984; Wood 1985: 175, 179–85; Hallager 1988: 93; Hansen 1994: 214.
27. See below, p. 130.
28. Lloyd 1967: 80–81; Macqueen 1968: 179–85; 1986: 39–41; Mellaart 1968; Hooker 1976: 128–31; Muhly 1974. See also Dickinson 1994: 253, 306.
29. Güterbock 1983: 133–34, 138; 1984: 116, 119. Of interest in this regard is a Mycenaean sword, discovered at Hatussa, bearing a dedicatory inscription of Tudkhaliya II (Hansen 1994).

30. It is not clear on what basis Arnuwadas laid claim to Alashia.
31. Güterbock 1983: 134.
32. Ibid.: 135.
33. Garstang and Gurney 1959: 111–14; Güterbock 1983: 135–37; 1984: 119–21.
34. On the identification of Milliwanda with Miletos, see Garstang and Gurney 1959: 80–81; Huxley 1968: 11–15; Mellink 1983.
35. Piyamaradus and Atpas resurface in a text sent by Manapa-Dattas, the beleaguered king of the Seha River Lands (Garstang and Gurney 1959). He complains that Piyamaradus has attacked the land of Laz-pas (Lesbos?) and has appointed Atpas over Manapa-Dattas. Furthermore, some of Manapa-Dattas's own soldiers, together with Hittite troops, have defected to Piyamaradus. See also Singer 1983: 209–13.
36. For an extensive bibliography of this text, see Steiner 1989.
37. Most recently, see Singer 1991: 173; Cline 1991B: 6 and the additional bibliography there.
38. Against his interpretation, see Singer 1991: 171 n. 56.
39. EA 38: 10–12.
40. See above, p. 128.
41. Linder 1970: 93–94; 1981: 39 fig. 38. This name was previously read mi-lim. They appear in EA 101: 4, 33, 105: 27, 108: 38, 110: 48(?), 111: 21(?), and 126: 63. Linder 1970: 93–94. Moran translates this term as "ships of the army."
42. Säve-Söderbergh 1946: 64–67. For an opposing view, see Lambdin 1953.
43. EA 101: 36.
44. Redford 1992: 243 n. 13 and additional bibliography; Artzy 1988: 186. Ramses II, apparently earlier in his career, also fought a sea battle against Shardanu ships. See below, p. 317.
45. Parkinson and Schofield 1993A; 1993B; 1995; Schofield and Parkinson 1994.
46. Furumark 1950; Mee 1978; 1982; 1986; Barber 1981; Davis 1992.
47. Hooker 1976: 110–16.
48. Davis 1992: 707.
49. We may presume that these groups were, or at least included, Mycenaeans. Stager (1991: 13–19; 1995) equates the Sea Peoples with the Mycenaeans. See articles in MEM; Karageorghis 1976: 58–94; 1982: 82–92; 1984; Karageorghis et al. 1988: 255–66; Dothan and Dothan 1992: 160–70, 238, 241, 257–59 pl. 22. See below, Chap. 8, n. 54.
50. See below, p. 292.
51. See below, pp. 176–77.
52. On bird-head devices, see below, pp. 177–97.
53. Larnax: Gray 1974: G19 no. 40a; Laffineur 1991: 61: b. Phylakopi sherd: Marinatos 1933: 172 no. 13.
54. Dakoronia 1990; 1991; 1993; 1995; 1996.
55. Furumark 1941: 337–40, 343 fig. 57: 42.
56. Ibid.: 245 fig. 27: 6, 8; 332 fig. 18.
57. Williams 1959; Morrison and Williams 1968: 37, 73 pls. 7: e–f, 8: a (Geom. 43, 44, Arch. 1); Casson 1995A: 71–74 figs. 70–71; Basch 1987: 182–83 figs. 384–86. Note, however, the possibility that the lunates on Kynos ship A may represent the backs of the oarsmen if they are involved in an operation that would require them to face the bow when rowing (Tilley 1992).
58. Several theories exist concerning the interpretation of the horizontal lines and rowers on Late Geometric ship depictions created by the Dipylon school in Athens during the end of the eighth century B.C. I follow here Casson's proposed interpretation. See particularly Kirk 1949: 123–31; Morrison and Williams 1968: 12–17; Casson 1995A: 71–74, 447 n. 73, fig. 69; Basch 1987: 161–70.
59. See below, pp. 166–77.
60. On the introduction of the brailed rig, see below, pp. 251–54.
61. Compare the structures in the bows of figures of ships from Enkomi and Hyria (Fig. 7.28: A, 30: A). On the discovery of the sherd containing the stern of this ship, see Dakoronia 1996: 162, 171 fig. 9.
62. Basch 1987: 172 figs. 354–56, 173 figs. 357–59.
63. See below, pp. 155–56.
64. Numerous arrowheads were among the weapons carried on board the Uluburun ship. See below, p. 307.
65. Bronze Age Aegean art almost invariably tends to represent a very shallow draw for the bow, with both arms portrayed in front of the torso (Wachsmann 1987: pls. 65, 66: C–D). On this ship, however, the archer's right arm is shown behind the torso. In the art of many cultures, this is the normal manner for representing the deep draw required when pulling the composite bow (Fig. 8.1; Yadin 1963: 186–87, 192, 200–201, 214, 216, 229, 235, 240, 334, 337–38, 346, 365–67, 382–93, 401–403, 407–10, 418–19, 422–25, 433, 435, 450, 453, 458, 460–61).

Although archers using various types of simple bows are recorded in Bronze Age Aegean art, generally speaking the bow does not seem to have been a preferred weapon of combat among the Minoans or Mycenaeans. Certainly, composite bows were not in common use among these peoples. Archery plays a relatively insignificant role in Homer, and only two composite bows are specifically mentioned: the bow of Pandarus, used in his unsuccessful attempt to kill Menelaus; and Odysseus's bow, with which he slew Penelope's suitors (Iliad IV: 105–26; Odyssey XXI; Balfour 1890: 226–27; 1921; Wachsmann 1987: 82–84). And Homer hopelessly misinterprets the process of constructing the composite bow of Pandarus, assuming that it was made by simply joining two wild goat horns together.

The Minoans, and probably the Mycenaeans also, exported to Egypt horns of the Cretan wild goat (agrimi). This was a vital component in the construction of the composite bows favored by the New

Kingdom Egyptians but presumably of little value in cultures that did not use this type of bow.

At least until they settled in Canaan, the Sea Peoples also seem to have shunned the composite bow. In the opening phase of the nautical battle depicted at Medinet Habu, Ramses III's archers were able to decimate the Sea Peoples because the latter lacked long-distance weapons (see below, p. 317). In fact, the only evidence for the use of the bow by the northern invaders in the Medinet Habu reliefs is a quiver attached to the side of a Sea Peoples' chariot depicted in the land battle (Nelson et al. 1930: pl. 32). But the Bible refers to archers at the Battle of Gilboa, in which Saul and Jonathan fell to the Philistines (I Samuel 31: 3). Either the Philistines had learned the use of the bow after their arrival at Canaan or they were using Canaanite auxiliaries.

66. Dakoronia 1996.
67. Korrés 1989.
68. Furumark 1941: 335, 333 fig. 56: 40: 2.
69. Svoronos 1914: 97; *PM* II: 242–46 fig. 142; Kirk 1949: 118; Vermeule 1964: fig. 43; Morrison and Williams 1968: 9, BA 2; Bass 1972: 22.
70. Before the discovery of these sherds, Sakellarakis (1971: 210), based on stylistic considerations, had correctly identified the stem device as bird-shaped.
71. See below, p. 144 and Fig. 7.29: A.
72. Casson 1995A: 85.
73. Morrison and Williams 1968: 9–10, pl. 1b (BA 2). Alternately, it bears comparison with the double hemispherical device attached to the quarter rudder loom on the Kynos A ship (Fig. 7.10).
74. Compare this to other palms depicted on Late Helladic pottery (Furumark 1941: 276–82 figs. 38–40).
75. Piet De Jong's reconstruction of this artifact was published upside down in relation to the ship, which was described as an "odd arrangement difficult to interpret—possibly suggesting plow or chariot with shaft" (Blegen et al. 1973: 16, ill. 108: a–d). Bouzek (1985: 170, 174 fig. 87.12) published the diadem with the ship right side up. See also Bouzek 1994: 230.
76. Alexiou 1970: 253–54; 1972: 90–98; 1973; Sakellarakis 1979: 110; Wachsmann 1981: 202–203 figs. 17–18; Aubert 1995.
77. Kirk 1949: 114–16 fig. 4; Morrison and Williams 1968: 28–29 pl. 4e (Geom. 19); Casson 1995A: 72 n. 12, fig. 74; Basch 1987: 163–65 figs. 328–30.
78. Compare Casson 1995A: figs. 65–66.
79. Basch 1987: 145–46 fig. 305.
80. Boardman 1967: 72, 73 fig. 6: 21, pl. 14: 21.
81. See below, pp. 190–91, 193–94.
82. Furumark 1941: 53 fig. 30.
83. Compare Furumark 1941: 281 fig. 40: 22a (palm tree), 286 fig. 42: 32, 293 fig. 45 (flower).
84. On the role of ships in the afterlife in Minoan and Mycenaean religion, see Laffineur 1991 and the additional bibliography there.

85. Sandars 1985: 130 fig. 85; Basch 1987: 141, 142 fig. 295.
86. Kirk 1949: 117; Morrison and Williams 1968: 10, BA 3.
87. Casson 1995A: 32; Bass 1972: 22; Basch 1987: 146–47 fig. 309. Previously, Basch (1975: 201–202 fig. 2) held that the left end was the bow.
88. Palmer 1871: pl. opp. 29; Jaussen et al. 1905: pls. 6–7; Rahmani 1980: 117 fig. 2.
89. Marinatos 1933: 172 no. 13. The galley is on a matt-painted sherd, apparently of Middle Cycladic date. (Personal communication, Mr. M. Wedde, February 20, 1995.) I thank Mr. Wedde for bringing this to my attention.
90. See below, p. 183.
91. Morricone 1975: 360–61 fig. 358; Sandars 1985: 135 fig. 92.
92. See below, pp. 176–77.
93. Laviosa 1972: 9–10.
94. Gjerstad et al. 1934: 484 no. 262, pl. 77—top row center; Sjöqvist 1940: fig. 20: 3; Furumark 1941: 335, 333 fig. 56: 40: 1; Casson 1995A: fig. 59. The ships are depicted with somewhat rounded hulls, a detail that has led some scholars to conclude that the ships represented are beamy merchantmen (Vermeule 1964: 258; Morrison and Williams 1968: 11 no. BA 8; Casson 1995A: 36). These ships are apparently taking part in a procession / race similar to that depicted at Thera.
95. Karageorghis 1960: 146, pl. 10: 7. Concerning the whorl-shell motif on Mycenaean vase painting, see Furumark 1941: 308–10, 311 fig. 51, 312. I thank Mr. M. Wedde for bringing these sherds to my attention and Professor G. F. Bass and Mr. C. Pulak for their insightful comments concerning them.
96. Furumark 1941: 237–42 fig. 25.
97. See above, pp. 117–18.
98. Schaeffer 1952: 102–104.
99. See above, pp. 69–76.
100. Basch 1987: 148 fig. 312: A.
101. Ibid.: 188, 190 fig. 398.
102. Blegen 1949; Basch 1987: 143–45 figs. 300–302. Blegen dates the tomb to the end of the Middle Helladic period, or the very beginning of the Late Helladic period. More recently, Buchholz and Karageorghis (1973: 94 no. 1168) assign the ship graffiti a Late Helladic III date.
103. Basch (1987: 143) interprets these as an "X-ray" view of the ships' frames seen through the hull.
104. Karageorghis 1976: 99 pls. 73–74; Basch and Artzy 1985.
105. On the Kition anchors, see below, pp. 273–74.
106. Karageorghis 1976: 58–94.
107. Basch and Artzy 1985: 332 fig. 8A.
108. The statement made by Basch and Artzy (1985: 326), that all the graffiti on the wall are facing left, is curious. In most cases there is no way of determining stem from stern. Graffiti "O" has a line descending

at an angle from its left extremity. If this is a quarter rudder, as seems probable, then it also is facing right.

109. Basch and Artzy 1985: 324, 328; Artzy 1987: 80.
110. Basch 1987: 141 fig. 293: 1.
111. See below, pp. 241–43.
112. Basch 1987: 250–51 fig. 529; van Doorninck 1982B: 279–80 fig. 5.
113. Compare Basch 1987: 329–30 figs. 703–12, 340 fig. 724.
114. Basch 1987: 141 fig. 293: 2.
115. Morrison and Williams 1968: 37; Casson 1995A: 49; Johnston 1985: 28, BA 19; Basch 1987: 141.
116. Morrison and Williams 1968: 11, BA 7.
117. Johnston 1985: 31, BA 22.
118. Ibid.: 32–33, BA 25; Basch 1987: 149–50 fig. 317.
119. For a more naturalistic depiction of a water bird head from a Late Helladic ship model, see Fig. 8.48.
120. Catling 1964: 52.
121. Yon 1971: 51–52.
122. For the possible identity of these lines, see below, pp. 190–91.
123. Pieridou 1965: 87 no. 108, pl. 10: 9.
124. Göttlicher 1978: 35 no. 149.
125. Johnston 1985: 29–30, BA 21.
126. Göttlicher 1978: 63 no. 332; Johnston 1985: 33–34, BA 26.
127. Louvre model: Westerberg 1983: 15–16 fig. 10 (no. 10); Haifa Maritime Museum model: Stieglitz 1972–75B: 44 fig. 1.
128. Göttlicher 1978: Taf. 7: 103.
129. Stieglitz 1972–75B.
130. Palaiologou 1989.
131. See below, pp. 156, 242–43. Dakoronia 1996.
132. See below, p. 185.
133. Hallager 1987; Palaima 1991A: 282–83.
134. Palaima 1991A: 277–78.
135. Ventris and Chadwick 1973: 336, 337; Palaima 1991: 281.
136. Ventris and Chadwick 1973: 374; Chadwick 1973: 519; Palmer 1963: 326–27; Palaima 1991: 281.
137. Harder to explain is the adoption of the Semitic word for "lion" by the Linear B scribes. See above, p. 40.
138. See below, pp. 303–307.
139. See above, p. 61.
140. Palaima 1991A: 288–89.
141. Ibid.: 274–76.
142. Ventris and Chadwick 1973: 356. Note that the Cape Gelidonya ship carried about a ton of copper (CG: 163). I thank Professor J. Chadwick for his comments on PY Ja 749 (personal communication).
143. See below, p. 333.
144. Uchitel 1988: 21–22.
145. See below, p. 307.
146. Bass 1986: 296; 1988A: 37; Pulak 1992: 11; in press. See below, p. 307.

147. Pulak (in press) argues convincingly for the presence of two Mycenaeans on board the Uluburun ship when she sank.
148. Coldstream 1977: 385; Morrison and Williams 1968: 26–28; Basch 1987: 162–63.
149. Basch 1987: 190–94; Basch and Artzy 1985: 326–27 fig. 13: A–G.
150. See above, Chap. 7, n. 49.
151. Casson 1995A: 55–56.
152. See below, pp. 241–43.
153. Linder 1992: 28, 34, and below, p. 366 n. 153.
154. See below, pp. 177–97.
155. Basch 1987: 164 fig. 328, 172 fig. 355, 173 fig. 357, 174 fig. 360, 176 fig. 368, 177 fig. 371 (?), 184 fig. 388: B.
156. Casson 1995A: 44–45 n. 10.
157. See below, pp. 159–60. Homer, describing the staff of Polyphémus used by Odysseus and his shipmates to poke out the Cyclops's eye, likens it to "the mast of a broad-beamed, black-hulled, 20-oared merchantman that sails the great sea" (Odyssey IX: 322–23; translation from Casson 1995A: 65). This may or may not reflect a Late Bronze Age reality.
158. Casson 1995A: 42 n.4.
159. Odyssey XIII: 113–15.
160. Kirk 1949: 126–27.
161. Casson 1995A: 331.
162. Hornell 1970: 202.
163. Professor J. R. Steffy, personal communication.
164. Van Doorninck 1982B: 283–85.
165. Professor L. Casson, personal communication.

Appendix: The Pylos Rower Tablets

1. Wachsmann in press D. Compare the situation at Ugarit reflected in KTU 2.47 and RS 20.238. See below, pp. 336–37 and 344. Shelmerdine (1987) suggests an interesting alternative interpretation based on a study of the changes in the architecture of the palace at Pylos. She sees there evidence for a slow decline as the result of the collapse of the palace-based economy. Such a scenario, if correct, does not preclude a final crisis that brought about the kingdom's destruction. In itself, however, Shelmerdine's reconstruction does not explain the need for the large fleet recorded in PY An 610. See also, Wright 1984.
2. See particularly Ventris and Chadwick 1973: 183–85, 357–58 (PY Jn 829); Chadwick 1976: 173–79; Palmer 1956; 1965: 143–54; Perpillou 1968; Baumbach 1983. On the possible evidence for human sacrifice in PY Tn 316, see above, p. 117.
3. Naville 1908: 2–5, pls. 153–54; Landström 1971: 130–31 fig. 383.
4. Casson 1995A: 65–68; 1995B. The Shipwrecked Sailor, in a clear allusion to an oared cargo ship, mentions that his vessel had a crew of 120. See above, p. 10.

5. Herodotus I: 163.

6. Ezekiel 27: 12; Basch 1987: 197.

7. Casson 1995A: fig. 92; Basch 1987: 308–309 fig. 650, 310 figs. 352, 354, 313 fig. 659, 314 figs. 660–61, 317 fig. 668, 318 fig. 669, 319 fig. 672. Sargon's artists erroneously depicted the rowers facing the bow, as if they were paddling.

8. Casson 1995A: figs. 86–87; Basch 1987: 259 fig. 559.

9. Herodotus VI: 41.

10. Herodotus I: 164. On pentekonters, see Höckmann 1995.

11. *ARAB* II: no. 326; see also nos. 239 and 309.

12. Barnett 1956: 91, 93 fig. 9; 1969: 6–7 pl. 1: 1.

13. Ezekiel 27: 8, 10.

14. See above, pp. 124–25. Palaima (1991A: 286), emphasizing the similarities between An 1 and *KTU* 4.40, limits the significance of the landholding terms in the rower tablets to the implication that "on the individual level, their (the rowers') service was obligatory in return for the use of land granted to them by the palace center of by or through the local communities."

However, the significance of this Ugaritic text itself, as Killen notes, is far from certain. It might equally refer to normal maritime activities or to a proportional military draft of oarsmen for the nautical defense of Ugarit. Thus, although the documents indicate a remarkably similar system of proportional call-up prevalent at Pylos and Ugarit, this only informs us *how*, but not *why*, the men were being called up.

15. Ventris and Chadwick 1973: 332–48 (Ta series); Palmer 1963: 338–63; Bennett and Olivier 1973: 230–31. Metal artifacts found during the excavations of Pylos, primarily of a fragmentary nature, appear among the plates of small finds in Blegen and Rawson 1966A: pls. 261–317.

16. On hoards and hoarding, see Knapp, Muhly, and Muhly 1988 and the additional bibliography there.

17. Blegen and Rawson 1966A: 350–51. A similar situation has been inferred for the demise of Kalavassos, in Cyprus, by its excavator, A. South-Todd. At this site Building X was not destroyed but rather abandoned, after all valuables had been removed. Only sherds and heavy storage jars were left behind.
V. Karageorghis believes that the fire that destroyed the building was set by its occupants. I thank Professor Karageorghis for bringing this potential parallel to my attention. (Personal communication, May 26, 1995.)

18. Blegen and Rawson 1966A: 424. Popham (1991) has now proposed an early date within the Late Helladic IIIB for the end of Mycenaean Pylos based on the site's enigmatic lack of fortifications. He has suggested a Proto-Geometric date for the ceramics found there, which Blegen attributed to the Late Helladic IIIC. Griebel and Nelson (1993) note the existence of a significant Geometric inhabitation at Pylos.

19. Archaeological surveys indicate a *minimum* population of about 50,000 for the kingdom of Pylos during the Late Helladic IIIB, with a dramatic drop in population in the following Late Helladic IIIC (McDonald and Simpson 1961: 257–58; 1969: 174–77; 1972A: 136–43). Chadwick (1972: 112–13), on the basis of the Linear B tablets from Pylos, proposes a population of between 80,000 and 120,000. These latter numbers do not appear at present to be supported by the archaeological evidence (McDonald and Simpson 1972B: 254–56).

20. I intentionally have not addressed here the question of the identity of the implied invaders of Pylos. For a recent review of the relations between Mycenaean Greece and the north, see Bouzek 1994.

Chapter 8: The Ships of the Sea Peoples

1. Wood 1991.

2. See above, pp. 128–30.

3. See below, p. 320.

4. See below, p. 324–325.

5. *BAR* IV: §566–68.

6. *KTU* 2.47, *RS* 20.18, *L.1*, *RS* 20.162, *RS* 20.238, and *RS* 34.129. See Astour 1965.

7. See below, *RS* 20.238, p. 344.

8. See below, *RS* 20.18, p. 343.

9. See below, *RS* 34.129, p. 343.

10. Anson Rainy notes (personal communication): Text *RS* 34.129 has strong Assyrian linguistic features, i.e., iṣ-bu-tu-šu-ú-ni (l.12). As an Assyrianized text, we would expect the signs with š would be used for s. So for ši-ka-la-iu-ú (ll.11 and 21) we could read Sik(k)alayū and for ši-ki-la (l.25) we could read Sik(k)ila. The vowel variation in the second syllable is puzzling but may be due to the presence of a short, indistinct vowel, like Hebrew shewa.
The phoneme in the Egyptian form ṯkrw (Sekels) can only be samech, never zayin or tsade. Therefore, the chance of equating the people in *RS* 34.129 with that Sea People is quite likely.

11. See above, pp. 128–30.

12. See below, *KTU* 2.47, pp. 336–37.

13. Assuming that the seven Sea Peoples' ships mentioned in *RS* 20.238 as having ravaged the Ugaritic coast were either penteconters, triaconters, or a combination of both, then the total fighting contingent that caused such great damage to Ugarit consisted of no more than between 210 and 350 fighter/rowers plus a handful of officers. See below, pp. 320–21.

14. Christensen 1972: 165.

15. Sandars 1985: 83.

16. Mazar 1985; 1990: 300–28; Dothan 1982; Dothan and Dothan 1992; Brug 1985; Stager 1991: 2–19; 1995.

17. On the Philistine culture in Israel, see particularly Dothan 1982; Dothan and Dothan 1992.

18. Casson 1995A: 38, 42 n. 4.

19. *BAR* IV: §77.
20. Nelson 1943.
21. On the representation of several stages of action in a single scene in Egyptian art, see Schäfer 1974: 227–30.
22. See above, p. 11–12.
23. Nelson 1929: 32–33.
24. See above, pp. 19, 22.
25. Nelson 1929: 22.
26. Ibid.: 22–31.
27. The masts of the ships in Figs. 8.8, 8.10–8.12, and 8.14 have been blackened to emphasize the manner in which the Egyptian artists depicted the listing of these ships as they sank. See below, pp. 317–19.
28. Casson 1995A: 37.
29. This negates Casson's (1995A: 38) assumption that these craft entirely lacked any decking.
30. For a similar depiction of a shipwrecked sailor sitting on his overturned galley, see Morrison and Williams 1968: 35 pl. 7 (Geom. 38).
31. Nelson et al. 1930: 9–10.
32. See below, p. 231.
33. For a color photograph of the scene, see Miller 1988: 538–39.
34. See above, Chap 7, n. 58. Casson 1995A: 51 n. 58.
35. Compare the brackets supporting the quarter rudders of Hatshepsut's Punt ships (Fig. 2.26).
36. Morrison and Williams 1968: 52–53 pls. 3c; 4c (i), 4e; 7d; Casson 1995A: 46.
37. See above, p. 37.
38. Casson 1995A: 37, 69. See below, pp. 251–54.
39. On the possible origins of the crow's nest, see pp. 252–53.
40. Ingholt 1940: 71, pl. 22: 2; Riis 1948: 48 fig. 25, 97 fig. 130B: 112, 105–106, pl. 12C (no. G 8, 551 [5B902]); Hencken 1968: 627.
41. Ingholt 1940: 69–84, pls. 21–26; Riis 1948.
42. Riis 1948: 200.
43. Hencken 1968A: 627. Note that Tubb (1995) proposes that double-pithos burials, particularly common at Tell es-Sacidiyeh, but also known from Israeli sites, may be indicative of a Sea People's group.
44. Artzy 1984; 1987.
45. The first publication of this graffito depicts only three ships (Artzy 1984: 60 fig. 1).
46. Compare, for example, Jones 1990: 24, 28 (Objs. 308, 312).
47. See above, pp. 145–48.
48. Schaeffer 1952: 71.
49. Ibid.: 87–88, 412.
50. Sandars 1985: 135 fig. 92, 137.
51. Ibid.: 92, 93 figs. 54: b, d; 94.
52. A comparable helmet, identified by Morgan (1988: 102 pl. 150) as "spiky hair," is worn by a combatant on a cornelian lentoid sealstone from Crete.
53. Casson (1995A: 348 and fig. 147 [center ship]) interprets this as a "pennant on a short pole socketed into the top of the stempost." This is not a ship's light in the form of a torch. Although ships carried lights in their stern, these were placed in lanterns (Casson 1995A: 247–48 n. 91–92).
54. Hencken 1968A: 568–70, 672; 1968B: 107–10, 115–16, 146–48; Kaul 1995; Wachsmann, 1996A. For a view of the Sea Peoples from an Egyptian perspective, see Redford 1992: 241–56. De Boer (1991) now suggests a possible Thracian connection for the Sea Peoples. Zaanger (1995) argues for them coming from the Troad. The origins of the Sea Peoples seem to be far more complex, however, and to have included a host of cultures, although a main component was probably Mycenaean. See above, Chap. 7, n. 49.

    Indeed, a hallmark of the Sea Peoples' coalition now appears to have been its ability to absorb into it a variety of cultural components. This is eloquently expressed by an Ugaritic text (*RS* 20.18) in which Eshuwara, the chief prefect of Alashia, informs the king of Ugarit that men and ships belonging to the latter's kingdom have committed undefined transgressions against Ugarit, suggesting that they had "gone over" to the enemy. See below, p. 343. In studying the Sea Peoples coalition, one receives the impression of a "snowball effect," in which various elements are continually being added until, at the end of the process, the cultural entity has become something more, and different, than the sum of its aggregate parts. Concerning the origins of the Sea Peoples from the standpoint of contemporaneous ship iconography, see Wachsmann, in press C.
55. Bouzek 1985: 178.
56. Culican 1970; Tushingham 1971.
57. Hencken 1968A: 537 fig. 486.
58. Marinatos 1933: 173 no. 16 n. 1, 218–19. These sherds have been lost.
59. Hencken 1968A: 519–31.
60. For further clarification, in Figures 8.50, 8.52: D, 8.55: A, C–D, and 8.56: B, copies of the bird-head device from Figure 8.41: A have been added to illustrate the direction of the head in each case. Similarly, in figure 8.49: A, copies of the bird-head device on one of the Kynos ships (Figs. 7.16; 8.61: C) have been appended at either side. In Figure 8.55: B, a copy of the device on the Skyros ship's stem is added (Figs. 7.21, 8.35).
61. Kirk 1949: 133; Artzy 1987: 80 n. 6; Basch 1987: 201.
62. Korrés 1989: 199–200, 202.
63. Furumark 1941: 253 fig. 30, 255 fig. 31 (nos. 36–52); Benson 1961; 1975; Dothan 1982: 201–202 figs. 61–63.
64. The festive, bird-shaped stem decorations portrayed on Late Bronze Age Minoan/Cycladic craft represent a swallow, as is evident from the bowsprit of one of the ships taking part in the festive race at Thera (Basch 1987: 107 figs. 192–93). These were apparently attached to the craft during festivities and were not a normal fixture on the bow. The Helladic ornament, on the other hand, represents a water bird and seems

to have been a permanent fixture on the stem- and sternposts of Helladic oared vessels. On the continuation of the bird motif on Iron Age Cypriot pottery, see Benson 1975.

65. Dakoronia 1991; 1996: 161–62, 169–70 pls. 3–4.

66. Kirk 1949: 118–19 fig. 6; Morrison and Williams 1968: 12 pl. 1: d (Geom. 1); Casson 1995A: 36 fig. 60; van Doorninck 1982B.

67. For other strongly recurved beaks, see also Figs. 8.42, 8.49: B.

68. See below, pp. 199–200.

69. Morrison and Williams 1968: pls. 1: e, 2: a, 4: c.

70. Casson 1995A: 57 n. 80, 58.

71. Morrison and Williams 1968: 73–74 (Arch. 2), pl. 8: b.

72. Ibid.: pls. 2: a, 4: a and c.

73. Broodbank 1989: 328.

74. Haddon 1937: 28.

75. Svoronos 1914: 127.

76. Hornell 1970: 271.

77. Bishop 1938: 415.

78. Hornell 1970: 272–73. On similar rituals in modern Portugal, see Filgueiras 1995.

79. Hornell 1970: 275.

80. Compare a somewhat similar figure painted on a Daunian dish from Siponto in southeastern Italy dating from the sixth or fifth century B.C. (Gimbutas 1989: 16 fig. 26: 8).

81. A better preserved, though less decorated, version of this motif is also known (*Nefer*: 10).

82. Egypt has been suggested as the ultimate source for the European bird and sun-disk design (Hopkins 1955: 78–80; 1957: 334–35), but this seems most unlikely.

83. Yon 1992: 400.

84. Casson 1995A: 348 n. 15.

85. Clarke 1920: 51.

Appendix: Homer's νηυσὶ κορωνίσιν

1. Thus the standard Greek lexicon translates κορωνίς as "*crook-beaked:* hence, generally, *curved* . . . . " *LSJ*[9], s.v. (p. 983). Likewise, Lattimore (1951) once translates "beaked" at *Iliad* VII: 229, but sixteen times renders it as "curved" or "curving," exemplifying the confusion I discuss below. Kurt, in his study of Homeric nautical terms, defines κορωνίς as "provided with crooked, beaklike stern" (1979: 39; my trans.).

2. Always in the dative plural; κορωνίσι (ν) occurs fifteen times in the *Iliad*, twice in the *Odyssey*.

3. Seabird: *Odyssey* v: 66–67, xii: 418 = xiv: 308. Crow: Hesiod, *Works and Days* 747. Chantraine (1970, s.v.) considers these birds to be the *Puffinus Kuhlii* and the *Corvus Corone*, respectively. See *LSJ*[9], s.v. I, for further references, as well as Thompson (1936: 168–73).

4. Door handle: *Odyssey* i: 441, vii: 90, xxi: 46, xxi: 138 = 165. Bow-tip: *Iliad* IV: 111.

5. See *LSJ*[9], s.v. II., with Revised Supplement (1996).

6. Aratus, *Phaenomena*, line 345; his archaizing language closely follows Homer's.

7. *LSJ*[9], s.v.

8. Nussbaum (1986) has shown that two distinct roots need to be differentiated for "head" (which I omit) and "horn."

9. κορωνίς surely means "horned" in Theocritus 25: 151: "ἐπὶ βουσὶ κορωνίσι" and Gow (1950: 205) translates "the horned kine." Most, however, have derived both this and κορωνός (see n. 10) from "curved" (horns). Theocritus archaized in language, and his usage here sheds light on Homer's κορωνίς (cp. below), although reliance on any such argument risks becoming circular.

10. "Horned" is the clearest meaning in the phrase "βοῦς . . . κορωνός" ("horned ox"), Archilochus 35: 1–2 (West 1989; cp. preceding note), despite the reliance of West (1989: 17) and *LSJ*[9] on the overly clever *Etymologicum Magnum* for a metaphorical meaning of "overarching."

11. Of ships' extremities, "νηῶν . . . ἄκρα κόρυμβα," at *Iliad* IX: 241 (Nussbaum 1986: 9). Casson (1971: 46 n. 19) understands this word as "peaks," i.e. from a root "head" (cp. above, n. 8).

12. Also a month-name at Knossos, perhaps named from a festival (*GDI* no. 5015, line 28).

13. Since they are usually of a different material, this may have fostered the supposed connection with birds' beaks, but neither "beak" nor "curve" seems the essential etymological element in the word for a seabird or crow, κορώνη (A).

14. So κορωνίζω, "bring to completion"; κορωνιάω and κορωνίης, both referring to arching one's neck (see *LSJ*[9], s.vv.). The Latin *cornu*, or "horn," can mean (like κορώνη [B]) "the tip of a bow" (*OLD*, s.v. definition 7[c]). A beak may perhaps be seen in this category, although the word is not related etymologically. For Homer's κορωνίς, Latacz suggests the definition "high-projecting [*hochaufragend*], that is, above the water-line" (1986: 120; my trans.). My suggestion is along the same lines, although I take the epithet to refer to the extremities of the stem or stern rather than to the stem and stern themselves.

15. "νεῶν ὀρθοκραιράων," *Iliad* XVIII: 3 and XIX: 344 (Casson 1971: 45, 49); elsewhere in Homer this adjective is an epithet of cattle.

16. Nussbaum (1986: 9); see above, n. 11.

17. See above, nn. 9, 10.

18. *LSJ*[9], s.v. κεραΐς (noun), used of Medea at Lycophron, *Alexandra*, line 1317; Chantraine 1970: 517.

19. The repetition of this epithet in seemingly hollow formulae does not mean that it had no meaning to Homer, nor that it need be of great antiquity.

20. The word denotes "wreath" (cp. below), "final flourish of the pen," "end," and a curved accent mark (the "hook" used to mark crasis, which resembles an

apostrophe mark). For references, beginning with Stesichorus, see *LSJ⁹*, s.v. II.

21. However, a distinction may have to be made between the Indo-European roots for "curved" and "round, crowning," which for convenience I have listed together in column B, above.

22. *OLD*, s.v. That is, semantically, it again combines roundness with the idea of termination, as a head or horn. *Corona* is said to have been borrowed directly from Greek, although the reason for this is not given (Ernout and Meillet 1967; Walde and Hofmann 1938). An exception in Latin is the word's architectural use for a straight crowning element, the cornice, where the sense of "crowning" dominates.

23. Stesichorus 187: 3 (Page 1962). In Welsh, *cor* means "circle" (*OLD*, s.v. "curvus").

24. For references, see above, n. 4.

25. "Crow" is an archaic English word for "doorknocker," after the medieval Latin *cornix* (*OED²*, s.v. "crow" [7]); similarly, Greek κόραξ (*LSJ⁹*, s.v. II.2).

26. κορωνιάω (verb) means "curve" in pseudo-Hesiod, *Scutum* 289 (a work of debated date); see *LSJ⁹*, s.v.

27. I wish to acknowledge the aid of the Thesaurus Linguae Graecae database of Greek texts (copyright TLG and the regents of the University of California).

Appendix: Additional Evidence

1. The sherd was found by the Leon Levy Expedition to Ashkelon. I thank Professor L. E. Stager for inviting me to publish this sherd and for his and Dr. Barbara Johnson's valuable comments. For a more detailed study of this sherd, see Wachsmann, in press E.

2. See, for example: (Minoan) Wachsmann 1987: pls. XLI–XLIII; (Mycenaean) Buchholz and Karageorghis 1973: 103 no. 1248f, 379 fig. 1248f; (Hittite) Gurney 1990: 24, 164. See also, Wachsmann 1987: 40 n. 81.

3. See above, Chap 7, n. 65.

4. Morrison and Williams 1968: pl. 8e; Basch 1987: 175 fig. 362, 193 fig. 411; Casson 1995A: fig 62.

5. Mazar 1985; Stager 1991: 9–18; 1995: 334–40.

6. Wreschner 1971.

7. Wreschner 1971: 218 fig. 1 no. 5, pl. 47: C.

8. Artzy 1991B; 1994.

9. Winkler 1939: 1–2, 7–9 and plan, sites 61–69; Winlock 1936: pl. I.

10. Basch 1994A.

11. Giddy 1987: 170–73.

12. Winlock 1936: 58.

Chapter 9: Shipwrecks

1. For a more detailed discussion of the cargoes of the Gelidonya and Uluburun wrecks, see below, pp. 303–307.

2. *Enalia* 1 (1990); Vichos, Tsouchlos, and Papa-

thanassopolous 1991; Papathanassopolous et al. 1992; Papathanassopolous, Vichos, and Lolos 1995; Parker 1992: 162 (no. 362); Saramandi and Moraïtou 1995. This excavation was directed by Dr. G. Papathanasopolous and Dr. Y. Vichos for the Hellenic Institute of Marine Archaeology.

3. Lolos 1991; 1995; Pennas and Vichos 1991; 1995; Pennas 1992; Lolos, Pennas, and Vichos 1995; Karageorghis 1993: 584–88. The site is currently under investigation by the Hellenic Institute of Marine Archaeology.

4. See below, p. 279.

5. Bass 1976; 1996: 54–59; Parker 1992: 402 (no. 1079); Margariti, in progress. The excavation was directed by Dr. G. F. Bass for the Institute of Nautical Archaeology.

6. Bass, Frey, and Pulak 1984: 272 fig. 1; Bass 1986: 270 ill. 1; Parker 1992: 439–40 (no. 1193).

7. Oxhide ingots received their name from the mistaken assumption that they had the value of an ox and that their strange shape represented the hide of an ox. Although this theory was abandoned long ago, the name remains (Seltman 1965: 7; *CG*: 69).

8. Pulak 1989: 8–9; 1990A: 12, 13 fig. 13; Bass 1996: 63.

9. Pulak 1991: 6–7; 1992: 8.

10. The excavation was directed by G. F. Bass and C. Pulak and is an Institute of Nautical Archaeology project.

11. On hull remains, see below, pp. 216–17.

12. Bass 1986: 293; Pulak 1988A: 33–34.

13. Weinstein, in Bass et al. 1989: 17–29.

14. The bronze globed pin, of a type usually dated to the end of the Mycenaean period, thus remains enigmatic in the context of the wreck (Pulak 1988A: 29 fig. 36, 34).

15. Pulak 1996A; in press; Kuniholm 1996; Kuholm et al. 1996. For an opposing view, see Renfrew 1996.

16. Mr. C. Pulak, in press. On the anchors and the *shofar*, see below, pp. 281, 283, 306.

17. Pulak 1992: 10 figs. 10–11; 1995: 53 Abb. 23.

18. Clamer 1980; *Israel Museum*: 118–20.

19. See above, p. 40.

20. See above, p. 128, 195. Yet a fourth possibility is that the figurine may have represented the wife or daughter of the ruler, as mentioned in the Amarna tablets (Bass, in press; Pulak, in press: n. 10). In that case it would represent an item of royal gift exchange.

21. Hornell 1943A; 1945. In Classical times the station of the tutelary deity was at the stern (Svoronos 1914: 98–101; Casson 1995A: 181–82, 347–48 figs. 146, 151.

22. Hornell 1945: 25.

23. Virolleaud 1931: 195, 199–201; Schaeffer 1939: 62–63; *KTU* 1.3; Caquot, Sznycer, and Herdner 1974: 68–73, 172–73, 176–78, 182–83, 188, 193–94, 199, 201–207, 227, 256–57, 319, 322, 324, 327, 359, 360–61, 363, 486, 529, 530, 539, and 542.

24. Schaeffer 1939: 62 pl. 32. Note, however, that some of

these were found crumpled and were being carried for remelting. It is not clear if the others were personal possessions or items of trade. See below, p. 306.

25. CG; Parker 1992: 108–109 (no. 208); Bass 1996: 25–35 and the additional bibliography there. On the discovery of the Gelidonya wreck, see Throckmorton 1960, 1962, 1967, 1987A.

26. See below, p. 217.

27. Bass 1967: 164.

28. Frost 1968: 424; Basch 1972: 51–52; Catling 1969: 85; McCann 1970.

29. Bass 1973: 36–37; 1991: 69.

30. Cadogan 1969: 188; Muhly 1970: 43 n. 180. See above, p. 39.

31. Ralph 1967.

32. Bass 1967: 120; 1991: 71–72.

33. Catling 1964: 292–94. Bass (1973: 35 n. 46 and additional bibliography; 1991: 71–73) accepts the possibility of a twelfth-century dating for the wreck, although he considers it unlikely.

34. Bass 1988: 4–5; Pulak 1988B: 13.

35. Hennessy and du Plat Taylor 1967.

36. Pulak 1988B: 13; Bass 1990A: 12.

37. The scarabs found on the wreck date to the thirteenth century (Nineteenth Dynasty), according to B. Brandle. In his opinion, there is a strong probability that the scarabs were made on the coastal region of Canaan and that the five scarabs formed a set. (B. Brandle, personal communication.)

38. See below, pp. 283, 285.

39. Wachsmann and Raveh 1981; in press; Parker 1992: 209 (no. 494).

40. Misch-Brandl, Galili, and Wachsmann 1985: 7, 9–10 pls. 1.1–1.2 and 6 (nos. 1–2, 5, 6); Wachsmann, in press A; in press B.

41. Misch-Brandl, Galili, and Wachsmann 1985: 9 and pl. 1 (no. 1); Wachsmann and Raveh 1984A; Wachsmann in press A.

42. Misch-Brandl, Galili, and Wachsmann 1985: 9 and pl. 1 (nos. 3–7); Raban and Galili 1985: 327–28 fig. 9.

43. Galili and Shmueli 1983; Misch-Brandl, Galili, and Wachsmann 1985: 9–10 pls. 2 and 3.3 (nos. 2, 3.3); Galili, Shmueli, and Artzy 1986; Parker 1992: 211–12 (no. 503).

44. Galili, Shmueli, and Artzy 1986: 27 fig. 2, 34–35.

45. Bass 1986: 273 fig. 3, 274; 1987: 695–96, 705, 707, 722; Pulak 1988A: 6; 1988B: 12. On the Uluburun anchors and possible reasons for the many groups of stone anchors found in the breaker zone, see below, pp. 281, 283, 293.

46. Misch-Brandl, Galili, and Wachsmann 1985: 8–10 (nos. 1.3–1.7, 3.1–3.2, 4; Raban and Galili 1985: 326–29; Parker 1992: 225 (no. 540).

47. Jonah 1: 4–5; Acts 27: 18; Throckmorton 1987B; Wachsmann and Raveh 1984A: 174. Compare the Rhodian Sea Law 3: 9, 22, 38, 43 (Ashburner 1909: cclii–ccliii, cclviii, 87, 102–103, 112, 116).

48. Parker 1976: 347; 1992: 312 (no. 816).

49. CG: 61 nos. 18–20, 56–74; 1986: 270–72 n. 7–8 and ill. 1; Pulak and Frey 1985: 19; Throckmorton 1987A: 32; Parker 1992: 54–55 (no. 42), 226–27 (no. 544).

50. Tantura Lagoon: Wachsmann 1995C: 6; Sibella 1995A: 13 fig. 1; 1995C: 13. Beit Yannai: Porat, Dar, and Appelbaum 1985: 256–57 figs. 137–38.

51. Galili 1985; 1987; Frost 1986B; Parker 1992: 288 (no. 741).

52. See below, pp. 272, 285–86.

53. Basch 1972: 50–52.

54. Bass 1991: 70–71.

55. See below, p. 307.

56. Casson 1995A: 344–45.

57. Jenkins 1980: 87–88 ills. 62–63; Johnstone 1981.

58. Bass 1986: 296; 1987: 722, 726; Pulak 1991: 8–9; 1992: 11; in press.

59. Jonah I: 4–6.

60. Jonah I: 3.

61. EA 35: 8–9, 16–17, 40–41.

62. See pp. 48, 295–96, 324.

63. See pp. 12–14, 128–30, 164, 313, 343.

64. See pp. 62, 276.

65. See below, Chap. 12.

Chapter 10: Ship Construction

1. Sayed 1980: 156–57 fig. 3, pl. 22: 5. The Red Sea site of Wadi Gawasis served as a port for trips to Punt during the Middle Kingdom (Sayed 1977; 1978; 1980; 1983). On the Wadi Gawasis stone anchors, see below, pp. 259–60, 286.

2. Sayed 1983: 36.

3. Haldane 1984: 13, 23, 56. Shallow (5 centimeters deep) mortise-and-tenon joints were used to connect individual planks of the strakes on the Pittsburgh boat (Haldane 1984: 50). The original tenons on the Dashur ships were probably 22–25 centimeters long by 7.5 centimeters wide and 1.8 centimeters thick along planking seams, while about half that size at the ends (Haldane 1993A: 218). The depth of mortises on Classical wrecks varies between 3 and 10 centimeters (Casson 1995A: 214–16).

4. Lipke 1984: 64. See also Haldane 1993A: 99–102.

5. Compare Haldane 1992A: pls. 118–19, 121, 123.

6. Pulak 1987: 129–31 ill. 73; 1988B: 14; Bass 1986: 275; 1987: 733; 1989B; 1996: 71.

7. Pulak 1990A: 9 fig. 2, 10; 1995: 53 Abb. 24; Steffy 1994: 36–37; Bass 1996: 71.

8. Bass et al. 1989: 12.

9. Pulak 1990A: 10; 1990B: 52.

10. Pulak 1993: cover, 4–5, 7, 8 figs. 4–5, 10–11; 1994: 9, 11, 12 figs. 7–9, 13; in press; Fitzgerald 1996: 9. Concerning the lack of evidence for frames at Uluburun, Pulak also notes that two Archaic period vessels, from Playa de la Isla (Mazarrón, Spain) and Marseilles (France) seem to have frames more widely

spaced than was typical of Mediterranean ships in later times. See Negueruela, et al. 1995: 196 figs. 11–12.

11. A single repair in one of the Lisht timbers has a peg that transfixes a tenon. See below, p. 220. Surprisingly, the most recent studies of the scant Uluburun hull remains, made after they were raised from the seabed, indicate that the tenons were chiseled remarkably deep (Fitzgerald 1996: 8–9). At times they are only 1.5 to 2 centimeters short of breaking through the opposite side of the plank. Another interesting characteristic of this hull is that tenons carved into a plank from opposite edges are consistently placed so close to each other that often one is cut by the other. This resulted in rectangular hollows 13–15 centimeters long and 1.5–2 centimeters thick over most of the length of the surviving hull.

   This system of placing pairs of mortise-and-tenon joints next to each other up the hull appears with regularity, spaced center-to-center about every 25 centimeters. This would seem to have weakened the structural integrity of the hull. Indeed, the reason for this system remains enigmatic. It has been hypothesized that this pattern facilitated keeping a specific standard distance between joints or, alternately, that the mortise-and-tenon joints represent a form of "exoskeleton" of "internal" frames.

12. Pulak 1989: 6; 1990A: 9–10.
13. Pulak 1989: 9; 1992: 5 fig. 1.
14. Pulak 1992: 11 fig. 12; 1995: 54 Abb. 25.
15. Pulak 1991: 8; 1992: 11.
16. See above, p. 41. Concerning merchant galleys, see Casson 1995B.
17. Pulak 1991: 5.
18. *CG*: 48–51.
19. *CG*: 48 fig. 46, 50–51 fig. 51 (Wd 3, 4).
20. Haldane 1993A: 94–95.
21. Haldane 1992A: 107; 1993A: 183–84, 256 n. 6, 258. See above, pp. 14–15. Only one example of a pegged mortise-and-tenon joint is known from pharaonic Egypt hull remains. See below, p. 220.
22. O'Connor 1991; Haldane 1992B; 1993A: 78–82.
23. Petrie, Wainwright, and Gardiner 1913: 24–25 pl. 9: 1–7; Vinson 1987: 39–81; Haldane 1993A: 58–71.
24. Frankfort 1941: 343.
25. Vinson 1987: 79, 81.
26. Haldane 1993A: 66–68.
27. Saad 1947: 111, pls. 40, 59; 1951: 41–42, pls. 59a–59b, 60, plans 16–18; 1969: 23, 74–75 pls. 105–108.
28. Emery 1954: 138 pls. 44–45.
29. For an overview, see Vinson 1987: 193–210.
30. On these and other Old Kingdom boat graves, including graves carved out of the rock or built out of brick in the shape of hulls, see Hassan 1946: 38–41, 56–69, 79–82; Edwards 1972: 133, 147–48, 164, 188–89; Jenkins 1980: 22, 26–28 figs. 14–15; Haldane 1993A: 132–57.

31. Nour et al. 1960; Landström 1970: 26–34; Jenkins 1980; Steffy 1994: 23–29.
32. Lipke 1984.
33. Jenkins 1980; Lipke 1984; Haldane 1993A: 89–118.
34. Recent research on the identification of timber used in the construction of Egyptian wooden coffins in the British Museum illustrates the wide variety of foreign timbers imported into the Nile Valley during Pharaonic times (Davies 1995). Cedar, however, was found to be the most commonly imported timber. Sidder, also known as jujube or Christ-thorn (*Ziziphus spina-christi*), was used much later in the stern part of the Galilee boat's keel (Werker 1990: 67, 69, 71 figs. 8.18–8.21; Steffy 1990: 30, 37; Wachsmann 1995A: 252).
35. See below, p. 254.
36. El Baz 1988; Miller 1988; Haldane 1993A: 119–30.
37. Haldane 1988A; 1992A; 1993A: 158–94.
38. Haldane 1993A: 171 fig. 8–10. In a scene of ship-building from the tomb of Niankh-khnum and Khnumhotep, a workman is carving what appears to be a short plank with a joggled edge (Moussa and Altenmüller 1977: Abb. 8.)
39. Haldane 1988A: 144 fig. 3; 1992A: 105 fig. 20; 1993A: 172–73 figs. 8–11.
40. Haldane 1990A: 135 fig. 1; 1993A: 172, 174 fig. 8–12, 175.
41. Haldane 1988A: 144 fig. 4; 1992A: 105 fig. 21.
42. Haldane 1992A: 105, 111 pl. 129; 1993A: 175 fig. 8–13.
43. Haldane 1988A: 147–48 figs. 6–7; 1992A: 106 pls. 106, 115c, 133; 1993A: 177–81, 184–89. Haldane identifies four additional "upper" timbers among the Lisht timbers.
44. Haldane 1992A: 106; 1993A: 185, 188 fig. 8–20. For the Meir models, see Belger 1895: 26 figs. 2–4; Reisner 1913: 1–7 nos. 4798–4801.
45. Lythgoe 1915: 147 fig. 2; Hayes 1953: 271; Johnson 1980A: 13 n. 30; Haldane 1992A: 106–107, 112 pl. 117; 1993A: 195–201.
46. de Morgan 1895: 81–83 pls. 29–30; Reisner 1913: 83–87 nos. 4925–26; Landström 1970: 90–93; Haldane 1984A; 1984B; 1993A: 202–39; Patch and Haldane 1990; Steffy 1994: 32–36.
47. Landström 1970: 90. See also Reisner 1913: 86–87.
48. Haldane 1993A: 229–33.
49. Haldane 1984A: 98–101; Patch and Haldane 1990: 41–42 fig. 24.
50. Patch and Haldane 1990: 40.
51. Ibid. 1990: 30.
52. Haldane 1992A: 103; 1993A: 240–49; Haldane and Haldane 1990: 23–24.
53. Haldane 1993A: 243 fig. 11–3, 244 fig. 11–4.
54. Simpson 1965.
55. Glanville 1931; 1932.
56. Glanville 1931: 109.
57. See above, pp. 10, 51–52.
58. Glanville 1931: 114.

59. Glanville 1932: 20 n. 43.

60. Clowes was a curator of the Science Museum, South Kensington. This museum contains an important collection of ship models that Clowes (1932) published.

61. Glanville 1932: 31–32. Italics added.

62. Glanville (1932: 33) notes of Clowes's conclusions, "One would be inclined to accept Mr. Laird Clowes' interpretation of the different parts of the boat without further question were it not for the difficulty of getting the meaning he requires out of *wnḫ*."

63. The *Tantura A* Shipwreck, dating to about the mid-fifth to mid-sixth centuries A.D., is presently the earliest recorded vessel from the Mediterranean Sea to have been constructed, at least up to the turn of the bilge, without mortise-and-tenon joints, and in a "frame-based" manner. On this shipwreck, see Wachsmann 1995C; 1995D; 1996B; Kahanov and Breitstein 1995A; 1995B; Sibella 1995A; 1995B; 1995C; Charlton 1995.

64. Glanville 1932: 10 n. 6; Jones 1988: 159 no. 34.

65. Glanville 1932: 31–32.

66. Caminos 1954: 163–64.

67. See below, *KTU* 4.338, pp. 337–38.

68. Virolleaud 1965: 130.

69. Caminos 1954: 159–60; Anastasi IV: 7: 9–8: 7.

70. Glanville 1932: 8 n. 1. On the reuse of ship timber in Egypt, see Haldane 1993A: 254–56.

71. A similar situation of wood starvation appears to have existed along the shores of the Sea of Galilee in the first centuries B.C.–A.D. (Steffy 1990: 37; Wachsmann 1995A: 141–47).

72. Herodotus II: 96. Translation from Casson 1995A: 14 n. 15. This part of the text is also known from a papyrus (Hunt 1911: 180 text 55).

73. Casson 1995A: 14–15 n. 15.

74. Wachsmann 1989: 188–89; Haldane 1990A; 1992A: 108; 1993A: 189; Haldane and Shelmerdine 1990.

75. Casson 1992A: 557 n. 17.

76. Porten 1968: 34.

77. This translation from Porten 1996: 115–22 (B11). For previous translations, see Cowley 1923: 88–97; Porten and Yardeni 1986: 99, 101.

78. Three Persian karsh weights have been found in Egypt. Their weight was established as 83.33–83.36 grams (Porten 1968: 66). Thus, about fifteen kilograms of linen cloth are required for the repair.

79. Casson 1990.

80. See above, pp. 206, 208, 211–12.

81. On shipbuilders (*ḥrš anyt*) in Ugarit, see Gordon 1956: 143; Rainey 1967: 84 n. 23.

82. *Diodorus Siculus* XVII: 46: 1.

83. Katzenstein 1973: 24.

84. *Hist. Nat.* VII: 209.

85. Exodus 26: 15–17, 19.

86. Levine 1969: 22–24.

87. Johnstone 1977.

88. Ezekiel 27: 5–6.

89. Feliks 1968: 79–81; Hareuveni 1984: 94, 121–22, 125–26.

90. Feliks 1968: 84–87; Hareuveni 1984: 94, 121, 125.

91. Ezekiel 27: 9. The term appears again in verse 27.

92. Nahum 2: 2.

93. II Kings 12: 6, 8.

94. Ventris and Chadwick 1973: 123, 298–99, 562; Lindgren 1973 (I): 175, (II): 100; Palaima 1991A: 287–88.

95. Killen and Olivier 1989: 322–U736; Palaima 1991A: 295–96.

96. Ventris and Chadwick 1973: 349; Chadwick 1973A: 503–505; Palmer 1963: 366–67; Bennett and Olivier 1973: 254, 256.

97. Van Effentere 1970.

98. Ibid.: 45–46.

99. Palaima 1991A: 296–301; 1991B; Hocker and Palaima 1990–91.

100. Casson 1995A: 46 n. 21; Meiggs 1985: 111–12.

101. Casson 1995A: 217–19. More recently, Marks (1991; 1996) has argued that Odysseus built his ship with lashed construction. Casson (1992B) objects to this interpretation.

102. Casson 1995A: 10 n. 27.

103. *Odyssey* IX: 382–88.

104. Lacau 1904.

105. Davies 1900: 30 pl. 13: 278.

106. Haldane 1992A: 105; 1993A: 50–51.

107. Edgerton 1922–23: 120.

108. Indonesian *prahus* still have their planks edge-joined with large wooden dowels (Horridge 1982: 10 fig. 5).

109. For a comprehensive listing of ship construction scenes in Egypt, see Vandier 1969: 660–88.

110. Mekhitarian 1978: 42.

111. Moussa and Altenmüller 1971: 27 pls. 18–19, 23.

112. See below, pp. 242–43.

113. Severin 1982: 56; italics added.

114. Boreux 1925: 250 fig. 75; Vandier 1969: 88 fig. 60.

115. Petrie 1892: 23; Vandier 1969: 664–66.

116. Petrie 1892: 26–27; Vandier 1969: 666.

117. Steindorff 1913: Tafs. 119–21; Landström 1970: 38–39 fig. 102; Jenkins 1980: 126–27 fig. 102; El Baz 1988: 538–39; Steffy 1994: 29–31, 33.

118. Hornell 1970: 48.

119. Landström 1970: 38.

120. For a model of such a vise, see Winlock 1955: 33 pls. 28–29, 68.

121. A carpenter is also depicted cutting mortises in a piece of wood in another scene from the tomb of Tí (Steindorff 1913: Taf. 133).

122. Duel et al. 1938: pl. 152; Rogers 1992: 10–11, 13; 1996: 40–52; Haldane 1993A: 55–56.

123. Compare this figure to the photo of a modern Egyptian shipwright in Miller 1988: 539.

124. Clarke (1920: 8) assumes that Khnumhotep's craft lacked an internal framework of vertical frames because there were none visible above the planking.

125. Edgerton 1922–23: 129; Landström 1970: 91; Haldane 1988A: 151.
126. Wreszinski I: 55. On the similarities and differences in the wall paintings of the two tombs, see Davies 1902 (I): 20–21, 36–40; Wachsmann 1987: 25–26.
127. Compare also Vandier 1969: 681 fig. 271: 2; Moussa and Altenmüller 1977: Abb. 8.
128. Bruyère 1933: 75; Vandier 1969: 683–84.
129. Wachsmann 1987: 18, 78 pl. 9: A–B.
130. Haldane 1992A: 107; 1993A: 184, 246.
131. Professor J. R. Steffy, personal communication.
132. The scene is described by Davies (1927: 70) and Klebs (1934: 193). For photographs, see Wreszinski I: 368–69.
133. Faulkner 1940: 9.
134. Newberry 1942.
135. For listing, see Jones 1988: 148–49 no. 79.
136. Sayed 1977: 170.
137. Sayed 1978: 71 n. 7.
138. Säve-Söderbergh 1946: 11–13; Kitchen 1971: 189–93.
139. *BAR* I: §429–33.
140. Apparently Henu built and outfitted the ship for the expedition to Punt but did not take part in the sea trip (*BAR* I: §433 n. c).
141. *BAR* I: §605.
142. *BAR* IV: §407. Concerning Ramses III's nautical expedition to the land of Atika, see above, p. 11.
143. This refers to the Indian Ocean, including the Red Sea (*BAR* IV: §407: c). See also Kitchen 1971: 189–90 n. 23.
144. For sources, see Newberry 1942: 64.
145. *ANET*³: 240.
146. To judge from Ovid's description of a shipwreck, even pegged mortise-and-tenon joinery could work loose during severe storms in the open sea (Casson 1995A: 202 n. 7).
147. Jenkins 1980: 55 fig. 31, 58 fig. 32, 71 figs. 42–43; El Baz 1988.
148. Basch 1972: 23–29.
149. Edgerton 1922–23: 135.
150. Severin 1982: 55; italics added.
151. Hornell 1970: 193 fig. 29: A–B, 217.
152. Severin 1982: 68.
153. Bon Porté I: Basch 1981A. Concerning this wreck, see also Liou 1974; Basch 1976C; 1981B; Joncheray 1976; Jestin and Carrazé 1980; Pomey 1981; Steffy 1994: 39–40, fig. 3–20. Giglio: Bound 1985: 51–61; 1991: 31–34; 1995: 65 Abb. 7, 67. Gela: Freschi 1989: 207–208. On the Maagan Michael Shipwreck similar ligatures, sewn through triangular holes, were used with pegged mortise-and-tenon joints to attach planks at the stem and the stern (Kahanov 1991: 7; Linder 1992: 31; Steffy 1994: 40–42, fig. 3–21a).
154. Hornell 1970: 192–93.
155. Coates 1985: 17.
156. Severin 1982: 56.
157. The pegs locking mortise-and-tenon joints on ancient Mediterranean ships were normally driven from inside the hull. Notable exceptions to this general rule were those pegs located in areas of the hull in which it would have been difficult—if not impossible—to swing a mallet as, for example, at the posts, or along the keel/garboard seams (Steffy 1985: 81; 1990: 33; 1994: 48, 56, 65). Steffy estimates that, on average, only about ten percent of the joint pegs were driven from outside the hull (Professor J. R. Steffy, personal communication).
158. Professor J. R. Steffy, personal communication.
159. See above, pp. 51–52.
160. On the wood joinery found in this tomb, see Ricketts 1960.
161. Sleeswyk 1980; Basch 1981B: 249.
162. See above, pp. 23–24.
163. Landström 1970: 107.
164. See above, pp. 52–53.
165. This is undoubtedly the case with a second terra-cotta model from Byblos that authentically copies another type of Egyptian Nile traveling ship, which could only have crossed the Mediterranean in the form of a model (Fig. 3.19). See above, pp. 53–54.
166. Landström 1970: 107.
167. See below, pp. 245–46.
168. Hornell (1938B) reports that the outrigger-*nuggars* of the Blue Nile have a large keel that is nearly flush with the exterior of the hull. Since this particularly broad hull type is specially adapted to shallow waters, it is likely that the keel protrudes inside the hull to prevent it from getting caught on sandbanks. Perhaps when the ancient Egyptians finally adopted the keel for use on their vessels, they positioned it amidships primarily protruding into the hull for the same reason. This reasoning would not explain the use of an internal keel on the ships of other cultures from the Mediterranean Bronze Age, however.
169. See above, p. 63.
170. Dakoronia, 1996: 159, 165 figs. 1–2, 166 figs. 3–4, 167 pl. I. I thank Dr. Dakoronia for making available a photograph of this model prior to its publication.
171. Basch (1987: 141 fig. 293: 1) considers at least one of these internal elements to be a keelson ("carlingue").
172. Severin 1985: 282 fig. 17.1.
173. Servin 1948: 64–65 fig. 9. For a photograph of this scene, see Davies 1900: pl. 25: a.
174. Morgan 1988: 129.
175. Shaw 1973: 157–85.
176. Marinatos 1974: 23 pl. 41: a–c.
177. Marinatos 1976: 17 pl. 24: a.
178. Marinatos 1971: 41–42 pls. 34: b, 35–37, 104–105. For an illustration of a modern reconstruction of the bed, see Doumas 1989: 59 fig. 39.
179. Mycenaean architecture also employed half-timbering, but in a somewhat different manner than in Minoan construction (Wright 1984: 27 n. 4; 1996). Timbers were secured to ashlar by means of mortises

cut in the stone to take wooden tenons or dowels (Wright 1984: pls. 8–9).

180. *PM* II: 629 fig. 394: 5, 630 fig. 393: d, i, j, 632; Platon 1971: 113, 128–29, 157–58; Wells 1974.

Appendix: Did Hatshepsut's Punt Ships Have Keels?

1. See above, pp. 216–17.
2. Haldane 1993A: 207; C. W. Haldane, personal communication.

Chapter 11: Propulsion

1. Note particularly tests carried out on the Japanese tanker *Shin Aitoku Maru* and Cousteau's *Alcyone* (*Time*, Oct. 20, 1980: 54; Jan. 7, 1985: 49).
2. See above, pp. 106–108; Landström 1970: 58 fig. 171; Wachsmann 1995B: 10–20.
3. Ballard 1920: 165. In one ship the oarsmen may be seen backing water (Figs. 2.16, 2.24; Faulkner 1940: 9).
4. Jarrett-Bell 1930.
5. See also Sølver 1936: 460–61.
6. See above, p. 29.
7. Landström 1970: 69.
8. Ibid.: 69 fig. 202; Goedicke 1971: 87.
9. Naville 1901: pls. 88–89.
10. Le Baron Bowen 1960A: 119–20.
11. Frankfort 1924: pl. 13; Casson 1964: ill. 15; 1995A: 12 fig. 6.
12. Borchardt 1913: 147 fig. 17; Greenhill 1966: 17 figs. 14–15, 27 fig. 21; Wachsmann 1985A.
13. Swiney and Katzev 1973: 351; Steffy 1985: 86–87; Eiseman and Ridgeway 1987: 16–17; Pulak and Townsend 1987: 38–39 fig. 7.
14. Casson 1995A: 21.
15. Faulkner 1940: 8 fig. 2; Vandier 1969: 932–33. A hogging truss was also used on Hatshepsut's obelisk barge, but, unfortunately, the upper part of the truss is missing. The determinative for an obelisk barge in the accompanying text does not indicate how the hogging trusses were tightened (Naville 1908: pl. 154).
16. Goedicke 1971: 107, 111, 113.
17. Naville and Hall 1913: 23.
18. Vandier 1969: 926, 991.
19. Kitchen 1973: 251–52; *SKHC*: xiv. Vinson (1993) notes several additional New Kingdom ship depictions that appear to depict brailed sails, some of which still retain the boom but have the sail furled to the yard.
20. Casson 1995A: 37–38.
21. Barnett 1958: 226.
22. Davies 1943: pls. 61, 68, 94; Landström 1970: 99 fig. 316, 101 fig. 319; Mekhitarian 1978: 80.
23. On the problem of the use of copybooks vis-à-vis Egyptian tomb painting (and in particular the ships on the Iniwia relief), see above, pp. 54–60.
24. Säve-Söderbergh 1946: 1–2.

25. Compare Landström 1970: 138 fig. 405.
26. See above, p. 140; Ezekiel 27: 7. Theophrastus (*Enquiry into Plants*, 4.8.4) and Pliny (*Natural History*, 13.22.72) refer to sails made of papyrus. For additional classical references, see Casson 1995A: 48 n. 41, 234 n. 43.
27. Pliny, *Natural History*, 19.3.16–19.3.18. See Winlock's (1955: 29–33 pls. 25–27, 66–67) description of the model of a shop in which linen is being prepared from flax, found in the Twelfth Dynasty tomb of Meket-rēᶜ.
28. McWilliams 1992.
29. Black and Samuel 1991: 224–25.
30. Rougé 1987; Schoefer, Cotta, and Beentjes 1987; Valansot 1987: 81, 83–84, 90; James 1988; Black and Samuel 1991: 220.
31. Benoit 1961: 178 fig. 94, pl. 30; Gianfrotta and Pomey 1980: 287–88.
32. Catling 1964: 262.
33. Ballard 1920: 169–70; Sølver 1936: 460.
34. Le Baron Bowen 1960A: 129; Casson 1995A: 273–74.
35. Katzev 1989: 8, 10; 1990: 254.
36. The *Kyrenia II* averaged a little less than three knots on both legs of a voyage from Greece to Cyprus and back (Katzev 1989: 4, 10; 1990: 245, 255). See Casson 1995A: 281–99.
37. Campbell 1964: 67; *EA* 81: 25–33, 41–47; 82: 41–46.
38. See Fitzgerald 1994: 211–14; Charleton 1996.
39. Shick 1988: 32 figs. 1–2, pl. 13: 2–3.
40. Compare Jones 1990: pl. 36: K.
41. I thank Mr. W. H. Charlton and Mr. M. Fitzgerald for much of the following information.
42. *Phoenix dactylifera*: rope from Hellenistic stone anchors found on the west shore of the Dead Sea (Hadas 1992; Shimony, Yucha, and Werker 1992). Pliny (*Natural History*, 13.7.30, 16.37.89) describes the use of date palm leaves for rope making.
43. *Hyphaena thebaica*: Cape Gelidonya shipwreck (du Plat Taylor 1967B: 160–62). This palm is not found north of Egypt or Sinai, indicating that the rope (or at least the raw materials used in making it) must have originated in that area.
44. *Stipa tenacissima*: Punic shipwreck at Marsala, on the Nemi ships, the Roman period wreck at Caesarea, and for the cordage used to fasten the hull of the first-century B.C. Commachio wreck (*Lilybaeum*: 93–97; Ucelli 1950: 268, 431 no. 440; Fitzgerald 1994: 211–14). For references by Classical authors to esparto grass used for cordage, see Casson 1995A: 231 n. 28.
45. *Linum usitatissimum*: Casson 1995A: 231 n. 27. Also, Varro (*On Farming*, 1.23.6) refers to flax in rope making.
46. *Phragmites communis*, var. *isiacus*: Cape Gelidonya; see above, Doum palm.
47. *Desmostachya bipinnata*: Cheops ship (Nour et al. 1960: 42, 44 pls. 32: B, 38: B, 41: A, 63: A–B, 64–65).
48. *Cannabis sativa*: Nemi ships (Ucelli 1950: 268); Casson 1995A: 231 n. 26.

49. *Cyperus papyrus*: Pliny, *Natural History*, 13.22.72; Casson 1995A: 231 n. 25.

50. Reisner 1913: 28 figs. 111–14, 29 figs. 116–17, 55 figs. 196–98, 59 fig. 210, 60 figs. 212–13, 65 fig. 232, 94 fig. 344; Jones 1990: pls. 13 (obj. 352), 23, 25, 33, 36.

51. Concerning the "internal keel," see above, pp. 241–46.

Chapter 12: Anchors

1. Frost 1963A; 1963B: 42–61.

2. Frost 1969B: 428; 1979: 138.

3. Frost 1973: 399.

4. Frost 1966: 55.

5. Frost 1963A: 7–10; 1963B: 50–51 and elsewhere.

6. Frost 1982B: 269.

7. *ANET*[3]: 91–92.

8. Frost 1984B.

9. Heltzer 1982: 189 nos. 9, 12. See below, *KTU* 4.689, pp. 339–40.

10. Herodotus II: 96.

11. Frost 1964; 1979: 139 pl. 1; Basch 1987: 47–48 figs. 72–74.

12. Galili 1985: 149.

13. Wachsmann and Raveh 1980: 258 figs. 4–5, 260. This shape apparently had a very long life, continuing at least well into the first millennium B.C. During its 1995 season of excavation, the INA/CMS Joint Expedition to Tantura Lagoon uncovered several stone anchors in the immediate vicinity of the *Tantura A* shipwreck. One of these anchors, which weighed 83.5 kilograms, had an asymmetrical appearance. It was found to be lying *on* Persian period ceramics, and thus cannot predate that horizon.

14. Frost 1982A: 162.

15. Frost 1989; 1995. Interestingly, pulleys are not depicted in these scenes, although they were certainly known when these ships were painted. A bas-relief of Ashur-nasirpal II (884–860/859 B.C.) clearly shows a pulley being used to raise a bucket, presumably of water, into a town besieged by the Assyrians (Gadd 1936: 144, pl. 4; Albenda 1972).

16. Frost 1979: 138–39; Basch 1985B: 466–67.

17. Casson 1995A: fig. 19.

18. Frost 1979: 138–40; Basch 1985B: 457–65; 1994B. Nibbi (1984: 247–53; 1992) argues for the use of stone anchors on the Nile.

19. Le Baron Bowen 1963.

20. Davies 1902 (II): 9.

21. Reisner 1913: 1 fig. 4, 27 fig. 107, pl. 30 (no. 4835).

22. Boreux 1925: 415 fig. 176; Vandier 1969: 762 fig. 297: 1.

23. Basch 1985B: 463 fig. 14.

24. Davies and Gardiner 1915: pl. 12; Mekhitarian 1978: 80.

25. Casson 1995A: 257–58.

26. Frost 1979: 141–47.

27. Borchardt 1907: 128–29 (Abb. 108).

28. Frost 1979: 143–47.

29. Frost 1969B: 430–31; Dunand 1950: pl. 14.

30. Frost 1969A: 241, 245 table 1: 11; 1991: 378–79 no. 9, pls. 4: 9, 5: 9a, 10; Schaeffer 1978: 372 fig. 2, 376 fig. 9, 380.

31. Sayed 1977: 150–69; 1978: 70–71 pl. 11: 1; 1980: 154–56 pls. 21: 2, 22: 1–2; Frost 1979: 147–51.

32. Frost 1979: 154; 1980.

33. Sayed 1980: 156; Frost 1979: 151.

34. Sayed 1978: 70–71; 1980: 156 pl. 22: 3–4; Frost 1979: 151–52.

35. Sayed 1980: 154 pl. 21: 1.

36. Nibbi 1992.

37. Bakr and Nibbi 1991.

38. Nibbi 1991; Frost 1993.

39. Conwell 1987; O'Connor 1987.

40. Nibbi 1993: 18–21; Bakr and Nibbi 1994.

41. Nibbi 1993: 19 fig. 22a.

42. Wachsmann 1986B.

43. The story behind the name is of some interest. Not knowing quite what to make of the stone, which at that time was unique, Bar Adon was reminded of a Yiddish folktale of a not-too-knowledgeable *melamed* (teacher) who was teaching the Bible to a class in a *cheder* (Jewish day school). They came to the sentence "Dan shall be a serpent in the way, a viper (*shfifon*) by the path, that bites the horse's heels so that his rider falls backwards" (Genesis 49:17). "What is a *shfifon*?" one of his more precocious pupils asked. Not knowing the answer but loath to show his ignorance, the teacher replied that it was obviously a *"meshugeneh* (crazy) fish." When asked why so, he replied that any fish that was "by the path" had to be crazy. Fish should be in the sea.

    The teacher of the story didn't know what a *shfifon* was, and Bar Adon, likewise, had no idea what the monolith was. He therefore called it a *shfifon*. In doing so, he coined a term that now refers to the entire group of these pierced stones and in its wider sense has entered the lexicon of Israeli archaeology to describe any unidentifiable artifact found during archaeological excavations and surveys.

44. The excavation was carried out by Dr. D. Bahat for the Israel Department of Antiquities and Museums.

45. Wachsmann 1986B: 546 fig. 5: D.

46. Nun 1977: 99–101.

47. Wachsmann 1990B.

48. Nun 1977: 93–97; 1993. See below, pp. 270–71.

49. Kochavi 1973; Wachsmann and Raveh 1980: 263 fig. 14.

50. Wachsmann 1986B: 549 fig. 8.

51. This was suggested to me by Mr. Uzi Avner. A second tomb built in the Middle Bronze Age I, lacking *shfifonim*, was subsequently excavated at Kibbutz Degania "A" (Yogev 1985).

52. For the chronology used here, see Mazar 1990: 108–10.

53. Hirschfeld 1992: 41–44; 1994.

54. Hebrews 6:19. The *shfifon* was found together with

the face of a saint painted on a fresco fragment dating to the eleventh to twelfth centuries A.D. (Ben-Arieh 1994).

55. For examples, see *SACI*.

56. Wachsmann and Raveh 1978: 282; 1980: 260, 258 figs. 4–5; 1984B: 239–40. In one case, a stratigraphic sequence of anchors was recorded on the seabed at Dor when the shank of a Byzantine iron anchor was found to be resting on a stone covering a pierced stone—either a stone anchor or a mooring stone. For additional photos of the anchor appearing in Fig. 12.20, see Figs. 12.3: C, 23).

57. Stieglitz 1972–75A; Ronen and Olami 1978: 27 no. 58: 2 and map (site 58). The anchors were found during a survey by the Undersea Exploration Society of Israel.

58. Frost 1979: 150; McCaslin 1980: 36–37 Figs. 22, 43; Basch 1985B: 453.

59. Nibbi 1984: 259.

60. Galili, Raveh, and Wachsmann 1982; Galili and Raveh 1988.

61. Note that the stone doorjambs of Jaffa's city gate are inscribed with the names and titles of Ramses II (Kaplan 1972: 79, 80 fig. 8, 81).

62. Raban and Galili 1985: 326–27; Galili, Sharvit, and Artzy 1994: 101, 105 fig. 20.

63. Hamilton 1935: 13. Concerning the date of Stratum V, see above, p. 48.

64. Balensi 1980 (I): 519.

65. Roger 1986: 5; *NEAEHL* 1: 14 (s.v. Abu Hawam, Tell).

66. Dr. J. Balensi, personal communication.

67. Professor M. Dothan, personal communication.

68. *SACI*; Elgavish 1968: 34–35 pls. 46, 16: 1.

69. Nun 1975; 1977: 96–97, 101; 1993: 12.

70. Fritsch and Ben-Dor 1961: 57, 54 fig. 9.

71. Wachsmann 1990A; 1995A: 335–37.

72. Stefanski 1989: 17 fig. 14.

73. MacGregor 1870: 341; Wachsmann 1995A: 340–41.

74. Schult 1966: Taf. 27: B.

75. Hadas 1989; 1989–90; 1992; 1993A. Concerning seafaring on the Dead Sea in antiquity, see Hadas 1993B. See above, Chap. 11, n. 42.

76. Frost 1969B.

77. Ibid.: pl. 3, figs. 23–28. The number six may have cultic significance. The Degania "A" tomb was built of six monoliths, two of which were *shfifonim*.

78. See below, pp. 273, 288.

79. See above, pp. 52–54.

80. Twenty-six stone anchors of "Byblian" shape have been recorded from along Israel's Mediterranean coast (Galili, Sharvit, and Artzy 1994). Of these, twenty-five were found along the Carmel coast. One anchor, from a matching pair found off Kfar Samir in the environs of Haifa, had an Egyptian-style L-shaped notch that had been chiseled out in antiquity, thus canceling its intended function (Galili, Sharvit, and Artzy 1994: 96 figs. 7–9). The reasons for this peculiarity remain enigmatic.

81. Ronen and Olami 1978: 10 and map (no. 21).

82. Frost 1966: 60.

83. Frost 1969A; 1991; Schaeffer 1978.

84. Frost 1991: 356, 375–82 pls. 1, 3, 6, 8.

85. Schaeffer 1978: 374 figs. 6–7.

86. Wachsmann and Raveh 1980: 258 fig. 4, 260.

87. Frost 1984A.

88. Frost 1970A: 14–17; Hult 1977; 1981: 42 no. F1254, 84 figs. 134–35, 89 fig. 140; Öbrink 1979: 19–20, 65 fig. 49, 71 figs. 94–95, 72 figs 102–102A; McCaslin 1978: 117–32, 137–38, figs. 265–83, 305–306; Envig and Åstrom 1975: figs. 15–16, 20, 33–34; Herscher and Nyquist 1975.

89. Green 1973: 166–68, 177.

90. Frost 1970A: 16 fig. 2, 17–19; 1982A, 1986C.

91. Frost 1986C: 282.

92. Frost 1970A: 22; 1986C: 287–88 pls. K–N.

93. Frost 1986C: 290–91.

94. Ibid.: 293.

95. Bass 1972: 32 fig. 25. Nikolaou and Catling 1968: pl. 24; Frost 1970A: pl. 6: 2–3; 1986C: 293, 297 fig. 7.

96. See above, p. 62.

97. Frost 1979: 144.

98. Gianfrotta and Pomey 1980: 299; Alpözen 1983: 63. On the anchors found on the Uluburun and Cape Gelidonya shipwrecks, see below, pp. 281, 283–85.

99. Haddon 1937: 297; van Nouhuys 1951; Campbell 1957; Wachsmann 1995A: 337, 339–40.

100. See above, p. 130.

101. Braemer and Marcadé 1953: 153 fig. 13, 154.

102. Pennas and Vichos 1991: 16. Concerning the site, see above, p. 205.

103. Papathanassopoulos et al. 1992: 15–21.

104. Frost 1963B: 46 pl. 8 (opp. p. 54); 1973: 400–401 no. 6; Pelon 1970: 141 pl. 7: 2; Poursat 1980.

105. Frost 1986C: 295.

106. *PM* IV: 650–53 fig. 635. For a color photo of the stone, see Sakellarakis 1979: 45 no. 26; Davaras 1980: 61–67.

107. Frost (1963B: 46) considers it an anchor.

108. Shaw and Blitzer 1983.

109. H. Blitzer, personal communication (1991).

110. Dr. J. Shaw, personal communication (1993). I thank Drs. Joseph and Maria Shaw for the information and illustrations and for their kind permission to incorporate it here. Dr. J. Shaw notes (1993) concerning H. Blitzer's attribution of the previous anchors as press weights that "while there is some ambiguity about use of some of the smaller pierced weights, the discovery of the two new anchors strengthens the case for S636, found on the hillside" (Fig. 12.46: D: a). For a thorough study of the anchors, see Shaw 1995.

111. Davaras 1980: 47–53.

112. Marinatos 1974: 19 pl. 29.

113. *AMM*: 82.

114. Maiuri 1923–24: 150 fig. 72; Buchholz and Karageorghis 1973: 49 no. 430.

115. Pulak 1990A: 12; 1991: 8–9 fig. 8; 1993: 4, 9 fig. 9, 10;

1995: 53 fig. 24, 54 fig. 26; Frey 1993–94: 21.

116. Bass 1987: 706–707; Pulak 1988B: 12.

117. Bass 1986: 271 ill. 2, 273 ill. 3; 1987: 705; Bass et al. 1989: 3 fig. 2; Pulak 1988A: 2 fig. 1; 1988B: 17 fig. 9; 1990A: 13 fig. 9.

118. Pulak 1991: 8.

119. The individual anchors weighed 121, 164, 171, 181.5, 204, and 207.9 kilograms respectively (Pulak 1992: 8, 9 fig. 6).

120. Pulak and Rogers 1994: 20, 21 fig. 7.

121. Paul describes lowering anchors to prevent a ship from running aground (Acts 27:29; see Throckmorton 1987B). One triangular pierced stone at Gelidonya was initially regarded as an anchor; however, in the end it was considered a natural stone (CG: 26, 45, 142).

122. Galili 1985; 1987; Frost 1986B.

123. Galili 1985: 146 table 1, 147.

124. Ibid.: 148 fig. 5.

125. Ibid.: 144 fig. 2, 150 fig. 6, 151–52.

126. Wadi Gawasis: Sayed 1980: pl. 22: 3; Naveh Yam: Fig. 12.29: 16; Uluburun: Fig. 14.1 (square N15).

127. Wallace 1964: 14.

128. This theory was suggested independently by Green (1973: 175).

129. Wallace 1964: 16.

130. Frost 1982B: 263–64. See also 1991: 369.

131. Casson 1995A: 252.

132. *Argonautica* I: 950; Frost 1966: 57; 1982A: 163–64.

133. Frost 1982A: 162, 166.

134. On holy anchors in the Classical period, see Svoronos 1914: 105–11; Davaras 1980: 54–58.

135. Bass 1989B: 25–26; Pulak 1988A: 33.

136. Sayed 1978: 71; 1980: 154.

137. Faulkner 1940: 9.

138. Frost 1986C: 291–93.

139. Frost 1963B: 43; 1969B: 434; Wachsmann and Raveh 1984A: 169–70 fig. 2; Wachsmann in press A.

140. Frost (1969B: 434) suggests an Ugaritic origin for this anchor.

141. Frost 1991: 370, 372.

142. Frost 1982B: 270–71 fig. 6.

143. Casson 1971: 252 n. 107, 255–56, 332–33.

144. Frost 1982A: 162.

145. Dickson 1959: 482: a.

146. Frost 1969A: 241. For additional anchors with square rope holes, see Figs. 12.33: 2, 6; 12.36: A: 2; 12.37: B, E; 12.38: F, I, N; 12.41; 12.44; 12.45: A; 12.46; 12.48; 12.52: A–B; 12.58.

147. Tusa 1973: 418 no. 11, figs. 14–15; Frost 1966: 61; 1986A: 362; Nibbi 1991.

148. See above, Chap. 11, n. 42.

149. Frost 1970A: 21–22.

150. Frost 1982A: 164–65; 1986C: 293–95; 1991: 358–67.

151. Frost 1982A: 165 fig. 3.

152. Frost 1986C: 294.

153. Wachsmann and Raveh 1980: 258 fig. 5, 260.

154. Frost 1986C: 288–89; 1991: 363, 376–77, 379–81, 383–84, 386.

Chapter 13: Navigation

1. Casson 1971: 270–73. Note, however, that Wenamun left Egypt for Byblos in early January and arrived there in early May of 1075 B.C. (Egberts 1991: 59–61, 67). Tjekkerbaal's messenger and gifts were sent to Egypt after his meeting with Wenamun in early June. The messenger returned in September or early October.

   Linear B text PY Tn 316 begins with the name of a month: *po-ro-wi-to-jo*. Palmer has suggested that the month was named *Plowistos* and meant "the month of sailing" (Palmer 1955: 10–12; 1963: 248, 254, 265; Bennett and Olivier 1973: 233; Chadwick 1976: 90, 179, 192). This apparently referred to a lunar month in the beginning of spring.

   A Midrash defines the sailing season as the period between the Jewish festivals of Shvuot and Sukkot; that is, roughly from May to September (Sperber 1986: 99–100). During the Middle Ages this nautical custom became statutory, and it became unlawful to sail outside of the sailing season (Ashburner 1909: cxlii–cxliii).

   Note, however, that a custom account from Egypt dating to 475 B.C., which was found palimpsest on the Ahiqar scroll from Elephantine, describes a relatively long sailing season stretching from February / March to November / December (Porten and Yardeni 1993: xx; Yardeni 1994: 69–70).

2. Main among these are (archaeological evidence): the ax head from the Adonis River, Egyptian anchors at Byblos and Ugarit; (textual evidence): Egyptian ships bringing wood, Thutmose III's organization of harbors, Amarna texts referring to Syro-Canaanite ships in Egypt, an Ugaritic text that mentions a ship wrecking while en route to Egypt (*KTU* 2.38), foreigners at Ugarit (Rainey 1967: 87–90), and Wenamun.

3. Beal 1992 and the additional bibliography there.

4. Wachsmann 1986A; 1987: 99–102. The following is a summary of these discussions.

5. *EA* 114: 49–53. Translation by Professor A. Rainey from Wachsmann 1986A: 101.

6. *EA* 114: n. 12.

7. *EA* 113: 35–44.

8. Holmes 1969: 159.

9. This was first suggested by Power (1929: 156).

10. See pp. 61–62, 338, 343–44.

11. See below, *KTU* 4.390, p. 339.

12. See above, pp. 273, 292; Schaeffer 1978: 379 fig. 12.

13. See above, p. 83.

14. See above, p. 83.

15. Vercoutter 1956: 417. See below, pp. 10, 308.

16. Heltzer 1988. See below, *RS* 16.238 + 254, p. 340.

17. See above, pp. 129–30.
18. Gelsinger 1972.
19. Bass 1986: 270–72 ill. 1.
20. Taylor 1957: 4.
21. See pp. 85–86, 307; Edel 1966: 33–60; Cline 1987; 1990; Wachsmann 1987: 95–99.
22. Merrillees 1972: 290.
23. This identification remains difficult and has been debated. It does not seem to fit in well with the rest of the list (Cline 1987: 3–4).
24. Redford (1982: 59–60) suggests that Eighteenth Dynasty toponym lists, and particularly that of Thutmose III at Karnak, were based on itineraries.
25. McGeehan Liritzis 1988: 243.
26. Wachsmann 1987: 121–22.
27. See above, p. 85.
28. Furumark 1950: 214, 223.
29. Casson 1995A: 272.
30. *ANET*³: 416.
31. Vercoutter 1956: 420–21.
32. Ibid.: (Thutmose III's Hymn of Victory) 51–53, (Rechmire) 56–57, (Tomb of Kenamun [T. 93] [?]) 81, (Abydos) 87–88, (Luxor) 91–92.
33. Bietak 1995.
34. The great Polynesian migrations followed the migratory paths of specific birds. The discovery of the Hawaiian Islands by Polynesians from Tahiti or the Society Islands probably resulted from the careful study of the migratory route of the golden plover. Hornell (1946: 144) notes, "The sailor-folk of the Society Islands would naturally reason that if birds could fly to this group from some distant land, they, in a large and well-found double-canoe could certainly sail to the land whence the birds came."
    Lewis (1975: 24) considers unintentional drift voyages, which took place continually in the Pacific, as a complementary category of inter-island discovery.
35. Evans 1925B; Pomerance 1975. In recent years, some scholars have argued for a direct route from Egypt to Crete in the Bronze Age (Watrous 1992: 177–78; Warren 1995: 10–11). In doing so, comparisons are made to similar voyages carried out in the seventeenth and eighteenth centuries A.D. Such comparisons, however, lack validity for Mediterranean ships of the recent past had hulls and sail systems specifically designed for sailing into the wind. This is a far cry from Bronze Age ships. These employed a single primitive boom-footed sail intended for sailing with stern winds and were built with hulls that, as we have seen, seem to show little concern for leeward drift (see above, pp. 216, 241–43, 245–46, 248–51, and Lambrou-Phillipson 1991: 13; Roberts 1995: 310).
36. *Odyssey* XIV: 252–58.
37. Ibid. XVII: 426.
38. Casson 1995A: 287 n. 75.
39. See below, p. 306.
40. Vercoutter 1956: 419–22 fig. 162; Bass 1987: 697–99; Pulak 1988A: 36–37.
41. White 1986A; Conwell 1987.
42. White 1986B: 76–79 figs. 26–34; 1990.
43. Casson 1950: 43–46; 1995A: 289 n. 91. The *Isis* reached Cyprus in seven days during a storm.
44. *LAE:* 51.
45. I Kings 9:27; II Chronicles 8:18. Ezekiel (27:8) also specifically mentions Tyrian pilots when comparing Tyre to a ship.
46. I Kings 22:48; II Chronicles 20:36–37.
47. When Lewis interviewed Oceanic navigators, he received answers in the stereotyped form in which they had originally been memorized. Any deviation from the original chain of memory caused the navigator to become confused. Lewis (1972: 11, 32) found that most of the highly trained navigators of modern Oceania were illiterate. See also Goodenough and Thomas 1987. On orientation in the ancient Near East, see Har-El 1981.
48. Lewis 1972: 2; 1976.
49. Hornell 1936: 373 fig. 267; Lewis 1972: 200 fig. 39, 203 fig. 40, 204 fig. 41.
50. Lewis 1972: 17.
51. Ibid.: 2.
52. Wachsmann 1987: 101–105, 122–25, 127–29.
53. Winlock 1955: pl. 33.
54. Pulak 1988A: 33 fig. 41. On later lead weights see Casson 1995A: 246 n. 85; Oleson 1988: 30–40 pl. 4 and the additional bibliography there.
55. On the use of birds in navigation, see Hornell 1946; Taylor 1957: 60–61, 72–74, 76–78, 246–47; Gatty 1958: 168–201; Hutchinson 1962: 101–102; Gladwin 1970: 180–81, 188, 195–200; Lewis 1972: 162–72; Tibbetts 1981: 246, 287–88, 443–44.
56. Genesis 8:6–12; *ANET*³: 94–95.
57. *OCSS*, s.v. "wind navigation."
58. *OCSS*, s.v. "wind rose."
59. Taylor 1957: 14–20, 37–38.
60. Weller 1913: 141–45 figs. 77–79; Taylor 1957: pl. 3.
61. Lewis 1972: 73–81.
62. See above, pp. 9–10.
63. Casson 1995A: 245 n. 83.
64. See below, p. 307.
65. Taylor 1957: 43; *OCSS*, s.v. "Navigation. Aratus of Soli."
66. Lewis 1972.
67. Ibid.: 1972: 45–82; Halpern 1985; Goodenough and Thomas 1987: 4–5; Irwin, Bickler, and Quirke 1990.
68. *LAE:* 51–52.
69. Psalms 48:7; Ezekiel 27:26.
70. *LAE:* 154. Wenamun probably departed from Byblos in April, 1074 B.C. (Egberts 1991: 62–67).
71. *War* III: 421–26.
72. *War* I: 409; see also *Antiquity* XV: 333.
73. Matthew 16:2–3.
74. *LAE:* 145–46.

Chapter 14: Sea Trade

1. Bass, Frey, and Pulak 1984; Pulak and Frey 1985; Bass 1986; 1987; Bass et al. 1989: 3 fig. 2; Pulak 1987; 1988A; 1989; 1990A; 1990B; 1991; 1992; 1993; 1994; 1995; in press; Pulak and Haldane 1988. The eleventh, and final, season of excavation took place during the summer of 1994.
2. See above, p. 41.
3. Pulak 1991: 8.
4. Concerning the ballast stones, see Bass 1986: 292; Bass et al. 1989: 10; Pulak 1988B: 13, 16; 1989: 5, 9; 1990A: 9, 12; 1991: 7; 1992: 8–10. On the Uluburun anchors, see above, pp. 281, 283.
5. Bass, Frey, and Pulak 1984: 273–75 figs. 2–5; Pulak and Frey 1985: 18, 22–23; Bass 1986: 275–77; 1987: 692, 703–705; Bass et al. 1989: 7, 9, 12; Pulak 1988A: 6–10 figs. 3–5; 1988B: 16–17 figs. 7–8; 1989: 5–6, 8–9 fig. 9; 1990A: 9, 11 fig. 7; 1991: 7; 1992: 9 fig. 8; 1993: 4–5, 9–10; 1994: 10. Ancient sources of tin have now been identified in the Bolkardağ mining district, about 100 kilometers north of Mersin (Bass 1987: 698–99; Yener and Özbal 1987; Yener, Özbal, Minzoni-Deroche, and Aksoy 1989; Yener et al. 1991; Yener and Vandiver 1993A, 1993B; Muhly 1993; Willies 1993).
6. CG: 64; 1985: 3; for a listing of other suggested identifications, see Wachsmann 1987: 53 n. 73. On the importing of tin to the Aegean from the Near East during the Middle Bronze Age, see above, p. 83.
7. Pulak 1992: 4. Many of the copper oxhide ingots in the middle rows were badly corroded, requiring the innovation of underwater conservation techniques (Pulak 1989: 8; Peachey 1990).
8. C. Pulak, personal communication. This figure does not include the weight of the many copper bun ingots found at Uluburun. On the iconographic evidence for oxhide ingots, see Bass 1967: 62–69; 1973: 30–31, 38 figs. 1–6. A stone mold for the casting of oxhide ingots was found at Ras Ibn Hani (Lagarce et al. 1983: 277–90). The copper for use in the mold must have been imported in the form of copper ores or ingots not of oxhide shape.

    Heltzer (1977) compares prices of metals at Ugarit and its neighboring kingdoms. He concludes that Ugarit acted as a middleman in the metals trade. The textual, archaeological, and iconographic evidence all argue for a significant Syro-Canaanite role in this trade.
9. Gale 1991: 228–31; Pulak, in press for summary of data.
10. Stos-Gale and Gale 1984; Gale 1991: 231–32; Stos-Gale and Macdonald 1991: 265–67.
11. Pulak 1991: 5; 1992: 5 fig. 1.
12. On lead in the Aegean during the Bronze Age, see Renfrew 1967; 1972: 317–19; Gale 1980; Stos-Gale and Macdonald 1991: 255–62, 267–70, 272, 275, 277.
13. Bass et al. 1989: 7, 23; Pulak 1990A: 10 fig. 3; 1991: 7.
14. Bass 1986: 281–82; 1987: 716–18; Pulak 1988A: 14; 1988B: 13–14; 1989: 6, 8–9; 1990A: 11; 1990B: 52; 1991: 6, 7 fig. 6; 1992: 8; 1993: 9–10; 1994: 10; in press; Pulak and Frey 1985: 23.
15. *Dalbergia melanoxylon.* Bass 1986: 282–85 ills. 18–19; 1987: 721–22, 726–27, 729; Bass et al. 1989: 9 fig. 17, 10–11 fig. 20 and n. 52; Pulak 1988A: 33; 1988B: 14–16; 1989: 5–6; 1990A: 9, 11, 12 fig. 8; 1991: 6–7; 1992: cover, 5, 8, 10; 1993: 5; 1994: 10; Pulak and Frey 1985: 23. On the use of hippopotamus and elephant ivory at Ugarit, see Caubet and Poplin 1987. On hippopotamus ivory depicted in Egyptian tomb paintings, see below, p. 310. For the identity of additional woods found on the wreck, see above, p. 217.
16. Bass 1986: 278–79; Bass et al. 1989: 11; Pulak 1988A: 11.
17. Haldane 1986; 1988B; 1990B; 1991; 1993B. Concerning Late Bronze Age trade in organic materials in general, see Knapp 1991.
18. *Pistacia terebinthus* var. *atlantica.* This was previously identified with the *Burseracaea* family, which includes frankincense and myrrh (Bass 1986: 277–78; 1987: 709, 726–27; Pulak 1988A: 10–11; 1989: 5, 7; 1990B: 52; 1995: 5; Haldane 1990B: 57; 1993B: 352–53). One small vial may indeed contain myrrh (Haldane 1991). Concerning the possible uses of terebinth resin in the Late Bronze Age, see below, pp. 308, 310.
19. Feliks 1968: 104–106; Haldane 1993B: 353.
20. Bass 1986: 278; Pulak 1989: 7; 1992: 7; 1994: 9, 13; Haldane 1986; 1988B; 1990B: 57–60; 1991; 1993B: 352–57.
21. *Sarcopoterium spinosum.* Bass 1987: 729; Bass et al. 1989: 8; Pulak 1991: 5; 1992: 5; Pulak and Haldane 1988: 4 fig. 4; Haldane 1990B: 58 59; 1993B: 356–57. In addition to the thorny burnet, a single branch, apparently also employed as dunnage, was found at the lower end of the preserved hull (Pulak 1994: 12).
22. Haldane 1991; Pulak 1994: 9.
23. Bass 1987: 730; Bass et al. 1989: 10.
24. Bass 1986: 285; Pulak 1988A: 10; 1989: 7. The fig seeds in the jars may be intrusive.
25. Pulak 1989: 7.
26. Haldane 1988B; 1993B; Pulak 1989: 7.
27. For references, see Wachsmann 1987: 75.
28. Bass et al. 1989: 9 n. 44; Pulak 1988A: 33; 1989: 8; 1990A: 9; 1991: 7; 1992: 8; 1993: 9; 1994: 10; Conwell 1987: 33 fig. 14.
29. Bass 1987: 729; Bass et al. 1989: 8; Pulak 1988A: 5 ns. 5–7; 1994: 12–13. The *opercula* of another type of as yet unidentified shell are mixed in with the predominant murex *opercula* in an approximate ratio of 1:10 (Pulak 1992: 7).
30. Pulak 1989: 6–7 fig. 6; 1991: 7; 1992: 8.
31. Pulak 1990A: 9; 1991: 6–7.
32. Bass, Frey, and Pulak 1984: 273; Bass et al. 1989: 12; Pulak 1988B: 14, 16; 1989: 7–8; 1990A: 10, 12; 1991: 7–8, 10 fig. 11; 1992: 10; 1993: 4; 1994: 9.

33. Pulak 1988A: 12 fig. 7, 13, 32.

34. Pulak and Frey 1985: cover; Bass 1986: 279–82; 1987: 710–11, 718–19. These include: (Cypriot) five milk bowls, three Base-ring II bowls, three White Shaved juglets, three Bucchero jugs, and (Syro-Canaanite) four lamps.

35. Cypriot pottery: Bass 1990C; Bass et al. 1989: 9; Pulak 1988B: 14–16 fig. 16; 1989: 6–8; 1990A: 9–10; 1991: 6–8; 1992: 4, 8–9, 11; 1993: 5, 9; 1994: 9. Pilgrim flasks: Bass 1986: 284–85; Bass, Frey, and Pulak 1984: 276–77 fig. 7; Bass et al. 1989: 8–9, 11–12; Pulak 1989: 9; 1990A: 9; 1991: 6–7. Lamps: Bass 1986: 285–86 ill. 22; Bass et al. 1989: 9; Pulak 1988B: 15; 1990A: 9; 1991: 8; 1992: 8–9, 11. Wall brackets: Bass, Frey, and Pulak 1984: 273, 276 fig. 6; Bass 1986: 275, 292 n. 139; Bass et al. 1989: 9; Pulak 1988A: 13; 1988B: 14; 1992: 11.

36. See above, p. 205. Cadogan 1972, 1979; Karageorghis 1979: 200; Pulak in press. More recently, Cypriot pottery is being found at Kommos in southern Crete (Watrous 1992: 156–59).

37. Bass 1986: 277 ill. 7; Bass, Frey, and Pulak 1984: 276–78 fig. 8; Bass et al. 1989: 8; Pulak and Frey 1985: 21; Pulak 1988A: 10–11; 1989: 7–8; 1990A: 11; 1991: 7. "Syro-Canaanite" is perhaps a more accurate definition for these amphoras. For studies of this jar type found in the Aegean, see Åkerström 1975; Yannai 1983: 66–68.

38. Bass 1986: 278 ill. 8; Pulak 1988A: 10–11.

39. Pulak 1988B: 14.

40. Bass 1986: 288–90 ill. 28; Pulak 1989: 5, 8; 1991: 8; 1992: 8, 10; 1993: 9; 1994: 10.

41. Bass 1986: 286–87, 289 ills. 25–26; 1987: 722; Bass et al. 1989: 2; Pulak 1988A: 24 fig. 27; 1988B: 13–15; 1989: 5–6, 8–9; 1990A: 9, 11; 1991: 6 fig. 4, 7; 1992: 8, 9 fig. 7, 10–11; 1993: 5, 9–10; 1994: 8, 9 figs. 2–3, 10, 12–13. Concerning beaded textiles in antiquity, see Barber 1991: 93, 140 fig. 4.20, 141, 154–56, 162, 171–74, 195, 200, 312, 313 n. 2, 314; 1994: 91, 183, 202, 204 fig. 8.7, 210, 212–14.

42. Bass 1986: 278, 289.

43. Bass et al. 1989: 11 fig. 21, 12; Pulak 1988A: 26–27 fig. 31; 1988B: 14–15; 1992: 10; 1993: 5.

44. *Odyssey* VIII: 430–32. Bass 1986: 286, 289 ill. 24; 1987: 714; Pulak 1995: 45 Abb. 3, 49 Abb. 8; Pulak and Frey 1985: 24.

45. Lolos (1990) suggests an Aegean origin for the cup.

46. Bass 1987: 702; Bass et al. 1989: 11–12 fig. 22.

47. Pulak 1991: 10.

48. Bass 1986: 287–90; 1987: 693, 718–19; Bass et al. 1989: 2, 4–6 figs. 3, 5–6; Pulak 1988A: 25–27 figs. 29–30; 1992: 11; 1995: 51 Abb. 16.

49. Bass 1986: 289–90, 293–94 pl. 17, fig. 4; 1987: 719; Bass et al. 1989: 4 fig. 4, 7; Pulak 1988A: 26–27 fig. 32; 1988B: 15 fig. 4; 1992: 11.

50. Pulak 1989: 8–9 fig. 8; 1990A: 10 fig. 5, 11; 1992: 5 figs. 2–3; 1993: 9, 10 fig. 10. Items of carved wood were also found (Pulak 1994: 9).

51. Pulak 1989: 8; 1990A: 9; 1991: 6 fig. 5, 7; 1992: 10; 1994: 12.

52. Pulak 1992: 7, 8 fig. 4.

53. Bass 1986: 290–91; 1987: 708; Bass et al. 1989: 7–8 fig. 12; Pulak 1988A: 32 fig. 40; 1992: 8; 1995: 50 Abb. 12; Smith 1987: cover.

54. Bass 1987: 722–26, 731–32; Pulak 1988A: 27–29 figs. 33–35; 1988B: 14 fig. 2; 1989: 5 fig. 2, 9; 1990A: 10 fig. 4; 1992: 8, 10 fig. 9; 1993: 5; 1994: 10; 15 fig. 13; Collon in Bass et al. 1989: 12–16 figs. 24–28; Weinstein in Bass et al. 1989: 17–29, figs. 29–30.

55. Pulak and Frey 1985: 24; Bass 1986: 283–85 ill. 20, 288 ill. 23, 291 ill. 29, 292–93 ill. 34; 1987: 714–15; Bass et al. 1989: 8 fig. 15, 9, 12 fig. 23; Pulak 1988A: 13 ills. 8–9, 14; 1988B: 14; 1989: 6 fig. 3, 8; 1991: 6; 1992: 8, 11; 1994: 10, 13, 16 fig. 16; 1994: 10.

56. Pulak 1992: 10 figs. 10–11; 1995: 53 Abb. 23; *Geographica 2*. See above, pp. 206, 208.

57. Pulak 1990A: 10, 11 fig. 6; 1992: 11; 1995: 52 Abb. 22; *Geographica 1*.

58. Pulak 1991: 4.

59. Bass 1987: 721; Bass et al. 1989: 5, 7–9 figs. 9, 13; Pulak 1988A: 32–33; 1988B: 13–15; 1989: 5–6, 8; 1990A: 9; 1991: 7; 1992: 8–11; 1993: 5, 8, 11 fig. 13; 1994: 9–10.

60. Pulak 1991: 10.

61. Bass 1986: 292 fig. 31; Bass et al. 1989: 7–9 fig. 14; Pulak 1988A: 30–32 figs. 37–38; 1988B: 14–15; 1989: 5, 6 fig. 4, 8; 1990A: 9–10; 1991: 6–7, 8 fig. 7; 1992: 7–8, 11; 1993: 5, 9; 1994: 10, 12, 16 fig. 15; 1995: 52 Abb. 19; 1996B.

62. Pulak 1988A: 31, 32 fig. 39a; Petruso 1987.

63. Bass 1987: 730–31; 1990B; Bass et al. 1989: 10–11 fig. 19; Pulak 1988A: 33; 1995: 50 Abb. 13; Payton 1991; Pendleton and Warnock 1990; Symington 1991; Warnock and Pendleton 1991.

64. The Alashian king writes to the Egyptian pharaoh (*EA* 37: 16–17): "And whatever [yo]u n[ee]d put down on a tablet so I can send (it) to you." Might he be referring to a diptych?

65. Pulak 1991: 5; 1992: 7. During the final, 1994 season at Uluburun, an additional diptych leaf was discovered (Pulak 1994: 11 fig. 6).

66. Bass 1986: 274, 282–83 ill. 17, 294; 1987: 703, 712–13, 716, 726; Bass et al. 1989: 7–8; Pulak 1988A: 20–24 figs. 20–26; 1988B: 13–14; 1989: 8; 1990A: 9; 1991: 5 fig. 2, 6 fig. 3, 7, 8 fig. 9; 1992: 7–8, 11; 1993: 11 fig. 13, 120; 1994: 15 fig. 14; 1995: 50 Abb. 11.

67. Pulak 1992: 9.

68. Later medieval statutes sometimes stipulated that ships had to carry weapons on board (Ashburner 1909: cxlvi).

69. Bass 1986: 274, 292–93 ills. 32–33; 1987: 722; Bass et al. 1989: 5, 7, 9 figs. 8, 10, and 18; and Pulak 1988A: 14–20 figs. 10–19; 1988B: 13; 1989: 5, 8; 1990A: 8 fig. 1, 9, 11–12; 1991: 7, 9 fig. 10; 1992: 7, 8 fig. 5, 11; 1993: 9–11.

70. Pulak 1989: 6–7 fig. 5; 1992: 10; 1994: 10.

71. Pulak 1988B: 14; 1989: 6; 1994: 10.

72. Bass 1987: 709, 720.
73. *EA* 33: 19–32; 35: 40–41; 36: 18; 37: 13–16, 19–27; 40: 16–20, 27–28.
74. *EA* 39: 14–20. Italics added.
75. Pulak 1994: 15; in press.
76. See below, pp. 327–29.
77. *CG*: 52–121. Fifteen of the oxhide ingots from the Cape Gelidonya shipwreck were examined with lead isotope and trace element analysis and were found to be made of Cypriot copper (Gale 1991: 227–28).
78. *CG*: 45 figs. 38–40, 73 fig. 91.
79. Ibid.: 44. The twigs were identified as immature oak (*Quercus* sp.) (Western 1967: 169). Bass (*CG*: 49) notes that this type of brushwood dunnage is mentioned in the *Odyssey*.
80. Schulman 1967; Hennessy and du Plat Taylor 1967: 124 fig. 133: P29, 125 no. P29; du Plat Taylor 1967A; *CG*: 132–42; Buchholz 1967.
81. Linder 1972. See *KTU* 4.390 below, p. 339.
82. Loret 1949: 49–61; Bass 1989A: 59–60.
83. Haldane 1990B: 57; 1993B: 353.
84. Davies 1943 (1): 28; Loret 1949: 23–25.
85. Loret 1949: 20–23.
86. Melena 1983: 91 n. 5; Chadwick 1976: 120–21; Bass 1987: 727.
87. Bass 1987: 727. Concerning evidence for the production of aromatics at Pylas, see Shelmerdine 1985.
88. Melena 1974: 53.
89. *ANET*³: 441. See also above, pp. 10, 296.
90. Vercoutter 1956: 44 n. 1 and the additional bibliography there. Interestingly, although Ipu-wer describes Byblos as an exporter of resins for embalming, Vercoutter observes the complete lack of evidence for this practice at Byblos itself. Note, however, that a grayish lump of unidentified resin was found in a Middle Bronze Age tomb at el Jisr, south of Tel Aviv (Ory 1946: 32–33).
91. Herodotus II: 87; Diodorus Siculus I: 83: 5.
92. Lucas 1962: 299.
93. Lucas 1931; 1962: 309.
94. There is only one example of this resin being identified on an ancient mummy (Lucas 1962: 321, 324). Fifty kilograms of terebinth resin were also found in a Twenty-sixth Dynasty tomb at Matarieh, near Cairo. It was placed between the walls of the monolithic limestone case and the sarcophagus that fit tightly inside it.
95. Nilsson 1950: 625–30.
96. Ibid.: 629. The discoveries at Tel el Dabᶜa emphasize the opportunities for elements of Egyptian ritual to have been absorbed by the Minoans.
97. Kurtz and Boardman 1971: 191; Taylour 1983: 65.
98. Persson 1938: 342–43, 349–50; 1942: 13–14; Hood 1971: 140 pl. 113.
99. Persson 1942: 171 figs. 1–3.
100. Ibid.: 34–35, 38.
101. Apollodorus III: 17–20; Persson 1938: 350–52; 1942: 9–24; Hood 1971: 92, 138.
102. Schliemann 1880: 296.
103. For a painting of the upper part of the body, see Schliemann 1880: 297 fig. 454.
104. *PM* II: 177 fig. 70; Wachsmann 1987: pl. 52: A.
105. Wachsmann 1987: 78–92.
106. Davies and Davies 1933: pl. 7.
107. Davies 1943: pls. 17–20, 23; Wreszinski I: 56.
108. Davies 1922: pl. 9.
109. Meiggs 1985: 59–60; Haldane 1993A: 26–33.
110. For a list of the woods imported into Egypt, see most recently Haldane 1993A: 33–39 and the additional bibliography there.
111. See above, pp. 9–10. The timber of Lebanon was valued by Asiatic and Egyptian rulers throughout ancient history. For an overview of the Lebanese timber in trade/tribute, see Meiggs 1985: 49–87.
112. Brunton and Caton-Thompson 1928: 62–63; Lucas 1962: 430.
113. *BAR* III: §94; *ANEP*: {110} and {288} (no. 331). Meiggs (1982: 67) considers them "highly stylized" cedar trees.
114. *LAE*: 149.
115. Ibid.: 151. Alternatively, this delay may have resulted from the difficulty in moving the logs during the winter months (Egberts 1991: 61–62 n. 34).
116. Rowe 1936: 288.
117. *LAE*: 149.
118. I Kings 5:9; II Chronicles 2:16; Sølver 1961: 29; Casson 1995A: fig. 92; Katzenstein 1973: 243; *ANEP*: no. 107.
119. *ANET*³: 243. The offerings were made to the goddess of Byblos. These expeditions to cut cedars were quite large. Tjekkerbaal sent 300 men and 300 cattle to cut the wood for Wenamun (*LAE*: 151). See above, p. 10.
120. *ANET*³: 243 n. 1.
121. *LAE*: 148–49.
122. See above, pp. 223–24.
123. Loret 1916: 47; Meiggs 1985: 405–409.
124. Glanville 1932: 9–10.
125. See above, p. 39.
126. *LAE*: 151.
127. Haldane 1993A: 236.
128. Vandier 1969: 681 fig. 271: 2; Moussa and Altenmüller 1977: Abb. 8.
129. See above, pp. 215–16.
130. See above, pp. 219–20, 222. Bennett 1939: 10, 13 n. 41.
131. Janssen 1975: 381–82.
132. *EA* 160: 14–19; 161: 56.
133. *EA* 36: 10, 13. See also *EA* 35: 27–29; 40: 6–15.
134. Lipinski's (1977) interpretation has been refuted by Knapp (1983), who suggests that the text deals with an Alashian wishing to purchase ships from Ugaritic merchants.
135. Schaeffer 1962: 142 (*RS* 19.20).
136. The king of Alashia asks the Egyptian pharaoh for an ox (*EA* 35: 23–26). Moran's (*EA* 35 n. 5) assumption that this refers to an *ox-shaped* object is negated by

the iconographic evidence. Horses and bulls appear as items of tribute/trade brought by Syro-Canaanites to Egypt in many Egyptian tombs: Rechmire (T. 100): Davies 1943: pl. 23; Menkheperresonb (T. 86) and Amenmose (T. 42): Davies and Davies 1933: pls. 7, 34–36; Amunezeh (T. 84): Davies and Davies 1941: pl. 13; Thannuny (T. 74): Mekhitarian 1978: 99; Nebamun (T. 90): Davies 1923: pl. 28; Huy (T. 40): Davies and Gardiner 1926: pl. 19; and two unnamed tombs (Ts. 91 and 119): Wreszinski I: 291, 340. See also Fig. 14.3.

137. Pulak 1989: 8.

138. See also Redford 1992: 221, 223.

139. Ezekiel 27:13; *Odyssey* XIV: 285–98; XV: 440–84; Herodotus I: 1; II: 54.

140. Davies 1927: 57.

141. Mekhitarian 1978: 33, 35, 64, 67, 94, 112, 127, 136.

142. Brothel scenes also appear on the "erotic papyrus" in Turin (Peck 1978: 94 fig. 21).

143. *EA* 113: 14; 155: 68.

144. *EA* 105: 14–17.

145. See above, pp. 311–12.

146. Note, however, that the stele of Antefoker makes repeated reference to the construction of "ships" for the voyage to Punt (Sayed 1977: 170). See above, p. 238.

147. See above, pp. 42–44.

148. Malamat 1971: 38. See below, *KTU* 4.647, p. 339.

149. *PM* II: 309; Buchholz 1973; Allen 1994, and the additional bibliography there.

Chapter 15: War and Piracy at Sea

1. Pliny, *Nat. Hist.*: VII: 58: 209.

2. Sandars 1978: 50 n. 14 and additional bibliography. The reference to *Tanis II* should be to pl. 2, no. 78.

3. Güterbock 1967: 78.

4. Presumably these were from the cities of Ugarit, Ura, and elsewhere. Compare *RS* 20.212 and *RS* 26.158, but note that the ship captain in *RS* 17.133 has a Hittite name. See below, pp. 323–24, 340–42.

5. Güterbock 1967: 80.

6. I thank Professor Lionel Casson for suggesting the latter interpretation to me (personal communication).

7. Yadin 1963: 251–52. Only two northern warriors are depicted carrying throwing spears. They stand to the left of the mast in ships N. 2 and N. 5 (Figs. 8.4, 7, 8, 12). This weapon may have been in use at Ugarit also (Rainey 1967: 90).

8. Casson 1995A: 38.

9. Brunner-Traut 1974.

10. Schäfer 1974: 169 fig. 159; Wachsmann 1987: 56 n. 100.

11. Strictly speaking, the masts cross the yards, indicating that they are being viewed from the stern.

12. Nelson (1929: 34) was the first to suggest that the grapnel was "thrown into the enemy rigging either to tear the sail or to overturn the light craft of the foe."

13. Ormerod 1978: 13.

14. *Thucydides* I: 5: 1.

15. Ormerod 1978: 18.

16. Ringler 1980: 20.

17. See above, p. 130

18. Ormerod 1978: 69–70.

19. Morrison 1980: 132.

20. Ziskind 1974: 137.

21. Ormerod 1978: 31.

22. *RS* 20.238 and *RS* 20.18; see below, pp. 343–44.

23. Christensen 1972: 165. See above, pp. 166, 168.

24. Marinatos 1974: color pl. 9; Ernstson 1985: 319 fig. 4; Doumas 1992: 78.

25. *Odyssey* X: 28–30; Ormerod 1978: 44–45.

26. Ormerod 1978: 43.

27. *EA* 101: 11–13; 105: 11–17.

28. *EA* 114: 15–20.

29. See above, pp. 10, 39–40, 313.

30. See above, pp. 208, 307.

31. Concerning the introduction of the ram on Greek galleys, see above, pp. 157–58.

Chapter 16: Sea Laws

1. Gordon (*UT* 19: 1443) considers the *rb-tmtt* to be the epithet of a war god, such as Reshef or Mat. Rainey (1967: 87 n. 118) identifies him as a "supervisor of prisoners." Virolleaud (1965: 82) considers him a pirate chief. Linder (1970: 46) recognizes in him an official of the king of Tyre, generally in charge of salvage but who had defected for some undetermined reason. Gordon's identification seems to fit the context best.

2. See below, *KTU* 2.38, p. 334. Linder 1970: 44.

3. Katzenstein 1973: 267–76; Linder 1981: 33 n. 14 and additional bibliography.

4. *ANET Suppl.*: 98.

5. See below, *RS* 17.133, pp. 340–41.

6. Fensham 1967.

7. Compare the Rhodian Sea Law 3: 10 (Ashburner 1909: 91).

8. On the location of Ura, see above, p. 295.

9. Fensham 1967: 224; Ashburner 1909. The Rhodian Sea Law may have formed the basis of the code of maritime laws of Oleron, enacted in the twelfth century A.D. by Eleanor of Aquitaine, who later married Henry II of England (*Oleron*). The law code was introduced to England by their son, Richard I, in 1190. In 1336 it was codified in the "Black Book of the Admiralty."

10. Ashburner 1909: ccix–ccxxxiv.

11. Ziskind 1974: 136. The person who swore the oath was the harbor captain, not the captain of the ship as Ziskind would have it (Nougayrol 1956: 118–19).

12. See below, pp. 337–38.

13. Pardee 1975A.

14. *LAE*: 155.

15. Ormerod 1978: 74–77.
16. *LAE*: 145.
17. Ashburner 1909: cxlv–cxlvi.
18. Ormerod 1978: 62–63.
19. *LAE*: 144.
20. Ibid.
21. Compare the Rhodian Sea Law 3: 3–4 (Ashburner 1909: 81–84).

22. *LAE:* 143.
23. Rhodian Sea Law 3: 13 (Ashburner 1909: 94).
24. *LAE:* 145 and above, p. 40.

Chapter 17: Conclusions

1. Liverani 1987: 70.

GLOSSARY OF NAUTICAL TERMS

BY FREDERICK M. HOCKER

abaft (prep.): behind.

aft (adv.): toward the stern.

amidships (adv.): in the middle of the vessel, midway between bow and stern or at the widest part of the vessel.

aphlaston (n.): curving ornament at the head of the sternpost; such an ornament is typical of Classical warships.

apical rope groove (n.): groove found at the apex of a stone anchor, used to seat the anchor rope.

astern (adv. or prep.): behind the vessel.

athwartships (adv.): lying or running in a direction across the vessel, at a right angle to the centerline.

backstay (n.): a stay (q.v.) running aft from the head of the mast to provide longitudinal support to the mast. The stay can be belayed on the centerline, often by attachment to the sternpost, or it can lead to one side. If the latter, there are normally pairs of backstays to balance the lateral stress.

baldachin (n.): a simple canopy, normally consisting of a curved roof supported on four pillars, typically found on Egyptian craft, where they are often used to shelter important persons. The baldachin may be fixed or portable.

ballast (n.): dense material, typically stone, placed low in the hold of a vessel to lower the center of gravity and increase stability.

batten (n.): thin strip of wood or fiber placed against the inner surface of planking at a seam, either to cushion seam ligatures or to act as caulking.

beam (n.): (1) width of a vessel amidships or at the widest point. Extreme beam is the overall width to the outside of planking, wales, rubrails, and so on, while molded beam is the width to the inside surface of the planking. (2) A transverse timber, straight or crowned, fastened at its ends to the sides of the hull: beams can act as thwarts or support decks.

beam shelf (n.): a stringer (q.v.) that supports the ends of deck beams.

belaying pin (n.): wooden pin for the temporary attachment of the free end of an element of the running rigging.

bireme (n.): a rowed vessel with two banks of oars on each side. In ancient biremes, the two banks were set at different levels.

boom (n.): spar used to spread the foot of a sail.

boom-footed rig (n.): type of square rig, common on certain ships of the Bronze Age, in which the foot of the sail is attached to a boom.

bow (n.): the end of the vessel toward the normal direction of travel; the "front" end.

bow patch (n.): circular, spoked device seen on the upper hull at the bow of Geometric ship representations.

brace (n.): element of the running rigging (q.v.) attached to the yardarm (q.v.) to adjust the angle of a square sail to the wind. They are used in pairs, one on each yardarm.

brail (or brailing line) (n.): line used to gather up a sail. In ancient square rigs, a number of brails were used to control the shape of the sail and trim it to suit the point of sail and existing wind conditions.

brailing fairlead (n.): ring, grommet, eye, or loop attached to the yard or sail to guide a brailing line.

bulwarks (n.): the topsides above the deck: may consist of a planked continuation of the side or may be only lightly planked or open.

butt end (n.): squared, unscarfed end of a timber, such as a plank or beam.

butt joint (n.): joint between the ends of two members in which neither member is scarfed or notched to receive the other; the timbers meet at butt ends.

caprail (n.): a railing atop the sheerstrake or bulwarks, normally defining the upper edge of the side of the vessel.

carling (n.): a longitudinal timber fixed to the beams but not to the sides of the vessel. It may be continuous or consist of short pieces between adjacent beams.

ceiling (n.): planking over the inboard surface of the frames.

chine (n.): angular join of bottom to side instead of a rounded bilge.

clamp (n.): a heavy stringer (q.v.) normally set opposite a wale. A clamp often supports deck beams, in which case it may be called a deck clamp. See also beam shelf.

cleat (n.): (1) small block of wood, nailed to the surface of another timber either as a fastening or a stop. (2) A block of wood with horns or ears, used for the belaying of running rigging.

clew (n.): either corner at the foot of a square sail (q.v.) or the after corner of a fore-and-aft sail (q.v.).

coracle (n.): small boat of wicker frame covered with animal hide.

crow's nest (n.): small platform attached to the mast near its head, used by lookouts, archers, or slingers as a vantage point.

crutch (n.): stanchion or prop that supports long spars, such as mast and yard, when they are not in use.

cutwater bow (n.): bow with a projecting forefoot somewhat resembling a waterline ram but not normally used as a weapon.

deck (n.): approximately horizontal platform across the interior of the hull, normally constructed of a layer of longitudinal planks fastened to or resting on a series of transverse beams.

deck beam (n.): a beam that supports a deck.

dieres (n., Greek): an oared vessel rowed by two groups of men: normally assumed to be synonymous with bireme (q.v.).

dovetail joint (n.): rigid joint, frequently used where two members join at a right angle, in which the end of one member is formed into a flared, shouldered face tenon that fits into a matching face mortise in the longitudinal edge of the second member.

dowel (n.): a wooden rod. In structural terms, it is used to align two timbers, normally edge-to-edge.

dugout (n.): a vessel carved from a solid log, normally in one piece. Extended dugouts have pieces, such as side planks, added to the dugout base; expanded dugouts are broadened by softening and spreading the sides of the hull.

edge-joined (adj.): joined edge-to-edge. Refers here to several methods of ancient Mediterranean hull construction in which adjacent planks were fastened to each other, either by lashing or wooden tenons, passing through their common edges.

floor (n.): the bottom of the vessel amidships.

floor timber (n., sometimes abbreviated to floor): the central component of a frame that crosses the keel (thus spanning the floor).

foot (of a sail, n.): the lower edge of a sail.

fore (adj.): pertaining to the bow or closer to the bow.

fore-and-aft rig (n.): a sailing rig in which the sail or sails are set with the plane of the sail parallel to the centerline of the ship instead of athwartships.

forecastle (n.): a raised structure built at the bow of a vessel.

forestay (n.): stay (q.v.) running forward from the head of the mast to provide longitudinal support to the mast. It is often attached at its lower end to the stem.

frame (n., also timber): a transverse reinforcing member, made up of one or more components, fastened to the interior surface of the exterior hull planking and sometimes to the keel.

furl (v.): to bundle up a sail when it is not is use. Square sails are often folded or rolled up and tied to the yard.

galley (n.): large seagoing vessel propelled primarily by oars.

gangway (n.): a narrow deck running either along the side of the vessel or down the centerline to connect small decks at the ends of the ship. It is often used on vessels with open holds or oared ships to allow the sailing crew to move around the ship.

garboard (n.): the strake nearest the keel, or the lowest side strake in some flat-bottomed vessels, such as the Cheops ship.

gripe (n.): a projecting fin, either part of or attached to the forward face of the stem below the waterline.

grommet (n.): loop made of rope or leather. It has many uses, such as for oarlocks or brailing rings.

halyard (n.): line for hoisting and lowering a sail: can be attached either directly to the sail or to a spar, such as a yard.

hawser (n.): heavy rope, normally used for mooring.

head (of a sail, n.): the upper edge of a sail.

helm (n.): the apparatus for steering the ship, as well as (more abstractly) the steering quality of the ship.

helmsman (n.): the crew member steering the vessel. This may be an official rank or position, or it may be just one of the many tasks performed by all members of a small crew in rotation.

hog (n. and v.): vertical distortion of the hull in which the ends droop and the middle rises.

hogging truss (n.): an arrangement of ropes (and sometimes props) connecting the ends of the ship and pulling them up, to counteract hogging.

hull (n.): the body of the vessel, consisting of the structural timbers that give the ship its shape and strength but excluding rigging, fittings such as windlasses, and the contents of the hold.

interscalmium (n. Latin, "between tholes"): the distance between thole pins or oarlocks in a rowed vessel.

joggle (v.): to cut a step, or a series of steps, in a timber to fit another; commonly used in ancient Egyptian ship construction.

kedge (v.): to pull a vessel through the water by carrying an anchor away from the vessel, dropping it, and hauling the vessel up to the anchor. This is most commonly done when the vessel is becalmed or in an attempt to free a grounded vessel. In later times, some vessels carried a special anchor, called a kedge anchor, designed specifically for this purpose.

keel (n.): central backbone timber, of sufficient cross-sectional area to offer significant longitudinal strength to the hull. In most cases, a portion of it projects below the bottom planking and offers lateral resistance.

keel plank (also plank keel, n.): centerline strake, often thicker than the adjoining garboards but not stiff enough to be considered a true keel.

keelson (n.): an internal centerline timber lying atop the frames, of sufficient length, cross-sectional area, and rigid fastening to add significantly to the longitudinal stiffness of the hull. The maststep may be cut into the keelson, or it may be a separate timber fastened to the upper surface of the timber.

L-shaped lashing mortise (n.): a lashing mortise (q.v.) in which one end of the mortise exits the interior plank surface and the other exits the plank edge.

lanyard (n.): (1) a length of light-to-medium line used for tightening stays. (2) A short length of light line attached to a small, portable object to prevent its being lost.

lashed construction (n.): the joining of structural components by wrapping them with several passes of rope or cord. This is also applied to a style of Egyptian shipbuilding in which planks are fastened to each other by several turns of heavy cord passing through a common mortise or series of common mortises. See sewn construction.

lashing mortise (n.): a mortise, open at both ends, through which lashing ropes or cords pass.

lateen rig (n.): a fore-and-aft rig (q.v.) in which a triangular sail is set on a diagonal yard raised on a mast.

launch (n.): a small boat, often used as a ship's boat.

leech (n.): the leeward edge of a sail. On a fore-and-aft sail it is always the after edge, but it may be either edge of a square sail, depending on how the sail is trimmed.

leeward (adv.): the side of a vessel or object that is away from the wind.

lift (n.): a line supporting the weight of a yard or a boom, normally running from the masthead to the yardarm, but may run to another part of the yard. See running lift, standing lift.

line (n.): rope or cord, especially a piece of cordage set up to do a specific job on board ship.

loom (n.): the part of an oar, usually square or cylindrical in section, between the blade and the handle.

luff (n.): the leading or windward edge of a sail. On fore-and-aft sails it is always the forward edge, but it may be either edge of a square sail, depending on how the sail is trimmed. (v.): to sail too high into the wind, so that the leading edge (luff) of the sail ceases to work effectively and starts to tremble or flap.

mast (n.): vertical spar fixed to the hull to carry sails, either directly or attached to other, movable spars.

mast cap (n.): a fitting attached to the head of the mast and supporting a number of sheaves, slots, or rings for rigging, such as lifts (q.v.). Such fittings were used on some Bronze Age vessels to handle the large number of lifts and other lines associated with certain versions of the square rig. See truck.

masthead (n.): the uppermost portion of the mast, above the highest position of the uppermost sail or yard. This area is used for the attachment of stays and other rigging.

mast partner (n.): a structure at deck level (or above the step in undecked vessels) to support the mast. The partner is primarily a transverse support but can also be used as a longitudinal support. The partner, combined with the rigging, transmits most of the driving force of the sail to the hull.

maststep (n.): a mortise to house the heel of a mast and/or the timber into which it is cut.

midships (adj): located or pertaining to amidships, as in the midships section.

monoxylon (n.): a dugout (q.v.) carved from a single tree.

moor (v.): to secure a vessel, temporarily or semipermanently, either by anchoring or by tying to other structures, such as a pier or wharf.

mortise-and-tenon joint (n.): an edge-to-edge planking fastening commonly used in the ancient Mediterranean. Each joint consists of a free tenon housed in mortises in opposing edges of a seam: in its fully developed form, the tenon is locked into each plank by a wooden peg driven through plank and tenon.

nuggar (n.): a small to medium-sized Nile vessel of the historic period characterized by edge-fastened planking and the absence of internal framing.

oar (n.): a long, narrow piece of wood having a broad blade at one end and a handle at the other, supported in a fixed mounting, such as a thole (q.v.) or oarlock (q.v.), and used to propel a vessel by pulling or pushing the handle, causing the blade to push against the water.

oarlock (n.): a mounting for an oar characterized by a vertical member both before and abaft the oar. In modern vessels, the oarlock is a U-shaped casting that pivots with the oar, but in older watercraft an oarlock can be as simple as a pair of thole pins.

oculus (n.): device in the form of an eye, often used as a decorative or apotropaic element on watercraft.

outrigger (n.): any structure that extends off one or both sides of a vessel. Such structures may support pontoons for added stability, as on Polynesian canoes, or tholes, as on modern rowing shells.

papyriform (adj.): having the shape of a bundle of papyrus reeds: normally used to describe Egyptian wooden vessels built in the same general shape as Nilotic reed rafts.

penteconter (n.): an ancient Greek warship rowed by fifty men, arranged in twenty-five pairs on a single level.

port (adj. or adv.): left side when facing forward.

protokeel (n.): a longitudinal centerline timber having some of the characteristics of a true keel (such as substantially greater scantlings than the adjoining planking) but lacking others (such as firm attachment to the rest of the hull structure).

quarter (n.): the side of the vessel at the stern.

quarter rudder (n.): a rudder (q.v.) instead of a steering oar (q.v.) fixed to the side of the hull at the stern; i.e., on the quarter (q.v.).

refit (v.): to repair or overhaul a vessel in a thorough, systematic way, often incorporating modifications and improvements.

rigging (n.): the system of cordage fitted to spars and sails to support and control them.

rowlock (n.): see oarlock.

running lift (n.): a lift (q.v.) that can be adjusted to support the weight of a yard or boom at any position.

running rigging (n.): lines attached to spars and sails that can be easily hauled or slacked to adjust the height and attitude of sails and spars.

scarf (n.): a joint in which timbers with parallel axes overlap longitudinally.

sewn construction (n.): any of a number of construction methods in which adjacent planks are fastened together by fiber stitching. The stitching may be continuous along the seam (in the manner of garment sewing), or it may consist of individual ligatures (in the manner of medical sutures).

sheave (n.): a pulley, set either in a separate housing (a block) or in a slot in a spar or hull component.

sheer (n.): the upper edge of the uppermost continuous strake of exterior planking. In many smaller vessels, this is the upper edge of the side. In larger vessels, the sheer, sometimes called the planksheer, may be below the bulwarks and other upper works. See sheerstrake.

sheerstrake (n.): the uppermost continuous strake of structurally significant planking; on vessels with light bulwarks, the sheerstrake may actually be at deck level.

sheet (n.): line attached to the clew (q.v.) of a sail and used for trimming the sail.

shell-based construction (n.): hull construction methods in which the shell of planking plays the primary role in determining the shape of the hull and provides the greater share of structural strength. Most ancient methods of construction were shell-based.

shell-first construction (n.): hull construction methods in which the shell of planking is the first major component erected, generally after the keel. The finished hull may be shell- or skeleton-based.

shroud (n.): a stay (q.v.) that provides transverse support to a mast; it runs from the masthead to the vessel's side.

sidereal compass (n.): a method of determining direction from the positions of rising and setting stars.

skeleton-based construction (n.): hull construction methods in which an internal framework, usually consisting of frames and stringers (q.v.), plays the primary role in determining the shape of the hull and provides the greater share of structural strength. Most ancient methods of construction evolved toward skeleton-based methods.

skeleton-first construction (n.): hull construction methods in which an internal framework is the first major component erected, generally after the keel. Such hulls are usually, but not always, skeleton-based.

Spanish windlass (n.): a device for exerting tension by twisting ropes strung between two fixed points.

spinnaker (n.): a large, baggy, triangular sail on modern yachts, set forward when sailing before the wind.

square sail (n.): a sail, normally set on a yard (q.v.) at right angles to the centerline of the vessel.

stanchion (n.): a vertical post supporting a load above.

standing lift (n.): a lift (q.v.) of fixed length that supports the weight of a yard or boom in only one position, generally when the yard is lowered.

standing rigging (n.): rigging of more or less fixed length, used to support a spar in a certain position. Although it may be adjusted slightly in use, it is not commonly hauled, slacked, or belayed with every change of sail.

starboard (adj. or adv): right side when facing forward.

stave (n.): one of the long, narrow pieces of wood used to build a cask or barrel. The term also applies to wooden members used in other forms of similar construction.

stay (n.): an element of the standing rigging (q.v.) that supports a mast. See forestay, backstay, shroud.

steering oar (n.): an oar used for steering. It pivots on a thole or oarlock and is used by sweeping it through the water to push one end of the vessel across the line of travel. It is less efficient than a rudder.

stem (n.): the upright backbone timber rising from the forward end of the keel or keel plank. It may denote either the specific timber into which the plank hooding ends are rabbeted in a complex assembly or the entire assembly.

stern (n.): the end of the vessel away from the normal direction of travel; the "back" end.

sternpost (n.): the upright backbone timber rising from the after end of the keel (keel plank). It may denote either the specific timber into which the plank hooding ends are rabbeted in a complex assembly or the entire assembly.

strake (n.): a continuous run of planking, made up of one or more planks joined or butted end-to-end.

stringer (n.): a heavy longitudinal timber, such as a clamp, on the interior of the vessel.

sweep (n.): a long, heavy oar, typically operated by two or more men.

tabernacle (n.): a mast partner (q.v.) designed to allow the mast to be stepped and struck by leaning it forward and backward, respectively.

tenon (n.): a tongue on the end of a member, or a separate element, designed to be housed in a mortise and used to join components.

thole (n.): a fixed pivot point for an oar, generally consisting of a pin or hook fixed to the side of the vessel. The oar may rest either before or abaft the thole.

thole bight (n.): a grommet of rope or leather to attach an oar to a thole. It can serve either to transmit the force of the oar to the hull (if the oar lies before the thole) or simply as a keeper, to prevent the oar from being lost if it is let go.

thole-board (n.): a strake or other longitudinal timber into which the tholes or oarlocks are fitted.

through-beam (n.): a beam (q.v.) that passes completely

through the sides of the vessel so that the ends are visible from outboard. This is often done in an attempt to fasten the beam securely to the side by notching it over a wale.

thwart (n.): a simple seat, consisting of a board set athwartships. In some vessels, the thwart may also act as a beam (q.v.) if properly fastened to the sides.

tiller (n.): a straight or curved piece fixed at an angle to the head of the rudder to give the helmsman leverage or to allow him to steer when the rudder head is out of normal reach.

toggle (n.): a short wooden bar, often with swelled ends, seized or spliced into the end of a rope to allow another rope, with a loop in its end, to be rapidly attached.

transom (n.): (1) a transverse timber in the stern, crossing the inner face of the sternpost assembly and holding the sides together. Sometimes called a transom timber to distinguish it from the flat, transverse plane forming the sterns of some vessels. (2) A flat, transverse plane forming the stern of the vessel.

treenail (n.): a wooden peg of substantial size used to fasten together two members, such as a plank and a frame.

trieres (n.): Greek oared warship rowed by three groups of oarsmen, probably set at three levels.

truck (n.): a sheave (q.v.), slot, or ring in the head of the mast to take a line for raising and lowering something. See mast cap.

truss (n.): an element designed to exert tension in a structure and provide it with rigidity. In ancient ships, rope trusses were sometimes run between the ends of the hull, either to compress the entire hull and thus increase its strength and rigidity through preloading or to pull the ends up and reduce hogging. See hogging truss.

truss girdle (n.): a girdle of ropes around a hull to hold the hull together or to provide a point of attachment for a truss.

tumble-home (n.): hull shape in which the upper parts of the hull lean inward, toward the centerline.

V-shaped lashing mortise (n.): a lashing mortise (q.v.) in which both ends of the mortise exit the same surface of the plank.

wale (n.): an exceptionally heavy strake.

waterline (n.): the imaginary line on the hull that marks the level of the water surface when the vessel is afloat. Some vessels have a waterline painted on or inscribed in the hull.

webbing (n.): a woven or plaited strap used in place of several turns of lashing in some ancient Egyptian hulls, such as the one at Lisht.

wind rose (n.): a diagram of geographic directions in which a series of points corresponds to the origins of known, prevailing winds. Common wind roses in the West are derived from ancient wind systems that divided the compass into eight or twelve points.

windlass (n.): a mechanical device for multiplying human force in hauling in ropes. It consists of a horizontal barrel of circular or polygonal section set in a fixed mounting, which is turned by bars set in holes in the barrel.

woolding (n.): a binding used to hold together a mast of composite construction.

yard (n.): a spar set athwartships on a mast to support a square sail.

yardarm (n.): the end of the yard, outboard of the sail, where controlling lines such as braces (q.v.) are attached.

BIBLIOGRAPHY

Abbreviations

AA = Archäologischer Anzeiger

AAAS = Annales archéologiques arabes syriennes

AASOR = Annual of the American Schools of Oriental Research

ABSA = Annual of the British School at Athens

ACTA² = Acta of the Second International Colloquium on Aegean Prehistory: "The First Arrival of Indo-European Elements in Greece." (Athens, April 5–11, 1971). Athens. 1972.

AE = Archaeologika Ephemeris

AEg = Ancient Egypt

AF = Altorientalische Forschungen

AfO = Archiv für Orientforschungen

AHw = Akkadisches Handwörterbuch. W. von Soden. Wiesbaden. 1958–81.

AJA = American Journal of Archeology

AJBA = Australian Journal of Biblical Archaeology

AJSLL = American Journal of Semitic Languages and Literatures

AMM = Aegean Maritime Museum. *Motion* (Olympic Airways magazine). (May 1990): 80–109.

ANE = The Aegean and the Near East: Studies Presented to Hetty Goldman. S. S. Weinberg, ed. Locust Valley. 1956.

ANEP = The Ancient Near East in Pictures Relating to the Old Testament. 2d ed. J. B. Pritchard, ed. Princeton. 1969.

ANET³ = Ancient Near Eastern Texts Relating to the Old Testament.(3d ed. with supp.). J. B. Pritchard, ed. Princeton. 1969.

ANET Suppl. = The Ancient Near East: Supplementary Texts and Pictures Relating to the Old Testament. J. B. Pritchard, ed. Princeton. 1969.

AO = Analecta Orientalia

AOAT = Alter Orient und Altes Testament

APATP = American Philological Association: Transactions and Proceedings

ARAB = Ancient Records of Assyria and Babylonia I–II. Reprint. D. D. Luckenbill, ed. New York. 1968.

AS = Anatolian Studies

ASAE = Annales du service des antiquités de l'Égypte

ASP = American Studies in Papyrology

AuOr = Aulor Orientalis

AV = Archaeologica Viva

AW = Archaeology under Water. K. Muckelroy, ed. New York. 1980.

BA = Biblical Archaeologist

BAR = Ancient Records of Egypt I–V. J. H. Breasted, ed. Chicago. 1906–1907. (1988 reprint.)

BARIS = BAR International Series

BASOR = Bulletin of the American Schools of Oriental Research

BASP = Bulletin of the American Society of Papyrologists

BASPR = Bulletin of the American School of Prehistoric Research

BATM = Bronze Age Trade in the Mediterranean. N. H. Gale, ed. (*SIMA* 90). Jonsered. 1991.

BCCSP = Bollettino del Centro Camuno di Studi Preisorici

BCH = Bulletin de correspondance hellénique

BibAR = Biblical Archaeology Review

BICS = Bulletin of the Institute of Classical Studies of the University of London

BIFAO = Bulletin de l'institut français d'archéologie orientale

BiOr = Bibliotheca Orientalis

BMMA = Bulletin of the Metropolitan Museum of Art

BMSP = B.P. Bishop Museum Special Publication

CAH = The Cambridge Ancient History³*: I: 1. Cambridge. 1970.

CAH = The Cambridge Ancient History³: II: 1. Cambridge. 1980.

Cd'AS = Cahiers d'archéologie subaquatique

Cd'É = Chronique d'Égypte

CG = Cape Gelidonya: A Bronze Age Shipwreck. (Transactions of the American Philosophical Society, n.s., 57: 8.) G. F. Bass. Philadelphia. 1967.

CO = *Canoes of Oceania*. A. C. Haddon and J. Hornell. Honolulu. 1975.

CQ = *Classical Quarterly*

CR = *A Colourful Record. MM 71 (1985): 119–28.*

CRAI = *Comptes-rendus de l'Académie des Inscriptions et Belles-Lettres*

CRB = *Cahiers de la revue biblique*

DD = Digging Diary. *Egyptian Archaeology* 1 (1991): 13–14.

EA = *The Amarna Letters.* W. L. Moran, ed. and trans. Baltimore. 1992.

EAEHL = *Encyclopedia of Archaeological Excavations in the HolyLand* I–V. M. Avi-Yonah and E. Stern, eds. Oxford. 1975–78. (English edition.)

EAL = *Egypt, the Aegean and the Levant: Interconnections in the Second Millennium B.C.* W.V. Davies and L. Schofield, eds. London. 1995.

EM = *Encyclopedia Miqrait* I–IX. M. D. Cassuto, H. Tadmor, and S. Ahituv, eds. Jerusalem. 1955–88. (In Hebrew.)

Enalia Annual = *Enalia, Annual of the Hellenic Institute of Marine Archaeology*

ESI = *Excavations and Surveys in Israel*

FDS = *From the Depths of the Sea.* (*Israel Museum Catalogue* 263, summer 1985.)

Galilee Boat = *The Excavations of an Ancient Boat in the Sea of Galilee* (*Lake Kinneret*). (*ʿAtiqot* XIX.) S. Wachsmann et al. 1990.

GDI = *Sammlung der griechischen Dialekt-Inschriften.* H. Collitz et al., eds. Göttingen. 1884–1915.

Geographica 1 = Geographica: From Bronze Age Wreck, "More of Everything." *NG* 181/5 (May 1992).

Geographica 2 = Geographica: Mystery Statue Surfaces on A Bronze Age Wreck. *NG* 183/5 (May 1993).

HA = *Hadashot Arkheologiot*

Herodotus = *Herodotus* I. Loeb Classical Library. A. D. Godley, trans. London. 1975.

HKN = *Hong Kong News: Dragon Boat Festival Has Colorful History.* Hong Kong Tourist Association. N.d.

HML = *High, Middle, or Low?* (Acts of an International Colloquiem on Absolute Chronology Held at the University of Gothenburg, August 20–22, 1987) I–II. P. Åström, ed. (*SIMAL*: Pocket-book 57). Gothenburg. 1987.

HS = *History from the Sea.* P. Throckmorton, ed. London. 1987.

HSBUA = *A History of Seafaring Based on Underwater Archaeology.* G. F. Bass, ed. New York. 1972.

IEJ = *Israel Exploration Journal*

IFAO, RA = *L'Institut française d'archaéologie orientale, Recherches d'archéologie, de philologie et d'histoire*

IHT = *International Herald Tribune*

IJNA = *International Journal of Nautical Archaeology*

ILN = *Illustrated London News*

INAN = *INA Newsletter*

INAQ = *INA Quarterly*

IPR = *In Poseidons Reich: Archäologie unter Wasser.* (*Zaberns Bildbände zur Archäolgie* 23). Mainz. 1995.

Israel Museum = *Treasures of the Holy Land: Ancient Art from the Israel Museum.* New York. 1986.

JAOS = *Journal of the American Oriental Society*

JARCE = *Journal of the American Research Center in Egypt*

JAS = *Journal of Archaeological Science*

JCS = *Journal of Cuneiform Studies*

JEA = *Journal of Egyptian Archaeology*

JESHO = *Journal of Economic and Social History of the Orient*

JFA = *Journal of Field Archaeology*

JHS = *Journal of Hellenic Studies*

JHS-AR = *Journal of Hellenic Studies, Archaeological Reports*

JIAN = *Journal international d'archéologie numismatique*

JMA = *Journal of Mediterranean Archaeology*

JNES = *Journal of Near Eastern Studies*

JRAI = *Journal of the Royal Anthropological Institute*

JRAS = *Journal of the Royal Asiatic Society*

JSSEA = *Journal of the Society for the Study of Egyptian Antiquities*

Khirokitia = *Fouilles récentes à Khirokitia (Chypre) 1977–1981: I–II. Recherche sur les Civilisations.* Paris. 1984.

Kition = *Excavations at Kition V: I: The Pre-Phoenician Levels, Areas I and II.* V. Karageorghis and M. Demas. Nicosia. 1985.

KTU = *The Cuneiform Alphabetic Texts from Ugarit, Ras Ibn Hani and Other Places (KTU).* Second, enlarged edition. (= *Abhandlungen Zur Literatur Alt-Syrien-Palästinas und Mesopotamiens,* Band 8.) M. Dietrich, O. Loretz, and J. Sanmartin, eds. Münster. 1995.

LAE = *The Literature of Ancient Egypt: An Anthology of Stories, Instructions, and Poetry.* W. K. Simpson, ed. R. O. Faulkner, E. F. Wente, Jr., and W. K. Simpson, trans. New Haven. 1972.

Lilybaeum = *Lilybaeum (Atti della Accademia Nazionale dei Lincei: Notizie Degli Scavi di Antichà.* Serie 8: 30.) H. Frost. Rome. 1981.

LSJ⁹ = *A Greek-English Lexicon.* 9th ed. with supp. H. G. Liddell, R. Scott, and H. S. Jones, eds. Oxford. 1968 (With Revised Supplement, 1996).

MA = *Marine Archaeology.* (Proceedings of the Twenty-third Symposium of the Colston Research Society at the University of Bristol, April 4–8, 1971.) (*Colston Papers* no. 32.) D. J. Blackman, ed. London. 1973.

MAdPT = *Marine Archaeology.* J. du Plat Taylor, ed. London. 1965.

MDIK = *Mitteilungen des Deutschen Archäologischen Instituts, Abteilung Kairo*

Mélanges = *Mélanges de l'Université Saint-Joseph, Beyrouth*

MEM = *The Mycenaeans in the Eastern Mediterranean.* (Acts of the International Archaeological Symposium at Nicosia, March 27–April 2, 1972.) 1973.

MIFAO = *Mémoires de l'institut française d'archéologie orientale du Caire*

MM = *The Mariner's Mirror*

MME = *The Minnesota Messenia Expedition: Reconstructing a Bronze Age Regional Environment.* W.A. McDonald and G.R. Rapp, Jr., eds. Minneapolis. 1972.

MMR = *Maritime Monographs and Reports.* National Maritime Museum, Greenwich.

MT = *The Minoan Thalassocracy: Myth and Reality.* (Proceedings of the Third International Symposium at the Swedish Institute in Athens, May 31–June 5, 1982.) R. Hägg and N. Marinatos, eds. Stockholm. 1984.

NASN = *Nautical Archaeology Society Newsletter*

NC = *La Nouvelle Clio*

NEAEHL = *The New Encyclopedia of Archeological Excavations in the Holy Land* 1–4. E. Stern, ed. Jerusalem. 1993.

NG = *National Geographic*

NGR = *National Geographic Research*

OA = *Opuscula Archaeologica*

OAth = *Opuscula Atheniensia*

OCSS = *The Oxford Companion of Ships and the Sea.* Oxford. 1976.

Odyssey = *The Odyssey.* 2 vols. Reprint. Loeb Classical Library. A. T. Murray, trans. Harvard. 1974–75.

OED² = *The Oxford English Dictionary.* 2d ed. Oxford. 1989. 1973.

OLA = *Orientalia Lovaniensia Analecta*

OLD = *Oxford Latin Dictionary.* P. G. W. Glare, ed. Oxford.1982.

Oleron = *OCSS:* s.v. Oleron, the Laws of

Or = *Orientalia*

OrA = *Oriens Antiquus*

PAP = *Proceedings of the American Philosophical Society*

PCA = *Pylos Comes Alive: Industry + Administration in a Mycenaean Palace.* C. W. Shelmerdine and T. G. Palaima, eds. New York. 1984.

PEQ = *Palestine Exploration Quarterly*

PGP = *Problems in Greek Prehistory.* (Papers Presented at the Centenary Conference of the British School of Archaeology at Athens, Manchester, April 1986.) E. B. French and K. A. Wardle, eds. Bristol.

PM = *The Palace of Minos* I–IV. A. Evans. London. 1921–64.

PPS = *Proceedings of the Prehistoric Society*

PRU = *Le palais royal d'Ugarit*

PZ = *Prähistorische Zeitschrift*

QDAP = *Quarterly of the Department of Antiquities in Palestine*

RA = *Revue archéologique*

RAssyr = *Revue d'Assyriologie*

RB = *Revue biblique*

RBCC = *The Relations between Cyprus and Crete, ca. 2000– 500 B.C.* (Acts of the International Archaeological Symposium at Nicosia, April 16–22, 1978.) Nicosia. 1979.

RDAC = *Report of the Department of Antiquities, Cyprus*

Rd'É = *Revue d'égyptologie*

Res Mycenaeae = *Res Mycenaeae.* (Akten des VII. Internationalen Mykenologischen Kolloquiums in Nürnberg vom 6.–10. April 1981.) A. Heubeck and G. Neumann, eds. Göttingen. 1983.

RH = *Revue de histoire de la philosophie et d'histoire générale de la civilisation.* N.S.

RlA = Reallexikon der Assyriologie. Berlin. 1928–

RRS = *Archéologie au Levant. Receuil Roger Saidah. Séries: Collection de la Maison de l'Orient méditerranéen* XII, *Serie archéologique* IX. Lyon. 1982.

RSO = *Ras Shamra-Ougarit*

SACI = Stone Anchors from the Coast of Israel. *Sefunim* 3 (1969–71): 92, pl. 9.

SAOC, OI = *Studies in Ancient Oriental Civilization, The Oriental Institute.* Chicago.

SBT = *Studien zu den Boğazköy–Texten*

SC = *Sociétés et Compagnies de commerce en Orient et dans l'océan Indien.* (Actes du huitième Colloque international d'histoire maritime, Beyrouth, 5–10 septembre 1966). M. Mollat, ed. Paris.

SCABA = *Sanctuaries and Cults in the Aegean Bronze Age.* (Proceedings of the First International Symposium at the Swedish Institute, Athens, May 12–13, 1980.) (*Acta Instituti Athensiensis Regni Sueciae,* series in 4°, 28.) R. Hägg and N. Marinatos, eds. Stockholm. 1981.

SDL = *Studi in onore di Professor Doro Levi. Antichità Cretesi* I (Universita di Catania, Instituto di Archeologica). Catania. 1973.

SIMA = *Studies in Mediterranean Archaeology*

SIMAL = *Studies in Mediterranean Archaeology and Literature*

SKHC = *Scenes of King Herihor in the Court: The Temple of Khonsu* I: Plates 1–110. (UC, OIP 100). By the Epigraphic Survey. Chicago. 1979.

SPB = *Sewn Planked Boats: Archaeological and Ethnographic Paper Presented to a Conference at Greenwich,* November 1984. (*BARIS* 276.) S. McGrail and E. Kentley, eds. Oxford. 1985.

SSCA² = *Second Symposium on Ship Construction in Antiquity.* (Summaries of lectures.) Delphi. 1987.

SSCA³ = *Third Symposium on Ship Construction in Antiquity.* (Summaries of lectures.) Athens. 1989.

SSCA⁴ = *Fourth Symposium on Ship Construction in Antiquity.* (Summaries of lectures). Athens. 1991.

SSCA⁵ = *Fifth Symposium on Ship Construction in Antiquity.* (Summaries of lectures.) Nauplion. 1993.

Thalassa = *Thalassa: L'Égée préhistorique et la mer.* (Actes de la troisième Recntre égéenne internationale de l'Université de Liège, Station de recherches sous-marines et océanographiques [StaReSO], Clavi, Corse [23–25 avril 1990].) R. Laffineur and L. Basch, eds. Liege. 1991.

Thera = *Thera and the Aegean World.* (Papers Presented at the Second International Scientific Congress, Santorini, Greece, August 1978.) C. Doumas, ed. London. 1978.

Thera II = *Thera and the Aegean World* II. (Papers and Proceedings of the Second International Scientific Congress, Santorini, Greece, August 1978.) London. 1980.

Thera III / 1 = *Thera and the Aegean World* III. (Papers and Proceedings of the Third International Congress, Santorini, Greece, September 3–9, 1989.) Vol. 1: *Archaeology.* D. A. Hardy, ed. London. 1990.

Thera III / 3 = *Thera and the Aegean World* III. (Papers and Proceedings of the Third International Congress, Santorini, Greece, September 3–9, 1989.) Vol. 3: *Chronology.* D. A. Hardy, ed. London. 1990.

Treasures = Treasures of Tutankhamun. Trustees of the British Museum. London. 1972.

Tropis I = (Proceedings of the First International Symposium on Ship Construction in Antiquity, Piraeus, August 30–September 1, 1985.) H. Tzalas, ed. Athens. 1989.

Tropis II = (Proceedings of the Second International Symposium on Ship Construction in Antiquity, Delphi, August 27–29, 1987.) H. Tzalas, ed. Athens. 1990.

Tropis III = (Proceedings of the Third International Symposium on Ship Construction in Antiquity, Athens, August 24–27, 1989.) H. Tzalas, ed. Athens. 1995.

Tropis IV = (Proceedings of the Fourth International Symposium on Ship Construction in Antiquity, Athens, August 29–September 1, 1991). H. Tzalas, ed. Athens. 1996.

Tropis V = (Proceedings of the Fifth International Symposium on Ship Construction in Antiquity, Nauplion, August 26–28, 1993.) H. Tzalas, ed. Athens. In press.

TUAS = Temple University Aegean Symposium 7. (Symposium sponsored by the Department of Art History, Temple University, with the theme "Trade and Travel in the Cyclades during the Bronze Age," March 5, 1982.)

TvA = Teva va Aretz. (English series.)

TUAT = Texte aus der Umwelt des Alten Testaments

UC,OIC = The University of Chicago, Oriental Institute Communications

UC,OIP = The University of Chicago, Oriental Institute Publications

UF = Ugarit–Forschungen

UR = Ugarit in Retrospect: Fifty Years of Ugarit and Ugaritic. G. D. Young, ed. Winona Lake. 1981.

UT = Ugaritic Textbook. (*AO* 38). C. H. Gordon. Rome. 1965.

VS = Valcamonica Symposium (Actes du Symposium International d'Art Préhistorique, Capo di Ponte [Edizioni del Centro]). 1970.

WA = World Archaeology

WO = Die Welt des Orients

Wreszinski = Wreszinski, W. Atlas zur altägyptischen Kulturgeschichte I–II. Leipzig. 1923–35.

ZA = Zeitschrift für assyriologie

ZÄSA = Zeitschrift für ägyptische Sprachen und Altertumskunde

ZDPV = Zeitschrift des Deutschen Palästina–Vereins

References

Abercrombie, T. J. 1977. Egypt: Change Comes to a Changeless Land. *NG* 151: 312–43.

Aboud, J. 1994. *Die Rolle des Königs und seiner Familie nach den Texten von Ugarit* (= *Forschungen zur Anthropologie und Religionsgeschichte,* Band 27.) M.L.G. Dietrich and O. Loretz, eds. Münster.

Abramovitz, K. 1980. Frescoes from Ayia Irini, Keos. Parts 2–4. *Hesperia* 49: 57–85, pls. 3–12.

Aharoni, Y. 1979. *The Land of the Bible: A Historigraphical Geography.* 2nd rev. and emended ed. A. F. Rainey, trans. and ed. London.

Ahlberg, G. 1971. *Fighting on Land and Sea in Greek Geometric Art.* (*Acta Instituti Athaniensis Regni Sueciae,* series in 4°, 16.) Stockholm.

Aitken, M. J. 1988. The Thera Eruption: Continuing Discussion of the Date: I: Resume of Dating. *Archaeometry* 30: 165–69.

Åkerström, A. 1975. More Canaanite Jars from Greece. *OAth* 11:186–92.

Albenda, P. 1972. A Syro-Palestinian (?) City on a Ninth century B.C. Assyrian Relief. *BASOR* 206: 42–48.

Albright, W. F. 1948. Exploring in Sinai with the University of California African Expedition. *BASOR* 109: 5–20.

Aldred, C. 1970. The Foreign Gifts Offered to Pharaoh. *JEA* 56: 105–16.

Alexiou, S. 1970. Mikrai Anaskaphai kai Perisulloge Arxaion eis Kreten. *Praktika tes en Athenais Archaiologikes Etaireias:* 252–55, pls. 354–55. (In Greek.)

———. 1972. Larnakes kai Aggeia ek Taphou Para to Gazi Irakleiou. *AE:* 86–98. (In Greek.)

———. 1973. Nea Parastasis Ploiou epi Minoikis Larnakos. In *Anatupon ek tou a Tomou ton Pepragmenon tou Gama Diethnous Kritologikou Sunedriou, En Rethumno, 18–23 September, 1971, Athens:* 3–12 pin. 1–2. (In Greek.)

——— n.d. *Minoan Civilization³.* Heraclion.

Allen, S. H. 1994. Trojan Grey Ware at Tel Miqne-Ekron. *BASOR* 293: 39–51.

Alpözen, O. 1983. The Bodrum Museum of Underwater Archaeology. *Museum* 35: 61–63.

Alt, A. 1951. Ägyptisch-Ugaritisches. *AfO* 15 (1945–51): 69–74.

Amiet, P. 1961. *La glyptique mésopotamienne archaïque.* Paris.

Amiran, R. 1972. A Cult Stele from Arad. *IEJ* 22: 86–88, pls.14–15.

Artzy, M. 1984. Unusual Late Bronze Age Ship Representation from Tel Akko. *MM* 70: 59–64.

———. 1985. Merchandise and Merchantmen: On Ships and Shipping in the Late Bronze Age Levant. In *Acts of the Second International Cyprological Congress.* T. Papadopoullos and S. Chatzestylli, eds. Nicosia: 135–40.

———. 1987. On Boats and Sea Peoples. *BASOR* 266: 75–84.

———. 1988. Development of War/Fighting Boats of the Second Millennium B.C. in the Eastern Mediterranean. *RDAC:* 181–86.

———. 1991A. Conical Cups and Pumice, Aegean Cult at Tel Nami, Israel. In *Thalassa:* 203–206, pls. 52–53.

———. 1991B. Cultic Ship Representation in Late Bronze Age Mediterranean. In *SSCA⁴.*

———. 1994. On Boats, on Rocks, and on 'Nomads of the Sea.' *C.M.S. News* 21: 2–3.

Ashburner, W. 1909. *The Rhodian Sea Law.* Oxford.

Astour, M. C. 1964. Greek Names in the Semitic World

and Semitic Names in the Greek World. *JNES* 23: 193–201.

———. 1965. New Evidence of the Last Days of Ugarit. *AJA* 69: 253–58.

———. 1970. Maʾḫadu, the Harbor of Ugarit. *JESHO* 13: 113–27.

———. 1973. Ugarit and the Aegean. *AOAT* 22: 17–27.

———. 1981. Ugarit and the Great Powers. In *UR*: 3–29.

———. 1995. La topographie du royaume d'Ougarit. In *La pays d'Ougarit autour de 1200 av. J.-C.: Histoire et archéologie.* (Actes du Colloque International, Paris, 28 juin–1ᵉʳ juillet 1993 = *Ras Shamra-Ougarit* 11.) M. Yon, M. Sznycer, and P. Bordreuil, eds. Paris: 55–71.

Aubert, C. 1995. Nouvelle interpretation du decor de la larnax de Gazi no 18985. In *Tropis* III: 31–42.

Baines, J. 1990. Interpreting the Story of the Shipwrecked Sailor. *JEA* 76: 55–76.

Bakr, M. I., and A. Nibbi. 1991. Three Stone Anchors from Tell Basta. *Rd'É*: 3–10, pl. 1.

———. 1994. A Stone Anchor Workshop at Marsa Matruh. *Discussions in Egyptology* 29: 5–22.

Baldacci, M. 1989. Review. *BiOr* 46: 110–20.

Balensi, J. 1980. Les fouilles de R. W. Hamilton à Tell Abu Hawam: Niveaux IV et V. 3 vols. (Ph.D. thesis, University of Strasbourg.)

Balfour, H. 1890. On the Structure and Affinities of the Composite Bow. *JRAI* 26: 210–20.

———. 1921. *The Archer's Bow in the Homeric Poems.* The Royal Anthropological Institute of Great Britain. London.

Ballard, G. A. 1920. The Sculptures of Deir el–Bahri. *MM* 6: 149–55, 162–74, 212–17.

———. 1937. Egyptian Shipping of About 1500 B.C. *MM* 23: 103–105.

Barber, E. J. W. 1991. *Prehistoric Textiles: The Development of Cloth in the Neolithic and Bronze Ages with Special Reference to the Aegean.* Princeton.

———. 1994. *Women's Work: The First 20,000 Years.* New York.

Barber, R. L. N. 1981. The Late Cycladic Period: A Review. *ABSA* 76: 1–21.

Barnett, R. D. 1956. Phoenicia and the Ivory Trade. *Archaeology* 9: 87–97.

———. 1958. Early Shipping in the Near East. *Antiquity* 32: 220–30, pls. 21–24.

———. 1969. Ezekiel and Tyre. *Eretz Israel* 9: 6–13, pls. 1–4.

———. 1973. New Data on Ancient Shipping in the Levant. (Unpublished lecture given at the First Archaeological Congress, August 1973, Jerusalem.)

Basch, L. 1969. Phoenician Oared Ships. *MM* 55: 139–62, 227–45.

———. 1972. Ancient Wrecks and the Archaeology of Ships. *IJNA* 1: 1–58.

———. 1975. Another Punic Wreck in Sicily: Its Ram, 1. A Typological Sketch. *IJNA* 4: 201–28.

———. 1976A. Radeaux minoens. *Cd'AS* 5: 85–97.

———. 1976B. One Aspect of the Problems Which Arise from the Interpretation of Representations of Ancient Ships. *MM* 62: 231–33.

———. 1976C. Le navire cousu de Bon Porté. *Cd'AS* 5: 37–42.

———. 1978. Le navire *mnš* et autres notes de voyage en Égypte. *MM* 64: 99–123.

———. 1981A. The Sewn Ship of Bon–Porté. *MM* 67: 244.

———. 1981B. Carthage and Rome: Tenons and Mortises. *MM* 67: 245–50.

———. 1983. Bow and Stern Appendages in the Ancient Mediterranean. *MM* 69: 395–412.

———. 1985A. The *Isis* of Ptolomy II Philadelphius. *MM* 71: 129–51.

———. 1985B. Anchors in Egypt. *MM* 71: 453–67.

———. 1986. The Aegina Pirate Ships of c. B.C. 1700. *MM* 72: 415–38.

———. 1987. *Le musée imaginaire de la marine antique.* Athens.

———. 1987A. The Interpretation of Ship Representations in Profile. The Case of the Aegina Ships of c. B.C. 1700. *MM* 73: 198–200.

———. 1994A. Un navire grec en Égypte à L'époque de Ulysse. *Neptunia* 195: 19–26.

———. 1994B. Some Remarks on the Use of Stone Anchors and Pierced Stones in Egypt. *IJNA* 23: 219–27.

Basch, L., and M. Artzy. 1985. App. 2: Ship Graffiti at Kition. In *Kition*: 322–36.

Bass, G. F. 1960–61. A Bronze Age Shipwreck. *Expedition* 3: 2–11.

———. 1961. The Cape Gelidonya Wreck: Preliminary Report. *AJA* 65: 267–76.

———. 1965. Cape Gelidonya. In *MAdPT*: 119–40.

———. 1972. The Earliest Seafarers in the Mediterranean and the Near East. In *HSBUA*: 12–36.

———. 1973. Cape Gelidonya and the Bronze Age Maritime Trade. *AOAT* 22: 29–38.

———. 1976. Sheytan Deresi: Preliminary Report. *IJNA* 5: 293–303.

———. 1985. Bronze Age Shipwreck . . . The Oldest and Most Valuable Ever Excavated in the Mediterranean. *NG* 167: 2–3.

———. 1986. A Bronze Age Shipwreck at Ulu Burun (Kaş): 1984 Campaign. *AJA* 90: 269–96, pl. 17.

———. 1987. Oldest Known Shipwreck Reveals Bronze Age Splendors. *NG* 172: 693–733.

———. 1988. Return to Cape Gelidonya. *INAN* 15/2 (June): 2–5.

———. 1989A. Civilization under the Sea: Treasures and Secrets Long Lost Are Now Being Returned to Land. *Modern Maturity* (April–May): 58–64.

———. 1989B. The Construction of a Seagoing Vessel of the Late Bronze Age. *Tropis* I: 25–35.

———. 1990A. Cape Gelidonya–Once More. *INAN* 16/4: 12–13.

———. 1990B. A Bronze-Age Writing-Diptych from the Sea off Lycia. *Kadmos* 29/2: 168–69.

———. 1990C. Proceedings: The Interpretation of

Shipwrecked Cypriot Artifacts. *AJA* 94: 337.

———. 1991. Evidence of Trade from Bronze Age Shipwrecks. In *BATM*: 69–82.

———. 1996. *Shipwrecks in the Bodrum Museum of Underwater Archaeology.* Ankara.

———. In press. Beneath the Wine Dark Sea: Nautical Archaeology and the Phoenicians of the Odyssey. In *Greeks and Barbarians.* J. E. Coleman and C. A. Walz, eds.

Bass, G. F., C. Pulak, D. Collon, and J. Weinstein. 1989. The Bronze Age Shipwreck at Ulu Burun: 1986 Campaign. *AJA* 93: 1–29.

Bass, G. F., D. A. Frey, and C. Pulak. 1984. A Late Bronze Age Shipwreck at Kaş, Turkey. *IJNA* 13: 271–79.

Bass, G. F., and P. Throckmorton. 1961. Excavating a Bronze Age Shipwreck. *Archaeology* 14: 78–87.

Baumbach, L. 1983. An Examination of the Evidence for a State of Emergency at Pylos c. 1200 BC from the Linear B Tablets. *Res Mycenaeae*: 28–40.

Beal, R. H. 1992. The Location of Cilician Ura. *AS* 42: 65–73.

Beaux, N. 1990. *Le cabinet de curiosités de Thoutmosis III: Plantes et animaux du «Jardin botaniques» de Karnak.* OLA 36. Leuven.

Belger, C. 1895. Deck, Ruderbänke und Mastbefestigung an ägyptischen Schiffsmodellen. *ZÄSA* 33: 24–32.

Ben-Arieh, R. 1994. A Wall Painting of a Saint's Face in the Church of Mt. Bernice. *BA* 57: 134–37.

Bennett, E. L., Jr., and J.-P. Olivier. 1973. *The Pylos Tablets Transcribed* I. (*Incunabula Graeca* 51.) Rome.

Bennett, E. L., et al. 1989. 436 raccords et quasi-raccords de fragments inédits dans KT 5. *Minos* 24: 199–242.

Bennett, J. 1939. The Restoration Inscription of Tut'anchamūn. *JEA* 25: 8–15.

Benoît, F. 1961. *Fouilles sous-marines: L'épave du Grand Congloué à Marseille.* (XIVe supplément à Gallia.) Paris.

Benson, J. L. 1961. A Problem in Orientalizing Cretan Birds: Mycenaean or Philistine Prototypes. *JNES* 20: 73–84, pls. 3–6.

———. 1975. Birds on Cypro-Geometric Pottery. In *The Archaeology of Cyprus.* N. Robertson, ed. Park Ridge: 129–50.

Berger, P. R. 1969. Die Alašia-Briefe Ugaritica 5, Noug. Nrn. 22–24. *UF* 1: 217–21, 357.

Berger, P. R. 1970. Zu den "akkadischen" Briefen Ugaritica V. *UF* 2: 285–93.

Bernal, M. 1987. *Black Athena* I. New Brunswick.

Betancourt, P. P. 1987. Dating of the Aegean Late Bronze Age with Radiocarbon. *Archaeometry* 29: 45–49.

Betts, J. H. 1968. Trees in the Wind on Cretan Sealings. *AJA* 72: 149–50.

———. 1973. Ships on Minoan Seals. In *MA*: 325–38.

Bietak, M. 1984. Problems of Middle Bronze Age Chronology: New Evidence from Egypt. *AJA* 88: 471–85.

———. 1988. Zur Marine des Alten Reiches. In *Pyramid Studies and other Essays Presented to I. E. S. Edwards.* J. Baines, T. G. H. James, A. Leahy, and A. F. Shore, eds. London: 35–40, pls. 5–9.

———. 1992. Minoan Wall-Paintings Unearthed at Ancient Avaris. *Egyptian Archaeology* 2: 26–28.

———. 1995. Connections Between Egypt and the Minoan World: New Results from Tell el Dabᶜa / Avaris. In *EAL*: 19–28, pls. 1–4.

Bishop, C. W. 1938. Long Houses and Dragon Boats. *Antiquity* 12: 411–24, pls. 1–4.

Black, E., and D. Samuel. 1991. What Were Sails Made of? *MM* 77: 217–26.

Blegen, C. W. 1949. Hyria. *Hesperia: Supplement* 8: 39–42.

Blegen, C. W., and M. Rawson. 1966A. *The Palace of Nestor at Pylos in Western Messenia* I: *The Buildings and Their Contents.* Pt. 1: *Text.* Princeton.

———. 1966B. *The Palace of Nestor at Pylos in Western Messenia* I: *The Buildings and Their Contents.* Pt. 2: *Illustrations.* Princeton.

Blegen, C. W., M. Rawson, L. W. Taylor, and W. P. Donovan. 1973. *The Palace of Nestor at Pylos in Western Messenia* III: *Acropolis and Lower Town Tholoi, Grave Circle, and Chamber Tombs Discoveries outside the Citadel.* Princeton.

Boardman, J. 1967. The Khaniale Tekke Tombs, II. *ABSA* 62: 57–75, pls. 7–17.

———. 1970. *Greek Gems and Finger Rings.* London.

Bodenheimer, F. S. 1949. *Animal Life in Biblical Lands: From the Stone Age to the End of the Nineteenth Century* I. Jerusalem. (In Hebrew.)

Borchardt, L. 1907. *Das Grabdenkmal des Königs Ne-User-Reᶜ.* Leipzig.

———. 1913. *Das Grabdenkmal des Königs S'a3hu–reᶜ* II. Leipzig.

———. 1981. *Das Grabdenkmal Des Königs Sa3hu–reᶜ: Band II: Die Wandbilder,* Text. Osnabrück. (Reprint, 1913.)

Boreux, C. 1925. *Études de nautique égyptienne: l'art de la navigation en Égypte jusqu'à la fin de l'Ancien Empire.* (*MIFAO* 50) Cairo.

Bound, M. 1985. Early Observations on the Construction of the Pre-Classical Wreck at Campese Bay, Island of Giglio. In *SPB*: 49–65.

———. 1991. The Giglio Wreck. (*Enalia Supplement* 1.) Athens.

———. 1995. Das Giglio-Wrack. In *IPR*: 63–68.

Bouzek, J. 1985. *The Aegean, Anatolia and Europe: Cultural Interrelations in the Second Millennium* B.C. (*SIMA* 39.) Göteborg.

———. 1994. Late Bronze Age Greece and the Balkans: A Review of the Present Picture. *ABSA* 89: 217–34.

Braemer, F., and J. Marcadé. 1953. Céramique antique et pièces d'ancres trouvées en mer à la Pointe de la Kynosoura (Baie de Marathon). *BCH* 77: 139–54.

Branigan, K. 1967. Further Light on Prehistoric Relations between Crete and Byblos. *AJA* 71: 117–21.

———. 1981. Minoan Colonialism. *ABSA* 76: 23–33.

Breasted, J. H. 1917. The Earliest Boats on the Nile. *JEA* 4: 174–76, 255, pls. 33–34, 54.

———. 1948. *Egyptian Servant Statues.* New York.

Broodbank, C. 1989. The Longboat and Society in the

Cyclades in the Keros–Syros Culture. *AJA* 93: 319–37.

———. 1992. Colonization and Culture in the Neolithic and Early Bronze Age Cyclades. *AJA* 96: 341.

———. 1993. Ulysses without Sails: Trade, Distance, Knowledge and Power in the Early Cyclades. *WA* 24: 315–31.

Broodbank, C., and T. F. Strasser. 1991. Migrant Farmers and the Neolithic Colonization of Crete. *Antiquity* 65: 233–45.

Brown, L. M. 1979. The Ship Procession in the Miniature Fresco. In *Thera*: 629–44.

Brug, J. F. 1985. *A Literary and Archaeological Study of the Philistines*. (*BAR International Series* 265.) Oxford.

Brunner–Traut, E. 1956. *Die altägyptischen Scherbenbilder*. Wiesbaden.

———. 1974. Aspective. In J. Schäfer, *Principals of Egyptian Art*. J. Baines, trans. Oxford: 421–46.

Brunton, G., and G. Caton–Thompson. 1928. *The Badarian Civilization and Predynastic Remains near Badari*. London.

Bruyère, B. 1933. *Rapport sur les fouilles de Deir el Médineh (1930)*. Cairo.

Buchanan, B. 1966. *Catalogue of Ancient Near Eastern Seals in the Ashmolean Museum* I. Oxford.

Buchholz, H.-G. 1959. Keftiubarren und Erzhandel im zweiten vorchristlichen Jahrtausend. *PZ* 37: 1–40.

———. 1967. The Cylinder Seal. In *CG*: 148–59.

———. 1973. Grey Trojan Ware in Cyprus and Northern Syria. In *Bronze Age Migrations in the Aegean*. R. S. Crossland and A. Birchall, eds. London: 179–87.

Buchholz, H.-G., and V. Karageorghis. 1973. *Prehistoric Greece and Cyprus*. London.

Buck, R. J. 1989. Mycenaean Human Sacrifice. *Minos* 24: 131–37.

Cadogan, G. 1969. Notices of Books: Bass (G. F.) and Others. Cape Gelidonya: A Bronze Age Shipwreck. *JHS* 89: 187–89.

———. 1972. Cypriot Objects in the Bronze Age Aegean and Their Importance. In *Praktika First Cypriot Congress*. Nicosia: 5–13.

———. 1973. Patterns in the Distribution of Mycenaean Pottery in the Eastern Mediterranean. In *MEM*: 166–74.

———. 1978. Dating the Aegean Bronze Age without Radiocarbon. *Archaeometry* 20: 209–14.

———. 1979. Cyprus and Crete c. 2000–1400 B.C. In *RBCC*: 63–68.

Caminos, R. A. 1954. *Late–Egyptian Miscellanies*. (*Brown Egytological Studies* 1.) London.

Campbell, E. F. 1964. *The Chronology of the Amarna Letters*. Baltimore.

Campbell, R. W. 1957. The Killick in Newfoundland. *MM* 43: 158–59.

Canney, M. A. 1936. Boats and Ships in Temples and Tombs. In *Occident and Orient: Gaster Anniversary Volume*. B. Schindler and A. Marmorstein, eds. London: 50–57.

Caquot, A., M. Sznycer, and A. Herdner. 1974. *Textes ougaritiques* I: *Mythes et légendes*. Paris.

Carpenter, R. 1958. Phoenicians in the West. *AJA* 62: 35–53.

Carter, H. 1933. *The Tomb of Tut–Ankh–Amun* III. London.

Caskey, J. L. 1964. Investigations in Keos, 1963. *Hesperia* 33: 314–35.

Casson, L. 1950. The *Isis* and Her Voyage. *APATP* 81: 43–56.

———. 1964. *Illustrated History of Ships & Boats*. Garden City.

———. 1966. Studies in Ancient Sails and Rigging. In *Essays in Honor of C. Bradford Welles* (*ASP I*): 43–58.

———. 1975. Bronze Age Ships. The Evidence of the Thera Wall Paintings. *IJNA* 4 : 3–10.

———. 1978. The Thera Ships. *IJNA* 7: 232–33.

———. 1989. *The Periplus Maris Erythraei*. Princeton.

———. 1990. Documentary Evidence for Graeco-Roman Shipbuilding (P. Flor. I 69). *BASP* 27: 15–19.

———. 1992A. The Nautical Imagery in *Anthologia Graeca* 10.23. *CQ* 12: 555–57.

———. 1992B. Odysseus' Boat (*Od.* 5.244–53). *IJNA* 21: 73–74.

———. 1995A. *Ships and Seamanship in the Ancient World*. Baltimore. (Reprint with Addenda and Corrigenda.)

———. 1995B. Merchant Galleys. In *Conway's History of the Ship: The Age of the Galley*. London: 117–26.

Catling, H. W. 1964. *Cypriote Bronzework in the Mycenaean World*. Oxford.

———. 1969. The Cypriote Copper Industry. *AV* 2: 81–88.

———. 1970. Cyprus in the Neolithic and Chalcolithic Periods. In *CAH**: 539–56.

———. 1973. The Achaean Settlement of Cyprus. In *MEM*: 34–39.

Caubet, A., and F. Poplin. 1987. Les objets de matière dure animale. Étude du matériau. In *Ras Shamra–Ougarit* III (*Le centre de la ville: 38ème–44ème campagnes* [*1978–84*]. Dir. M. Yon.): 273–306.

Chadwick, J. 1958. *The Decipherment of Linear B*. Cambridge.

———. 1972. The Mycenaean Documents. In *MME*: 100–16.

———. 1973A. Part III: Additional Commentary. In M. Ventris and J. Chadwick, *Documents in Mycenaean Greek*²: 385–524.

———. 1973B. A Cretan Fleet? In *SDL*: 199–201.

———. 1976. *The Mycenaean World*. London.

———. 1979. The Minoan Origin of the Classical Cypriote Script. In *RBCC*: 139–43.

———. 1987A. The Muster of the Pylian Fleet. In *Tractata Mycenaea*. (Proceedings of the Eighth International Colloquium on Mycenaean Studies, Ohrid, September 15–20, 1985.) P. H. Ilievski and L. Crepajac, eds. Skopje: 75–84.

———. 1987B. *Linear B and Related Scripts*. Berkeley.

———. 1988. The Women of Pylos. In *Texts, Tablets and Scribes: Studies in Mycenaean Epigraphy and Economy Offered to Emmett L. Bennett, Jr.* (*Minos*, supp. no. 10.) J. P. Olivier and Th. G. Palaima, eds. Salamanca: 43–95.

Chantraine, P. 1970. *Dictionnaire étymologique de la langue grecque* II. Paris.

Charlton, W. H., Jr. 1995. The Rope. *INAQ* 22/2: 17.

———. 1996. Rope and the Art of Knot-Tying in the Seafaring of the Ancient Eastern Mediterranean. (M.A. thesis, Texas A&M University).

Chen, A. 1989. The Thera Theory. *Discover* 10/2: 76–83.

Cherry, J. F. 1981. Pattern and Process in the Earliest Colonization of the Mediterranean Islands. *PPS* 47: 41–68.

———. 1990. The First Colonization of the Mediterranean Islands: A Review of Recent Research. *JMA* 3: 145–221.

Christensen, A. E. 1972. Scandinavian Ships from Earliest Times to the Vikings. In *HSBUA:* 159–80.

Clamer, C. 1980. A Gold Plaque from Lachish. *Tel Aviv* 7: 152–62.

Clarke, S. 1920. Nile Boats and other Matters. *AEg:* 2–9, 40–51.

Clarke, S., and R. Engelbach. 1990. *Ancient Egyptian Construction and Architecture.* (Unabridged repub., 1930). New York.

Cline, E. 1987. Amenhotep III and the Aegean: A Reassessment of Egypto-Aegean Relations in the Fourteenth Century B.C. *Or* 56: 1–36, pls. 1–4.

———. 1990. An Unpublished Amenhotep III Faience Plaque from Mycenae. *JAOS* 110: 200–12.

———. 1991A. Orientalia in the Late Bronze Age Aegean: A Catalogue and Analysis of Trade and Contacts between the Aegean and Egypt, Anatolia and the Near East. (Ph.D. diss., University of Pennsylvania.) University Microfilms: Ann Arbor.

———. 1991B. A Possible Hittite Embargo Against the Mycenaeans. *Historia* 40: 1–9.

Clowes, G. S. L. 1932. *Sailing Ships: Their History and Development as Illustrated by the Collection of Ship Models in the Science Museum.* London.

Coates, J. F. 1985. Some Structural Models for Sewn Boats. In *SPB:* 9–18.

———. 1987. Interpretation of Ancient Ship Representations. *MM* 73: 197.

Coldstream, J. N. 1977. *Geometric Greece.* London.

Coleman, J. E. 1985. "Frying Pans" of the Early Bronze Age Aegean. *AJA* 89: 191–219, pls. 33–37.

Conwell, D. 1987. On Ostrich Eggs and Libyans: Traces of Bronze Age People from Bates' Island, Egypt. *Expedition* 29/3: 25–34.

Coulton, R. L. 1977. Preserved Aboriginal Canoes in Western Canada. *MM* 63: 248–52.

Cowley, A. 1923. *Aramaic Papyri of the Fifth Century B.C.* Oxford.

Crossland, R. A. 1980. The Mystery of Ahhiyawa. *ILN* 268 (no. 2986, September): 85–86.

Culican, W. 1970. Problems of Phoenicio–Punic Iconography: A Contribution. *AJBA* 1/3: 28–57.

Cunchillos, J. R. 1983. Le pronom démonstratif *hn* en Ugaritique. Son existence, son histoire, ses rapports avec les autres démonstratifs et avec l'article. *AuOr* 1: 155–65.

———. 1986. Par une pluie torrentielle la moitié dela flotte se trouva à Tyr et l'autre moitié à Akre. Une lettre ougaritique du roi de Tyr au roi d'Ugarit (*KTU* 2.38). *Sefarad* 46: 133–41.

———. 1989. Correspondance: *Textes ougaritiques* II: *Textes religieux, rituels, correspondance.* Paris: 241–421.

Dakoronia, F. 1990. War-Ships on Sherds of LH III C Kraters from Kynos. In *Tropis* II: 117–22.

———. 1991. Kynos . . . Fleet. In *SSCA*⁴.

———. 1993. Homeric Towns in East Lokris: Problems of Identification. *Hesperia* 62: 115–27.

———. 1995. War Ships on Sherds of LH III Kraters from Kynos? Editor's Note. In *Tropis* III: 147–48.

———. 1996. Kynos . . . Fleet. In *Tropis* IV: 159–71.

Danelius, E., and H. Steinitz. 1967. The Fishes and other Aquatic Animals on the Punt–Reliefs at Deir El–Bahri. *JEA* 53: 15–24.

Daressy, G. 1895. Une flotille phénicienne d'après une peinture égyptienne. *RA* 27: 286–92, pls. 14–15.

Davaras, C. 1976. *Guide to Cretan Antiquities.* New Jersey.

———. 1980. Une ancre minoenne sacrée? *BCH* 104: 47–71.

Davies, N. de G. 1900. *The Mastaba of Ptahhetep and Akhethetep at Saqqara* I: *The Chapel of Ptahhetep and the Hieroglyphs.* London.

———. 1901. *The Mastaba at Ptahhetep and Akhethetep at Saqqara* II: *The Mastaba. The Sculptures of Akhethetep.* London.

———. 1902. *The Rock Tombs of Deir el Gebrâwi* I–II. London.

———. 1905A. *The Rock Tombs of Amarna* II: *The Tombs of Panehesy and Meryra II.* London.

———. 1905B. *The Rock Tombs of Amarna* III: *The Tombs of Huya and Ahmes.* London.

———. 1908. *The Rock Tombs of El Amarna* V: *Smaller Tombs and Boundary Stelae.* London.

———. 1920. *The Tomb of Antefoker.* London.

———. 1922. *The Tomb of Puyemre at Thebes* I–II. NewYork.

———. 1923. *The Tombs of Two Officials of Thutmose IV.* London.

———. 1927. *Two Ramesside Tombs at Thebes.* New York.

———. 1930. The Egyptian Expedition: The Work of the Graphic Branch of the Expedition. *BMMA* 25 (pt. 2, December): 29–42.

———. 1933. *The Tomb of Neferhotep at Thebes.* New York.

———. 1935. The Egyptian Expedition 1934–35: The Work of the Graphic Branch of the Expedition. *BMMA* 30 (sect. 2, November): 46–57.

———. 1943. *The Tomb of Rech–mi–rē' at Thebes* I–II. New York.

———. 1948. *Seven Private Tombs at Kurnah.* London.

Davies, N. de G., and A. H. Gardiner. 1915. *The Tomb of Amenemhet* (no. 82). London.

———. 1926. *The Tomb of Ḥuy: Viceroy of Nubia in the Reign of Tutʿankhamūn* (no. 40). London.

Davies, N. de G., and R. O. Faulkner. 1947. A Syrian Trading Venture to Egypt. *JEA* 33: 40–46, pl. 8.

Davies, N. M., and N. de G. Davies. 1933. *The Tombs of Menkheperresonb, Amenmose and Another.* London.

———. 1941. Syrians in the Tomb of Amunedjeḥ. *JEA* 27: 96–98, pl. 13.

Davies, W. V. 1987. *Catalogue of Egyptian Antiquities in the British Museum* VII: *Tools and Weapons* I: *Axes*. London.

———. 1995. Ancient Egyptian Timber Imports: Analysis of Wooden Coffins in the British Museum. In *EAL*: 146–56, pls. 31–32.

Davis, J. L. 1980. Minoans and Minoanization at Ayia Irini, Keos. In *Thera* II: 257–60.

———. 1992. Review of Aegean Prehistory I: The Islands of the Aegean. *AJA* 96: 699–756.

De Boer, J. 1991. A Double Figure-Headed Boat-Type in the Eastern Mediterranean and Central Europe during the Late Bronze Ages. In *Thracia Pontica* IV (Sozopol, October 6–12, 1988). Sofia: 43–50.

De Cervin, G. B. R. 1977. The Thera Ships: Other Suggestions. *MM* 63: 150–52.

———. 1978. A Further Note on the Thera Ships. *MM* 64: 150–52.

Deilaki, E. 1987. Ship Representations from Prehistoric Argolis (MH Period). In *Tropis* II: 123–26.

Demargne, P. 1964. *Aegean Art: The Origins of Greek Art*. London.

de Moor, J. C. 1971. *The Seasonal Pattern in the Ugaritic Myth of Baᶜlu According to the Version of Ilimilku*. Neukirchen-Vluyn.

———. 1979. Contributions to the Ugaritic Lexicon. *UF* 11: 639–53.

de Morgan, J. 1895. *Fouilles à Dahchour, mars–juin 1894*. Vienne.

———. 1903. *Fouilles à Dahchour en 1894–1895*. Vienna.

Desborough, V. R., d'A. 1964. *The Last Mycenaeans and Their Successors: An Archaeological Survey c. 1200–c. 1000 B.C.* Oxford.

———. 1972. *The Greek Dark Ages*. London.

Desroches-Noblecourt, C. 1963. *Tutankhamen*. Boston.

DeVries, K., and M. L. Katzev. 1972. Greek, Etruscan and Phoenician Ships and Shipping. In *HSBUA*: 38–64.

Diamant, S. 1979. A Short History of Archaeological Sieving at Franchthi Cave, Greece. *JFA* 6: 203–17.

Dickinson, O. 1994. *The Aegean Bronze Age*. Cambridge.

Dickson, H. R. P. 1959. *The Arab of the Desert*³. London.

Dietrich, M., and O. Loretz. 1966. Zur ugaritischen Lexikographie (I). *BiOr* 23: 127–33.

———. 1977. Eine Matrosenliste aus Ugarit (*KTU* 4.40), zu ug. ǵr "Gesamtheit" und ǵr ON. *UF* 9: 332–33.

———. 1978. Das "Seefahrende Volk" von Šikila (*RS* 34.129). *UF* 10: 53–56.

———. 1984. Ugaritisch 'ṯr, aṯr, aṯryt und aṯrt. *UF* 16: 57–62.

———. 1985. Historisch-chronologische Texte aus Alalah, Ugarit, Kamid el Loz/Kumidi und den Amarna Briefen. In *TUAT* 1 *Rechts- und Wirtschaftsurkunden. Historisch-chronologische Texte*. Gütersloh: 505–20.

———. 1986. Akkadisch *siparru* "bronze," ugaritisch *spr*, ǵprt und Hebräisch *spr*, ᶜprt. *UF* 17: 401.

———. 1987. Die ugaritischen Gefässbezeichnungen *ridn* und *kw*. *UF* 19: 27–32.

———. 1990. Schiffshandel und Schiffsmiete zwischen Byblos und Ugarit (*KTU* 4.338: 10–18). *UF* 22: 89–96.

Dietrich, M., O. Loretz, and J. Sanmartín, 1973. Zur ugaritischen Lexikographie (VII). *UF* 5: 79–104.

———. 1974A. Zur ugaritischen Lexikographie (XI). *UF* 6: 19–38.

———. 1974B. Zu *PRU* 5,106 (= *RS* 18.25), 10–15. *UF* 6: 473.

———. 1975A. Die keilalphabetischen Belege für *bcr* I und *bcr* II. *UF* 7: 554–56.

———. 1975B. Guer urgaritischen Lexikographic (13). *UF* 7: 157–69.

Dijkstra, M. 1975. Does Occur the Verb *hbṯ* in *CTA* 4.III.21? *UF* 7: 563–65.

———. 1976. Two Notes on *PRU* 5, no. 60. *UF* 8: 437–39.

———. 1989. Marginalia to the Ugaritic Letters in *KTU* (II). *UF* 21: 141–52.

Dijkstra, M., and J. C. de Moor. 1975. Problematical Passages in the Legend of Aqhâtu. *UF* 7: 171–215.

Dikaios, P. 1969. *Enkomi* I: *Excavations 1948–1958: The Architectural Remains, The Tombs*. Mainz.

———. 1971. *Enkomi* II: *Excavations 1948–1958: Chronology, Summary and Conclusions, Catalogue and Appendices*. Mainz.

Dodd, E. 1972. *Polynesian Seafaring*. (*The Ring of Fire* II). New York.

Dossin, G. 1939. Les archives économiques du palais de Mari. *Syria* 20: 97–113.

Dothan, T. 1982. *The Philistines and Their Material Culture*. Jerusalem.

Dothan, T., and M. Dothan. 1992. *People of the Sea: The Search for the Philistines*. New York.

Doumas, C. 1967. Le Incisioni Rupestri di Nasso, nelle Cicladi. *BCCSP* 3: 111–32.

———. 1970. Remarques sur la forme du bateau égéen à l'âge du Bronze Ancien. In *VS*: 285–90.

———. 1982. The Minoan Thalassocracy and the Cyclades. *AA*: 5–14.

———. 1983. *Thera: Pompeii of the Ancient Aegean*. London.

———. 1989. *Santorini: A Guide to the Island and Its Archaeological Treasures*. Athens.

———. 1992. *The Wall Paintings of Thera*. A. Doumas, trans. Athens.

Driver, G. R. 1932. The Aramaic *Papyri* from Egypt: Notes on Obscure Passages. *JRAS*: 77–90.

Duel, P., et al. 1938. *The Mastaba of Mereruka* II. Chicago.

Dunand, M. 1937. *Fouilles de Byblos* I: *1926–1932* (*Atlas*). Paris.

———. 1939. *Fouilles de Byblos* I: *1926–1932* (*Text*). Paris.

———. 1950. *Fouilles de Byblos* II: *1933–1938* (*Atlas*). Paris.

———. 1954. *Fouilles de Byblos* II: *1933–1938* (*Text*). Paris.

du Plat Taylor, J. 1967A. The Stone Objects. In *CG*: 126–30.

———. 1967B. The Basketry and Matting. In *CG*: 160–62.

du Plat Taylor, J., M. V. Seton Williams, and J. Waechter. 1950. The Excavations at Sacke Gözü. *Iraq* 12: 53–138.

Dussaud, R. 1914. *Les civilisations préhelléniques*. Paris.

———. 1937. L'influence orientale en Crète. *Syria* 18: 233–34.

Eccles, E. 1939–40. The Seals and Sealings. In R. W. Hutchinson, Unpublished Objects from Palaikastro and Praisos, II. *ABSA* 40: 43–49.

Edel, E. 1966. *Die Ortsnamenlisten aus dem Totentemple Amenophis III*. Bonn.

Edgerton, W. F. 1922–23. Ancient Egyptian Ships and Shipping. *AJSLL* 39: 109–35.

———. 1926–27. Ancient Egyptian Steering Gear. *AJSLL* 43: 255–65.

Edwards, I. E. S. 1972. *The Pyramids of Egypt*. Harmondworth. (Reprint, 1947.)

Egberts, A. 1991. The Chronology of *The Report of Wenamun*. *JEA* 77: 57–67.

Eiseman, C. J., and B. S. Ridgway. 1987. *The Porticello Shipwreck: A Mediterranean Merchant Vessel of 415–385 B.C.* College Station.

El Baz, F. 1988. Finding a Pharaoh's Funeral Bark. *NG* 173: 512–33.

Elgavish, J. 1968. *Archaeological Excavations at Shiqmona* I: *The Levels of the Persian Period: Seasons 1963–1965*. Haifa.

Emanuele, P. D. 1977. Ancient Square Rigging, with and without Lifts. *IJNA* 6: 181–85.

Emery, W. 1954. *Excavations at Sakkara: Great Tombs of the First Dynasty* II. London.

Envig, O. T., and P. Åström. 1975. *Hala Sultan Teke* II: *The Cape Kiti Survey*. (*SIMA* 45: 2). Göteborg.

Erman, A. 1927. *The Literature of the Ancient Egyptians*. London.

Ernout, A., and A. Meillet. 1967. *Dictionnaire étymologique de la langue latine*. 4th ed. Paris.

Ernstson, J. 1985. The Ship Procession Fresco: the Pilots. *IJNA* 14: 315–20.

Evans, A. 1900–1901. The Palace of Knossos: Provisional Report of the Excavation for the Year 1901. *ABSA* 7: 1–120.

———. 1925A. The Ring of Nestor. *ABSA* 45: 1–75, pls. 4–5.

———. 1925B. The Early Nilotic, Libyan and Egyptian Relations with Minoan Crete. *JRAI* 55: 199–228.

———. 1936. Some Notes on the Tal Atchana Pottery. *JHS* 56: 133–34, pls. 6–7.

Faulkner, R. O. 1940. Egyptian Seagoing Ships. *JEA* 26: 3–9 and pls. 2–4.

———. 1964. *A Concise Dictionary of Middle Egyptian*. Oxford.

Faure, P. 1968. Toponymes créto–mycéniens dans une liste d'Aménophis III. *Kadmos* 7: 138–49.

Feliks, J. 1968. *Plant World of the Bible*. Ramat Gan. (In Hebrew.)

Fensham, F. C. 1967. Shipwreck in Ugarit and Ancient Near Eastern Law Codes. *OrA* 6: 221–24.

Février, J. G. 1935. Les origines de la marine phénicienne. *RH*10: 97–125.

———. 1949–50. L'ancienne marine phénicienne et les découvertes récentes. *NC* 1–2: 128–43.

Filgueiras, O. L. 1995. Some Vestiges of Old Protective Ritual Practice in Portuguese Local Boats. In *Tropis* III: 149–66.

Fitzgerald, M. A. 1994. The Ship. In *The Harbours of Caesarea Maritima: Results of the Caesarea Ancient Harbour Excavation Project 1980–1985* II: *The Finds and the Ship*. J.P. Oleson, ed. (BAR International Series 594). Oxford: 163–223, pls. 29–44.

———. 1996. Continuing Study of the Uluburun Shipwreck: Laboratory Research and Analysis. *INAQ* 23/1: 7–9.

Foster, K. P. 1988. Snakes and Lions: A New Reading of the West House Frescoes from Thera. *Expedition* 30/2: 10–20.

Foucart, G. 1924. *La belle fête de la vallée*. (*BIFAO* 24.)

Frankel, D. 1974. A Middle Cypriote Vessel with Modelled Figures from Politiko, *Lambertis*. *RDAC*: 43–50.

Frankfort, H. 1924. *Studies in the Early Pottery of the Near East* I: *Mesopotamia, Syria, and Egypt and Their Earliest Interrelations*. London.

———. 1926. Egypt and Syria in the First Intermediate Period. *JEA* 12: 80–99.

———. 1939. *Cylinder Seals*. London.

———. 1941. The Origin of Monumental Architecture in Egypt. *AJSLL* 58: 329–58.

Freedman, L. R. 1977. Studies in Cuneiform Legal Terminology with Special Reference to West Semitic Parallels. (Ph.D. diss., Columbia University.)

Freschi, A. 1989. Note techniche sul relitto greco arcaico di Gela. In *Atti della IV rassegna di archeologia subacquea*. Giardini Naxos 1989: 201–10.

Frey, D. A. 1993–94. Treasures of the Sponge Divers: Twenty Years Later, the INA Still Follows Turkey's Sponge Divers to the Wrecks of Antiquity. *Sea History* 68: cover, 18–22. (Reprinted with additional color photographs in *Aramco World* 44/3[1993]: cover, 2–9.)

Fritsch, C. T., and I. Ben–Dor. 1961. The Link Expedition to Israel, 1960. *BA* 24: 50–58.

Frost, H. 1963A. From Rope to Chain: On the Development of the Anchor in the Mediterranean. *MM* 49: 1–20.

———. 1963B. *Under the Mediterranean*. London.

———. 1964. Egyptian Anchors. *MM* 50: 242.

———. 1966. Stone–Anchors as Indications of Early Trade Routes. In *SC*: 55–61.

———. 1968. Review: *Cape Gelidonya: A Bronze Age Shipwreck* by G. F. Bass. *MM* 54: 423–24.

———. 1969A. The Stone Anchors of Ugarit. *Ugaritica* 6: 235–45.

———. 1969B. The Stone Anchors of Byblos. In *Mélanges* 45: 425–42.

———. 1970A. Some Cypriot Stone–Anchors from Land and from the Sea. *RDAC*: 14–24, pl. 6.

———. 1970B. Bronze-Age Stone-Anchors from the Eastern Mediterranean: Dating and Identification. *MM* 56: 377–94.

———. 1973. Anchors, the Potsherds of Marine Archaeology: On the Recording of Pierced Stones from the Mediterranean. In *MA*: 397–406.

———. 1979. Egypt and Stone-Anchors: Some Recent Discoveries. *MM* 65: 137–61.

———. 1980. Egypt and Stone-Anchors (*MM* 65: 2), a Correction. *MM* 66: 30.

———. 1981. Cordage. In *Lilybaeum*: 93–100.

———. 1982A. On a Sacred Cypriote Anchor. In *RRS*: 161–66.

———. 1982B. The Birth of the Stocked Anchor and the Maximum Size of Early Ships: Thoughts Prompted by Discoveries at Kition Bamboula, Cyprus. *MM* 68: 263–73.

———. 1984A. Chapitre 15: Khirokitia: Une pierre d'ancrage. In *Khirokitia*: 125–26, pl. 30.

———. 1984B. Gilgamesh and the "Things of Stone." *RDAC*: 96–100.

———. 1985. Ancient Egyptian Anchors: A Focus on the Facts. *MM* 71: 348.

———. 1986A. Stone-Anchors: Criteria for a Corpus. In *Thracia Pontica* III (Sozopol, October 6–12, 1985). Sofia, 1986: 354–69, 520.

———. 1986B. Comment on "A Group of Stone Anchors from Newe Yam" (*IJNA* 14: 143–53). *IJNA* 15: 65–66.

———. 1986C. App. 1: The Kition Anchors. In *Kition*: 281–321, pls. A–N.

———. 1989. Where Did Bronze Age Ships Stow Their Anchors? In *SSCA*[3].

———. 1991. Anchors Sacred and Profane: Ugarit-Ras Shamra, 1986: The Stone Anchors Revised and Compared. In *Ras Shamra-Ougarit VI: Arts et Industries de la pierre*. Paris: 355–410.

———. 1993. Stone Anchors: A Reassessment Reassessed (*MM*, 79, 1[1993], 5–26). *MM* 79: 449–58.

———. 1995. Where did Bronze Age Ships Keep Their Stone Anchors? In *Tropis* III: 167–75.

Furumark, A. 1941. *The Mycenaean Pottery: Analysis and Classification*. Stockholm.

———. 1950. The Settlement of Ialysos and Aegean History ca. 1550–1400 B.C. *OA* 6: 150–271.

Gaál, E. 1974. Osiris-Amenophis III in Ugarit (*nmry mlk ʿlm*). In *Studia Aegyptiaca* I: *Recueil d'etudes dédiées à Vilmos Wessetzky à l'occasion de son 65è anniversaire*. L. Kakosy, ed. Budapest.

Gaballa, G. A. 1976. *Narrative in Egyptian Art*. Mainz.

Gadd, C. J. 1936. *The Stones of Assyria: The Surviving Remains of Assyrian Sculpture, Their Recovery and their Original Positions*. London.

Gale, N. H. 1980. Some Aspects of Lead and Silver Mining in the Aegean. In *Thera* II: 161–95.

———. 1991. Copper Oxhide Ingots: Their Origin and Their Place in the Bronze Age Metals Trade in the Mediterranean. In *BATM*: 197–239.

Galili, E. 1985. A Group of Stone Anchors from Newe Yam. *IJNA* 14: 143–53.

———. 1987. Corrections and Additions to "A Group of Stone Anchors from Newe–Yam" (*IJNA* 14: 143–53). *IJNA* 16: 167–68.

Galili, E., and K. Raveh. 1988. Stone Anchors with Carvings from the Sea off Megadim. *Sefunim* 7: 41–47, pl. 5.

Galili, E., and N. Shmueli. 1983. Notes and News: Israel. *IJNA* 12: 178.

Galili, E., K. Raveh, and S. Wachsmann. 1982. Stone Anchors from the Megadim Coast. *HA* 80–81: 9–10. (In Hebrew.)

Galili, E., J. Sharvit, and M. Artzy. 1994. Reconsidering Byblian and Egyptian Stone Anchors Using Numeral Methods: New Finds From the Israeli Coast. *IJNA* 23: 93–107.

Galili, E., N. Shmueli, and M. Artzy. 1986. Bronze Age Cargo of Copper and Tin. *IJNA* 15: 25–37.

Gardiner, A. 1961. *Egypt of the Pharaohs*. Oxford.

———. 1969. *Egyptian Grammar*. London.

Gardiner, A. H., and T. E. Peet. 1952. *The Inscriptions of Sinai* I: *Introduction and Plates*. London.

———. 1955. *The Inscriptions of Sinai* II: *Translations and Commentary*. London.

Gardner, P. 1891A. Boat-Races among the Greeks. *JHS* 11: 90–97.

———. 1891B. Boat-Races at Athens. *JHS* 11: 315–17.

Gargallo, P. 1961. Anchors of Antiquity. *Archaeology* 14: 31–35.

Garstang, J. 1907. *The Burial Customs of Ancient Egypt*. London.

Garstang, J., and O. R. Gurney. 1959. *The Geography of the Hittite Empire*. London.

Gaster, T. H. 1938. A Phoenician Naval Gazette: New Light on Homer's Catalogue of Ships. *PEQ* 70: 105–12.

Gatty, H. 1958. *Nature Is Your Guide*. London.

Gelsinger, B. E. 1972. The Mediterranean Voyage of a Twelfth-Century Icelander. *MM* 58: 155–65.

Gianfrotta, P. A., and P. Pomey. 1980. *Archeologia sub-acquea: storia, techniche, scoperte e relitti*. Milano.

Giddy, L. L. 1987. *Egypt Oasis: Baḥariya, Dakhla, Farafra and Kharga During Pharaonic Times*. Warminster.

Giesecke, H.-E. 1983. The Akrotiri Ship Fresco. *IJNA* 12: 123–43.

Gillmer, T. C. 1975. The Thera Ship. *MM* 61: 321–29.

———. 1978. The Thera Ships: A Re-analysis. *MM* 64: 125–33.

———. 1985. The Thera Ships as Sailing Vessels. *MM* 71: 401–16.

Gimbutas, M. 1972. Pre-Hellenic and Pre-Indo–European Goddesses and Gods: The Old European Pantheon. In *ACTA*[2]: 82–98.

———. 1989. *The Language of the Goddess*. San Francisco.

Gjerstad, E., et al. 1934. *The Swedish Cyprus Expedition* I: *Finds and Results of the Excavations in Cyprus 1927–1931: Text and Plates*. Stockholm.

Gladwin, T. 1970. *East Is a Big Bird*. Cambridge.

Glanville, S. R. K. 1931–32. Records of a Royal Dockyard of the Time of Thutmose III: Papyrus British Museum 10056. *ZÄSA* 66: 105–21; 68: 7–41.

———. 1972. *Catalogue of Egyptian Antiquities in the British Museum* II: *Wooden Model Boats*. R. O. Faulkner, rev. London.

Goedicke, H. 1971. *Re-used Blocks from the Pyramid of Amenemhet I at Lisht*. (Publications of The Metropolitan Museum of Art, Egyptian Expedition 20.)

———. 1975. *The Report of Wenamun.* Baltimore.

Gonen, R. 1984. Urban Canaan in the Late Bronze Period. *BASOR* 253: 61–73.

———. 1992. The Late Bronze Age. In *The Archaeology of Ancient Israel.* A. Ben-Tor, ed. New Haven: 211–57.

Goodenough, W. H., and S. D. Thomas. 1987. Traditional Navigation in the Western Pacific. *Expedition* 29/3: 3–14.

Gordon, C. H. 1954. Ugarit and Caphtor. *Minos* 3: 126–32.

———. 1956. Ugaritic Guilds and Homeric DHMIOERGOI. In *ANE:* 136–43.

———. 1965. *Ugaritic Textbook.* (Especially the glossary.) Rome.

Göttlicher, A. 1978. *Materialien für ein Korpus der Schiffsmodelle im Altertum.* Mainz am Rhein.

Gow, A. S. F., ed. 1950. *Theocritus* I. 2d ed. Cambridge.

Gray, D. 1974. *Seewessen.* (*Archaeologia Homerica* 1G). Göttingen.

Green, J. N. 1973. An Underwater Archaeological Survey of Cape Andreas, Cyprus, 1969–70: A Preliminary Report. In *MA:* 141–78.

Greenhill, B. 1966. *The Boats of East Pakistan.* (2d reprint, with additional notes [1966] from *MM* 43/2–3.)

———. 1976. *Archaeology of the Boat.* London.

Griebel, C., and M. C. Nelson. 1993. Post-Mycenaean Occupation at the Palace of Nestor. *AJA* 97: 331.

Gurney, O. R. 1990. *The Hittites.* London.

Güterbock, H. G. 1967. The Hittite Conquest of Cyprus Reconsidered. *JNES* 26: 73–81.

———. 1983. The Hittites and the Aegean World: Part 1. The Ahhiyawa Problem Reconsidered. *AJA* 87: 133–38.

———. 1984. Hittites and Akhaeans: A New Look. *PAP* 128: 114–22.

Guzzo Amadasi, M. G. 1982. Il vocabolo *mḥz/mḥz* in Ugaritico e Fenicio. *Materiali lessicali ed epigrafici* I: 31–36.

Hadas, G. 1989. ʿEin Gedi Shore. *HA* 94: 68. (In Hebrew.)

———. 1989–90. ʿEin Gedi Shore. *Excavations and Surveys* 9: 80–81

———. 1992. Stone Anchors from the Dead Sea. *ʿAtiqot* 21: 55–57.

———. 1993A. A Stone Anchor from the Dead Sea. *IJNA* 22: 89–90.

———. 1993B. Where was the Harbour of ʿEn-Gedi Situated? *IEJ* 43: 45–49.

Haddon, A. C. 1937. *The Canoes of Melanesia, Queensland and New Guinea.* (*BMSP* 28.) *CO.*

Hadjidaki, E., 1993. Excavation of the Classical Ship at Alonnesos. In *SSCA⁵.*

———. 1995. Ein Schiffswrack aus klassischer Zeit vor der Insel Alonnisos, Griechenland. In *IPR:* 69–71.

Haldane, C. W. 1984A. The Dashur Boats. (M.A. thesis, Texas A&M University.)

———. 1984B. A Fourth Boat from Dashur. *AJA* 88: 389, pl. 54.

———. 1986. The Contributions of Archaeobotanical Analysis to the Interpretations of Shipwrecks. (Report submitted in partial fulfillment of the requirements for the degree of Master of Science in Bioarchaeology of the University of London in 1986; Institute of Archaeology, London.)

———. 1988A. Boat Timbers from El–List: A New Method of Ancient Egyptian Hull Construction. Preliminary Report. *MM* 74: 141–52.

———. 1988B. The Ulu Burun Wreck. *NASN* (January).

———. 1990A. Egyptian Hulls and the Evidence for Caulking. *IJNA* 19: 135–36.

———. 1990B. Shipwrecked Plant Remains. *Biblical Archaeologist* 53/1: 55–60.

———. 1991. Organic Goods from the Ulu Burun Wreck. *INAN* 18/4: 11.

———. 1992A. The Lisht Timbers: A Report on Their Significance. In D. Arnold, *The Pyramid Complex of Senwosret at Lisht: The South Cemetaries at Lisht.* (Publications of the Metropolitan Museum of Art, Egyptian Expedition 25.) New York: 102–12, pls. 115–33.

———. 1992B. "A Pharaoh's Fleet": Early Dynastic Hulls from Abydos. *INAQ* 19/2: 12–13.

———. 1993A. Ancient Egyptian Hull Construction. (Ph.D. diss., Texas A&M University.)

———. 1993B. Direct Evidence for Organic Cargoes in the Late Bronze Age. *WA* 24: 348–60.

Haldane, C. W., and D. D. Haldane. 1990. The Potential for Nautical Archaeology in Egypt. *INAN* 17/1: 22–25.

Haldane, C. W., and C. W. Shelmerdine. 1990. Herodotus 2.96.1–2 Again. *CQ* 40: 535–39.

Haldane, D. D. 1984. *The Wooden Anchor.* (M.A. thesis, Texas A&M University.)

Hallager, E. 1987. The Inscribed Stirrup Jars: Implications for Late Minoan IIIB Crete. *AJA* 91: 171–90.

———. 1988. Aspects of Aegean Long-Distance Trade in the Second Millennium B.C. In *Momenti precoloniali nel mediterraneo antico.* E. Acquaro, L. Godart, F. Mazza, and D. Musti, eds. Rome: 91–101.

Halpern, M. D. 1985. The Origins of the Carolinian Sidereal Compass. (M.A. thesis, Texas A&M University.)

Hamilton, R. W. 1935. Excavations at Tell Abu Hawam. *QDAP* 4: 1–69 and pls. 1–39.

Hammond, N. 1993. Newsbriefs: Minoans in Egypt. *Archaeology* 46/1: 20.

Hankey, V. 1979. Crete, Cyprus and the South–Eastern Mediterranean ca. 1400–1200 B.C. In *RBCC:* 144–57.

———. 1981. The Aegean Interest in el Amarna. *JMAA* 1: 38–49.

———. 1987. The Chronology of the Aegean Late Bronze Age. In *HML:* 39–59.

———. 1988. Review: *Aegeans in the Theban Tombs,* by S. Wachsmann. *JHS* 108: 260–61.

———. 1993. Egypt, the Aegean and the Levant. *Egyptian Archaeology* 3: 27–29.

Hansen, J. 1992. The Introduction of Agriculture into Greece: The Near Eastern Evidence. *AJA* 96: 340–41.

Hansen, O. 1994. A Mycenaean Sword from Boğazköy-Hattusa Found in 1991. *ABSA* 89: 213–15.

Harden, D. 1962. *The Phoenicians.* New York.

Har–El, M. 1981. Orientation in Biblical Lands. *BA* 44: 19–20.

Hareuveni, N. 1984. *Tree and Shrub in Our Biblical Heritage.* H. Frenkley, trans. Kiryat Ono.

Harris, H. A. 1972. *Sport in Greece and Rome.* Ithaca.

Hartmann, B., and J. Hoftijzer. 1971. Ugaritic *hnk–hnkt* and a Punic Formula. *Le Muséon* 85: 529–35.

Hassan, S. 1946. *Excavations at Giza* VI: I: *The Solar-Boats of Khafra, Their Origin and Development, Together with the Mythology of the Universe Which They Are Supposed to Traverse.* Cairo.

Hassan, S. 1954. The Causeway of Wnis at Sakkara. *ZÄSA* 80: 136–39, Tafs. 12–13.

Hayes, W. C. 1953. *The Scepter of Egypt* I. New York.

———. 1980. Egypt: Internal Affairs from Thutmose I to the Death of Amenophis III. In *CAH*: 313–416.

Heimpel, W. 1987. Das untere Meer. *ZA* 77: 22–91.

Heltzer, M. 1974. On the Akkadian Term *rēšu* in Ugarit. *Israel Oriental Studies* 4: 4–11.

———. 1976. *The Rural Community in Ancient Ugarit.* Wiesbaden.

———. 1977. The Metals Trade of Ugarit and the Problem of Transportation of Commercial Goods. *Iraq* 39: 203–11.

———. 1978. *Goods, Prices and the Organization of Trade in Ugarit.* Wiesbaden.

———. 1979. Some Problems of the Military Organization of Ugarit (Ugaritic *ḫrd* and Middle Assyrian *ḫurādu*). *OrA* 18: 245–53.

———. 1982. *The Internal Organization of the Kingdom of Ugarit: Royal Service System, Taxes, Royal Economy, Army and Administration.* Wiesbaden.

———. 1988. Sinaranu, Son of Siginu, and the Trade Relations between Ugarit and Crete. *Minos* 23: 7–13.

Hencken, H. 1968A. *Tarquinia, Villanovans and Early Etruscans* I–II. (*BASPR* 23.) Cambridge.

———. 1968B. *Tarquinia and Etruscan Origins.* New York.

Hennessy, J. B., and J. du Plat Taylor. 1967. The Pottery. In *CG*: 122–25.

Henrichs, A. 1980. Human Sacrifice in Greek Religion: Three Case Studies. In *Le sacrifice dans l'antiquité.* J. Rudhardt and O. Reverdin, eds. Geneva: 195–235 (236–242 = discussion).

Herdner, A. 1963. *Corpus des tablettes en cunéiformes alphabétiques découvertes à Ras Shamra–Ugarit de 1929 à 1939.* Paris.

———. 1969. Review: *Syria* 46: 130–32.

Herscher, E., and A. Nyquist. 1975. A Site of an Ancient Anchorage? In *Hala Sultan Teke* II: *The Cape Kitti Survey* (*SIMA* 45: 2) by O. T. Engvig and P. Åstrom. Göteborg: 22, figs. 48–49.

Higgins, R. 1967. *Minoan and Mycenaean Art.* London.

Himmelhoch, L. 1990–91. The Use of the Ethnics *a-ra-si-jo* and *ku- pi-ri-jo* in Linear B Texts. *Minos* 25–26: 91–104.

Hirschfeld, N. 1990A. Incised Marks on Late Helladic Late Minoan III Pottery. (M.A. thesis, Texas A&M University.)

———. 1990B. Fine Tuning: An Analysis of Bronze Age Potmarks as Clues to Maritime Trade. *INAN* 17/1: 18–21.

Hirschfeld, Y. 1992. *A Guide to Antiquity Sites in Tiberias.* Jerusalem.

———. 1994. The Anchor Church at the Summit of Mt. Berenice, Tiberias. *BA* 57: 122–33.

Hocker, F., and T. G. Palaima. 1990–91. Late Bronze Age Aegean Ships and the Pylos Tablets Vn 46 and Vn 879. *Minos* 25–26: 297–317.

Höckmann, O. 1995. Some Thoughts on the Greek Pentekonter. In *Tropis* III: 207–20.

Hoftijzer, J. 1979. Une lettre du roi de Tyr. *UF* 11: 383–88.

———. 1982. Une lettre du roi Hittite. In *Von Kanaan bis Kerala. Festschrift für Prof. Mag. Dr. Dr. J. P. M. v.d. Ploeg O.P. zur Vollendung des siebzigsten Lebensjahres* (*AOAT* 211). Neukirchen-Vluyn: 379–87.

———. 1983. Ugaritische brieven uit de tijd van de ondergang van de stad. In *Schrijvend Verleden. Documenten uit het Oude Nabije Oosten vertaald en toegelicht.* K. R. Veenhof, ed. Leiden-Zutphen: 94–99.

Hoftijzer, J., and W. H. van Soldt. 1991. Texts from Ugarit Concerning Security and Related Akkadian and West Semitic Material. *UF* 23: 189–216.

Holmes, Y. L. 1969. The Foreign Relations of Cyprus during the Late Bronze Age. (Ph.D. diss., Brandeis University.) University Microfilms: Ann Arbor.

———. 1973. Egypt and Cyprus: Late Bronze Age Trade and Diplomacy. *AOAT* 22: 91–98.

———. 1975. The Foreign Trade of Cyprus During the Late Bronze Age. In *The Archaeology of Cyprus: Recent Developments.* N. Robertson, ed. Park Ridge: 90–110.

Hood, S. 1971. *The Minoans: Crete in the Bronze Age.* London.

———. 1978. *The Arts in Prehistoric Greece.* Norwich.

Hooker, J. T. 1976. *Mycenaean Greece.* London.

———. 1985. Minoan and Mycenaean Settlement in Cyprus: A Note. In *Praktika tou Diethnous Kypriologikou Synedriou* (Leukosia, 20–25 Apriliou 1982.) Nicosia: 175–79.

Hopkins, C. 1955. Oriental Evidence for Early Etruscan Chronology. *Berytus* 11: 75–84.

———. 1957. Oriental Elements in the Hallstatt Culture. *AJA* 61: 333–39, pls. 97–100.

Hornell, J. 1936. *The Canoes of Polynesia, Fiji, and Micronesia.* (*BMSP* 27.) CO.

———. 1937. Egyptian Shipping of about 1500 B.C. *MM* 23:105–107.

———. 1938A. Boat Processions in Egypt. *Man* 38: 145–46 and pls. I–J.

———. 1938B. The Outrigger-Nuggar of the Blue Nile. *Antiquity* 12: 354–59, pls. 1–2.

———. 1939–40. The Frameless Boats of the Middle Nile I–II. *MM* 25: 417–32; 26: 125–44.

———. 1943A. The Prow of the Ship: Sanctuary of the Tutelary Deity. *Man* 43: 121–28, pl. F.

———. 1943B. The Sailing Ship in Ancient Egypt. *Antiquity* 65: 27–41.

———. 1945. The Palm Leaves on Boats' Prows of Gerzian Age. *Man* 45: 25–27, pl. B.

———. 1946. The Role of Birds in Early Navigation. *Antiquity* 20: 142–49.

———. 1947. Naval Activities in the Days of Solomon and Ramses III. *Antiquity* 21: 66–73.

———. 1950. *Fishing in Many Waters*. Cambridge.

———. 1970. *Water Transport*. Newton Abbot. (Reprint, 1946.)

Horridge, G. A. 1978. *The Design of Planked Boats of the Moluccas*. (MMR 38–1978) Basildon.

———. 1982. *The Lashed-lug Boat of the Eastern Archipelagoes, the Alcina MS and Lomblen Whaling Boats*. (MMR 54.)

Huehnergard, J. 1986. Note brève **šanāʾiš. *RA* 80: 191.

———. 1987. *Ugaritic Vocabulary in Syllabic Transcription*. Atlanta.

———. 1989. *The Akkadian of Ugarit*. Harvard Semitic Series 34.

Huffmon, H. B. 1966. The Treaty Background of Hebrew *yādaᶜ*. *BASOR* 181: 31–37.

Huffmon, H. B., and S. B. Parker. 1966. A Further Note on the Treaty Background of Hebrew *yādaᶜ*. *BASOR* 184: 36–38.

Hughes, D. D. 1991. *Human Sacrifice in Ancient Greece*. London.

Hult, G. 1977. Stone Anchors in Area 8. In *Hala Sultan Teke* III: *Excavations 1972*. (SIMA 45: 3.) Göteborg: 147–49.

———. 1981. *Hala Sultan Teke 7: Excavations in Area 8 in 1977*. (SIMA 45: 7.) Göteborg.

Hunt, A. S. 1911. *Catalogue of the Greek Papyri in the John Rylands Library, Manchester* I. Manchester.

Hutchinson, R. W. 1962. *Prehistoric Crete*. Harmondsworth.

Huxley, G. L. 1968. *Achaeans and Hittites*. Belfast. (Reprint.)

Iakovides, Sp., 1973. Rhodes and Aḫḫiyawa. In *MEM*: 189–92.

———. 1981. A Peak Sanctuary Ceremony in Bronze Age Thera. In *Temples and High Places in Biblical Times*. A. Biran, ed. Jerusalem: 54–60.

Immerwahr, S. A. 1960. Mycenaean Trade and Colonization. *Archaeology* 13: 4–13.

———. 1977. Mycenaeans at Thera: Some Reflections on the Paintings from the West House. In *Greece and the Eastern Mediterranean in Ancient History and Prehistory*. (Studies presented to Fritz Schachermeyer on the occasion of his eightieth birthday.) K. H. Kinz, ed. Berl 173–91, 289–92, pls. A–D.

Ingholt, H. 1940. *Rapport préliminaire sur sept campagnes de fouilles à Hama en Syrie (1932–1938)*. Copenhagen.

Irwin, G., S. Bickler, and P. Quirke. 1990. Voyaging by Canoe and Computer: Experiments in the Settlement of the Pacific Ocean. *Antiquity* 64: 34–50.

Israel, F. 1995. Études de grammaire Ougaritique. La dernière phase de la langue. In *Le pays d'Ougarit autour de 1200 av. J.-C.: Histoire et archéologie*. (Actes du Colloque International, Paris, 28 juin–1er juillet 1993 = *Ras Shamra-Ougarit* 11.) M. Yon, M. Sznycer, and P. Bordreuil, eds. Paris: 255–62.

Izre'el, S. 1991. *Amurru Akkadian: A Linguistic Study* I–II. Harvard Semitic Studies 41.

Jacobsen, T. W. 1993. Maritime Mobility in the Prehistoric Aegean: Some Practical Considerations. In *SSCA*⁵.

James, B. 1988. The Secrets of a Mummy Unwrapped. *IHT* (Thursday, March 24): 5.

Janssen, J. J. 1961. *Two Ancient Egyptian Ships' Logs*. Leiden.

———. 1975. *Commodity Prices from the Ramesside Period: An Economic Study of the Village of Necropolis Workmen at Thebes*. Leiden.

Jarrett-Bell, C. D. 1930. Rowing in the Eighteenth Dynasty. *AEg*: 11–19.

———. 1933. Ancient Ship Design: Based on a Critical Analysis of the Twelfth Dynasty Barge. *AEg*: 101–11.

Jaussen, A., R. Savignac, and H. Vincent. 1905. 'Abdeh. *RB*: 74–89.

Jean, C.-F., and J. Hoftijzer. 1965. *Dictionnaire des inscriptions sémitiques de l'ouest*. Leiden.

Jenkins, N. 1980. *The Boat beneath the Pyramid*. London.

Jestin, O., and F. Carrazé. 1980. Mediterranean Hull Types Compared 4. An Unusual Type of Construction. The Hull of Wreck 1 at Bon Porté. *IJNA* 9: 70–72.

Johnson, J. 1980. *Maroni de Chypre*. (SIMA 59.) Göteborg.

Johnson, S. B. 1980A. Two Wooden Statues from Lisht. Do They Represent Sesostris I? *JARCE* 17: 11–20.

Johnston, P. F. 1982. Bronze Age Cycladic Ships: An Overview. In *TUAS*: 1–8.

———. 1985. *Ship and Boat Models in Ancient Greece*. Annapolis.

Johnstone, P. 1973. Stern First in the Stone Age? *IJNA* 2: 3–11.

———. 1980. *The Sea–craft of Prehistory*. London.

Johnstone, W. 1977. Biblical Hebrew *Wāwîm* in the Light of Phoenician Evidence. *PEQ* 109: 95–102.

———. 1981. Signs. In *Lilybaeum*: 191–239.

Joncheray, J.-P. 1976. L'épave grecque, ou étrusque, de Bon Porté. *Cd'AS* 5: 5–36.

Jones, D. 1988. *A Glossary of Ancient Egyptian Nautical Titles and Terms*. London.

———. 1990. *Model Boats from the Tomb of Tut'ankhamūn*. (Tut'ankhamūn's Tomb Series 9.) J. R. Harris, gen. ed. Oxford.

Kahanov, Y. 1991. An Investigation of the Maʿagan Michael Ship. *C.M.S. News* 18: 6–7.

Kahanov, Y., and S. Breitstein. 1995A. A Preliminary Study of the Hull Remains. *INAQ* 22/2: 9–13.

———. 1995B. Tantura Excavation 1994: A Preliminary Report on the Wood. *C.M.S. News* 22: 11–13.

Kaiser, O. 1970. Zum Formular der in Ugarit gefundenen Briefe. *ZDPV* 86: 10-23.

Kantor, H. 1992. The Relative Chronology of Egypt and Its Foreign Correlations before the First Intermediate Period. In *Chronologies in Old World Archaeology*. R. W. Erich, ed. Chicago: 3–21.

Käpitan, G. 1984. Ancient Anchors: Technology and Classification. *IJNA* 13: 33–44.

Kaplan, J. 1972. The Archaeology and History of Tel Aviv-Jaffa. *BA* 35: 66–95.

Karageorghis, V. 1960. Supplementary Notes on the Mycenaean Vases from the Swedish Tombs at Enkomi. *OAth* 3: 135–53, pls. 1–14.

———. 1976. *Kition: Mycenaean and Phoenician Discoveries in Cyprus.* London.

———. 1979. Some Reflections on the Relations between Cyprus and Crete during the Late Minoan IIIB Period. *RBCC*: 199–203.

———. 1982. *Cyprus from the Stone Age to the Romans.* London.

———. 1984. Exploring Philistine Origins on the Island of Cyprus. *BibAR* 10/2: 16–28.

———. 1993. Le commerce cypriote avec l'occident au bronze récent: quelques nouvelles découvertes. *CRAI* (avril–juin): 577–88.

Karageorghis, V., and J. des Gagniers. 1974. *La céramique chypriote de style figuré, âge du Fer (1050–500 Av. J.-C.)* 1–2. Rome.

Karageorghis, V., et al. 1988. *Excavations at Maa-Palaeolkastro 1979–1986* 1–2. Nicosia.

Katzenstein, H. J., 1973. *The History of Tyre: From the Beginning of the Second Millennium* B.C.E. *until the Fall of the Neo–Babylonian Empire in 538* B.C.E. Jerusalem.

Katzev, M. 1989. Voyage of Kyrenia II. *INAN* 16/1: 4–10.

———. 1990. An Analysis of the Experimental Voyages of Kyrenia II. In *Tropis* II: 245–56.

Kaul, F. 1995. Ships on Bronzes. *The Ship as Symbol in Prehistoric and Medieval Scandinavia.* O. Crumlin-Pedersen and B. Munch Thye, eds. (Publications from the National Museum, Studies in Archaeology and History 1.) Copenhagen: 59–70.

Kenna, V. E. G. 1960. *Cretan Seals: With a Catalogue of the Minoan Gems in the Ashmolean Museum.* Oxford.

———. 1967–68. The Seal Use of Cyprus in the Bronze Age II. *BCH* 91: 552–77; 92: 142–56.

———. 1969. *The Cretan Talismanic Stone in the Late Minoan Age.* (*SIMA* 24.) Göteborg.

Kennedy, D. H. 1976. Cable Reinforcement of the Athenian Trireme. *MM* 62: 159–68.

———. 1978. A Further Note on the Thera Ships. *MM* 64:135–37.

Kenyon, K. M. 1960. *Excavations at Jericho I: The Tombs Excavated in 1952–1954.* London.

Kestemont, G. 1977. Remarques sur les aspects juridiques du commerce dans le Proche-Orient du XIVè siècle avant notre ère. *Iraq* 39: 191–201.

Kilian, K. 1988. Ausgrabungen in Tiryns 1982/1983: Bericht zu Den Grabungen. *AA*: 105–51.

Killen, J. T. 1983. PY An 1. *Minos* 18: 71–79.

Killen J. T., and J.-P. Olivier. 1989. *The Knossos Tablets. Fifth Edition.* (*Minos* Suppl. 11.) Salamanca.

Kirk, G. S. 1949. Ships on Geometric Vases. *ABSA* 44: 93–153, pls. 38–40.

Kitchen, K. A. 1971. Punt and How to Get There. *Or* 40: 184–207.

———. 1973. *The Third Intermediate Period in Egypt (1100–650* B.C.*).* Warminster.

———. 1978. Review: *The Sea Peoples and Egypt,* by Alessandra Nibbi. *JEA* 64: 169–71.

———. 1983. Review: *Ancient Egypt and Some Eastern Neighbors,* by Alessandra Nibbi. *PEQ* 115: 77–79.

———. 1987. The Basics of Egyptian Chronology in Relation to the Bronze Age. In *HML* 1: 37–55.

Klebs, L. 1934. *Die Reliefs und Malerein des nuen Reiches.* Heidelberg.

Klengel, H. 1974. "Hungerjahre" in Ḫatti. *AF* 1: 165–74.

Knapp, A. B. 1983. An Alashiyan Merchant at Ugarit. *Tel Aviv* 10: 38–45.

———. 1991. Spice, Drugs, Grain and Grog: Organic Goods in Bronze Age East Mediterranean Trade. In *BATM*: 21–68.

———. 1993. Thalassocracies in Bronze Age Trade: Making and Breaking a Myth. *WA* 24: 332–47.

Knapp, A. B., J. D. Muhly, and P. M. Muhly. 1988. To Hoard Is Human: Late Bronze Age Metal Deposits in Cyprus and the Aegean. *RDAC*: 233–62.

Kochavi, M. 1973. A Built Shaft–Tomb of the Middle Bronze Age I at Degania "A." *Qadmoniot* 4/2 (22): 50–53. (In Hebrew.)

Korrés, G. S. 1989. Representation of a Late Mycenaean Ship on the Pyxis from Tragana, Pylos. In *Tropis* I: 177–202.

Kühne, C., and H. Otten. 1971. *Der Šaušgamuwa–Vertrag.* (*SBT* 16.) Wiesbaden.

Kuniholm, P. I. 1990. Overview and Assessment of the Evidence for the Date of the Eruption of Thera. In *Thera* III/3: 3: 13–18.

———. 1996 *Aegean Dendrochronology Project December 1996 Progress Report.* (The Malcolm and Carolyn Wiener Laboratory for Aegean and Near Eastern Dendrochronology).

Kuniholm, P. I., *et al.,* 1996. Anatolian Tree Rings and the Absolute Chronology of the Eastern Mediterranean, 2220–718 B.C. *Nature* 381: 780–82.

Kurt, C. 1979. *Seemännische Fachausdrücke bei Homer.* Göttingen.

Kurtz, D. C., and J. Boardman. 1971. *Greek Burial Customs.* Ithaca.

Lacau, P. 1904. *Sarcophages antérieurs au Nouvel Empire* I–II. (*Catalogue général des Antiquités égyptiennes du Musée du Caire.*) Cairo.

Laffineur, R. 1983A. Iconographie mycénienne et symbolisme guerrier. *Art et fact, Revue des historiens d'art, des archéologues, des musicologues et des orientalistes de l'Université de lEtat à Liège* 2: 38–49.

———. 1983B. Early Mycenaean Art: Some Evidence from the West House in Thera. *BICS* 30: 111–22.

———. 1984. Mycenaeans at Thera: Further Evidence. In *MT:* 133–39.

———. 1991. La mer et l'au-delà dans l'Égée préhistorique. In *Thalassa:* 231–38, pl. 61.

Lagarce, J., E. Lagarce, A. Bounni, and N. Saliby. 1983. Les fouilles à Ras Ibn Hani en Syrie (Campagnes de 1980, 1981, et 1982). *CRAI* (Avril–Juin): 249–90.

Lallemand, H. 1923. Les assemblages dans la technique égyptienne et le sens originel du mot *menkh*. *BIFAO* 22: 77–98.

LaMarche, V. C., Jr., and K. K. Hirschboeck. 1984. Frost Rings in Trees as Records of Major Volcanic Eruptions. *Nature* 307: 121–26.

Lambdin, T. O. 1953. The Miši-People of the Byblian Amarna Letters. *JCS* 7: 75–77.

Lambrou-Phillipson, C. 1991. Seafaring in the Bronze Age Mediterranean: The Parameters Involved in Maritime Travel. In *Thalassa*: 11–19, pl. 1.

———. 1993. Ugarit: A Late Bronze Age Thalassocracy? The Evidence of the Textual Sources. *Or* 62: 163–70.

Landström, B. 1970. *Ships of the Pharaohs*. Garden City.

Lang, M. L. 1969. *The Palace of Nestor at Pylos in Western Messenia* 2: *The Frescoes*. Princeton.

Latacz, J. 1986. Review of C. Kurt 1979. *Kratylos* 31: 110–24.

Lattimore, R., trans. 1951. *The Iliad of Homer*. Chicago.

Laviosa, C. 1972. La Marina Micenea. *Annuario della Scuola Archeologica di Atene* 47–48 (1969–70; n.s. 31–32). Rome: 7–40.

Le Baron Bowen, R. 1960A. Egypt's Earliest Sailing Ships. *Antiquity* 34: 117–31.

———. 1960B. Man's Earliest Sails. *MM* 49: 144–46.

———. 1962. Egyptian Sails of the Second Millennium B.C. *MM* 48: 52–57.

———. 1963. Egyptian Anchors. *MM* 49: 304.

Lehmann, G. A. 1979. Die Šikalāju—ein neues Zeugnis zu den "Seevölkern"—Heerfahrten im späten 13. Jh. v. Chr. (*RS* 34.129). *UF* 11: 481–94.

Levine, M. 1969. *The Tabernacle: Its Structure and Utensils*. Tel Aviv.

Lewis, D. 1975. *We, the Navigators*. Honolulu.

———. 1976. "Hokulèa" Follows the Stars to Tahiti. *NG* 150: 512–37.

Liddell, H. G., and R. Scott. 1953. *A Greek-English Lexicon*. (Reprint, 1953.) Oxford.

Linder, E. 1970. The Maritime Texts of Ugarit: A Study of Late Bronze Age Shipping. (Ph.D. diss., Brandeis University.) University Microfilms: Ann Arbor.

———. 1972. A Seafaring Merchant–Smith from Ugarit and the Cape-Gelidonya Wreck. *IJNA* 1: 163–64.

———. 1973. Naval Warfare in the El–Amarna Age. In *MA*: 317–24.

———. 1981. Ugarit, a Canaanite Thalassocrasy. In *UR*: 31–42.

———. 1992. Excavating an Ancient Merchantman. *BibAR* 18/6: 24–35.

Lindgren, M., 1973. *The People of Pylos: Prosopographical and Methodological Studies in the Pylos Archives* I–II. *Boreas* (*Uppsala Studies in Ancient Mediterranean and Near Eastern Civilizations*: 3–21 Uppsala.

Liou, B. 1974. Note provisoire sur deux gisements gréco–étrusques (Bon Porté A et Pointe du Dattier). *Cd'AS* 3: 7–19.

Lipiński, E. 1967. Recherches Ugaritiques. *Syria* 44: 253–87.

———. 1971. Épiphanie de Baal–Haddu, *RS* 24.245. *UF* 3:81–92.

———. 1977. An Ugaritic Letter to Amenophis III Concerning the Trade with Alašiya. *Iraq* 39: 213–17.

Lipke, P. 1984. *The Royal Ship of Cheops*. (*BARIS* 125.) Greenwich.

Lipschitz, O. 1972. Notes and News: Timnᶜa. *IEJ* 22: 158, pl. 27.

Liverani, M. 1970. *Kbd* nei testi amministrativi ugaritici. *UF* 2: 89–108.

———. 1979A. Ras Shamra-Histoire. *Supplément au Dictionnaire de la Bible* 9. Paris, coll. 1295–1348.

———. 1979B. La dotazione dei mercanti di Ugarit. *UF* 11: 495–503.

———. 1987. The Collapse of the Near Eastern Regional System at the End of the Bronze Age: The Case of Syria. In *Center and Periphery in the Ancient World*. M. Rowlands, M. Larsen, and K. Kristiansen, eds. Cambridge: 66–73.

———. 1995. Le fin d'Ougarit: quand? pourquoi? comment? In *Le pays d'Ougarit autour de 1200 av. J.-C.: Histoire et archéologie*. (Actes du Colloque International, Paris, 28 juin–1ᵉʳ juillet 1993 = *Ras Shamra-Ougarit* 11.) M. Yon, M. Sanycer, and P. Bordreuil, eds. Paris: 113–17.

Lloyd, S. 1967. *Early Highland Peoples of Anatolia*. London.

Lloyd, S., and J. Mellaart. 1965. *Beycesultan* II. (*Occasional Publications of the British Institute of Archaeology at Ankara* 8.) London.

Lolos, G., C. Pennas, and G. Vichos. 1995. Der Shiffsfund von Kap Iria (Golf von Argos). In *IPR*: 59–62.

Lolos, Y. 1991. Underwater Surface Investigation of the Wreck of the Late Bronze Age at Point Iria: Part 2: The Pottery and Its Ramifications. *Enalia* 3 (1–2): 17–25. (In Greek.)

———. 1990. The Gold Chalice from the Late Bronze Age Wreck at Akroterion (Ulu Burun) in Lycia. *Enalia* 1: 8–9.

———. 1995. The 1991 Underwater Survey of the Late Bronze Age Wreck at Point Iria: Part 2: The Pottery. *Enalia Annual 1991* (English Edition) 3: 9–16.

Long, C. R. 1974. *The Ayia Triadha Sarcophagus: A Study of Late Minoan and Mycenaean Funerary Practices and Beliefs*. (*SIMA* 41.) Göteborg.

Loret, V. 1916. Quelques notes sur l'arbre âch. *ASAE* 16: 33–51.

———. 1949. *La résin de térébinth* (sonter) *chez les anciens Égyptiens*. (*IFAO, RA* 19.) Cairo.

Lucas, A. 1931. Cedar-Tree Products Employed in Mummification. *JEA* 17: 13–21.

———. 1962. *Ancient Egyptian Materials and Industries*⁴. J. R. Harris, rev. London.

Lythgoe, A. M. 1915. Excavations at the South Pyramid of Lisht in 1914. *AEg*: 145–53.

McCann, A. N. 1970. Review: *Cape Gelidonya: A Bronze Age Shipwreck*, by G. F. Bass. *AJA* 74: 105–106.

McCaslin, D. 1978. The 1977 Underwater Report. In *Hala Sultan Teke* IV. (*SIMA* 45: 4). Göteborg: 97–157.

McCaslin, D. E. 1980. *Stone Anchors in Antiquity: Coastal Settlements and Maritime Trade–Routes in the Eastern Mediterranean ca. 1600–1050 B.C.* (*SIMA* 61.) Göteborg.

McCoy, F. W., and G. Heiken. 1990. Anatomy of an Eruption: How a Terrifying Series of Explosions Reshaped the Minoan Island of Thera. *Archaeology* 43/3: 42–49.

McDonald, W. M. 1967. *Progress into the Past.* New York.

McDonald, W. A., and R. H. Simpson. 1961. Prehistoric Habitation in Southwestern Peloponnese. *AJA* 65: 221–60.

———. 1969. Further Explorations in Southwestern Peloponnese: 1964–68. *AJA* 73: 123–77.

———. 1972A. Archaeological Exploration. In *MME*: 117–47.

———. 1972B. Perspectives. In *MME*: 240–61.

McGeehan Liritzis, V. 1988. Seafaring, Craft and Cultural Contact in the Aegean during the Third Millennium B.C. *IJNA* 17: 237–56.

MacGregor, J. 1870. *The Rob Roy on the Jordan, Nile, Red Sea & Gennesareth, &c.* London.

Macqueen, J. G. 1968. Geography and History in Western Asia Minor in the Second Millennium B.C. *AS* 18: 169–85.

———. 1986. *The Hittites and Their Contemporaries in Asia Minor.* London.

McWilliams, K. 1992. A Sail for the Kinneret Boat Model. *INAQ* 19/3: 7.

Maddin, R., T. S. Wheeler, and J. D. Muhly. 1977. Tin in the Ancient Near East: Old Questions and New Finds. *Expedition* 19: 35–47.

Maiuri, A. 1923–24. Jalisos: Scavi della missione archeologica italiana a Rodi I–II. *Annuario della Scuola archeologica di Atene:* 6–7: 83–341.

Malamat, A. 1971. Syro-Palestinian Destinations in a Mari Tin Inventory. *IEJ* 21: 31–38.

Manning, S. W. 1988A. The Bronze Age Eruption of Thera: Absolute Dating, Aegean Chronology and Mediterranean Cultural Interrelations. *JMA* 1: 17–82.

———. 1988B. Dating of the Santorini Eruption. *Nature* 332: 401.

———. 1989. The Santorini Eruption: An Update. *JMA* 2: 301–13.

———. 1990. The Thera Eruption: The Third Congress and the Problem of the Date. *Archaeometry* 32: 91–100.

———. 1991. Response to J. D. Muhly on Problems of Chronology in the Aegean Late Bronze Age. *JMA* 4: 249–62.

Margariti, R. In progress. The Shipwreck at Sheytan Deresi and the Minoan Connection in the Eastern Aegean. (M.A. thesis, Texas A&M University.)

Marinatos, N. 1984. *Art and Religion in Thera: Reconstructing a Bronze Age Society.* Athens.

———. 1988. The Imagery of Sacrifice: Minoan and Greek. In *Early Greek Cult Practice.* (Proceedings of the Fifth International Symposium at the Swedish Institute at Athens, June 26–29, 1986.) R. Hägg, N. Marinatos, and G. C. Nordquist, eds. Stockholm: 9–20.

———. 1993. *Minoan Religion: Ritual, Image, and Symbol.* Columbia.

Marinatos, S. 1933. La marine créto–mycénienne. *BCH* 57: 170–235.

———. 1971. *Excavations at Thera IV (1970 Season).* Athens.

———. 1974. *Excavations at Thera VI (1972 Season), Text and Plates.* Athens.

———. 1976. *Excavations at Thera VII (1973 Season).* Athens.

Mark, S. E. 1991. *Odyssey* 5.234–53 and Homeric Ship Construction: A Reappraisal. *AJA* 95: 441–45.

———. 1993. A Study of Possible Trade Routes Between Egypt and Mesopotamia, ca. 3500–3100 B.C. (M.A. thesis, Texas A&M University.)

———. 1996. *Odyssey* (5.234–53) and Homeric Ship Construction: A Clarification. *IJNA* 25: 46–48.

———. In press. *From Egypt to Mesopotamia: A Study of Predynastic Trade Routes.* (*Studies in Nautical Archaeology* 4.) College Station.

Martin, G. T. 1991. *The Hidden Tombs of Memphis: New Discoveries from the Time of Tutankhamun and Ramesses the Great.* London.

Masson, O. 1956. Documents Chypro-Minoens de Ras Shamra. *Ugaritica* 3: 233–50.

———. 1969. Documents Chypro-Minoens de Ras Shamra. *Ugaritica* 6: 379–92.

———. 1974. *Cyprominoica.* (*SIMA* 31: 2.) Göteborg.

Mazar, A. 1985. The Emergence of the Philistine Material Culture. *IEJ* 35: 95–107.

———. 1990. *Archaeology of the Land of the Bible: 10,000–586 B.C.E.* New York.

———. 1992. The Iron Age I. *The Archaeology of Ancient Israel.* A. Ben-Tor, ed. New Haven: 258–301.

Mee, C. 1978. Aegean Trade and Settlement in Anatolia in the Second Millennium B.C. *AS* 28: 121–56.

———. 1982. *Rhodes in the Bronze Age: An Archaeological Survey.* Warminster.

———. 1986. A Mycenaean Thalassocracy in the Eastern Mediterranean? In *PGP*: 301–306.

Meiggs, R. 1985. *Trees and Timber in the Ancient World.* Oxford.

Mekhitarian, A. 1978. *Egyptian Painting.* S. Gilbert, trans. New York.

Melena, J. L. 1974. KI-TA-NO en las tablillas de CNOSO. *Durius* 2: 45–55.

———. 1983. Olive Oil and Other Sorts of Oil in the Mycenaean Tablets. *Minos* 18: 89–123.

Mellaart, J. 1968. Anatolian Trade with Europe and Anatolian Geography and Culture Provinces in the Late Bronze Age. *AS* 18: 187–202.

Mellink, M. J. 1983. The Hittites and the Aegean World: Part 2. Archaeological Comments on Ahhiyawa-Achaians in Western Anatolia. *AJA* 87: 138–41.

Merrillees, R. S. 1968. *The Cypriote Bronze Age Pottery Found in Egypt.* (*SIMA* 18.) Göteborg.

———. 1972. Aegean Bronze Age Relations with Egypt. *AJA* 76: 281–94.

———. 1973. Mycenaean Pottery from the Time of Akhenaton in Egypt. In *MEM*: 175–86.

———. 1974. *Trade and Transcendence in the Bronze Age Levant.* (*SIMA* 39.) Göteborg.

———. 1986. Political Conditions in the Eastern Mediterranean During the Late Bronze Age. *BA* 49: 42–50.

———. 1987. *Alashia Revisited.* (*CRB* 22.) Paris.

Meshel, Z. 1971. *Southern Sinai.* Jerusalem. (In Hebrew.)

Michael, H. N., and P. P. Betancourt. 1988A. The Thera Eruption: Continuing Discussion of the Date: II: Further Arguments for an Early Date. *Archaeometry* 30: 169–75.

———. 1988B. The Thera Eruption: Continuing Discussion of the Date: II: Further Arguments for an Early Date. *Archaeometry* 30: 180–81.

Millard, A. 1995. The Last Tablets of Ugarit. In *Le pays d'Ougarit autour de 1200 av. J.-C.: Histoire et archéologie.* (Actes du Colloque International, Paris, 28 juin–1ᵉʳ juillet 1993 = *Ras Shamra-Ougarit* 11.) M. Yon, M. Sznycer, and P. Bordreuil, eds. Paris: 119–24.

Miller, G.I. 1980. Studies in the Juridical Texts from Ugarit. (Ph.D. diss., John Hopkins University.)

Miller, P. 1988. Riddle of the Pyramid Boats. *NG* 173: 534–50.

Misch–Brandl, O., E. Galili, and S. Wachsmann. 1985. Finds from the Late Canaanite (Bronze) Period. In *FDS*: 7–11 and pls. 1–7.

Montet, P. 1928. *Byblos et l'Égypte: Quatre campagnes de fouilles à Gebail 1921–1922–1923–1924.* Text and Plates. Paris.

Morgan, L. 1988. *The Miniature Wall Paintings of Thera: A Study in Aegean Culture and Iconography.* Cambridge.

———. 1990. Island Iconography: Thera, Kea, Milos. In *Thera* III/1: 252–66.

———. 1995. Minoan Painting and Egypt: The Case of Tell el Dab'a. In *EAL*: 29–53.

Morricone, L. 1975. Coo–Scavi e scoperte nel "Serraglio" in località minori (1935–43). *Annuario della Scuola Archeologica di Atene*: 50–51 (1972–73; n.s. 34–35): 139–396.

Morris, S. P. 1989. A Tale of Two Cities: The Miniature Frescoes from Thera and the Origins of Greek Poetry. *AJA* 93: 511–35.

Morrison, I. A. 1980. Structure under Water: Many Types of Submergence. In *AW*: 132–33.

Morrison, J. S., and R. T. Williams. 1968. *Greek Oared Ships: 900–322 B.C.* Cambridge.

Moussa, A. M., and H. Altenmüller. 1971. *Old Kingdom Tombs at the Causeway of King Unas at Saqqara: The Tomb of Nefer and Ka-Hay.* Mainz am Rhein.

———. 1977. *Old Kingdom Tombs at the Causeway of King Unas at Saqqara Excavated by the Department of Antiquities: Das Grab des Nianchchnum und Chnumhotep.* Mainz am Rhein.

Muhly, J. D. 1970. Homer and the Phoenicians. *Berytus* 19: 19–64.

———. 1974. The Hittites and the Aegean World. *Expedition* 16/2: 2–10.

———. 1991. Egypt, the Aegean and Late Bronze Age Chronology in the Eastern Mediterranean: A Review Article. *JMA* 4: 4: 235–47, 256–62.

———. 1993. Early Bronze Age Tin and the Taurus. *AJA* 97: 239–53.

Müller, W. 1904. Neue Darstellungen "mykenischer" Gesandter und phönizischer Schiffe in altägyptischen Wandgemälden. *Mitteilungen der Vorderasiatischen Gesellschaft* 9: 113–80, Tafs. 1–4.

Naville, E. 1898. *The Temple of Deir el Bahri* III: *End of the Northern Half and Southern Half of the Middle Platform.* London.

———. 1901. *The Temple of Deir el Bahri* IV: *The Shrine of Hathor and the Southern Hall of Offerings.* London.

———. 1908. *The Temple of Deir el Bahri* VI: *The Lower Terrace, Additions and Plans.* London.

Naville, E., and H. R. Hall. 1913. *The XIth Dynasty Temple at Deir el-Bahri* III. London.

Negbi, O. 1976. *Canaanite Gods in Metal: An Archaeological Study of Ancient Syro–Palestinian Figurines.* Tel Aviv.

———. 1979. The "Miniature Fresco" from Thera and the Emergence of Mycenaean Art. In *Thera*: 645–56.

Negbi, O., and S. Moskowitz. 1966. The "Foundation Deposits" or "Offering Deposits" of Byblos. *BASOR* 184: 21–26.

Negueruela, I., J. Pinedo, M. Gómez, A. Miñano, I. Arellano, and J. S. Barba. 1995. Seventh-Century B.C. Phoenician Vessel Discovered at Playa de la Isla, Mazarrón, Spain. *IJNA* 24: 189–97.

Nelson, H. H. 1929. The Epigraphic Survey of the Great Temple of Medinet Habu (Seasons 1924–25 to 1927–28). *Medinet Habu 1924–28.* (*UC,OIC* 5.) Chicago: 1–36.

———. 1943. The Naval Battle Pictured at Medinet Habu. *JNES* 2: 40–45.

Nelson, H. H., et al. 1930. *Medinet Habu* I: *Earlier Historical Records of Ramses III.* (*UC,OIP* 8). Chicago.

Newberry, P. E. 1893. *Beni Hassan* I. London.

———. 1894. *El Bersheh* I: *The Tomb of Tehuti-Hetep.* London.

———. 1938. Three Old–Kingdom Travellers to Byblos and Pwenet. *JEA* 24: 182–84.

———. 1942. Notes on Seagoing Ships. *JEA* 28: 64–66.

Nibbi, A. 1975A. Egyptian Anchors. *JEA* 61: 38–41.

———. 1975B. *The Sea Peoples and Egypt.* Park Ridge.

———. 1979. Some Remarks on the Assumption of Ancient Egyptian Sea-Going. *MM* 65: 201–208.

———. 1984. Ancient Egyptian Anchors: A Focus on the Facts. *MM* 70: 247–66.

———. 1991. Five Stone Anchors from Alexandria. *IJNA* 20: 185–94.

———. 1992. A Group of Stone Anchors from Mirgissa on the Upper Nile. *IJNA* 21: 259–67.

———. 1993. Stone Anchors: The Evidence Re-Assessed. *MM* 79: 5–26.

Niemeier, W.-D. 1990. Mycenaean Elements in the Miniature Fresco from Thera? In *Thera* III: 267–84.

———. 1991. Minoan Artisans Travelling Overseas: The Alalakh Frescoes and the Painted Plaster Floor at Tel Kabri (Western Galilee). In *Thalassa*: 189–201, pls. 46–51.

Nikolaou, K., and H. W. Catling. 1968. Composite Anchors in Late Bronze Age Cyprus. *Antiquity* 42: 225–29, pl. 34.

Nilsson, M. P. 1950. *The Minoan–Mycenaean Religion and Its Survival in Greek Religion.²* Lund.

Nougayrol, J. 1956. *Textes accadiens des archives sud* (*PRU* IV). Paris.

———. 1960. Nouveaux textes accadiens de Ras Shamra. *CRAI:* 163–71.

Nour, M. Z., Z. Iskander, M. S. Osman, and A. Y. Moustafa. 1960. *The Cheops Boats* I. Cairo.

Nun, M. 1975. Ancient Anchors from the Sea of Galilee. *TvA* 17/4: 26–28.

———. 1977. *Sea of Kinneret: A Monograph.* Tel Aviv. (In Hebrew.)

———. 1993. *Ancient Stone Anchors and Net Sinkers from the Sea of Galilee.* Ein Gev.

Nussbaum, A. J. 1986. *Head and Horn in Indo-European.* Berlin.

Oates, J. 1993. Trade and Power in the Fifth and Fourth Millennia B.C.: New Evidence from Northern Mesopotamia. *WA* 24: 403–22.

Öbrink, U. 1979. *Hala Sultan Teke V: Excavations in Area 22, 1971–1973 and 1975–1978* (*SIMA* 45: 5.) Göteborg.

O'Connor, D. 1987. Egyptians and Libyans in the New Kingdom. *Expedition* 29/3: 35–37.

———. 1991. Boat Graves and Pyramid Origins. *Expedition* 33/3: 5–17.

Oleson, J. P. 1988. Ancient Lead Circles and Sounding–Leads from Israeli Coastal Waters. *Sefunim* 7: 27–40.

Olivier, J.–P. 1975. Le disque de Phaistos: Édition photographique. *BCH* 99: 5–34.

Onassoglou, A. 1985. *Die ›Talismanischen‹ Siegel.* (*Corpus der minoischen und mykenischen Siegel,* Beiheft 2.) Berlin.

Oppenheim, A. L. 1973. A Note on *ša rēši. The Journal of the Ancient Near Eastern Society of Columbia University* 5: 325–34.

Ormerod, H. 1978. *Piracy in the Ancient World: An Essay on Mediterranean History.* Liverpool. (Reprint, 1924.)

Ory, J. 1946. A Middle Age Tomb at El Jisr. *QDAP* 11: 31–42, pls. 12–14.

Otten, H. 1975. *Puduḫepa. Eine hethitische Königin in ihren Textzeugnissen.* Wiesbaden.

Owen, D. I. 1981. An Akkadian Letter from Ugarit at Tel Aphek. *Tel Aviv* 8: 1–17, pls. 1–2.

Page, D. L. 1962. *Poetae Melici Graecae.* Oxford.

———. 1976. *History and the Homeric Iliad.* Berkeley.

Palaima, T. G. 1989A. Ideograms and Supplementals and Regional Interaction among Aegean and Cypriote Scripts. *Minos* 24: 30–54.

———. 1989B. Cypro-Minoan Scripts: Problems of Historical Context. In *Problems of Decipherment* (*Bibliothèque des cahier de l'Institute de Luinguistique de Louvain* 49). Louvaine-La-Neuve: 121–87.

———. 1991A. Maritime Matters in the Linear B Tablets. *Aegaeum* (*Annals d'archéologie égéene de l'Université de Liège*) 7: 273–310, pl. 63.

———. 1991B. Textual Background to Fred Hocker's Paper at *Thalassa* ᵗᵐ II. (Unpublished sheets supplied to participants of the conference: September 23, 1991.)

Palaima, T. G., P. B. Betancourt, and G. H. Myer. 1984. An Inscribed Stirrup Jar of Cretan Origin from Bamboula, Cyprus. *Kadmos* 23: 65–73, pl. 1.

Palaiologou, H. 1989. Aegean Ships from the Second Millennium. In *Tropis* I: 217–28.

Palmer, E. H. 1871. The Desert of Tíh and the Country of Moab. *Palestine Exploration Fund Quarterly Statement* 3: 3–73.

Palmer, L. R. 1955. A Mycenaean Calendar of Offerings (PY Kn 02). *Eranos* 53: 1–13.

———. 1956. Military Arrangements for the Defence of Pylos. *Minos* 4: 120–45.

———. 1963. *The Interpretation of Mycenaean Greek Texts.* Oxford.

———. 1965. *Mycenaeans and Minoans: Aegean Prehistory in the Light of the Linear B Tablets.* New York.

Papathanassopolous, G. 1991. Dokos Excavation '89: The Early Helladic Wreck at Dokos and the Prehistoric Settlement. *Enalia* 1: 34–37.

Papathanasopolous, G., et al. 1992. Dokos: 1990 Excavation. *Enalia Annual* (English Edition) 2: 6–23.

Papathanassopoulos, G., Y. Vichos, and Y. Lolos. 1995. Dokos: 1991 Campaign. *Enalia Annual 1991* (English Edition) 3: 17–37.

Pardee, D. 1974. The Ugaritic Text 147(90). *UF* 6: 275–82.

———. 1975A. The Ugaritic Text 2106: 10–18 a Bottomry Loan? *JAOS* 95: 612–19.

———. 1975B. The Preposition in Ugaritic. *UF* 7: 329–78.

———. 1976. The Preposition in Ugaritic. *UF* 8: 215–322.

———. 1977. A New Ugaritic Letter. *BiOr* 34: 3–20.

———. 1980. La lettre de *pnht* et de *yrmhd* à leur maître. *AAAS* 29/30 (1979–80): 23–36.

———. 1981. A Further Note on *PRU* V no 60, Epigraphic in Nature. *UF* 13: 151–56.

———. 1987. Epigraphic and Philological Notes. *UF* 19: 199–217.

———. 1988. *Les textes para-mythologiques de la 24è campagne (1961)* (*Ras Shamra-Ougarit* IV). Paris.

Park, H. W. 1977. *Festivals of the Athenians.* London.

Parker, A. J. 1976. News: Italy, International Congress of Underwater Archaeology. *IJNA* 5: 347–48.

———. 1992. *Ancient Shipwrecks of the Mediterranean & the Roman Provinces.* (*BAR International Series* 580.) Oxford.

Parker, S. B. 1967. Studies in the Grammar of Ugaritic Prose Texts. (Ph.D. diss., John Hopkins University.)

Parkinson, R., and L. Schofield. 1993A. Mycenaeans Meet the Egyptians at Last. *The Art Newspaper* 24 (January): 10.

———. 1993B. Akhenaten's Army? *Egyptian Archaeology* 3: 34–35.

———. 1995. Images of Mycenaeans: A Recently Acquired

Painted Papyrus from El-Amarna. In *EAL*: 125–26, pl. 8.

Parrot, A. 1937. Les peintures du palais de Mari. *Syria* 18: 325–54.

———. 1953. *Mari: Documentation photographique de la mission archéologique de Mari.* (Collection des ides photographiques 7.) Neuchatel.

———. 1958. *Mission archéologique de Mari* II: *Le Palais: Peintures murales.* Paris.

Patch, D. C., and C. W. Haldane. 1990. *The Pharaoh's Boat at the Carnegie.* (The Carnegie Museum of Natural History.) Pittsburgh.

Payton, R. 1991. The Ulu Burun Writing-Board Set. *AS* 41: 107–10.

Peachey, C. 1990. Taking Conservation Underwater at Ulu Burun. *INAN* 17/3: 10–13.

Peck, W. H. 1978. *Egyptian Drawing.* New York.

Pelon, O. 1970. *Fouilles exécutées à Mallia* III: *Exploration des maisons et quartiers d'habitation (1963–1966).* Paris.

Pendlebury, J. D. S. 1930. Egypt and the Aegean in the Late Bronze Age. *JEA* 16: 75–92.

———. 1939. *The Archaeology of Crete.* London.

Pendleton, M., and P. Warnock. 1990. Scanning Electron Microscopy Analysis of the Ulu Burun Diptych. *INAN* 17/1: 26–27.

Pennas, H. 1992. Point Iria Wreck. *Enalia Annual* (English edition) 2: 39–41.

Pennas, H., and Y. Vichos. 1991. Underwater Surface Investigation of the Wreck of the Late Bronze Age at Point Iria: Part I: Underwater Investigation. *Enalia* 3 (1–2): 8–16. (In Greek.)

———. 1995. The 1991 Underwater Survey of the Late Bronze Age Wreck at Point Iria: Part I: The Underwater Survey. *Enalia Annual 1991* (English Edition) 3: 4–9.

Perpillou, J.-L. 1968. La tablette PY An 724 et la flotte pylienne. *Minos* 9: 213–18.

Persson, A. W. 1938. Tombs. Frödin, O., and A. W. Persson, *Asine: Results of the Swedish Excavations, 1922–1930.* Stockholm: 336–431.

———. 1942. *The Religion of Greece in Prehistoric Times.* Berkeley.

Petrie, W. M. F. 1892. *Medum.* London.

———. 1896. *Naqada and Ballas.* London.

———. 1921. *Corpus of Prehistoric Pottery and Palettes.* London.

Petrie, W. M. F., and G. Brunton. 1924. *Sedment* I. London.

Petrie, W. M. F., G. A. Wainwright, and A. H. Gardiner. 1913. *Tarkhan* I *and Memphis* V. London.

Petrocheilou, A. 1984. *The Greek Caves.* Athens.

Petruso, K. M. 1987. Marks on Some Minoan Balance Weights and Their Interpretation. *Kadmos* 17/1: 26–42.

Pieridou, A. 1965. An Early Cypro-Geometric Tomb at Lapethos. *RDAC*: 74–111, pls. 10–15.

Pini, I., 1987. Zum "Ring des Minos." In *Eilapine: Tómos timetikos gia tov Kathegeté Nikoláu Platona.* G. Orphanou and N. Giannadakis, eds. Hierakleion: 441–55.

Platon, N. 1971. *Zakros: The Discovery of a Lost Palace of Ancient Crete.* New York.

Platon, N., 1984. The Minoan Thalassocracy and the Golden Ring of Minor. In *MT*: 65–73.

Pomerance, L. 1975. The Possible Rôle of Tomb Robbers and Viziers of the Eighteenth Dynasty in Confusing Minoan Chronology. In *SDL*: 21–30, pls. 4–5.

Pomey, P. 1981. L'épave de Bon–Porté et les bateaux cousus de Méditerranée. *MM* 67: 225–43.

Popham, M. 1988. The Historical Implications of the Linear B Archive at Knossos Dating to Either c. 1400 B.C. or 1200 B.C. *Cretan Studies* 1: 217–27.

———. 1990. Pottery Styles and Chronology. In *Thera* III/3: 27–28.

———. 1991. Pylos: Reflections on the Date of Its Destruction and on Its Iron Age Reoccupation. *Oxford Journal of Archaeology* 10: 315–24.

Porada, E. 1948. *Corpus of Ancient Near Eastern Seals in North American Collections* I. *The Collection of the Pierpont Morgan Library.* (The Bollingen Series 14.) Washington.

———. 1984. The Cylinder Seal from Tell el–Dabᶜa. *AJA* 88: 485–88, pl. 65: 1–3.

Porat, Y., S. Dar, and S. Applebaum. 1985. *The History and Archaeology of Emek Hefer.* Tel Aviv. (In Hebrew.)

Porten, B. 1968. *Archives from Elephantine.* Berkeley.

———. 1996. *The Elephantine Papyri in English: Three Millennia of Cross-Cultural Continuity and Change.* Leiden.

Porten, B., and A. Yardeni. 1986. *Textbook of Aramaic Documents from Ancient Egypt* 1: *Letters.* Jerusalem.

———. 1993. *Textbook of Aramaic Documents from Ancient Egypt* 3: *Literature, Accounts and Lists.* Winoan Lake.

Porter, B., and R. L. B. Moss. 1960. *Topographical Bibiography of Ancient Egyptian Hieroglyphic Texts, Reliefs and Paintings* I: 1 *The Theban Necropolis: Private Tombs.* Oxford.

———. 1979. *Topographical Bibliography of Ancient Egyptian Hieroglyphic Texts, Reliefs, and Painting* 3. *Memphis.* Oxford.

Poursat, J.-C. 1980. Appendice: Les ancres du quartier Mu. B. Detournay, J.-C. Poursat, and F. Vandenabeele. In *Fouilles exécutées à Mallia: Le quartier Mu II: Vases de pierre et de métal, vannerie, figurines et reliefs d'applique, éléments de parure et de décoration, armes, sceaux et empreintes.* Paris: 235–38.

Power, E. 1929. The Ancient Gods and Language of Cyprus Revealed by the Accadian Inscriptions of Amathus. *Biblica* 10: 129–69.

Pritchard, J. B. 1951. Syrians as Pictured in the Paintings of the Theban Tombs. *BASOR* 122: 36–41.

Prytulak, M. G. 1982. Weapons on the Thera Ships? *IJNA* 11: 3–6.

Pulak, C. M. 1987. A Late Bronze Age Shipwreck at Ulu Burun: Preliminary Analysis (1984–85 Excavation Campaigns). (M.A. thesis, Texas A&M University.)

———. 1988A. The Bronze Age Shipwreck at Ulu Burun,Turkey: 1985 Campaign. *AJA* 92: 1–37.

———. 1988B. Excavations in Turkey: 1988 Campaign. *INAN* 15/4: cover, 13–17.

———. 1989. Ulu Burun: 1989 Excavation Campaign. *INAN* 16/4: cover, 4–11.

———. 1990A. Ulu Burun: 1990 Excavation Campaign. *INAN* 17/4: cover, 8–13.

———. 1990B. The Late Bronze Age Shipwreck at Ulu Burun, Turkey: 1989 Excavation Campaign. In *Underwater Archaeology Proceedings from the Society for Historical Archaeology Conference.* T. L. Carrell, ed. Tucson: 52–57.

———. 1991. The Late Bronze Age Shipwreck at Ulu Burun, 1991 Field Season: "Ingot Summer." *INAN* 18/4: cover, 4–10.

———. 1992. The Shipwreck at Ulu Burun, Turkey: 1992 Excavation Campaign. *INAQ* 19/4: cover, 4–11, 21.

———. 1993. The Shipwreck at Uluburun: 1993 Excavation Campaign. *INAQ* 20/4: cover, 4–12.

———. 1994. 1994 Excavation at Uluburun: The Final Campaign. *INAQ* 21/4: 8–16.

———. 1995. Das Shiffswrack von Uluburun. In *IPR*: 43–58.

———. 1996A. Dendronological Dating of the Uluburun Ship *INAQ* 23/1: 12–13.

———. 1996B. Analysis of the Weight Assemblages from the Late Bronze Age Shipwrecks at Uluburun and Cape Gelidonya, Turkey. (Ph.D. dissertation, Texas A&M University).

———. In press. The Uluburun Shipwreck. In *Res Maritimæ 1994: Cyprus and the Eastern Mediterranean: Prehistory Through the Roman Period* (18–22 October 1994, Nicosia, Cyprus).

Pulak, C. M., and C. Haldane. 1988. Ulu Burun: The Late Bronze Age Shipwreck: The Fourth Excavation Campaign. *INAN* 15/1: 1–4.

Pulak, C. M., and D. A. Frey. 1985. The Search for a Bronze Age Shipwreck. *Archaeology* 38/4: 18–24.

Pulak, C. M., and E. Rogers. 1994. The 1993–1994 Turkish Shipwreck Surveys. *INAQ* 21/4: 8–16.

Pulak, C. M., and R. F. Townsend. 1987. The Hellenistic Shipwreck at Serçe Limanı, Turkey: Preliminary Report. *AJA* 91: 31–49.

Quibell, J. E. 1908. *Excavations at Saqqara (1906–1907).* Cairo.

Raban A., and E. Galili. 1985. Recent Maritime Archaeological

Research in Israel: A Preliminary Report. *IJNA* 14: 321–56.

Radwan, A. 1973. Amenophis III dargestellt und angerufen als Osiris (*wnn nfrw*). *MDIK* 29: 71–76.

Rahmani, L. Y. 1980. Palestinian Incense Burners of the Sixth to Eighth Centuries C.E. *IEJ* 30: 116–22.

Rainey, A. 1963. A Canaanite in Ugarit. *IEJ* 13: 43–45.

———. 1966. New Tools for Ugaritic Study. *Leshonenu* 30: 250–72. (In Hebrew.)

———. 1967. *A Social Structure of Ugarit.* Jerusalem. (In Hebrew.)

———. 1971. Observations on Ugaritic Grammar. *UF* 3: 151–72.

———. 1974. The Ugaritic Texts in Ugaritica 5. *JAOS* 94: 184–94.

———. 1978. *El Amarna Tablets 359–379: Supplement to J. A. Knudtzon, Die Amarna Tafeln* (2d ed.). (*AOAT* 8). Neukirchen–Vluyn.

———. 1995. Unruly Elements in Late Bronze Canaanite Society. In *Pomegranates and Golden Bells: Studies in Biblical, Jewish, and Near Eastern Ritual, Law, and Literature in Honor of Jacob Milgrom.* D. P. Wright, D. N. Freedman, and A. Hurvitz, eds. Winona Lake: 481–96.

Ralph, E. K. 1967. Appendix 1: Carbon–14 Dates for Wood. *CG*: 168.

Raphael, M. 1947. *Prehistoric Pottery and Civilization in Egypt.* New York.

Redford, D. B. 1982. A Bronze Age Itinerary in Trans Jordan (Nos.89–101 of Thutmose III's List of Asiatic Toponyms). *JSSEA* 12: 55–74.

———. 1992. *Egypt, Canaan and Israel in Ancient Times.* Princeton.

Reese, D. 1992. Tale of the Pigmy Hippo. *Cyprus View* 6 (July): 50–53.

———. 1993. Folklore and Fossil Bones: The Pygmy Mammal of Cyprus. *Terra Nova* 42/3: 319–21.

Rehak, P. 1996. Aegean Breechcloths, Kits and the Keftiu Paintings. *AJA* 100: 35–51.

Reisner, M. G. A. 1913. *Models of Ships and Boats.* Cairo.

Renfrew, C. 1967. Cycladic Metallurgy and the Aegean Early Bronze Age. *AJA* 71: 1–20, pls. 1–10.

———. 1972. *The Emergence of Civilization.* London.

———. 1996. Kings, Tree Rings and the Old World. *Nature* 381: 733–34.

Renfroe, F. 1992. *Arabic-Ugaritic Lexical Studies* (= *Abhandlungen zur Literatur Alt-Syrien-Palästinas*, Band 5). Münster.

Reynolds, C. G. 1978. The Thera Ships. *MM* 64: 124.

Ribichini, S., and P. Xella. 1985. *La terminologia dei Tessili nei testi di Ugarit* (= *Collezione di Studi Fenici* 20). Rome.

Ricketts, M. 1960. Appendix B: Furniture from the Middle Bronze Age. K. Kenyon, *Excavations at Jericho* I: *The Tombs Excavated in 1952–4.* London: 527–34.

Riis, P. J. 1948. *Hama: les cimetières a cremation.* Copenhagen.

Ringler, D. 1980. To go a'Viking. *Oceans* 13: 18–26.

Roberts, O. T. P. 1995. An Explanation of Ancient Windward Sailing: Some Other Considerations. *IJNA* 24: 307–15.

Roger, H. 1986. Tel Abu Hawam. The End. *Kolbotek* [weekend magazine of *Kol Haifa*] 239 (October 17, 1986): 5–28.

Rogers, E. 1992. Boat Reliefs in the Tomb of Tí and Mastaba of Mereruka. *INAQ* 19/3: cover, 8–11, 13.

———. 1996. An Analysis of the Tomb Reliefs Depicting Boat Construction from the Old Kingdom Period in Egypt. (M.A. thesis, Texas A&M University.)

Ronen, A., and Y. Olami. 1978. *The Archaeological Survey of Israel* I: *Atlit Map.* Jerusalem. (In Hebrew.)

Rose, M. 1993. Newsbriefs: Vintage Wreck. *Archaeology* 46/4: 21.

Rothenberg, B. 1972. *Timna: Valley of Biblical Copper Mines.* London.

Rothenberg, B., et al. 1988. *The Egyptian Mining Temple at Timna.* (*Researches in the Arabah 1959–1984* 1.) London.

Rougé, J. 1987. La momie contenait-elle les fragments d'une voile? In *Autopsie d'une momie égyptienne du Museum de Lyon.* (*Nouvelles archives du museum d'histoire naturelle de Lyon* 25.) Lyon: 91–96.

Rowe, A. 1936. Addendum A: Axe-Head of the Royal Boat-Crew of Cheops (or Saḥew-Rā [?]). In A. Rowe, *A Catalogue of Egyptian Scarabs, Scaraboids, Seals and Amulets in the Palestine Archaeological Museum.* Cairo: 283–88.

Rutkowski, B. 1978. Religious Elements in the Thera Frescoes. In *Thera:* 661–64.

———. 1986. *The Cult Places of the Aegean.* New Haven.

Saad, Z. Y. 1947. *Royal Excavations at Saqqara and Helwan (1941–1945).* Cairo.

———. 1951. *The Royal Excavations at Helwan.* Cairo.

———. 1969. *The Excavations at Helwan: Art and Civilization in the First and Second Egyptian Dynasties.* Norman.

Saadé, G. 1995. Le port d'Ougarit. In *Le pays d'Ougarit autour de 1200 av. J.-C.: Histoire et archéologie.* (Actes du Colloque International, Paris, 28 juin–1er juillet 1993 = *Ras Shamra-Ougarit* 11.) M. Yon, M. Sznycer, and P. Bordreuil, eds. Paris: 211–25.

Sakellarakis, J. A. 1971. Ivory Boats from Mycenae. *AE:* 188–233. (In Greek.)

———. 1979. *Herakleion Museum: Illustrated Guide to the Museum.* Athens.

Sakellarakis, J. A., and E. Sapouna-Sakellaraki. 1991. *Archanes.* Athens.

Sakellarakis, Y., and E. Sapouna–Sakellaraki. 1981. Drama of Death in a Minoan Temple. *NG* 159: 205–22.

Sakellariou, A. 1980. The West House Miniature Frescoes. In *Thera* II: 147–53.

Sandars, N. K. 1985. *The Sea Peoples: Warriors of the Ancient Mediterranean 1250–1150 B.C.* London. (Rev. ed.)

Sanmartín, J. 1988A. Glossen zum ugaritischen Lexikon (V). *Studi epigrafici e linguistici* 5: 171–80.

———. 1988B. Notas de lexicografia Ugaritica. *UF* 20: 265–75.

Saramandi, T., and A. Moraïtou. 1995. Conservation of the Ceramic Finds from the Dokos Wreck. *Enalia Annual 1991* (English Edition) 3: 38–44.

Sasson, J. M. 1966. Canaanite Maritime Involvement in the Second Millennium B.C. *JAOS* 86: 126–38.

Säve–Söderbergh, T. 1946. *The Navy of the Eighteenth Egyptian Dynasty.* Uppsala.

———. 1957. *Four Eighteenth Dynasty Tombs.* Oxford.

Sayed, A. M. A. H. 1977. Discovery of the Site of the Twelfth Dynasty Port at Wadi Gawasis on the Red Sea Shore. (Preliminary report on the excavations of the faculty of arts, University of Alexandria, in the Eastern Desert of Egypt–March, 1976.) *Rd'É* 29: 140–78.

———. 1978. The Recently Discovered Port on the Red Sea Shore. *JEA* 64: 69–71.

———. 1980. Observations on Recent Discoveries at Wâdî Gâwâsîs. *JEA* 66: 154–57, pls. 21–22.

———. 1983. New Light on the Recently Discovered Port on the Red Sea Shore. *Cd'É* 58: 23–37.

Schaeffer, C. F. A. 1939. *The Cuneiform Texts of Ras Shamra-Ugarit.* (The Schweich Lectures of the British Academy, 1936.) London.

———. 1952. *Enkomi–Alashia.* Paris.

———. 1962. Fouilles et découvertes des XVIIIe et XIXe campagnes, 1954–1955. *Ugaritica* 4: 1–150.

———. 1973. Remarks and Conclusions. In *MEM:* 285–89.

———. 1978. Remarques sur les ancres en pierre d'Ugarit. *Ugaritica* 7: 371–78.

Schaeffer–Forrer, C. F. A. 1978. Ein Steinanker vom Mittelmeer auf der Heuneburg? *Ugaritica* 7: 384–88.

Schäfer, H. 1908. *Priestgräber und andere Grabfunde vom Ende des alten Reiches bis zur griechischen Zeit vom Totentempel des Ne–user–rê.* Leipzig.

———. 1974. *Principles of Egyptian Art.* J. Baines, trans. Oxford.

Schliemann, H. 1880. *Mycenæ: A Narrative of Researches and Discoveries at Mycenæ and Tiryns.* New York.

Schneider, H. 1993. The Rediscovery of Iniuia. *Egyptian Archaeology* 3: 3–5.

Schoefer, M., D. Cotta, and A. Beentjes. 1987. Les étoffes de rembourrage: du chiffon au vêtement et à la voile de bateau. In *Autopsie d'une momie égyptienne du Museum de Lyon.* (*Nouvelles archives du museum d'histoire naturelle de Lyon* 25.) Lyon: 77–80.

Schofield, L., and R. B. Parkinson. 1994. Of Helmets and Heretics: A Possible Egyptian Representation of Mycenaean Warriors on a Papyrus from El-Amarna. *ABSA* 89: frontispiece, 157–70, pls. 21–22.

Schulman, A. R. 1967. The Scarabs. In *CG:* 143–47.

Schult, H. 1966. Zwei Häfen aus römischer Zeit am Toten Meer. *ZDPV* 82: 139–48, Tafs. 26 31.

Seltman, C. 1965. *Greek Coins: A History of Metallic Currency and Coinage Down to the Fall of the Hellenistic Kingdoms².* London.

Servin, A. 1948. Constructions navales égyptiennes: Les barques de papyrus. *ASAE* 48: 55–88.

Severin, T. 1982. *The Sinbad Voyage.* London.

———. 1985. Constructing the Omani Boom *Sohar*. *SPB:* 279–87.

Shaw, J. W. 1973. *Minoan Architecture: Materials and Techniques.* Annuario 49 (n.s. 33). Rome.

———. 1995. Two Three-Holed Anchors from Kommos, Crete: Their Context, Type and Origin. *IJNA* 24: 279–91.

Shaw, J. W., and H. Blitzer. 1983. Stone Weight Anchors from Kommos, Crete. *IJNA* 12: 91–100.

Shaw, M.C. 1980. Painted 'Ikria' at Mycenae. *AJA* 84: 167–79.

———. 1982. Ship Cabins of the Bronze Age Aegean. *IJNA* 11: 53–58.

Shelmerdine, C. W. 1984. The Perfumed Oil Industry at Pylos. In *PCA:* 81–95.

———. 1985. *The Perfume Industry of Mycenaean Pylos.* (*SIMA* Pocketbook 34.) Göteborg.

———. 1987. Architectural Change and Economic Decline at Pylos. *Minos* 20–22: 557–68.

Shick, T. 1988. Naḥal Ḥemar Cave: Cordage, Basketry and Fabrics. ʿAtiqot 18: 31–43.

Shimony, C., R. Yucha, and E. Werker. 1992. Ancient Anchor Ropes from the Dead Sea. ʿAtiqot 21: 58–62.

Sibella, P. 1995A. The Ceramics. INAQ 22/2: 13–16.

———. 1995B. Notes on the Architectural Marble. INAQ 22/2: 13–16.

———. 1995C. Ceramics from the First Excavation Campaign in Tantura Lagoon at Dor, Israel: Fall 1994. C.M.S. News 22: 13–14.

Simmons, A. H. 1988. Test Excavations at Akrotiri–Aetokremnos (Site E), an Early Prehistoric Occupation in Cyprus: Preliminary Report. RDAC (pt. 1): 15–24.

———. 1991. Humans, Island Colonization and Pleistocene Extinctions in the Mediterranean: The View from Akrotiri Aetokremnos, Cyprus. Antiquity 65: 857–69.

Simmons, A. H., and D. S. Reese. 1993. Hippo Hunters of Akrotiri. Archaeology 46/5: 40–43.

Simpson, W. K. 1965. Papyrus Reisner II. Boston.

Singer, I. 1983. Western Anatolia in the Thirteenth Century B.C. According to the Hittite Sources. AS 33: 205–17.

———. 1991. Appendix III: A Concise History of Amurru. In S. Izre'el, Amurru Akkadian: A Linguistic Study I–II. Atlanta: 134–95.

Sivan, D. 1990. Is There Vowel Harmony in Verbal Forms with Aleph in Ugaritic? UF 22: 313–15.

Sjöqvist, E. 1940. Problems of the Late Cypriote Bronze Age. Stockholm.

Sleeswyk, A. W. 1980. Phoenician Joints, coagmenta punicana. IJNA 9: 243–44.

———. 1983. On the Location of the Land of Pwnt on Two Renaissance Maps. IJNA 12: 279–91.

Smith, K. C. 1987. '86 in Review: Research of Staff and Students Spans Thirty-one Millennia of Maritime Enterprise. INAN 13/4: 1–6.

Smith, S. 1992A. Tribute to a Statesman: Dragon Boat Racing in Yueyang, China. The World & I (October): 671–79.

———. 1992B. Friendship through Paddling: East Meets West on the Water. The World & I (October): 662–69.

Smith, W. S. 1958. The Art and Architecture of Ancient Egypt. Bungay.

———. 1965. Interconnections in the Ancient Near East. New Haven.

Sølver, C. V. 1936. Egyptian Shipping of about 1500 B.C. MM 22: 430–69.

———. 1961. Egyptian Sea–Going Ships, about 2600 B.C. MM 47: 24–30.

Spencer, J. E. 1976. Junks of Central China: The Spencer Collection of Models at Texas A&M University. College Station.

Sperber, D. 1986. Nautica Talmudica. Ramat Gan.

Stager, L. E. 1991. Ashkelon Discovered. Washington.

———. 1995. The Impact of the Sea Peoples in Canaan (1185–1050 B.C.E.). In The Archaeology of Society in the Holy Land. T. E. Levy, ed. New York: 331–48, 583–85.

Stefanski, Y. 1989. Ḥanot Minim (Khan Minya). HA 93: 15–17. (In Hebrew.)

Steffy, J. R. 1985. The Kyrenia Ship: An Interim Report on Its Hull Construction. AJA 89: 71–101, pl. 21.

———. 1987. The Kinneret Boat Project: Part II. Notes on the Construction of the Kinneret Boat. IJNA 16: 325–29.

———. 1990. The Boat: A Preliminary Study of Its Construction. Galilee Boat: 29–47.

———. 1994. Wooden Ship Building and the Interpretation of Shipwrecks. College Station.

Steffy, J. R., and S. Wachsmann. 1990. The Migdal Boat Mosaic. In Galilee Boat: 115–18.

Steindorff, G. 1913. Das Grab des Tí. Leipzig.

Steiner, G. 1989. "Schiffe von Ahhijawa" oder "Kriegschiffe" von Amurru im Šauškamuwa-Vertrag? UF 21: 393–411.

Stieglitz, R. R. 1972–75A. Inscribed Egyptian Stone Anchors. Sefunim 4: 42–43 and pl. 6: 1–2.

———. 1972–75B. An Ancient Terra–Cotta Ship from Cyprus. Sefunim 4: 44–46.

———. 1979. Commodity Prices at Ugarit. JAOS 99: 15–23.

———. 1981. A Physician's Equipment List from Ugarit. JCS 33: 52–55.

———. 1984. Long-distance Seafaring in the Ancient Near East. BA 47: 134–42.

———. In press. Phoenician Ship Equipment and Fittings. In Tropis V.

Stos-Gale, Z. A., and C. F. Macdonald. 1991. Sources of Metals and Trade in the Bronze Age Aegean. In BATM: 249–88.

Stos-Gale, Z. A., and N. H. Gale. 1984. The Minoan Thalassocracy and the Aegean Metal Trade. In MT: 59–63.

Svoronos, J. N. 1914. Stylides, ancres hierae, stoloi, akrostolia, embola, proembola et totems marines. JIAN 16: 81–152.

Swiney, H. W., and M. L. Katzev. 1973. The Kyrenia Shipwreck: A Fourth-Century B.C. Greek Merchant Ship. In MA: 339–55.

Symington, D. 1991. Late Bronze Age Writing Boards and Their Uses: Textual Evidence from Anatolia and Syria. AS 41: 111–23.

Tammuz, O. 1985. The Sea as Economic Factor: Aspects of the Maritime Connections of the Eastern Mediterranean Coastal Populace, from the Amarna Age to the Decline of the Assyrian Empire, According to Written Documents. (M.A. thesis, Hebrew University, Jerusalem.) (In Hebrew.)

Taylor, E. G. R. 1957. The Haven Finding Art: A History of Navigation from Odysseus to Captain Cook. New York.

Taylour, L. W. 1983. The Mycenaeans. London.

Televantou, C. A. 1990. New Light on the West House Wall-Paintings. In Thera III/1: 309–26.

Theocares, D. R. 1958. Iolkos, Whence Sailed the Argonauts. Archaeology 11: 13–18.

Thomas, C. G. 1993. *Myth Becomes History: Pre-Classical Greece. (Publications of the Association of Ancient Historians* 4). Claremont.

Thompson, D'A. W. 1895. *A Glossary of Greek Birds.* Oxford. (Reprint, 1936.)

Thomson, D. F. 1939. The Tree Dwellers of the Arafura Swamps: A New Type of Bark Canoe from Central Arnhem Land. *Man* 39: 121–26.

Throckmorton, P. 1960. Thirty–three Centuries under the Sea. *NG* 117: 682–703.

———. 1962. Oldest Known Shipwreck Yields Bronze Age Cargo. *NG* 121: 697–711.

———. 1967. The Discovery. In *CG*: 14–20.

———. 1987A. Sailors in the Time of Troy. In *HS*: 24–33.

———. 1987B. Shipwrecks and St. Paul. In *HS*: 78–80.

Tibbetts, G. R. 1981. *Arab Navigation in the Indian Ocean before the Coming of the Portuguese.* London.

Tilley, A. 1992. Rowing Astern: An Ancient Technique Revived. *IJNA* 21: 55–60.

Tilley, A. F., and P. Johnstone. 1976. A Minoan Naval Triumph? *IJNA* 5: 285–92.

Todd, I. A. 1987. Chronology, Foreign Relations and Comparisons. In *Vasilikos Valley Project 6: Excavations at Kalavasos-Tenta* I. (*SIMA* 71: 6.) Göteborg: 173–85.

Troev, T. 1989. Sur une barque de papyrus à travers les millénaires. *Loisirs en Bulgarie* 3: 33–35.

Tropper, J. 1990. *Der Ugaritische Kausativstamm und die Untersuchung zum S-Stamm und zu den umstrittenen nichtsibilantischen Kausativstämmen des Ugaritischen.* (= *Abhandlungen zur Literatur Alt-Syrian-Palästinas,* Band 2). Münster.

———. 1994A. Zur Grammatik der ugaritischen Omina. *UF* 26: 457–72.

———. 1994B. Die enklitische Partikel -*y* im Ugartischen. *UF* 26: 473–82.

Tubb, J. N. 1995. An Aegean Presence in Egypto-Canaan. In *EAL*: 136–45, pls. 25–30.

Tusa, V. 1973. Ancore, antiche nel Museo di Palermo. In *MA*: 411–37.

Tushingham, A. D. 1971. God in a Boat. *AJBA* 1/4: 23–28.

Tzalas, H. 1989. On the Obsidian Trail with a Papyrus Craft in the Cyclades. In *SSCA*³.

———. 1990. "Kyrenia" II in the Fresco of Pedoula Church, Cyprus: A Comparison with Ancient Ship Iconography. In *Tropis* II: 323–27.

———. 1995. On the Obsidian Trail: With a Papyrus Craft in the Cyclades. In *Tropis* III: 441–69.

Tzamtzis, A. I. 1987. "Papyrella": Remote Descendant of a Middle Stone Age Craft? In *SSCA*².

Ucelli, G. 1950. *Le navi di Nemi.* Rome. (2d ed.)

Uchitel, A. 1988. The Archives of Mycenaean Greece and the Ancient Near East. In *Society and Economy in the Eastern Mediterranean (c. 1500–1000 B.C.).* (Proceedings of the International Symposium held at the University of Haifa from April 28 to May 2, 1985.) M. Heltzer and E. Lipinski, eds. (*OLA* 23). Leuven: 19–30.

Valansot, O. 1987. Histoire de fil et de trame: documents

techniques. In *Autopsie d'une momie égyptienne du Museum de Lyon.* (*Nouvelles archives du museum d'histoire naturelle de Lyon* 25.) Lyon: 81–90.

Vandier, J. 1969. *Manuel d'archéologie égyptienne* V: *Bas-reliefs et peintures: Scènes de la vie quotidienne.* Paris.

Van Doorninck, F., Jr. 1982A. The Anchors. *Yassi Ada* I: *A Seventh-Century Byzantine Shipwreck.* G. F. Bass and F. H. Van Doornink, Jr., eds. College Station, Tex.: 121–43.

———. 1982B. Protogeometric Longships and the Introduction of the Ram. *IJNA* 11: 277–86.

Van Effenterre, H. 1970. Un navire mycénien (?). In *SC*: 43–53.

———. 1979. Cretan Ships on Seal-Stones: Some Observations. In *Thera*: 593–97.

Van Nouhuys, J. W. 1951. The Anchor. *MM* 37: 17–47.

Van Seters, J. 1964. A Date for the "Admonitions" in the Second Intermediate Period. *JEA* 50: 13–23.

Van Soldt, W. H. 1989. Labels from Ugarit. *UF* 21: 375–88.

———. 1990. Fabrics and Dyes at Ugarit. *UF* 22: 321–57.

———. 1991. *Studies in the Akkadian of Ugarit: Dating and Grammar.* (*AOAT* 40.) Neukirchen-Vluyn.

———. 1994. The Topography and the Geographical Horizon of the City-state of Ugarit. In *Ugarit and the Bible.* (Proceedings of the International Symposium on Ugarit and the Bible, Manchester, September 1992.) (= *Ugaritische-Biblische Literatur,* Band 11). G. Brooke, A. H. W. Curtis, and J. F. Healy, eds. Münster: 363–82.

Ventris, M., and J. Chadwick. 1973. *Documents in Mycenaean Greek.*² Cambridge.

Vercoutter, J. 1951. L'Égée et l'Orient au deuxième millénaire av. J.-C. *JNES* 10: 205–12.

———. 1956. *L'Égypte et le monde égéen préhellénique.* Cairo.

Vermeule, E. 1964. *Greece in the Bronze Age.* Chicago.

———. 1981. *Aspects of Death in Greek Art and Poetry.* Berkeley.

———. 1983. Response to Hans Güterbock. *AJA* 87: 141–43.

Verreet, E. 1988. *Modi Ugaritici. Eine morpho-syntaktische Abhandlung über das Modalsystem im Ugaritischen.* (= *OLA* 27). Leuven.

Vichos, Y., N. Tsouchlos, and G. Papathanassopoulos. 1991. Première année de fouille de l'épave de Docos. In *Thalassa*: 147–52, pls. 41–44.

Vinson, S. M. 1987. Boats of Egypt before the Old Kingdom. (M.A. thesis, Texas A&M University.)

———. 1993. The Earliest Representations of Brailed Sails. *JARCE* 30: 133–50.

Virolleaud, C. 1931. Un poème phénicien de Ras Shamra. *Syria* 12: 191–224, pls. 38–43.

———. 1937. Etats nominatifs et pièces comptables provenant de Ras Shamra. *Syria* 18: 159–73.

———. 1941. Textes administratifs de Ras-Shamra en cunéiforme alphabétique. *RAssyr* 37 (1940–41): 11–44.

———. 1965. *Le Palais royal d'Ugarit* V: *Textes en cunéiformes alphabétiques des archives Sud, Sud-Ouest et du Petit Palais.* Paris.

Wachsmann, S. 1977. Letters to the Editor. *IJNA* 6: 266–67.

———. 1980. The Thera Waterborne Procession Reconsidered. *IJNA* 9: 287–95.

———. 1981. The Ships of the Sea Peoples. *IJNA* 10: 187–220.

———. 1982. The Ships of the Sea Peoples. (*IJNA* 10.3: 187–220): Additional Notes. *IJNA* 11: 297–304.

———. 1985A. A Square Sail at Cairo. *MM* 71: 230–32.

———. 1985B. Review: *Stone Anchors in Antiquity: Coastal Settlements and Maritime Trade Routes in the Eastern Mediterranean ca. 1600–1050 B.C.*, by D. E. McCaslin. *MM* 71: 483–85.

———. 1986A. Is Cyprus Ancient Alashiya? New Evidence from an Egyptian Tablet. *BA* 49: 37–40.

———. 1986B. *Shfifons:* Early Bronze Age Anchor-Shaped Cult Stones from the Sea of Galilee Region. In *Thracia Pontica* III (Sozopol, October 6–12, 1985). Sofia 1986: 395–403, 542–54.

———. 1987. *Aegeans in the Theban Tombs.* (*OLA* 20). Leuven.

———. 1988. The Galilee Boat: Two-Thousand–Year-Old Hull Recovered Intact. *BibAR* 14/5: 18–33.

———. 1989. Seagoing Ships and Seamanship in the Late Bronze Age Levant. (Ph.D. diss., Hebrew University, Jerusalem.)

———. 1990A. The Anchors. In *Galilee Boat:* 107–10.

———. 1990B. First Century C.E. Kinneret Boat Classes. *Galilee Boat:* 119–24.

———. 1995A. *The Sea of Galilee Boat: An Extraordinary 2000 Year Old Discovery.* New York.

———. 1995B. Earliest Mediterranean Paddled and Oared Ships to the Beginning of the Iron Age. In *Conway's History of the Ship: The Age of the Galley.* London: 10–35.

———. 1995C. The 1994 INA/CMS Joint Expedition to Tantura Lagoon. *INAQ* 22/2: cover, 3–8.

———. 1995D. Return to Tantura Lagoon. *C.M.S. News* 22: 9–11.

———. 1996A. Bird-Head Devices on Mediterranean Ships. In *Tropis* IV: 539–72.

———. 1996B. Technology Before Its Time: A Byzantine Shipwreck from Tantura Lagoon. *The Explorers Journal* 74/1: 19–23.

———. In press A. Haḥotrim: The Excavation Report: Part 2: The Artifacts. In *ᶜAtiqot.*

———. In press B. Haḥotrim: The Excavation Report: Part 4: Conclusions. In *ᶜAtiqot.*

———. In press C. Were the Sea Peoples Mycenaeans? The Evidence of Ship Iconography. In *Res Maritimæ 1994: Cyprus and the Eastern Mediterranean: Prehistory Through the Roman Period* (October 18–22, 1994, Nicosia, Cyprus).

———. In press D. The Pylos Rower Tablets Reconsidered. In *Tropis* V.

———. In Press E. Of Ships, Birds and Sea Peoples. In *The Sea Peoples: New Historical and Archaeological Perspectives.* E. Oren, ed.

Wachsmann, S., and K. Raveh. 1978. Underwater Investigations by the Department of Antiquities and Museums. *IEJ* 28: 281–83.

———. 1980. Underwater Work Carried Out by the Israel Department of Antiquities. *IJNA* 9: 256–64.

———. 1981. An Underwater Salvage Excavation near Kibbutz ha-Ḥotrim. *IJNA* 10: 160.

———. 1984A. Concerning a Lead Ingot Fragment from ha-Ḥotrim, Israel. *IJNA* 13: 169–76, 340.

———. 1984B. A Concise Nautical History of Dor/Tantura. *IJNA* 13: 223–41.

———. In press. Haḥotrim: The Excavation Report: Part 1: The Discovery and Excavation. In *ᶜAtiqot.*

Wainwright, G. A. 1939. Some Sea Peoples and Others in the Hittite Archives. *JEA* 25: 148–53.

Walde, A., and J. B. Hofmann. 1938. *Lateinisches etymologisches Wörterbuch* I. 3rd ed. Heidelberg.

Wall, S. M., J. H. Musgrave, and P. M. Warren. 1986. Human Bones from a Late Minoan IB House at Knossos. *ABSA* 81: 333–88.

Wallace, H. 1964. Ancient Anchors: Taking Stock. *Triton* 8: 14–17.

Walters, H. B. 1903. *Catalogue of the Terracottas in the Department of Greek and Roman Antiquities, British Museum.* London.

Ward, W. H. 1910. *The Seal Cylinders of Western Asia.* Washington.

Warnock, P., and M. Pendleton. 1991. The Wood of the Ulu Burun Diptych. *AS* 41: 107–10.

Warren, P. 1966. A Stone Receptacle from the Cave of Hermes Kranaios at Patsos. *ABSA* 61: 195–96, pl. 43a.

———. 1980. Minoan Crete and Ecstatic Religion: Preliminary Observations on the 1979 Excavations at Knossos. In *SCABA:* 155–67.

———. 1984. Knossos: New Excavations and Discoveries. *Archaeology* 37: 48–55.

———. 1987A. Absolute Dating of the Aegean Late Bronze Age. *Archaeometry* 29: 205–11.

———. 1987B. The Ring of Minor. In *Eilapine: Tómos timetikos gia tov Kathegeté Nikoláu Platona.* G. Orphanou and N. Giannadakis, eds. Hierakleion: 485–500, figs. 1–20.

———. 1988A. The Thera Eruption: Continuing Discussion of the Date: III: Further Arguments against an Early Date. *Archaeometry* 30: 176–81.

———. 1988B. *Minoan Religion as Ritual Action.* Göteborg.

———. 1995. Minoan Crete and Pharaonic Egypt. In *EAL:* 1–18.

Warren, P., and V. Hankey. 1989. *Aegean Bronze Age Chronology.* Bristol.

Watrous, L. V. 1992. *Kommos III: The Late Bronze Age Pottery.* Princeton.

Wedde, M., 1990. The "Ring of Minos" and Beyond: Thoughts on Directional Determination on Aegean Bronze Age Ship Iconography. *Hydra* (Working Papers in Middle Bronze Age Studies) 7: 1–24.

Weingarten, J. 1982. The Use of the Zakro Sealings. *Kadmos* 21: 6–13.

Weller, C. H. 1913. *Athens and Its Monuments.* New York.

Wells, H. B. 1974. The Position of the Large Bronze Saws of Minoan Crete in the History of Tool Making. *Expedition* 16/4: 2–8.

Wente, E. F., and C. C. Van Siclen III, 1976. A Chronology of the New Kingdom. In *Studies in Honor of George R. Hughes* (SAOC, OI 39). Chicago: 217–61.

Werker, E. 1990. Identification of the Wood. In *Galilee Boat*: 65–75.

Wesselius, J. W. 1980. Some Regularities in the Ugaritic Administrative Texts. *UF* 12: 448–50.

West, M. L. 1989. *Iambi et Elegi Graeci*. 2d ed. Oxford.

Westerberg, K. 1983. *Cypriote Ships from the Bronze Age to c. 500 B.C.* (*SIMA*, Pocket–books, 22.) Göteborg.

Western, A. C. 1967. Appendix 2: Identification of the Wood. In *CG*: 169–69.

Whitaker, R. E. 1972. *A Concordance of the Ugaritic Literature*. Cambridge.

White, D. 1986A. Excavations at Bates' Island: A Late Bronze Age Egyptian Trading Station. *AJA* 90: 205–206.

———. 1986B. 1985 Excavations on Bates' Island, Marsa Matruh. *JARCE* 23: 51–84.

———. 1990. Proceedings: The Third Season at Marsa Matruh, the Site of A Late Bronze Age Station on the Northwest Coast of Egypt. *AJA* 94: 330.

Wiener, M. 1984. Crete and the Cyclades in LM I: The Tale of the Conical Cups. In *MT*: 17–26.

———. 1987. Trade and Rule in Palatial Crete. In *The Function of the Minoan Palaces*. (*Proceedings of the Fourth International Symposium at the Swedish Institute in Athens, June 10–16, 1984*.) R. Hägg and N. Marinatos, eds. Stockholm: 261–68.

———. 1990. The Isles of Crete? In *Thera* III: 128–60. (Privately distributed copy with errata corrected; for errata see *Nestor* 18: 8 [November 1991].)

Wilde, H. 1953. *Le tombeau de Tí II: La Chapelle. Première partie*. Le Caire.

Williams, R. T. 1959. Addenda to "Early Greek Ships of Two Levels." *JHS* 79: 159–60.

Willies, L. 1993. Appendix: Early Bronze Age Working at Kestrel. *AJA* 97: 262–64.

Winkler, H. A. 1939. *Rock Drawings of Southern Upper Egypt* II. London.

Winlock, H. E. 1936. *Ed Dākhleh Oasis: Journal of a Camel Trip Made in 1908*. (*The Metropolitan Museum of Art, Department of Egyptian Art* V). New York.

———. 1955. *Models of Daily Life in Ancient Egypt*. Cambridge.

Wood, B. G. 1991. The Philistines Enter Canaan: Were They Egyptian Lackeys or Invading Conquerors? *BibAR* 17: 44–52, 89–92.

Wood, M. 1985. *In Search of the Trojan War*. New York.

Wooley, L. 1953. *A Forgotten Kingdom: Being a Record of the Results Obtained from the Excavation of Two Mounds, Atchana and Al Mina, in the Turkish Hatay*. London.

———. 1955. *Alalakh: An Account of the Excavations at Tell Atchana in the Hatay, 1937–1949*. (*Reports of the Research Committee of the Society of Antiquaries of London*, 18.) London.

Woolner, D. 1957. Graffiti of Ships at Tarxien, Malta. *Antiquity* 31: 60–67.

Worcester, G. R. G. 1956. The Origin and Observance of the Dragon Boat Festival in China. *MM* 42: 127–31.

———1971. *The Junks & Sampans of the Yangtze*. Annapolis.

Wreschner, E. 1971. Prehistoric Rock-Engravings in Nahal ha-Me`arot, Mount Carmel. *IEJ* 21: 217–18, pls. 46–47.

Wright, J. C. 1984. Changes in Form and Function of the Palace at Pylos. In *PCA*: 19–29.

———. 1996. Hittite Influences in Mycenaean Architecture: Half-Timbering. Abstract submitted for *TEXNH: Craftsmen, Craftswomen, and Craftsmanship in the Aegean Bronze Age*. (Philadelphia, Pennsylvania, April 18–21, 1996.)

Xella, P. 1982. Die Ausrüstung eines kanaanäischen Schiffes. *WO* 13: 31–35.

———. 1990. "Arsenic et vieilles dentelles," encore sur la terminologie des textiles à Ugarit. *UF* 22: 467–74.

Yadin, Y. 1963. *The Art of Warfare in Biblical Lands*. Jerusalem.

Yamada, M. 1992. Reconsidering the Letters from the "King" in the Ugarit Texts: Royal Correspondence of Carchemish? *UF* 24: 431–46.

Yannai, A. 1983. Studies on Trade between the Levant the Aegean in the Fourteenth to Twelfth Centuries B.C. (Ph.D. diss., Linacre College, Oxford.)

Yardeni, A. 1994. Maritime Trade and Royal Accountancy in an Erased Customs Account from 475 B.C.E. on the Ahiqar Scroll from Elephantine. *BASOR* 293: 67–78.

Yener, K. A., and H. Özbal. 1987. Tin in the Turkish Taurus Mountains: The Bolkardağ Mining District. *Antiquity* 61: 220–26.

Yener, K. A., and P. B. Vandiver. 1993A. Tin Processing at Göltepe, an Early Bronze Age Site in Anatolia. *AJA* 97: 207–38.

———. 1993B. Reply to J. D. Muhly, "Early Bronze Age Tin and the Taurus." *AJA* 97: 255–62.

Yener, K. A., H. Özbal, A. Minzoni–Deroche, and B. Aksoy. 1989. Bolkardağ: Archaeometallurgy Surveys in the Taurus Mountains, Turkey. *NGR* 5/3: 477–94.

Yener, K. A., et al. 1991. Stable Lead Isotope Studies of Central Taurus Ore Sources and Related Artifacts from Eastern Mediterranean Chalcolithic and Bronze Age Sites. *JAS* 18: 541–77.

Yogev, O. 1985. Degania "A." *ESI* 4: 20–21.

Yon, M. 1971. *Salamine de Chypre II: La Tombe T. I du XIème s. av. J.-C.* Paris.

———. 1992. Ducks' Travels. In *Acta Cypria* 2. P. Åstrom, ed. Jonsered: 394–407, pls. 1–2.

Zaccagnini, C. 1970. Note sulle terminologia metallurgica di Ugarit. *OrA* 9: 315–24.

———. 1990. The Transition from Bronze to Iron in the Near East and the Levant: Marginal Notes. *JAOS* 110: 493–502.

Zangger, E. 1995. Who Were the Sea Peoples? *Aramco World* 46/3: 20–31.

Ziskind, J. R. 1974. Sea Loans at Ugarit. *JAOS* 94: 134–37.

Cycladic frying pans, 70–71, 74, 76, 106, 109, 193

cypress wood, 217, 227

Cypriot seals, 66

Cypriot ships, 61–67, 254, 350nn1–47; anchors of, 62, 273–74, 292; archaeological evidence on, 62; iconographic evidence on, 62–67; propulsion of, 250; textual evidence on, 61–62

Cypro-Minoan script, 61, 83

Cyprus, 151–52, 185, 328, 329, 330; sea routes of, 295–96; Syro-Canaanite ships in, 49–51; trade in, 313. *See also* Alashia

Dagon, Temple of, 273

Dakaronia, F., 131

Dashur, 29, 220–22, 227, 245, 312

Davies, N. de G., 32, 44, 55, 257–58, 310, 313

Dead Sea, 271

De Cervin, G. B. R., 106

decks: of Cypriot ships, 62; of Egyptian ships, 25, 29; of Minoan/Cycladic ships, 94, 96, 105; of Mycenaean/ Achaean ships, 142, 156; of Sea Peoples ships, 172, 174; of Syro-Canaanite ships, 54

Degania, 265

Deir el Bahri, 18–29, 32, 247, 250, 288, 314, 327, 330. *See also* Punt ships

de Morgan, J., 220

Demosthenes, 324

Deveboynu Burnu, 209, 297

dieres, 132–33, 156, 174

Diodorus Siculus, 226, 239, 308

Dirmil, 186

Dokos, 205, 279

Dor, 48, 163, 164, 209, 265, 266, 272, 273, 292

double-ended craft, Aegean, 76–77

doves, 113

dragon boats, 74–75, 109–10, 116, 195

duck ornaments, 196

dugouts, 32, 229–30, 351n26

dummy anchors, 262, 264, 271–73

Dunand, M., 52, 53, 54

Dussaud, R., 62

Eccles, E., 102

Edgerton, W. F., 11, 14, 228, 239

Egypt: Alashia and, 130; Cypriot ships in, 61–62; Graeco-Roman shipbuilding in, 226; Miniature Frieze influenced by, 105–106; Minoan/Cycladic contacts with, 85–86; peace treaty with Hatti, 333; sea routes of, 295–96, 297–99; trade in, 9, 308, 310–13, 327, 329, 332

Egyptian ships, 9–38, 254, 327–28, 330, 345–47nn1–171; anchors from, 11, 26, 256–62, 266, 272, 288; archaeological

evidence on, 11; construction of, 215–26, 238–39, 241–42; Cypriot ships compared with, 64; iconographic evidence on, 11–32, 227–38; of Middle Kingdom, 18, 32–33, 36, 52–54; Minoan/Cycladic ships compared with, 97; Mycenaean/Achaean ships compared with, 144, 156; of New Kingdom, 18–32, 35–36; of Old Kingdom, 12–18, 24–25; propulsion of, 248, 251, 252–53; Sea Peoples ships and, 163, 166–75; size of, 23, 345n16; Syro-Canaanite ships and, 10, 12–14, 15, 39, 40–41, 42–47, 47, 49, 52, 53, 241; textual evidence on, 9–11, 223–26; war and, 317–19

Eileithyia cult cave, 353n96

Ein Gedi, 271, 292

E-ke-ra₂-wo, 124

El, 208

Elephantine Papyrus Cowley No. 26, 224–26

embalming, 308–10, 332, 374n90

Emery, W., 219

Enenkhet, 19

Enkomi, 50, 51, 98, 118, 142, 143, 147, 155, 156, 176, 177, 185, 201

Esarhaddon, 323

Eshuwara, 343, 360n54

Euboea, 209

Eusebius, 226

Evans, A., 83, 99, 101, 106, 116, 120, 279

Eye of Horus, 14, 24–25

Ezekiel, 160, 226, 227, 300

faenus nauticum, 324

fanlike devices, 148, 176

Faulkner, R. O., 24, 27, 29, 31, 44, 45, 238, 248, 250

feather helmets, 142, 177

Fensham, F. C., 323

fertility cults, 74, 109, 116, 329

Février, J. G., 52, 53

fire-dog ornaments, 186

First Dynasty boat graves, 219

fish ornaments, 19, 22, 71, 74, 77, 102

forecastles: of Egyptian ships, 25, 38; of Mycenaean/Achaean ships, 137, 144, 147, 150, 156

forestays, 28, 137, 143

Forrer, E., 128

Fortesta, 186

frames, 364n10; of Cheops ships, 220; of Mycenaean/Achaean ships, 148, 149, 150; tripartite, 220

Franchthi Cave, 69

Frankfort, H., 218

Frost, H., 209, 255, 256–57, 259, 271, 272, 273, 274, 287–88, 290, 292

frying pans, 70–71, 74, 76, 106, 109, 193

Furumark, A., 298

Gaballa, G. A., 12, 23

Galili, E., 211, 285–86

garboards, 216

Gardiner, A. H., 33–36

garlands, 88, 101, 119

Gazi, 138–39, 145, 148, 150, 157, 185, 191

Gela, 240

Gerzean ships, 248

Giglio, 240

Gilgamesh epic, 256

Gillmer, T. C., 106, 107

Glanville, S. R. K., 223–24, 312

Goedicke, H., 40

Gordon, "Chinese," 75

Graeco-Roman shipbuilding, 226

graffiti: of Aegean ships, 71, 73; of birds/ bird-head devices, 185, 202–203; of Egyptian ships, 32–38; of Mycenaean/ Achaean ships, 143, 144–45, 147–48, 152; of Sea Peoples ships, 176; of Syro-Canaanite ships, 48, 49–50

grain, sheaves of, 111

grapnel, 317, 319, 332, 375n12

Greek ships, 101, 187–89, 196, 328; anchors from, 279; Mycenaean/Achaen trade with, 154; wrecks of, 205

Grey Minyan Ware, 314

Grünwald, 178

Gulf of Eilat, 11

Haddon, A. C., 193–94

Hagia Triada sarcophagus, 71, 104–105, 115, 120

Hahotrim, 209, 288

Hala Sultan Teke, 49–51, 273–74

Haldane, C. W., 218–19, 220, 222–23

halyards, 330; of Egyptian ships, 27, 28; of Minoan/Cycladic ships, 96–97; of Mycenaean/Achaean ships, 137, 141–43; of Sea Peoples ships, 175; of Syro-Canaanite ships, 45, 47, 51

Hama, 175–76, 178

Hamilton, R. W., 267, 270

Hand One (Pylian scribe), 127

Harkhuf, 19

"Harvesters Vase," 115, 120

Hathor, Temple of, 32

Hatshepsut, 85, 159, 297; obelisk barge of, 26, 41, 367n15; Temple of, 18, 23. *See also* Punt ships

Hatti, 333

Hattusilis, 129

hawser weights, 286–87

helmets, 142, 143, 177

helmsmen, 28, 31, 132, 134, 153

Heltzer, M., 256

Hencken, H., 178

Henu, 19, 238

Herihor, royal galley of, 251, 252

Hermes Kranaios, cave of, 355n171

Herodotus, 114, 157, 159, 160, 223, 224, 227, 256, 257, 308

Hesychius, 200
Heteb, 324
hippopotamus ivory, 306, 310
Hippus of Tyre, 226
Hishulei Carmel, 209
Hittites, 128–30, 317, 329
Hocker, F. M., 227
hogging trusses, 248–50; of dragon boats, 74; of Egyptian ships, 14, 15, 18, 24, 25–26, 228, 242, 346n55; of Hatshepsut's obelisk barge, 367n15; hybridism in, 56; lack of on Syro-Canaanite ships, 45; of Punt ships, 246
Holmes, Y. L., 295
Holy Tabernacle, 227
Homer, 39, 95, 128, 149, 157, 186, 199–201, 227, 299, 300, 356n65, 358n157, 361–62nn1–27
Hood, S., 116
Horemheb, 251
Hornell, J., 29, 77, 158, 194–95, 197, 206, 229, 239, 240
horse-head devices, 139
hulls: of Aegean ships, 69, 71–73, 227; construction of, 215–23; of Cypriot ships, 62, 63, 64, 66–67; of Egyptian ships, 23–24, 29–31, 32, 33–34, 35, 36, 37, 38, 215–23; of Minoan/Cycladic ships, 90, 94, 96, 104; of Mycenaean/Achaean ships, 131, 137, 138, 141, 142, 143, 144–45, 148, 149, 152, 153, 156; of Sea Peoples ships, 171–72, 176; of Syro-Canaanite ships, 42, 44, 45, 48, 49, 50, 51, 54
human sacrifice, 113–17, 354n157, 354n159
Hungary, 178
Hutchinson, R. W., 99, 101
hybridism, 55–60
Hyksos, 39, 253
Hyria, 144, 155, 156

Ialysos, 281
Iappa-Addi, 314, 321
Ibnadušu, 164
iconographic evidence: on Aegean ships, 69–80; on anchors, 256–58; on Cypriot ships, 62–67; on Egyptian ships, 11–32, 227–38; on Minoan/Cycladic ships, 85–105; on Mycenaean/Achaean ships, 130–53; on Sea Peoples ships, 166–76; on ship construction, 227–38; on Syro-Canaanite ships, 42–51
Idrimi, 40
ikria, 94, 96, 99, 101, 111, 118
Ikria Wall Paintings, 101
incense, 305, 306, 332
Indian ships, 194–95, 197
"Indictment of Madduwatas," 129, 130
Iniwia, tomb of, 54–60, 328, 350n119
Institute of Nautical Archaeology (INA), 208, 283
international trade, 154–55

interregional trade, 154–55
Iolkos, 80
Ipy, tomb of, 183, 238
iron anchors, 258
iron nails, 226, 239–40
Isidis Navigium, 354n132
Israel, 201–203, 226–27, 329; anchors from, 262–71, 331; shipwrecks in, 208–209
Israel National Maritime Museum, 152
Italy, 195

Ja 749, 154
Ja 829, 154
Jarrett-Bell, C. D., 29, 223, 247
Jehoshaphat, 299
Jericho, 241
Jesus, 301
jewelry, 303–305, 306
Johnstone, P., 107
Jonah, 212
Josephus, 301
juniper wood, 227, 298

Kabri, 84
kalla dhoni, 197
Kambos, 122
Kamose, 39, 42, 253, 312
Käpitan, G., 255
Karatepe, 186–87
Karnak, 274, 328
Kassite seals, 307
Kato Zakro, 243
Katsamba, 86
Kazaphani, 63, 66, 67, 242, 250, 328, 330
Kbn ships, 238
Kea, 86, 87
keel-planks, 216, 217, 222, 245
keels: of Aegean ships, 69, 73; of Cypriot ships, 63, 64, 66; defined, 245; of Mycenaean/Achaean ships, 134, 145, 148, 149, 150, 151, 153, 156, 158; proto-, 242; of Punt ships, 241, 242, 245–46, 367nn1–2; of seagoing ships in Late Bronze Age, 241–43; of Sea Peoples ships, 175; of Syro-Canaanite ships, 45, 52, 53
Keftiu, 51–52, 298, 328
Kehotep, mastaba of, 258
Kenamun, tomb of, 42–45, 47, 50, 51, 52, 56, 57, 60, 217, 248, 253, 300, 305, 306, 313, 314, 328, 330
Kennedy, D. H., 106
Keos, 104
Keros-Syros culture, 70, 75
Kfar Samir, 208, 209, 267
Khaniale Tekke, 138, 144
Khan Minya, 270–71
Khasekhemi, 9
Khenty-khety-wer, 238
Khirbet Kerak, 262. See also Tel Beit Yerah
Khirokitia, 273
Khnumhotep, 19, 37; tomb of, 231–32

Khonsu, Temple of, 251
Khui, tomb of, 19
Kibbutz Beit Zera, 262
Kibbutz Hahotrim, 208
Kibbutz Naveh Yam, 209
Kibbutz Shaar ha-Golan, 262
kidnapping, 212
Killen, J. T., 126
killicks, 275
Kinneret, 270
Kirk, G. S., 140, 157–58
Kition, 41, 152, 176, 185, 203; anchors from, 255, 272, 273–74, 283, 288, 290, 292; graffiti of, 147–48
Knossos, 61, 83, 86, 154, 243; anchor from, 279; fleet and officers at, 127–28
knots, 28, 254; sacral, 120–21
Kofinas, 105
Kolona, 88, 94, 95, 103
Kom el Hetan, 84, 297
Kommos, 279, 280
Korrés, G. S., 185
Kothar-wa-Khasis, 84
KTU 2.38, 334
KTU 2.39, 334–35
KTU 2.42, 335–36
KTU 2.46, 336
KTU 2.47, 336–37
KTU 4.40, 41, 126, 337
KTU 4.81, 337
KTU 4.338, 324, 337–38
KTU 4.352, 338
KTU 4.370, 338–39
KTU 4.390, 339
KTU 4.394, 339
KTU 4.421, 339
KTU 4.647, 339
KTU 4.689, 41, 256, 339–40
Kynos, 151, 153, 155, 156, 157, 243; birds/bird-head devices at, 185, 186, 191, 202; Mycenaean/Achaean ships at, 131–37
Kynos A (ship graffito), 131–34, 156, 172, 174, 176
Kyrenia II, 253–54, 367n36

Labaia, 40
Lacau, P., 227
lacing, 44. See also lashings
ladder design, 131, 133, 148, 151
Laffineur, R., 95
Laganda tomb, 177
Lallemand, H., 227
Lambertis, 62
Lamu Archipelago, 240
Landström, B., 18, 28, 38, 222, 230, 241, 242, 248
"La Parisienne," 121
Lapithos, 151–52
larnax, 131, 137–38, 139
lashings: of Cheops ship, 14–15, 219–20; of Egyptian ships, 14–15, 27, 218, 222,

Rhodian Sea Law, 324, 325, 376n9

rhytons, 104, 116

Rib-Addi, 10, 130, 254, 295, 296, 314, 321

rigging: of Aegean ships, 109; of Egyptian ships, 28; in Miniature Frieze, 96–98; of Minoan/Cycladic ships, 96–98, 101–102, 109; in Minoan seals, 101–102; of Mycenaean/Achaean ships, 140, 141; of Sea Peoples ships, 175; of Syro-Canaanite ships, 45, 48, 49. *See also* boom-footed rigs

Ring of Minos, 354n136

Rod el ᶜAir, 32–38

rope, 254, 271, 283, 288–92, 367n42, 367n43, 368n44, 368n45

rope grooves, 283, 285, 286, 288, 331

rope ladders, 45, 51

Rothenberg, B., 11

round ships, 145, 147, 153, 157, 176

Rowe, A., 11, 310

rowers: of Egyptian ships, 24, 31; of Mycenaean/Achaean ships, 132, 137, 141, 154, 155–56; of Syro-Canaanite ships, 41

rowers' galleries: of Mycenaean/Achaean ships, 138, 140, 144, 145, 149, 151, 155–56, 157; of Sea Peoples ships, 176

rower tablets, 123–27, 159–61, 329, 359n14

RS 16.238 + 254, 340

RS 17.133, 340–41

RS 20.18, 343

RS 20.162, 341

RS 20.212, 341

RS 20.238, 344

RS 20.255A, 341–42

RS 26.158, 342

RS 34.129, 343

RS 34.135, 342

RS 34.145, 342

RS 34.147, 342–43

RS L.1, 343–44

rudders. *See* quarter rudders

Rujm el Baḥr, 271

Rumania, 178

running lifts: of Egyptian ships, 27, 28; of Minoan/Cycladic ships, 97

Saad, Z. Y., 219

Sacke Gözü, 111

sacral clothing, 120

sacral knots, 120–21

Sahure, 10, 11, 12–15, 18, 19, 23, 26, 28, 44, 218, 256, 312

sails, 248–54, 328, 330, 331; of Aegean ships, 118, 251, 252; of Egyptian ships, 27–28, 251, 252–53; of Minoan/Cycladic ships, 96, 97, 108, 109; of Mycenaean/Achaean ships, 134, 137, 139–40, 143–44; of Sea Peoples ships, 175, 176, 251, 252; square, 248, 253

Sakellariou, A., 111

sand-anchors, 255

Sandars, N. K., 164, 177

sandstone anchors, 281, 283

Saqqara, 173

Sasson, J. M., 39, 53, 62

Satu Mare, 178

Säve-Söderbergh, T., 9, 39, 44, 45, 47, 130

saws, two-handled, 243

Sayed, A. M. A. H., 288

scarabs, 306, 363n37

"Scene on the Brook," 120

Schaeffer, C. F. A., 49, 176, 273

Schäfer, H., 29

Schliemann, H., 310

screens, 50, 51, 56, 156

SCUBA, 205

Scylla, 116

sea laws, 323–35, 332, 375–76nn1–24

seals, 306–307; Cypriot, 66; Enkomi, 176; Kassite, 307; Mesopotamian, 111; Mycenaean, 211–12; steatite prism, 102; Tell el Dabᶜa, 42, 51; Ugaritic, 49. *See also* Minoan seals

Sea of Galilee, 262, 264, 271

Sea Peoples ships, 27, 29, 31, 52, 130, 148, 163–97, 202, 204, 329–30, 333, 359–61nn1–85; archaeological evidence on, 166; composite bow and, 357n65; cultures influencing, 360n54; iconographic evidence on, 166–76; Mycenaean/Achaean ships compared with, 133, 134, 137, 139, 141, 142, 144, 152, 155, 156–57, 176–77; piracy and, 320; propulsion of, 251, 252; Syro-Canaanite ships and, 40, 51, 164, 175, 252; textual evidence on, 163–66; war and, 317

sea routes, 295–99, 331

sea trade. *See* trade

Sebekhotep, tomb of, 310

Sekel, 163, 324

Sennacherib, 159–60

Sennefer, tomb of, 253

Senufer, 10, 11, 310–12

Senusret III, 222

Serabit el Khadem, 32–33

Seraglio, 141

Sesostris I, 36, 220, 223

Sesostris II, 273

Seti I, 55

Severin, T., 228, 239

sewn ships, 218

Shaft Grave IV, 88

Shardanu ships, 317

Shaushgamuwa Treaty, 129, 130

sheer: of Aegean ships, 73; of Cypriot ships, 63; hybridism in, 56; of Syro-Canaanite ships, 44, 48, 49

sheets, 28, 45, 96

shell-first ship construction, 224, 226, 239

Sheytan Deresi, 205–206

shfifonim, 262–65, 292, 331, 368n43, 369n54

ship construction, 215–46, 363–68nn1–180; ancillary materials in, 217–23; iconographic evidence on, 227–38; primary materials in, 215–17; shell-first, 224, 226, 239; skeleton-first, 224, 239; textual evidence on, 223–27

ship models, 328; Aegean, 69–70, 73, 74; *askoi*, 140, 151–52, 156, 185, 201; bronze, 104; Byblos, 241–42; Cypriot, 62–67; lead, 69–70, 73, 74; limestone, 105; metal, 54; Minoan/Cycladic, 104–105; Mycenaean/Achaean, 140, 148–53, 151–52; Syro-Canaanite, 54; wooden, 44. *See also* terra-cotta ship models

ship sizes: Cheops ships, 219; Egyptian ships, 23, 345n16; Syro-Canaanite ships, 41

shipwrecks, 205–12, 330, 362–63nn1–65; anchors on, 208, 281–86; ethnic identification problems, 211–12; evidence of trade from, 303–307; laws on dealing with, 323–24; sites of, 205–11; willful, 323–24

shrouds, 176, 250, 254, 330; of Cypriot ships, 350n38; of Minoan/Cycladic ships, 102; of Syro-Canaanite ships, 45, 51

Shukku, 323, 324, 340–41

Shuppululiuma II, 317

sidder, 219, 364n34

"Siege Rhyton," 88, 114, 116, 354n153

Siginu, 340

Sikila, 163, 164

Sinai, 32–33, 327

Sinaranu, 296, 331, 340

Sinda, 329

sinn, 290

skeleton-first ship construction, 224, 239

Skyros, 137, 139–40, 145, 183, 187

slaving, 212, 313

smiting-god statuettes, 41–42, 348n40

Sneferu, 9

Sohar, 228, 229, 239, 243

Solima, 77, 190

Solomon, 299, 327

Solomon Islands, 71, 77, 190

solub e res, 194

solub wok-wak, 194

Sølver, C. V., 14, 15, 26, 28, 253

Somes River, 178

Somner, F., 129

sons of Ugarit, 333

sounding weights, 299, 300

Sphoungaras, 101

spurs, 150, 151, 156, 157, 158

square hawser holes, 288–92

square sails, 248, 253

stanchions: of Cheops ship, 220; of Cypriot ships, 64; of Egyptian ships,

stanchions (contd.)
    28–29, 31, 33, 34, 36, 37, 38; of
    Minoan/Cycladic ships, 95; of
    Mycenaean/Achaean ships, 132–33,
    137, 138, 145, 149; of Syro-Canaanite
    ships, 44, 51, 54
stays, 101–102; fore, 28, 137, 143
steatite prism seal, 102
steering oars: of Aegean ships, 73; of
    Egyptian ships, 15, 28, 29, 33, 34, 36,
    37, 38; of Mycenaean/Achaean ships,
    157; of Sea Peoples ships, 175; of Syro-
    Canaanite ships, 51, 53, 54
Steffy, J. R., 158, 227
Steiner, G., 129
stellar navigation, 300
stemposts: of Cypriot ships, 62; of
    Egyptian ships, 24–25, 31; of
    Mycenaean/Achaean ships, 137, 138,
    140, 144, 149; of Syro-Canaanite ships,
    44, 50, 51
stems: of Aegean ships, 74, 77; of Cypriot
    ships, 63; of Mycenaean/Achaean
    ships, 134, 137, 145, 149, 151, 152, 153,
    156; of Sea Peoples ships, 175; of Syro-
    Canaanite ships, 54
sternposts: of Cypriot ships, 62, 63, 66; of
    Egyptian ships, 34, 36; of
    Mycenaean/Achaean ships, 137, 139,
    142, 143, 144, 152; of Syro-Canaanite
    ships, 44, 50, 51
sterns: of Aegean ships, 73–74; of Cypriot
    ships, 63; horizontal device on
    Miniature Frieze, 73–74, 106, 108, 109,
    111; of Minoan/Cycladic ships, 88, 90,
    104, 106, 108, 109, 111; of Mycenaean/
    Achaean ships, 144, 145, 149, 152, 156;
    of Syro-Canaanite ships, 54
stick charts, 299
Stieglitz, R. R., 266
stone anchors, 209–10, 216, 217, 256–58,
    265–71, 273–74, 275–79, 331
strakes, 216, 217, 227
Sudanese Nilotic craft, 239–40
Surata of Acco, 40
sycamore wood, 219, 222
Syria, 178, 273
Syro-Canaanite coast, 48–49, 226–27;
    Mycenaean/Achaean ships and, 129;
    sea routes of, 295–97
Syro-Canaanite ships, 39–60, 254, 327–28,
    330, 347–50nn1–120; anchors of, 41,
    257, 266; archaeological evidence on,
    41–42; characteristics of, 51;
    construction of, 217, 226–27; Cypriot
    ships compared with, 66; Egyptian
    ships and, 10, 12–14, 15, 39, 40–41, 42–
    47, 49, 52, 53, 241; hybridism in, 55–
    60; iconographic evidence on, 42–51;
    Minoan/Cycladic ships compared
    with, 97; propulsion of, 248, 250, 253;
    Sea Peoples ships and, 40, 51, 164,

175, 252; ships misinterpreted as, 52–
    60; sizes of, 41; textual evidence on,
    39–41, 226–27; trade and, 39–40, 155,
    308, 310, 312, 314, 329; tutelary
    goddesses of, 206; wrecks of, 212
Syros, 70

Tabaria, 288
"Tale of the Shipwrecked Sailor," 10, 32,
    299, 300, 359n4
"Tale of Wenamun." See Wenamun
talismanic seals, 99–101, 103, 119
Tanagra, 148–49
Tantura A shipwreck, 365n63, 368n13
Tantura Lagoon, 209
Tarkhan planks, 218–19
Tartous, 288
Tarxien, 73
tassels, 71, 74, 77, 88
"Tawagalawas Letter," 129
"Teachings of Merikare, The," 298
Tel Beit Yerah, 262, 264, 265
Tel Ein Gev, 270
Tell Abu Hawam, 48–49, 51, 253, 267, 270
Tell Atchana, 84
Tell Basta, 257, 261
Tell el Dabᶜa, 42, 51, 85, 298
Tel Shiqmona, 270
Temple of Amun, 55, 62, 310
Temple of Baal, 259, 273
Temple of Dagon, 273
Temple of Hathor, 32
Temple of Hatshepsut, 18, 23
Temple of Khonsu, 251
Temple of the Obelisks, 271
Temple of Userkaf, 259
tenons, 217, 219, 220, 222
terebinth resin, 305, 308–310, 332, 372n18,
    374n94
terra-cotta ship models: Aegean, 70–73,
    74, 76–77; birds/bird-head devices of,
    185, 191, 201; Cypriot, 62, 63–66;
    Minoan/Cycladic, 104; Mycenaean/
    Achaean, 148–50, 152, 157, 158; Syro-
    Canaanite, 50, 51, 52–54
textual evidence: on Aegean ships, 227;
    on anchors, 256; on Cypriot ships, 61–
    62; on Egyptian ships, 9–11, 223–26;
    on Minoan/Cycladic ships, 83–84; on
    Mycenaean/Achaean ships, 123–30;
    on Sea Peoples ships, 163–66; on ship
    construction, 223–27; on Syro-
    Canaanite ships, 39–41, 226–27
Theban tombs, 85–86, 297
theft in harbor, 324–25
Theocritus, 200
Thera, 86–99, 157, 328–29; anchors from,
    280–81; destruction of, 352n1; human
    sacrifice at, 113–17. See also Miniature
    Frieze
Tholos Tomb 1, 137

Throckmorton, P., 205
through-beams, 24, 31, 52, 54
Thucydides, 320
Thutmose I, 306
Thutmose III, 10, 39–40, 51, 55, 85, 86,
    223, 239, 241, 297, 308, 310, 312, 313,
    314, 321, 327, 330, 352n1
T(161), tomb of, 173–74, 227, 229–31
tillers: of Aegean ships, 73; drawings of
    on anchors, 265–66; of Egyptian ships,
    28–29, 31, 34, 36, 37, 38; of
    Mycenaean/Achaean ships, 137; of
    Sea Peoples ships, 171, 176; of Syro-
    Canaanite ships, 44, 47, 51
Tilley, A. F., 107
timbers: of Aegean ships, 227; of
    Egyptian ships, 223, 224; trade in,
    310–13
tin ingots, 303
Tiryns, 150, 156, 157, 183, 201
Tjeker, 164
Tjekkerbaal, 11, 12, 40, 310, 311–12, 314
toggles, 248
tomb paintings, 212, 310. See also specific
    sites
"Tower of the Winds," 300
Tower Temple, 271
trade, 9, 39–40, 303–15, 327, 329, 331–32,
    372–75nn1–149; Aegean ships and, 76;
    convoys of ships in, 314;
    international, 154–55; interregional,
    154–155; invisible items in, 313;
    manufactured materials in, 306;
    Mycenaean/Achaean ships and, 154–
    155; organic materials in, 305–306;
    personal items and ship's equipment
    in, 306–307; port scenes and
    recreation ashore, 313; prestige items
    in, 306; raw materials in, 303; Sea
    Peoples ships and, 163; in timber and
    ships, 310–13
Tragana, 139, 144, 145, 151, 157, 185, 191,
    201
traiectito pecunia, 324
traveling gods, 206
treenails, 228, 235–38
Trésor de bronzes, 253
triaconters, 157
Trianda, 84
tripartite frames, 220
tripod masts, 15, 18, 250
Tudkhaliya II, 356n29
Tudkhaliya IV, 129, 323, 329, 340
Turkey: anchors from, 274; birds/bird-
    head devices at, 186; shipwrecks in,
    205–208, 209
turquoise, 32
Tutankhamen, 24, 29, 31, 206, 242, 245,
    312
tutelary deities, 206–208, 307
two-handled saws, 243
Tylissos, 86

Typhis, 287
Tyre, 226, 227

Uchitel, A., 154
Ugarit, 253; destruction of, 332; sea routes of, 295, 296; supplies dragoman for Minoans at Mari, 83; Syro-Canaanite ships in, 41, 49, 51
Ugaritic alphabetic script, 334–40
Ugaritic seals, 49
Ugaritic ships, 226, 255, 272, 273, 274, 283, 290, 292
Ugaritic texts, 317, 328, 333–44; in Akkadian language, 340–43; on Cypriot ships, 61; on Egyptian ships, 224; on Minoan/Cycladic ships, 84; on Mycenaean/Achaean ships, 154; on piracy, 320; on a seaborne invasion, 343–44; on Sea Peoples ships, 163–64; on shipwreck laws, 323–24; on Syro-Canaanite ships, 39; on trade, 313; in Ugaritic alphabetic script, 334–40
Uhhazitis, 129
Uluburun, 42, 44, 66, 154, 155, 205, 206, 209, 211–12, 226, 243, 245, 300, 328, 330; anchors from, 259, 281–83, 285, 286, 288, 290, 293, 331; construction of ships at, 216–17; evidence of trade from, 303–308; piracy and, 321; sea routes of, 297
Unas, 12, 14, 15–18, 28, 250, 256, 257
Uni, 9, 300
unpegged mortise-and-tenon joinery, 215, 218, 227, 228, 239, 330; examples of, 229–35
Ura, 295
Urnfield culture, 137, 178, 330
Useramun, tomb of, 312
Userkaf, Temple of, 259
Utnapishtim, 300

Van Effenterre, H., 99, 227
Vathyrkakas, 66
vegetation cults, 111–13, 116, 329
Velem St. Vid, 178
Vercoutter, J., 298, 299
Versailles effect, 84
Vikings, 164, 320
Villanovan art, 178, 183
Vinson, S. M., 218
Virolleaud, C., 224
Vn 865, 227
volutes, 178
V series of texts, 127–28, 227

Wadi Gawasis, 32–33, 215–16, 238, 239, 257, 259, 260, 286, 312, 327, 331
Wadi Hammamat, 19, 41
Wadi Tumilat, 238
Waḥpremakhi, 224–26
wales: of Cypriot ships, 63, 66; of Mycenaean/Achaean ships, 132, 150; of Sea Peoples ships, 175
Wallace, H., 286–87
wall paintings, 84, 85, 97, 101, 297–98, 328, See also specific sites
war galleys, 133
Warren, P., 116
warships, 317–19, 332, 375nn1–31; dragon boats as, 75, 110; oared, 155–58
waterborne processions/races: in Aegean, 117–20; of Mycenaean/Achaean ships, 143. See also under Miniature Frieze
weather lore, 300–301
We-da-ne-u, 124
wedged stiches, 240–41
weight-anchors, 255, 272, 274, 283
Weinstein, J., 206
Wenamun, 11, 12, 40–41, 61–62, 163, 164,

206, 212, 300–301, 310, 311–12, 314, 324–25, 332, 370n1
Westerberg, K., 62, 67
West House, 86, 87, 101, 115, 118, 243
White Painted I fabric, 151
White Painted II Ware, 62
White Painted IV Ware, 62
Wiener, M., 84
Williams, R. T., 140
wind roses, 300
Winkler, H. A., 203
Wolley, L., 84
wood. See acacia wood; cedarwood; cypress wood; juniper wood; Lebanese cedar; meru-wood; sidder; sycamore wood
wooden anchors, 271, 288
wooden ship models, 44
Wreschner, E., 202

Yadinu, 336–37
Yam Kinneret, 264
Yannai, A., 41–42
yards, 330; of Aegean ships, 80; of Egyptian ships, 27, 28, 37, 252–53; of Minoan/Cycladic ships, 96–97; of Mycenaean/Achaean ships, 130, 134, 139, 143; of Sea Peoples ships, 175; of Syro-Canaanite ships, 45, 47, 48, 49, 51, 253
Yarim-Lim, 84
Yon, M., 196

Zakynthos, 124
Zau, tomb of, 257
Zawiet el Meitin, 229
Zeus, 116
Zimri-Lim, 83
Ziskind, J. R., 324